APR   1995

TWENTIETH-CENTURY

ITALIAN DRAMA

■

TWENTIETH-CENTURY

ITALIAN DRAMA

■

AN ANTHOLOGY

THE FIRST FIFTY YEARS

Edited by

Jane House and
Antonio Attisani

COLUMBIA UNIVERSITY PRESS
NEW YORK

■

COLUMBIA UNIVERSITY PRESS

New York   Chichester, West Sussex

Copyright © 1995 Columbia University Press
All rights reserved

Library of Congress Cataloging-in-Publication Data
Twentieth–century Italian drama, an anthology: The First Fifty
Years / edited by
Jane House and Antonio Attisani.
v. cm.
Includes bibliographical references.
ISBN 0–231–07118–3 (alk paper) : $39.50
1. Italian drama—20th century—Translations into English.
I. House, Jane. II. Attisani, Antonio, 1948–   .
PQ4244.E5A67   1994   94–29111
852′.91208—dc20   CIP

All copyright information can be found at the back of the book.

Columbia University Press wishes to express its appreciation of
assistance given by the Pushkin Fund in the publication of this
translation.
∞
*Casebound editions of Columbia University Press books are printed
on permanent and durable acid-free paper.*

PRINTED IN THE UNITED STATES OF AMERICA

C 10 9 8 7 6 5 4 3 2 1

■

Contents

ONE

TWO

THREE

FOUR

TEN

ELEVEN

TWELVE

THIRTEEN

The idea for this anthology emerged during a fall 1987 conference on Italian theater I organized when I was director of the Theater Project at Columbia University's Institute on Western Europe. At that time, Antonio Attisani and I undertook to work together on an English language anthology of Italian drama that would include important works and represent the lively diversity of Italian dramatic literature of the twentieth century. We envisioned an anthology in two volumes. The present volume represents the first part of this anthology and includes plays written from the beginning of the century to the post–World War II period.

The selections in this volume illuminate developments in Italian drama in the first part of this century, a period that has been neglected on this side of the Atlantic and, indeed, in all English-speaking countries. The exceptions are Luigi Pirandello, Eduardo De Filippo, and Ugo Betti, whose plays still stimulate great interest today. We especially hope that younger readers and students will now be introduced to the major movements in the Italian theater and of the richness of Italian dramatic literature in the first half of this century. In addition, they will see how Italian drama has moved beyond the commedia dell'arte and *commedia erudita* and the comedies of Carlo Gozzi and Carlo Goldoni.

If some twentieth-century Italian playwrights such as Pirandello and De Filippo are "geniuses" of theater, as Eric Bentley has shown,[1] others not so well known have explored the frontiers of our modern age, an age of machines, telecommunications, computer chips, neuroses, psychoses, anomie, city living, disintegration of the family unit, and loss of faith. Indeed, Marinetti and the Italian futurists were leaders in profoundly affecting concepts about what art is and what it should do throughout Western and Eastern Europe.

The two hundredth anniversary of Goldoni's death occurred in 1993, making this an appropriate time to look back at Italian drama in the first half of the century. In doing so, we can see that the comedic legacy was still very much evident in the work of Eduardo De Filippo, Massimo Bontempelli, Achille Campanile, Italo Svevo, and Ettore Petrolini. In addition, however, Italian drama, never previously celebrated for tragic writers on the order of Shakespeare, Marlowe, Calderone, Racine, or Pushkin, could now boast writers who reflected the agonies of the modern age. In Federigo Tozzi, Pier Maria Rosso di San Secondo, Luigi Pirandello, Ugo Betti, and Alberto Savinio, Italy had writers who presented with great delicacy of feeling the tragic aspect of the human condition and humanity's longing for an ideal world.

In this volume we have collected twelve plays (including five one-acts), one variety act, and three futurist *sintesi*, or sketches. Most are new translations of plays by writers whose dramatic works are completely unknown to English readers. They have been selected with a view to introducing the reader to important developments in twentieth-century Italian theater, drama, and literature: the aesthetic-mystical or symbolist movement, futurism, cabaret and variety theater, *teatro grottesco*, Pirandello's theater of ideas, *realismo magico*, the Catholic strain of drama, cabaret and variety theater, psychological realism, and a post–World War II strain of existentialist drama. We were also interested in bringing to the attention of the English reader writers already familiar to them as novelists, but whose dramatic works have remained obscure—in particular Alberto Savinio, otherwise known as Andrea De Chirico, brother to the famous painter, Giorgio De Chirico. All the writers we present have merited entries in Italy's own history of Italian literature, *Letteratura Italiana: I contemporanei*.[2]

For the most part, we present the plays in chronological order. The anthology begins with Gabriele d'Annunzio. While the lyrical, pastoral tragedy *La figlia di Iorio* is often considered his finest dramatic work, space limitations precluded our selecting that play to represent the decadent or symbolist school of playwriting prevalent at the turn of the century. Instead we have chosen *A Spring Morning's Dream*, a one-act play that was a vehicle for Eleonora Duse as well as Sarah Bernhardt. While the play had been translated into English before, we felt that a new translation was necessary. D'Annunzio's choice of words and his extraordinary and often violent images can turn dangerously cloying in the wrong hands, and we believe ourselves extremely fortunate to have been able to have Anthony Oldcorn breathe new life into this play. He has created a fine and true translation that captures the sonorities of the original.

Variety theater was flourishing in the major cities at the turn of the century, and we have included *Fortunello*, a variety sketch by Ettore Petrolini, who was of Roman origin, and *Via Toledo by Night*, a full-length play by Raffaele Viviani, a Neapolitan. Viviani developed this play from a number of his variety sketches. Music was an essential part of variety theater, and the musical scores for both pieces are included. We can look upon these variety stars as the performance artists of their day. They left a lasting impression on Filippo

T. Marinetti and the futurist movement. While futurist plays by many different writers abound, we have selected three *sintesi,* syntheses or synthesized plays, by Marinetti to illustrate this influential movement. One of the three, *Connecting Vessels,* never translated into English before, is an example of a futurist simultaneous setting.

The period following World War I saw the rise of Pirandello as a dramatist. He has eclipsed other major Italian playwrights whose plays were produced between the end of World War I and the mid-1930s, a time in which Mussolini and his Fascist Party also rose to power. We wish now to introduce some of these writers to the English reader. One is Pier Maria Rosso di San Secondo, a lyrical writer whose *Puppets of Passion!* we have selected as an example of the Italian *teatro grottesco.* Frederick May has called this play "possibly the most important, because deeply probing and subtle, exponent of the [*grottesco*] form."[3] Another is Massimo Bontempelli, here representing *realismo magico,* whose sophisticated characters in *Dea by Dea* Anthony Oldcorn has brought to life with a style and wit reminiscent of Noel Coward. The humorist Achille Campanile's *The Inventor of the Horse* is an exceedingly funny satire on the pretensions of the academic scientific community. Federigo Tozzi, novelist and playwright, is the moody and mystical black sheep of this group. *The Casting* is a difficult play, an exploration of the behavior of a deeply troubled personality and his bourgeois family. Italo Svevo achieved fame as the author of the novel *The Confessions of Zeno* very late in his life. He is still relatively unknown as a dramatist, and we have here included *With Gilded Pen,* a four-act play that, although unfinished, has been successfully produced in Italy and France in recent years and that explores the themes of power and money when a woman holds the purse strings.

And then there is Pirandello who was in his early forties and had already gained distinction as a writer of fiction when Nino Martoglio directed his first play, *La morsa* (*The Vise*) in 1910.[4] Although Pirandello started out with a strong antitheatrical prejudice, he was gradually drawn more toward theater. In the mid-1910s he focused increasingly on writing plays, and from 1925 to 1928 he managed the Teatro d'Arte. This experience with directing led him to respect and value the art of staging plays and the power of the theater. The one-act play *Why?* (1892), probably his earliest play, remained unproduced until 1986 and is often neglected in listings of Pirandello's works, but we present it here because it reveals both his early interest in the idea of the relativity of truth and his ability to create a lively script around that idea. The play also deals with the subject of male jealousy, a theme that is picked up and developed further in Pirandello's mature work *Tonight We Improvise,* the third and final play in the trilogy Pirandello wrote using the structure of a play within a play, the other two being *Six Characters in Search of an Author* and *Each in His Own Way.* Returning to his Sicilian roots and following a practice that was quite usual to him, Pirandello drew the plot of the inner play in *Tonight We Improvise* from his own short story "Leonora, Addio!," a tragic tale of a Sicilian husband's jealousy.[5] Using the production of this play within the play as a jumping-off point, Pirandello returns to themes he examined (the relationship between theater and reality, between actor and character, between director and actor) and techniques he used (changing the performance space, actors breaking out of character) in the first two plays in the trilogy. Because *Tonight We Improvise* is the least known work of the trilogy, we hope that our presenting it here will give it new life. This translation by J. Douglas Campbell and Leonard G. Sbrocchi has already been successfully produced in Canada.

The Neapolitan Eduardo De Filippo, who was born in 1900 and died in 1984, had a vibrant career as an actor, playwright, and director both before and after World War II. To represent his work in the first half of the century we have chosen *The Nativity Scene,* a play that went through many stages of creation. Since it exists in a number of different versions, we have asked Paola Quarenghi to enlighten us in a special introductory essay about the development of the script and the reasons why such a superb comic writer kept it in flux. We have also thought to provide the potential financially strapped producer with an alternative last act, the author's own, which reduces the number of actors required to mount the play.

The last two playwrights represented in the volume are Ugo Betti and Alberto Savinio. Although Alberto Savinio was making an international name for himself well before World War I, we have placed him at the end of the book with Betti because the two plays selected to represent their work are set in the post–World War II period, and both are full of feelings of desperate longing and confusion, especially on the part of women. In *Crime on Goat Island,* Betti touches on the existential anguish created by the horrors of the war. The play trembles with repressed sexuality: amoral actions lead to murder and despair. The desperation and confusion in Alberto Savinio's *Emma B. Widow Jocasta* centers on a woman whose husband has either died or left her and who lives half in a world of dreams, waiting for the return of her son as if he were her lover. These plays, we believe, are a fitting representation of the gloom in the aftermath of the war.

For readers interested in exploring other works of these playwrights or books and articles on Italian theater, we have included a bibliography at the end of the volume. It must be emphasized that this bibliography is intended for English readers and does not include many fine and important works written in Italian.

Notes

1. Eric Bentley, ed., *The Genius of the Italian Theater* (New York: New American Library, 1964).

2. (Milan: Marzorati, 1969).

3. "Italy," *The Oxford Companion to the Theatre,* 3d ed. (London: Oxford University Press, 1967), p. 811.

4. *La morsa* was entitled *L'epilogo* when it was published in *Ariel* in 1898.

5. See Luigi Pirandello. *Tonight We Improvise and "Leonora, Addio!,"* trans. with introduction and notes by J. Douglas Campbell and Leonard G. Sbrocchi (Ottawa: Canadian Society for Italian Studies, Biblioteca di Quaderni d'italianistica, 1987). *Tonight We Improvise* in this anthology is reprinted from this work.

Acknowledgments

A work of this size depends on the cooperation and assistance of many people. We must first thank, indeed we cannot thank enough, all the translators, who devoted many hours to their labors of love. As the editor in charge of translation, Jane House is particularly obliged to Daniel Gerould, teacher, colleague, and friend, for introducing her to the one-act play *Why?* and suggesting she translate it, for his concern and his careful reading of the manuscript, and for his always helpful and perceptive comments; to Eric Bentley who suggested including *Tonight We Improvise* as the Pirandello entry; and to the Marta Abba Estate for giving us permission to do so; to Allen Mandelbaum who led her to Anthony Oldcorn, who, in addition to his contribution of three marvelous translations often gave her the benefit of his wise counsel; and to Ruth Cuker for constantly prodding her to complete this work. But most of all, we will always be indebted to Elliot Zupnick who, with typical foresight, encouraged, supported, and believed in this project from its very beginnings, when he was director at Columbia University's Institute on Western Europe, until the book reached its final stages.

We are also grateful to Massimo Malucelli, Marilyn Firment, and Susan Altabet for their help with some of the music and to the Pushkin Players, among them especially Sarah Melici, and students at Lehman College, The City University of New York, for bringing to life for the first time some of the characters in the English translations of these plays. Of the many scholars whose works we have consulted we would particularly like to acknowledge Peter Bondanella whose entries in the *McGraw-Hill Encyclopedia of World Drama* were indispensable.

Finally, we would like to express our

appreciation to the various staff members of Columbia University Press, particularly to Jennifer Crewe, our editor, for her counsel and encouragement in the preparation of this manuscript. For the valuable assistance they rendered at the Press, we are also indebted to Leslie Bialler, Adam Tibbs, Anne McCoy, and Ursula Bollini.

We would be extremely remiss were we not to mention essential financial assistance received at the very beginning of the project from Ansaldo North America; Cassa di Risparmio di Torino; E.N.I.; Fiat U.S.A., Inc.; The Institute on Western Europe, Columbia University; The Italian Cultural Institute, New York.

Between 1870 and 1900 the most innovative works on the Italian stage were those written in the tradition of naturalism, known in its Italian version as *verismo*. The renowned Italian actress Eleonora Duse triumphed in Emile Zola's *Teresa Raquin* in 1879. In 1891 Duse introduced Italians to the works of Ibsen by playing Nora in *A Doll's House*. By the end of the decade, particularly as a result of the actor Ermete Zacconi's numerous productions, Italians had seen many versions of Ibsen in their own language. Italian *verismo* writers had also had their showing. In 1884 Duse performed in Giovanni Verga's adaptation of his short story *Cavalleria rusticana*. By 1900 audiences had seen the harsh reality of peasant life in the dramas of both Verga and Luigi Capuana, the crueler aspects of bourgeois life in plays by Marco Praga and Gerolamo Rovetta and in the last works of Giuseppe Giacosa, and depictions of the new urban proletariat in the works of Carlo Bertolazzi and Luigi Illica. But by this time *verismo* writers had become mannered. Giacosa today, for example, is remembered more for his great success as a collaborator with Luigi Illica on the librettos for Giacomo Puccini's three operas *La Bohème* (1896), *Tosca* (1900), and *Madam Butterfly* (1904) than for his late *verismo* plays such as *Come le foglie* (*Like Falling Leaves*).

At the turn of the century the Italian stage reflected the values and interests of the new bourgeois classes who were prepared to be emotionally moved—but only if the passions were diluted into a comforting and comfortable morality. This attitude affected not only the playwrights' sensibilities but every aspect of Italian theater. In 1902, for example, Roberto Bracco reported that "In Rome, as well as in Milan and Turin and Naples, a wider base of pop-

■

Introduction: Social and

Theatrical Contexts of Italian

Drama, 1900 to 1950

ANTONIO ATTISANI

■

ular support for the theater creates natural limits; if they did not have their usual enervating choice of plays, the public would not come to the theater. Thus, the demand for a minimum of ten different plays each month; thus, the endless waste of energy."[1] At that time Ugo Ojetti, a playwright and critic, described the incredible confusion caused by the commercial exploitation of theater spaces, which were used not only for dramatic and musical shows but also for political meetings, children's parties, operettas, and boxing matches.[2] This multifunctional approach detracted from the idea of theater as a serious activity and relegated written drama to a minor and unprofitable, albeit prestigious, role. In addition, the audiences, increasingly attracted by the excitement of new theatrical effects, were less sensitive to the artistic aspects of the theater: the arts of acting, staging, and playwriting.

Theater artists became more and more aware of the necessity to preserve these arts. They realized that touring companies needed to be rescued from their difficult working conditions and their vast repertories and that the uniqueness of each theatrical production needed to be respected. For example, sets had to be newly designed for each production and not, as was standard practice, assembled from painted flats belonging to a variety of different shows.

Various attempts were made to create permanent theaters subsidized by government funding. Following the example of Antoine's Théâtre Libre in Paris, Domenico Lanza established the short-lived Teatro d'Arte in Turin in 1898 where he eliminated the "silly little prompter's dome" and replaced the footlights with floodlights. A few years later, in 1900, the actor Ermete Novelli set up a semipermanent theater in Rome called Casa di Goldoni, but it was not successful, and he was forced to go back to touring. Even an affirmed critic like Edoardo Boutet accepted the challenge and inaugurated the Stabile Romana in 1905.

Meanwhile, a new theatrical perspective, poetic and tragic in nature, and with an anti-*verismo* outlook, was emerging. This perspective was particularly represented by works produced together by the poet Gabriele d'Annunzio and the actress Eleonora Duse, who, significantly, had once been an enthusiastic supporter of *verismo*. In 1894 she met d'Annunzio and began a tormented relationship with him. In 1897 she performed his one-act play *Sogno d'un mattino di primavera* (*A Spring Morning's Dream*) in Paris; this production marked the stage debut of the already famous writer. Duse played Isabella, driven to insanity by lying all night with her dead lover, whom "the duke" (presumably her husband, although d'Annunzio never explicitly says so) had brutally murdered. Thus d'Annunzio drove the familiar theme of the bourgeois triangle to its limits, and his play is essentially a lament over the tragic conclusion of the adulterous trio. A second dream play, *Sogno d'un tramonto d'autunno* (*Dream of an Autumn Sunset*), although written in 1897, had to wait until 1905 for its first Italian production, which starred Teresa Franchini. D'Annunzio's next play, *La città morta* (*The Dead City,* 1898), premiered in Paris with Sarah Bernhardt as the blind Anna.

Most important, Duse and d'Annunzio developed a project they were not able to realize in their own day but that would be the topic of conversation for several decades. Their plan, which d'Annunzio described in his novel *Il fuoco* (*The Flame of Life,* 1900) and which he claimed was inspired by the Hellenic theater, seventeenth-century madrigal writers, and Wagner, involved erecting a festival theater in the Albano hills near Rome one similar to those of ancient Greece. This "temple to the Tragic Muse," as d'Annunzio called it, was to be a laboratory for worldwide reform of the theater. In their vision, the temple would allow for a new kind of interaction between poets, actors, and the public; it would foster productions where the word would be fused with music and dance, and it would help form new generations of actors. This utopian project was opposed to commercial, bourgeois theater. D'Annunzio wished to promote the virtues of poetry in a theatrical system dominated by "urban theaters where, in suffocating heat which reeks with all sorts of impurities, before a crowd of guzzlers and prostitutes, actors traffic their wares."[3]

While Duse and the celebrated actor Ermete Zacconi collaborated on several Italian tours between 1899 and 1901 in an effort to promote d'Annunzio's work, they only had some success with *La Gioconda* (*Gioconda,* 1899) and *La città morta,* which they presented in Italian for the first time in 1901. D'Annunzio achieved his first international success as a playwright with *Francesca da Rimini* (1901). Here, for the first time, he abandoned prose and created a tragedy in verse. After *Francesca da Rimini,* historical tragedies in verse became as fashionable as they once were in the seventeenth and eighteenth centuries.

In 1904 d'Annunzio produced what is considered his masterpiece, *La figlia di Iorio* (*The Daughter of Iorio*). The staging of the work, however, marked the break-up of his relationship with Duse, who relinquished her role to Irma Grammatica. The following years were extremely busy, and d'Annunzio wrote four new tragedies, introducing some important stylistic innovations: a kind of irony, for example, reminiscent of Henry James and an experimentation with the language of tragedy that anticipated Eugene O'Neill and T. S. Eliot. D'Annunzio dedicated himself fiercely to theater until 1909, the year in which his *Fedra* (Phaedra) was poorly received. Misfortune followed. A financial crisis forced him to put his house up for auction, and in 1911 his works were banned by the ecclesiastical authorities. The poet fled to Paris, where he remained until 1915. In exile, he remained as active as he had been in Italy, and he even turned to writing for the cinema. However, his most memorable works from this period are musical scripts written in French and developed in collaboration with such composers as Claude Debussy, (*Le Martyre de Saint Sébastien,* 1911) and Ildebrando Pizzetti (*La Pisanelle; ou, La mort parfumée* [Pisanella; or, fragrant death], 1913). Vsevolod Meyerhold's sojourn in Paris fortuitously led to the Russian director's staging of *La Pisanelle* in 1913.

The repertory of Italian theaters in the early twentieth century reflected prevailing literary trends, or rather, features of these trends were isolated and adapted to create commercial products for a wide audience. As we have noted, d'Annunzio's project for theatrical reform met with little success, but his *Francesca da Rimini* was popular and instigated a flood of historical dramas overflowing with sentimental feeling and unrealistic, bombastic heroes that represented the other side of the petite bourgeoisie in the Giolitti era. Among these minor authors, some of whom deserve to be remembered not only for their skillfully written scripts but also for their high visibility at the time, one finds Sem Benelli, whose *Cena delle beffe* (Tricksters' banquet, 1908) was an old favorite for at least two generations of actors, including John Barrymore who performed in an English adaptation of the play entitled *The Jest.*[4]

The most popular commercial theater was undoubtedly vaudeville and the French *po-chades,* short sketches freely adapted and rewritten by Italian actor-playwrights. These adaptations were extremely popular in the dialect theater. In Naples, Eduardo Scarpetta made good use of them. Scarpetta, once the student of Antonio Petito, the last great Pulcinella, and natural father to Eduardo, Titina, and Peppino De Filippo, realized that new scripts had to be written to satisfy a large public comprised of different social classes. After a few totally independent experiments, he found a good formula in reworking French texts, and he had several decades of success at his theater, the San Carlino.

The new bourgeois public was not a homogeneous entity, however, and it supported various forms of theater. For example, one could find echoes on the stage of the hot ideological debate over the crisis of positivism and the spread of a new spiritualism. In a similar way, nationalist imperialist sentiments and even some radical, antibourgeois positions were popularized for the more informed public in the dramas of Enrico Annibale Butti, Enrico Corradini, and Vincenzo Morello. Another trend, usually described as intimate and crepuscular but more succinctly called self-pitying, included the dulcet works of Fausto Maria Martini and Ercole Luigi Morselli; they were very successful in the 1910s and 1920s, as was the sentimental and basically nationalistic play *Addio giovinezza!* (Goodbye youth!, 1911) by Sandro Camasio and Nino Oxilia.

During the first two decades of the twentieth century, the last glimmers of nineteenth-century *verismo,* written in both standard Italian and dialect, could be found in the works of Marco Praga, Sabatino Lopez, Salvatore di Giacomo, and Augusto Novelli. They achieved a certain popularity in that they answered the needs of the most serious and most well-educated sector of the bourgeois public.

Certain critics, including Silvio d'Amico in *Tramonto del grande attore* (Decline of the great actor, 1929), claimed that the Italian theater did not keep pace with the changing styles of playwriting and stage practice that had affected the rest of Europe from the time the Théâtre Libre was founded in Paris in 1887; and some have suggested that it took such directors as Luchino Visconti and Giorgio Strehler in the 1950s to bring Italy into step. Recent historical studies, however, show that there was indeed a great deal of exchange between Italy and other countries and that Italians were well aware of important theatrical innovations and changing theories of theater. The tradition of the star actor touring company, for instance, made it possible for audiences and critics to compare France's Rachel to Adelaide Ristori, Sarah Bernhardt to Eleonora Duse, and for Stanislavsky to discover the great Italian actors Ernesto Rossi and Tommaso Salvini as well as Eleonora Duse, whom he considered a realistic actress of enormous power.

Moreover, many Italian critics, producers, and directors followed theatrical trends in the rest of Europe. One need only look at Antonio Gramsci, Silvio d'Amico, Piero Gobetti, Adriano Tilgher, and, of course, Anton Giulio Bragaglia, who had an omnivorous appetite for producing plays from all over the world. One should also note the actor-manager and playwright Dario Niccodemi, whose Parisian apprenticeship led him to carry out some of the first Italian experiments in directing. And it was not uncommon for Italians

to sojourn in other European cities, especially, but not exclusively, in Paris, witness d'Annunzio, Filippo T. Marinetti, Alberto Savinio, and Pier Maria Rosso di San Secondo among
many others. Indeed, it was in Paris that Marinetti founded the futurist movement.

Futurism arrived on the scene at the end of the first decade of the twentieth century.
Arising in opposition to other forms of theater, futurism propounded a new aesthetic and
a new outlook on every aspect of living, including food and fashion. Marinetti published
the first futurist manifesto in Paris in 1909. Many other manifestos followed, including
two that are important in the context of futurist theater: *Manifesto del teatro di varietà* (Manifesto of the variety theater, 1913) and *Manifesto del teatro sintetico futurista* (Manifesto of
synthetic futurist theater, 1914). In calling for a synthetic, dynamic, alogical, nonrealistic
theater that could involve several scenes happening simultaneously on stage, the futurists
hoped to destroy the traditional aesthetics of the theater. Their early theatrical output
consisted of about fifteen *sintesi* written by Marinetti, Emilio Settimelli, Bruno Corra,
Remo Chiti, Francesco Balilla Pratella, Paolo Buzzi, and Umberto Boccioni. This collection of two-minute scenes was performed throughout Italy by various companies, including the Berti-Masi company, a professional theater company. Audiences were provoked,
and the performances turned into grand happenings. Shrewd observers of audience reactions, the futurists themselves were very often the ones who initiated the audience protests
against their work. Futurism had an impact in other countries, and from the 1920s on
longer, more serious works appeared that were of greater literary value, as was true in
Marinetti's case.

Paralleling their interest in theater, the futurists recognized the communicative power
of the circus and of variety theater. The great comedian of variety theater, Ettore Petrolini,
both influenced and in turn was influenced by futurism, as is evident in his sketches and
characters and his delight in word games.

However, the futurists' finest artistic achievements can be claimed by several exponents
of the movement primarily interested in theater's visual aspects: set design, pantomime,
and dance. Fortunato Depero is remembered, above all, for having designed the sets for
Le chant du rossignol (The nightingale's song, 1916) by Stravinsky in Paris and for his own
Balletti plastici (Plastic ballets, 1918). Depero eliminated the painted backdrop, replacing
it with *mobili architetture cromatico-luminose* or, in other words, mobile set pieces of geomet-
rical design that could be transformed through the use of light. The greatest artist in this
field was Ettore Prampolini who supported the idea of a *scenotecnica* where the stage designer would not just be a painter but would make use of all the modern possibilities on
stage—electric lights, constructed costumes, and set pieces. Prampolini later promoted
the creation of *architetture elettromeccaniche,* electrically propelled set pieces that could be
brought to life through lighting. In 1921 he designed the sets and costumes of the Futurist
Synthetic Company, then he collaborated for a long time with Bragaglia at the Teatro degli
Indipendenti in Rome as well as with Achille Ricciardi on Ricciardi's Teatro del Colore.
In 1927 he founded the Teatro dello Pantomima Futurista and began to travel to Paris quite
often. He created sets for opera and ballet, collaborating with such people as Aurel M.

Millos, André Gide, Jean Cocteau, Paul Hindemith, and Bela Bartòk. Prampolini's creative energy never flagged, and in the 1940s he agreed to work with some of the first modern Italian directors such as Enrico Fulchignoni and Giulio Pacuvio.

It must be noted that the futurists used theater for propagandistic purposes, for the proclamation of their vision of the world. It was the most effective medium to reach an audience that did not read and that was beginning to attend the cinema and listen to the radio, media that in themselves were of interest to the futurists. In fact, it was in the 1910s, at a time when silent film was essentially a reproduction of mime, that people began asking themselves whether theater could, or even should, survive now that there was the alternative of the moving picture, which was drawing larger audiences all the time. Before World War I, the Arturo Ambrosio studio and Giovanni Pastrone's Itala-Film company, both in Turin, were in the forefront of movie making. Pastrone's 1914 epic, *Cabiria,* for which d'Annunzio wrote the screenplay and which had an unprecedented budget of over one million dollars, achieved enormous international success and influenced both Cecil B. De Mille and D. W. Griffith. Audiences had never seen anything like the spectacular crowd scenes in this film. It is not surprising that compared to film theater was considered to be in decline and obsolete. The first important Italian theoretical discussion of cinema, a book by Sebastiano Arturo Luciani entitled *L'antiteatro,* was published in 1926.

Nowadays, the futurists, if they were still active, would focus on television. That the movement undervalued formal theater language and quality of performance in its early stages may be explained by its strong emphasis on its message. Notwithstanding the seeming importance of Marinetti and futurism as exponents of the Fascist regime, the regime did not actually prize the futurists' weltanschauung and used their movement as an expedient in Fascist propaganda.

While the futurists were making their early attempts to deal a deathblow to old theatrical forms in the early 1910s, some playwrights were developing who had less destructive aims, among them Pirandello and playwrights writing in a style that came to be known as *teatro grottesco.* The year 1916 saw the openings of Luigi Pirandello's *Pensaci Giacomino!* (Think about it, Giacomino!) and *La maschera e il volto (The Mask and the Face)* by Luigi Chiarelli. In 1917, Pirandello's *Così è (se vi pare) (It Is So [If You Think So])* and *Il piacere dell'onestà (The Pleasure of Honesty)* were performed along with *Scala di seta* (Silken staircase) by Chiarelli; then in 1918 there was Rosso di San Secondo's *Marionette, che passione!,* translated here as *Puppets of Passion!,* and Luigi Antonelli's *L'uomo che incontrò se stesso* (The man who met himself); in 1919 Enrico Cavacchioli gave us *L'uccello del paradiso* (The bird of paradise), and in 1921, a decisive year in the history of Italian theater, came the premiere of *Six Characters in Search of an Author,* which, to judge from the reactions of critics and the public, was close to terrifying.

The *teatro grottesco,* to which most of these works belong, is so named for its characteristic reactions to the bourgeois drama: an analytical breakdown of the human passions, a skeptical and ironic tone, and a grotesque portrayal of human beings moving like puppets at the mercy of fate. The *grottesco* playwrights sought to have the audience question certain aspects of the predominant culture. They reexamined the traditional love triangle, which had previously been used to provoke hilarity or pathos. Their ironic tone broke the mode of conventional playwriting; sometimes a choruslike character was added to the plot, one who oversees events without taking part in them and who seems to break the fourth wall, thus estranging the audience and stimulating them to keep a critical distance. *Grottesco* playwrights aimed at creating more than simple entertainment; in wishing to provoke discussion, they offered multiple points of view on events as well as multiple meanings.

The most radical and revolutionary aspects of the *teatro grottesco* disappeared during the Fascist period. Some of its characteristics were taken up by others, such as Bertolt Brecht, although this was usually coincidental and not due to direct exchange. During the Fascist period in Italy, many authors, in good or bad faith, chose to make use of comforting myths and confused visions of utopia; for example, few plays written during that time included an estranging character. The *grottesco* period brought an end to the grandiloquent type of leading actor. The quick-witted character who was seen playing an estranging role in the grotesque theater appeared in the form of the *raisonneur* in Pirandello's unique dramas.

As mentioned above, 1921 was a pivotal year because of the appearance of Luigi Pirandello's *Six Characters in Search of an Author* directed by Niccodemi. The first performances were met with tremendous critical dissension. At first, audience and critics found the text awful and considered the play a terrible piece of entertainment, but then the production triumphed and gave Italians something worth thinking about. The play was a theatrical event signaling a total theatrical revolution not only because it dealt with the main issues of the time but also because it exploded them, so to speak, into a philosophical discussion of truth and fiction, of life, imagination, and reality, with such artistic power that even today this play or the idea of a play within a play makes us meditate on problems that still remain unresolved. Pirandello's ultimate aim was not to display the social background and psychology of his characters but to create "figures" that reflect deeper thoughts and problems.

In *Six Characters in Search of an Author,* theater is the absolute protagonist: the bare stage is dominated by a stereotypical company of professional actors who, although soulless, have a haughty pride in their profession. Then the Six Characters arrive from outside, with their hopeless pretension of giving theatrical form to real life. It becomes quite clear that there is a discrepancy between the "demand of the theater," the need to tell a story, and the aesthetic conventions and ideological limitations that circumscribe that demand. Pirandello was not thinking of theater in the abstract but as a social institution in the Europe of his time. The discrepancy is distressing, the problem demands a solution. The Six Characters know that theater is not life, but they have hope anyway—just as today we all hope—that the stage will succeed in giving shape to ideas, forces, and perhaps even mysteries holding sway over humankind. Their tragic appeal has affected all subsequent revolutions in the theatrical arts.

During the 1920s, in reaction to the show business of theater, a number of small permanent theaters were formed inspired both by earlier efforts in this vein and by the German *Kammerspielen* and analogous English enterprises. Among these Pirandello's Teatro d'Arte must especially be noted. The Sicilian playwright felt he had to become both artistic and managing director of this experiment; thus, he put himself in a position he described as "absurd," one that would put to the test his antitheatrical pronouncements of the preceding years, when he had accused theater professionals of betraying and trivializing written works.

Pirandello's theatrical adventure spanned three seasons, from 1925 to 1928; during this period he supervised about fifty productions, bearing almost complete responsibility for them, from choosing the texts to directing the actors, from shouldering the economic burdens of financial management and raising public funds to handling the difficult task of finding space. It is a story of failure insofar as his dream of a "unique" theater—an art theater within the market system, a theater that would be permanent and free of ideological conditioning, and therefore independent—was concerned. The regime, which only gave him half-hearted support, and the prevailing impresario system of production, which was hostile to his efforts, have both been blamed for this failure. However, Pirandello's efforts are still remembered as an extraordinary experiment, above all because they revealed his directorial abilities. Besides making shrewd use of new ideas in lighting and set design, Pirandello succeeded in realizing, if only for a little while, his idea of a philosophical theater.

The Teatro d'Arte presented in its repertory such works as *Nostra Dea,* translated here as *Dea by Dea,* by Massimo Bontempelli, an enthusiastic supporter of Pirandello, and plays by Marinetti, Savinio, and many others; nevertheless, most of the repertory consisted of various texts by Pirandello. While staging his own works, Pirandello also used the authorial power of a director to rewrite *Six Characters in Search of an Author* and create the text we know today. His rewrites were influenced by Georges Pitoëff's staging of the play for its Paris premiere. Pitoëff emphasized the otherworldly nature of the Six Characters by having them arrive in an elevator. This choice shocked Pirandello, and in his revisions he clarified the relationship between the actors and the Six Characters by differentiating them more.

While Pirandello's experience as artistic and administrative director was extremely important, though not typical, in the light of Italian history, the most experimental of the little theaters was Anton Giulio Bragaglia's Teatro degli Indipendenti. Bragaglia's outlook was shaped by the futurist movement, which he strongly supported in its beginnings. In 1922 he founded his own theater, which he intended as a permanent laboratory where aspiring directors could experiment and learn their craft. He used amateur actors for the most part, welcomed new authors, and also introduced both classic and modern plays from abroad.

Among Bragaglia's many theoretical treatises, the most notable is *Del teatro teatrale; ossia, Del teatro* (About theatrical theater; or, about theater, 1929), in which he revealed himself to be a strong believer in the visual elements of the stage. He claimed that "the audience that comes to the theater knows the cinema and, therefore, it demands much more from the stage than what it used to demand in the past."[5] For this reason he emphasized the work of the director (whom he still described as one who "mounted" a work "on the stage"). He considered the director the true author of the production. Bragaglia is remembered also for the generosity he displayed in giving young people the chance to prove themselves.

Not everyone agreed with Bragaglia regarding the role of the director. Silvio d'Amico took a completely opposite position and accused Bragaglia not only of being an unprofessional dilettante but also of not recognizing the primary value of the text and, therefore, the subordinate role of the director vis-à-vis the playwright or the poet. D'Amico and Bragaglia exchanged harsh words, and their controversy turned into a legal battle when one accused the other of defamation of character. Their argument was paradigmatic. In those decades of change, the whole of Italian theater oscillated between these two currents of thought, and leading exponents of the two positions could be found in two great foreign directors, Max Reinhardt and Jacques Copeau.

Max Reinhardt first conquered Italian audiences and critics during the 1932 tour of his production of Goldoni's *Arlecchino, Servant of Two Masters*. This was followed in 1933 by his *féerie* production of *A Midsummer Night's Dream* in the Boboli Gardens, Florence, and in 1934 by *The Merchant of Venice*. Meanwhile, Jacques Copeau, a living legend who fled the French theatrical system, staged *La rappresentazione di Santa Uliva* in Florence's Santa Croce cloister (1935), *Savonarola* by Rino Alessi in Florence's Piazza della Signoria (1935), and *As You Like It* (1938). Copeau was d'Amico's inspiration. Beginning in 1933, d'Amico developed his theory about a new form of "Italian directing" that would merge respect for the text with meticulous care for the stage's visual elements (movement, lights, set, costumes).

During those same years, the Fascist regime was exerting more and more control over the theater. In general, actors were tolerated only if they used an old-fashioned rhetorical style, and if they did, they were often honored. The regime also suppressed the use of regional dialects in favor of a flat, dull, and "functional" language. This policy had a major effect on the dialect playwrights, among them Raffaele Viviani and Eduardo De Filippo, who, along with Pirandello, were important Italian playwrights during this period. Since Viviani's language was specifically rooted in the life of the Neapolitan poor, it could not be "Italianized" without being drained of its essential nature; his company was effectively confined to minor regional theaters. Meanwhile, Eduardo De Filippo, who cannot be accused of yielding to Fascism, found that by "Italianizing" his plays he could reach more of the general public and more critics. An outspoken critic of the regime's antidialect program was Gordon Craig. Craig, who lived and worked in Italy for over twenty years, greatly admired actors in the dialect theater. He considered them authentic "supermarionettes" and defended them in a private audience with Mussolini in 1934, a meeting that left both men annoyed and frustrated.[6]

Increasing government intervention was concrete evidence of the Fascist effort to rationalize the theater and to restore a "sublime drama." A newly formed bureaucracy was in position to control what happened on stage in hundreds of ways. In 1931 censorship powers were arrogated by the Department of Internal Affairs. Meanwhile the process of making the government and the Fascist Party homogeneous was already underway. In 1935 the Ministero della Cultura Popolare (Department of Popular Culture), or Minculpop, was established; it became the central supervising body of Italian theater and also functioned as a think tank, generating the idea of a popular nationwide theater that would focus on the classics and directing. The postwar generation, while criticizing its source, would later adopt this idea.

Although the Fascists held a tight rein on the newly instituted system of government subvention of theaters, discouraging any foreign and dialect productions, they did not succeeded in creating their own theater. An outstanding example of the pomposity and uselessness of the "sublime drama" they wished to promote can be found in Gioacchino Forzano and Benito Mussolini's *Cesare* (*Caesar,* 1939–40), performed in 1940, just as Italy was about to enter the war. The Fascist leader had already collaborated with Forzano on *Campo di Maggio* (1930) and *Villafranca* (1932).

Despite the deadening effect of the Fascist regime on theater, it was in the Fascist period that certain ideas were formulated and institutions developed that would have an impact on the future of Italian theater. The Fascists made a major effort to create a popular theater with the Carri di Tespi (Thespian carts), large outdoor mobile theaters that traveled throughout Italy and the Italian empire between 1929 and 1942, performing plays and lyrical works and paying little attention to the quality of their productions. The audience was largely comprised of members of the Dopolavoro (Afterwork) organizations, a Fascist institution organizing free time for workers in all categories: factory workers, railway workers, teachers, and so on. In spite of government support and the involvement (which was limited to the theoretical level) of many people, the experiment did not last. It confirmed that theater for the masses could be used to promote either rightist or leftist ideologies and that theater for propaganda purposes is always detrimental to artistic values.

Perhaps a positive outgrowth of this theater for the masses was the Roman manifesto "For a Theater of the People," created at the fall of Fascism in 1943 and signed by theater people such as the critic, director, and historian Vito Pandolfi, the directors Orazio Costa and Gerardo Guerrieri, and the writer Diego Fabbri. The manifesto addressed the theater's moral and social duties; foremost among those were its obligations to be affordable, to educate audiences, to be disciplined, and to emphasize artistic aims rather than commercial ones.

It was under the Fascist regime that, mainly through the efforts of Silvio d'Amico, plans were initiated to face the crisis in Italian theater. Since the 1910s and especially since the advent of sound in 1929–30, the cinema had increasingly been appropriating both audiences and theater spaces. It became obvious that noncommercial theater needed to be supported by the state if it was going to survive. With the assistance of Mussolini's government, Silvio d'Amico organized the October 1934 Volta Conference and invited Pirandello to chair it. The participants were international theater people invited to talk about the future of theater around the world and to discuss Italian theatrical reform, the creation of an Italian national theater subsidized by the state, and the definition of the new role of the director.

Thus Pirandello, who at the end of his career was skeptical about the relationship between art and power, as can be seen in his last work *I giganti della montagna* (*The Mountain*

Giants, 1929–36), presided over a conference on theater that was sponsored by the Fascist state. At the conference, he met with the most prominent figures in the theater of his time: Bontempelli, Bragaglia, Marinetti, Prampolini, Rosso di San Secondo, Guido Salvini, Adriano Tilgher, Walter Gropius, Maurice Maeterlinck, Alexander Tairov, Jacques Copeau, William B. Yeats, Gerhardt Hauptmann, and various others. Gordon Craig, who was a member of the audience at the conference, realized that the real purpose of the convention was to garner support for d'Amico's project, to obtain regular government assistance for the creation, production, and distribution of theater.[7] Indeed, in the following year, the National Academy of Dramatic Art was founded, and d'Amico was made director of his dream child. One of the academy's functions was to train students to be professional directors. The first person entrusted with this job was the Russian actress and director, Tatiana Pavlova, and after her would come Guido Salvini.

D'Amico continued to play the role of mediator, neither supporting one side nor the other when there were differences of opinion but rather advocating a melding of diverse innovative ideas, which he hoped would not clash with either the political or religious powers. His personal intervention on Pirandello's behalf with the future Pope, Cardinal Montini, was perhaps decisive in preventing the playwright's excommunication. In the 1930s and 1940s he was able, thanks to this strategy, to achieve his aims, first, under the Fascists and, later, under the new democratic, postwar government. This is not to say that d'Amico's position was ambiguous or that he colluded with Fascism—quite the contrary. He opposed the idea of theater either as an instrument for the promotion of cultural conformity or as innocuous entertainment. He dedicated himself to the colossal task of creating a concept of theater that while adhering to Catholic tenets, was not to be sworn to them. To understand the scope of his thinking, one need only look at his weighty *Storia del teatro* or his monumental *Enciclopedia dello spettacolo,* a thirteen-volume work, the only one of its kind in the world, which he edited in the postwar years.

In a 1932 article in the magazine *Scenario,* the linguist Bruno Migliorini was the first to propose definitions for *regia* (directing) and *regista* (director) and, given his intelligent and convincing arguments in favor of using these words, they were immediately incorporated into the Italian language. While d'Amico quite rightly argued that directing has always existed in some form, it was only with Richard Wagner, the Duke of Saxe-Meiningen, and André Antoine that a person called the director assumed new responsibilities in interpreting the meaning of a theatrical work.

In the wake of protodirectors, such as Dario Niccodemi and Virgilio Talli, and of Bragaglia and Pirandello in their experimental theaters, it was d'Amico's academy that set down the fundamentals of directing during its early years of operation. Pavlova came to Italy in 1921, at a time when spectators and even critics were confusing staging with stage design; they did not understand who the "clumsy little man [was] who [came] out on stage, at the end, along with the actors, to acknowledge the applause."[8] Pavlova was an actress in Russian theater and film before and during the early years of the Russian revolution. She knew such famous people as Stanislavsky, Yevgeny B. Vakhtangov, and Nikolai N. Evreinov. As the head of the directing department of the newly formed academy, she was therefore in a position to offer the students solid training in the tasks and responsibilities of the director. She also applied her experience to her work with various companies of her own, which she directed from the early 1920s to the 1950s. She insisted that the director should coordinate all the components involved in a stage production: music, lighting, sets, costumes, and the actors' movements. Guido Salvini took over her teaching position from 1938 to 1944. Salvini came from a theatrical family and was both a director and set designer. He showed a great sensitivity to the demands of outdoor performances and had a talent for directing large groups of performers.

However, Pavlova and Salvini were still focused on innovations regarding the management of the entire working process in the theater, not specifically on the function of the director of a stage production. For Pavlova and Salvini, the director was not yet a theatrical author, someone guided by a particular aesthetic or an overriding idea in selecting and adapting texts. They were, nevertheless, in their positions at the academy, the teachers of Italy's first true modern directors.

The 1939–40 season was marked by several events of symbolic significance. While Zacconi was giving his great farewell performance in an old-fashioned production of *Apologia di Socrate* (Socrates' apologia), based on Plato's dialogues, the first modern Italian directors—Costa, Fulchignoni, and Pacuvio—were making their debut. Orazio Costa, a 1937 graduate of the academy who had also studied with Jacques Copeau in Paris, directed the company of the Academy of Dramatic Art in *Il mistero della natività* (The mystery of the nativity), a collection of medieval texts. He declared that his aesthetics were based on Catholic principles and inspired by Copeau. The stage was bare, separated from the audience by a scrim. A choral group standing on the apron of the proscenium stage disappeared when an Annunciation scene was illuminated behind the scrim. In Costa's conception, the text was a kind of litany or prayer and the theater a temple. His preference for theater as an auditory event, in which the vocal work on each speech had priority over the work on character, was evident.

Enrico Fulchignoni, a Sicilian doctor and a friend of Bragaglia's, staged *Piccola città* (*Our Town*) by Thornton Wilder first at Bragaglia's Teatro delle Arti (1938–39) and then in Milan's Teatro Nuovo (1940). He, too, chose to use a bare stage. Windows were indicated by projections on the backdrop, and the cemetery was suggested by a set of chairs. Wilder's stage manager in Fulchignoni's interpretation became a kind of director-shaman figure or animator of a psychodrama.[9]

Giulio Pacuvio made his directing debut in 1940 with *Murder in the Cathedral* by T. S. Eliot. He eliminated the curtain and the prompter's box and connected the pit to the stage by a short flight of stairs that extended the width of the stage and was reminiscent of the stairs connecting the priests' presbytery to the worshipers' benches. Pacuvio displayed his faith in a kind of poetic theater that required a ritual format for its realization and a homogeneous community for its audience.

Those who understood the accomplishments of these three directors considered them dazzling innovators. One person who understood them was the young Vito Pandolfi, then a critic. Signing himself *"Il corifeo"* in the magazine *Roma fascista* in 1940,[10] he pointed out that the three directors all conceived of directing in the same way; the director's function was not simply to illustrate the text but to decode it, to fulfill it completely, to guide the actors and make them feel safe. The three directors also chose similar themes and formal structures. The works selected were meditations on life and death. And they all reflected Giovanni Gentile's[11] idea that the director is the one to give a production its spiritual life, to make it something alive and vibrant for contemporary audiences.

Costa, Fulchignoni, and Pacuvio did not stand completely alone in their particular approaches to directing. Other directors with a similar outlook were emerging elsewhere. In Milan, for instance, during the late 1930s and the war years, Paolo Grassi and Giorgio Strehler came to the fore in the Corrente company. While the group had a predilection for the plays of the Sicilian writer Beniamino Joppolo, they also staged many other works. Riding the wave of curiosity and eclecticism typical of those years when the end of Fascism seemed imminent and people were looking forward to radical changes, their readings and experimental stagings followed one another in a frenzy of activity. Grassi, as the Corrente group's director and theoretician, attempted to find a way into theater spaces that the more liberal arm of Fascism had opened up. He and Strehler would become the founders of Milan's Piccolo Teatro (Little Theater) in 1947, Grassi as managing director and Strehler as artistic director.

Vito Pandolfi finished his courses at the academy in 1939 and in 1941 directed his first piece, a collage of texts featuring Pulcinella. In 1942, drawing on the works of Ernest Hemingway[12] and of Saint Teresa of Avila, he wrote and directed *The Dance of Death*. In directing the work, he attempted to realize Adolphe Appia's ideas about rhythmic space and was inspired by André Masson's and Pablo Picasso's drawings and paintings of bullfights. His various theoretical allusions to Edmund Husserl, Søren Kierkegaard, Friedrich Nietzsche, and even Antonin Artaud, whose *Theater and Its Double* he had read, added further nourishment to a highly imaginative production that did not fail to make an impression on the spectators. In 1943 he staged a *Beggar's Opera,* which was inspired by both John Gay and Brecht; set in the 1920s, the play made clear references to Fascism. The cast included a young and acrobatic Vittorio Gassman. The production was closed down, despite ovations on its opening night, but the authorities could not prevent Pandolfi from continuing to be provocative in productions reflecting the outlook of an atheistic existentialist, such as his 1943 staging of *Life Is A Dream* by Calderón de la Barca—not in its play version but in the version Calderón wrote as an *auto-sacramental*.

Giorgio Strehler began as an actor and did not make his directorial debut until 1943 when he presented three one-act plays by Pirandello: *The Man with the Flower in his Mouth, At the Gate, Dream (But Perhaps Not)*. Luigi Veronesi's abstract scenery and the actors' colorful, clownish wigs were particularly noted. The first part of Strehler's career was quite extraordinary for the tremendous energy he expended in producing a vast repertory and for the leading role he played in the theater of a modern postwar Italy undergoing reconstruction.

A quick review of the plays Strehler directed during his first three years at the Piccolo Teatro, 1947–1950, provides ample proof of his extraordinary energy and of his eclectic repertory: Pirandello's *The Mountain Giants* and *Tonight We Improvise,* Aleksander N. Ostrovsky's *The Storm,* Fyodor Dostoevsky's *Crime and Punishment* as adapted by Gaston Baty, Shakespeare's *Richard II, Richard III, The Tempest,* and *The Taming of the Shrew,* T. S. Eliot's *Murder in the Cathedral,* Carlo Goldoni's *Arlecchino, servitore di due padroni (Arlecchino, Servant of Two Masters),* Carlo Gozzi's *Il corvo* (The crow), Anton Chekhov's *The Seagull,* Maxim Gorky's *Lower Depths,* Thornton Wilder's *The Skin of Our Teeth,* Bontempelli's *Gente del tempo* (Period folk) adapted by Ivo Chiesa, Albert Camus' *The Just,* Henri Becque's *The Parisian Woman,* Henrik Ibsen's *Little Eyolf,* and Savinio's *Alcesti di Samuele,* which was followed by Goldoni's *La putta onorata* (The respectable girl) in Venice and *Sofonisba* by Giambattista Trissino.

Strehler's soaring star was somewhat dislodged from its course by the scathing criticism that met the opening night performance of *Alcesti di Samuele* by Alberto Savinio on January 1, 1950. Strehler was subsequently forced to moderate his directorial experiments, to select a less eclectic repertory, and generally to follow safer paths. His productions of Brecht demonstrated his social commitment, and in them he experimented further with language.

Luchino Visconti, self-taught director of the 1943 film *Obsession,* began his career as a theater director in 1945 with Jean Cocteau's *Les parents terribles,* a production he financed himself. He then began to alternate contemporary French and American plays with works by Pierre-Augustin Caron de Beaumarchais, Shakespeare, Chekhov, and Goldoni. He proved his commitment to realism in superior productions, achieved largely by exercising strict control over his actors and over the stage picture; he kept an eye on every detail of production and made use of the best technology available.

In the early postwar period in Italy, Costa and Visconti represented two opposing ideals in the conflict over directing. But while an ideal can have an impact on the imagination, it often makes little difference in everyday life. And, in effect, both Costa's and Visconti's visions were too extreme for their time given the political environment and the economic prospects of postwar Italian theater. Of course, no one could stop these directors from working, but their impact was neutralized because they were treated as exceptions. Other outstanding directors included Ettore Giannini, Gerardo Guerrieri, Ruggero Jacobbi, and, as already mentioned, Pandolfi, Fulchignoni, and Pacuvio. They were either marginalized and reduced to silence, or they were forced to change careers.

Those who remained—Giorgio Strehler, Gianfranco de Bosio, and Luigi Squarzina, who functioned as artistic directors of the first public theaters in Italy—suffered political and economic censorship. In addition, theater in southern Italy and all other dialect theater came to be considered second-class and was pushed aside. Even Eduardo De Filippo, the great proponent of Neapolitan theater, began "Italianizing" his dialogue in the 1930s.

De Filippo can be viewed as a descendant of the Italian tradition of the actor-author, a tradition that continued with artists such as Dario Fo, Carmelo Bene, Paolo Poli, and later, Carlo Cecchi, Leo de Berardinis, and others. This tradition and its modern variations will be considered in a second volume.

Translated by Jane House and Daniela Cavallero

Notes

1. Roberto Bracco, article in *Corriere di Napoli,* collected in *Tra le arti e gli artisti* (Naples, 1919).

2. Ugo Ojetti, article in *Pegaso,* one of numerous journals he edited over the years.

3. James Gordon Bennett, "Talks with Gabriele d'Annunzio," *New York Herald,* Paris edition, October 10, 1897, p. 5.

4. (New York: French, 1939).

5. Anton Giulio Bragaglia, *Del teatro teatrale; ossia, Del teatro* (Rome: Tiber, 1929), p. 16.

6. "Correspondence F. Orestano," Collection Edward Gordon Craig, Département des arts du spectacle of the Bibliothèque Nationale de Paris. Cited in Gianfranco Pedullà, "Edward Gordon Craig e la mancata riforma del teatro italiano" (Edward Gordon Craig and the lost chance of reforming the Italian theater), *Il castello di Elsinore* 4, no. 10 (1991): 42–43.

7. Pedullà, "Edward Gordon Craig," p. 36ff. For further information about the Volta Conference and Italian theater in the first part of the century, see also Franca Angelini, *Teatro e spettacolo nel primo Novecento* (Theater and spectacle in the early 1900s) (Rome: Laterza, 1988).

8. Tatiana Pavlova, "Dal copione alla ribalta" (From script to stage), *La Lettura,* Rome (May 1, 1931).

9. Claudio Meldolesi, *Fondamenti del teatro italiano: La generazione dei registi* (Foundations of Italian theater: The generation of directors) (Florence: Sansoni, 1984), pp. 44–46.

10. Il corifeo [Vito Pandolfi], "Regia," *Roma fascista,* Rome (September 4, 1940).

11. Giovanni Gentile (1875–1944) was a major Italian philosopher between the two wars, along with Benedetto Croce. His philosophy consisted of a reform of Hegel and was called actualism. His philosophy was influential only in Italy and only during the period in question here, but his mystic idealism influenced many young Italian intellectuals. He was an adherent of the Salò Republic and was murdered by anti-Fascist partisans.

12. See Claudio Meldolesi, *Fondamenti del teatro italiano,* p. 75, note 64.

ONE

GABRIELE

D'ANNUNZIO

Introduction

Gabriele d'Annunzio was born in Pescara on March 12, 1863. His gifts as a writer and poet became apparent at an early age, and he received the first public acknowledgment of his work in the Roman journal *Fanfulla della Domenica* (May 2, 1880). In 1881 he enrolled in the Faculty of Letters at the University of Rome, where he joined the literary milieu and was invited into Rome's fashionable circles. He collaborated on several reviews and wrote society columns. In 1883 he married Maria Hardouin of the noble Gallese family who would bear him three sons: Mario, Gabriele, and Veniero. While writing about the theater in society magazines, he wrote *La cantata di calen d'aprile* (Song of the kalend of April), which was not a play but incorporated dialogue. His most successful works before meeting Eleonora Duse were his poetry, his lyrical works, and his novels: *Il piacere* (*The Child of Pleasure*), *Giovanni Episcopo* (*Episcopo and Company*), and *L'innocente* (*The Victim*).

After meeting Duse in Venice in 1894 and learning that she was bored with her repertory, d'Annunzio took it upon himself to create "modern tragedy." His theatrical adventures began in 1897 with *Sogno d'un mattino di primavera* or *A Spring Morning's Dream,* which is presented here. In 1898 the poet and the actress began to maintain separate abodes across the street from one another in Settignano, a village near Florence. *Il fuoco* (*The Flame of Life,* 1900), a novel, grew out of this relationship; in it, d'Annunzio also imaginatively described his theatrical project for an outdoor theater in Rome. The d'Annunzio-Duse association ended in 1904, shortly before the triumph of d'Annunzio's verse drama *La figlia di Iorio* (*The Daughter of Jorio*).

In 1911, following financial embarrassment and the banning of his work, d'Annunzio went into voluntary exile in Paris, where he lived until 1915. During that time he wrote in French and Italian for the stage and cinema although he considered film a minor form for the writer. His dramatic output stopped in 1914 with *Il ferro,* (The sword; published as *The Honeysuckle*). During World War I, he called for Italian intervention against Germany. His patriotic speeches to the troops and his bravery at the front won him various military honors and made him an Italian war hero. Between 1919 and 1920 he headed the occupation of Fiume, a city of Istria considered to have been unjustly taken away from Italy during the peace negotiations following the war. D'Annunzio eventually settled down in a villa at Gardone Riviera, on Lake Garda. He made the villa and its gardens into a monument to the heroism of Italians and the estate became known as *Il Vittoriale degli italiani.* In 1927 Gioacchino Forzano, the Fascist playwright and director who would coauthor several plays with Mussolini, mounted a memorable production of *La figlia di Iorio* in the gardens of Il Vittoriale. In 1937 d'Annunzio was nominated president of the Royal Academy of Italy. He died at Gardone Riviera on March 1, 1938.

Two factors have contributed to the difficulty of reading d'Annunzio's work. The first is his language. D'Annunzio struggled with a language undergoing change. The language of all Italians had been rooted in dialects for centuries. However, at the turn of the century an attempt was being made to create a language that would unify a nation with an imperial dream. D'Annunzio rejected a simplified everyday language and strove to create a "classical" one. He yearned for a language that was sublime, imperial, and ecumenical, as Latin once was. D'Annunzio's linguistic labors went through various phases or trial periods, and he experimented relentlessly with different verse forms. As a result, his writing is alien to succeeding generations who have grown up with a simplified functional language, the language of the mass media. The second difficulty is that prejudice against d'Annunzio as a reactionary and decadent figure has led to a belittlement of his work as a playwright. In fact, an objective assessment of his theatrical output was undertaken only recently, and there still exist few complete studies that restore him to his proper place in the pantheon of twentieth-century theater.

As often happens, theater practitioners preceded scholars in reexamining d'Annunzio as a playwright. The reevaluation of d'Annunzio that rejected the standard view of him as the mouthpiece for Fascist ideas was due, first, to the insights of three directors who staged his work in the 1970s and 1980s and, second, to a 1989 collection of scholarly papers entitled *Gabriele d'Annunzio: Grandezza e delirio nell'industria dello spettacolo* (Gabriele d'Annunzio: Grandeur and delirium in the theatrical industry).[1] The directors referred to above—Aldo Trionfo, Giancarlo Cobelli, Roberto De Simone—staged memorable productions of *Giovanni Episcopo, La città morta,* and *La figlia di Iorio,* which enlightened many young people. The scholars, whose thirteen papers appeared in the collection already cited, argued that it was necessary to reassess d'Annunzio's place in the history of theater and to rethink the ways in which his works should be staged. Valentina Valentini[2] recognizes d'Annunzio as one of the originators of contemporary theater because he created a ritualistic style of drama. Silvana Sinisi discusses *Le martyre de Saint Sébastien* (1911), a mystery play in French and in verse written for the dancer Ida Rubinstein, with music by Claude Debussy and sets and costumes by Leon Bakst.[3] She reveals the breadth of experimentation in this total theater piece: d'Annunzio united poetry, music, dance, and figurative art, fused Greco-Roman, Asiatic, and Judeo-Christian figures and legends with mystic medieval themes and paganism, and even went so far as to stimulate the audience's senses by combining colored lights and sound with olfactory stimuli (incense, aromas, perfumes).[4]

Several scholars addressed the topic of d'Annunzio and the role of the director. Paolo Puppa writes, "Of course, d'Annunzio often calls for spectacular solutions, demanding such a variety of techniques, such accuracy, such a superabundance of multimedia that he anticipates the central role of the *director,* which only took hold [in Italy] during the period following World War II."[5] According to Paolo Bosisio,[6] d'Annunzio's most significant work comprised his experiments in directing and his attempts to modernize the Italian stage. As a director d'Annunzio loved grandiosity and large casts but at the same time he demanded "perfection in everything down to the smallest detail."[7] He gave preliminary readings of his plays, those he was going to stage, to the actors; they were accomplished at one sitting, without interruption, and were both ceremonial and majestical, showing great confidence in the stage event.

A Spring Morning's Dream evokes a Pre-Raphaelite atmosphere. Two colors are held in balance in this "tragic poem," as d'Annunzio called it, the life-giving green of spring and the blood red of death. Duse played Isabella, the young woman who has been driven mad after lying all night with her murdered lover in her arms. She appears in two of the five scenes. The actress interpreted Isabella as living in a dream. Her gestures and her costume of green voile made her seem ethereal and weightless. Cesare Molinari's examination of Duse's personal script[8] has shown that despite Duse's objections a large part of her final monologue or "song" was probably cut. Additional markings in the script pinpoint the passages and stage directions Duse interpreted as signposts for the emotional changes in her character or, in other words, for giving theatrical and organic form to the text. It has been deduced that Duse brought a great deal of physical expression to the text, thereby creating a strong sense of truth—which was almost unbearable for many spectators.

Shortly after the first production at the Théâtre de la Renaissance in Paris on June 15, 1897, Sarah Bernhardt, one of Duse's greatest rivals, performed Isabella in a French translation of the play.

A. A.

Trans. J. H.

Notes

1. *Gabriele d'Annunzio: Grandezza e delirio nell'industria dello spettacolo,* Atti del Convegno Internazionale di Torino, 21–23 Marzo 1988, Centro Regionale Universitario per il Teatro del Piemonte (Genova: Costa & Nolan, 1989).

2. Valentina Valentini, "L'attore virtuale e l'attore reale nel teatro di Gabriele d'Annunzio," (The virtual actor and the real actor in Garbiele d'Annunzio's plays) in *Gabriele d'Annunzio: Grandezza e delirio nell'industria dello spettacolo,* pp. 186–212.3. Opened at the Châtelet, Paris, May 22, 1911.

4. Silvana Sinisi, "Il San Sebastiano di d'Annunzio" (d'Annunzio's Saint Sebastian), in *Gabriele d'Annunzio: Grandezza e delirio nell'industria dello spettacolo,* pp. 107–21.

5. Paolo Puppa, "Mitologie teatrali nella scena dannunziana: Dal *Fuoco* alla *Fedra*" (Theatrical mythologies on the Dannunzian stage: From *Flame* to *Phaedra*), in *Gabriele d'Annunzio: Grandezza e delirio nell'industria dello spettacolo,* p. 40.

6. Paolo Bosisio, "Gabriele d'Annunzio: La regia teatrale e l'allestimento scenico" (Gabriele d'Annunzio: Theatrical directing and staging), in *Gabriele d'Annunzio: Grandezza e delirio nell'industria dello spettacolo,* pp. 141–70.

7. Ibid., p. 157.

8. Cesare Molinari, *L'attrice divina* (Rome: Bulzoni, 1985), pp. 181–83.

■

A SPRING MORNING'S DREAM

A Tragic Poem

(Sogno d'un mattino di primavera, 1897)

Translated by Anthony Oldcorn

■

PÀNFILO'S SONG[1]

Per una ghirlandetta
Ch'io vidi, mi farà
Sospirar ogni fiore.

Al mio giardin soletta
La mia donna verrà
Coronata da Amore.

Ha nome Simonetta
La donna che sarà
Regina del mio core.

Per una paroletta
Il mio cor non saprà
Mai più che sia dolore.

O Amore, aspetta, aspetta!
Chi non ama, amerà;
Ti lauderà Signore.

---

1. In the Italian original, Pànfilo's song, whose first three lines are those of a ballad by Dante, is a good example of d'Annunzio's "variations on a theme."—Trans.

Diman l'avrai soggetta
La fera che non sa
Qual sia lo tuo valore.
Per una ghirlandetta!

—

Al for a garlande faire
That ones my love did weare,
I sigh for each flower.

Al in my garden faire,
She shal Love's garlande weare,
Alone for an hour.

Quene is the maiden faire:
Simone that name doth beare,
Quene of my heart.

Al for a word from her
My heart shal never beare
Sorrow or smart.

Prithee, my love, forbeare:
Love-not true love shal sweare,
Praise Love her Lord.

Ere long Love's servant were
She who would never heare
Of Love's worth a word.
Al for a garlande faire!

Dramatis Personae

THE MADWOMAN [ISABELLA] BEATRICE

VIRGINIO

THE DOCTOR

TEODATA

SIMONETTA

PÀNFILO

The curtain opens on a vast loggia, bright and peaceful, in an ancient villa in Tuscany, the Villa Armiranda. A row of stone columns overlooks the garden, giving the loggia the appearance of the wing of a cloister. In each of the two lateral walls is a door with a sculptured architrave, flanked by two statues on pedestals. Through the slender arches, whose sole ornament is the swallow's nest, a garden is visible, divided by quickset hedges of cypress and box, out of which grow, at regular intervals, dense evergreen alaternus bushes clipped in the shape of round urns. In the middle of the garden stands a stone wellhead. Over it a wrought-iron grapevine, its tendrils and grape clusters rusty, serves as a device for lowering the wellbuckets. To the right and left, along the garden walls, extend jutting roofs in whose shelter young citrus trees thrive in large reddish clay pots arranged in rows on stepped benches. Beyond the gate at the back, one can see wild uncultivated woodland, and in it the play of the morning sunlight, a vision of untrammeled strength and joy. On the portico, at the bases of the columns, stand a large number of pots of flowering lilies-of-the-valley, their green infinitely tender in its childlike delicacy in contrast with the seasoned old hedges. All the grace of the early spring is diffused over the austere and gloomy spectacle presented by the symmetrical forms of the dark evergreens. As a result, the garden conjures up the human image of a careworn face crowned with a garland of fresh flowers.

Scene 1

Below the loggia, **PÀNFILO** *the gardener is busy pruning a young orange tree, fresh from the greenhouse and just about to blossom, which stands in a pot atop an upturned capital. The young housekeeper* **SIMONETTA** *stands next to him following the work of his expert hands with bemused and fascinated eyes.* **PÀNFILO** *(sings):*

> Al for a garlande faire
> That ones my love did weare,
> I sigh for each flower.

> Al in my garden faire
> She shal Love's garlande weare,
> Alone for an hour . . .

Tomorrow the whole garden will be in bloom . . . Myriads of flowers . . . I never saw a finer season. The bees will have plenty of nectar to suck this year at Villa Armiranda! The humming under the shelters is deafening. Bees and swallows busy all over the place: beehives and swallows' nests . . . What's on your mind, Simonetta. Your garland?

SIMONETTA *(shaking off her languor):* What garland?

PÀNFILO: Your wedding garland.

SIMONETTA: Lucky you, Pànfilo, you always have a smile on your lips! I was just about to fall asleep on my feet. I can hardly keep my eyes open. Last night there wasn't much sleep to be had at Villa Armiranda . . . And now, with all those bees making their golden murmur . . . Oh, I'd love to go to sleep down there in the long grass till noon. Lucky you!

PÀNFILO: You spent a sleepless night, did you? On account of Donna Isabella? Was she on edge?

SIMONETTA: She never got a minute's rest. I stayed with her for hours and hours, on the terrace, in the moonlight, braiding and unbraiding her hair. Every now and then she would ask me if I could see her hair getting white . . . It was a cool night, and she was freezing in that thin dress, her teeth were chattering. What a pitiful sight! Whenever I managed to persuade her to go inside, she would get up, take a few steps toward the door; then, all of a sudden, she'd start shaking with fear. And she'd cry out: "No, no . . . He's there, he's there, behind the door . . ." Oh, if you could only hear her voice at times like that! You start thinking there really is somebody behind the door . . . We stayed like that until daybreak . . . Moonlight like I never saw before . . . The owls hooting . . . It made my blood run cold . . . Donna Beatrice came down too. She stood there in tears, by the railing . . .

PÀNFILO: Poor creature! I feel sorrier for her than I do for the madwoman, seeing her sacrificed like that . . . with no one to love her . . .

SIMONETTA: Love, is that all you think about?

PÀNFILO: What about you? (*pause*)

SIMONETTA: Just look where love gets you!

PÀNFILO: When it's not blessed.

SIMONETTA: Let it be blessed then! I'm speaking for Donna Beatrice . . .

PÀNFILO: For Donna Beatrice? That young gentleman, then, who comes here on horseback . . .

SIMONETTA: I don't know, I don't know.

PÀNFILO: Who is he? Don't you know?

SIMONETTA: It's his brother . . .

PÀNFILO: Brother? Whose brother?

SIMONETTA: The dead man's brother.

PÀNFILO: The dead man's?

SIMONETTA: The brother of the man who was killed, in Donna Isabella's room at Poggio Gherardi, by the duke . . .

PÀNFILO: Oh, I see. And now he comes . . .

SIMONETTA: I don't know.

PÀNFILO: I saw him the other morning roaming about in the woods. He looks very young, not much more than peach fuzz on his cheeks. He had tied his horse to a tree, and he seemed to be waiting for somebody, to be on the lookout for somebody. Does he come to see Donna Beatrice?

SIMONETTA: I don't know.

PÀNFILO: But doesn't the spilled blood come between them? Weren't the two brothers in love with the two sisters once upon a time?

SIMONETTA: Maybe . . . I don't know . . .

PÀNFILO: Tell me, is it true that the other one was killed in the arms of Donna Isabella, right there in her arms, in her bosom, while he was sleeping; and she was all drenched with his blood, and she spent the whole night with the corpse in her arms, and next morning she was crazy?

SIMONETTA: Ask the old woman. She knows everything.

PÀNFILO: And now his brother . . . But is Donna Beatrice in love with him? Was she waiting for him to come back? She was sobbing last night with the owls . . . Poor creature! Aren't there ever times when she confides in you?

SIMONETTA (*listening*): Do you hear a voice? It's the doctor. He's talking to the old woman on the stairs . . . I'm off.

PÀNFILO: Where are you off to? Be a good girl! Come into the greenhouse. Listen to me once in a while. I have something to tell you . . . Simonetta! Simonetta!

(*He follows her, as she goes off down the garden between the cypress hedges.*)

Scene 2

Through the door on the left, the old housekeeper, **TEODATA**, *enters, accompanied by the* **DOCTOR**.

TEODATA: It's the spring, it's the spring . . . It brings everything back to life. Even the blood blooms again. All it took the other day was the sight of a red rose.

DOCTOR: That color must be kept out of her sight, Teodata.

TEODATA: It caught us off-guard. Nobody knew it was there, hidden in the rose garden, among all the white ones. It even hoodwinked the gardener. The poor soul cried out when she saw it and started trembling all over; her eyes dilated again with all the horror of that night . . . Then she plucked it and put it in her bosom and folded her arms over it . . . And she spoke words which pierced my heart . . . Yesterday she insisted on lying down at the edge of the fishpond and trailing her hair in the water to steep it like a bundle of flax . . . She can feel the stain on her again . . . Ah, how can I forget? Her hair, her hair especially was sodden with it, matted together with clotted blood, and we just couldn't wash it out . . . She kept laughing and laughing in the bath as we scrubbed her, she laughed without stopping, without taking a breath. I can still see her, I can still hear her . . . Oh, I'll hear it forever, that laughter, that shriek . . . It was like the chain on a wellbucket that keeps running out without ever hitting the bottom . . . Our hands were like ice.

DOCTOR: You were there; you know everything . . . Did you ever see his brother at the time, that young man who came . . . ?

TEODATA (*in a tone of almost maternal tenderness*): Virginio?

DOCTOR: Oh, his name is Virginio? He came to see me, to talk to me . . .

TEODATA: I know, I know.

DOCTOR: Has he talked with you too?

TEODATA: Yes, with me too.

DOCTOR: He arrived unannounced, all keyed up, his horse lathered in sweat, as if to call me to the bedside of someone who was dying . . . It was as if he had come from far, far away, over rivers and woods . . . I had never seen him before. At first, when I saw him standing there in front of me without speaking, with those sapphire blue eyes all ablaze, I was seized with a strange feeling of awe. I don't know why, but the first thing that came to my mind was that he was a child of the Spring . . . You know: it was in that visiting room of mine, where all I see every morning are my poor pale-faced patients with their complaints . . . I could sense the presence of a life-giving force, as one senses the presence of a thousand spores in each breath of wind that wafts across the open countryside . . . I know you understand me. Nothing is hidden from your divining heart . . . We two are old, but no one is more fitted than us to perceive the light of youth . . . Oh, what a light that is! He was saturated with fresh sunlight, his whole being was compounded of pristine and feverish beauties. There was something so "new" about him, something indescribable: he was—how shall I put it—like a human child the Spring had given birth to . . . In that one moment, as he stood there before me without speaking, I grasped all of the rapture of the world. In his silence he spoke the things that only grass, wind, and water can express . . . Perhaps he could find some miraculous word to say to this poor lost soul.

TEODATA (*with a glimmer of hope*): Do you think he could? Oh, could he? He has asked to see her . . . He could, could he, Doctor? . . .

DOCTOR: When he asked to see her, it was as if he were saying: "Let me work the miracle!" He came from far off, at full gallop, through the springtime, as if driven by an unshakable faith. It was as though he had been sent to accomplish some gesture that would brook no delay. He must have dreamed long and deep to have such faith in the occult power of his dream . . . And he must have loved immensely . . . (*pause*) And yet, he is the brother of the man who was killed. He can only see her through a veil of blood, his own blood . . . Does he carry some secret inside him? Tell me.

TEODATA: Oh, what sorrow!

DOCTOR: Tell me.

TEODATA: It is a great sorrow.

DOCTOR: He too? Was he in love with her too?

TEODATA: Oh yes, I know; perhaps I am the only one who does know . . . More than once on summer nights at Poggio Gherardi I would hear his desperate sobbing on the far side of the rose hedge ravaged by his frenzied hands . . . I have seen him spend an entire night, stock-still like a statue, against the wall, his eyes glued to a lighted window . . . I have seen him kneel upon the ground she had trodden as she passed and kiss with his lips the blades of grass that bore the trace of her footsteps. How pitiful, how touching! He knew this old woman had guessed his secret; he could sense that a mother's heart was suffering his anguish, and he didn't dare speak, but his eyes became gentle, almost filial, when they met mine . . . Those dear childlike eyes scorched by so cruel a fever! They were so enormous, some days, they seemed to consume his entire face. At times like that, it was as if his soul would leap up out of his limbs like a flame from tinder-dry firewood . . . It seemed as though every flicker of his eyelids would make his whole body quiver, like the wind that douses and fans the flames of a bonfire . . .

DOCTOR: What images, Teodata! Who is it prompts you to speak that way? You missed nothing . . . You never miss anything . . . Life reveals itself to you in lightning flashes, as it does to a seer . . . (*pause*) And you've spent all these years patiently reading at the bedside of an invalid! Books haven't weakened your eyesight! . . . And tell me, wasn't she aware of it? And what about his brother? Tell me.

TEODATA: I don't know . . . I've always had a suspicion in the back of my mind . . . I will never forget the day we came upon him unexpectedly in a deserted corner of the park. I was walking Isabella in the park, alone. She was on edge, anxious, already prey to a dark foreboding, but I could sense too that she was fascinated by the fate she could not avoid, in the grip of the fever of her passion and guilt, heedless of any way out, drawn on by a kind of terrible craving toward that pool of blood already glimmering in the dark so close at hand . . . A rustling in the leaves betrayed the presence of someone stumbling through the tangled underbrush. It was Virginio. Isabella recognized him and called out his name. He stopped a short distance from her, and I realized she was trembling. Perhaps she understood; perhaps she could still feel those searing eyes on her, even though she herself was on fire. He didn't look like a human being, he looked like some wood-spirit, a creature wild and gentle at the same time, weaned on the juices of those roots witches strain into their love philters. His torn clothes and his hair were besprinkled with leaves, berries, thorns . . . as if he had had to defend himself angrily against the encroachment of the branches. He was panting and trembling beneath Isabella's gaze, and he seemed to shrink, as if he wanted the untamed earth to swallow him up. No sooner did he hear the sound of the first question she asked him than he took to his heels, plunging blindly into the thicket like a startled buck. And that was the last we saw of him. The silence all around us was total. The leaves still trembled on the branches he had crashed through as he fled. She looked at me in bewilderment. Had she understood? Or was that apparition—which had nothing about it to prove it was real—was it forever confused with the violent dream that possessed her? And that unbroken silence all around us, a deathly silence. I'll never forget it. (*pause*)

DOCTOR: Oh! what a maelstrom of life swirled beneath your soul in that silence! How could you forget it?

TEODATA (*thinking back*): It was the end of September. Some of the leaves were already dead or dying. I remember: she had gone on a little way ahead; a dead twig got caught in the hem of her dress and began to scrape along the ground. Then, all at once, a sob rose up in my throat. The face of her dying mother came back to me, repeating: "Watch over her, watch over her, Teodata!" On the threshold of death, her mother had sensed the mysterious danger that lay in wait for this timid and headstrong soul. And she kept repeating: "Watch over her, watch over her!" And I failed to watch over her, I was unable to save her. She's been engulfed in the blood she adored, neither dead nor alive.

DOCTOR: Who knows! Who knows! Maybe she is alive, with a life deeper and vaster than ours. She's not dead; she has made her descent into absolute mystery. We are not familiar with the laws her life obeys now. But they are divine laws, I'm certain of that.

TEODATA: She is further from us than if she were in a tomb.

DOCTOR: And yet, Teodata, sometimes she's so close that she seems to pluck with her musical fingers certain chords within us which would sleep forever if she did not rouse them.

TEODATA (*going to the door and listening*):   Is she still asleep? (*pause*)

PÀNFILO (*voice off, singing at the end of the garden*):

> Quene is the maiden faire:
> Simone that name doth beare,
> Quene of my heart . . .

TEODATA: She's asleep. Seeing her sleep, no one would ever know the curse that is on her, would he? If I look at her when she's asleep, it's as if I were seeing her face pure once again on its virginal pillow. Her brow is still suffused with that aura of supreme melancholy. It was her most beautiful feature when she was still in her mother's house waiting for a sign from her destiny.

DOCTOR: It's true. It's as if her former soul returns at times to float upon her sleep like a rootless flower upon becalmed waters.

TEODATA: I sometimes think her eyes are looking at me through diaphanous lids, with their old innocent expression. Oh, if only she could wake up completely renewed! Could she, perhaps; could she, Doctor?

DOCTOR: It could happen. Perhaps nothing inside her has been really destroyed, nothing really deformed. Don't you have the impression that at times her face lights up with something like the light of a transfiguration?

TEODATA: Oh yes, the miracle, the miracle! If Virginio were to see her, talk to her . . .

DOCTOR: He will see her.

TEODATA: When?

DOCTOR: This morning, maybe; soon.

TEODATA: Will she know him? What will she say to him? What will he say to her? What dream did he dream?

DOCTOR: A marvelous dream, that's for sure.

TEODATA: Some extraordinary illusion must have inspired his life since that autumn morning when he came to the door to receive his brother's pale corpse.

DOCTOR (*with a start*):   Did he come to the door himself?

TEODATA: Virginio himself, with two servants, shortly after daybreak, as soon as he got the news. The body was handed over wrapped in a sheet. I could see him from a window. He uncovered his brother's face and looked at him for what seemed like an age, then he kissed him on the forehead, for so long it seemed he could no longer tear his lips from the frigid brow. He followed the two servants across the park through the mist, as they carried the body to his mother. Oh, if he had heard the shrieks of the madwoman who had held his murdered brother in her arms all night and had been steeped in his blood down to the last drop. Oh, if he had seen how daubed she was! . . . (*pause*) What dream can he have dreamed after that?

DOCTOR (*becoming impassioned*):   A marvelous dream, Teodata, into which all the rapture of the world flooded in inexhaustible torrents—a divine and youthful dream in which death and life became one and the same thing, infinitely greater and more beautiful than either life or death themselves . . . Oh, I know what it's like, I know what it's like . . . You know what it's like . . . You remember . . . One April day, when our hearts were a wellspring of joy, we too once felt all our strength suddenly ebb from us, melt away, disperse to the very ends of the horizon like an evanescent mist, leaving us in a void like a languorous dying. And then all at once, from the ends of the horizon, flooding back upon us, what felt like a legion of hurricanes, reinforced with a thousand fresh energies, fervent with all the spirits of spring, mighty with all the powers of the earth, flashing and thundering through a sky too narrow to hold them; and our souls under their onslaught dilated beyond human limits, and our every thought converted into a thought of pure beauty, the proudest of our dreams tempting our will like a miracle not needing the slightest effort . . . Oh yes, I know what it's like . . . That's how it feels, that's how it feels . . . When he appeared before me, he seemed to have come from far, far away, carried on the whirlwind of that power, over rivers and woods, to perform a miracle. What miracle? What is it he wants? What is he seeking? Perhaps not even he knows. For him she is intangible, inaccessible, beyond that veil of blood . . . I don't believe he can live any longer without seeing her once more, even if it's only for a moment. And he will see her, and nothing will be accomplished, and all that immense impetuous force will dissipate like a drop of water.

TEODATA (*wearily*):   Nothing will be accomplished. What about our hope? The hope that was beginning to stir?

DOCTOR: We must wait . . . This is a terrible and holy moment, Teodata. He will stand there before her with his hidden love, fashioned of tears, silence, frenzy; he will behold her, consecrated by his brother's blood, borne aloft in a mystery more mournful than death; and with a religious gesture he will lay at her feet, like a sublime offering, that love of his, that dream of his . . . And she will speak some gentle childlike words. And hearing her he will think perhaps that he is dying . . .

TEODATA (*consumed with anxiety*):   But what if she were to be released from her madness? What if the miracle were to occur? What then?

DOCTOR: What then? Perhaps she would no longer be able to live. Perhaps neither of them would be able to live any longer . . .

TEODATA (*starting and listening*):   His horse neighed in the wood.

VOICE OF PÀNFILO (*singing, down at the end of the garden*):

> Al for a word from her
> My heart shal never beare
> > Sorrow or smart.
> Al for a garlande faire.

DOCTOR: Perhaps she's awakened.

TEODATA (*going toward the door, keeping her voice down*):   She's at the top of the stairs. She's coming down.

(**PÀNFILO'S** *song can still be heard, fading away over the cypress hedges.*)

Scene 3

THE MADWOMAN *appears on the threshold wearing a delicate green dress. She steps forward into the room almost furtively, smiling a vague indestructible smile.*

MADWOMAN: "Al for a garlande faire!" (*She walks slowly toward the* DOCTOR, *still smiling, holding out her hands.* TEODATA *moves to one side, then disappears through the door.*) Did you hear, Doctor, did you hear Pànfilo's song?

> Al for a word from her
> My heart shal never beare
> Sorrow or smart.
> Al for a garlande faire.

Did you hear it? It's a lovely song, Doctor, but . . .

DOCTOR (*taking her hands*): Were you asleep earlier? When I got here you were asleep by the window ledge. Such a peaceful sleep!

MADWOMAN: You saw it, didn't you? You saw it flying back and forth over my forehead? I felt it flying back and forth in my sleep. The white butterfly. When I opened my eyes, it had settled on the window ledge. Oh, if only I'd had a veil within reach to catch it in! It flew away, it disappeared out into the sunlight . . . (*She puts her fingers to her forehead, painfully.*) It's as if it had flown away from here . . . I miss it, here; I miss it, here . . . look. Oh, what a shame! I slept so well when I could feel its little wings beating, beating . . . You saw it, didn't you, Doctor? My sleep was so peaceful, so peaceful, you say . . . I dreamt I was a flower on the water.

DOCTOR: It will come back when you close your eyes again . . .

MADWOMAN: Oh, how hard it is to close my eyes, Doctor! Sometimes I think I don't have any eyelids. Did you ever hear about the princess whose eyelids fell off like two sodden leaves because she had cried too much; and then her eyes were naked day and night? Last night I . . . (*A white flash of terror goes over her face.*)

DOCTOR (*interrupting, taking her hands again, drawing her into a strip of sunlight beneath one of the arches*): Come over here in the sun! Let me look at you! You're all radiant this morning, all fresh and clean: just like in your dream, a flower on the water . . . And your dress is the color of tiny new leaves. My lady Spring!

MADWOMAN (*looking at herself*): Do you like my dress? I told Beatrice: "Make me a green dress, a very pale shade, so that when I go through the woods the tiny little green leaves won't be afraid of me." And Beatrice gave it to me, and this morning I'm wearing it for the very first time. Do you like it? Now I can lie down under the trees that are budding: they won't notice me. I'll be like the simple grass at their feet; I'll fool them with my silence. Perhaps I'll find out some of their secrets, if they think they're alone. I'll overhear what they say . . . (*She laughs a short childlike laugh.*) Then I told Beatrice: "I'll give you a nice dream in exchange." And so this morning I put on this dress and I sat down by the window ledge to dream a nice dream. The first dream was really for Beatrice. I dreamt that the husband she's waiting for was finally here. She doesn't know yet . . .

Last night, she was crying . . . Oh, how she was crying! Because she doesn't know yet . . .

> *Al for a garlande faire!*

(*She smiles in the direction of the gate, at the vision of the deep wood.*)

Have you seen her? Have you talked to her? Did she tell you about the moon's tricks?

DOCTOR: What tricks?

MADWOMAN: When the moon sees me, she likes to play tricks with my imagination. But I don't get upset. Oh, no. Because she's so gentle when she bathes me in her milk . . . She's as gentle as a nurse playing with her baby . . . (*She breaks off and puts her forefinger to her lips to enjoin silence.*) Do you hear that silvery tinkling? (*She remains silent for a few moments, bending over like someone tuning an instrument.*) How faint it is! Can you hear it?

DOCTOR: It's the humming of the bees.

MADWOMAN: Oh, no, no . . . You can't hear it.

DOCTOR: I'm an old man. My hearing's not as sharp as it used to be.

MADWOMAN: Your hair is white, Doctor. Mine . . . is not white. (*Once more, a flash of terror steals across her face.*) And I've done all I could to make it white! Only yesterday I held it in the water for a full hour, steeping it like flax. And all last night Simonetta beat it with her hands, beneath the moon . . . Doctor, have you ever seen linen on an August night, fresh from the scutchmill, how white it is? From a distance it's as white as snow. So I asked Simonetta: "Then is it as white as those bundles of flax in the yard at Laudomia?" But she answered something different. Simonetta always answers something different . . . She doesn't listen; she always has something else on her mind . . . So I asked her: "Do you see that white peacock on the balcony railing?" Yes, that's it, I was going to tell you about the moon's tricks . . . I could see a beautiful white peacock on the railing. Do you know the story of Madonna Dianora here at the Villa Armiranda? Didn't I ever show you the portrait of her by Desiderio da Settignano: that little bust made out of marble so golden and delicate it looks like petrified honey? It used to be up in my room, but now Teodata has taken it away, because every time I would see it I'd start to weep . . . I'd take it on my knees and I'd hold it (it wasn't too heavy), and I could see her face and neck wearing away under my fingers more and more each day. Oh, what a face! If you could only see it! It's like a half-opened almond shell with the tender fruit showing inside it. All encased in the smooth hair, as if in a husk, as far down as the chin, and the hair gathered up in a net . . . Just looking at it is enough to bring the tears to your eyes . . . Teodata was afraid I'd wear it out if I kept on crying and stroking it, so she took it away!

DOCTOR: You mustn't weep. Teodata can't bear to see you weep . . .

MADWOMAN: I wasn't crying because I was sad, not because I was sad . . . I was crying because I envied her fate. Do you know the story of Madonna Dianora?

DOCTOR: Vaguely. I don't remember all the details . . .

MADWOMAN: She was in love with a young man, Palla degli Albizi. On moonless nights, from the railing of that loggia, she would throw a silken ladder down to him in the garden, finespun as a spiderweb, tough as a coat of mail. Oh, I know how she would lean over the railing and offer up her face to his burning lips, the soft exposed almond of her face, half encased in its golden shell . . . But one night Messer Braccio caught her, pulled up the conniving ladder, and made a halter of it for her bent neck. And Dianora hung from the railing all night, under the eyes of the stars, mourned by the nightingales. At daybreak, when the bells at Impruneta began to chime, someone saw a white peacock fly away east from Villa Armiranda; and Messer Braccio found his halter empty. Since then, every so often, a white peacock visits the villa. When it alights, it is quieter and softer than a snowflake . . . I have seen it. I thought it had come back last night. And I said to Simonetta: "Do you see that white peacock on the balcony? It's the ghost of Madonna Dianora returning to the scene of her passion." And then the peacock began sobbing like a human creature; and that sobbing was a sword in my breast. And I said: "Oh peacock, oh Dianora, sweet soul, why do you weep? You mustn't weep, just think of your fate, dear sister of times that are no more. You did not see your lover die in your arms, you did not feel yourself smothering in his blood. Instead all of a sudden your throat was gripped tight by the same rope he had climbed to reach your mouth, that mouth from whose small white teeth all the light of the stars shone down upon his desire. Isabella alone must weep, only Isabella, who envies you . . ." And the white shape came nearer, and its tears bathed my hands, and a voice said: "It's me, it's Beatrice." Oh, you mustn't weep either! I have a dream of joy for you.

(*Impulsively, she stretches out her arms toward the sun; then she sways, dazzled by the light; she puts her arm around one of the columns, leans a cheek against it, and stays like that for several seconds, her eyes half-closed, panting a little.*)

DOCTOR (*in a pitying tone*): You mustn't excite yourself like that . . . You mustn't upset yourself . . . You said earlier that you wanted to be peaceful and quiet under the harmless trees . . . You must surrender yourself to the color of your dress, then, and be happy like a creature of the spring . . .

MADWOMAN (*in a hushed and mysterious voice*): Do you hear that silvery tinkling? It is the myriad and myriad little bells of the lilies-of-the valley tinkling in the breeze that stirs them. Do you hear them? (*She bends toward the mass of flowers, listening.*) It sounds like that fleeting tinkle you hear passing through the silent rooms of a house where someone is about to die. (*Pause. She gets up suddenly, with a start.*) A horse neighed in the woods. (*She leans out anxiously toward the garden with her eyes fixed on the gate at the end.*) A horse is neighing . . . Someone's here . . . The bridegroom! . . . Beatrice! Beatrice!

DOCTOR (*restraining her, uncertain what to do*): Don't call her!

MADWOMAN: Why not? Where's Beatrice?

DOCTOR (*hesitating*): Someone's here . . . Maybe she's out there . . .

MADWOMAN (*joyfully*): Has she already gone out to meet her bridegroom? So she's already with him. Oh, my dream did not lie! She's happy, after so much weeping. She's happy. I won't call her; I'll never call her again. You're right . . . I mustn't call her. If she were to look back for a moment, she would lose a moment of joy. I won't call her

. . . But I would still like to see her; I would like to see her new face, to hear her new voice. And her dear little face like the exposed white almond kernel . . . Maybe now it's all flushed. (*She smiles.*) What could I do to see her without being seen? (*She peers out toward the closed gate, through which she can see the deep wood and the play of sunlight in it.*) I will go into the wood, very quietly, without letting the gate creak. I will put on a mask of leaves, I will cover my hands with leaves. That way, I'll be all green. I can duck under the low branches, I can slip between the bushes, without being seen. I know where Beatrice will take her bridegroom . . . I know a place that she knows too . . . A magic circle in the forest. Perhaps Madonna Dianora used to go there too . . . It's like a sacred cup, a cup made of bark into which the forest pours its wine of forest scents, its purest and strongest wine, which is not for everyone's lips. Whoever drinks of it, if alone, is intoxicated and falls asleep, in a prodigious dream, in which all the roots of the forest are felt to be growing out from the most secret places of the heart. But if one isn't alone . . . (*She breaks off, suddenly distressed, overwhelmed. Her voice becomes strangled.*) There was a cup just like it, in the depths of another forest . . . It became red in autumn . . . And we never drank of it again.

DOCTOR (*in an effort to break in on that terrible thought*): Did you hear? The horse neighed again.

MADWOMAN (*drawing herself up again*): Yes, yes . . . It's neighing after them as they go off . . . Look, Doctor, look. Tell me whether Isabella and the tree are as one.

(*She runs out to the little orange tree, which is already caught by the rays of the sun. She puts her head in among the leaves. She turns toward the old man, sitting on the rim of the pot, and, holding the ends of two of the branches one in each hand, she bends them in, crossing them over her neck. She remains like this, mingled with the foliage, with her face almost covered. In the process, the wide sleeves of her dress slip down, leaving her arms bare to the elbows.*)

DOCTOR: Yes, you are as one.

MADWOMAN: I see everything green, as if my eyelids were two transparent leaves. All the veins of the leaves are silhouetted against the sunlight. The flowers are just about to blossom: like countless little half-open vials exhaling their perfume. Oh, a tiny little leaf, right next to my mouth! It's all shiny, as though it were covered with wax; my breath seems to melt it . . . How delicate and tender! I can feel it on my tongue like a consecrated wafer . . .

DOCTOR (*with an almost religious fervor, coming closer and leaning toward the living tree*): Blessèd, oh blessèd be this spring communion! May peace descend upon your spirit! Peace and freshness: all the freshness of new-sprouted leaves! Blessèd be this dress which your good sister gave you! Wear it, wear it always. Perhaps tomorrow it will blossom. May it be blessèd!

MADWOMAN: How fatherly your voice sounds! And how far-off! It's incredible how far-off everything sounds, as though I were underneath the bark: the murmur of the bees, the twittering of the swallows, and that tinkling . . . Your voice is never off key. Your words always blend in with a natural chorus, in the air, around whomever hears you. All becomes calm and pure. There are times when I would like to sit at your feet as I would at the foot of a hill, or at the mouth of a river, to receive some mysterious infinite largess.

DOCTOR: May all the blessings in the world descend upon your head and fill your soul! It is as though you too were born this instant, like that tiny leaf that is opening at the touch of your breath. I can see something childlike and divine in your eyes as they peep at me through the branches . . .

MADWOMAN: So I can become as one with the trees, the bushes, and the grass! Beatrice will pass next to me, she will brush me with her foot, without knowing me. I will see her by the side of the husband my dream has given her, all beauteous with love, all radiant with hope, after so many tears. And he will say to her . . . I know, I know the words which reveal life to those who languish and are dying. The whole world vanished like a cloud when his lips fell silent and was reborn with a word, transfigured into a miracle of joy . . . Oh! (*She lets out a cry.*) A drop of blood . . . (*With a cry of terror she breaks free of the bush, leaping forward. A branch breaks off.*) A drop of blood . . . (*Terrified, she stares at a red spot on her bared arm. A violent shiver runs through her.*)

DOCTOR (*taking her arm, reassuringly*): Don't be afraid, don't be afraid! It's not blood . . . It's just a harmless little insect that landed on your arm . . . Look: a ladybug. It's a good omen: a sign of good luck . . . Don't tremble like that! It's nothing. There now, it's gone. You see.

MADWOMAN (*still shivering, full of anguish*): It's everywhere, everywhere . . . I see it everywhere: all over me, all around me . . . Oh, Doctor, don't let me see it any more! Take this terrible thing away! . . . I thought I was pure, there, among the leaves . . . I can't, I can't . . . In the woods too, yesterday, I saw some trees, with a stain on them . . . where I was passing . . .

DOCTOR: Those were the trees marked for felling.

MADWOMAN: And red drops everywhere in the bushes . . . where I was passing . . .

DOCTOR: Those were the blackthorn berries.

MADWOMAN: I can't, I can't . . . (*She touches the hair at the back of her neck, at the temples, with a shudder, then looks at her hands.*)

DOCTOR (*taking her hands*): The lilies-of-the-valley are less white than your hands.

MADWOMAN (*staring at the broken branch hanging from the tree*): I broke off a branch! (*She goes over to the pot and bends over it in a gesture of pity and remorse.*) Oh look, what a cruel wound! It's all wet with sap. All the tree's strength will ebb out through this gash . . . And it's my fault, all my fault!

DOCTOR: Don't worry. The wound will heal. The tree will grow another branch.

MADWOMAN: But what about this one?

DOCTOR: Weave it into a garland.

(*The **MADWOMAN**'s face lights up with a childlike smile. She breaks off the branch and bends it, continuing to smile.*)

MADWOMAN:
> Al for a garlande faire
> That ones my love did weare
> I sigh for each flower!

I'll make a garland for Beatrice. Look. There are leaves and flowers on the branch: flowers that haven't yet opened. They will open on Beatrice's brow. Who'll give me a thread, a golden thread? Simonetta!

DOCTOR: Look, here comes Simonetta through the garden. I'll go now . . . Someone's waiting . . . Perhaps there's a blessing in store for you . . . Weave your garland!

MADWOMAN (*with a curtsy, smiling, suddenly gay*): Good day, my dear Doctor! (*Her eyes follow the old man as he goes over to the door on the right.*)
> Al for a word from her
> My heart shal never beare
> Sorrow or smart.
> Al for a garlande faire!

(*Repeating the words of the song, she walks slowly between the cypress hedges to meet* **SIMONETTA**. *She signals the housekeeper to open the gate, goes with her into the wood, and disappears from sight.*)

Scene 4

Enter **BEATRICE** *through the door to the right. She steps cautiously, like someone spying, peering out toward the gate through which the* **MADWOMAN** *has disappeared. She signals to the visitor, who has stopped uncertainly in the doorway.* **VIRGINIO** *comes hesitantly toward her. His whole appearance betrays his terrible anxiety. Both stand side by side for several seconds without speaking, staring at the entrance to the wood.*

VOICE OF PÀNFILO (*singing at the bottom of the garden*):
> Prithee, my love, forbeare:
> Love-not true love shal sweare,
> Praise Love her Lord.
>
> Ere long Love's servant were
> She who would never heare
> Of Love's worth a word . . .

BEATRICE (*in a hesitant, trembling voice*): She went into the wood . . . She was holding a branch . . . Maybe she'll see your horse . . . Maybe she'll come back. Listen! The horse is neighing. Did you hear it? (*She gives a start. Pause.* **VIRGINIO** *remains at her side, waiting, motionless.*) Maybe she'll come back . . . If she comes back, if she comes, will you stay here? Do you want her to find you here? . . . Are you ready for that? Or don't you think you'd better give up this risky ill-fated scheme?

VIRGINIO (*without changing position, choking with anxiety*): I must see her.

(*Pause.* **BEATRICE** *takes a step or two into the garden, between the cypress hedges, still looking.*)

BEATRICE: She's not coming back . . . Sometimes she stays in the wood for hours on end. She has a favorite place where she goes. She asked me for a green dress. She said: "Make me a green dress, a pale shade of green, so that, when I go in the woods, the tiny new leaves won't be afraid of me." She's so touching! She can say such sweet child-like things, somehow they make you feel sad and happy at the same time, like someone smiling through tears. (*Pause. She motions the visitor to a bench between two columns.*) Would you like to sit down here? (*They sit down next to each other on the stone bench.* **VIRGINIO**, *in the grip of an inner turmoil, seems unable to open his lips. He is pale and staring.*) How sweet the lilies-of-the-valley smell, and the white roses, and the daffodils! But a lot of flowers have been banished from the Villa Armiranda, so she won't see them . . . The gardener has to have eyes at the back of his head. Did you hear him singing? He's always singing; he makes up the words as he goes along. He sings and keeps a sharp lookout. But even he's not infallible. Soon it will be the poppy season. They spring up unexpectedly in the grass like a brushfire. Teodata thinks we should mow the grass before it gets too high . . . (*pause*) Do you have many flowers at Fontelucente?

VIRGINIO: Lots of roses.

BEATRICE: Your mother really loved flowers. Does she still love them?

VIRGINIO: All she loves now is her grief.

BEATRICE (*hesitantly*): Does she still suffer a great deal?

VIRGINIO (*looking her in the face, touched perhaps by the tone of her voice*): Like on the very first day!

BEATRICE: Aren't you her consolation?

VIRGINIO: She's not interested in consolation. All she wants is to brood over her grief. She loves it as she once loved the son who was taken from her.

BEATRICE: Here we never forget her name in a single one of our prayers. A humble and devout thought goes out to her every day.

VIRGINIO: She is grateful for your thoughts, and she reciprocates.

BEATRICE: She does not curse anyone then?

VIRGINIO: Ah, you don't know her heart!

BEATRICE: Has she forgiven?

VIRGINIO: For her, the gentle and heroic creature who bore supreme witness to her love in that interminable bloodbath is eternally blessed.

BEATRICE: Nothing was kept from her then?

VIRGINIO: For a soul like hers, no deception can compare in beauty to the terrible truth.

BEATRICE: And does she know you have come to Villa Armiranda?

VIRGINIO: She knows; she's waiting for me to return. She knows I have come to see Isabella. She will kiss the eyes that have seen her; she will seek her image in their depths . . . Don't you see? She knows that for one sole creature in the entire world Giuliano is not wholly dead; because that creature still feels upon her something of him, something living and warm and uncancelable, something that drives her to distraction . . . Don't you see? She has a desperate longing to see her, to touch her, to embrace her, to hold her in her arms, to speak to her, to question her; but she knows it would be her death, that her heart would stop beating at the first touch, at the first word . . . To be closer to her, to have the illusion of communicating with her through a blossoming garden, sparked by who knows what hope, who knows what expectation, she has come back to our villa at Fontelucente, which has lain practically abandoned for years. Every evening she climbs up to the highest terrace and looks in the direction of Villa Armiranda and prays . . . She prays for you too.

BEATRICE: For me?

VIRGINIO: She knows what you've sacrificed. She knows that you have given yourself up body and soul to this labor of pity and sorrow, living here as if in a cloister . . . For you she feels a mother's tenderness. She told me: "If Beatrice would only decide to come to Fontelucente some day!" Do you remember? You used to come to the Villa of the Cedars sometimes . . .

BEATRICE: I remember.

VIRGINIO: Couldn't you come to Fontelucente some day to grant my mother's wish?

BEATRICE: Yes, one day . . . (*Her voice is faint. She can no longer conceal the agitation that has come over her little by little in the course of the conversation, an agitation already betrayed by the blushes that from time to time have stolen over her delicate cheeks.*) . . . one day I'll come . . .

VIRGINIO: I'll take you there myself. It's not very far. My mother will come half-way to meet you. Perhaps she will manage a smile again when she sees you. She never smiles any more.

BEATRICE: Yes, one day I'll come, whenever you tell me . . . Two walking griefs will meet and recognize one another. Maybe they'll smile. (*Pause. Sitting side by side, they both bow their heads.*) Oh, but which grief is the crueler? At least she knows he's in peace in the grave. And I too, I know that *she* is in a deep dark grave—my sister—but she's still alive, pulsing and bleeding unstanch- able blood. I know she's on the other side, cut off, beyond recall. And yet her living eyes gaze at me imploringly; and I can't call her back, I can't draw her to me!

VIRGINIO: What about your hope? (*They look each other in the face, both prey to the same unspeakable emotion. With an involuntary gesture,* **VIRGINIO** *gets up and turns toward the wood.* **BEATRICE** *follows suit. Pause.*)

BEATRICE (*sitting back down*): She's not coming back . . . She's wearing her green dress this morning, and she's forgotten everything else. Perhaps she's happy for a moment. It's such a clear morning, each and every one of us feels he could be reborn . . .

VIRGINIO (*as if feeling his former exhilaration return to course through his veins*): Everyone feels he is about to seize the secret of beauty and joy in some mysterious way . . . Here you are in what amounts to a cloister: how can you understand? I rose at daybreak, up there on the hill, while the stars were still twinkling in the sky. Down in the valley, still plunged in shadow, I watched the river turn rosy, as though the dawn were bathing in its waters: waters so infinite and intimate they seemed to engulf and nourish my soul. Borne on the wind, I quaffed the heady spirits of all things that are renewed and, as a bourdon to the countless melodies which poured from the birds' nests, I could hear the deep and holy breathing of the Mother who nourishes each blade of grass, as well as our human thoughts. All sorrow and all desire were transformed within me into a force of inexpressible boldness and alacrity. And I spurred on my mount toward a goal, not knowing whether it was inside myself or at the farthest edge of the world. And the still dark figures of my past life were lighted with a prodigious glare, as unrecognizable as the statues in a burning temple. And I felt within me no horror of that death; on the contrary, it seemed as beautiful to me as a victim sacrificed upon an altar I could not approach, and all the blood that was spilled flowed back into my veins to swell my fraternal heart, to love again, to love again, with a purer and more distant love . . .

(*The* **MADWOMAN** *appears in the gateway at the back, on the boundary dividing garden and wood. She pauses secretively. Her face is covered with a mask of leaves, her hands are wrapped with stalks of grass. Mysterious, silent and green, like some strange plantlike apparition, she comes forward toward the loggia—unseen by the others—between the cypress hedges.*)

BEATRICE (*turned toward the visitor, trembling and spellbound, not understanding*):   And was this cloister the goal of your impassioned ride? This cloister, home to insanity and grief?

VIRGINIO: You are surprised . . . Ah, you cannot understand!

BEATRICE: If I could understand . . . (*She breaks off with a start, hearing the furtive footsteps approaching.*) She's coming. She's here . . .

(*Pale and anxious, both pairs of eyes are fixed on the silent green apparition. For several seconds there is complete silence, interrupted only by the swallows' cries, the murmur of the bees, a breath of wind.*)

Scene 5

The **MADWOMAN** *pauses beneath the arch, hesitating. In one hand, hanging down by her side, she holds the garland made from the broken branch. Her eyes are smiling, her teeth shining, through the mask of leaves. Staring at her,* **VIRGINIO** *stands stock-still, as if spell-bound, while* **BEATRICE** *makes as if to move toward her.*

BEATRICE: Isabella!

MADWOMAN: I am not Isabella. (*She takes a step forward.*) I am not Isabella. The green things took me for one of them. They are not afraid of me any more . . . We were waiting for you in the wood. We thought you would pass by, side by side, talking of your happiness. We wanted to be infinitely gentle, gentler than we had ever been before, beneath your feet, above your heads . . . Why did you disappoint us? We may never be so glad and lovely again; we may never again be so young and so light-hearted. We were all quivering in unison, with a delicious neverending tremor, for the sun was playing with us. He was playing with us like an excited child, touching us with a thousand golden fingers, with a thousand warm and nimble fingers, without ever doing us harm. His games were endless, fresh, and ever different. Oh, how he would excite us, without our ever getting tired, as though our joy could keep growing and growing and growing; and we all quivered in unison, with a sustained tremor, as if we were about to break into sudden peals of unheard laughter . . . Oh, why didn't Beatrice chance by at that moment with her husband?

(**VIRGINIO** *and* **BEATRICE** *look at each other. The* **MADWOMAN** *takes another step toward them. At the back* **SIMONETTA** *appears in the gateway and is about to enter the garden. But* **PÀNFILO**, *who has been watching from behind the hedge, goes toward her. For a few moments, they remain on the boundary; then they go off and are lost to sight in the wood.*)

In exchange for a green dress, Isabella promised Beatrice a golden dream. And a dream was dreamed by the window ledge, while Pànfilo sang a song about a garland. And in the dream was the bridegroom who came riding through the spring toward this garden. And when she awoke, Isabella carried the annunciation on her lips. But Beatrice, perhaps from that very railing by which she wept last night, having seen from far off the bridegroom her soul awaited, had already flown to meet him on the outstretched wings of her soul. Poor dove! Poor dove! (*She approaches her sister tenderly and touches the hair on her temples with her grass-wreathed hands.*)

BEATRICE (*choking with anguish*): Oh, Isabella, what are you saying?

MADWOMAN (*turning to the visitor*): Look at her, sir: how pure she is! She seems to have sprung up out of all the grief of our house, like a spring of water from a mountain in labor. She is transparent. You may place in her all that you have most precious, and you will see it shine forever inviolate in the depths of her clarity. In all the wide land there is no stream clearer, no stream in which it is sweeter to freshen one's lips or one's hands. She is as perennial as the wellspring that rises from the depths of the mountain. I commend her into your hands. She must never weep again. In each one of her tears is the lost essence of some unopened flower that might have bloomed and brought joy. She must never weep again. I will never again see her at dusk, leaning on the railing, listening to the bells that make the whole valley moist and blue like her eyes . . . Will you take her far away, sir? Very far from here?

BEATRICE (*agonized, beseeching*): Isabella, Isabella, stop saying these things! You don't understand, you don't understand . . .

MADWOMAN: Oh, don't be sorry for Isabella, don't be sad because she's left all alone! She has the dress you gave her and, on account of that, some creature will love her: some creature young and tender as you are, Beatrice. Farewell . . . (*She breaks off, remembering the garland she has in her left hand by her side. She holds it up.*) You see? While I was dreaming for you by the windowledge, Pànfilo was singing about a garland . . . You know that song:

> All for a garlande faire
> That ones my love . . .

You know the song. Now take this garland I made for you out of a branch I broke off. Alas, one can't make a garland without breaking off a branch! Look there: the wound is still fresh. (*She points to the tree with which she earlier became as one. She places the garland on* **BEATRICE**'s *bowed head. She steps back with a light and noiseless step, as if she were shod with moss. It is as if the mystery of the forest she is about to reenter were diffused over her green figure. Her voice becomes hushed.*) Farewell, farewell. I am no longer Isabella . . . Will you walk through the woods later? We will be waiting, we will be waiting . . .

(**BEATRICE** *looks desperately at* **VIRGINIO**, *removing the garland and letting it fall to the ground. Then she runs after the* **MADWOMAN** *to stop her.*)

BEATRICE: Isabella, listen to me, listen! You don't understand, you don't understand . . . It's not the way you say . . . Come, come here . . . (*She takes the* **MADWOMAN** *by the hand and leads her up to* **VIRGINIO** *who seems to be turned to stone.*) Don't you recognize him? Look at him, look at him carefully . . . Don't you know him? Don't you remember him? Take a good look at his face . . . (*With a sudden gesture, the* **MADWOMAN** *tears the mask of leaves from her face and leans toward the young man, her eyes fixed and dilated.*) Don't you recognize him? It's Virginio . . . Virginio, his brother . . .

(*The* **MADWOMAN** *starts. Suddenly she takes the young man's head between her hands. Pale and bent over backwards as if he were about to collapse and die, he closes his eyes. She stares at his head with a terrible intensity, and then lets him go with a cry, when she feels his head growing heavy in her hands.*)

MADWOMAN: Oh, he's dying, he's dying too . . .

BEATRICE: No, no . . . Don't you see him? Don't you see him?

MADWOMAN: I felt the weight of death in my hands once again.

BEATRICE: No, no . . . Look at him! Don't you see? He's standing in front of you. Don't you see him?

MADWOMAN (*blind with terror by now*): Who? Who? Giuliano? Who is standing in front of me?

BEATRICE: His brother . . . Virginio . . . Don't you recognize him? There he is! Look at him! Look at him properly!

MADWOMAN: His brother? What is his brother doing here? What has he come for? (*Her eyes that had wandered stare at the young man once again, with an expression of frenzied terror. She steps back, tearing off the stalks of grass that bind her hands, looking at her bare hands, looking at her body again and touching it as if she felt herself stained again. Madness floods over her.*) Why did he come? To take him back? To snatch him from me? To take him back to his mother? . . . Back to his mother, in that state: without blood, without a drop of blood left! All his blood is on me . . . I'm covered with it . . . Look, look at my hands, look at my arms, my bosom, my hair . . . I'm smothered in his blood . . . Oh, don't let her curse me, don't let his mother curse me! Oh, you tell her, you tell her not to curse me; tell her what I did for her dying son . . . I never forsook him. If the wound didn't go all the way through him and into me, if it didn't pierce my heart too, oh, tell her not to curse me for that! I died a thousand times in a single hour. My whole body is an agonizing wound; I myself don't have a drop of blood in my veins . . . I'm not alive; tell her I'm no longer alive . . . I felt his death enter my flesh, like a heavy frost, and I felt my bones bow beneath its weight . . . That is what dying is, that is what dying is! But tell her that her son didn't suffer, tell her that he fell blissfully asleep, in my arms . . . Oh, tell her I was able to give him bliss without bounds, obliviousness of the world, the ultimate consolation! He had closed his eyes in bliss on my breast, and he never opened them again. Me, I opened mine to find him gasping for breath . . . His mouth poured over me all the blood of his heart, pure and ardent as a flame, and it smothered me. My hair was saturated; all my bosom was flooded; and I was completely immersed in that stream that seemed as if it would never let up . . . Oh, how full his veins were, and with what hot blood! All of it I received, over my flesh and over my soul, down to the last drop; and the wild cries that rose to my lips I suffocated by grinding my teeth, so that no one would hear them, so that no one would come to separate me from him, to take him from my arms, to put him in a coffin . . . Tell her, tell his mother I did this; tell her not to curse me. And tell her it was almost a joy, almost a joy this smothering in hot blood, still alive, still pulsing, still mingled with his soul . . . But then afterward, afterward . . . How can the shudder of death be compared with the first shudder that ran through my bones when I felt the warmth ebbing out of the body I clasped? And I clasped it again, and I held it to me, and little by little I felt it grow cold against my breast, become icy, stiffen, become heavy as stone, as iron, become a true corpse, an alien thing, forever deaf, forever distant, which nothing can bring back to life, never again, never again . . .

(*Her knees begin to shake so violently that she falls to the ground.* **BEATRICE**, *who had been covering her face with her hands, hears her fall and runs toward her sister, holds her up, tries to help her to her feet.* **TEODATA**, *who had come into the doorway and was weeping silently, also runs over to support her.*)

MADWOMAN (*still stretching her hands out beseechingly to* **VIRGINIO**, *whose anguish prevents him from either moving or speaking*):   Oh, tell her, tell her this, tell her not to curse me! Bear me away too in the same coffin, bury me too with him, since I'm no longer alive! Oh, you can't bury him properly if you don't bury me with him, because all his blood is on me, all that was his life is on me . . . (*She frees herself violently from the hands that are trying to help her to her feet.*) No, no . . . Leave me alone! Leave me alone! Don't touch me! They are trying to get me into the water . . . No, no; I don't want to, I don't want to! Leave me like this! I want to stay like this, I want his mother to see me like this . . . (*She is overcome with sudden weakness, as if she were about to faint. She leans over to one side and touches the floor with her temple.*) buried like this . . .

(*The* **DOCTOR**, *who has already entered by the door on the left, signals to the two women to move away from her prostrate form. Then he leads* **VIRGINIO**, *gently, to the bench where he was previously sitting next to Beatrice.* **VIRGINIO** *sits down, hiding his face in his hands.* **BEATRICE** *goes slowly toward him. The* **DOCTOR** *bends over* **ISABELLA**, *who seems almost to have fallen asleep, and touches her. She appears to wake up, her mind a blank. Her mouth contracts as though her jaws were sore. Her hands wander bewilderedly over her temples, her cheeks, her lips.*)

DOCTOR (*bending over her*):   Were you going to go to asleep? Why go to sleep here? A white butterfly flew by; it's headed for the wood . . . Didn't you say earlier that you wanted to lie down under the trees, to be like the simple grass at their feet? Would you like me to take you down there, under the tiny new leaves! You and the trees, and the bushes, and the grass are as one . . . Would you like me to take you down there?

MADWOMAN (*looking about her with glazed, bewildered eyes*):   Yes, yes . . . down there, down there . . . to sleep . . . with the little leaves . . .

(**TEODATA** *exits soundlessly through the door she came in by, bowed beneath the weight of her grief.* **BEATRICE**, *still standing by the bench, helps* **VIRGINIO** *to his feet. Together they exit through the other door. On the threshold* **VIRGINIO** *turns back to look at* **ISABELLA** *who is still on her knees; then he disappears. There is complete silence, broken only by the swallows' cries, the murmur of the bees, a breath of wind.*)

DOCTOR: Come along then . . . Give me your hands. (*He puts out his hands to help her up.*)

MADWOMAN: I don't have the strength, Doctor . . . Wait a little while longer, I beg you! I was down there earlier, I think . . . I was down there . . . like the grass . . . Someone trampled me . . . I'm sure someone trampled me . . . Wait, I beg you! Perhaps I'll get up . . . (*She continues to gaze about her. Her gaze falls on the orange tree.*) Oh, Doctor, look at all the bees round that plant! They're all ready to suck. They're waiting for the flowers to open . . . I'd like to have a honeycomb . . . (*Continuing to look round, she catches sight of the mask of leaves and the fallen wreath.*) And those leaves over there? And that garland? (*A flash of recognition appears to cross the confused darkness of her mind.*) Where is Beatrice? Where is Beatrice? (*Once again her hands wander bewilderedly over her temples, her cheeks, her lips. Her mind is still a blank. She drags herself over to the garland, looks down at it, and smiles her vague childlike smile.*)

  Al for a garlande faire!

CURTAIN

TWO

FILIPPO TOMMASO MARINETTI

Introduction

Filippo Tommaso Marinetti was born in Alexandria, Egypt, in 1876 and died in Bellagio, Italy, in 1944. He established a reputation as a poet, playwright, journalist, and novelist, and he was the dynamic leader and guiding spirit of the Italian futurist movement, which he, along with other artists, founded in 1909. This movement had its strongest impact in the 1910s and continued until World War II, profoundly influencing modern theater, art, and literature. It is with the new futurist dramatic forms—the manifestos, *parole in libertà, serate,* and *sintesi*—that Marinetti left his mark on the theater.

Marinetti made his literary debut in 1898 when his poem "L'Echanson" appeared in the bilingual Milanese journal *Anthologie-Revue.* His collaboration on numerous literary journals brought him frequently to Paris where he eased into French literary circles. His early work as a poet—"La Conquête des étoiles," "La Momie sanglante," "Destruction," "La Ville charnelle"—shows the influence of Stéphane Mallarmé, Charles Baudelaire, Maurice Maeterlinck, Emile Verhaeren, and of the turn-of-the-century decadent symbolist school. In 1904 he founded the journal *Poesia* to introduce the symbolist aesthetic to Italy. Italian literature was, according to Marinetti, mired in classicism and the past. At this time he began working closely with the Italian anarchic symbolist poet Gian Pietro Lucini to introduce the concept of free verse to Italian writers. It was this idea that would lead to the development of the futurist *parole in libertà* (words in freedom). Other important influences were Enrico Annibale Butti, who helped introduce Ibsen to Italy, and Mario

Morasso who, in celebrating the industrial world and the machine, represented the Italian strain of machinist literature.

Marinetti wrote two full-length plays before founding the futurist movement. *Le Roi Bombance* (1905), inspired by Jarry's *Père Ubu* but in no way comparable, uses a gastronomical metaphor to explore the relationship between the ruling elite and starving, rebellious subjects. It was inspired by the failure of the 1904 general strike in Milan, which to Marinetti signified the tragic victory of idealist individualism over the passive, nostalgic, and brutal masses. Heavy-handed in its symbolism, the play presents a pessimistic view of the human condition; it shows Marinetti's obsession with the powerful influence of the past on the present. This obsession played an important role in the development of his futurist philosophy. In the play, the Vampire *savant* exclaims, "The future, that's the only religion! . . . When you regret something . . . that's already a germ of death you're carrying around with you."

The plot of *Poupées electriques* (Electric dolls, 1909) stems from the bourgeois theater but introduces robot characters who live with a married couple, Marie and Jean, and who are the "alogical synthesis" of the deadening forces that are part of their lives. The theme of the play is again—but this time on a more intimate level—the difficulty of escaping the past.

By 1909 there was a significant change in Marinetti's writing. While an anarchistic defiance of the cosmos still inspired him, his earlier images of dynamic communion with the ocean—possibly growing out of an early trauma when he came close to drowning—were replaced by images of the intoxicating sensations of speed; and images of the vitality of liquid elements by those of the vitality of technology. Marinetti's relationship with the machine was not always an easy one. He was not interested in the social progress the technological revolution would bring but in the inebriating effect of speed and the sometimes frightening experience of the power of the machine.

On February 20, 1909, *Le Figaro* published Marinetti's "Foundation and Manifesto of Futurism" in which he proclaimed his revolutionary aim of abolishing the past and its established institutions. He and his futurist friends, who were artists of all kinds—Aldo Palazzeschi, Francesco Balilla Pratella, Luigi Russolo, Paolo Buzzi, Umberto Boccioni, Emilio Settimelli, Bruno Corra, Enrico Prampolini, Fortunato Depero—were to publish hundreds more of such manifestos in subsequent years. This movement, which continued into the 1940s, influenced the culinary arts, music, painting, sculpture, dance, cinema as well as the theatrical arts in Italy, Europe, the United States, and Russia. In the theater it had two major poles: the futurist *serata* or evening and the futurist *sintesi,* or theater of synthesis.

The first futurist *serata* was at the Politeama Rossetti in Trieste on January 12, 1910. Marinetti and his followers subsequently traveled to many cities throughout Italy holding these *serate.* They consisted of a mixture of politics and art and prefigured the 1960s phenomenon of the happening. Paintings were exhibited, speeches made, films shown, manifestos declaimed, music played. The evenings often intentionally provoked the audience to violence. Once, in response to having an orange thrown at him, Marinetti peeled it and ate it. It was part of his futurist program to abolish the traditional relationship between performer and audience and to provoke the audience out of its conventional comfortable role.

In "The Variety Theater" manifesto of November 21, 1913, Marinetti drew on nightclubs, circuses, and music halls as inspiration for futurist theater. He extolled the speed, invention, simultaneity, and dynamism of these forms, the short numbers, the nonpsychological, nonliterary, primitive approach to entertainment, the elements of surprise, improvisation, and spectacle, and the fluidity of the boundaries separating actors from spectators. In line with his idealization of war, danger, and violence, he praised the variety theater for encouraging acts of heroism and feats of strength.

During these years, Marinetti developed the concept of *parole in libertà,* which carried Lucini's ideas of free verse one step farther by eliminating any rules regarding versification, spelling, syntax, spatial distribution of words on a page, and typography. *Parole in libertà* were presented as theatricalized performances; for instance, Marinetti's *Zang-Tumb-Tumb* (1914) describes the siege of Adrianople during the Balkan War. These performances began in 1914 at the Gallerie Sprovieri in Rome and Naples. They were different from the *serate* in that costumes, sets, sound, and music were used for dramatic effect, and multiple performers were often involved. Marinetti called them "dynamic and synoptic declamations."

Marinetti also had a significant influence on the theater with his futurist *sintesi.* Marinetti's aim with the *sintesi* was brevity of expression—transmitting the essentials of a five-act play in a few scenes, for instance—simultaneity, and the elimination of the fourth wall and psychological playwriting. During 1915–16, acting companies, among them Ettore Petrolini's, toured Italy presenting a program of these short pieces. Marinetti's are among the best. Inanimate objects and body parts become the dramatic focus in *They Are Coming* (*Vengono*) and *Feet* (*Le basi*); in the former, a precursor to Ionesco's *The Chairs,* animated chairs take on a menacing aspect. *Simultaneità,* a good example of his idea of theatrical simultaneity, comprises two different scenes that penetrate each other. A bourgeois family spends an evening quietly around a table. Meanwhile, in their midst but unseen by them, a beautiful call girl grooms and dresses herself and receives several visitors. She then breaks the invisible wall by walking over to the table and telling the family to go to bed. Marinetti explained that the call girl represented the peaceful family's inner feelings about luxury, adventure, disorder, and waste, which they experienced as anguish, desire, or regret.

Marinetti explores the idea of simultaneity again in *I vasi comunicanti,* translated here as *Connecting Vessels.*[1] Moving from the battle field, to a city square, to a funeral parlor, three sets are fused into one by battling soldiers searching for an enemy who defeats them. Written in 1916, this *sintesi* on a realistic level reflects Marinetti's preoccupation with the war. As has already been indicated, Marinetti and many other futurists glorified war as a means to achieve national greatness. The stage picture can also be read in symbolic terms: the soldiers are the blood of life, battling for existence in the body's blood vessels. When all the walls have been broken down, one has reached the ultimate battle ground, the battle with death, here represented by the soldiers moving toward the wings. They do not get far. Death beats us all, always.

The full-length plays of Marinetti's later period, such as *Il tamburo di fuoco* (The drum of fire, 1922), *Prigionieri* (Prisoners, 1925), and *Vulcano* (Volcano, 1926) are inventive allegories but somewhat heavy-handed. *Tamburo,* set in an unidentified place and time, tells the mysterious story of Kabango, a black prophet, who meets defeat and betrayal when he tries to save his people. In *Vulcano,* which was directed by Pirandello for the Teatro d'Arte in March 1926—with Marta Abba in the title role and set designs by Enrico Prampolini— a competition takes place between a poet, a pyrotechnist, the moon, and Mount Etna. Only in *Il suggeritore nudo* (The naked prompter), *Locomotivi,* and *Simultanina*—all written in 1928—was Marinetti able to recover the bite of his futurist experimental pieces.

Regarding the ties of the futurists to the politics of Fascism—about which much has been written—Antonio Gramsci wrote to Leon Trotsky in 1922, when the second wave of futurism was gathering, that "Actually, monarchists, communists, republicans, and fascists participate in the futurist movement."[2] Marinetti's own relationship to the Fascist Party fluctuated. As one might expect, his devotion to the anarchic revolutionary principles of futurism often caused him to be at loggerheads with Mussolini, and in 1920 he quit the Party, claiming it was reactionary and *passéist.* However, he returned to it in 1923/24, and although he never became as deeply involved again and, in fact, in 1938 condemned the Fascist anti-Semitic policies, he was able to justify his participation in the regime despite evidence that Mussolini's rule was growing steadily more and more repressive in the 1920s and 1930s. This paradoxical tie should not, however, lead us to deny either the originality of his work or the enormous influence it had on the development of the theater.

J. H.

Notes

1. First published in *Teatro futurista sintetico,* a supplementary edition to *Gli Avvenimenti* 2, no. 15 (April 2–9, 1916). This collection of *sintesi* was republished as *Teatro sintetico futurista* (Milan: Coll. Biblioteca Teatrale, Istituto Editoriale Italiano, n.d.).

2. Cited in Giovanni Lista, *Marinetti* (Paris: Seghers, coll. poètes d'aujourd'hui, 1977), p. 135. The quotation is translated from the French by Jane House.

■

CONNECTING
VESSELS

A Theatrical Synthesis

(I vasi comunicanti, 1916)

Translated by Jane House

■

The stage is divided into three by two partitions.

—The first area (to the left): Brightly lit room. A catafalque in the center, surrounded by flaming candles, praying priests, numerous weeping relatives.

—The second area (center stage): A street; in front of the tavern door, a table and a bench on which is seated a woman.

—The third area (to the right): The countryside; trenches a short distance upstage from the footlights.

As the curtain rises, in the first area, the priests are muttering prayers and the relatives moan: "aiaiaiaiaiai." *Suddenly, from among the relatives* **A VOICE** *cries:* Thief! *And the* **PICKPOCKET** *separates from the group and escapes, comes downstage toward the footlights, skirts the first partition, enters the second area, and sits down next to the* **WOMAN** *on the bench. He has a drink and talks to her. Meanwhile, a* **CROWD OF SOLDIERS** *come down the street toward the footlights.*

A SOLDIER (*to the thief*):   Come and join us!

THE THIEF: Okay, I will! To die for my country! (*He gets up.*)

THE WOMAN (*holding him back*):   What? But we're so in love and so completely happy. Why are you leaving me now? (*She cries.*)

(*The thief pushes the woman away and mixes in with the soldiers; skirting the second partition, they enter the third area and occupy the trenches.*)

AN OFFICER: Fire! Fire! (*gunfire, then*) Forward! Bash down that wall! Keep going!

(*The soldiers come out of the trenches, run upstage, knock down the second partition, crowd into the second area, and cross over it.*)

THE OFFICER (*in front of the first partition*):   Bash down this wall too, we've got to outflank the enemy!

(*The soldiers knock down the first partition as well, invade the first area and cross over it noisily, turning over the catafalque and the candles, throwing the relatives into confusion. Having reached the wings on the left, they suddenly fall over backward, shot down, all in a row.*)

CURTAIN

■

THEY ARE
COMING

Drama of Objects

(Vengono, 1915)

Translated by Victoria Nes Kirby

■

Luxurious room, evening. A large lighted chandelier. Open French windows (upstage left) that open onto a garden. At left, along the wall, but separated from it, a large rectangular table with cover. Along the wall on the right (through which a door opens), a huge and tall armchair beside which eight chairs are aligned, four to the right and four to the left of the armchair.

A **MAJORDOMO** *and* **TWO SERVANTS** *in tails enter from the left door.*

THE MAJORDOMO: They are coming. Prepare. (*exits*)

(*The* **SERVANTS,** *in a great hurry, arrange the eight chairs in a horseshoe beside the armchair, which remains in the same place, as does the table. When they have finished, they go and look out the door,*[1] *turning their backs to the audience. A long minute of waiting. The* **MAJORDOMO** *reenters, panting.*)

THE MAJORDOMO: Countermand. I am very tired . . . Many cushions, many stools . . . (*exits*)

(*The* **SERVANTS** *exit by the right door and reenter loaded down with cushions and stools. Then, taking the armchair, they put it in the middle of the room and arrange the chairs (four on each side of the armchair) with the chairs' backs turned toward the armchair. Then they put cushions on each chair and on the armchair and stools before each chair and, likewise, before the armchair.*

The **SERVANTS** *go again to look out the French windows. A long minute of waiting.*)

THE MAJORDOMO (*reenters, running*): Briccatirakamekame. (*exits*)

(*The* **SERVANTS** *carry the table to the middle of the room, arrange the armchair (at the head of the table) and the chairs around it: then, leaving and reentering from the right door, they rapidly set the table. At one place, a vase of flowers; at another, a lot of bread; at another, eight bottles of wine. At other places, only a knife, fork, and spoon . . . one chair must be leaning against the table, with its rear legs raised, as is done in restaurants to indicate that a place is reserved. When they have finished, the* **SERVANTS** *go again to look outside. A long minute of waiting.*)

THE MAJORDOMO (*reenters, running*): Briccatirakamekame. (*exits*)

(*Immediately, the* **SERVANTS** *replace the table, which remains set, in the position it occupied when the curtain went up. Then they put the armchair in front of the French windows, at a slant, and behind the armchair they arrange the eight chairs in Indian file diagonally across the set. Having done this, they turn off the chandelier. The set remains faintly lit by the moonlight that is coming in through the French windows. An invisible reflector projects the shadows of the armchair and chairs on the floor. The very distinct shadows (obtained by moving the reflector slowly) visibly lengthen toward the French windows.*

The **SERVANTS,** *wedged into a corner, wait trembling with evident agony, while the* **CHAIRS** *leave the room.*)

---

1. *La porta*: Marinetti apparently means the French windows. —Trans.

■

FEET

(Le basi, 1915)

Translated by Victoria Nes Kirby

■

A curtain edged in black should be raised to about the height of a man's stomach. The public sees only legs in action. The actors must try to give the greatest expression to the attitudes and movements of their lower extremities.

1.

Two Armchairs

(*one facing the other*)

A BACHELOR
A MARRIED WOMAN

HIM: All, all for one of your kisses! . . .
HER: No! . . . Don't talk to me like that! . . .

2.

A MAN WHO IS WALKING BACK AND FORTH

MAN: Let's meditate . . .

3.

A Desk

A SEATED MAN WHO IS NERVOUSLY MOVING HIS RIGHT FOOT

SEATED MAN: I must find . . . To cheat, without letting myself cheat!

3a.

A MAN WHO IS WALKING SLOWLY WITH GOUTY FEET
A MAN WHO IS WALKING RAPIDLY

THE RAPID ONE: Hurry! Vile passéist!
THE SLOW ONE: Ah! What fury! There is no need to run! He who goes slowly is healthy . . .

4.

A Couch

THREE WOMEN

ONE: Which one do you prefer?

ANOTHER: All three of them.

A Couch

THREE OFFICIALS

ONE: Which one do you prefer?

ANOTHER: The second one.

(*The second one must be the woman who shows the most legs of the three.*)

5.

A Table

A FATHER
A BACHELOR
A YOUNG GIRL

THE FATHER: When you have the degree, you will marry your cousin.

6.

A Pedal-Operated Sewing Machine

A GIRL WHO IS WORKING

THE GIRL: I will see him on Sunday!

7.

A MAN WHO IS RUNNING AWAY
A FOOT THAT IS KICKING AT HIM

THE MAN WHO IS GIVING THE KICK: Imbecile!

Introduction

Ettore Petrolini (born in Rome, January 13, 1884; died in Rome, June 29, 1936) made his name in the variety theater at the beginning of the twentieth century. By 1913 he had performed all over Italy as well as in Paris, New York, and Latin America. The Italian variety theater is said to have been instituted when "Salone Margherita" was inaugurated on November 20, 1890, in the vaults beneath the new Galleria Umberto I in Naples. Others opened soon thereafter in major Italian cities.

While the variety theater had a certain discipline in its organizational structure—a series of "numbers" following each other in order of increasing importance—no limitation or restriction was placed on the inventiveness of the performers, whether they were acrobats, jugglers, singers, musicians, dancers, magicians, contortionists, comics, or other artists. They could be as bizarre and as audacious as they wished. The futurists greatly admired variety theater, and F. T. Marinetti exalted it in his manifesto, "The Variety Theater" (1913).

This form of entertainment was certainly influenced by the French *café-chantants,* such as the Moulin Rouge, but it also had its own origins in Italy: in popular song, puppet theater, open air entertainment, and the circus; in popular festivals such as the Piedigrotta; in the *commedia* tradition—which the great Pulcinella, Antonio Petito (1822–76), and his pupil Eduardo Scarpetta (1853–1925), modernized by introducing contemporary types and situations into the repertory—and in the *periodica,* a very popular form of private entertainment for the petite bourgeoisie at the turn of the century. The *periodica* imitated the musical and literary salons of

■

THREE

ETTORE
PETROLINI

■

the aristocracy. Out of these *periodiche* came many comic variety stars of the 1890s including Nicola Maldacea, Gennaro Pasquariello, and Elvira Donnarumma.

Great comic artists were of prime importance to the variety theater and they had to have superb technique. The impression they made had to be immediate since each sketch or *macchietta* lasted only a few minutes. These sketches often included music and song. Indeed, many lyricists and composers began to write for variety artists. Among the most famous of them were Salvatore Di Giacomo and Ferdinando Russo, who were also playwrights. It was Russo who wrote the words to Maldacea's sketch of the *viveur,* an affected aristocratic type, full of nervous ticks, which Maldacea introduced at the Salone Margherita. This sketch was really a parody of the audience members themselves. It would be developed further by Petrolini and Raffaele Viviani. Other popular sketches were those of the *guappo,* a term used to describe the local kingpin, and the *scugnizzo* or street urchin.

Petrolini began performing his sketches in variety theaters in Rome in 1903; he parodied the *caffè-concerto* world in the sketch *Giggi er Bullo* (Giggi the hoodlum), nineteenth-century acting traditions in *Amleto* (Hamlet) and *Cyrano de Bergerac,* silent movie divas such as Lydia Borelli in *Ma l'amor mio non muore* (But my love never dies), operas in *Pensaci* (Think about it), and Dannunzian rhetoric in *Serenata pedestre* (Pedestrian serenade). He even parodied variety theater sketches themselves in *Il danzadero* (The Dancedero), *Il prestidigitatore* (The magician), and *Il guappo* (The kingpin). Two of his most popular pieces were *Fortunello* (Fortunello) and *I salamini* (Sausages).

Petrolini's use of mechanical effects, parody, and satire as well as the anti-Dannunzian stance he exhibited in many of his variety sketches made him a favorite of the futurists, with whom he had extensive contact; he collaborated with them, and they often wrote pieces for him. He inspired, directly or indirectly, many of their published writings on the art of acting, for example, Bruno Corra and Marinetti's piece, "La risata italiana di Petrolini" (Petrolini's Italian laugh), in *L'Italia futurista* (2, no. 20, July 1, 1917). Corra wrote a number of additional articles praising Petrolini's acting genius.

Along with the companies of other Italian actors, including those of Annibale Ninchi, Lorenzo-Falconi, Ettore Berti, and Gualtiero Tumiati, Petrolini toured Italy with futurist *sintesi* during World War I. After the war, in 1921, when he toured South America, he included two futurist pieces in his repertory: the Bruno Corra and Emilio Settimelli *sintesi* entitled *Grey + Red + Violet + Orange,* and the one-act play he wrote with Francesco Cangiullo entitled *Radioscopia di un duetto* (Radioscopy of a duet). In this play, first performed at the Naples Politeama in 1918, the action happens in a variety theater; both the onstage and backstage areas, separated by a scrim, are simultaneously visible to the audience.

In the 1920s Petrolini moved toward performing his own full-length dramatic works— *Gastone* (Gastone), *Benedetto tra le donne* (Benedict, blessed, among women), *Chicchignola* (Chicchignola)—and those of other writers (Pier Maria Rosso di San Secondo, Luigi Chiarelli); he also adapted contemporary plays (Luigi Pirandello, Sacha Guitry, Renato Simoni) and works by Shakespeare and Molière.

It should also be noted that Petrolini was a film actor and writer. The films he acted in during the early 1910s, the great age of Italian silent movies, are not preserved, nor are *Mentre il pubblico ride* (While the public laughs), the 1919 adaptation of *Radioscopia,* and *Il cortile* (The courtyard, 1930). However, his performances can still be seen in his adaptation of Molière's *Il medico per forza* (The doctor in spite of himself, 1931), directed by Carlo Campogalliani, and in *Nerone* (Nero, 1930), directed by Alessandro Blasetti. *Nerone* was based on Petrolini's own script and features his one-act play of the same name as well as a Pulcinella farce and two variety sketches: *Fortunello* and *Gastone.*

Fortunello, dating from 1915, was based on a children's cartoon character. While the scenery and Petrolini's performance would very probably have varied over the years, we are fortunate to have a partial recording of the sketch in *Nerone.* Here, the backdrop, painted in childlike manner, represents a suburban scene. A little pathway leads up to a two-storied featureless house; one wall has been "rubber-stamped" with the letters "Kl." Beside the house stand a telephone pole and some huge, colorful flowers. Fortunello has a weird appearance: on top of his bald pate sits a tin can; concave plastic molds make his eyes appear to bulge; two furry antenna, one protruding from each temple, wave around as he moves; and an appendage gives his nose a crusty look. The costume consists of patched brown pants, green jacket with black velvet collar, spotted yellow vest, and overly large shoes.

This creature, this cross between man and insect, this Fortunello, bursts onto the stage like a woundup toy, flinging up his arms and legs as he bounces forward with each stride. Having planted himself before the pathway to his house, Petrolini/Fortunello, without attempting to make any sense of the words, begins to sing. He follows a relentless, mechanical rhythm and barely pauses for breath. Petrolini's performance was probably toned down for *Nerone* where the movement is limited—Fortunello is primarily seen in close-up from one angle. On stage, however, Petrolini/Fortunello has been described as growing increasingly manic and seemingly out of control. Corra and Marinetti considered this sketch one of Petrolini's *chefs d'oeuvre.* We are including the music Petrolini used in a recording of the sketch. In order to preserve the rhythm and rhyme of the original a few liberties have been taken in the English translation.

J. H.

■

FORTUNELLO

Tale of an Idiot

(Fortunello, 1915)

Translated by Jane House

■

I'm a typical fellow: aesthetic,
asthmatic, synthetic,
lymphatic, cosmetic.
I love the Bible, the tibia, and Libya
sweet baby booties
sensible beauties
such dear silly goosies
I'm exhilarated
Concentrated
Acquitted "for no crime committed."
I've a special passion for the North Pole. Virginal wax.
Nebuchadnezzar. Butter from Lodi. La fanciulla del
West. Fly paper. Heavy cavalry. Shoelaces. Aeronautical
cookery. Playing the lottery. Acetylene and osso buco.
I am: Homerical
Hysterical
Generical
Chimerical
Clysterical
But of all the things I am
I cannot poss'bly speak
I try 'n I'm a sham
so now I'll attempt to sing.

A man I am, so gracious 'n bello
I am Fortunello.
A man I am, so fearless 'n sane
I am an aeroplane.

A man I am, oh so derisible
I am a dirigible.
A man I am, who likes to play god
I am a lightning rod.
A man I am, with such a proud head
I am Mahommed.
A man I am, without any flaw
I am the 404.
A man I am, whom they can't duplicate
I am a son illegitimate.
A man I am, who'll never fade
I am the son of the housemaid.
A man I am, with no priggery
I am coffee made with chicory.
A man I am, gynaegetical
I am a stroke apoplectical.
A man I am, as plain as snow
I am an Eskimo.
A man I am, of little worth
I am neutral on earth.
A man I am, without a coda
I am a pagoda.
A man I am, quite condescending
I am an accident portending.
A man I am, of the confederation
for which I suffer humiliation.
A man I am, who weighs a gram
I am a radio-telegram.
A man I am, from Istanbul
I am full of bull.
A man I am, a petty meany
I am Petrolini.
A man I am, a Jack of all trades
I am terrific at charades.

But of all the things I am
I cannot poss'bly speak
I try 'n I'm a sham
so now I'll attempt to sing.

And since I am not nothing
I leave their feathers ruffling.
If I had a little pretension
I'd pocket an English pension.
If I were a Minister
I would be most sinister.

IIf I had a nose for news—oh
I would be like Caruso.
f in hope I were living
I would surely die a-singing.
If I were a beautiful lady
I still would want my baby.
If I hadn't a falsetto
I'd be Rigoletto.
If I had gloves that were gray
I'd go to Paris every day.
If I were a big-assed barbarian
I'd be Austrohungarian.
If I had a palandra
I'd be like Salandra.[1]
If I were less buffo
I'd be Titta Ruffo.[2]
If I had a yard of dental floss
I'd free my teeth of all their dross.
If I were the Father in heaven
I'd be rolling sixes and sevens.
If on my head there were a helmet
my name it'd be Helmut.
If I were a cantatrice
I'd show off my fleece.
If I had some bread that's sliced
I'd eat salami hot and spiced.
And when I were full enough
I would auction off the stuff.
And when it got bone-stiff
I could play a riff.
And when I'm dry 'n sick
I'll go for a salt lick.
And when I join the clerical gentry
I will have secret entry.
And like all vulgar flirts
I will wear skirts.
And like all wedded Joans
I'll have my monthly moans.

---

1. Antonio Salandra (1853–1931), conservative politician, president of the Council in 1914.—Trans.

2. A famous Italian baritone (1877–1953).—Trans.

If my grandpa had a fleece
grandma would have a piece.
If my grandma had a piece
my nephew would be my niece.

But of all the things I am
I cannot poss'bly speak
I try 'n I'm a sham
so now I'll attempt to sing.

If each day I do a purge
I am great Petersburg.
If the purging is very bad
I am Petrograd.
If I were a cocotte
I'd sure be hot to trot.
To avoid a pretty pass
I'll burn his palliasse.
I'll never make a silver hake
I am a beefsteak.
In being sly I'm at my ease
I am a good sneeze.
If I trip up the town with my wit
I am a nitwit.
If the motor makes me shake
I am an earthquake.
If I'm heading for the sewer
I'm a rotten swine for sure.
And if this creates a crisis
I am bronchitis.
If I had more sympathy
I'd sure have less antipathy.
If I had more antipathy
You can bet I'd have less sympathy.
And if I have not yet mentioned
I am the aforementioned.
And if I have not yet signed
I am the undersigned.
To mischief I love to pander
Since I am a commander.
I save my money without contrition
I am a politician.
I am for a socialistic nation
I am a grand purgation.

A man I am, a melancholic
I am a bitter tonic.
If I were from the outskirts of Rome
it would cost a lot to drive it home.
So bandy it and proclaim
that idiot is my name.

But of all the things I am
I cannot poss'bly speak
I try 'n I'm a sham
so now I'll attempt to sing.

Music for Fortunello

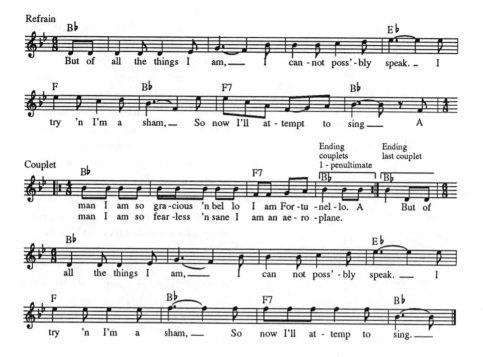

Refrain

Bb   Eb

But of all the things I am, — I can-not poss'-bly speak. _ I

F   Bb   F7   Bb

try 'n I'm a sham, — So now I'll at - tempt to sing — A

Couplet

Ending couplets 1 - penultimate   Ending last couplet

Bb   F7   [Bb   [Bb

man I am so gra-cious 'n bel lo   I am For -tu -nel - lo. A   But of
man I am so fear -less 'n sane I   am an ae - ro -plane.

Bb   Eb

all the things I am, — I can not poss' - bly speak. — I

F   Bb   F7   Bb

try 'n I'm a sham, — So now I'll at - temp to sing. —

■

FOUR

RAFFAELE

VIVIANI

■

Introduction

Raffaele Viviani (born January 9, 1888, in Castellammare di Stabia; died March 22, 1950, in Naples) grew up around popular entertainment such as puppet opera, variety theater, and circuses. His father managed the seaside Arena Margherita, where second-rate Pulcinellas performed, and produced plays, including *La mano nera* (The black hand), an American drama, and *Around the World in Eighty Days,* in Naples at various Masaniello theaters.[1] Viviani had his stage debut at the age of four. At seven, he performed variety acts, singing popular songs, alone and in duet with his sister, Luisella, and Vincenzina Di Capua. His father's death in 1900 left the family—widow, daughter, and son—destitute. Struggling to earn a living as performers, Luisella and Raffaele Viviani had to leave school.

In 1904 Viviani obtained employment in a variety theater of good standing, the Perella Theater, in the Basso Porto area of Naples. Here he began to make his reputation with two contrasting sketches. One was *Il scugnizzo* (The street urchin), for which Giovanni Capurro wrote the lyrics and Francesco Buongiovanni the music. Viviani, singing in a hoarse voice, emphasized the sad spirit of the indigent boy and modeled his costume on reality. The other was *Fifì Rino* (1905), a comic sketch of a Dannunzian aristocrat performed in marionette style, for which Viviani created the words and music. In 1908 Viviani was performing six original realistic melologues, or sketches with words and music, playing all the parts himself, at major variety theaters such as the Eden in Naples and the Jovinelli in Rome, and he was invited to perform in three films.

That he used the ordinary man as inspiration, transforming himself in voice, body, and facial expression into the characters, rep-resented a significant departure from those variety performers inspired by the comic, im-provisational spirit of the commedia dell'arte. In his sketches Viviani represented people from the whole Neapolitan social scale with a sense of realism that could come only from close observation; given the exigencies of variety theater, he had to change from one char-acter to the next in an instant. By 1912 his fame had spread throughout Italy and to France and Hungary.

As a result of the closing of variety theaters after the defeat of the Italian army at Capo-retto in 1917, Viviani was pressed into forming his own company, a company that per-formed plays and musicals, and into writing scripts for and acting in the legitimate theater. Mr. Del Piano, a retired engineer and theater lover, offered him the Teatro Umberto in Naples, which became Viviani's base for the next four years. He began by presenting one-act musical pieces drawn from his sketches. Between 1917 and 1919 he created and pro-duced seventeen musical plays, which are considered by many his liveliest work. A large number include their Neapolitan settings in the title: Via Toledo, Via Partenope, Porta Capuana, Santa Lucia Nova, Piazza Municipio. The protagonists are both the public place and the people who inhabit it. The people and situations change quickly in an almost cine-matographic rhythm. These early plays often have no dramatic resolution; they are replete with songs, comic duets, choral action, jokes, and *lazzi* (gags). It is important to note, however, that Viviani rehearsed all stage action very carefully and never allowed his actors to improvise during performances.

In his depiction of the Neapolitan lower classes and his fidelity to the Neapolitan dialect, Viviani was following the lead of Antonio Petito (1822–76), one of the greatest Pulcinel-las, as well as that of Neapolitan playwrights such as Pasquale Altavilla, Eduardo Scarpetta, Salvatore Di Giacomo, and Ferdinando Russo. What is unique in Viviani's vision and what brought him great popularity is the nonromantic, nonsentimental depiction of the lives of the Neapolitan poor—a bitter yet comic vision that caught the attention of Maxim Gorky and Vladimir Ivanovich Nemirovitch-Danchenko. The Neapolitan speech of his characters is terse, caustic, realistic. Although his stage world includes aristocrats, the upper middle classes, shopkeepers, and policemen, his focus is on the needy proletariat, the margin-alized: vagabonds, urchins, traveling street vendors, prostitutes, gypsies, pimps, racke-teers, migrant workers, and so on.

His company became well known throughout Italy and, like many other Italian compa-nies, toured South America. He adapted Pirandello's plays *La patente* (The patent) and *Pensaci, Giacomino!* (Think it over, Giacomino!) into Neapolitan and worked with Ugo Betti to adapt one of Betti's plays for Ettore Petrolini, a project that never reached fruition.

Viviani wrote over sixty-five plays, only one of them in standard Italian. In comparison to the one-act plays of 1917–19, his plays of the 1920s and 1930s are longer, more com-plex, and have stronger dramatic threads, but while he shifted focus to the individual and began to use a more psychological approach to character development, he retained—and would always retain—his concern for the unfortunate of the world. To this period belong the two tragedies *I pescatori* (Fishermen, 1925) and *Gli zingari* (Gypsies, 1926) as well as

Circo equestre Sgueglia (Sgueglia equestrian circus, 1922) and *La musica dei ciechi* (Music of the blind, 1927).

In the late 1920s he began to write dramas with clear social criticism such as *Nullatenenti* (Have-nots, 1928), *I vecchi de San Gennaro* (Old people of San Gennaro, 1933), and *La tavola dei poveri* (The table for the poor, 1931), which was made into a film in 1932. It was his clear social criticism that would get him into trouble with the Fascists. In 1926 a law was instituted prohibiting dialect theater because it supposedly destroyed the unity of Italian culture. This law was applied more severely to Viviani's work than to that of other writers in dialect such as Angelo Musco, Cesco Baseggio, Ettore Petrolini, and Eduardo De Filippo because the Fascists considered Viviani's dramatic vision and his recurring theme of a suffering populace demeaning to Italians. This invidious censorship was applied by the Ministry of Popular Culture, which arranged the tours for all theater companies in Italy. The Ministry denied him access to major theaters in important cities and relegated his company to the marginal theaters, for short runs of one to three days, in unpopular seasons, such as mid-August. In 1942 it refused to allow Viviani to tour the bombarded areas of Naples, his hometown, with other companies. His protests against this censorship were met by official silence.

Although he was tired and sick after the war, Viviani continued to write, revising old scripts and preparing new works: *I dieci comandamenti* (The ten commandments, 1947) and *I sette peccati* (The seven deadly sins, 1949). After his death in 1950, his son Vittorio, together with the actor Nino Taranto, began to produce revivals of Viviani's work on stage and television. The Neapolitan playwright and director Giuseppe Patroni-Griffi presented several Viviani works at the Aldwych Theatre, London, for the 1968 International Festival.

The play we present here, *Via Toledo by Night,* is a quasi-picaresque piece. The title refers to the night life on Via Toledo, which crosses Naples from Piazza San Ferdinando to Piazza Dante. This major artery was opened in 1536. It was renamed Via Roma in 1870 but is still referred to as Toledo. The street has been the subject of writings by Roberto Bracco and Salvatore Di Giacomo. Viviani sets each of the seven scenes of the play in a different quarter of the city through which Toledo passes. Two groups are contrasted in the play: the wealthy free-livers who are able to indulge themselves in the Neapolitan nightlife and those who struggle to make a living in the cold night air.

The music to *Via Toledo by Night* is published here as an appendix to the text. Each Roman numeral corresponds to a section of music. The Italian text of the songs has been translated in the body of the work; in the translation every effort has been made to remain faithful to the words of the original while retaining the rhythm of the Italian and the appropriate number of syllables. In this piece Viviani made intelligent use of Italian popular music as well as contemporary European and American musical styles. The Coachman's song (XVIII), which was originally written in 1912, is reminiscent of the American cakewalk and ragtime music; this is very appropriate because the Coachman is in constant contact with tourists. The Rag Man's song, one of the play's most haunting numbers, begins with a song (VII), moves to a long *mélologue,* which is half spoken, half sung (VIII and IX), then returns to the song, ending with a couplet from the popular Neapolitan tune "The

Sand and Sea" (X). The words "din din mbò, din din mbà" heard throughout are nonsense words used purely for rhythmic and phonetic effect. Rusella the Grass Seller and her lover, Pascalino, are the most positive and hopeful characters passing through *Via Toledo by Night;* their duet (XI) is full of sweetness and gentle love, giving us a fleeting glimpse of happiness in what is, overall, a dark vision of life.

The first performance of the play took place at Teatro Umberto, Naples, on January 9, 1918. It had various titles in Neapolitan, at first '*A notte* (Night) or '*A strada* (The street), and then *Tuledo 'e notte* (Toledo by night). Raffaele Viviani interpreted four parts: the Pizza Maker, the Rag Man, Filiberto Esposito, and the Coachman, all of them characters he had created for the variety theater. Other actors were Tecla Scarano as Bambinella, a part Viviani's sister Luisella Viviani would also play; Grigi Pisano as Tummasino; and, alternating as Leopoldo Coletta, Salvatore Costa and Cesare Linguiti; Linguiti was one of the oldest members of Viviani's troupe.

Unless otherwise indicated, the notes to the play were provided by the editors in the original Italian.

J. H.

Notes

1. See Vittorio Viviani, *Storia del teatro napoletano* (Naples: Guida, 1969), pp. 807–10.

■

VIA TOLEDO BY NIGHT

A One-Act Play with Music

(Via Toledo di notte, 1918)

Prose and Verse Translated by Martha King
Lyrics adapted by Marilyn Firment

■

Setting: Naples 1918

Characters

LEOPOLDO COLETTA, coffee vendor

SCARRAFONE or **COCKROACH**, old news vendor

CIENTEPELLE or **COWBELLY**, cooked meat vendor

FURMELLA or **GOLDBRICK**, idler

TUMMASINO, the Millionaire

THE PIZZA MAKER

FRITZ

GASTONE

RUSELLA, the couch grass seller

PASCALINO, the little baker

THE RAG MAN

MARGHERITA

INES

FILIBERTO ESPOSITO

BRIGADIER BRIGHELLA

OFFICER GUARDASCIONE

MIMÌ, café waitress

NICOLA, night watchman

GNAZIO, driver for hire

MARIO

FLORA

PIERRETTE

EDGARDO

GEORGETTE

FERNANDA

FILUMENA, the Fat One

MARIA, the Nuisance

TITINA

PAPELE MARIUOLO

DON AITANO, the Consumptive

PEPPINO SFATICATO

CRISTINA, the Minor

AFFUNZINO, the Stutterer

THE ORGAN GRINDER

PRELUDE — MUSIC I[1]

Scene 1

Curtain up.

Via Toledo, at the corner of Vico Berio, near Piazza San Ferdinando. Late at night, winter. SCAR-
RAFONE,[2] *the old news vendor, is shivering in a corner at right. At left two men are on the ground
playing a card game: one is* CIENTEPELLE,[3] *the cooked-meat vendor—who has a little pushcart
nearby—and the other player is* FURMELLA,[4] *a young idler.*

A CRY (*of* LEOPOLDO COLETTA, *the itinerant coffee vendor*): "Coffee for sale! Coffee, cigars, cigarettes, rum and anise! Leopoldo Coletta is here. Ready to serve you. Come
get your coffee!"

SCARRAFONE (*gives his "cry"*): "The Italian Daily! Rome Tribune! Final edition! Naples
Courier!"

ANOTHER CRY (*far away, nostalgic: the snail and boiled mussels vendor*) "Mussels from Taranto!
Lovely snails . . ."

(TUMMASINO *the Millionaire enters. He is a young pimp, with a manner somewhere between
arrogant and chivalrous. He is called "the millionaire" strictly for his verbal ostentation. In reality
he is a poor man. He is wearing a short jacket with the collar turned up against the cold. His hands*

---

1. Music note: The Roman numerals in the text refer to the musical pieces found at the end of
the play. Regarding the songs, the body of the text contains the English translation of the lyrics; the
Neapolitan lyrics have been retained in the music itself. However, care has been taken in translation
to match the rhythm and stress of the original Neapolitan lyrics so that those wishing to sing the
songs or perform the play may substitute the English lyrics with ease. [J. H., ed.]

2. Scarrafone, or cockroach, here is a nickname meaning a very ugly man.—Trans.

3. Cientepelle (one hundred skins). Tripe.—Trans.

4. Furmella: the name of a game.—Trans.

are in his pockets. He comes from Piazza San Ferdinando⁵ and, after a glance at the street corner, makes a gesture of contempt. He asks **SCARRAFONE** *about someone.*)

SCARRAFONE: Who? Ines! I don't know her!

TUMMASINO (*responds with a brief nod of greeting; he looks again at the street corner and mutters*): . . . No doubt she's joined a nunnery!

(*And he goes over to the players.* **LEOPOLDO** *enters carrying a brazier with a copper coffeepot in one hand, and a large square basket in the other.*)

LEOPOLDO (*repeats his cry*): "Coffee for sale! Coffee, cigars, cigarettes, rum and anise! Leopoldo Coletta is here. Ready to serve you. Come get your coffee!" (*He stops right front.*)

TUMMASINO (*to the players in a superior tone*): What's the ante?

CIENTEPELLE (*looks up at him square in the face, irritated*): Six soldi.

FURMELLA (*smiling deferentially*): Thirty centesimi.

TUMMASINO (*with a tone that admits of no reply*): Give me a nickle.⁶

CIENTEPELLE: Why should I?

TUMMASINO: That's the racket!

CIENTEPELLE (*annoyed*): Take all six.

TUMMASINO: Four belong to me. (*He bends down to collect the four soldi and puts them in his pocket.*)

FURMELLA (*through his teeth*): What a swell guy!

CIENTEPELLE (*boiling with indignation, after shuffling the deck of cards, to* **FURMELLA**): Cut!

FURMELLA (*"cuts" the deck, with a sigh. And the two begin to play again.*)

TUMMASINO (*goes over to Leopoldo*): Good evening, Liopo'.

LEOPOLDO: Oh! The distinguished Don Tommasino! Aren't we the lucky ones.

TUMMASINO: Gimme a cigarette.

LEOPOLDO: (*hands him one*) Where've you been? We haven't seen you lately.

TUMMASINO: Taking the air at San Francisco prison.

LEOPOLDO: At San Francisco? What for?

TUMMASINO: For nothing! Swindle, assault and battery, and bearing illegal arms.

LEOPOLDO (*ironically serious*): Well, for such trifles they arrest an honest man?!

TUMMASINO: What can ya do? When the law gets on your back there's no arguing! (*He lights the cigarette.*)

LEOPOLDO: May I heat up the coffee for you?

---

5. San Ferdinando: square with church of same name, near the theater of San Carlo and Piazza Trieste and Trento.—Trans.

6. Nickle: an old coin worth twenty centesimi.—Trans.

TUMMASINO: No. What have I done to deserve that? Ya wanna ruin what little health I got left?

LEOPOLDO: You want coffee? You can have it. I made it fresh today with sediment only a week old.

TUMMASINO: Oh, yeah?

LEOPOLDO: My word of honor. As an expression of my regard.

TUMMASINO: So let's have this offering!

LEOPOLDO (*prepares the coffee*).

SCARRAFONE (*gives his cry*): "The Italian Daily! Final edition! Just out!"

CIENTEPELLE (*stretching his numb legs while* **FURMELLA** *shuffles the cards*): What's the score?

FURMELLA: Ten for you, and one for me!

CIENTEPELLE (*rubbing his hands with satisfaction*): Shuffle! Shuffle!

FURMELLA (*angrily*): Cut!

CIENTEPELLE (*"cuts" the deck. The game begins again*).

MUSIC II

THE PIZZA MAKER'S CRY "Get 'em while they're good and hot! Pizza!" (*from offstage.*)

(*The* **PIZZA MAKER** *enters, blowing a flat whistle. He is toting a large warming oven on his head.*) (*Music breaks*).

LEOPOLDO (*to the* **PIZZA MAKER**): Hey, haven't you gone home yet?

THE PIZZA MAKER: . . . How can I go home before I sell these pizzas? Should I take them home to sleep with me? (*He looks around and gives his cry.*) "Swimming in oil!" (*He blows the whistle again.*)

MUSIC III

LEOPOLDO (*winks at the vendor, laughing.*)

THE PIZZA MAKER (*gives his cry*): So hot they're burning me . . .

TUMMASINO (*bitingly*): Get outa here!

MUSIC IV

THE PIZZA MAKER:

> Went out early in the evening:
> Walked the streets for five long hours!
> (*Pizza warmer's like a freezer*)!
> (*Points to the warmer. Gives his cry.*)
> "Good and hot!"

LEOPOLDO (*ironically*):
> Right! In this weather!

THE PIZZA MAKER (*laughs in spite of himself*):
> They're not pizzas, they're leather pieces.
> If I don't sell 'em, I cut them up,
> And sell you laces for your shoes.
> (*He continues with his cry.*)
> "They're fresh and wholesome!"

SCARRAFONE (*breaking into laughter*):
> Sure!

THE PIZZA MAKER (*justifying himself*):
> They are pizzas made in wartime:
> made of sawdust and of bran:
> you need a saw to cut them up!
> (*His cry again.*)
> "Get your pizzas! I'm moving on!"

TUMMASINO (*crossly*):
> Then get going. Are you still here?

THE PIZZA MAKER (*bitterly*):
> That's just fine for one who's eaten;
> what do you care if someone starves!

(*Music breaks*).

LEOPOLDO (*looks at the pizza maker in sympathy.*)

MUSIC V

THE PIZZA MAKER (*gives his cry*):
"Get 'em while they're good and hot! Pizza! Oh! Pizza!"

(*The vendor wanders around blowing his whistle.*)

LEOPOLDO (*hands the coffee to Tummasino*): Here you are, sir.

CIENTEPELLE (*to Furmella*): You've made four points! (*Shuffles the cards.*)

FURMELLA: And the one I had makes five! Five to ten! Thanks to the Madonna! (*He rubs his hands in satisfaction.*)

CIENTEPELLE (*crossly*): Cut! (*The game continues.*)

TUMMASINO (*sips the coffee, spits it out and turns to Leopoldo in disgust*): Phew! I could throw it in your face. I had such a nice taste in my mouth and now you've ruined it!

LEOPOLDO: Is it too strong?

TUMMASINO: Get lost. This is the stuff that poisoned Christ!

THE PIZZA MAKER (*quits blowing because the whistle is acting up.*)

(*Music breaks*).

   (*To* **SCARRAFONE**, *laughing.*) See? Even the whistle's got a cold!

SCARRAFONE: My "Italian Daily" has had a toothache all day.

THE PIZZA MAKER (*makes a gesture as though to say, What an exaggeration! and gives his cry*):   "Yeah, so hot they're burning me!"

TUMMASINO: So throw 'em on the ground. (*referring to the pizzas*)

THE PIZZA MAKER (*looks at him.*)

TUMMASINO: Leopo', ya shouldn't 'a give me this coffee! (*He gives back his cup.*)

THE PIZZA MAKER (*looks at* **SCARRAFONE**, *who is laughing; he begins again.*) "Well, I'm moving on . . . "

TUMMASINO: Then get a move on.

THE PIZZA MAKER: ". . . Well, I'll soon be gone . . . "

TUMMASINO: Then get going!

THE PIZZA MAKER (*the interruption makes him stammer nervously*):   Y-y-young man, let me do my work. All right? I got a lot of worries on my mind and all you can think about is making fun of me!

TUMMASINO: No one wants your pizzas now!

THE PIZZA MAKER: No one wants them right now? They can eat them tomorrow! The day after tomorrow . . . a month from now . . . a year from now . . . or when we have another war . . .

SCARRAFONE (*ironically*):   . . . or in a couple of centuries!

THE PIZZA MAKER: The pizzas last in here! (*He points to the warmer.*) Are they going to run away? (*pause*) So, you don't know my plan? Well! Once I kept two pizzas for three months and I transformed 'em. The lard and cheese I smeared on 'em became like little fish. And I sold 'em! I sold 'em!

TUMMASINO: . . . You sold 'em!

THE PIZZA MAKER: The guy who ate 'em even thanked me. He got drafted, and they discharged him right away. Not fit for military service!

SCARRAFONE (*laughing*):   He had stomach cancer!

LEOPOLDO (*to the pizza maker*):   What can you do? Today pizza's past its time . . .

THE PIZZA MAKER (*offended*):   Oh, Liopo', why should two old merchants quarrel?

TUMMASINO (*commiserating with him*):   "Merchants"!?

THE PIZZA MAKER (*to* **LEOPOLDO**):   Pizza, if you don't know it, has been ruined by the goings on in Europe! Or else it'd be selling all over the world right now!

LEOPOLDO: What's that got to do with it?

THE PIZZA MAKER: Oh, Liopo'! (*as if to say: how dumb can you be?*) What's the war done? It's turned life upside down. Those who were up are down, and those who were down are up; and in all this reshuffling what happened to the pizza lovers? They've vanished!

(*pause*) Then what's the collapse of the exchange rate done? It's made the pizza collapse, too. The exchange rate went up, and pizza went down!

LEOPOLDO: I don't get it.

THE PIZZA MAKER: What is pizza? Something to eat, no? Made with flour, no? And the flour, where does that come from? From abroad!

TUMMASINO: Oh, yeah . . . it's very expensive . . .

THE PIZZA MAKER: And also pizza took a dive because its price went up. Before, with two soldi, you could get a nice pizza with cheese, lard, tomato, mozzarella. You could smell the aroma! Oh, what consolation! Now for a lira and a half you get a little nothing (*He shows how small.*), and when you get a whiff of it you drop dead! (*The others laugh.*) And why's that? Because, after all, the ingredients aren't as good as they were before! (*to* **LEOPOLDO**) Do you know that at the allies conference in Genoa they talked more about pizza than anything else? Anyway, despite everything, my wife who—like me— always has her hands in the dough, she, even in this crisis, has a weakness for stuffed pizza . . . Once I used to go home and ask her: "Woman, what d'ya want for supper?" "Oh, make me a stuffed pizza with something in it like ricotta, salame, eggs, mozzarella . . ." And now that times have changed, she still has the same idea. "Woman, what d'ya want for supper?" "Oh, make me a stuffed pizza with something in it like ricotta, salami, eggs, mozzarella . . ." "Hang on! You can still have the pizza, but you're gonna have to wait for the stuffing till the prices come down!" (*Everyone laughs.*)

TUMMASINO (*incredulous*): Yeah!

THE PIZZA MAKER: Jesus! They said that food's supposed to be cheaper an' be as good as before.

TUMMASINO: What does that mean?

THE PIZZA MAKER: Why, isn't pizza food?

LEOPOLDO: Yeah, you're right!

THE PIZZA MAKER: Can you tell me your coffee's like the coffee before the war?

LEOPOLDO: Yes, it's the still the same!

THE PIZZA MAKER: Exactly the same?

LEOPOLDO (*nods*): Yeah!

THE PIZZA MAKER: Like what you've got here?

LEOPOLDO: Never mind: the quality's the same! (*Everyone laughs.*)

THE PIZZA MAKER: Well, so long. (*Gives his cry.*)

MUSIC VI

THE PIZZA MAKER:

"Get 'em while they're good and hot! Pizza here!
Oh! Pizza!"

(*He exits blowing his whistle.*)
(*Music breaks.*)

CIENTEPELLE (*with a gesture of irritation, pretends to rip the cards*): These lousy cards have changed!

FURMELLA (*very happy*): I got another five points and now we're even!

CIENTEPELLE (*very nervous; barely restraining himself*): Cut! (*The game continues.*)

TUMMASINO (*to* **LEOPOLDO**): What do I owe ya?

LEOPOLDO: Two soldi for the cigarette and one for the coffee: three soldi.

TUMMASINO (*with his superior air*): You'll get it tomorrow.

LEOPOLDO (*not pleased*).

TUMMASINO: I don't want to break my coin!

LEOPOLDO (*through his teeth*): Like it was a gold piece!

TUMMASINO (*looks around again nervously; he turns to* **LEOPOLDO**): . . . Seen a woman with hair on her head?

LEOPOLDO (*joking*): No, I saw one with a beard go by.

TUMMASINO: . . . The one with all the hair: Ines . . .

LEOPOLDO: Do I know dear Ines?

TUMMASINO (*bitterly*): Oh, well! I'm goin' fishing!

LEOPOLDO: Lotsa luck! (**TUMMASINO** *hurries out.*)

FURMELLA (*euphoric*): Score! (*plays*) Score! Oh! Oh! Score! (*to* **CIENTEPELLE** *ironically*) . . . are you gonna give up . . . ?

CIENTEPELLE (*violently throws the cards in the air*): Jeez! (*to* **FURMELLA**, *contemptuously*) Cut! (*He stands up.*)

FURMELLA: What? Giving up?

CIENTEPELLE (*giving him a shove*): Cut! Or I'll throw these cow guts in your face.

FURMELLA (*silently picks up the cards.*)

CIENTEPELLE (*starts to leave.*)

FURMELLA (*calls him back*): Hey!

CIENTEPELLE: I'm not playing!

LEOPOLDO (*sarcastically*): I see Montecarlo's closed!

CIENTEPELLE (*angrily*): What nerve! Look how bad I lost!! (*To* **SCARRAFONE**) But how could he win ten to one?

SCARRAFONE: Cientepelle, how much did you lose?

CIENTEPELLE (*biting his lip*): What a day! What a wasted day! That's what it was!

LEOPOLDO: Did you lose a lot?

CIENTEPELLE: I can't break the habit! I can't break . . .

SCARRAFONE: Can't you tell me how much you lost?

CIENTEPELLE: I'm a jerk! A jerk and a sap! I lost three soldi!

SCARRAFONE: Just look at that! (*in an ironical tone of superiority*) Here we bet all of a half lira!

LEOPOLDO: Those two are high rollers! (*He laughs.*)

CIENTEPELLE (*takes his pushcart and goes toward San Ferdinando, crying*): "Sheep's feet! Pig's feet! Chewy tripe! Snout! They melt in your mouth! Sheep's feet! Pig's feet!" (*He exits.*)

FURMELLA (*finishes counting the cards*):   Thirty-eight, thirty-nine . . . One card's missing!

(*He looks around for it.* **GASTONE** *and* **FRITZ** *enter, two very elegant gentlemen in overcoats, top hats, and canes. They are having an animated discussion.*)

FRITZ: . . . I'm never going back to that club again! How did the baron score nine eleven times in a row at "baccarat"?

SCARRAFONE (*gives his cry*):   "The Morning! The Afternoon! The Evening!" (*The two pay no attention to him.*) "The whole day!" (*He strolls around bored, stamping his feet on the ground to keep warm.*)

GASTONE (*to* **FRITZ**):   But listen, you shouldn't have plunged in like that . . .

FRITZ: Why not?

GASTONE: You shouldn't have taken such a chance!

FRITZ: Oh, Christ! I'd already lost three thousand lire. I was trying to recoup . . .

SCARRAFONE (*starts up his cry again*):   "The Rome Tribune! The Daily Italian!"

GASTONE (*going up to the coffee vendor*):   Leopo', give me a pack of cigarettes. But not like those ten dried out twigs you sold me last night. (*to* **FRITZ**) Say, do you want any?

FRITZ: Didn't you get some? They'll do for me, too.

GASTONE (*between his teeth*):   He's made me cashier!

FURMELLA (*to* **SCARRAFONE**, *indicating* **FRITZ**):   His pal's broke!

LEOPOLDO (*gives the cigarettes to* **GASTONE**. *He asks*):   Do you both want coffee?

GASTONE (*disgustedly*):   Yuk! It's disgusting, made with chicory!

LEOPOLDO (*with subtle irony*):   No, I used to make it with chicory. But now I make it with crushed chestnuts. I even tried to make it with beans, but it came out too light, so I had to add some black soot to make it darker . . .

GASTONE (*handing him some money*):   Sure, very funny! Here are two lire. Give me the change.

LEOPOLDO: . . . And you say it's chicory! (*He digs in his pocket for the change; then he turns to* **SCARRAFONE**.) Hey, can you change these two lire?

SCARRAFONE: What do you think?

LEOPOLDO (*to* **FURMELLA**):   You got change?

FURMELLA: Never had two lire. (*He keeps counting his cards.*)

SCARRAFONE (*to* **LEOPOLDO**):   See the grass seller on the corner!

LEOPOLDO (*goes to the corner of Vico Berio and calls loudly*):   Ruse'!

FURMELLA: . . . Thirty-eight, thirty-nine . . . Still thirty-nine and that's it! (*to* **FRITZ** *in a confidential tone*) Well, what can you do? It's the luck of us gamblers . . .

FRITZ (*offended, to* **GASTONE**):   Do you know this bum?

FURMELLA: It cost me a card to win three soldi! Now I don't have a full deck! (*He goes away muttering.*)

FRITZ: . . . Three soldi! I lost eight thousand lire! (*pause*) Oh, well, eight thousand lire, more or less . . . Gastone, lend me two soldi for the newspaper.

GASTONE: Whatever you say. (*He gives it to him.*)

FRITZ (*to* **SCARRAFONE**) "Italian."

(*He buys the newspaper.* **RUSELLA**, *the couch grass seller, enters: she is very young, with an open, honest face. She is carrying two bundles of couch grass under her arm.*)

RUSELLA (*to* **LEOPOLDO**): Who wants me?

LEOPOLDO: No one. I called you to change these two lire for me.

RUSELLA (*annoyed*): You'll get what you deserve someday! (*She begins to count her change.*)

FRITZ: Oh, Gastone, look how cute the grass seller is!

GASTONE: A real pretty girl. (*He goes up to the girl and strokes her cheek.*)

RUSELLA (*indignant*): Hey, you! What do you think you're doing? Do you want the money in your face?

LEOPOLDO (*softly to* **SCARRAFONE**, *laughing*): Now the aristocracy is going to get it!

GASTONE: Oh, take it easy, little girl. I was only teasing.

RUSELLA: Teasing? Do it to your sister! Yuk, look what I have to put up with! (*to* **LEO-POLDO**) . . . Just because we're all here at night in the street, they think that makes us all alike . . .

GASTONE: But . . .

RUSELLA (*counts the money out nervously*): Four! Eight, twelve, sixteen and four, twenty. Here! (*She hands the money to* **LEOPOLDO** *and goes off down the street with a determined step that makes her clogs resound.*)

LEOPOLDO (*goes up to* **GASTONE**, *barely able to keep from laughing*): Here's your change! (*He gives it to him.*)

FRITZ: . . . Gastone, you've made a fool of yourself!

GASTONE: (*seriously*): Know what I just realized? If I ever get married, I'll marry a grass seller!

FRITZ: Yeah! (*As if to say: you don't say so!*)

GASTONE: But you saw how modest she is . . .

(*They exit.*)

LEOPOLDO (*continues to laugh along with* **SCARRAFONE**.)

Scene 2

Via Toledo, the corner of Ponte di Tappia. Some minutes later. A coatless young man, with a woolen scarf around his neck, is waiting on the sidewalk. He is **PASCALINO**, *the little baker.*

LEOPOLDO'S CRY "Coffee for sale! Coffee, cigars, cigarettes, rum and anise! Leopoldo Coletta is here, ready to serve you. Come get your coffee!" (*He enters and stops on the sidewalk.*)

PASCALINO: Good evening, Liopo'!

LEOPOLDO (*cordially*): Good evening, Pascali'!

PASCALINO: Have you seen Rusella?

LEOPOLDO: A minute ago, at the corner of Vico Berio. Oh, you should have been there!

PASCALINO: Why's that?

LEOPOLDO: A gentleman dared to touch your girlfriend, and she really gave it to him!

PASCALINO: Good for her!

LEOPOLDO: Are you waiting for her here?

PASCALINO: Yes. (*pause*) Leopo', it's cold. Know what you can do? Give me a little cup of dirty water . . .

LEOPOLDO: Dirty water? (*He prepares the coffee.*)

MUSIC VII

(*Sadly, from far off, from the maze of streets of Ponte di Tappia comes the voice of the* **RAG MAN**.[7])

THE CRY OF THE RAG MAN:

> *We were a group of a hundred sixteen beggars;*
> > *e ndin ndin mbò . . .*

(**SCARRAFONE** *enters with a bundle of newspapers under his arm.*)

SCARRAFONE (*greeting* **LEOPOLDO** *with a hand gesture*): Hey, good evening! (*Gives his cry.*) "The Italian! The Tribune! The Rome!"

THE CRY OF THE RAG MAN: . . .

> *we drew by twos on a deck of cards to see*
> > *e ndin ndin mbà . . .*

LEOPOLDO (*to the news vendor who is leaving*): Hey, Scarrafo'!

SCARRAFONE: Yo!

LEOPOLDO: Keep to the wall so no one smashes you!

SCARRAFONE (*exits*).

THE VOICE OF THE RAG MAN:

> *which of us would be the president;*
> > *e ndin ndin mbò . . .*

LEOPOLDO (*giving the coffee to* **PASCALINO**): See if it's good and sugary.

PASCALINO (*takes a sip*).

THE VOICE OF THE RAG MAN: . . .

> *My luck held out—it went of course to me!*
> > *e ndin ndin mbà!*

(*The little* **RAG MAN** *enters, pale, thin, shoeless, with a tattered coat barely covering his chilled skin; he has a large basket over his right arm and is holding a lantern in his left.*)

---

7. The rag man, called *sapunariello,* diminutive of *sapunaro:* rag man. One who goes through the streets with a basket on his arm, trading homemade laundry soap for rags.—Trans.

(*Music breaks.*)

THE RAG MAN (*upon seeing the others, he playfully poses like a statue*):   The troubadour!

PASCALINO (*teasing*):   Here we go again!

THE RAG MAN (*holds up the lantern to look at him*):   Oh, yeah! Look who's talking. (*to* **LEO-POLDO**) Ya get it, Leopoldo? It's always so beautifully satisfying . . .

LEOPOLDO: What's that?

THE RAG MAN: To play the game with one hundred and sixteen beggars and come out president!

LEOPOLDO (*sarcastically*):   President of the Cabinet!

PASCALINO: Imagine how envious everyone is!

THE RAG MAN (*scornfully*):   I'll have to wear a good luck charm against the evil eye! (*He sighs.*) What can you do! When tight-fisted fortune says no, it's all over!

MUSIC VIII

Look, what a cruel wind blows off the mountain
and comes sweeping down at any minute!
If only I had a little fur coat now,
I'd be sitting pretty, I'd kill this wind!

But tired to death, bare and dead from hunger,
how can I kill this wind, can you tell me?
It'll go just the other way, oh, Lordy:
maybe one day the wind will kill me!

(*Music breaks.*)

LEOPOLDO: Come here, sit down!

PASCALINO: Warm yourself a little!

THE RAG MAN (*sits on his basket near Leopoldo's brazier; he rubs his hands, making a wry face*):   Go on, this is colder than I am!

MUSIC IX

Meanwhile the deputy and all the guards
make a sweep of the common folk and low life!
Low life? You hear? That's what they call it!
What? That, you should know, is the good life!
Those are the people who eat and who drink,
with carriages, theater, country outings;
with hookers and etcetera etcetera . . .
And that is the bad life? Don't believe it!
The real low life, the one that's authentic,

is the one I lead! This dreadful misery!
This is the low life! And yet the others,
such as are called the "fancy dandies,"
have the satisfaction to get lugged off
to jail; and I, nothing. Oh, well, so goes life!

(**PASCALINO** and **LEOPOLDO** break into laughter.)

No, don't laugh, it's nothing to laugh about,
that really is the comfortable life:
because prison is a nice government
employment that they get. It's real soft!
There in rain, or stormy night or thunder,
you have the prisoner's garb to cover you,
soup, a bed, and so forth . . . And finally,
in the summer you can say: "I'm in the cooler!"
because inside there it's really cool,
at that place they call "San Francisco."

(*Music breaks.*)

PASCALINO: But you've got your freedom and you complain?

THE RAG MAN (*suddenly serious*): Freedom? You want ta see what freedom looks like? Take a look at freedom! (*He stands and turns around, showing his tattered coat that reveals his naked lower back.*) See how wonderful freedom is?

PASCALINO (*puts a hand on his shoulder.*)

THE RAG MAN (*sits down again*): Damn whoever's the cause of all this!

LEOPOLDO (*in a tone half-serious, half-facetious*): The blame all goes to the commissioner of street sweepers who has turned the streets of Naples into an arcade and destroyed the tobacco industry!

THE RAG MAN: Exactly! Before Labriola you could find butts like this. (*He shows the size with his thumb and forefinger.*) Now who gives 'em to you any more? Smokers are economical today and don't toss their butts away like they used to! And then, with the invention of those newfangled cigarette holders they even smoke the ashes! (*pause*) But this is a wonderful discovery for mankind; and one a' these days we'll all go on strike!

LEOPOLDO: Really?

THE RAG MAN: Really?! I'm a man of character! Because I have the courage to walk around a butt seven, eight times, and do nothing! I don't pick it up!

PASCALINO: Bravo!

THE RAG MAN (*he spies a bottle of anise in Leopoldo's basket. To the coffee vendor*) Look over there, over there . . .

LEOPOLDO (*turns to look where he is pointing.*)

THE RAG MAN (*takes the bottle and drinks, then puts the bottle back.*)

LEOPOLDO (*turns to him questioningly.*)

THE RAG MAN (*with a gesture of indifference*):   It's gone, it's gone!

PASCALINO (*laughs silently.*)

THE RAG MAN (*takes a pipe from his basket, lights it from the lantern, crosses his legs, and smokes.*)

PASCALINO: How comfortable you look!

THE RAG MAN (*looks at* **LEOPOLDO** *and his itinerant shop; and with irony*):   It might be the Café d'Italia!

LEOPOLDO (*facetiously*):   But what do you need?

THE RAG MAN: What do I need? Everything I don't have! (*pause*) Besides there I pay for the eats, and here the eats are free. This weather's eating me alive! (*Shivers from the cold.*) Oh! Someone left the door open! (*to* **LEOPOLDO**) . . . Look over there, over there . . .

LEOPOLDO (*turns as before; and the other again takes a quick swallow of anise; then, as before, the coffee vendor turns to find out what the* **RAG MAN** *was pointing at.*)

THE RAG MAN: It's gone, it's gone . . .

PASCALINO (*gives a call*):   Rusella!

RUSELLA (*runs in, responding to the call*):   Goodness! Have you been here long?

PASCALINO: Where have you been?

RUSELLA: Behind the street getting six bundles of couch grass for the coachman! His poor horse was starving!

(*The two young people stand aside chatting lovingly and then they slowly exit.*)

MUSIC X

(*The patrol enters, led by* **BRIGADIER BRIGHELLA** *who is talking with officer* **GUARDASCIONE**. *The police come down from Montecalvario and head for Ponte di Tappia, where they disappear.*)

THE RAG MAN (*raises his eyes to heaven; sighs*):
    Another day has dawned right in my face!
    And what have I to show for it? Zero!

(*He gets up, looks in his basket with a sense of distrust.*)

    A night of rummaging round Mercato and Vecaria,
      did I find a piece of old rag! Not even one!

Fortune, fortune! Stick out your head so I can spit in your face! (*Looks at the lantern: it has gone out.*)
    I had a lantern but it's gone out;
      now I'll close up the shop and bon soirée!

> And go along home to my one-eyed wife,
> who keeps that one eye on me!

LEOPOLDO (*ironically*):   She really lucked out, didn't she!

THE RAG MAN (*Taking up the song again*):

> If fortune ever took care of the poor,
> e ndin ndin mbò,
> I'd have some food and bottles full of wine
> e ndin ndin mbò,
> But lady luck had something else in store
> e ndin ndin mbò,
> and she has made this empty basket mine!
> e ndin ndin mbà!

(*Reciting, he takes the basket and lets his torn sleeve dangle.*)

A sleeve in the Mary Stuart style! (*pause*)

> Now I get it: it's the Eternal Father
> who holds the wheel of this world in hand,
> and makes it turn like this . . . like this . . .
>   like this . . .
> (*He makes a circular gesture forward.*)
> Sooner or later he gets tired . . . And then swings
> it like this . . . like this . . . like this . . .
> (*He makes a circular gesture backward.*)
>   I'll wait here for . . .
>   the world to turn a little my way!

(*He sighs, looks at the bottle of anise; to* **LEOPOLDO**):   Look over there, over there . . .

(*But this time* **LEOPOLDO** *catches him in the act and makes him put the bottle back.*)

LEOPOLDO: Oh! Look here! If you don't get outa here . . .

THE RAG MAN (*laughs*):   Hey, excuse me if I've been a little too chummy . . .

LEOPOLDO (*quickly*):   Why do you care? You got the best of it!

THE RAG MAN: A very happy and holy night! (*He picks up his lantern and, going away, gives his cry.*)

> "Sand and sea,
> and a farewell to thee!"

(*He exits.*)

(*Music breaks.*)

LEOPOLDO (*shouts after him, like a good wish*):   Keep up your spirits! God helps the cheerful man!

Scene 3

Via Toledo, Commercial Bank building. A few minutes later.

LEOPOLDO'S CRY: "Coffee for sale! Coffee, cigars, cigarettes, rum and anise! Leopoldo Coletta is here. Ready to serve you! Come get your coffee!"

(**PASCALINO** *and* **RUSELLA** *enter arm in arm heading toward San Ferdinando. They stop, overcome by tenderness.* **LEOPOLDO** *enters, moving slowly toward the two lovers.*)

PASCALINO: . . . How long will it be? February, March, April, and May: another four months and we'll be happy!

RUSELLA (*happy*): We'll be married in May!

PASCALINO: When the roses are in bloom!

RUSELLA: We'll be married in May!

LEOPOLDO (*ironically*): When the donkeys' bray! (*exits*)

MUSIC XI

PASCALINO:

Rusella mia!
You're my rose:
you're lovely and sweet like a flower!

RUSELLA:

My Pascalino,
I could die of joy!
In just a few more months I'll be your bride!
But with no dowry . . .

PASCALINO:

Who needs a dowry?
You are all the treasure that I need!

RUSELLA:

Oh, my dearest love,
you speak with such nobility!

PASCALINO:

It's a lie
that lots of money makes a love more strong!
We've everything we need to start our life,
with health and flowering youth!

RUSELLA:

> It gives me joy to know I'll be your wife.

(*The* **PATROL** *again crosses the street, going toward the streets of* "*Sopra i Quartieri*.")

PASCALINO: (*takes* **RUSELLA'S** *hands in his. He kisses them*).

RUSELLA:

> Here's a secret I'll tell you.
> I've started sewing my trousseau.

PASCALINO:

> You're so clever!

RUSELLA:

> But cotton's all I have——no lace or silken embroidery.

PASCALINO:

> But beauty is simplicity.
> Your smile is all the ornament you need!

RUSELLA:

> Oh, my dearest love. You speak with such nobility.

PASCALINO:

> It's a lie
> that silk and satin make a love strong!
> Love based on wealth and luxury
> will not endure!
> We have a love that's true,
> good and pure!

RUSELLA:

> Oh, my dearest love,
> you speak with such nobility!

PASCALINO:

> It's my love for you that gives me this ability——
> Love, real love, has found my heart.

PASCALINO and RUSELLA:

> And only death can make us part.

(*They exit.*)
(*Music breaks.*)

Scene 4

"Sopra i Quartieri"[8] *Piazzetta of the Trinità degli Spagnoli, with the façade of the church of the same name. A few minutes later.*

LEOPOLDO'S CRY: "Coffee for sale! Coffee, cigars, cigarettes, rum and anise! Leopoldo Coletta is here. Ready to serve you! Come get your coffee!"

(**LEOPOLDO** *enters and stops at the corner of the street leading to Toledo. He knocks at the door of a street level apartment; a woman in nightclothes opens the door, hands him a copper coffee container that he pours into his own container. The door closes.*)

LEOPOLDO (*revives the flame of the brazier, stirs the coffee in the container. He is suddenly disturbed.*): Wait, there's something in here! (*He removes a card from the receptacle.*) A two of diamonds! The card that bungler Furmella lost! (*He looks at it.*) A piece is missing. I don't know if it's still inside . . . or was always like this! (*Shrugs his shoulders.*) Oh, well! (*He continues stirring.*)

MUSIC XII

(*A* **WOMAN'S VOICE** *is heard. It's the voice of a prostitute who is singing a sad ditty.*)

THE VOICE:
> Like a leaf
> the wind blows from a tree
> that flies from here to there
> and then to obscurity,
> so I wait
> not knowing where I'll go,
> but with unhappy heart wondering where
> the wind will blow.

(*She enters. It is* **MARGHERITA**, *dark, with large expressive eyes.*)
(*Music breaks.*)

MARGHERITA (*sighing*): They wrote that song for me! (*Goes up to the coffee vendor.*) Liopo', give me a coffee.
LEOPOLDO: Oh, Donna Margheri', how's it going?
MARGHERITA: A little better . . . (*She sips the coffee he hands her.*)
LEOPOLDO: Any news of Don Peppeniello?

---

8. A latticework of streets and alleyways above Via Toledo, once the area where the Spanish troops were quartered. — Trans.

MARGHERITA: I don't know anything . . . It was supposed to be a quick trial. But it's been a year and a half, and it hasn't moved.

LEOPOLDO: The train must be a little slow! (*He laughs.*)

MARGHERITA (*she also laughs, though against her will*): Yeah! That express train turned into a local on the way!

LEOPOLDO: But why was he arrested?

MARGHERITA: He lifted a silver crucifix from a shop.

LEOPOLDO (*half serious, half joking*): Think of that! They send you to prison now for being too good a Catholic! It's hopeless: there's no religion any more!

MUSIC XIII

(INES, *called* BAMBINELLA, *enters. She is no longer young, but her glitzy elegance and the air of superiority with which she shows off make this woman a still attractive street walker.*) (*Music breaks.*)

INES: Hey, Margari', good t' see ya!

MARGHERITA: Hey, Ines, how ya doing? How's it going?

INES: So so. Not bad! (*She lights a cigarette, smokes.*)

MARGHERITA: What do you mean! Not bad? You look great!

INES: Oh, well, everyone knows me . . .

MUSIC XIV

INES:

> The name's Bambinella
> I'm very well known in this part of town
> dancing all night to the hurdy-gurdy tunes
> in the back streets of Napoli.
>
> And if patrols of police should come by
> I turn on my heels and away I fly!
> If they should catch me and bring me in
> it's just a formality.
>
> I might start to flirt
> and then I might lift up my skirt,
> I can do just as I please
> I have all the cops on their knees.
>
> They turn into boys,
> and they think of me as a toy,
> and just as soon as they have me,
> they have to let me go!

(**FILIBERTO ESPOSITO** *enters. He is* **INES'S** *young protector. Pale, frail, but elegant in his own way, in a very tight pea-green suit, with a white silk scarf around his neck. He approaches his woman, takes the cigarette from her mouth, takes two or three puffs, and gives it back to her.*)

FILIBERTO (*to* **LEOPOLDO**):   Coffee! (**LEOPOLDO** *prepares it.*)

INES (*to* **MARGHERITA**):

> There are some people who make me laugh
>   when they tell me to look out for myself!
> I'm making love with the man on top . . .

FILIBERTO (*puts his hand to his hat in greeting and smiles*): Thanks!

INES:

> . . . and I spend a lot just to make him look swell.
>   I'm getting deeper and deeper in debt,
>   but I'm making money so let it go.
>   I have a good-looking man beside me . . .

FILIBERTO (*pleased, to* **LEOPOLDO**, *who hands him the coffee*):   She exaggerates!

INES:

>   . . . bringing respect to me.
>   Girls walking by night
>   need some protection alright . . .

FILIBERTO:

> . . . Someone who's strong and who always
>   knows how to win in a fight!

(*Drinks the coffee, finds it bitter; to* **LEOPOLDO**):   Sugar! (*He bends to take it from the basket, stirring the coffee.*)

INES:

>   Nightly—about now
>   he likes to start up a row!
>   He beats me up—but he loves me,
>   and hides it from the world.

(*Music breaks.*)

FILIBERTO (*still finding the coffee bitter he takes more sugar; he bends over to take even more, but* **LEOPOLDO**, *annoyed, lifts the basket up to him.* **FILIBERTO** *stirs the coffee and throws the spoon roughly in the brazier.*)

LEOPOLDO: Look at that! He throws it in the china cabinet!

FILIBERTO (*sips, then goes to offer some to* **INES**, *who sips it; he finally gives the cup back to* **LEO- POLDO**):   Take it, and write down fifty-three soldi!

LEOPOLDO (*annoyed, through his teeth*):   Oh, it has to reach two thousand before you pay!

FILIBERTO (*clicks his tongue in disgust. He bends to take the bottle of anise from* **LEOPOLDO'S** *basket and pours some in his mouth. A drop of anise splashes in one eye. Irritated by the burning he gives a kick at* **LEOPOLDO** *who protests; then he takes a gulp of anise. Unable to stand it, he spits it into the basket, and gives the bottle back to the coffee vendor who swears.*)

MARGHERITA (*to* **INES**):   . . . Want me to give you some advice? Think about yourself!

FILIBERTO (*adjusts the front of his jacket haughtily.*)

LEOPOLDO (*through his teeth, looking at him*):   Oh, he thinks he's Christ himself!

FILIBERTO (*begins to cough.*)

INES (*turns up the collar of his jacket*):   See, you do have a little cough! Put your coat on!

FILIBERTO (*giving her a shove*):   When did a tough guy ever wear a coat?

MUSIC XV

INES (*to* **MARGHERITA**):

> It's been three months now that I've been his nurse,
> I've done all that I can to make him well.
> Lucky the doctor is hot for me,
> so it's cost me nothing for medical care.
> They might arrest him—they've got a warrant.

FILIBERTO:

> Dead or alive they'll take me away.

INES (*to* **FILIBERTO**):

> Now don't you worry and don't be afraid,
> I'll always be here for you!

MARGHERITA:

> Go see the brigadier,
> tell him what he wants to hear.
> And while you're turning your trick
> he'll make his escape on the quick.

INES:

> When he holds me tight
> and makes love to me through the night
> then I am happy to do
> all his dirty work for him!

(*She embraces* **FILIBERTO** *who continues to cough.*)
(*Music breaks.*)

MARGHERITA (*comes up to* **LEOPOLDO**):   How much do I owe you?

LEOPOLDO: One for the coffee, and twelve for the cigarettes: thirteen soldi.

MARGHERITA (*hands him the money*):   Give me change for a lira.

LEOPOLDO: Right away! (*He digs in his pocket for the change.*)

MARGHERITA: (*looking left, gives a shout*):   The cops!

(*She runs toward Largo delle Baracche.*)

LEOPOLDO: *I've lost another thirteen soldi!* (*He goes away, crying out in a cursing tone.*) "Coffee, cigars, cigarettes, rum and anise! Leopoldo Coletta is here. Ready to serve you. Come get your coffee!" (*He turns toward Via Speranzella.*)

FILIBERTO (*in the meanwhile has given* **INES** *his gun.*)

INES (*hides it under her dress. The* **PATROL** *enters*).

FILIBERTO (*greeting the brigadier jokingly*):   Distinguished Signor Brighella!

BRIGHELLA: Oh? (*with a little smile*) Do you know me?

INES: Well, naturally . . .

GUARDASCIONE: Pst. Quiet, you!

FILIBERTO: (*gives his lover a dirty look.*)

BRIGHELLA (*to* **FILIBERTO**):   What are you doing out so late?

FILIBERTO (*smiling*):   You see, she suffers from asthma. I'm having my wife take a little air. (*He introduces her.*)

INES: Yes sir, I'm his . . .

GUARDASCIONE: Quiet, you!

FILIBERTO: (*to* **INES**, *harshly*):   Shut up! (*pause*) What do you want a protector for—just to waste money? (*He asks her with a furtive gesture about the gun. She reassures him.*)

BRIGHELLA (*he has taken a notebook and pencil from his pocket*):   Identification.

FILIBERTO: (*hesitates*).

INES (*under her breath*):   Tell him your name!

BRIGHELLA: What is your name?

FILIBERTO: Filiberto Esposito.

BRIGHELLA (*writes it down*).

FILIBERTO: . . . Known as "The Nice Guy."

BRIGHELLA: I asked you your name.

FILIBERTO: Filiberto Esposito.

BRIGHELLA: Good!

FILIBERTO: . . . Known as "The Nice Guy."

BRIGHELLA (*impatiently*):   That will do! (*pause*) I don't want to know if you're a nice guy or not! (*quietly to* **GUARDASCIONE**) Do you know him?

GUARDASCIONE (*shakes his head no.*)

BRIGHELLA (*writes something else in his notebook.*)

FILIBERTO (*whispers to* **INES**):   The gun?

INES (*in a whisper*):   It's underneath . . .

BRIGHELLA: . . . Age?

FILIBERTO (*reflects.*)

BRIGHELLA: Age? (*pause*) Look, how old are you?

FILIBERTO: Twenty-five, twenty-six, twenty-seven . . .

BRIGHELLA (*sarcastically*): Sure! Twenty-eight, twenty-nine . . . (*hard*) Can you tell me how old you are?

FILIBERTO: Oh, hold on . . . I know I'm two years younger than my sister Matalena, who's the first. She must be . . . How old can she be?

BRIGHELLA: You want me to tell you?

FILIBERTO (*calculates*): . . . She was thirteen when she left home . . . Then eight years as a hooker, and that makes twenty-one . . . Two in the slammer and that makes twenty-three . . . Five years with a street sweeper and that makes twenty-eight . . . Then, for me, make it twenty-six.

BRIGHELLA (*ironically*): "Make it twenty-six." (*Writes it.*) Your father?

FILIBERTO (*asks* **INES** *again about the gun with a quick look*).

BRIGHELLA: Hey! Your old man?

FILIBERTO: You do it.

BRIGHELLA: God! "You do it"?! (*to* **GUARDASCIONE**) Unknown (*He writes.*) Your mother?

INES: Oh, his mother, sir, was a martyr: she died in prison . . .

GUARDASCIONE: Quiet, you!

FILIBERTO (*irritated, to the woman*): Now I'm cutting out! Then you won't have me to represent you!

BRIGHELLA (*to* **GUARDASCIONE**) Did you get that? "Father unknown, mother died in prison . . ." An exemplary family. (*He smiles, then to* **FILIBERTO**.) How do you support yourself?

FILIBERTO: I work for myself. My wife . . .

BRIGHELLA: Your wife supports you?

FILIBERTO: My wife can testify . . .

INES (*ready to speak.*)

BRIGHELLA: I'm not interested. (*pause*) Then what's your line of work . . . ?

FILIBERTO: I work just like you work . . .

BRIGHELLA (*impatiently*): What do you do?

FILIBERTO: I'm a salesman.

BRIGHELLA: What kind of work? What do you sell?

FILIBERTO: I sell whatever comes along; I take it and I sell it.

BRIGHELLA: . . . But are you with a firm, with a house? What company are you with?

FILIBERTO: . . . It's a private house, not a firm. A small house . . .

BRIGHELLA: I get it, I get it . . . (*pause*) And you say you're a salesman?

FILIBERTO: Yes.

BRIGHELLA: What do you represent?

FILIBERTO: Nothing!

INES (*giving him a shove*):   Hey!

FILIBERTO: . . . Do I know what I represent?

BRIGHELLA: I know! (*He writes.*) Address?

FILIBERTO (*pointing to his suit*):   Only this.

BRIGHELLA: Address . . .

FILIBERTO: I told you: only this. Isn't it good enough?

BRIGHELLA (*raising his voice*):   Where do you live?

FILIBERTO: Oh?! (*as though to say: now I understand*) Largo delle Baracche.

BRIGHELLA: Number?

FILIBERTO: It's the only door on the block.

BRIGHELLA (*finishes writing and puts the notebook back in his pocket*):   All right! Tomorrow we'll check to see if the information is correct or not.

INES: No, sir, that's the pure and holy truth.

GUARDASCIONE: Quiet, you!

FILIBERTO: No, let her talk, she's not lying. And besides I have my surveillance paper here, where you can . . . (*He takes it from the inner pocket of his jacket, looks at it rapidly.*) . . . No, this is the expired one.

INES (*irritated with* FILIBERTO):   You haven't had it renewed yet?

FILIBERTO: I haven't had time!

BRIGHELLA: Oh, yeah? You're under police surveillance and you're on the street at this hour?

FILIBERTO: I have a special permit from the officer in charge.

BRIGHELLA: Give it here! (*He takes the document and makes a sign for* GUARDASCIONE *to search* FILIBERTO, *then he reads.*)

GUARDASCIONE (*rapidly searches* FILIBERTO.)

FILIBERTO (*cannot stand still. He laughs and crouches with the officer when he bends over to feel his legs.*)

GUARDASCIONE (*repeats the search; the other laughs louder, suddenly crouching*):   Hey! (*The officer is annoyed.*) Do you have to act up?

FILIBERTO: But I'm ticklish . . .

INES: Take it easy . . .

GUARDASCIONE (*with pungent irony*):   Don't worry. I won't wear out your Nice Guy! (*to* BRIGHELLA) Nothing!

BRIGHELLA (*gives the document back to* FILIBERTO *with a hard look*).

FILIBERTO (*lifts his hat*):   Anything else?

BRIGHELLA (*goes off, without answering, at the head of the patrol.*)

FILIBERTO (*covertly watches the officers in the distance, then gestures to* INES *to give him the gun.*)

INES (*raises her dress and gives him the weapon.*)

FILIBERTO (*puts a cigarette in his mouth.*)

MUSIC XVI

(*In the meantime a man wrapped in a cloak has entered.* INES *goes up to him plying her trade, while* FILIBERTO *goes to one side and lights the cigarette. Then* INES *and the* MAN *go away arm in arm toward Via Speranzella.* FILIBERTO, *with an ironic little smile, throws away the match and goes out the opposite way.*)
(*Music breaks.*)

Scene 5

Via Toledo, corner of Vico Rotto San Carlo, with a view of Piazza San Ferdinando in the background. A little while later. LEOPOLDO *has stopped on the sidewalk at left, under the luminous "Il Mattino" sign.*

LEOPOLDO (*gives his cry*): "Coffee, cigars, cigarettes, rum and anise!" (*Enter* MIMÌ, *café waitress, in a worn tuxedo jacket and package under her arm.*)

MIMÌ: Hey, God bless, Liopo'!

LEOPOLDO (*cordially*): Hey, Mimì, let God do it? Where are you working?

MIMÌ: The Gran Café d'Europa on Pertusillo Lane!

LEOPOLDO: Oh?! (TUMMASINO *enters. He looks around impatiently.*)

TUMMASINO: She's not here! (*He exits.*)

MIMÌ: Yes, but I'm leaving tomorrow! You know what I earned as head waitress? Thirteen soldi!

LEOPOLDO: And you're complaining?

MIMÌ: No, I'm dancing! You really picked the right job!

LEOPOLDO: What are you talking about?! More people don't pay me than do! (TUMMASINO *comes in again and goes to* LEOPOLDO.)

TUMMASINO: *Gimme another cigarette. Three soldi and two are five . . .*

LEOPOLDO (*quietly to* MIMÌ) See? See? See? See? (*gives the cigarette to* TUMMASINO.) Here you are, sir.

(TUMMASINO *lights the cigarette and puffs hard.* MARGHERITA *enters and goes over to* LEOPOLDO.)

MARGHERITA: Liopo', take this money . . . (*lifts her skirt to take some change from her stocking*)

TUMMASINO (*surprised, calls her*): Margari'!

MARGHERITA (*gaily*) Hey! Tummasi'! You're out of jail?

TUMMASINO: . . . Listen . . .

MARGHERITA: Wait, I have to give thirteen soldi to Liopoldo.

TUMMASINO: Never mind . . .

MARGHERITA: What do you mean?

TUMMASINO: Never mind! (*to* LEOPOLDO) Put it on my account!

LEOPOLDO: God's will be done!

MARGHERITA (*to* LEOPOLDO):   We're even! (*and she begins to talk in a lively way with* TUM-MASINO)

MIMI (*to* LEOPOLDO, *laughing*):   You have such nice customers!

TUMMASINO (*to* MARGHERITA):   And Ines?

MARGHERITA: Oh! Forget about her! She's in love with Filiberto now!

TUMMASINO: Filiberto? (*pause*) But is he a moneymaker?!

MARGHERITA: What can I tell you? All I know is that Ines is ahead one hundred percent by being with him, and, you know . . . she loves him!

TUMMASINO: Oh, yeah? (*They talk.*)

MIMI: Well, be good, Liopo'.

LEOPOLDO: You going home?

MIMI: What can I do? I'm dead tired. On my feet since early morning! I'm going to retire!

LEOPOLDO: Retire?

MIMI (*jokingly*):   . . . I'm going to bed. (*exits*)

TUMMASINO (*to* MARGHERITA):   Listen, I want to talk to her . . .

MARGHERITA: What do you want to do? Why do you want to make a fool of yourself?

TUMMASINO (*with a sardonic laugh*):   Filiberto? (*swaggers*) The guy ain't born yet who can make a fool outa me. (*pause*) Go tell her I want to see her!

MARGHERITA: If I find her . . .

TUMMASINO: Find her! I'll be on Toledo!

MARGHERITA (*exits.*)

(NICOLA, *the night watchman, enters with his mastiff, Leone. He begins checking the shop doors.*)

NICOLA (*speaking to his dog*):   Lio', your master's pride and joy, did you understand me good? While I'm checking the shops on Toledo, you be busy doing something else. Look at me: you go down to San Giacomo and, with the excuse that you're sniffing the ground, investigate the city hall square. Then pretend to be lost and turn on to Guantare Street.[9] And if you see someone suspicious, run tell me!

TUMMASINO (*patting the dog as it leaves*):   He even knows what time it is!

LEOPOLDO: What an intelligent animal, Don Nico'!

NICOLA (*flattered*):   Oh, not to knock him, but he can't talk!

LEOPOLDO: What does that matter? He's your dog; that's enough!

MUSIC XVII

(*A carriage with the top down enters.* GNAZIO, *the coachman—ruddy complexioned, a sly little old fox—is in the seat.*)

---

9. Via Guantai Vecchi and Via Guantai Nuovi make up the center of the Neapolitan glove industry.—Trans.

GNAZIO: Ho! (*The nag stops. The Coachman gets out and invites a couple of lovers to descend:* **MARIO** *and* **FLORA**.)

MARIO (*strikes a match and reads the carriage meter*): Three and sixty! (*becoming angry*) How can that be? A four lire supplement?!

GNAZIO: Why not? Did you expect to pay less than four lire for a room by the sea?!

(*Music breaks.*)

MARIO (*restrained by* **FLORA**): That's indecent!

GNAZIO: Indecent? Indecent is what you did!

MARIO (*gives him the money and exits indignantly with* **FLORA**.)

GNAZIO (*looking at the money*): Five lire? For using my carriage for a hotel!

NICOLA (*to* **GNAZIO**): Why are you always grousing?

TUMMASINO: You should be a coachman . . .

GNAZIO: Yeah. And see if we aren't always in the wrong!

MUSIC XVIII

GNAZIO:

> A signorina came up to me:
> "Coachman! Hurry! Quick! To the station!"
> "It's a good thing," I said to myself,
> "I've fallen into a bit of luck!"

(*Pretends to get into the seat and urge the horse on.*)

> "Hah! Hah!" Nothing!

LEOPOLDO:

> What is it?

NICOLA:

> What happened?

LEOPOLDO:

> He doesn't want to go?

GNAZIO:

> No sir!
> "Hah! Hah! Hah!"

(*Pretends to tickle the horse with the handle of the whip.*)

TUMMASINO:

> What did you do?

GNAZIO:

>A little
>tickle under his belly!
>"Hah! Hah!

(*Gives the impression that the carriage is moving, and he imitates the worried voice of the passenger.*)

>"Hurry! Or you'll make me miss
>the fast train at twenty past three!
>Hurry! Hurry! Because we have only
>fifteen minutes to spare!"
>"Where do you have to go?"
>"To Rome."
>"Oh, but there's still the train
>that leaves for Rome tomorrow morning . . ."
>"No!
>Are you crazy? Pull up now! Pull up now!
>Let me out of here!"
>"That's impossible!
>This animal can't make stops just because
>someone has an inspiration!"
>"Hurry! Hurry! tomorrow morning
>I have to, want to, must be in Rome!"
>"So, Signorina, why don't we go
>to Rome in my ever-ready carriage?!"

TUMMASINO (*breaks into laughter*):

>Oh, that's really incredible!
>That horse of yours could never make it!

GNAZIO:

>What, "Not make it?" You know what you're saying?
>That horse went from Porta Capuana
>to the station in one fell swoop—nonstop!

(*The* **OTHERS** *laugh.*)

NICOLA:

>And after that, then what happened?

GNAZIO:

>And after that, I: "Hah! Hah! Hah!"

(*Pretends to set off at a trot; again takes up the voice of the passenger*).

>"Hurry! We've only got six minutes!"
>"I'm going as fast as I can!"

"Stop trying to put something over on me,
whip your horse to make it go faster!"
"What? Whip it? For heaven's sake, signori' . . .
Treat this beauty bad and most likely you'll
not make the day after tomorrow train!
But you can count on one thing, Miss,
if this train should happen to pull out
of the station a couple of hours late
we'll make it for sure . . ."

TUMMASINO:

Oh, what trouble she had to go through,
that pitiful signora!

GNAZIO:

And all at once: "Mario! Mario!
Hold it! Pull up! Stop now!"

(*Pretends to stop abruptly, at the command.*)

"Whoa!"

(*Music breaks.*)

GNAZIO: (*imitates* **MARIO'S** *affected voice*) "Flora, like this! Leaving?" "Yes, because my husband Cornelio is waiting in Rome!" "Let him wait, stay with me tonight." "Ah, dear fool, what are you making me do!" "What you've always done!" "Well, climb up, get on, coward!" "Hurry, coachman, turn at Santa Lucia; and then, up to Posillipo, at a gallop!

LEOPOLDO: At a gallop?!

GNAZIO: It's a manner of speaking! (*imitates* **MARIO'S** *voice*) "Hurry, raise the top!" (*to those present*) Understand?

TUMMASINO: Oh, well, what can you do? It's all part of your business!

GNAZIO: And then, I . . . "At once, sir"! (*Describes the raising of the top; then he pretends to climb into his seat, to look inside at the two lovers embracing; and then, with an almost spiteful expression, imitates the way he made the additional charge on the meter.*)

NICOLA (*surprised*): That is all extra?

GNAZIO: Eh! (*As if to say: Exactly. He pretends to move on with the horse*) "Hah!"

MUSIC XIX

GNAZIO: "Hah!" (*Pretends to trot. Then turns, showing that the two inside are hugging and kissing.*) "Hah!" (*Pretends to urge the horse.*) "Hah!" (*Repeats this several times, with increasing emphasis to show what is going on inside the coach . . . In the end, as though stopping the horse, and as though speaking to* **MARIO**) "Well, sir, did you make it or not? (*imitating* **MARIO'S** *voice*) "No, take us back to Via Toledo . . ." . . . . Well, I come here and he puts four lire in my hand! Go to hell, you and your mother! (*The others break into laughter. Then a small mixed choir of happy voices is heard. They are prostitutes and free-livers.*)

THE CHOIR:

> The night is silent—it's cold but you don't feel it,
> when there's a willing woman by your side . . .
> The streets are dead, but we have come to life.
> While others sleep we're masters of the town.
> And with the sunrise,
> we'll abdicate to workers unenlightened,
> but we'll be back when they are sleeping.
> Back to our streets and to the pleasures of the night.
> The night is silent—It's cold but you don't feel it . . . no.

(*The group enters. The prostitutes are* **PIERRETTE**, **GEORGETTE**, *and* **FERNANDA**; *the free-livers,* **GASTONE**, **FRITZ**, *and* **EDGARDO**.)

(*Music breaks.*)

GNAZIO (*at attention*): Gentlemen, do you want a carriage?

GEORGETTE (*to* **GASTONE**): What should we do? Go home?

GASTONE: Whatever you want!

PIERRETTE: No, let's go to our bar, the "Caffettuccio"!

EDGARDO: Who wants to wander around all night. Let's go to bed!

FRITZ: Uh, are we chickens, going to bed at this hour?

PIERRETTE: It's really not chic to go to bed at three!

GNAZIO (*to* **LEOPOLDO** *and* **NICOLA**): That's why we stay up all night.

FERNANDA: Let's go, so we can have a coffee!

GEORGETTE: Yes, yes, let's go to the "Caffettuccio."

GNAZIO: Miss . . . (*He winks at* **GEORGETTE**, *pointing to* **LEOPOLDO**.)

GEORGETTE (*equivocating, offended*): You bastard, how dare you . . .

GNAZIO: What do you think I meant? I was pointing out the coffee vendor . . .

LEOPOLDO: Sir, do you want a really good cup of coffee?

FRITZ: Well?

LEOPOLDO: Then get one here.

FRITZ: Yuk! (*makes a gesture of disgust*)

GASTONE: He wanted to sell us coffee earlier . . .

FRITZ: We'd be dead by now . . .

GNAZIO: No, sir: this is really a good cup of coffee: it's cleansing! (*He laughs.*)

GEORGETTE: Well, let's make up our minds!

GASTONE: It's all the same to me, let's go. Anyway, I get up at eight in the evening . . .

EDGARDO: That's fine for you, but the cock crows in the morning for me. I have to be up by noon. If the bar was nearby . . . but to go as far as Piazza Vittoria!

FERNANDA: Let's take carriages . . .

EDGARDO: But there's only one.

GNAZIO: Don't worry, we'll make only one trip. The horse is up to it.

PIERRETTE: And where will we sit?

GNAZIO: What?

PIERRETTE (*laughing*): Where will we sit?

GNAZIO (*to* **LEOPOLDO**, *enticed*): . . . Keep quiet: she's all excited. She's lost her head . . .

LEOPOLDO (*giving him a shove*): Are you going or not?

GNAZIO: Look, sir. You'll be comfortable: four inside and two on the driver's seat.

TUMMASINO: And where will you sit?

GNAZIO: On the horse! (*He laughs.*)

LEOPOLDO: And then it'll take a couple of oxen to pull it!

NICOLA: Sir, if my dog was here, he could go call a couple of carriages for you!

TUMMASINO (*joking*): No, if the watchman's dog was here, he could carry you on his back!

GNAZIO (*mocking*): No, if the dog was here, he would make four cups of espresso all by himself!

PIERRETTE (*to* **EDGARDO**): Oh, well, let's go home! Anyway, it's clear that as long as I'm with you, I'm out of circulation.

GNAZIO: Shall we go, sir?

FERNANDA (*to* **PIERRETTE** *and* **EDGARDO**): Yes, you take the carriage, we want to walk a little bit more!

PIERRETTE (*looking the nag over*): Tell me, does this horse go?

GNAZIO: Go? This is an airplane!

FRITZ: In fact, you can see his wings . . .

GNAZIO: No, sir, those are the animal's ears!

GEORGETTE (*to* **PIERRETTE** *and* **EDGARDO**): We wish you good night!

PIERRETTE: And we wish you good fun!

GASTONE: Ah, no, no. The good wishes go the other way around. Good night to us and good fun to you . . .

EDGARDO: No, I wish myself good sleep!

GNAZIO (*has looked at the horse closely; he seems discouraged.*)

PIERRETTE: Tell me, what's the matter?

GNAZIO: The horse is stuck to the ground!

NICOLA: He's starving!

GNAZIO: He always does this to me, the bastard! He's an obstructionist! (*looks at the nag's belly*) What can I do now? Damn!

EDGARDO: What's wrong?

GNAZIO: The girth-strap is broken! (*The men laugh.*) Miss! (*to* **PIERRETTE**) Do you have a piece of string?

PIERRETTE: Not likely!

GNAZIO (*to* **GASTONE**): A belt?

GASTONE: I'm wearing suspenders.

GNAZIO: A shoe lace?

FRITZ: Come on . . .

GNAZIO (*to* **LEOPOLDO**, *alluding to the gentlemen*):   They don't have anything! I don't know what kind of gentry they are!

(*He takes his belt from his trousers, and tries to fix the strap on the horse's belly.*)

FERNANDA (*laughing*):   We're off to a good start!

FRITZ: Eddie, now I understand; we'll get to bed before you!

PIERRETTE: Goodbye, Fernanda, Goodbye, Georgette . . . (*She climbs into the carriage.*)

FERNANDA: Ciao!

GEORGETTE: May the Madonna protect you!

EDGARDO: We're going on a long journey! (*He climbs into the carriage.*)

GASTONE: Eddie, write me when you get there!

GNAZIO (*occupied with seeing the two passengers into the carriage, wants to call* **EDGARDO**, *who is laughing with* **PIERRETTE**; *turns to the men*) Can he write?

LEOPOLDO (*ironically*):   No, he's always wrong!

GASTONE: Edgardo!

GNAZIO: Don Eduardo!

EDGARDO: What is it?

GNAZIO: Why did you get on? (*to the others*) Huh, he's getting on! (*to* **EDGARDO**) Come on down, go up front, and pull on the horse's halter a little . . . (*He pushes the carriage, but without result.*) What's the young lady's name?

FERNANDA: Pierrette.

GNAZIO: Miss Piertit . . . (*They all laugh.*) You come down and pull, too! "Hah! Hah!" (*to* **LEOPOLDO**) He does it to be mean . . . (*He pretends to beat the horse; then to the men.*) Gentlemen, please help push from behind!

GASTONE (*laughing with the others*):   Are you crazy?

TUMMASINO: Wait, I'll give you a hand . . .

GNAZIO: Once he gets started he'll keep going . . .

TUMMASINO (*pushes the carriage, helped by* **NICOLA** *and* **LEOPOLDO**) So! So!

GNAZIO (*gets into the driver's seat. Cracks the whip, takes the reins.*) Hah! (*The horse moves, the carriage finally leaves.*)

MUSIC XX

(*The men wave goodbye to* **EDGARDO** *and* **PIERRETTE** *with great flourishes, then exit singing.*)

CHORUS:

> The night is silent . . .

(*Music breaks.*)

Scene 6

Via Toledo, corner of Via Corsa. A little later.

LEOPOLDO: "Coffee, cigars, cigarettes, rum and anise!"

(**NICOLA** *is heard whistling for his dog. Silence.* **NICOLA** *enters. He is very nervous.*)

NICOLA: That idiot! He's probably broken his leg on the way back!

LEOPOLDO: Who?

NICOLA: Leone! Who knows what he's doing? He's reading the signs over the stores . . .

LEOPOLDO: But why ever, what grade's he in at school? (*He laughs.*)

NICOLA: Don't be a fool! (*panting, as if he was talking to the dog*) Hell, I'm not going to wait for you! (*pause*) Leopo', do me a favor, when he comes, tell him that in half an hour I'll be waiting on Piazza Dante. If he wants to go home, I've left the key in the usual place. He knows where it is! (*He exits.*)

LEOPOLDO (*shouting after him, with sarcasm*): Shall I tell him to fix dinner, too?! Should I have him put the wine to cool?!

NICOLA'S VOICE: You're always kidding! (*Silence.* **INES** *is heard singing.*)

MUSIC XXI

INES'S VOICE:

> *Love, everlasting love—don't you believe it.*
> *No, don't believe a word the bastards tell you,*
> *'cause ev'ry one of them, they will deceive you.*
> *Men have a hundred lies, a thousand hearts.*
> *Women are trusting souls, they live for love.*
> *They fall for ev'ry lie, blind with "amore."*
> *But then he breaks her heart and she suffers,*
> *when the ingrate don't love her anymore!*

(**TUMMASINO** *enters and waits, with an expression of evil joy.*)

INES (*appears, starts to cross the street; stops, surprised*): Tummasino!

TUMMASINO: Finally. (*pause*) Can we offer you a cup of coffee?

LEOPOLDO (*to himself*): Oh, Christ!

INES: Thanks, don't go to any trouble.

TUMMASINO: A spot of anise?

LEOPOLDO: Don Tummasi', make yourself at home! (*to himself*) Then, with the excuse he doesn't have change, he won't pay me!

TUMMASINO (*to* **INES**, *insisting*): What do you say?

INES: Anise warms me up.

TUMMASINO: Would you like a pack of cigarettes?

LEOPOLDO: Okay! (*decided*) That does it! (*Takes his things and goes away.*) "Coffee, cigars, cigarettes, rum and anise! Leopoldo Coletta is here. Ready to serve you. Come get your coffee!" (*exits*)

MUSIC XXII

TUMMASINO:

> *Oh, lord, yes, it's made me very happy*
> *that you have found yourself another lover!*
> *Do me one favor and keep it to yourself*
> *so I won't have to save face with the neighbors,*
> *by cutting you to pieces with my knife.*

INES:

> *And just you try it! You know prison's nasty,*
> *Why would you go throw away your freedom?*

TUMMASINO:

> *And what do I care? For a man to be a man*
> *he's got to look out for himself. Every man for himself.*
>
> *And in no time flat I'll find another lover:*
> *I've fifty women waiting in reserve.*
> *One is a beauty, and one is fascinating;*
> *and each of them just wants to be my servant,*
> *to have the thrill of being near to me!*
> *So many women! I can't help it I'm so handsome.*
> *You're not leaving? It's your loss!*
> *Just turn the corner and I'll give a little wink*
> *and watch the girls fall at my feet like a deck of cards.*
>
> *Oh—one more thing—that silk scarf that I gave you—*
> *you'll have to give it back (it cost three lire!).*
> *It's not a thing a gentleman would ask*
> *but if I don't the neighbors will be asking*
> *"How come you let Ines keep all your gifts?"*
> *And while we're at it, you have six berets of mine*
> *and a bottle of brilliantine!*
> *It's really not nice, but then nothing lasts forever—*
> *(Haven't paid for them yet!)*

(*Music breaks.*)

INES: You'll get back everything.

TUMMASINO: All right. (*pause*) However, never let it be said that Tummasino the millionaire will stand for this insult! Because he won't!

INES (*startled*): Hey! Oh! Will you stand for it or won't you? You're just making a big noise because you found me alone . . . But if Filiberto was here you wouldn't dare talk like that!

TUMMASINO: Who's this Filiberto? I'm going home to get my Browning, and then I'll be back!

INES: And hurry back to Largo delle Barracche where you can talk to him!

TUMMASINO: I'll talk to him, to you, to the bandit Musulline, to the statue of Garibaldi! But who is he? (*He goes away gesturing.*)

INES (*shrugs her shoulders and exits*).

Scene 7

"Sopra i Quartieri," Largo delle Baracche. **INES** *is waiting, smoking impatiently. Light filters through from the doors of the indistinct houses. The cry of* **LEOPOLDO** *is heard.*

LEOPOLDO'S CRY: "Coffee, cigars, cigarettes, rum and anise!"

FILIBERTO'S VOICE: Ines! Ines!

INES: Filibe'!

FILIBERTO (*enters in high spirits*): Ines, I'm so happy . . . !

INES: Oh! happy! Tummasino is out of prison!

FILIBERTO: Who's Tummasino? (*scornful*) Tummasino! Too bad for him! He gets out of prison to go to the hospital! Funny!

INES: What happened?

FILIBERTO: I met my lawyer. And know what he said? Funny! I've been put on notice!

INES (*remains indifferent.*)

FILIBERTO: Don't you understand? My career! At twenty-six, already given warning! I'm five years ahead. And at this rate, at twenty-nine, thirty . . . house arrest: accelerated course!

INES (*with slight disappointment*): But you're already under police surveillance, what do you care about the warning?

FILIBERTO: I can see you're an ignoramus. The warning is official confirmation of the danger of an individual. It's like a technical license. Besides, could I refuse the thoughtfulness of the police commissioner? (*He kisses her.*) Now, go call your friends so we'll have lots of people to celebrate my promotion. We have to drink a toast!

INES (*calling*) Mari'! Filume'! Cuncetti'! Margari'! Cristi'! (*Different doors suddenly open and the* **STREET WALKERS** *come out.*)

MARGHERITA: What's going on?

INES (*explains the significance of the "ceremony" to her friends.* **LEOPOLDO** *enters*).

LEOPOLDO (*gives his cry*): "Coffee, cigars, cigarettes, rum, and anise."

FILIBERTO: Leopo', stay right there!

MUSIC XXIII

FILIBERTO: (*announces*) My friends!

(*Filiberto's friends enter in their racketeers' attire.*)

THE FRIENDS (*removing their hats*): Good evening! Greetings, Filibo'!

FILIBERTO (*to* **INES,** *showing off*): See how many came for me?!

(*Takes off his hat.*)

THE FRIENDS (*take off their hats again.*)

FILIBERTO (*introduces the women and men*): Don Aitano, the Consumptive. My better half. Affunzino, the Stutterer. Maria the Nuisance. Peppino Sfaticato.[10] Papele Mariuolo. Cristina, the Minor. Fatso. Margherita. Titina.

AITANO (*bowing to* **MARGHERITA**): I already know Margherita. I have a weakness for her.

(*Shakes her hand gallantly. Pause.*)

AFFUNZINO: What an honor!
Tonight is truly a gathering of the finest fl-flowers of-of-of the weaker a-and the stronger sex!

LEOPOLDO (*aside, heavily sarcastic*): Honesty and hard work!

TUMMASINO (*enters, taking off his hat*): Gentlemen of the court!

AFFUNZINO (*effusive, while the others tip their hats*):Distinguished Don Tummasino!

MARGHERITA (*quietly to* **INES,** *who trembles at the sight of* **TUMMASINO**): Call him over . . . (*Pointing at* **FILIBERTO.**)

INES (*angrily*): Why not? Tummasino should be taught a lesson!

FILIBERTO (*to* **INES**): What's going on?

INES (*feigning*): Nothing

FILIBERTO (*gives her the gun*): Here!

INES (*hides it in her blouse.*)

AFFUNZINO (*pointing out* **TUMMASINO** *to* **FILIBERTO**): You . . . Do you know each other?

FILIBERTO: It hasn't been my good fortune . . .

AFFUNZINO (*introducing the two men who look at each other coldly*): Fi-Filiberto Esposito . . . Tu-Tu-Tu . . . Tummasino the millionaire!

LEOPOLDO (*aside*): He owes me eighteen soldi!

FILIBERTO: I am so happy to meet you.

TUMMASINO: And I'm happy many times over!

---

10. *Aitano* means active, helpful, and *sfaticato* just the opposite.—Trans.

(*They shake hands.*)

AFFUNZINO (*pointing at Filiberto*):   He's just been pu-put on notice.

TUMMASINO: This promotion is something to celebrate, and if your friends will allow me I'd like to do the honors . . .

FILIBERTO: But look, don't go to any trouble . . .

TUMMASINO: It's the least I can do . . .

FILIBERTO: (*gestures as though insisting.*)

TUMMASINO (*with a superior air*):   Liopo', coffee for everyone!

(*The men tip their hats as a sign of thanks.*)

LEOPOLDO (*as though the roof had caved in*):   May you all drop dead!

(*He begins preparations half-heartedly.*)

FILIBERTO (*to* **INES**, *aside, pointing at* **TUMMASINO** *who is circulating among the group of men and women*):   Have you ever seen anyone so polite?

INES: Forget it, that's Tummasino!

FILIBERTO (*looks ferocious.*)

MARGHERITA (*to herself*):   Oh, God!

FILIBERTO (*to* **INES**):   Is that him . . . ?

INES: That's him!

FILIBERTO (*takes a tough-guy stance, goes up to the men and declares*)   No coffee for me!

(*And returns beside* **INES** *and* **MARGHERITA**.)

AFFUNZINO: N-no coffee for anyone!

LEOPOLDO (*who is about to pour the first two cups, starts with joy*):   Ah! It's a miracle!

TUMMASINO (*leaves the group and comes with a menacing air toward* **FILIBERTO**.)

MARGHERITA (*to herself*):   Here we go!

TUMMASINO (*to* **FILIBERTO**, *with a little smile*):   Listen, a little earlier I offered you coffee, you didn't want it. I say . . . I say . . . why?

(*And he turns to talk to the men.*)

FILIBERTO (*dumbfounded, to* **INES**):   Listen, basically, he is saying . . . "You didn't want it. Why?" What do you think?

INES (*egging him on*):   Go on, tell him!

FILIBERTO (*aloud, boldly, remaining, however, near the two women*):   Because coffee makes me nervous!

(*Turns his back to* **TUMMASINO** *who makes an angry gesture.*)

TUMMASINO: Oh, yeah? All right!

(*He talks animatedly with the others, going upstage.*)

FILIBERTO (*to* INES): Where'd he go?

INES: He's right behind you. Now he's coming to grab you . . .

FILIBERTO: Me? What for? He's threatening me?

INES: Be brave!

FILIBERTO: I'll cut his face up now right and left.

TUMMASINO (*comes forward with a fierce frown.*)

FILIBERTO (*goes up to meet him face to face.*)

LEOPOLDO: Now we're going to have a cock fight.

TUMMASINO: Speak.

FILIBERTO: Go on, you speak.

TUMMASINO: You speak.

FILIBERTO: Speak.

TUMMASINO: Go on! I'm used to being spoken to before I speak.

FILIBERTO: I've always let speak, and then I spoke about what was said.

TUMMASINO (*impatient*): Speak.

FILBERTO: Speak. You speak, I say.

TUMMASINO: Really, I have nothing to speak about.

FILIBERTO: Neither do I!

TUMMASINO (*between his teeth, in a huff*): You're worthless!

(*He returns to the others.*)

(*Music breaks.*)

FILIBERTO (*to* INES): I mortified him . . . How did it seem to you?

INES: . . . You were a little weak!

FILIBERTO: . . . But does he have to insult me . . . Did he insult me?

AFFUNZINO (*in a loud voice*): Well, here, my sirs, the incident is closed!

FILIBERTO: What incident? Amongst ourselves . . .

TUMMASINO: Don't stand on ceremony, whatever you want . . . (*He points to* LEOPOLDO.)

LEOPOLDO (*annoyed*): Oh, here we go again!

INES (*very nervous*): Thanks, thanks.

FILIBERTO: Thanks, don't go to any trouble.

TUMMASINO (*looking him in the eye, with ill-disguised challenge*): At your service. (*And he turns his back.*)

INES (*to* FILIBERTO, *crossly*): See what proud words he uses? Go on!

FILIBERTO (*again acts the tough; to* AFFUNZINO, *alluding to* TUMMASINO): Did he insult me?

AFFUNZINO: No, sir.

FILIBERTO (*turns to the women*): . . . He didn't insult me yet!

INES (*annoyed*): Yeah! (*Enter the* ORGAN GRINDER, *dragging the instrument by the handles, like a donkey.*)

AFFUNZINO (*to the group*): Well, here's the organ grinder! (*to the man*) Professor, play a waltz.

MUSIC XXIV

(*The* **ORGAN GRINDER** *starts playing the instrument with a crank. The couples begin to dance.* **FILIBERTO** *asks* **MARGHERITA** *to dance.*)

LEOPOLDO (*gives his cry*): "Coffee, cigars, cigarettes, rum, and anise! Leopoldo Coletta is here. Ready to serve you."

TUMMASINO (*going up to* **INES**): May we have the honor of this dance?

INES: You have to get Filiberto's permission!

TUMMASINO (*violently*): Filiberto's not worth the bother! (*grabs the woman and makes her dance*)

INES (*manages to free herself from his grasp. She is very upset. Grabs* **FILIBERTO** *by his arm.*) Did you hear that? Tummasino said you aren't worth the bother!

FILIBERTO: . . . Did he insult me?

INES (*through her teeth*): And how! He wanted to dance with me without asking you first!

FILIBERTO (*cocky*): Silence!

(*Music breaks.*)
(*The couples stop.*)

FILIBERTO (*to* **TUMMASINO**): Friend, one moment, please. (*The party divides into two groups: on one side* **TUMMASINO** *and the men, on the other* **FILIBERTO** *and the women.*)

LEOPOLDO (*worried*): Now all hell is about to break loose!

FILIBERTO (*in the tone of one wanting to make an announcement*): Listen . . . Not to take away from a good friend here with us, who has done time . . . (*He points to* **AFFUNZINO**.)

AFFUNZINO: Please, after you . . . (*Tips his hat.*)

FILIBERTO: . . . I did twelve years in the slammer. (*The men make gestures of interest, and listen carefully.*) . . . Therefore, you'll be frank, I'll be frank. We are two franks.

LEOPOLDO (*sarcastically, aside*): Even fewer, even fewer . . .

TUMMASINO: Well?

FILIBERTO (*loudly*): . . . Which . . .

TUMMASINO (*turns to the fellows*): What's he talking about?

FILIBERTO: . . . I'm obliged to point out that you have committed an indelicate act of enormous gravity, and I . . . (*He rushes forward with hands raised.*)

TUMMASINO: But what . . . (*He is also prepared to rush forward, but the friends restrain him.*)

FILIBERTO (*stepping backward, pushing* **INES** *and* **MARGHERITA** *forward, then, seeing his rival calm down, takes up his previous position, forcing his way among the women.*) Get outa the way! (*And acts as though he wants to slap them. He feels around; to* **INES**.) . . . I don't have my gun, how can I protect myself?!

INES (*gives him the gun*).

FILIBERTO (*puts it in his vest pocket, with the handle carefully showing; he goes boldly forward, as though to launch a bloody offensive against his adversary*):   . . . Consequently . . .

TUMMASINO (*quivers with fury*). .

AITANO: Easy does it . . . (*He takes hold of him.*)

TUMMASINO: But he insulted me . . .

AFFUNZINO: Wha'd he say?

TUMMASINO: What? He called me a "con's queen."

FILIBERTO: Consequently, before dancing with my woman . . . (*takes off his hat; and orders*) Caps! And hats! (*All the men remove their hats.*)

LEOPOLDO (*aside, mocking*):   The Holy Saints are passing by!

FILIBERTO: . . . You should have had the decency to ask her manager; because, if you don't know it, this woman (*points to* **INES**) is an agent of my business concern. And you, instead of considering me worthy of every regard, have tried my patience, and I'm going to break your . . . (*threatens again*)

TUMMASINO: What's with you . . . (*He starts forward, is restrained.*)

FILIBERTO (*returns to hide behind* **INES** *and* **MARGHERITA** *; and then comes rapidly forward again, as if he wanted to tear free from their hold. He seems wild.*) Get outa the way! Get outa the way or I'll start with you! (*Arranges the gun in his pocket, with the barrel pointing upward.*)

LEOPOLDO (*aside*):   He has positioned the anti-aircraft artillery!

INES (*in a fury, to* **FILIBERTO**):   Well, when . . . ?!

FILIBERTO: . . . To summarize . . .

TUMMASINO: Oh, I've had it! (*throws himself at* **FILIBERTO**)

A WOMAN'S SHOUT (*suddenly*):   The cops!

MUSIC XXV

(*The* **ORGAN GRINDER** *begins to play again. The couples join and start to dance.* **FILIBERTO** *hides the gun between his legs and dances as well as he can with* **INES**. **AFFUNZINO** *throws his weapon into* **LEOPOLDO**'s *basket, who protests. The others follow suit.*)

AFFUNZINO: Take care of these! (*that is, the guns.*)

LEOPOLDO: But . . .

AFFUNZINO: Take care of these!

(*The dance starts up again.* **BRIGHELLA, GUARDASCIONE,** *and the other officers of the patrol enter. The women, excited by the waltz, surround the officers, trying to force them to dance.*)

LEOPOLDO (*tries to slink away; gives his cry*):   "Coffee, cigars, cigarettes, rum, and anise!" (*But he is stopped by the officers and searched. They find the guns and take him. The unfortunate man loudly protests his innocence.*)

INES (*seeing danger ahead, that is, the stubborn resolve of the police, starts running away and shout-*

ing): Margari'! (*While the women still try to appease some of the officers, others run off after the fleeing suspects.*)

BRIGHELLA (*pushes* **FILIBERTO**) Come on! Come on!

FILIBERTO: Just a minute . . . I'm a gentleman . . . A little respect . . .

(*The* **ORGAN GRINDER** *keeps playing, laughing scornfully.*)

CURTAIN

Music for Via Toledo by Night

I
PRELUDIO

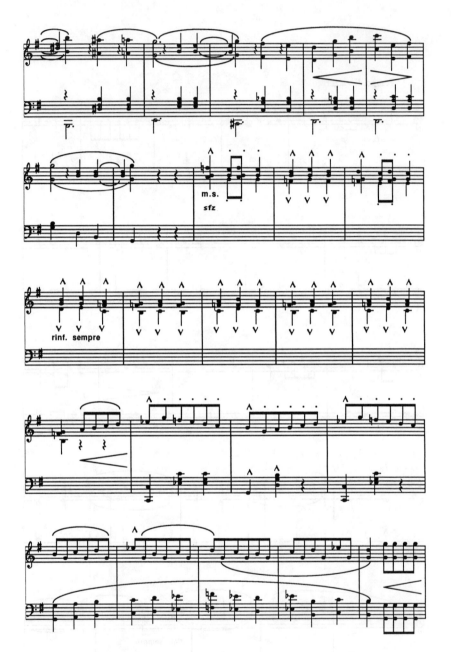

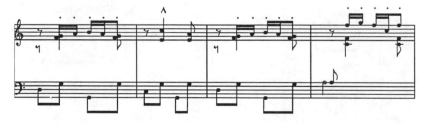

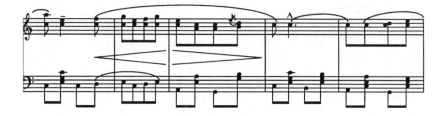

Allegro

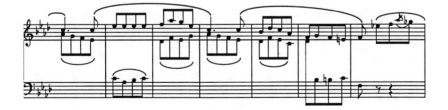

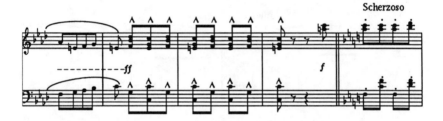

Scherzoso

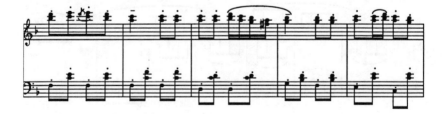

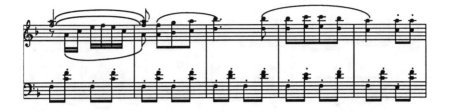

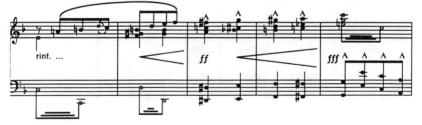

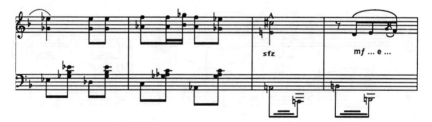

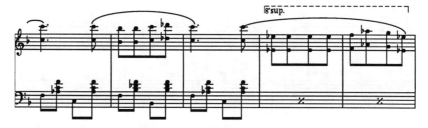

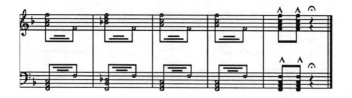

II

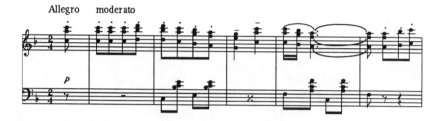

III

Allegro moderato

IV

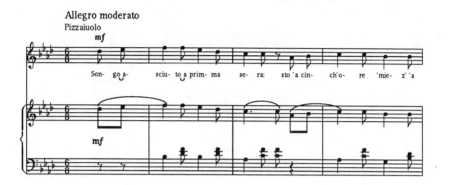

Allegro moderato
Pizzaiuolo
mf

Son- go a- sciu- to a prim- ma se- ra: sto 'a cin- ch'o- re 'mie- z' a

vi- a! Chi- stu ruo—— to è na sur- bet- te——ra!

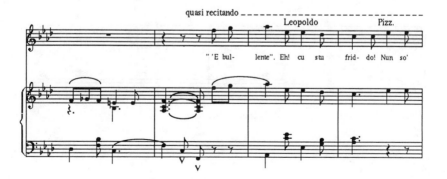

quasi recitando _

Leopoldo   Pizz.

" 'E bul- lente". Eh! cu stu frid- do! Nun so'

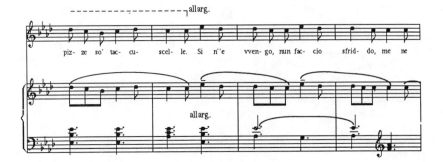

piz- ze so' tac- cu- scel- le. Si n''e vven- go, nun fac- cio sfrid- do, me ne

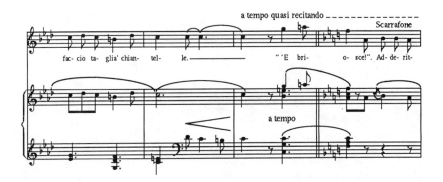

fac- cio ta- glia' chian- tel- le.———— "'E bri- o- sce!". Ad- de- rit-

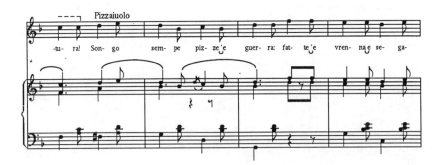

-tu- ra! Son- go sem- pe pìz- ze 'e guer- ra: fat- te 'e vren- na e se- ga-

V

"voce" Pizzaiuolo
liberamente

"'A ten- go ca- ve- ra e chi- n'a- li- - - - ce!——'O pez- za'!".——

Allegro moderato

mf

p

pp

VI

"voce" Pizzaiuolo
liberamente

"'A ten- go ca- ve- ra e chi- n'a- li—— ce!—— 'O pez- za'!".——

Allegro moderato

mf   allontanandosi

ppp

VII

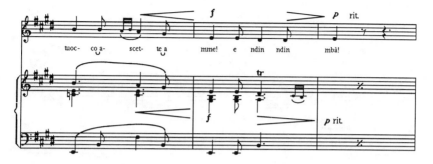

tuoc- co a- scet- te a mme! e ndin ndin mbâ!

VIII
MELOLOGO

Moderato

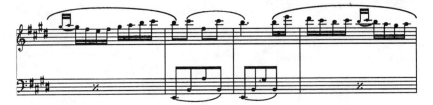

IX
MELOLOGO

X
MELOLOGO

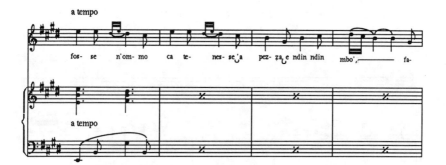

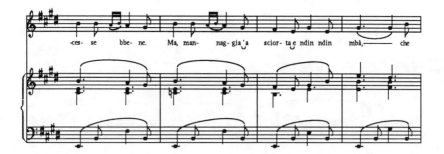

vvuo' fa' bbe- ne si na ddie- ce 'e pez- za e ndin ndin mbò,... —— mo

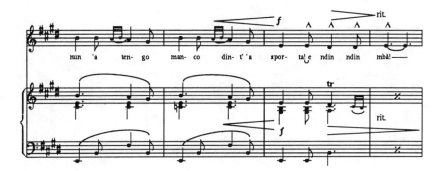

nun 'a ten- go man- co din- t' 'a spor- ta! e ndin ndin mbà! ——

Lentissimo

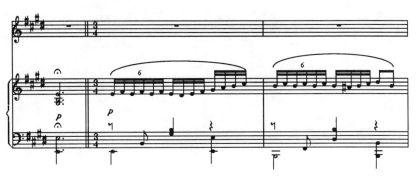

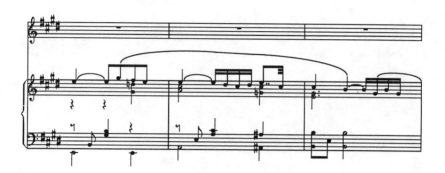

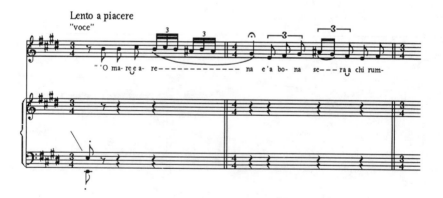

Lento a piacere
"voce"

" 'O ma-re e a- re———————— na e' a bo- na se——— ra a chi rum-

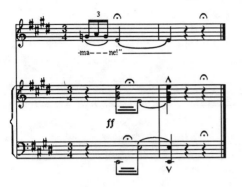

XI

Quant' al- le- gri- a: p' 'a ggioia se pò mu- ri'! 'A n'a- ti quat- te

mi- se fac- cio 'a spo- - - - sa! Ma sen- za do- te...

che vò di' 'a ric- chez- - -za? si puor- te ll'o- ne- stà, puor- te 'a bel-

XII

-ten- ta ———————— ad- do' mme por- ta 'o vien- to, sbat- ten- no 'a ccà e 'a

llà! ————————

XIII

Moderato (in uno)

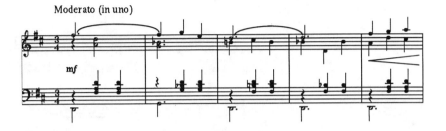

XIV

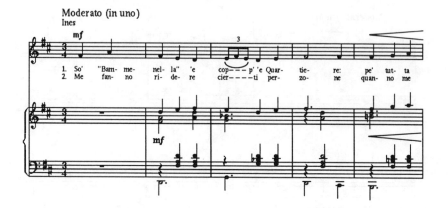

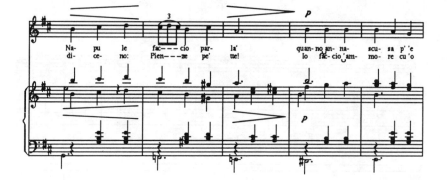

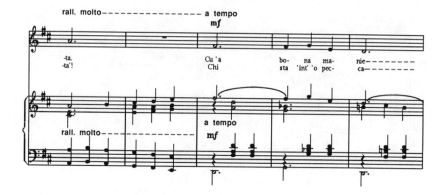

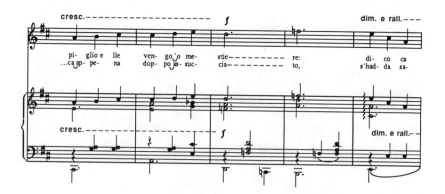

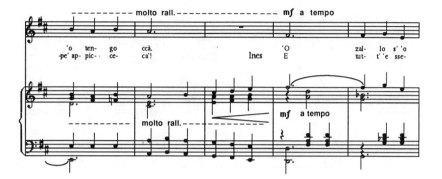

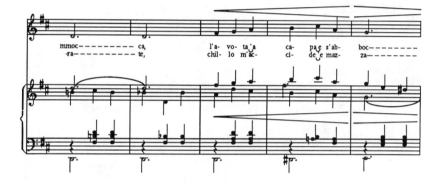

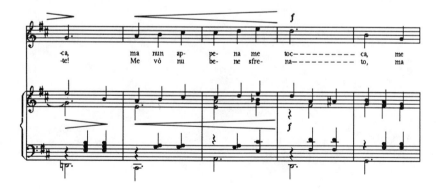

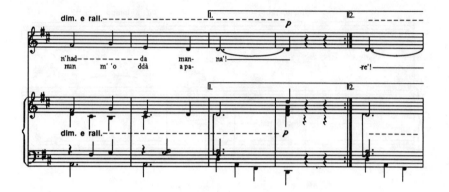

XV

Moderato (in uno)

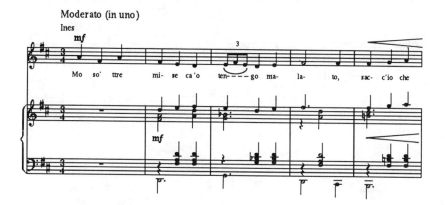

Mo so' ttre mi- se ca 'o ten——go ma- la- to, sac- c'io che

spen- go pe' far—lo sa- na'! Pe- rò 'o dot- to- re cu

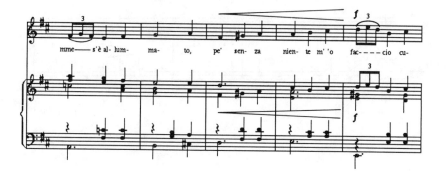

mme——s'è al- lum- ma- to, pe' sen- za nien- te m' 'o fac——cio cu-

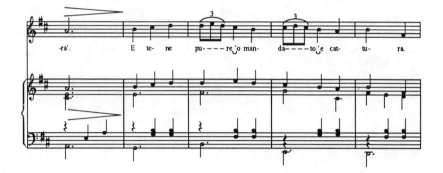

-ra'. E te- ne pu----re o man da----to 'e cat- tu- ra.

Filiberto   Ines

Prie- sto a 'mbu- lan- za me ve--- ne a pi- glia'. Ma nun da'

ret- ta, sta sen---- za pa- u- ra, pe' tte ce ston- go io

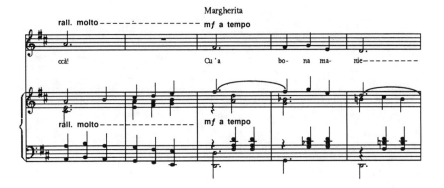

occà! Cu 'a bo- na ma- nie- - - - - - - -

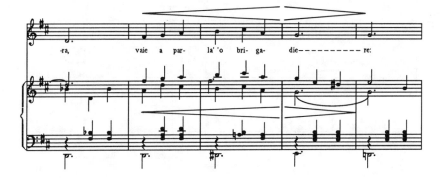

-ra, vaie a par- la' 'o bri- ga- die- - - - - - - - re:

men- tre lle vin- ne 'o me- stie- - - - - - - - re, is- so s' 'a

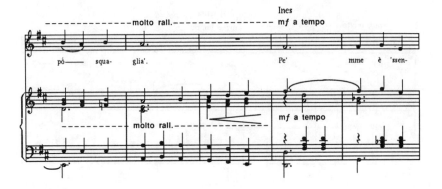

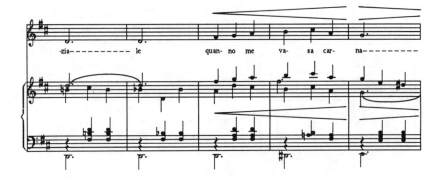

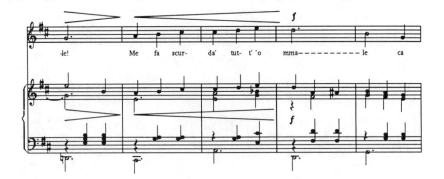

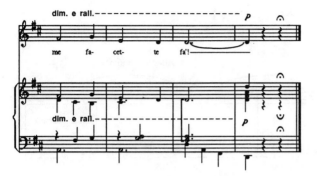

XVI

XVII

Allegretto scherzoso

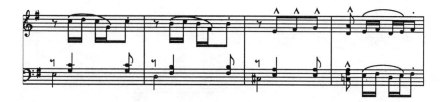

XVIII

Adagio

XIX

Adagio

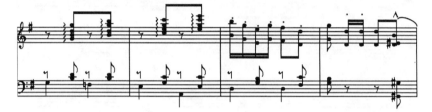

Lyrics:
re- stia- mo noi pa- dron del- la cit- tà.——— Al- l'al- ba
re- stia- mo noi pa- dron del- la cit- tà.——— Al- l'al- ba

po- i, riap- pa- re il so- le e scom- pa—- ri- a- mo no- i,———
po- i, riap- pa- re il so- le e scom- pa- ria- mo no- i,———

— per ri- tor- na- re a far- vi- ta gio- io- sa, quan- do chi ha la- vo-
— per ri- tor- na- re a far- vi- ta gio- io- sa, quan- do chi ha la- vo-

XX

XXI
STORNELLO

Moderato

Ines (voce fuori scena)

Am- mo- re am- mo- re no, nun lu cre- di———— te,—— nun lu cre-di- te a

chi——— sto 'nganna- to———— re,—— ca ll'uom- me- ne mo quan——- te ne ve-

-di——————— te—— te- ne- no cien- te fac- cie mil- le co- re;——

la fem- me- na scu- r'es———sa! e lu ssa- pi————— te,—— tut- to se cre-de e

le——- sto don' am- mo——— re,—— quan-no l'ha mi- so ll'om——- mo in-t' 'a li

ppe———— ne,—— lu sca- ru-scen- te nun la vò cchiú be- ne!——

XXII

Allegro
Tummasino

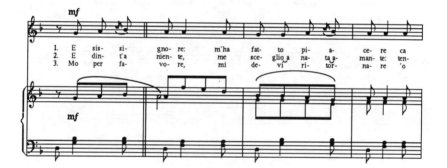

1. E sis- si- gno- re: m'ha fat- to pi- a- ce- re ca-
2. E din- t'a nien- te, me sce- glio a na- ta a man- te: ten-
3. Mo per fa- vo- re, mi de- vi ri- tor- na- re 'o

t'hē tru- va- to a n'a tu 'nnam- mu- ra- to!— Ma, pe' fa- vo- re, al-
go a cin- quan- ta fem- me- ne 'e ri- ser- va.— C'è l'av- ve- nen- te, al ce-
faz- zu- let- to 'e se- ta (sta tre lli- re!)— Cer- to un si- gno- re non

-me-no 'in-t' 'o quar- tie- re, nun fa' ac-ca- pi' ca m'hē li- cen- zi- a- to, si
sta l'af- fa- sci- nan- te; e o- gnu- na 'e che- sta mme fa- ces- se 'a ser- va, p' 'o
se lo fa ri- da- re, ma io me lo pi- glio poi per non sen- ti- re: "ll'og-

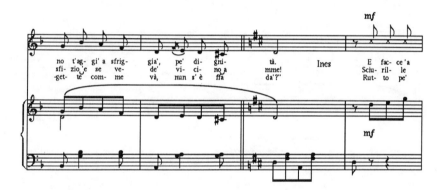

no t'ag- gi' a sfrig- gia', pe' di- gni- tà.   Ines   E fac- ce 'a
sfi- zio 'e se ve- de' vi- ci- no a mme!   Sciu- ril- le
-get- te com- me và, nun s' è ffa da'?"   Rut- to pe'

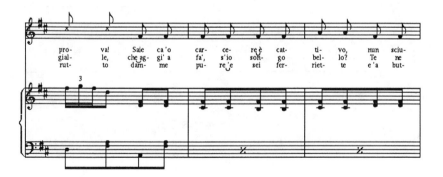

pro- gial- va! Sai e ca 'o car- ce- re è cat- ti- vo, nun sciu-
le, che ag- gi' a fa', s'io son- go bel- lo? Te ne
rut- to dam- me pu- re 'e sei fer- riet- te e 'a but-

-par- te 'a lib- ber- ta! —————— Tummasino E a che mi gio— - - -va? Quan-do
vaie? peg- gio pe' tte! —————— Vu- tan-no 'e spal- - - -le, dop-po
-te- glia 'e bril- lan- tè! —————— Cer- to, fa brut— - - -to, ma 'e ri-

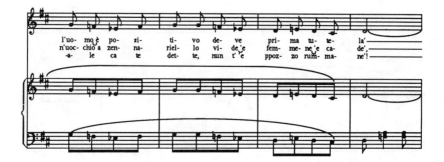

l'uo- mo è po- si- ti- vo de- ve pri- ma u- te- la '
n'uoc- chio a zen- na- riel- lo vi- de 'e fem- me- ne 'e ca- de ',
-a- le ca- te det- te, nun t' e ppoz- zo rum- ma- ne '!

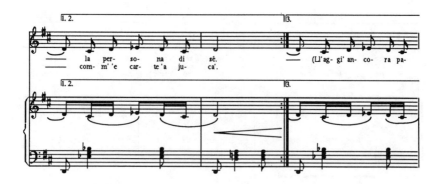

la per- so- na di sé.
com- m' e car- te 'a ju- ca'.   (Ll'ag- gi' an- co- ra pa-

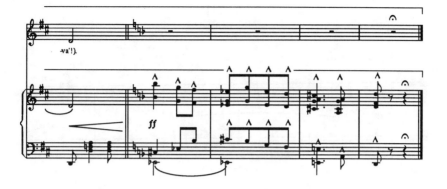

XXIII
MELOLOGO

Moderato (in tre)

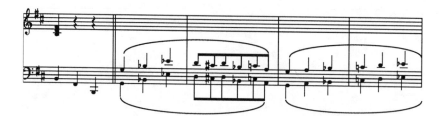

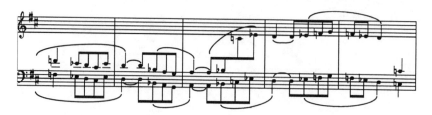

Adagio

Moderato

XXIV

Tempo di valzer (in uno)

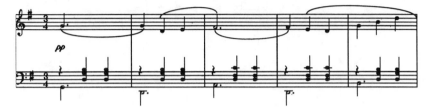

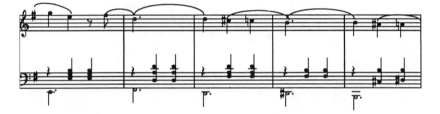

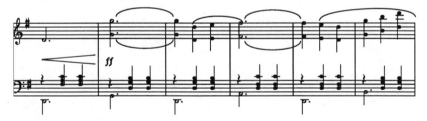

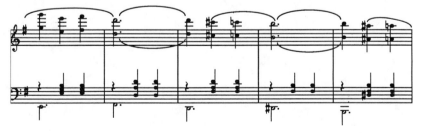

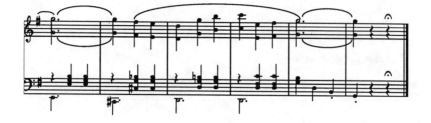

XXV

Tempo di valzer (in uno)

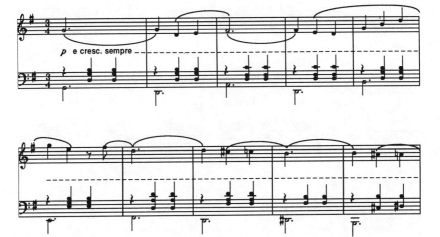

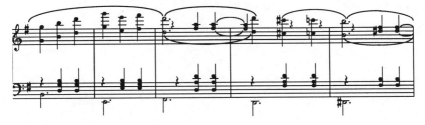

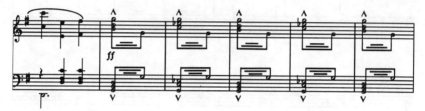

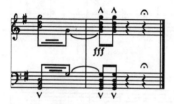

Introduction

Pier Maria Rosso di San Secondo (born November 30, 1887; died November 22, 1956) came from a noble Sicilian family of Norman descent. He wrote over thirty-five full-length plays and more than twenty one-acts. Dramatic critics have linked his work to movements in northern Europe, such as German expressionism, to symbolism and futurism, and to late nineteenth-century Sicilian art. He is best remembered as an outstanding representative of the grotesque school.

Rosso di San Secondo grew up in Sicily and then went to the University of Rome to earn a diploma in law. During these years before World War I, he wrote short stories and plays and took part in the city's literary and artistic life. He made his debut as a playwright with *La sirena ricanta* (The siren sings again, 1908), no longer extant, which was performed by the Italian Drama Company for Grand Guignol Repertory. Meanwhile, with a law diploma in his pocket, he began to work on various literary journals such as *Lirica*. In 1911 a collection of experimental one-act plays appeared in print under the title *L'occhio chiuso: Sintesi drammatiche* (The closed eye: Dramatic syntheses). In what is perhaps the most interesting play, *L'occhio chiuso,* he personifies an eye and an eyelid, a technique that was used by the last wave of symbolist poets whose works Marinetti published in *Poesia* before the foundation of futurism.

After serving as a soldier during World War I, Rosso di San Secondo returned to Rome and to writing. He worked on the journal *Idea nazionale* and then, along with Federigo Tozzi, edited the Sunday supplement of *Messaggero,* which published some

■

FIVE

PIER MARIA ROSSO DI SAN SECONDO

■

of his short stories. In 1917 his first novel, *La fuga* (Flight) came out, with a preface by Luigi Pirandello. Pirandello had encouraged Rosso di San Secondo in his literary pursuits ever since he was a young university student, and the two had become close friends. The following year, Pirandello persuaded Virgilio Talli, one of Italy's finest early directors, to stage *Marionette, che passione!*, here translated as *Puppets of Passion!*, which would bring Rosso di San Secondo almost overnight success and identify him with the Italian *teatro grottesco*.

While the phenomenon of the grotesque in its generic sense has no geographic or temporal specificity and can be found, for instance, in the paintings of Hieronymus Bosch and Pieter Brueghel, in tales by Ernst Theodor Amadeus Hoffmann and Edgar Allen Poe, and in the theater in Leonid Andreyev's *The Black Maskers* and Arthur Schnitzler's *The Green Cockatoo,* as well as in Shakespeare, the term has been applied to a specific group of Italian writers. Early signs of the grotesque in Italian theater can be seen in plays by the futurist poet Enrico Cavacchioli: *Ranocchie turchine* (Blue frogs, 1909) and *La campana d'argento* (The silver bell, 1914). Major dramatic works that have been identified with this movement include *The Mask and the Face* (1916) by Luigi Chiarelli, Pirandello's *Il berretto a sonagli* (*Cap and Bells*) (1917), Cavacchioli's *L'uccello del paradiso* (Bird of paradise, 1918), and Luigi Antonelli's *L'uomo che incontro se stesso* (The man who met himself, 1918). Rosso di San Secondo's *Puppets of Passion!* is an outstanding example of this school.

Giovanni Lista, in his exhaustive groundbreaking study, *La scène futuriste,*[1] has suggested that futurist and Italian grotesque writers drew their inspiration from the same source. Both of these movements were reacting to the political and economic crises of the early twentieth century. In the early stages of their work, circa 1910, both the futurists and those who would be identified with the grotesque movement, were motivated by a dislike for the aesthetics of d'Annunzio and his disciples: the overblown rhetoric, the all-powerful Dannunzian hero, the artificial style. They were also reacting against the wearisome cliché plot of the adulterous triangle in French-inspired bourgeois drama, among whose proponents they listed Giuseppe Giacosa, Marco Praga, Dario Niccodemi, Roberto Bracco, Sem Benelli, Sabatino Lopez, and Ercole Morselli.

Gigi Livio, in his introduction to *Teatro grottesco del novecento* (Twentieth-century grotesque drama),[2] drew a comparison between the futurists and the *teatro grottesco*. The futurists, he suggests, unleashed their destructive impulses in their desire to break the old molds of the adultery theme, psychological character analysis, and stage "naturalism," which they considered a fraud. Most importantly, they committed themselves to creating a new theatrical language and to adapting to a future new world order in politics and economics.

The grotesque writers, on the other hand, did not venture so far; their spiritual crisis was deeply felt. Rather than breaking completely with the old forms, they parodied them; they exposed to ridicule the bourgeois convention of the triangle. Their protagonists were puppets who mouth words and cannot master themselves. They may be disassociated and act out multiple roles or have doubles or other selves. *Puppets of Passion!* begins after three characters have experienced major emotional crises in their lives. They each claim to be suffering deeply the pangs of passion for an absent lover, and yet they rush into new triangular relationships. The sublime is mixed with the ridiculous. The grotesque writers' intent is to unnerve and disquiet their audience. There is to be no self-satisfied or good-humored laughter. The laughter produced is a bitter one. The tone is ironic and tragicomic. In these plays there is a sense of alienation from society, of the world as madhouse, bordering on the surreal. But the ideas they promote are intended to violate bourgeois sensibilities, not to destroy the existing order.

Virgilio Talli's production of *Puppets of Passion!* opened in Milan at Teatro Manzoni on March 4, 1918. The Woman in the blue fox was played by Maria Melato, a prominent actress who often worked with Talli. As a result of Talli's production, *Puppets of Passion!* was translated and presented in Germany and Czechoslovakia and in Paris by Aurélien-Marie Lugné-Poë on May 24, 1923. In May of 1926 Marta Abba and Camillo Pilotto played the leading roles when the play was produced at Pirandello's Teatro d'Arte.

With the help of Anton Giulio Bragaglia and Antonio Valente, Virgilio Talli directed two more plays by Rosso di San Secondo in 1919. By that time modernized equipment facilitated the use of stage lighting to carry out ideas that had long since been proposed by the futurists, by the dancers Loïe Fuller and Valentine de Saint-Point, and by the color theorist Achille Ricciardi. Thus, Rosso di San Secondo's *Per fare l'alba* (For the dawn) and *La bella addormentata* (Sleeping beauty) proved to be receptive ground for Talli's experiments in set design and lighting.

In 1934 Rosso di San Secondo was awarded the first prize for literature from the Italian Academy on Pirandello's recommendation. His plays were produced internationally and, in Italy, they were staged by such directors as Tatiana Pavlova, Ettore Petrolini, and Maria Melato. He continued to write plays until 1954. In 1955, shortly before he died, he received the Melpomene prize for *Il ratto di Proserpina* (The rape of Persephone), an adaptation of the Greek myth. The play is set in Sicily and New York, the latter being chosen as the scene of Pluto's modern hellish domain.

J. H.

Notes

1. (Paris: Editions du CNRS, 1989).
2. (Milan: Mursia, 1965).

■

PUPPETS
OF PASSION!

(Marionette, che passione!, 1918)

Translated by Jane House

■

Characters

PRELUDE

THE WOMAN IN THE BLUE FOX

THE MAN IN GRAY

THE MAN IN MOURNING

THE SINGER

HE WHO WAS NOT TO HAVE COME

THE TELEGRAPH OFFICE GUARD

AN OFFICE BOY FROM CITY HALL

THE CLERK WHO DOES NOT APPEAR

1ST WORKER

2D WORKER

A MAN

A WOMAN

A YOUNG GIRL

A TELEGRAPH OFFICE BOY

A BRIDEGROOM

A BRIDE

1ST BALLERINA

2D BALLERINA

A MAID

1ST WAITER

2D WAITER

A PROSTITUTE

A DANDY

Place: A Sunday afternoon and evening, in Milan.

ADVICE TO THE ACTORS: This play has many pauses filled with despair. It is advisable to reveal the hysteria of the subtext only during the silent moments. Furthermore, although the characters' suffering makes the play seem disjointed at times, the tone should be one of tragic, not comic, humor. In their profoundly human suffering, the three protagonists are like puppets, and passion is their pull-string. However, they are still human beings: human beings reduced to puppets and, therefore, profoundly pitiable.

PRELUDE[1]

A long Sunday afternoon, the streets are empty, the stores shuttered closed; a gray and desolate sky looms above the urban squalor.

Most people, freed from their jobs, are busy with their families or with loving relationships in the warmth of soberly conducted lives. However, the lost of the world, the homeless, the vagabonds, while they've rubbed shoulders unawares perhaps a dozen times during the week's mad rush of activity, now, on this desolate Sunday afternoon, as they drift along, waiting for it to stop raining, will suddenly find each other—beneath a theater arcade perhaps, or on the threshold of a cafe, at the deserted corner of the Stock Exchange, in the lobby of the post office; or even in the sleepy telegraph office where the heavy silence is occasionally broken by the footsteps of those few who come to send messages.

Because they are living organisms of electric sensitivity, they will notice each other, feel each other's presence, immediately size each other up; and, if their despair is stronger than the contempt each has for the other's miseries, which are so similar to their own, then a graze of the elbow will suffice—or a slight gesture of the hand, a tap of the umbrella, a glove let fall, a sigh, a word shooting up or dying in the throat—to puncture the pose of reserve and allow them to indulge in an orgy of confession; after the first *mea culpa,* they'll start weaving the threads of a most pitiful plot; within an hour, they'll be enmeshed in the web of a grotesque tragedy—which they create from nothing. They will suffer agonies, moan, and prostrate themselves as if they really were at the bottom of an abyss; and then finally collapse, bones aching, broken, overcome, worn out, but ready to begin everything all over again tomorrow: poor, wild, caged beasts, eternally flinging their longing for a fuller, more passionate life against those inflexible barriers of human potential! . . .

Black out. Lights up on Act 1.

ACT 1

The waiting room of Milan's central telegraph office, on a Sunday afternoon. It's dark. The glass partition with shuttered counters, only two of which are open, slants across and up the stage. One assumes that an entrance exists upstage somewhere although none is visible. To the right, walls with public announcements, posters, placards.

Downstage, toward the left, there is a large table for writing telegrams. Further back, toward the

---

1. The prelude has been adapted from Rosso di San Secondo's much longer prologue. —Trans.

right, a small table, for the guard. Silence and solemnity. Outside the weather is gloomy: it's drizzling.
The entire act should be spoken in low tones with long pauses.

Scene 1

When the curtain rises, the **GUARD** *is dozing at his table; little by little he lets his head fall onto his*
chest, gives a start and continues dozing. The **MAN IN GRAY** *is sitting at the big table. He is thickset*
and has an open face; his full head of hair is swept back; he twists it nervously, now with one hand now
with the other, accompanying the gestures with movements of his legs, which he keeps crossing and
recrossing. He puts down the pen, lights a cigarette, smokes big mouthfuls, puts it out, tries again to
write, again puts down the pen, shifts his weight first to one side then the other, stares at the ground,
the tips of his shoes; taps his forehead, his nose, his chin, clasps his hands; shrugs his shoulders, makes
the movements of a man who is talking to himself. A very long pause.

    AN OFFICE BOY FROM CITY HALL *enters, his trousers and his raincoat dripping. He walks*
along the glass wall reading the signs without comprehension. Finally he heads for the **GUARD,** *unbut-*
tons his raincoat, and opens the bag slung over his shoulder.

OFFICE BOY (*to the* **GUARD**): Hey, excuse me! (*The* **GUARD** *wakes up.*) I've got govern-
    ment telegrams. (*He takes out several pink forms.*)
GUARD (*irritated, because he's been woken up too brusquely*): For me? That window over there.
OFFICE BOY: The government window is closed.
GUARD: You think they all stay open on Sunday? There's just those two windows today,
    for everything, private and government.
OFFICE BOY: Take it easy. I didn't know.

(*He goes to one of the open windows, hands over his telegrams. The* **GUARD** *gets up, stretches, walks*
slowly around the room, walks upstage, then turns and walks toward the proscenium. The sound of the
official stamping of papers is heard from the office. The **OFFICE BOY** *puts something in his bag, closes*
it, buttons up his coat again, heads for the exit.)

CLERK (*calling him back, unseen*): Hey! Psst!
GUARD: Hey! They're calling you.

(*The* **OFFICE BOY,** *who was just about to exit, returns to the window, talks submissively for a moment*
with the clerk, then moves again toward the exit. The **GUARD** *has remained at his post. After having*
observed the **MAN IN GRAY** *from a distance for a while, he calls out; because the latter doesn't hear*
him at first, he has to repeat himself.)

GUARD: Listen, Mister . . . Mister!
MAN IN GRAY: Huh? . . . Talking to me?
GUARD (*gets up, and while he's walking toward him, says slowly*): I'm sorry, it's my job to tell
    you that this area is for writing telegrams only.
MAN IN GRAY: And just what do you think I'm writing?
GUARD: Oh, fine! If that's what . . . I said something because it's my job . . . and you
    have been sitting there for . . .

MAN IN GRAY: There's no law against thinking about a telegram for two hours, is there
. . .

GUARD: When the place is empty . . . Like today . . . Sunday . . . no, please go ahead
. . . There's nothing wonderful about being inside this place. If you fall asleep, the damp
gets into your bones. It's very unpleasant . . . It's been raining for eight days! (*He rubs
his hands, blows on them, sits down again. Pause. The* **MAN IN GRAY** *lights another cigarette.
The* **GUARD**, *almost to himself, sleepy, lumpish*) Oh, yes, telegrams! Folks have had a good
lunch, and squeezed in a delicious snooze: then, toward evening, they'll pour into cafes
beneath the arcades where little orchestras'll play in the cozy warmth, or they'll go to
the theater . . . The middle classes all go to matinees . . . on Sunday, most theaters
have two shows . . .

(*Murmuring, he falls asleep. Pause.*)

Scene 2

The **MAN IN MOURNING** *enters upstage, comes down toward the table, eyes the* **MAN IN GRAY**, *sits
opposite him, takes a form, resolutely writes out a telegram, but when he's finished, rereads it, and
instead of standing up to take it to the window, he puts it back on the table, frowns, remains motionless,
thinking. A long pause. The two gentlemen look at each other surreptitiously, then they each become
absorbed again in their own private anguish.* **TWO WORKERS** *enter.*

1ST WORKER (*to the* **GUARD**): A form please.

GUARD: There are lots over there, on the table!

(*The* **1ST WORKER** *goes and sits at the table. The* **2D WORKER** *follows.*)

2D WORKER (*in a low voice*): It would be better if he didn't know about his death . . .

1ST WORKER: But sooner or later . . . He's really not a baby. (*He writes, then reads it to his
friend, still in a low voice.*) Pained soul . . .

2D WORKER (*interrupting*): Put "suffering" at least.

1ST WORKER: Okay, "suffering." (*Corrects it, then begins again.*) "Suffering soul announce
decease your uncle Domenico. Come. Be brave."

(*The* **2D WORKER** *shrugs his shoulders, resigned. Then the* **1ST AND THE 2D WORKERS** *go to the
window and pass over the telegram. The usual pounding of the stamp is heard, then the clinking of
coins in payment. As the* **TWO WORKERS** *are heading for the exit, The* **WOMAN IN THE BLUE
FOX** *enters.*)

Scene 3

The **WOMAN IN THE BLUE FOX** *walks uncertainly toward the table. She is thin, elegant, un-
affected, has a blue fox around her neck. Dressed for walking, almost for travel. Dark, with reddened
eyes, perhaps from crying; gloves to the elbow. She places the dripping wet umbrella in a corner, comes
to sit at the table, closer to the* **MAN IN MOURNING** *than to the* **MAN IN GRAY**. *She takes a pen,
gets ready to write, but does not. Pause. The three of them look at each other.*

MAN IN MOURNING (*tears up his telegram, throws it in the wastepaper basket, rises, picks up his umbrella, seems to want to leave, but then puts down his umbrella, sits at the table again, removes his hat, leans toward the* **WOMAN IN THE BLUE FOX**, *and, as if to justify himself*):   It's so often difficult to compose a telegram.

WOMAN IN BLUE FOX (*shudders, looks at him, responds almost mechanically*):   Yes, that's true. It's often difficult, yes.

MAN IN MOURNING: For you too? . . .

WOMAN IN BLUE FOX: For me too . . . (*Stares listlessly into space. Pause. Prepares to write, dwells on it, then gives up. The* **MAN IN MOURNING** *does the same. The* **MAN IN GRAY** *lights another cigarette.*)

(*Silence.*)

MAN IN MOURNING (*quietly, but with trembling voice and the intensity of a madman*):   And to think that it could be so easy to write it, hand it over, and pay for it . . . It could be there where it's going in an hour.

WOMAN IN BLUE FOX (*in a low voice still, dully*):   In an hour? Is an hour enough?

MAN IN MOURNING: Of course, mark it urgent . . .

WOMAN IN BLUE FOX: What?

MAN IN MOURNING: See: in the space where it says "Directions" write: "Urgent." You pay more, but within an hour . . .

WOMAN IN BLUE FOX (*still in a low voice, dully*):   Really . . . in an hour . . .

(*Pause.*)

MAN IN MOURNING (*with his head in his hands*):   But, you see, it doesn't get written. And an entire day goes by instead.

(*Pause.*)

WOMAN IN BLUE FOX (*still in a low voice, as in a stupor*):   It's important to find the right style . . .

MAN IN MOURNING: You think? Just a question of style? . . .

WOMAN IN BLUE FOX: Sorry: I'm speaking for myself, I . . .

(*Pause.*)

MAN IN MOURNING: We always know ourselves best; but that could apply to me too. I need to find the right style . . .

(*The* **MAN IN GRAY** *coughs. The other two watch him for a moment, lower their eyes, as though mortified.*)
(*Pause.*)

MAN IN MOURNING (*leaning close to the* **WOMAN IN THE BLUE FOX**, *still softly and somewhat crazed*):   Excuse me: who are you sending a telegram to? (*The* **WOMAN IN THE BLUE FOX** *gives him a frightened, suspicious look. She says nothing.*) I'm not just asking out of curiosity, really. I can see you're in a bad way.

WOMAN IN BLUE FOX: Yes.

MAN IN MOURNING: I am too.

(*Pause.*)

WOMAN IN BLUE FOX: A tragedy?

MAN IN MOURNING: Horrible.

WOMAN IN BLUE FOX: I would prefer that: better death, I think, than to be eternally chained.

MAN IN MOURNING: What chain?

WOMAN IN BLUE FOX: Oh, I don't know! . . . that's what I call it.

MAN IN MOURNING: Please call it whatever you like. Perhaps I'm chained too.

WOMAN IN BLUE FOX: But your tragedy has already happened! . . . Death resolves everything, sir . . .

MAN IN MOURNING: Ah, because you see me in mourning. I'm dressed in mourning, yes. But she isn't dead. She's alive.

WOMAN IN BLUE FOX (*as though understanding, but still dully*): Ah! . . .

(*Pause.*)

MAN IN MOURNING: You see, I was resolved to live as though she were dead. Instead . . .

WOMAN IN BLUE FOX: You wanted to send her a telegram . . .

MAN IN MOURNING: Exactly. You should laugh at me . . . Don't you see? . . . Sending her a telegram, after she's treated me like dirt! . . .

WOMAN IN BLUE FOX: Your wife? You . . . once . . . you still . . . You love her, really?

MAN IN MOURNING: I'm a miserable wretch. Passionately! . . . Passionately . . .

(*Two tears run down the furrows in his cheeks, fall onto the paper.*)
(*Pause.*)
(*The* **MAN IN GRAY** *coughs; while pretending to write, he is keeping an ear open to the conversation between the two strangers.*)

WOMAN IN BLUE FOX (*startled by the coughs, looks at him, feigns indifference; settles down; slowly draws the glove off her right hand.*)

(*Pause.*)

(*Then to the* **MAN IN MOURNING**, *softly*): Don't cry. Be brave. If you only knew . . .

MAN IN MOURNING: You too, poor lady? . . .

WOMAN IN BLUE FOX: Better to die, I told you . . . (*From time to time she has been stroking her cheek with her fur, as though wanting to ease some ache in her head. She repeats the gesture.*)

MAN IN MOURNING: Do you feel sick? A pain?

WOMAN IN BLUE FOX: My whole head . . . and my jaw . . . my neck . . . my back . . . A dreadful journey last night . . . I feel dazed; like a village idiot! . . . And then . . .

MAN IN MOURNING: And then what? . . .

WOMAN IN BLUE FOX: He beat me! . . . He abused me . . . I can't take it anymore! . . . I couldn't take it any more! . . .

MAN IN MOURNING: Husband? . . . No? . . .

WOMAN IN BLUE FOX (*indicates no. Pause.*): And see, instead . . . After two days of trying to get away . . .

MAN IN MOURNING: You want to send him a telegram? . . . Oh! . . . Oh! . . .

Scene 4

THE SINGER *enters from upstage. Immediately the* **WOMAN IN THE BLUE FOX** *regains her composure. She moves away from the* **MAN IN MOURNING**, *who understands and pulls back too.*

SINGER (*walks over to the* **WOMAN IN THE BLUE FOX**, *bends over her, and says softly*): Sorry, darling, I can't wait any longer. I must stop by the theater and then go home.

WOMAN IN BLUE FOX: You go on, go on. I still haven't found the form . . . I'll find it . . . Then I'll come right back.

THE SINGER: Take a carriage, you don't know Milan. It's pouring. I'm sure you don't remember the number . . . or even the street . . .

WOMAN IN BLUE FOX: I remember . . . I remember . . . Corso Magenta . . . number . . .

THE SINGER: Twenty-eight. I'd better write it down for you. (*She writes.*) "Magenta . . . number . . . twenty-eight." And let me say it once again: don't send a telegram. You mustn't. You'll see . . . He'll come looking for you, I'm sure.

WOMAN IN BLUE FOX: Yes, perhaps. . . if I don't find the right form . . . I won't . . . I'll come right back home.

THE SINGER: Ciao, darling, come home soon.

(*She takes a good look at the* **MAN IN GRAY**, *and then at the* **MAN IN MOURNING**, *and exits, her high heels clicking.*)

Scene 5

MAN IN MOURNING (*after a pause*): Your girlfriend gave you good advice. Don't send the telegram.

WOMAN IN BLUE FOX: What about you, then? . . .

MAN IN MOURNING: Yes, right, I'm crazy too! It's incredible. To be so weak. If you don't send a telegram, I won't either. You'll be my strength.

(*They compose themselves upon suddenly hearing others entering.*)

Scene 6

A MAN, A WOMAN, AND A YOUNG GIRL *enter looking very cheerful. They linger a moment to whisper happily together, then* **THE MAN** *walks over to the table and sits. He writes the telegram, then turns toward the* **WOMAN** *and the* **YOUNG GIRL** *to show them what he wrote.*

MAN (*still whispering, but more distinctly and loud enough to be heard*): See: I pretended the baby is announcing its own birth.

WOMAN: How sweet!

YOUNG GIRL: Oh, what a charming idea!

MAN: At first they won't understand. Ha! Ha! (*reading*) "New born, I send you a loving kiss. I feel terrific."

YOUNG GIRL: Oh lovely! Oh, that's wonderful!

WOMAN: That's very funny.

(*The* **MAN** *goes to the window, hands over the paper. We hear the usual pounding of the stamp and clinking coins.* **THE MAN, THE WOMAN, THE YOUNG GIRL** *exit, still whispering and smiling.*)

Scene 7

MAN IN MOURNING (*again approaching the* **WOMAN IN THE BLUE FOX**): Did you hear that? There are happy people in this world. A newborn baby.

WOMAN IN BLUE FOX: Do you have any children?

MAN IN MOURNING: No. I used to be sad about it. But now, in my misery, I'm relieved.

WOMAN IN BLUE FOX: Liberate yourself then; forget her; you're a man!

MAN IN MOURNING (*with his fists tightly clenched and tears flowing down his cheeks*): Yes, yes, I must forget her. But what about my home! I was a homebody! Work and home. That bitch! That bitch! She's destroyed me. She's gone, understand, gone away with some bastard! . . . My home! Where can I find a home now? . . .

WOMAN IN BLUE FOX: So have you run away too? Have you only just arrived in Milan?

MAN IN MOURNING: Of course. Think about it. How could I stay there? In a small country town. With my house completely empty.

WOMAN IN BLUE FOX: Look for one here. Forget that one . . . You'll see . . . little by little. You'll regain your self-respect . . . pick up your life again . . .

MAN IN MOURNING: Yes, yes, I'll do that, certainly. But some other soul has to help me! . . . How can one manage all alone? . . . I'm an engineer: I'll easily find work in Milan . . . But it's another matter to regain my peace of mind, my tranquillity! . . .

WOMAN IN BLUE FOX: Be brave. You're young: you'll be able to start over . . .

(*Pause.*)

MAN IN MOURNING: Do you live near your friend?

WOMAN IN BLUE FOX: I'm staying with her: furnished apartments for performing artists . . . As for a house, me, I've never had one . . . She's a good friend, she's suffered a lot. But she's strong now, she's got her armor back on, and she's doing everything she can to help me.

MAN IN MOURNING: Did you say artist? In the theater?

WOMAN IN BLUE FOX: Yes, she's a singer.

MAN IN MOURNING: And you? . . .

WOMAN IN BLUE FOX: Me? . . . I used to be. Then he took me off the stage . . .

MAN IN MOURNING: Hoping to find some peace . . . tranquility? . . .

WOMAN IN BLUE FOX: I found neither! I don't know what the words mean. I was much happier when I was singing. (*She is seized by a tremor of anguish, immediately suppresses any sobs in her handkerchief. She cries, dries her tears, ashamed.*)

MAN IN MOURNING: Be brave. What can I say to comfort you? What can I do to help you?

(*He bows his head to hide his eyes, which are filling with tears. Both of them suddenly compose themselves, because the* MAN IN GRAY *coughs again and lights another cigarette.*)
(*Pause.*)

MAN IN MOURNING: Listen . . . I think it's destiny that we met. Our experiences are so similar. Do you want to help me? Do you want me to help you?

WOMAN IN BLUE FOX: But how? How can I possibly?

MAN IN MOURNING (*softly still, but anguished, desperate*): You forget him, I'll forget her. You've been crushed like me. Let's be friends. No one can understand your pain better than I. No one can understand mine better than you. Let's save each other.

(*Pause.*)
(*They've drawn closer, and they're not looking at each other any more: then, slowly they raise their eyes, look at each other, and stay like that for a while without saying a word. They separate again. The* MAN IN MOURNING *again tears up his telegram. She picks hers up and rereads it, keeps holding it, uncertain about what to do.*)

(*Pause.*)

(*The* MAN IN MOURNING, *after having glanced at the* MAN IN GRAY *to check on him, leans toward her and whispers:*)

MAN IN MOURNING: You want to?

(*The* WOMAN IN THE BLUE FOX *trembles. She does not respond. The* MAN IN MOURNING *after having again glanced at the* MAN IN GRAY *to check on him, again leans toward her and quickly*) Shall we try it?

(*Silence.*)
(*The* GUARD *has risen. He walks upstage a few steps, turns back, sits again. The* MAN IN GRAY *pretends to write. The* MAN IN MOURNING *again glances at the* MAN IN GRAY, *then at the* GUARD, *who is yawning and dozing off; turned on, excited, his voice trembling, he repeats:*)

MAN IN MOURNING: Shall we try it?

(*Pause.*)

WOMAN IN BLUE FOX (*trembling*): What are you saying?

MAN IN MOURNING (*urgently, as if suddenly obsessed*): Yes, yes, I'm really serious. Just like that! In a moment of strength! Me and you. Together. I'm serious. You'll see. We'll take an apartment for two. We'll pretend we've always been together. We'll pretend even to each other. I'll order myself to work. We'll demand that we love each other . . . Little by little we'll forget. I'll give you anything you want: I'll adore you, I will! You don't know how devoted I can be. Let's chain ourselves together: let's save each other . . . Do you want to? (*He takes one of her hands behind the table. She trembles.*) Tear up that telegram. Tear it up. (*The* **WOMAN IN THE BLUE FOX**, *with her free hand, crumples the telegram, but she remains seated, obtuse. The* **MAN IN MOURNING** *puts on his hat, picks up his umbrella; then he raises her, crooking an arm beneath her armpit.*) Come with me. We'll talk on the way. It's destiny that we've met.

MAN IN GRAY (*bursting out before the woman lets herself be pulled away, but in a low voice*): One moment, please. I have a few words to say before you go. I was supposed to write a telegram too. I didn't write it and I'm not going to write it. I decided against doing so fifteen minutes ago. However, I stayed on to listen to you. Yes, I admit it. You were my only concern. Really, I was afraid for you. Listen to me. What you're about to do is crazy, idiotic, awful. And useless, above all. In all sincerity, let me warn you against it. Then you can go away together, if you still think that's best.

(*The* **MAN IN GRAY** *has uttered these words in a sharp, metallic voice. He seems like a perfectly reasonable man, in fact terribly logical. Only his eyes have a glassy look that gives warning of his abnormal state of mind. The* **MAN IN MOURNING** *is stunned. The* **WOMAN IN THE BLUE FOX** *has lowered her eyes to the table and remains with her head bowed.*)
(*Silence.*)
(*The* **MAN IN MOURNING** *sits down again automatically. The* **MAN IN GRAY**, *after a pause, speaks again.*)

MAN IN GRAY: You see? A stranger, such as I, has only to prick your conscience . . . and right away you fall to pieces . . . But really, people, don't feel ashamed with me. I'm not a police inspector nor am I the coroner at an inquest: nor were you about to commit any crime. It's just that I'm as wretchedly unhappy as you, and as I listened to you from this side of the table, I felt rage and pain and anguish in seeing my own misery reflected in both of you. But also from seeing you fall slowly into a trap of self-deceptive thinking that I'm intimately familiar with—beginning to believe that tying yourself to someone else will make you forget—folly . . . acts of folly, my friends . . . Trust me, I've been on the verge of committing many such acts myself! Yes, why shouldn't I tell you about it? Yes. You see before you a man who has thought about them all; they've all danced around in my head on trains, in hotel rooms, in the streets of foreign cities, in forests, on the open plains, in the mountains, wherever I've fled . . . to escape . . . Then I realized that my passion was indestructible, that I had to let it wear away very slowly. Ha! ha! you people are novices! . . . You're still coming here to the telegraph office, believing that you're going to send a telegram. Yes, I still come here too, I know, but only when I feel I can no longer bear it. And now I'm like a father bringing his little boy to the coffee shop to buy him an ice cream. I bring him here, to the telegraph office, my unreasonable child, to make him happy. I let him sit down. I let him delude himself a bit. And when it's over, I take him by the hand, good as gold, and lead him away. But

I know from the start that I'll never ever try to contact that woman again. And if an ache for her gnaws away at me inside, gnaws away, goading me constantly, implacably, all the better! Gnaw, gnaw away; we all die when the hour comes. But as for acts of folly, no, my friends, no, those we need not commit . . . (*brief pause*)

However, if you want to, go ahead and do it anyway. But I warn you that, come tomorrow, you'll feel disgusted with yourselves. Go on! Take an apartment together! Try to be man and wife! . . . You may not feel like thieves and ashamed right away; for one month, let's say, or two or even three you may be able to keep on deluding yourselves that you're helping each other overcome your passion, but later on things will turn bad, that's sure. Later on you'll loathe each other; and in the end one of you will murder the other. Go on, go away together anyway, if you want to. See what happens. You think you can treat your soul the same way you treat a servant. But why? It's not a servile thing! . . . You think you can do what you want with it. Go on, just try it, my friends . . .

(*Silence.*)

(*All three remain immobile, under tremendous tension. The* **GUARD** *moves away from his post, walks slowly upstage, stretching and yawning.*

WOMAN IN BLUE FOX (*rearranges herself, then rises resolutely. She murmurs almost inaudibly*): Good evening, gentlemen.

(*She goes directly to the door, and exits. Pause. The* **MAN IN MOURNING** *and the* **MAN IN GRAY** *remain seated face to face but do not look at each other. Soon the* **MAN IN MOURNING** *adjusts his overcoat, puts on his cap, rises, takes his umbrella, turns to leave, takes a few steps, turns back.*)

MAN IN MOURNING (*facing the* **MAN IN GRAY**, *pointing with his index finger, in a low voice, but enunciating each syllable*): That's just fine. What you said is quite right. However, none of us can be sure, my dear sir, neither I, nor you, nor the lady, that we won't commit some folly that's infinitely more dangerous. Good evening.

(*He walks determinedly upstage and exits.*)

Scene 8

The **MAN IN GRAY** *remains quite still then shrugs his shoulders and gesticulates as though he's talking to himself.*

TELEGRAPH BOY (*enters briskly, raincoat dripping; goes toward the window and in a loud voice*): Ten telegrams not delivered. They're to stay here in the office. (*hands them over, and to the* **GUARD**, *exiting*) Dreadful weather! . . .

GUARD (*continuing his rounds, comes downstage to the proscenium, walks behind the* **MAN IN GRAY**, *watches him grimacing again. He stops close to the chair where the Woman in the blue fox was seated, bends down, and picks up a long glove.*): A glove. (*The* **MAN IN GRAY** *has buttoned up his overcoat. He stares at the glove the* **GUARD** *has put on the table, picks it up, examines it. The* **GUARD**, *smiling ironically*) It's certainly not yours.

MAN IN GRAY: I'm not saying it is. But I recognize it.

GUARD (*putting the table in order, the forms in their place, the pens in the inkwells*): Here's an address someone forgot. (*reading*) "Corso Magenta, number twenty-eight." Recognize that too?

MAN IN GRAY (*taking the sheet of paper*):   I recognize it.

(*He wraps the glove in the sheet of paper, puts it in his pocket, picks up his umbrella, and walks off as* THE NEWLY MARRIED COUPLE *enter.*)

Scene 9

THE NEWLY MARRIED COUPLE *linger near the entrance and chatter a bit, in low voices. Then they cross to the table and the* GROOM *writes the telegram, while the* BRIDE *reads the words, one by one, as he indicates them to her.*

BRIDE (*not making out a word and pointing to it*):   What's that?

GROOM: Send . . . Ha, see? . . . Send money . . . (*The* BRIDE *laughs slyly. The* GROOM *reads softly:*) "Trip Turin Milan, great. Tilde terrific, enthusiastic beautiful city. Tender hugs kisses. Send money."

(*They go to the window, hand it over. Single official pounding of the stamp, payment. They exit joking. The* GUARD *watches them go with an ironic look.*)

(*Pause.*)

MAN IN MOURNING (*reenters, comes downstage as if looking for someone; then, to the* GUARD): Please, that man in gray . . . Has he left?

GUARD (*surly*):   You can see for yourself no one's here.

MAN IN MOURNING (*is rather put out*):   Fine. (*exits resolutely*)

GUARD (*alone, sitting down again and yawning*):   The telegraph office, on Sunday; so what did we get: government telegrams, births, deaths, weddings . . . and then . . . complete muddles.

(*He dozes off again.*)

CURTAIN

ACT 2

A sitting room in an apartment building with furnished rooms for rent. Upon first glance, it gives the feeling of a junk room. The furnishings have become threadbare through overuse: small easy chairs, sofa, curtains, faded carpets. The furniture lacks style. A door upstage, one to the right. To the left a piano, and beside it, a stool piled with sheet music; upstage, to the right, a whatnot with a mirror; downstage, to the right, a desk.

It's evening, one hour after Act 1. The central lights are lit.

Scene 1

The **WOMAN IN THE BLUE FOX** *is lying supine on the sofa.*

SINGER (*standing, bending over her, stroking her, giving support*): Listen, I'm your friend, I can understand your pain, I've felt it myself. Listen, go and rest. Try to sleep. Time is the best medicine. You were right not to send a telegram. You need to be patient. There, there. (*Lifts her up. The* **WOMAN IN THE BLUE FOX** *seems worn out. She gets up as though drunk.*)

Unbutton your clothes and just lie down on the bed. In a little while I'll have to get dressed and go off to the theater. If you want, you can come with me. I'll get you a seat. If you don't want to see the show, you can wait in my dressing room. I only sing in the first two acts, so I'll be free early. We'll go and eat together. If not, wait for me here; we'll eat here, even better. So, whatever is best for you. But now, go and rest. (*leads her to the door on the right, makes her go in*) Nice and quiet, okay? (*The* **WOMAN IN THE BLUE FOX** *disappears. The* **SINGER** *goes upstage, opens the door, and calls out:*) Ninna! The dress! Haven't you ironed it yet?

(*While she's at the door,* **BALLERINA I** *appears, in dishabille.*)

BALLERINA I: Excuse me. Sorry. Do you have any envelopes and writing paper?

SINGER: As many as you want. There on the desk. (**BALLERINA I** *goes to the desk, rummages around, finds several sheets of paper and an envelope.*) That many sheets for just one envelope? Ah, it's that blessed boyfriend, so many things to say to him . . .

BALLERINA I: You'll see . . . once I've decided to write . . . I'm sorry . . . you know, I went out to buy a box, without realizing that today was Sunday and the stores are closed.

SINGER: Oh, go on! Don't be silly! (*calling toward the upstage door*) Ninna! The dress! Ninna!

BALLERINA I: She's been two hours ironing it. (*brief pause*) You know what?

SINGER: What?

BALLERINA I: Mrs. Geralli told me she'll be teaching dance and for next year she's engaged by La Scala. Just think, with *her* crooked legs!

SINGER: She's dreaming.

BALLERINA 2 (*appearing in the doorway*): Can I come in? (*She enters, also in dishabille.*) I can't stay in that room of mine any more. It's raining there like outside. The walls are seeping water. (*The* **SINGER** *and* **BALLERINA I** *laugh.*) Oh, yes, you can laugh, it's okay for you. I'm going to look for another house. Can you lend me two hairpins? I should have bought some; I don't know how I'm going to keep my hair up tonight.

SINGER: I'll get them for you later. Right now I don't want to disturb my girlfriend. She's resting.

BALLERINA I: Stay away! She has a bad case!

SINGER: How did you know? . . .

BALLERINA I: I could see.

BALLERINA 2: It's obvious. (*changing tone, to the* **SINGER**) You know what Mrs. Finzi told me?

SINGER: What?

BALLERINA 2: That you have a spring engagement at Dal Verme. Is that true?

SINGER: Maybe.

BALLERINA 1: You're so mysterious.

SINGER (*goes upstage as before and calls*): Ninna! (*The* **MAID** *appears, carrying a red dress.*) Finally. Let's see it.

MAID: It's like new. It came out beautiful. (*She lays the dress out on the sofa.*)

SINGER (*looks it over carefully*): What about the ribbons? They need to be attached.

MAID: They're all done. It'll only take a minute.

BALLERINA 1 (*looking it over*): You're going to wear it tonight?

BALLERINA 2: It's miraculous. I don't recognize it.

(*Knocking is heard at a door.*)

> **BALLERINA 1**: Who's that scratching at the door?
>
> **BALLERINA 2**: It's the front entrance.
>
> **BALLERINA 1**: Why don't they ring the bell?

MAID: Why? Because there's no light on the outside stairs, as usual. I'll go and open up. (*She exits for a moment. The* **TWO BALLERINAS** *stand in the upstage door, curious.*)

> **BALLERINA 1**: Who is it?
>
> **BALLERINA 2**: Who is it, Ninna?

Scene 2

The **MAN IN GRAY** *enters through the upstage door, taking off his hat, as the* **TWO BALLERINAS** *separate, astonished. The* **MAID** *follows him and remains on the threshold.*

SINGER (*sitting on the sofa next to her dress, intent on arranging the folds, turns, and seeing the* **MAN IN GRAY**, *frowns, and is also astonished; without even getting up*): Excuse me . . . but you . . . are you looking for someone . . . ?

MAN IN GRAY: Looking? . . . Well, really . . . That is . . . To tell the truth, for a while I haven't been looking for anything.

BALLERINA 1 & 2: Ha! ha! ha! (*They laugh.*)

MAN IN GRAY (*impassive*): Really, because I'm convinced that he who looks . . .

BALLERINA 1 & 2: . . . finds.

MAN IN GRAY: No, wrong. Does not find.

BALLERINA 1 & 2: Ha! ha! ha! (*They laugh.*)

MAN IN GRAY (*to the* **BALLERINAS**): Artistes?

BALLERINA 1: At your service.

MAN IN GRAY: Singing? (**BALLERINA 2** *indicates no.*) Acting? (**BALLERINA 1** *indicates no.*) Legs?

BALLERINA 2 (*stung*): Dance, if you don't mind.

MAN IN GRAY: On the contrary, see, I'm always dancing myself.

SINGER: Well, sir, how can we help you then? (*suddenly, as if remembering*) Oh, but you, an hour ago . . .

MAN IN GRAY: Precisely.

SINGER: At the telegraph office.

MAN IN GRAY: Right. (*to the* **BALLERINAS** *and the* **MAID**) Do you mind?

BALLERINA 1: Of course not.

BALLERINA 2: We were just going. (**BALLERINA 1** *and* 2 *exit with the* **MAID**.)

Scene 3

MAN IN GRAY: Your girlfriend left suddenly, without realizing that she forgot something . . .

(*He takes the glove out of his pocket and brings it over to the* **SINGER**.)

SINGER: Oh, thank you. It was very sweet of you to bother.

MAN IN GRAY: Well now, come on! You know it's only an excuse. I would have come anyway, even if the Woman in the blue fox hadn't left something behind.

SINGER: You know, you are a very strange person.

MAN IN GRAY: Me? Not at all! I'm not myself. There's another person leading me where he wants to go: I follow because I can't do otherwise. But, believe me, I'm being indulgent. He hasn't resigned himself . . . and he keeps on looking. I know he won't find anything. But . . . what do you want . . . I let him do it . . .

SINGER: Listen, sir, you've been very kind; but I'm waiting for an explanation. Tell me honestly: Are you looking for something?

MAN IN GRAY: Honestly, I can't tell you. And you know why? Because a little while ago, I, me, myself, in a fit of passion, said one shouldn't look for anything, that it's stupid to look, senseless, criminal . . . Now, after preaching such a good sermon . . . should I openly confess to wanting to dig for trouble?

SINGER: Oh, really now, I don't believe you mean to lead me in circles. But if you do, I warn you I have no time to waste.

MAN IN GRAY: Don't fly into a temper. Oh, damn it! Dear God, listen to me.

(*Short pause.*)

Alright, let me explain, then, that the two of them, they were just about to rush into an abyss; or rather, to get out of the abyss which they were in, they were falling into a much deeper one. Think of it: each of them gnawed by their own separate passion, and they were going to get together to help liberate each other . . .

SINGER: But who? You haven't told me who it is you're talking about.

MAN IN GRAY: Your friend, for goodness sake, and that other man, the Man in mourning.

SINGER: Who was at the telegraph office as well . . .

MAN IN GRAY: Precisely.

SINGER (*surprised*):   Really? My God, the poor girl has been driven mad, by passion, and pain . . .

MAN IN GRAY: I told her the same thing: it's madness, dear lady, complete madness . . .

SINGER: Thank you so much, my dear sir. I'm grateful to you for warning me! I'll take better care of her. Thank you. (*Extends her hand as if to say goodbye.*)

MAN IN GRAY (*without proffering his*):   Oh, no! You want me to leave? That shows real confidence in men! Think about it, madam, you can't possibly believe that a fully self-possessed man, who finds himself at the telegraph office for personal reasons, would bother to come and warn you that your friend and another man . . . etc. etc., just like that, for no reason, out of the kindness of his heart!

SINGER: Well . . . I suppose . . . But then what should I think?

MAN IN GRAY: Two things: that the man is not fully self-possessed, or that he has a second motive.

SINGER: You really strike me as very strange, as I've already told you.

MAN IN GRAY: So guess. Second . . .

SINGER: If you have a second motive, you can leave now and not talk about it any more.

MAN IN GRAY (*bursting out, no longer quasi-ironical, in a tortured tone*):   And if I were to tell you that I'm in pain, that I'm racked with pain, writhing with it, neither more nor less than your friend, like that other man, the one in mourning, and that using the pretext I gave you, I came here like a beggar, like a wretch to beg and beseech and implore: "Lady, some charity for this poor thirsty man, give him a little passion, give him a little pleasure, distract him with a little bit of bliss, so that he can forget that other woman, that murderous, that treacherous demon woman. This poor bastard cannot take it any more, he's tearing at his heart-strings with his nails. Liberate him, liberate him, the poor devil is dying." Ha! ha! ha!

But no. Ha! ha! No, dearest lady, after that sermon in the telegraph office! . . . They'd say . . . ha! ha! they'd say I'd done it so that that man, that vulture . . . ha! ha! . . . would let go his prey . . . Isn't that right? . . . isn't that right? . . . It's funny . . . funny . . . Go on, laugh . . .

SINGER (*bewildered, terrified*):   Sit down, sir, calm down. Of course, the anguish is terrible, I know! . . .

MAN IN GRAY (*sitting down*):   Don't be frightened; I've come back to normal. You see? . . .

(*A pause.*)

(*He looks at the Singer.*) You understand. So you've been on the rack too. (*in a tone between irony and despair, as before*) Look, because you haven't yelled at me for having come here looking for your friend . . . Will you allow me? (*takes her hand and kisses it*)

SINGER (*rises, indignant*):   What is this? You've just been talking so wisely about your passion . . . you've just declared that you're not looking for anything anymore because you know you can't find it . . .

MAN IN GRAY: Don't get angry now. I told you myself a few minutes ago that I'm caught in a terrible game. It's horrible, but I can't escape! . . . . Sit down, I beg you; fundamentally,

you see . . . if, one caress . . . what's one little caress to you? Your hand is soft and delicate; your slender body suggests an unusual wealth of talent in love: all of you stretches
upward like a stalk from your nervous little feet to the flower of your blond hair crowning
your pearly brow; ears of pearl, pearls around your neck, beneath the sky-blue splendor
of your eyes . . . Sweetheart . . . sweetheart, I beg you, stroke me . . .

SINGER (*shoving him violently onto the sofa*):   That's enough, now, I say. I'm sympathetic,
yes . . . compassionate, even. But that's all. And I'm neither a bashful bourgeoise, nor
an untouched flower. I could make an effort perhaps and, on a whim, yield up all those
treasures you mention, to some man. But that, lo and behold, you come here, and ask
me to make love to you, just like that, standing there on your two feet, just to help you
forget your misfortunes . . . Well, that's a bit much really!

MAN IN GRAY (*regaining his composure and rising*):   Look . . . precisely. Didn't I maybe tell
you myself you should laugh? Laugh. Go on, laugh!

SINGER: I'm not going to laugh, because I understand. However, I assure you that you're
not the first person to find himself on the torture rack. Really! Everyone's been there!
Some are able to grin and bear it, until it's over, and others not: you, for example. And
you're doing yourself no good in making such a sad spectacle of yourself. It's degrading;
you're humiliating yourself.

MAN IN GRAY (*bowing deeply*):   A well-deserved lesson. You are a wise teacher.

(*The door on the left opens.*)

Scene 4

WOMAN IN BLUE FOX (*appears in the door on the left; amazed to see the* **MAN IN GRAY**):   You!

MAN IN GRAY (*to the* **SINGER**):   See? She recognizes me.

WOMAN IN BLUE FOX: The Man in gray from the telegraph office.

MAN IN GRAY: I bet that when she heard my voice from inside there, she thought I was
the Man in mourning.

WOMAN IN BLUE FOX: Actually, I did not expect to find you.

MAN IN GRAY: But the other man.

WOMAN IN BLUE FOX: Not him either.

MAN IN GRAY: Don't lie.

SINGER (*to her girlfriend*):   Go back and rest, darling. You would find this man bewildering.

MAN IN GRAY: Don't worry, my blond friend. (*to the* **WOMAN IN THE BLUE FOX**) See? A
few minutes and I'm on intimate terms with your sweet lady hostess. (*proffering his hand
to the* **SINGER**) Look: I promise you that I'll be very good. I swear it. I'm a man of honor
and integrity.

SINGER (*giving him her hand*):   I believe you. But I must get dressed. I live by work and I
have to sing tonight.

MAN IN GRAY: Wonderful! I'll see you to the theater. Go and dress then. I'll wait for you.

WOMAN IN BLUE FOX: Go on. I'll stay with the gentleman. I've something to ask him.

SINGER (*about to lose patience*):   Good heavens!

MAN IN GRAY (*to the* **SINGER**):   Keep calm, I tell you. I'm perfectly under control.

SINGER (*takes her dress on one arm*):   Well, that's good!

(*She crosses to the exit on the left. On the threshold she turns. Unseen by her girlfriend, she makes a warning gesture to the* **MAN IN GRAY**, *who reassures her with a movement of his head. She exits.*)

Scene 5

WOMAN IN BLUE FOX (*with her friend barely out of the room, she runs over excitedly to the* **MAN IN GRAY**):   Sir, I understood perfectly what you said in the telegraph office. I'm so grateful to you, yes, yes, I'm truly grateful . . . I didn't send a telegram, I stopped listening to that other wretched man . . . But words are words! . . . And now, since you are so wise, can't you tell me what I should do? I can't bear it any more: I've gone mad! (*bursting into tears*) And I loved him, I loved him with every fiber of my being! I would have gone through anything for him! I tried to guess his thoughts, his wishes; by the time he opened his mouth I'd already satisfied his every desire . . . Oh God! . . . Oh God! . . . Maybe I gave him too much . . . maybe he'd had too much of me . . . He cheated on me, yes, yes . . . I'm sure of it . . . and when I got upset and screamed and cried . . . he beat me. And I was supposed to tolerate that! You understand, tolerate it? . . . Oh, no, escape! I escaped! Wasn't I right to escape?

MAN IN GRAY: Escape, but of course! Oh, heavens, that's a natural reaction! And so simple . . .

WOMAN IN BLUE FOX: Ah, good, you agree with me! I did the right thing then?

MAN IN GRAY: Of course. I escaped too, you see. A little while back. A year ago!

WOMAN IN BLUE FOX: Yes, but now what do I do? . . . What do I do? . . . I can't live without him . . . I can't! . . . What should one do? Please tell me.

MAN IN GRAY: Oh, well, that's the problem! Calm down, dear. Oh, damn it, there is something . . .

WOMAN IN BLUE FOX: Really? That's a relief. Think about it for me, I beg you. I can't.

MAN IN GRAY (*in the tone used to calm little children*):   Now, let's see . . . So you . . .

(*The upstage door is thrown open and the* **MAN IN MOURNING** *appears.*)

Scene 6

MAN IN MOURNING (*entering*):   I knew it! I guessed right! You're a phony! A complete impostor! Oh, what a sermon you gave in the telegraph office! And then to come here and take advantage of this poor woman's vulnerability. (*mimicking the* **MAN IN GRAY**) "You're committing a heinous crime!" "Watch out, tomorrow you'll feel ashamed, like thieves!" "Go away, then, if you have the courage!" Impostor! Phony! Charlatan! Oh, you'll pay for this! I want to die! I can't go on living. But you'll pay for it first! Making me a laughingstock! Think I'm a cheat like you? I'm a man suffering the pains of hell! I'm walking on the brink! I could kill you. (*He seems to reach for a revolver. The* **WOMAN IN THE BLUE FOX** *gives a piercing scream, and collapses onto the sofa.*)

SINGER (*rushing in from the left, half-dressed*): Oh my God! What's happened? (*With the* **TWO MEN**, *she bends over her friend, unfastens her bodice.*) Some eau de cologne . . . smelling salts . . . Call my maid . . .

MAN IN MOURNING (*rushes upstage and calls*): Maid! Hey there! Ma'am!

MAN IN GRAY (*disappears through the door on the left and reenters with the eau de cologne*): Here, I found it . . . (*The* **MAID** *enters upstage.*)

MAN IN MOURNING: Quick, find a doctor!

MAN IN GRAY (*to the* **MAN IN MOURNING**): Come on! How you do exaggerate! What do you mean, a doctor! She's coming round.

MAN IN MOURNING (*through his teeth*): You'll see if I'm exaggerating. You'll pay for this.

SINGER (*kneeling in front of her friend*): Good! That's good! There now, that's the spirit! . . . It's alright, dear!

BALLERINA 1 (*from upstage*): What happened?

BALLERINA 2 (*from upstage*): What happened?

MAID: Should I go for the doctor or not?

(*They're all gathered around the* **WOMAN IN THE BLUE FOX**.)

SINGER (*continues to give encouragement*): Come on, there now. It's nothing . . . (*rises after a bit, letting out a sigh*) Ah, that's better! People, don't stand over her. (*to the* **BALLE-RINAS**) What are you doing here, sweethearts?

BALLERINA 1: Nothing, nothing. We're going.

BALLERINA 2: We came in to help. We're going. (*They leave.*)

SINGER (*to the* **MAID**): Ninna, you can go. (*The* **MAID** *exits.*)

Scene 7

SINGER: Gentlemen, is that any way to behave? Do you want to kill her? . . . And you seem like two such nice men . . . She's so vulnerable . . . (*To her* **FRIEND** *who is sitting up on the sofa, bewildered, staring into space.*) Do you feel better, dear?

MAN IN MOURNING: It's not my fault. This man, whom I don't know, this faker . . . (*The* **MAN IN GRAY** *laughs.*) You see? He has the effrontery to laugh, because he still doesn't believe that I have it in me to get a thorough explanation out of him! In short, this phony . . .

WOMAN IN BLUE FOX (*moaning, distressed*): Please! . . . Please! . . . For goodness sake! . . . I beg you . . .

SINGER: Do you hear that or not, gentlemen? Do you hear that? Do you still want to continue this? (*to the* **MAN IN MOURNING**) I can assure you that the gentleman in gray is neither a faker, nor an impostor. He is in pain just like you, like her . . .

MAN IN MOURNING: What do you mean, in pain! Then why is he laughing? He's putting us on! Look! He's laughing!

SINGER (*to the* **MAN IN GRAY**): Stop laughing now, you! Why are you laughing if you're consumed by despair?

MAN IN MOURNING: What do you mean, despair! . . . Consumed! . . . He's joking . . . But I'll give him a joke soon!

SINGER (*to the* **MAN IN GRAY**): Cry! Go on. Like you did a little while ago! You've got a lot to cry about! . . . Let the gentleman in mourning see that you're crying inside; and what tears! . . .

MAN IN GRAY: No, on the contrary! I want to laugh, because my future killer is convinced that I'm joking! And I am joking. Yes, I am joking. We're all joking. Ha! ha! ha! It's funny; it's wonderful. The piano . . . let's have music. Let's dance. Get the ballerinas.

WOMAN IN BLUE FOX (*leaps up; begins to laugh and laugh and laugh*): Ha! ha! ha! ha! ha!

MAN IN GRAY: That's good. (*doing some dance steps*) Let's dance. (*to the* **MAN IN MOURNING**) You dance too, even though you're in mourning.

SINGER (*with a shout*): Stop! this is madness. (*to her girlfriend*) My friend, darling, sweet . . . No, don't do that, you're killing yourself, poor darling!

(*The* **WOMAN IN THE BLUE FOX** *after having laughed and laughed and laughed, collapses on the sofa again and bursts into tears.*)

MAN IN GRAY (*more soberly, to the* **MAN IN MOURNING**): So now, tell me . . . you're joking too, aren't you? But you're worse. You're joking, believing you're serious. If you weren't joking you wouldn't be here. A man like you, your soul still filled with your wife, your nose still full of the scent of her, a woman who's no longer yours, who ran away, who at this very moment is with somebody else. Yes, a man like you must certainly be joking if he makes a scene over a woman he met two hours ago. Come on then, tell me who's joking, me or you!

SINGER: That's enough, I beg you, gentlemen. All three of you are suffering. That's the truth. (*to the* **MAN IN GRAY**) Fasten my dress. It's still open in the back. Aren't you lucky to be doing me this favor! (*goes to the mirror*)

MAN IN GRAY: Very lucky. (*fastening her dress*) You smell like a flower. What a temptation! If it weren't for the gentleman in mourning and your friend . . .

SINGER: What would you do?

MAN IN GRAY: I would touch my lips to your delicious back.

SINGER: I give you permission, provided you're good afterwards.

MAN IN GRAY (*kisses her*): Ah, you would make a sweet little mother! (*The* **MAN IN MOURNING** *clenches his fists. But the* **WOMAN IN THE BLUE FOX** *smiles.*)

SINGER (*still turned toward the mirror*): Finished?

MAN IN GRAY: Wait, there are more down below. These snaps are never ending. I'll kneel down, it'll be easier.

SINGER: That way you can fasten me up and worship me!

MAN IN GRAY: Yes, I'll fasten you up and worship you. (*He has knelt down and is doing it. However, when he's finished, he embraces her legs and rises with her in his arms.*)

SINGER (*with a scream*): Aah!

MAN IN GRAY: Where do you want to go? To the theater? I'll carry you there!

SINGER (*still in his arms, supporting herself with her hands on his head, notices that her friend is* *smiling*): What a strange fellow! (*to the* **MAN IN MOURNING**) Come on now, you too, smile a little . . . Just a little . . . Go on.

MAN IN GRAY: Go on, killer . . . (*The* **MAN IN MOURNING** *laughs nervously.*)

SINGER: Oh, at last!

MAN IN GRAY (*releases his hold so that the* **SINGER** *slides down to the ground, but grasps her again immediately so that she has to give him a kiss*): Many thanks indeed.

SINGER: Be good, now, children. Listen to me. Let's do this . . . (*in a maternal tone, to the* **MAN IN MOURNING**) You come here, sit down next to my friend. (*Goes and takes him by the arm, makes him sit.*) You, on this side, here. (*The* **MAN IN GRAY** *obeys.*) And I'll stay here, in front of all of you. Well now, my chicks, I have to go to the theater. I'll be free early tonight. So, if you promise to be good, I propose that all three of you go together and get a table at a lovely restaurant I know about, and wait there for me. Okay? . . .

MAN IN GRAY: Most willingly.

WOMAN IN BLUE FOX: However, we mustn't talk about anything.

MAN IN MOURNING: I can't . . . I'm not used to . . .

SINGER: But of course you are. Be good! You'll see, it'll be just fine. You'll get to be friends. You already are. Isn't that right?

MAN IN GRAY (*to the* **MAN IN MOURNING**): Give me your hand. (*The* **MAN IN MOURNING** *hesitates, then extends it to him.*)

SINGER: Oh! God be praised! (*She rises.*) I'm going to get my fur coat. (*She exits to the left. They have all risen.*)

WOMAN IN BLUE FOX: Please, let's be friends. Be kind to me.

MAN IN GRAY (*taking her right hand*): Kind? Devoted, adoring! . . .

MAN IN MOURNING (*taking her left hand*): I beg your forgiveness.

(*He kisses her hand. The* **MAN IN GRAY** *kisses her right hand.*)

CURTAIN

ACT 3

A little room set apart, in a swanky restaurant. The ceiling has stuccowork in a floral design with gold filament and a central chandelier. The walls are in yellow silk, quite plain. A passageway upstage to the right is hidden by a silk drape, also yellow. There is a hidden door to the left, also covered by a drape. Two square tables, very white, sparkle with crystal, one to the right, one to the left.

About two hours after Act 2.

Scene 1

When the curtain rises, the three characters have only just entered. The men have put their cloaks and hats in the anteroom; the woman still has her blue fox draped around her shoulders.

1ST WAITER: Will this suit you?

MAN IN GRAY: Excellent. Although we only need one table. That one. (*indicates the one on the left*) The other one could get in the way later. Remove it.

1ST WAITER: How could I allow that, sir? . . . The owner of the . . .

MAN IN GRAY: I see. Well then . . . (*Thinks a bit; then, to the* **MAN IN MOURNING** *and the* **WOMAN IN THE BLUE FOX**) Help me settle this problem. Or we'll have some uninvited dinner guests.

WOMAN IN BLUE FOX: Oh, I don't know what to tell you . . . I'm in such a daze! . . .

MAN IN MOURNING: Me too; I don't feel well! . . .

MAN IN GRAY: Let's think.

MAN IN MOURNING: Isn't there another private room with only one table?

1ST WAITER: There is, but it's already taken.

MAN IN GRAY (*as if he's found the answer*): Very well, then. (*to the* **WAITER**) You'll arrange the four chairs at this table (*indicates the table to the right*) so that their backs are leaning against the place settings, as if they were sleepy. In fact, take away one place setting so that there are only three.

1ST WAITER: Then you wish to leave, and return later?

MAN IN GRAY: I haven't explained it yet: the table we'll be using will be that one (*pointing to the table on the left*). Take a place setting away from this one, and lean three chairs against the three settings that are left.

1ST WAITER: You're expecting three more people?

MAN IN GRAY: Precisely. They may come, they may not. In any case, whether they come or not, we'll take care of the bill. Okay?

1ST WAITER: Anything you say. (*He lifts off the fourth place setting from the right-hand table and takes away the chair, which he places near the wall: he leans the other three chairs against the remaining three place settings.*) Like that?

MAN IN GRAY: Like that. (*to the* **WOMAN IN THE BLUE FOX**) Why not take a seat meanwhile? (*Pulls out a chair from the table on the left. The* **WOMAN IN THE BLUE FOX** *sits so that the audience can see her face.*) For you, my friend. (*Indicates the seat on the woman's right. The* **MAN IN MOURNING** *sits down. The* **MAN IN GRAY**, *sitting on the woman's left:*) And now, a request.

1ST WAITER (*who is about to take away the fourth place setting from the table where they're sitting*): Can I take away this fourth place?

MAN IN GRAY: No, don't do that. We're waiting for a woman, the only person you can permit to come in here. We've left instructions at the front desk. You and your partner should bar entrance to anyone else.

1ST WAITER: What about the three people you've invited for the other table?

MAN IN GRAY I'm not sure they'll be coming. (*to his two table companions*) Isn't that right? Do you think they'll come? I know we're two men and one woman, but it's unlikely the opposite will happen, two women coming to this restaurant with one man.

1ST WAITER (*amazed*): Really it . . .

MAN IN GRAY: Anyway, they'll eat with us in fantasy; it's the same thing. We'll pay their bill. Since we're in no hurry, we'll chat before ordering dinner.

1ST WAITER: As you wish. (*He exits.*)

Scene 2

WOMAN IN BLUE FOX (*trembling*): Gentlemen, this is a nightmare, these three invited guests who won't be coming. I can't bear it.

MAN IN MOURNING (*an outburst, to the* **MAN IN GRAY**): How could you! We came here to forget, and you bring on the ghosts! Let's get rid of that table!

MAN IN GRAY: Come on, we're not babies! It's only my silly joke. Do you really expect our three tormentors to suddenly make an entrance? . . . Let's have a good laugh about it . . . Think about it! Our two women arm in arm with this lady's man, all of them here to give us the coup de grâce! . . . No such luck! . . . Instead, we can be sure they barely remember us any more; while we're still crazy about them and have the sudden urge to cover their table with flowers . . . In fact . . . (*He rises and rings the bell.*)

WOMAN IN BLUE FOX: What are you doing?

MAN IN MOURNING: Another fiendish joke?

MAN IN GRAY: Let's have some fun. Didn't we come here to have fun?

2D WAITER (*enters*): May I help you?

MAN IN GRAY: I'm astonished that a first rate place like this doesn't ply its customers with huge bunches of flowers. Go and get some immediately, a mixture of different kinds . . .

2D WAITER: I hope I can find some somewhere. (*He exits.*)

Scene 3

PROSTITUTE (*peeps in and enters followed by the* **DANDY**. *Eyeing the empty table*): We could sit here.

MAN IN GRAY: I'm very sorry, but it's taken, as you can see.

PROSTITUTE: Baby, we're jinxed tonight! (*She exits.*)

DANDY (*following her*): Patience, kitten, sweetheart. We'll find . . .

2D WAITER (*coming back with an assortment of flowers*): This is all I could come up with.

MAN IN GRAY: That's wonderful. (*to the* **WAITER**, *who is about to put the flowers on their table*) No, they're not for us. Give them here, and in the meantime bring us a mixed antipasto and a bottle of your best champagne.

2D WAITER: As you wish. (*He exits.*)

MAN IN GRAY (*standing, holding the flowers*): This is just what we needed. (*going over to the empty table*) Your paramour, dear lady, you just have to give him . . . Here we are: red carnations. Let's put him in the middle, between the two women. Perfect: his place awaits him: there. (*places the red carnations in the middle*) What about you? (*to the* **MAN IN**

MOURNING) You'll give your lady . . . you'll give her . . . My God . . . pansies. What could be better? . . . (*places them on the left place setting*)

MAN IN MOURNING (*bursting out, with a sob in his voice*):   And what about that viper who's made you so crazy that you've turned horribly cruel, what will she get? Come on, what? Tell us, go on . . .

MAN IN GRAY (*laughing*):   Me? Here we are: chrysanthemums. (*places them on the right hand setting*) Could there be any lovers more fulfilled than we three?

(*The **2D WAITER** comes in with the antipasto and the champagne. The **MAN IN GRAY** sits down in his chair. The **MAN IN MOURNING** falls exhausted into his. The **2D WAITER** serves and pours.*)

2D WAITER: If you wish to order for later . . . I will notify the first waiter.

MAN IN GRAY: We don't want anyone to disturb us for now, as you know.

(*The **2D WAITER** exits staring, amazed, at the empty table with the flowers on it.*)

WOMAN IN BLUE FOX: It's hot . . . It's so hot in here! . . . I'm going to take off my fox.

MAN IN GRAY: Take it off. (*He helps her off with the fox and places it on the empty chair.*) The heat will ease up, you'll see. Now let's drink to us and to the absentees. (*He raises his glass, and because the other two do not follow suit:*) Come on, has my little joke really made you so sad? Please, sir, cheer up, I want to be your friend, like a good boy! That's right, thank you. (*He clinks with the **MAN IN MOURNING** once the latter decides to raise his glass. Then to the **WOMAN IN THE BLUE FOX**:*) You too, lovely lady, don't make me feel guilty; I'm a fool, it's true, but I don't wish you any harm. Oh, well done, and without a tremble! (*He clinks glasses with the woman too. They drink.*) You'll see. Little by little, as we warm up, we'll forget our misfortunes . . . In fact, in an hour, when we'll have drunk a bit more, they'll seem so ridiculous to us, we'll wonder why we suffered so. Believe me, dear friends, that's how it will be. (*to the **WOMAN IN THE BLUE FOX***) When your blond friend joins us in a little while, she won't even recognize us. We'll be laughing and happy, floating on a cloud in seventh heaven. (*pouring*) Drink . . . drink up.

WOMAN IN BLUE FOX (*turning toward the **MAN IN MOURNING***):   My head is beginning to spin.

MAN IN MOURNING (*kind, fatherly, taking her hands, patting them*):   No, sweetheart, no. I admit now that our friend is right: we must force ourselves to be happy. A slightly spinning head is nothing. I'm feeling better now.

WOMAN IN BLUE FOX (*letting go the hands of the **MAN IN MOURNING** and stroking her throat and her chest*):   Yes, truthfully, it is nice. I don't know, I'm beginning to feel good . . .

MAN IN GRAY: My efforts are finally being rewarded. Thank you for the acknowledgment . . . and I drink to your passion. (*He drinks.*)

MAN IN MOURNING (*livening up*):   I'm so happy to have met you at the telegraph office! (*He drinks.*)

WOMAN IN BLUE FOX: Me too, very happy! (*She drinks.*)

MAN IN GRAY: You'll see. We'll fall madly in love with each other, all three of us. We'll stay together forever. We'll still have to fight off sadness and depression for a little while. But then our life as a threesome will reenergize us. We'll be terribly anxious to enjoy ourselves, to taste life to the fullest. We'll travel, we'll go abroad, to Europe, then to America, then perhaps to Australia, and, who knows, maybe India, China, and Japan . . . The three of us together always . . . I have got quite a lot of my inheritance left still. We'll spend it all, wildly. But on our travels we'll collect more treasure! Without even lifting a finger we'll have unlikely opportunities, with gold miners in California, pearl fishers in India! . . . We'll have faith in life. A woman always inspires a man and sets his imagination on fire. (*to the* **MAN IN MOURNING**) I beg you, don't be jealous; we've lost our own, but we're so lucky to have found this divine creature! . . . (*He kisses the hand of the* **WOMAN IN THE BLUE FOX**.)

WOMAN IN BLUE FOX (*to* **MAN IN MOURNING**): He seems to know how to lift our spirits. I'm glad to see you smile.

MAN IN MOURNING (*smiling*): I don't know how, but that man's words are winning me over. I'm beginning to see a light at the end of the tunnel.

MAN IN GRAY (*rings the bell*): If our blond friend joins us, we won't have any champagne to offer her. We must order some more.

(*A noisy quarrel explodes behind the curtain.*)

Scene 4

1ST WAITER (*from offstage*): I'm telling you that you cannot come in here! It's a private party.

HE WHO WAS NOT TO HAVE COME: What do you mean! I've gone through all the hotels, and the restaurants, theaters, and bars in this city! . . . Do you think you're going to stop me going in here? . . .

WOMAN IN BLUE FOX (*turns pale, begins to tremble*): It's him!

MAN IN MOURNING: Who?

MAN IN GRAY: Who?

WOMAN IN BLUE FOX: Yes, him! him!

1ST WAITER (*from offstage*): How dare you be so insolent! You may not pass through!

WOMAN IN BLUE FOX: Oh my God! oh my God! (*She has risen, not knowing what to do.*)

MAN IN GRAY: Be brave. When in dire straits, follow the usual strategy. The curtain. (*leads her behind the curtain of the concealed door*) There, don't move! (*Goes to sit down. To the* **MAN IN MOURNING**.) And we . . . we'll feign ignorance! . . .

HE WHO WAS NOT TO HAVE COME (*offstage*): I've had enough of this, now! You bore me!

(*The* **WAITER** *almost tumbles in, recoiling from a shove.* **HE WHO WAS NOT TO HAVE COME** *enters.*)

1ST WAITER (*enraged, to the two seated men*): Gentlemen, he used violence on me. I did try to stop him.

HE WHO WAS NOT TO HAVE COME (*tall, strong; overcoat buttoned up, hat in hand, umbrella. To the* **WAITER**): Well done. Now you can go. (*The* **WAITER** *remains irresolute, then exits.*)

Scene 5

HE WHO WAS NOT TO HAVE COME (*sniffs the air repeatedly, dilating his nostrils, and shrugging his shoulders. As though to himself*): No, it's not my imagination. (*Then to the two who have remained seated and are feigning imperturbability.*) So you gentlemen get a private room in a restaurant just to have a tête-à-tête with each other . . .

MAN IN GRAY: Oh . . . well . . . You know . . . you can often get so anxious that you come early . . . And then, of course, you have to wait . . .

HE WHO WAS NOT TO HAVE COME: And now you'd like to convince me that the woman hasn't come yet! (*sniffs the air*) Oh no, my dear sir. She's here alright.

MAN IN GRAY: Oh, come on, you can't pretend to be such an extraordinary connoisseur! Sniffing the air! . . . Well, damn it! . . . In a restaurant like this, every woman coming in . . .

HE WHO WAS NOT TO HAVE COME: I would recognize the scent I'm talking about, sir, not only here, but in a greenhouse. (*banging his fist on the table*) I've had enough! Where is she? . . . What a hellish day! I've ransacked all Milan.

MAN IN GRAY: How very sad! I sympathize, sir! . . . But, in this case, you're mistaken.

HE WHO WAS NOT TO HAVE COME: Mistaken?

MAN IN MOURNING (*jumping up, seized by an attack of nervous trembling*): Mistaken! Mistaken! How dare you take the liberty of coming in here and . . . and . . . without even knowing them, disturbing two gentlemen who for their own reasons . . .

HE WHO WAS NOT TO HAVE COME (*whose eyes have been searching high and low all over the room gives the* **MAN IN MOURNING** *a derisive signal to be silent*): Shut up! (*Walks coldly over to the empty chair, takes the blue fox, lifts it up and, lets it dangle.*) What about this? (*The* **MAN IN MOURNING** *is rendered speechless.*)

MAN IN GRAY (*making a final stab*): Well? So what about it?

HE WHO WAS NOT TO HAVE COME: What about it? . . . I'll tell you what! It cost three hundred and some lire, barely ten days ago, at Toldi's, in Garibaldi Street, Turin. Do you want to see? (*He shows the* **MAN IN GRAY** *the label on the blue fox.*) Alright?

MAN IN MOURNING (*shaken*): Listen, sir, who knows what you're imagining! . . . But we swear, on our word of honor as gentlemen . . .

MAN IN GRAY (*without losing his sangfroid*): And there, you see? (*indicating the other table*) You were invited too, an imaginary guest, it's true, but a place has certainly been reserved for you. If you don't believe me, ask the waiter. Indeed, you can find your seat very easily. Red carnations, between the pansies and the chrysanthemums. One could easily envy you your position, considering that the romantic melancholy of pansies is symbolic of the grieving heart of a husband who cannot bring himself to hate his unfaithful wife—quite possibly the case of this gentleman here! . . .—and that, oh my God, chrysanthemums look more funereal on a plate than on a tomb: a lover—you can easily see who—a lover who has written his own tombstone! . . .

HE WHO WAS NOT TO HAVE COME: I only see that by some stroke of luck, I've come to the right place. (*He goes toward the hidden door, raises the curtain. Behind it, deathly white,* stands the **WOMAN IN THE BLUE FOX**. *She closes her eyes and, as though unable to stand any longer, collapses against his chest.*) There now, sweetheart, don't you get into your usual twitch, and I don't want to make a scene about how I've wasted a whole night on the train and all day going all over everywhere. If there are any accounts to settle, we'll do it at home. (*He places the blue fox on her shoulders, buttons up her jacket.*) If I'm at fault, you shouldn't get even by doing something much worse.

MAN IN MOURNING (*almost in tears*): No wrong done. Ask her friend, the singer.

MAN IN GRAY: It's not necessary; he's a clever man. He already understands who we are, we two.

HE WHO WAS NOT TO HAVE COME: Two unhappy fellows, that's certain. Good night, gentlemen!

(*He leads off the* **WOMAN IN THE BLUE FOX**. *As she staggers past the table with the flowers, she is able to reach out and take the red carnations. As they exit, she places them inside the overcoat, next to the chest, of* **HE WHO WAS NOT TO HAVE COME**.)

Scene 6

MAN IN MOURNING (*sways a moment as if about to fall, then runs upstage*): No! No! Don't leave! . . .

MAN IN GRAY (*stopping him*): What are you doing? What are you saying?

MAN IN MOURNING (*withdrawing, tired*): Gone . . . Gone . . . She's gone away giving him the carnations! . . .

MAN IN GRAY: Only the carnations? She'll give him everything now, her soul, her body, her life! . . . Oh, hell, if the woman who betrayed you were to arrive, suddenly, unexpectedly, changed and begging your forgiveness . . . just pansies? . . . wouldn't you give her the blood in your veins?

MAN IN MOURNING (*collapsing into his chair like a puppet whose strings have been released*): Yes, yes . . . it's true . . . (*bursts into tears, hopeless*)

MAN IN GRAY (*stepping toward the table with the flowers, to himself*): As for me, now . . . if you'll allow me . . . (*taking the chrysanthemums*) there, outstripping them all, the chrysanthemums! . . . (*He strews them on the floor as if it were a coffin.*)

MAN IN MOURNING (*still between sobs*): Better to end it all . . . to die . . .

MAN IN GRAY (*still to himself*): I'm considering it.

MAN IN MOURNING (*still between sobs*): But having the courage to do it! . . . The courage to shatter this dreadful life! . . .

MAN IN GRAY (*like an echo*): Why courage? . . . What do you need it for! . . . Poor man! You've still enough of your heart left to gnaw away at! . . . Me . . . I devoured mine a long time ago! . . .

MAN IN MOURNING: And I've tried my best, you know! . . . I've tried . . .

MAN IN GRAY: I know. But you're still not fully mature. Just wait . . . wait. (*As he speaks, he slowly takes his wallet from his pocket, takes out a little paper packet, opens it, goes to the table* *and pours the contents into a glass of champagne, tapping the paper so that all the powder will fall out.*) When you've tried everything . . . you'll see, it'll be easy for you. Oh, so, so easy, you see! . . . It's all trial and error until finally there's no other way, no escape to the right or to the left, no escape . . . Then you'll chatter a lot . . . A lot . . . like me. You'll be desperate for conversation . . . for words . . . You'll hear your own voice as if it were the voice of someone else, of some dreadfully boring ham actor . . . It'll seem as if the air is entering your empty chest and making you whistle puffs of nonsense . . . When you're reduced to pumice stone . . . well . . . then it'll be like nothing to . . . (*swallows it in one gulp*) Like that. Who are you killing? . . . Nobody.

MAN IN MOURNING (*gazes at him bewildered and admiring, then in a dazed voice*): So . . . you? . . . That's it? . . .

MAN IN GRAY: I've never been over there . . . Still, I hope . . . (*extends his hand*) Goodbye then. My regards to the blond when she comes. Now there's a creature I would have liked to meet again! Uhm, you must tell her of my happy memory! (*Very short pause. Hitting his forehead.*) I forgot! . . . I haven't time to pay the bill now! . . . You'll have to take care of it . . . I'm so sorry . . . There's a hitch, beyond my control! . . . (*He exits hurriedly.*)

Scene 7

MAN IN MOURNING (*remains in his chair, stupefied, gazing into space, repeating dazedly*): That's it . . . It's all over! . . .

(*Pause. One hears someone passing behind the curtain and singing to himself. More prostitutes pass by laughing loudly. Pause. More bursts of laughter, clattering of silverware and dishes. Pause.*)

SINGER (*from offstage*): Through there?

1ST WAITER (*from offstage*): Here, ma'am, please come this way.

SINGER (*enters gaily onto the stage, but perceiving that the **MAN IN MOURNING** is alone, her face clouds over, and she stands confused*): Where are the others?

MAN IN MOURNING (*replies first with a motion of his hand, then in a weary voice*): Uh! Gone . . .

SINGER: What? Why?

MAN IN MOURNING (*dazed*): It's all over! . . . He came . . . and she, dragged off.

SINGER: I knew it! And the other man?

MAN IN MOURNING (*shrugs his shoulders*): It's all over! . . . (*points to the empty packet still lying on the table*)

SINGER (*understanding*): My God! . . . Really? . . . (*makes a small move for the exit*) We've got to go after him, try to find him! We've got to . . .

MAN IN MOURNING (*clinging to her, prey to another attack of despair*): Help me instead! . . . Help me to live! . . . (*bursts into tears as he founders like a wrecked ship onto the table.*)

SINGER (*pale, and remembering the other man*): What a terrible shame! . . . Maybe I could have loved him! . . .

CURTAIN

SIX

FEDERIGO
TOZZI

Introduction

Federigo Tozzi was born in Siena on January 1, 1883, the youngest and the sole survivor of seven children. During his lifetime, he received scant attention for his literary works and still less for his plays. Only after his early death at the age of thirty-seven did critics begin to see him as heir to Verga. One must take into account, moreover, that his literary activity was limited to a single decade, 1908–1920, in the middle of which World War I devastated Italy and Italian culture.

Tozzi was raised by an epileptic mother and a peasant father who achieved some wealth as the owner of a restaurant in Siena. His mother's death in 1895 left him practically alone since he had a turbulent relationship with his physically abusive father. He began his studies in higher education but did not do well and abandoned them in 1902. When his father died in 1908, he liquidated the restaurant, sold one of his father's farms, married the woman he had met through a "lonely hearts" column, and moved to the second family farm in Castagneto where he spent seven very intense years writing.

Between 1911 and 1914 he earned recognition in intellectual circles, collaborating on journals such as Ettore Cozzani's *L'Eroica*. Tozzi moved away from the socialist stance he had espoused during his early years in favor of symbolism and the Dannunzian aesthetic, both of which he would later abandon in his search for meaning. His youth was certainly influenced by medieval mysticism, particularly the revelations and ecstasies of Saint Catherine of Siena as she had written them down in her journal. In 1913 he and Domenico Giuliotti founded the journal *La Torre* as an "organ of Italian spiritual reaction." Two important collections of his poetry appeared during this early period: *La zampogna verde* (The green bagpipe, 1911) and *La città della Vergine* (The city of the Virgin, 1913). His novel *Con gli occhi chiusi (Eyes Shut)*[1] was written in 1913, but it was not published until 1919.

At the end of 1914 Tozzi moved to Rome, where he socialized with Giuseppe Prezzolini, Goffredo Bellonci, Antonio Baldini, and Dario Niccodemi, among others, and where he earned the respect and assistance of Luigi Pirandello and the critic Giulio Antonio Borgese. While still living in Rome, Tozzi worked as press aide for the Italian Red Cross and then wrote for the daily newspaper *Il Messaggero*. He died of pneumonia on March 21, 1920. *Tre croci* (Three crosses), a novel that is considered his masterpiece, was published shortly before his death.

While Tozzi wrote several short plays between 1908 and 1910, it was with *La Pippa*—an adaptation of a Boccacciesque tale by Anton Francesco Grazzini, aka Lasca—that he made his entrance into the world of the theater. After Tozzi wrote the first version by himself in 1909, he began to collaborate with Angelo Maria Tirabassi. The two authors created several different versions together—*La dote della Pippa* and *La vergine del Mugello*—but when they could not interest any producers, Tozzi removed his name. The fourth version, *La vergine dell'Antella*, was signed only by Tirabassi, although Tozzi retained author's rights. The play was at last successfully produced in 1913; it was subsequently adapted for the Neapolitan, Sicilian, and Milanese dialects, according to the practice of the time, and turned into a play with music.

Tozzi's other plays include two sketches of peasant life, the one-act drama *La famiglia* (The family, 1909–10) and *Gente da poco* (Poor folk, ca. 1915), a full-length play; two plays based on tales by Boccaccio: *L'uva* (Grapes, 1914), a one-act comedy, and *Le due mogli* (The two wives, 1916), a clown piece in three acts. The latter was produced by the well-known Borelli-Beltramo company in 1918. Florence was reserved in its reception of the piece; reviews in Milan were so savage that Tozzi wrote an open letter stating: "I agree completely with the public and the critics. I'm not putting up a front, I'm speaking quite sincerely and out of respect for myself as a writer."[2] Despite the Milanese critics, the Borelli-Beltramo company continued to produce the piece, even after Tozzi's death, something they would not have done had they not had some success with it.

During World War I the Società del Teatro Ambulante (Itinerant Theater Society), a war initiative, commissioned two plays from Tozzi, *L'amico* (The friend) and *La bandiera* (The flag), which was written in dialect. Both were patriotic one-act plays scheduled to be produced at the front. Eventually *I due figli* (Two sons), another one-act, replaced *La bandiera*, which was considered unsuitable.

When he died, Tozzi was completing revisions on his last play, *L'incalco* or *The Casting*, the three-act Oedipal drama that is presented here. It was published posthumously[3] together with the novel *Gli egoisti* (The egotists)—a pertinent coupling since the themes of searching for an old order in a modern world and reconciliation are present in both. *The Casting* can be seen as a play of social criticism, a study of a young man's search for identity in a modern world confronting the old order; in Virgilio's family, the patriarch is the domineering figure. Unable to escape, Virgilio withdraws further and further from reality. His reconciliation is brought about at great cost in the final moments of the tragedy. The play was first performed on June

4, 1930, in Rome by the Teatro dei Giovani. Critics, who were out in force, even those from the Italo-American New York press, were, for the most part, approving. Silvio d'Amico wrote a long article in *La Tribuna* counteracting the then current critical position that Tozzi was another Verga. Verga, he suggested, "uses the most simple, coarse, present-day, spoken expressions: a verist form in other words. Tozzi, however, at least in this drama, is precisely the opposite of a verist. He reaches to the center of the soul whose torment he wishes to reveal by using detached and isolated words."[4]

The details of Tozzi's life—his precarious health, his epileptic mother, his unhappy relationship with his father, his adherence to socialism and then his abandonment of that political position in 1913, his provincial life, his attachment to and his disgust with landed property and his interest in mysticism, particularly Madonna figures—undoubtedly affected his work. All these elements are embodied in his writing. Tozzi was also influenced by many literary figures: certainly d'Annunzio, Verga, and the Russian novelists (above all Dostoevski), among others. Given that until 1914 he lived far from the most advanced intellectual circles, it is quite understandable that he was only beginning to define himself as a writer during the last years of his short life, the years he was living in Rome.

The novel *I ricordi di un impiegato* (Memories of a clerk), which was begun in 1910 and published in 1920 after many revisions, is considered a minor work, but its form is revelatory. The timid, egotistical protagonist, who is estranged from reality and who is an object of scorn, has many of the author's traits, traits also found in the protagonist of *Con gli occhi chiusi*. The autobiographical underpinnings are sharper in *Il podere* (The farm), published in 1921, where the self-effacement of the protagonist, his disputes over the value of "things" and his attempt to dispossess himself in order to achieve freedom represent the problems of the world and of his generation. And in *Tre croci*, his masterpiece, Tozzi achieves remarkable and disquieting effects by intertwining universal themes and using a syntax and language drawn from the spoken Tuscan dialect.

The lack of appreciation for his plays during his lifetime was due, most of all—as it was for various other great Italian authors, from Italo Svevo to Alberto Savinio to Carlo Emilio Gadda—to the fact that they could not be adapted to the rigid stage practices and the hyperrealism typical of the time.

A. A.

Trans. by J. H.

Notes

1. Tozzi changed his original title, "Ghisola," after submission to the publisher.

2. Federigo Tozzi, "Rara avis," *Corriere della sera*, Milan, December 1918, after the opening of the play on December 16, 1918.

3. (Rome: Mondadori, 1923).

4. Silvio d'Amico, *La Tribuna*, Rome, June 6, 1930; reprinted in Glauco Tozzi, "Notizie sul teatro," in Federigo Tozzi, *Teatro*, vol. 3 of *Opere* (Rome: Vallecchi, 1970), p. 673.

■

THE CASTING

A Drama in Three Acts

(*L'Incalco*, 1919)

Translated by Mimi Gisolfi D'Aponte
and Jane House

■

Dramatis Personae

ENZO POGGI, a tall, thin, nervous man of about
fifty-five, with a very elegant, grizzled beard, which
is not as carefully groomed as one would expect
from a man of his years.

FLORA, his wife, ten years younger than he.
It's obvious that she used to be an exceedingly
beautiful woman.

VIRGILIO, his son, a clean-shaven, intense young
man of twenty-one; a bit eccentric.

SILVIA, his daughter, extremely beautiful, and still
very young.

GUIDO BARDI, Silvia's husband, a few years older
than she.

MARIO GERELLI, Virgilio's friend, three years
older than he; clean-shaven too and always
immaculately dressed.

SOME SERVANTS and a **GARDENER** at the Poggi
estate, non-speaking roles

Time: Around 1919

The Setting

The set for Acts 1 and 2 depicts the ground floor of a large villa. The set for Act 3 is on an upper floor. A portion of the gardens can be seen through the large entranceway in the center of the set for Acts 1 and 2. The villa is furnished in a very modern way; the characters are dressed in the latest fashion.

ACT 1

Scene 1

VIRGILIO *is stretched out on the sofa with several cushions under his head. At the curtain's rise he wakes up and begins to speak.* **MARIO** *is seated nearby holding a leather-bound book.*

VIRGILIO (*affable but preoccupied*):   Did I sleep long?

MARIO (*moving closer to him, with affection*):   Almost an hour and a half.

VIRGILIO: So you were bored?

MARIO (*smiling at him*):   I've been reading the whole time. If you had been awake, that would have been impossible.

VIRGILIO (*has risen and walks about the room*):   Did anyone from my family come in while I was asleep?

MARIO (*reassuring him*):   No, no one. The servant brought tea, but I sent him away. (*with great solicitude*) So, what do you want to do now?

VIRGILIO: If I listened to my thoughts, I wouldn't have faith in myself either. (*bitterly*) Don't ever tell anyone about these attacks. They'd make me see a doctor. I'm still a bit dizzy—as if I really were ill.

MARIO: Rest some more.

VIRGILIO (*forcefully, almost rudely*):   It won't happen again. Now I need to speak to my father. He has to understand that he should take me very seriously. I must take advantage of these moments. After these attacks, I feel strong and able to speak my mind. Every-thing I have to say to him becomes clear. Why can't I do what I want? Doesn't my father understand that I can't love him if he doesn't let me go when I wish to go? Why does he want to hold on to me? You're the only one who can come with me, if you want to, and if you're feeling as strong as I am.

MARIO: If you want to convince him, you'll have to do it gradually.

VIRGILIO: And if he doesn't understand, do I have to stay here and sacrifice my whole life to his villa?

MARIO: The villa is yours too. Some day it'll be all yours.

VIRGILIO: Yes, but I want him to live a long time. Then he'll see who I am. If only I'd left last year! It's precisely because I've been here forever that I'm ashamed to stay here, don't you see? I can't bear it any longer.

MARIO: Your going would make everyone very unhappy, especially your mother.

VIRGILIO: Well, it makes me unhappy being forced to stay here! I'm young! What have I done up to now? Nothing. And I'm getting to feel old here. I once had a dream about a man with a yellowing face fixed in a horrible expression. All he had to do was come up to people with that face of his and they turned into him. He came toward me, and I wanted to run away, escape. My heart was beating, I thought I was dying. But I couldn't run, and I felt as if I were turning yellow and dirty like him. And now it's the same thing. I'm young, but I feel like weeping—why? (*sadly*) I don't know what is wrong with my mind.

MARIO: Try to decide things more calmly. Don't create obstacles for yourself.

VIRGILIO: Obstacles are only created by a weakness in will power. Perhaps the problem is only inside me. I can't worry about other people. Don't you see—I can't take other people's advice any more. I've got to be alone. Just because they've given me life, they think they own me. If I've been born, that means I ought to be free. Who cares about this villa, about these gardens! These sad moods that come over me get darker and longer each time. I keep feeling like crying, for some sorrow that never goes away. (*vehemently*) If only they'd let me do what I want to do!

MARIO (*with enthusiasm and conviction*): I will come with you!

VIRGILIO (*after calming down a bit*): Yes, you'll come with me; and so, we need to pack, just the bare essentials. Nothing more. (*gaily*) Should we bring some books along? No! No! (*laughing*) I'll never read again! (*with affection, confident*) Neither will you.

MARIO: Don't be so impatient! Let's think about it for another day or two. (*as if making a spur-of-the-moment confession*) I am committed to someone.

VIRGILIO (*very surprised and then in a curt tone*): I don't want to know who she is, but I will ask if you really love her.

MARIO (*a bit confused and ashamed*): Yes.

VIRGILIO (*firmly and clearly*): Then don't leave her. When one loves, one doesn't leave the beloved.

MARIO: I don't want to lose your friendship.

VIRGILIO: You said there's someone you love. In your position, I wouldn't leave either.

MARIO: But your mother loves you.

VIRGILIO (*as if struck*): Perhaps I'm crazy. What will she say when I'm at the front door, about to leave without ever turning back. Because that's how one has to do it. And *you* mustn't stop me. You have to talk to her before I go. (*concerned*) Then she won't say anything. (*passionate*) I'll always think of her. I'll love her more than ever. But in order to love her, I must first be what I want to be. She must understand that. It's her obligation to understand. (*more firmly*) And that should be a great joy for her. I will love her so much, because she won't force me to stay here. I'll make her so proud! When she's convinced of that, she'll be the first to open the door for me. And you would leave the woman you love unless you were sure she loved you enough to understand you.

MARIO: Both women will suffer and there's no way around it. I'm not sure which of them will suffer more. Do we have the right to make them suffer?

VIRGILIO (*upon reflection*): No, we don't.

MARIO: I must tell you who I'm in love with. I should have told you a long time ago.

VIRGILIO (*not listening*): You're right; we need a few days to think. I feel so sad; it's as if I were dying, and I'm not good for anything in this mood! This sadness is like a shroud; just when it seems to be lifting it envelops me even more. Even being young seems useless! I feel my youth slipping away as if it were running ahead of me. It's as if my life has passed me by, as if I've looked out the window and seen forty or fifty years, which seemed infinite, rush by in a moment. I've lost my youth. I won't ever leave this house.

When I was a boy, running in the park made me feel immortal; infinity was my friend! I will stay here. I'll do what they want me to do. (*with irony*) It's better that way.

MARIO: What has happened to you? Can a few words turn all your shining visions into gloom? Were they only spongy dreams which you've squeezed dry?

VIRGILIO (*with a youthful sense of the tragic*): Nothing else. And something else is transparently clear now. What you call dreams, and perhaps that's what they are, will not come back. (*disheartened*) I must give in to the will of others; they are stronger than I am. Have you noticed how quickly the cypresses have grown, the ones my father planted along the road to the villa? They were forced to grow for no other reason than that he planted them there. And that is what he can say about me. When there's a bit of wind, it moves the treetops; in a storm, they seem to be taking off; and then, afterwards, there they are, still in the same spot. The wind dies down, and there they are, more firmly rooted than ever. Look at them; aren't they beautiful! (*with sarcasm*)

MARIO (*surprised*): Just because I stopped to think for a moment and didn't immediately agree with your plan, you're not imagining that I don't have the highest regard for our friendship?

VIRGILIO (*defensive*): Don't scold me. Perhaps tomorrow I will feel stronger than ever.

MARIO: And I'll still be here for you. (*demonstratively*) Because I am limited and mediocre. I need you. I can't even try to get out of the house without an enormous effort, if you don't pressure me. Even just now, reading that book, it was impossible to follow what I was reading. My mind wanders and my thoughts hover around something I don't seem to totally grasp.

VIRGILIO (*taken aback by these words*): Well, I have to get hold of myself. I'm expecting my father. He's been wanting to speak to me for over a week now about family business and things he has in mind for me. He'll be here soon, I'm sure. He asked that I wait for him here. You'll have to leave now. Come back tomorrow. I'll expect you.

(**MARIO** *exits.*)

Scene 2

Enter **ENZO**.

ENZO (*immediately seeking to win his son over*): Am I disturbing you?

VIRGILIO (*with affection but very withdrawn*): On the contrary, I'm ready to listen with the most affectionate attention a son can offer. But, this time, I will also speak up for myself.

ENZO (*objecting immediately*):   This is not the right moment. You won't want to argue. I'm here to put an end to any argument.

VIRGILIO: I would like that.

ENZO: Please don't be stubborn because this evening I'm prouder than ever of you and of our entire family, (*meaningfully*) including your sister and your brother-in-law.

All day long I've been waiting to tell you things that will prove my affection for you.

VIRGILIO: Then I hope you'll also understand my need to speak to you about myself.

ENZO (*sharply*):   I love you, but I expect obedience. Do you think a father can love a son who is always against him?

Once, when I was engaged to your mother, I stamped on all the presents she had given me for two years. Later, I asked myself what had possessed me; it seemed a sacrilege. I was almost terrified of my insanity and malice. But a stronger passion for your mother was born out of my repentance. Now, after so many years of marriage, my sense of family is stronger than ever. I've been worried that you and I and your mother don't love each other enough, or as much we should, from the moral point of view. And this troubles me a great deal! When I think about it, I feel that same terror as when I crushed your mother's gifts underfoot.

You must feel my tenderness for you, and you must realize that none of us should ever undermine any part of our family.

I want to feel that you are my son. I'm not asking for anything more.

VIRGILIO: And what will you give me in return, you and my mother, if I say yes?

ENZO: You'll get from us exactly what you give. Can you possibly hesitate? (*with increasing affection*) Why don't you embrace me? Why don't you thank me, when I'm asking so little of you? You're my own flesh and blood.

VIRGILIO (*his head down but raising it more and more with each word*):   That's true, but I also want to begin a life, and I can't wait any longer.

ENZO: No one can live according to his own will. Indeed, we should ask for God's mercy if we've ever threatened the family's wellbeing by looking elsewhere for our fulfillment.

VIRGILIO: You're always talking about God. How does God come into this discussion?

ENZO: I'll tell you, although your arrogant attitude warns me not to.

Do you see those portraits of my ancestors? You tell me, wouldn't they seem just like all the other portraits that you find in junk shops, if I didn't know that they are portraits of my own people? And looking at them, I can think of myself as part of an abstract family, endowed with feelings and emotions. Isn't it true that if it weren't for our feelings, it would be impossible to know who we are when we talk to each other?

VIRGILIO: When you talk to me like that it makes me feel that you don't want to acknowledge that I exist.

ENZO: Think about it carefully. We inherited many things from our parents that never ceased to exist, that are neither dead nor alive, but still live on in us. And so it's possible to feel completely at one with those who are no longer living.

(*Again overcome by fury*) And you want to judge your father?

VIRGILIO: I believe it my right. I'm old enough now to know whether you're right or wrong.

ENZO: That's your arrogance speaking.

VIRGILIO: That's not true! When will I be old enough?

ENZO (*with growing fury*): Never, never! I will not allow you to speak to me in this way! It's contrary to God's law and to mine.

VIRGILIO: My law exists too. It was born with me, and I'm claiming it.

ENZO: I know how to keep you in your place. Get out of my sight.

VIRGILIO: Give me the money that has caused all these arguments and I will.

ENZO: My money? You're mad! Really mad! You'll never see me again. You'll only get my money when I'm dead! (*walking around the room and shouting as though he were alone*) He's young: I'm old. But must I give him my place? He's got his youth! He's young!

VIRGILIO (*having given this some consideration*): Let's try, please, to understand each other. You cannot force me to get along with my sister's husband! That's what this entire argument is about. Let's be clear about this. We've never admitted it before, but that's the real problem. Until a week ago you were the guardian of my uncle's legacy, and now it's to be divided between me and my sister. Or rather, to be more exact, between me and my brother-in-law, because you'll be consigning her share to him. And that's what you would like me to do with mine.

You want me to be tied to him and to you, but more to him, my entire life. You don't want me to have my share to use as I please. Because for you money counts more than we do. So, to placate you, I must submit to all your views and permit you to control what is mine.

ENZO: But it's to your advantage! If we stay together financially, and that's the only way to do it, you'll be the beneficiary.

VIRGILIO: No. I don't want to grow old here. I don't want to be obliged to feel grateful to my sister's husband in any way. And isn't he the one who's convinced you to treat me this way? You never pay any attention to what I tell you, but whatever he tells you turns out to be absolutely perfect and wonderful for everybody.

And that's another reason why I want to be sure I never have to share anything with him. I'd rather lose what's mine than do that. You want to give everything to him? Do it then. But he'll have to account to *me* for it. So you see, I don't wish to oppose you; I'm simply defending myself at all costs against him, because he is my enemy. And he's going to have to answer to me.

ENZO: Don't divide what I'm trying to unite.

VIRGILIO: I'd prefer to leave here empty-handed, rather than having these fights with you. Tell him that! I'll work. You think I don't know how to work?

ENZO: But you can live like a gentleman here.

VIRGILIO: What do I care about that? What I earn on my own will be enough for me to live on, and I'll be the one in control. But I'll certainly never forgive him. Tell him that! You've more faith in him than in me!

ENZO: You're my son, and you owe me love! Get out. I hope God will make you see the light!

(**VIRGILIO**, *not wishing to fight any more, exits by one of the side doors, which are covered by ornate drapes.*)

Scene 3

ENZO (*not beaten*): In half an hour, my whole life has changed forever!

Scene 4

Enter **FLORA**, *who came running when she heard the shouting.*

FLORA: The fighting in this house is dreadful. We're always at each others' throats!

ENZO (*looking at her*): What does loving someone mean? He offended me, so wasn't it natural for me to react in kind? There's no dignity left in being his father. If I had felt superior to my family when I was twenty, I could never have acted against my own blood. There must be a way of coming to some sort of agreement. If I feel my heart drop when my son wants to leave, then I must oppose him in every way possible.

FLORA: You're the only one among us who can see these things clearly! I have absolute faith in your judgment.

ENZO (*with compelling irony*): But not everyone agrees with you! (*agitated again*) Why should I allow what's mine to be taken away? Nothing is more mine or of me than him. What if my instinct for family is rooted in a sense of property, it's still the sweetest feeling nature has given me, isn't it?

What could possibly replace it, when after so many years I've come to believe in it more and more?

I remember when Virgilio was small. Whenever our eyes met, from the time he was a baby, I knew he was mine, and that feeling grew. And why should things change now, just because he's grown? How can my heart accept such a contradiction?

FLORA: Perhaps we'll still be able to make him mend his ways. He's still so young! We needed other people too back then, remember?

ENZO: But he's different; believe me. He's different! If you really think you can bring him around, go ahead and try! (*anxiously*) Go on, go after him!

(**FLORA** *exits in the same direction as* **VIRGILIO**.)

Scene 5

ENZO: It seems easier to kill him than to let him leave. Better to kill him than see him killed through his own mistakes.

I wish I loved him less!

Scene 6

Enter SILVIA.

ENZO (*almost frightened*):   Who is it?

SILVIA (*she has entered from the far door which, as we've described, opens onto the gardens. She's hesitant.*): It's me.

ENZO (*going toward her with a springing step*):   What a surprise! . . . The joy of seeing you almost pains me. But why do you look so upset?

SILVIA (*trying to cover it*):   It's nothing! I thought Mamma would be here too.

ENZO: We'll call her immediately. (*sadly dejected*) I needed not to be alone any more either.

SILVIA (*justifying herself*):   I didn't want to come, but I found myself here against my will.

ENZO (*surprised and trying to quiz her*):   You didn't want to come?

SILVIA: No. (*She cries.*)

ENZO: What's the matter? Why are you crying?

SILVIA: Because I've had to leave Guido. I was the weaker one, even though I've been the rebel!

ENZO (*almost assaulting her*):   What are you saying? I forbid you to utter such words; you make me shudder!

SILVIA (*reproaching him*):   So, doesn't it matter to you that I'm your daughter?

ENZO (*still aggressive*):   Tell me the truth. Quickly. Without going in circles. Have you really left Guido?

SILVIA (*trying to respond in a lively manner*):   Yes.

ENZO: You're admitting it! So it's his fault then? (*fatherly but autocratic*) What has he done to you? Be careful, now, be fair. (*authoritatively*) I believe he's a gentleman. I believe he's like me. (*threatening her*) Take care. And explain what happened, without leaving anything out. Hurry up!

SILVIA (*trembling and trying to turn away*):   Now you're frightening me. You're not letting me say what I need to say.

ENZO: So I have that effect on you? I wouldn't have believed it. That means you're not really at peace with yourself. You had better be careful.

SILVIA (*her mind made up*):   I'll tell you everything.

Scene 7

FLORA *reenters.*

FLORA (*upset*):   What's the matter?

SILVIA (*embracing her*):   Nothing, Mamma! Let me stay with you! Don't ask me anything. Just keep me here with you. Pretend I'm still a child. It's the only thing that will make me feel better.

FLORA (*to her husband*):   What's the matter with her?

ENZO (*agitated and avoiding any response because he wants to get to the bottom of things on his own*): Nothing; nothing important. It's nerves. I can't stand female nerves.

SILVIA (*dreamily*): My head feels so hot! (*trying to stand up straight so that her mother won't have to support her*) And I don't want to cry! I want to be happy.

ENZO: She'll be alright.

FLORA (*to get* **SILVIA** *away from* **ENZO**): Come to my room, Silvia.

SILVIA: I'm coming, Mamma!

(**FLORA** *and* **SILVIA** *leave through the door opposite the one* **VIRGILIO** *used.* **ENZO**, *now alone, comes to a decision. He goes to call* **VIRGILIO**. **VIRGILIO** *enters.*)

Scene 8

ENZO: Virgilio.

VIRGILIO (*misunderstanding*): Papa, let's not talk about it anymore. I'm sorry we can't come to an understanding. I want to love you, and I've forgotten everything.

ENZO (*forcefully*): Not I! You say you want to love me! Why don't you then? But this doesn't concern you and me. I'm going to test you, and I want to be sure that you've had nothing to do with it.

Silvia has left her husband. She's here with your mother.

VIRGILIO (*happy*): She's here?

ENZO: I order you to go and speak with Guido yourself. Tell him to come here. I must know what this is all about.

VIRGILIO (*refusing to obey*): Silvia will explain it herself.

ENZO: She's too much like you!

VIRGILIO: Let her do what she thinks best.

ENZO: So you want them to separate then; because you hate her husband?

VIRGILIO: I wouldn't oppose a separation if it's necessary.

ENZO: Nothing is necessary. One must act according to a moral law which both your sister and her husband must submit to. I remain inflexible on this point. I will not allow my daughter to leave her house like this. Perhaps it's nothing. But even if it's not, I know how to get to the bottom of this and root out the problem. I've had experience with this before. And instead of opposing me, you're going to help me.

VIRGILIO: Your experience may give you insight, but it may not help others, judging from how you treat me when you're convinced you're acting for my own good.

ENZO: That's because you believe you're different from everyone else.

VIRGILIO: Everyone is different from everyone else.

ENZO: That's not true. And Silvia's beside herself. Perhaps you put her up to it.

VIRGILIO: I think she's done the right thing. I'm sure of it. And I'd like to tell her that.

ENZO (*enraged*): You go tell her. Do what you want. In fact, let me send her in to you. Then I'll have a better idea of what I'm dealing with.

(*He exits to fetch* **SILVIA**.)

Scene 9

SILVIA *enters.*

SILVIA (*still upset*):   I thought I would be stronger!

VIRGILIO: Our parents don't understand us any more. But you couldn't have come at a better moment for both of us.

SILVIA (*uncertain*):   But what if we're in the wrong?

VIRGILIO (*persuasively*):   I don't think we are. At our age, even if we're wrong, it's always for the best, because we act with a sincerity they no longer possess.

SILVIA: So are you in pain too?

VIRGILIO: Yes, in a great deal of pain. (*worried*) More than ever. I was talking with our father before you came over.

SILVIA: But you don't know something I've kept secret from you, something I should have told you right away.

VIRGILIO (*tenderly*):   Will you go on keeping it a secret? Don't you trust me? You see that with them it's impossible. You know I'm right.

SILVIA (*almost pompous*):   I'll tell you everything. (*completely sincere*) Although modesty still holds me back.

VIRGILIO: Tell me everything, or it'll be impossible for us to love each other. Trust me.

SILVIA: They think it's something silly, something trivial. They know I'm suffering, but they can't guess why.

VIRGILIO (*elated*):   So you're safe. Talk quickly.

SILVIA: You think I love Guido? I don't.

VIRGILIO (*thoughtful*):   Since when?

SILVIA: I don't know: since our life together put my feelings to the test. Anyway, on the pretext of a quarrel over something really silly, and knowing that our father was about to pressure you to sign the contracts he drew up with Guido, I ran to see you.

VIRGILIO (*becoming elated again*):   You're doing the right thing, and I'll take responsibility for saying so. If our parents heard us, they could never understand how good it feels to tell each other everything like this. I'm the only one you can speak your heart to. (*pressing her*) Go on.

SILVIA (*slightly fierce and catching* **VIRGILIO'S** *excitement*):   I want to be free to love someone else.

VIRGILIO (*self-important*):   Who?

SILVIA (*attempting to surmise what her brother thinks of her*):   Why do you ask his name?

VIRGILIO (*calmly*):   Because you have to tell me.

SILVIA (*impulsively*):   You're right. I'll tell you.

VIRGILIO (*prompting her*):   Do I know him?

SILVIA: He is a friend of yours.

VIRGILIO: I have only one close friend.

SILVIA: He's the one.

VIRGILIO (*happy*): I hadn't guessed. You could have told me right away. I'm happy about it. You will love him. You're free to love him. Better him than somebody else. But you have to admit, now, that the marriage has to be annulled immediately because our feelings, if they exist, count for more than any laws. You never wanted to admit that with your head, but now you've come to the same conclusion with your heart.

SILVIA (*desperate*): I'm irreversibly chained to Guido.

VIRGILIO: Why?

SILVIA: You know that I am going to be a mother.

VIRGILIO: I know.

SILVIA: You can see for yourself that I've done wrong.

VIRGILIO: Love can only be exchanged for love, and not for anything else. Any love that's even minimally part of an obligation ought not to be.

And is it necessary, just because you're going to be a mother, that you love your husband?

SILVIA: I didn't used to think so, but now that I've run away from him with the idea of never returning, I feel that it's not right.

VIRGILIO: The child will be all yours.

SILVIA: That's not true. With a child there's a feeling that can't be annulled.

VIRGILIO: But you just said you don't love him!

SILVIA: They're two different things. I would like to be in love with the father of my child.

VIRGILIO: Don't have second thoughts before taking the decisive step. How can you possibly live with your husband?

SILVIA (*sobbing*): I don't know.

VIRGILIO: You must love. It's your right. Listen to me; *I*'m telling you this.

SILVIA: But I shouldn't love another man.

VIRGILIO: If you turn back, I won't be able to go through with my plans either. With you near me, I feel capable of anything.

It's like the call of my youth; I can't think of any other way of putting it. I feel I can't live here any more. I must go away to become a man. Which, for them, seems outrageous.

SILVIA: But it's not always possible to do what we want. Do you remember . . . after school . . . how you never wanted anyone to know which way you'd come home? And then, after overhearing the violent arguments you had with father over that, I hid my feelings and my toys from Mamma. There was no way I would have told her what was going on in my head. Even though I wasn't thinking anything bad! I was a very good girl; I used to cry so easily.

VIRGILIO: Well, we were lucky then! We weren't afraid of anything!

SILVIA: That's how it should be. But it's not that way now.

VIRGILIO: That's not true! Spirit is all we need.

SILVIA: But perhaps I've become adult like them now.

VIRGILIO: But at our age we should be making our own decisions. Without worrying about anyone else. The two of us will be strong together. You will love Mario. You will do what your heart tells you.

SILVIA (*crying again*):   Even your generosity won't be enough to help me.

VIRGILIO: My generosity? I don't want you to say that. And I don't want to be generous.

SILVIA: You are good when you think you're bad. I think I'm honest, and it's not true. You say they're prejudiced, but you yourself are afraid of hearing certain words. You can't get beyond them.

VIRGILIO (*with a bitter smile*):   So we'll become like them?

SILVIA: They love us.

VIRGILIO: That's not enough! I don't want to give in to them, just because they love us.

SILVIA: And what if I don't feel capable of leaving my husband?

VIRGILIO (*having turned to the entrance, he sees* **GUIDO BARDI** *coming from the gardens and is obviously annoyed*):   There he is. He's coming to look for you.

SILVIA: Let me face him alone. And this will all be over. It's not too late.

VIRGILIO: No. Go hide in my room. Let me talk to him first. Don't deny me that, if you love me. I'm going to face him right now so he won't meet the others first.

(**VIRGILIO** *almost forces* **SILVIA** *into his room, and then he goes to meet* **GUIDO**.)

Scene 10

VIRGILIO: Silvia and I have talked.

GUIDO (*trying to avoid answering him*):   Where is she?

VIRGILIO (*a bit solemn and pompous*):   And now we need to talk.

GUIDO: Did she explain herself to you? (*unhappy and hostile*)

VIRGILIO (*insolent*):   She doesn't have to explain herself to anyone. That's what we decided.

GUIDO: And what did you say to her? I'm astounded that she could make such a sudden decision that would offend and hurt me so much. Let me talk with her immediately. I beg you. You must help me. You can help me more than anyone else.

VIRGILIO: Listen, pay close attention. It's essential. Both Silvia and I are ready for anything.

GUIDO: But it's a trivial matter, I hope. A misunderstanding I've discovered in time. You have nothing to reproach me with about Silvia. She couldn't have a better husband.

VIRGILIO: Tell me then, and don't be shy. Tell me what your life together has been like these past few months.

GUIDO (*trying to explain*):   Nothing out of the ordinary. Only it seemed I wasn't succeeding in understanding her any more. She was becoming capricious. Please don't object to my using that word. But why didn't she speak to me first? I've done everything I can to live in harmony with her!

VIRGILIO: Don't be surprised that you haven't succeeded. Everything's finished between you and my sister.

GUIDO (*becoming more and more irritated the longer he talks with* **VIRGILIO**): How dare you talk like that. You're in no position to judge.

VIRGILIO: Actually I'm not judging. I'm simply approving of whatever Silvia does.

GUIDO (*impatient*): Let me speak to her. It's outrageous that you won't let me speak to her this instant.

VIRGILIO: Answer me, and you will see it's more expedient for you to speak to me. Have you nothing to criticize in my sister's conduct?

GUIDO: She's the one woman I truly admire. I don't have to tell you that.

VIRGILIO: I assume then, if that's true, that you hold her in the highest esteem.

GUIDO: And who could value her more than I?

VIRGILIO (*quietly*): I could.

GUIDO: Stop provoking me!

VIRGILIO (*containing himself*): I will, for now.

GUIDO: And now why don't you explain what right you have to behave this way. I've come to find Silvia. So let me see her. Or else I'm prepared to take other measures. And I'll demand an explanation of anyone who tries to interfere.

VIRGILIO: I see that you're suffering, and therefore I'm ready to listen to you.

GUIDO: I am not merely suffering! I'm astounded that in a house where I've always been welcome, as I deserve to be, I am suddenly being treated like this.

VIRGILIO: Don't raise your voice. Otherwise you will force me to do the same.

GUIDO: As you wish.

VIRGILIO (*without giving him any time to think*): Do you love my sister?

GUIDO: That's enough of that.

VIRGILIO: Careful.

GUIDO: So then had Silvia and you already come to some agreement?

VIRGILIO: Of sorts; practically. Tell me if you love my sister. I'm asking you for the second time.

GUIDO (*disdainfully*): You are still too young to understand, and you have no idea what you're asking me.

VIRGILIO: I'm telling you that if you love my sister, you must let her stay where she is! If you don't love her, then go ahead and force her to go home with you.

GUIDO (*trying to go into the other room*): What nonsense!

VIRGILIO (*blocking his way*): Silvia will never go back to you.

GUIDO: And who told you that?

VIRGILIO: If you could even begin to understand, we could become friends. You are good to Silvia, and I do understand your feelings. That's why I want to be fair and impartial, although I have every reason to treat you in another manner altogether.

GUIDO: I'm warning you that this conversation of ours may have unhappy consequences, especially for Silvia.

VIRGILIO: If that's a threat, you're not a good man. Listen: I see I've made you unhappy, and I would have liked to have spared you that.

GUIDO (*resigned and very sad*):   But does Silvia love me? Is it possible that she can change so from one day to the next?

VIRGILIO: You might have been aware of that sooner.

GUIDO: I love her with every fiber of my being. More than before.

VIRGILIO: I see that it will not be as easy for Silvia to free herself from you as I would have hoped.

GUIDO (*anguished*):   Free herself from me! But then she must have feelings I know nothing about!

VIRGILIO: Unfortunately, yes. I think the differences are irreparable. (*sincerely*) It's painful for me as well.

GUIDO: What differences?

VIRGILIO: I don't know how much I should reveal. But what if my sister were already in love with someone else?

GUIDO: That's impossible. I have no doubt about her honesty. I warn you: you're hurting me deeply, perhaps more than you imagine, but you are slandering Silvia!

VIRGILIO (*with affecting sincerity*):   I see you're distressed, and that's why I'm not telling you anything more.

GUIDO: I realize that you are incapable of grasping the significance of your own words.

VIRGILIO: I think you're making a big mistake.

GUIDO: This is madness.

VIRGILIO (*sincerely still*):   Forgive me, Guido. Don't think I'm not sorry. I wish I could be in your place; but it's my duty. It's useless for you to speak to the rest of my family. Talk to me. I beg you on Silvia's behalf as well.

GUIDO: You're malicious and hateful.

VIRGILIO: This had to be said.

GUIDO: I don't deserve this, and I refuse to accept it.

VIRGILIO (*with feeling*):   And what do you plan to do?

GUIDO (*resolutely*):   My duty. Where's Silvia?

VIRGILIO: I'm telling you again, you shouldn't even ask to see her.

GUIDO: Get out of the way. I'm not putting up with your nonsense any longer. Let me pass.

VIRGILIO: Leave, and don't come back. I'm ordering you to leave. Fight with me, but leave my sister alone.

GUIDO: I've already begged too much. Things don't happen this way between gentlemen. I'll get even for this. Now it's I who'll be rejecting your sister, if from what you've told me, she's even the slightest bit at fault.

VIRGILIO: That doesn't seem likely!

(**GUIDO** *leaves through the gardens.*)

Scene 11

Enter **SILVIA**.

SILVIA (*trying to join her husband*):   Let me go! It's too much. I couldn't stand it any longer.

VIRGILIO (*surprised, but with vigor*):   Are you sorry?

SILVIA: I shouldn't have gone along with you this far.

VIRGILIO (*scornfully*):   Let him go.

(*He forces his sister to stay.*)

ACT 2

Scene 1

VIRGILIO *and* **MARIO**.

VIRGILIO (*happily, but somewhat worried*):   Everything is going the way I wanted. It couldn't go better! What a lift Silvia gave me when she came! I didn't think she would decide so soon.

I've made her stay in the house; now she won't have time to turn back.

MARIO: But I'm afraid something will go wrong.

VIRGILIO: No it won't! My father has been warned. Anyway, it's always better to be honest. As long as another attack doesn't hit me, I'll be fine. If it should, you must stay here and answer for me until I return to my senses, because I can't let them think I've changed my mind. But you don't have enough confidence in me either.

MARIO (*reproaching him*):   You're so full of mistrust, and you're wrong.

VIRGILIO (*gently*):   Then why haven't you told me who the lady is who loves you! Why must I prompt you?

MARIO: I don't have the courage to ask your forgiveness. Has *she* told you?

VIRGILIO: In a beautiful heartfelt moment; without my having to ask her.

MARIO: You must forgive me. But I never dared; I was afraid of losing your friendship. I never stopped feeling that way. Rather than that, I would have preferred to renounce my love for Silvia.

I believe she's still in her husband's power, and I don't know whether she'll ever be mine.

VIRGILIO: She's been waiting for you to tell me everything.

MARIO: I'm so confused, I don't know what part to play.

VIRGILIO: You should get used to being like me.

MARIO: We're too different, even though we are good friends.

VIRGILIO: But didn't you realize how important it was to tell me everything?

MARIO: You're right.

VIRGILIO: I am right, but I have to forgive you. And I'll always help you. And I really want to. It's a kind of mission I have, as your friend. Only you must be absolutely sure that you and Silvia really love each other. If your love is really pure it will deepen our friendship even more and prove my father wrong, and any others who laugh at us.

How long have you loved her?

MARIO: It's been more than a year. But when it really began I can't say. If I had to pinpoint the first time I lost myself gazing into your sister's eyes, I couldn't. But I loved her the moment I met her here at your house. All the same, we immediately decided to see each other only rarely. You see, then, how much I love her.

VIRGILIO: You couldn't love her less.

MARIO: Do you think I'm worthy of her?

VIRGILIO: As you are of my friendship.

MARIO: Without ever saying it in so many words, we agreed completely to keep our feelings chaste. And now your sister need no longer feel uncertain.

VIRGILIO (*worried again*): But why should we feel so uneasy just because we want to live our lives our own way? Why, when I am determined to follow my plans, do I still feel I'd be happier if I had my father's support? I'd like to go and find him and say: "Don't you realize that you shouldn't deny your son anything he asks? But instead, you force me to treat you like my worst enemy!" But if I were to speak honestly, we would never reach an understanding. Sometimes my thoughts seem to come from some harmful instinct. And I'm always on edge, never calm. But if I *do* make mistakes, as my father says, why doesn't he teach me how *not* to make them?

The three of us will all go away together. I'm feeling strong again. Let's not talk anymore. I'll go and tell Silvia now. She must be awake. She was tired yesterday evening after that talk with our parents, who know everything now; she seemed to have a fever.

MARIO: They must have insulted her!

VIRGILIO: But we can be proud we've gone about this in our own way. I feel completely in the right. And how much better it is to have this feeling of freedom that idiots and old people never experience.

MARIO: With you everything is possible.

VIRGILIO: With me? I don't deserve any credit. And you don't have the courage to confess that we're friends just because you are in love with Silvia.

MARIO: We'll defend her from everyone.

VIRGILIO: And they say we're deluded!

MARIO: They'll learn, from now on.

VIRGILIO: Not even one more day inside these walls!

MARIO: It seems like a dream.

VIRGILIO: And compare this with the way things have been.

MARIO: It's not the same thing any more.

VIRGILIO: If we didn't do this, we'd lose our self-respect. Remember, we're men and we're young!

MARIO: When we come back, everything will be different; it's inevitable.

VIRGILIO: Yesterday my father talked to me about our ancestors. You see? There they are. Don't they seem like dummies who should go jump out the window? They're almost asking for a kick, each and every one of them. Ancestors indeed!

MARIO: They *are* comical.

VIRGILIO: My father and mother are the only ones missing.

MARIO: Why don't you call Silvia right now?

VIRGILIO: She loves you, and our entire future hangs on that.

MARIO: They'll say she's a fallen woman.

VIRGILIO: They've already said it.

MARIO: The only thing they know how to do is finding evil where it doesn't exist. There should be more women like her!

VIRGILIO: All the same, they love her better than me, because they think she's weaker.

MARIO: For them, showing obedience means sacrificing oneself. I owe my rebirth to your friendship. I no longer feel weak-willed. I've often felt I lacked initiative, but now my inner nature has changed all by itself.

VIRGILIO: Each of us need only respect his own conscience. Everything hangs on that rule. Who knows whether they didn't rebel just like us in their youth? I'm sure that we have a lot in common.

MARIO: You're a man with no illusions.

VIRGILIO: I'm so completely happy that I feel destined to do everything I want.

Scene 2

Enter **FLORA.**

FLORA: Virgilio!

VIRGILIO: Mother!

FLORA: Are you still blinded by stubborn pride?

VIRGILIO: Absolutely.

FLORA: If it hadn't been for me, your father would have already disowned you. If I hadn't restrained him, he would long since have come to tell you that he no longer considers you his son. He doesn't love you any more. But you have time to ask his pardon. My devotion will save you. Go and speak to him like an obedient son. I hope I can spare you his punishment.

VIRGILIO: And what do you both demand of me?

FLORA: Nothing but your respect. Is that too much to ask? You ought to thank heaven that we love you so much.

VIRGILIO: You don't understand how much harm you're doing me.

FLORA: How can we possibly harm you? God has deprived you of reason.

VIRGILIO: Mother, you shouldn't put yourself between us. Leave everything to me.

FLORA (*dignified and stern*): And is this your friend who is taking your side?

VIRGILIO: Since I'm not alone, you might admit that perhaps you're in the wrong, not me.

FLORA: What does he know? (*turning to* **MARIO**) Tell me what you really think, seeing that I'm so upset. How do you have the nerve to lead Virgilio on like this? What sort of a friend are you?

MARIO (*respectfully*): Signora, he will speak for himself.

FLORA: I am terrified. You'll be the death of me yet. You'll always have to live with guilt.

Listen to me, Virgilio. Don't you recognize your mother any more? What have you got against me? And what harm has your father done you? Where do you want to go? What will you do without your parents? Listen to me, if you're my son.

VIRGILIO (*tenderly*):   It would have been better if you hadn't come.

FLORA: You'll never find peace. No one will want to be with you.

MARIO: Signora, I am a true friend.

FLORA: You cannot possibly understand what this is doing to me.

MARIO: Let Virgilio do as he wishes.

FLORA: Never. Do you think that I can act as reprehensibly as he does?

MARIO: He loves you.

FLORA: That's no way to love one's parents.

VIRGILIO: Nor one's children.

FLORA: Every word you say is hateful.

VIRGILIO: I don't believe it. I don't want to believe it.

FLORA: And you'll have to pay the consequences for what you are doing.

VIRGILIO: Naturally. In fact, if someone wanted to prevent it, I'd be unhappy.

FLORA: Come to your senses. You know that if it weren't for your father, life would lose all meaning for me. And I would be terribly afraid.

VIRGILIO: You only want one thing; for me to stop being who I am.

FLORA: Now you are going too far!

VIRGILIO: Why do you humiliate me by assuming I'm incapable of fulfilling my plans? You see that Silvia had to leave her home too. You're the ones who are driving us away.

FLORA: I could quite easily kill myself if I weren't so completely attached to your father! You'd like Silvia to lose herself too. But I'm keeping her with me!

VIRGILIO: Be careful that you don't destroy me.

FLORA: You'll learn the error of your ways.

VIRGILIO: And you're willing to strike the blow.

FLORA: For your own good and to save Silvia's honor.

VIRGILIO: And you think it would be good for her to submit to your tyranny? (*to* **MARIO**) Tell her the real truth yourself. Make her see!

FLORA: God willing, you'll see it yourself. Unless you mend your ways, you'll always be without family. Lose us, and you'll never be able to find another. (*to* **MARIO**) And you, who claim to be my son's friend, can't you refrain from shaming Silvia?

VIRGILIO: He is loyal. Like me.

FLORA: Loyal to himself, but not to others.

VIRGILIO: You like to contradict everything. But doesn't it occur to you that it might be God himself who is breaking Silvia's bonds for good? Don't you always say that everything happens according to the will of God?

FLORA: But not these things.

VIRGILIO: Only the things you like?

FLORA: Yes; because I never act against my conscience. Having a mother is a divine gift. Since even my love has no influence, there's no hope left for you. One should be willing to die for one's parents if that's necessary. But all that's being asked is that you show some respect and have some scruples. Go to your father and beg his forgiveness.

VIRGILIO: Is that all you've taught me, both of you? Obedience? Did nothing else ever matter to you?

Why do you never have even one kind word to say to me?

FLORA: You've been seduced by the emptiness of your own talk. I'm your mother and that should be enough to make you come to your senses. Your father has good reason to be angry.

VIRGILIO: My being honest is good too. And whenever a man speaks frankly, that's good.

FLORA: Your insensitivity has no limits.

VIRGILIO (*warmly*): I'll leave you alone, so as not to make you any more unhappy. There's nothing that grieves me more than that.

FLORA: Honor thy father and mother: that's the first commandment.

VIRGILIO: That's an entirely different question.

(**VIRGILIO** *and* **MARIO** *go out through door leading to the gardens.*)

Scene 3

Enter **ENZO**. **FLORA** *is extremely dispirited.*

ENZO: Are you convinced?

FLORA: I didn't believe he could sink so low.

ENZO: What did you expect when he's with his sister's lover from morning to night?

FLORA: I didn't want to believe what I was hearing. But be more gentle with Silvia.

ENZO: She is our shame.

FLORA: Perhaps she's the one least responsible.

ENZO: Your warm heart is deluding you.

FLORA: I've nothing else left.

ENZO: But I know how to wash this house clean.

FLORA: We'll lose them both.

ENZO: And to think that we raised them!

FLORA: I'm so humiliated. I'm even ashamed to look into your eyes.

ENZO: We'll be avenged and that will bring them back to us.

FLORA: But how can we do it alone?

ENZO: Leave it to me. I'm not afraid to do what I have to do.

FLORA: He couldn't have hurt me more if he had broken me into pieces.

ENZO: He'll be broken himself; that's the law.

FLORA: A daughter who says to her mother: I don't love my husband any more!

ENZO: We'll see if she says the same thing in a little while.

FLORA: If only you could bring her back to herself! But when a sin like that has been committed, one has to be as good as God. And never remember it. That will be my duty.

ENZO: I'll let you handle it as long as I see her trembling before you.

FLORA: Don't hurt her too much; remember her condition.

ENZO: She must cry.

FLORA: But listen to her first. It seems impossible that she won't find a way back to being herself again.

ENZO: I know what she will say.

FLORA: I can tell that she's really been suffering!

ENZO: That's not enough. If I don't put my foot down, your son with his theatrics will succeed in shaming us too, and in front of the world. And I'm answerable for that.

FLORA: Everything must be kept secret.

ENZO: I'll break his will to leave home.

FLORA: What will become of Silvia?

ENZO: She's not our concern, not since she crossed the threshold of this house.

FLORA: God sent her here on purpose. What if she hadn't come here?

ENZO: I know what has to happen. (*He calls out.*) Silvia!

Scene 4

SILVIA *comes through one of the two side doors without speaking; she leans against the drapes on the door.* **ENZO** *and* **FLORA** *sit side by side waiting for her.*

FLORA (*sweet but austere*): Please come in.

ENZO (*unyieldingly stern*): I've sent for Guido. He should be here soon. I hope that he comes. (*seeing her with her head down*) You've never had to hang your head in shame before.

SILVIA: If I came back to this house the way I used to as a young girl, and told you everything without being forced to, it shows that I didn't intend to behave badly or do anything without your knowing it.

ENZO: That's not enough.

FLORA: How will you convince your husband of that?

SILVIA: First, I have to convince myself.

ENZO: But you belong to him, not to yourself.

FLORA: Don't create a distance between you that doesn't exist.

SILVIA: But what about my feelings?

ENZO: What are your feelings?

SILVIA: I know what they are, unfortunately.

ENZO: And they can probably be changed.

FLORA (*more calmly*): It's up to you.

SILVIA: No one, not even you, can force me to do something that is repugnant to me.

FLORA: Remember that God's judgment is eternal. Your parents represent God. You'll have to account to Him. You don't realize that once I made the same mistake you're making.

ENZO (*to* **FLORA**, *exploding but full of tenderness*): Keep quiet! You should not reveal, even to your children, something that happened privately between us, before they were even born. It's none of their business. Your daughter shouldn't have heard that. Your life of loving virtue and pure devotion gives you an exalted place in my heart and in this house, always. What happened counts for less than a minute in many years of love. You have an exacting conscience, but it was unnecessary. It's Silvia's duty to learn everything through you, even how a woman breathes.

FLORA: I was teaching her how one speaks before God.

ENZO: You take first place in my family. And my family is the mold that I've shaped with my own hands, which neither shake nor tremble. Our children must also be conscious of our virtues. Their characters must pour easily, without cracks, into this form, which I will pass on to them before I die. And the casting must be perfect. Your daughter must give in.

SILVIA: You must advise me.

ENZO (*still unrelentingly stern*): I demand complete obedience from you.

SILVIA (*submissively*): I have always obeyed you.

ENZO: What will you tell your child? You won't be a good mother.

SILVIA: Must I worry about my child?

FLORA: Absolutely.

SILVIA: He'll have to respect me.

ENZO: As you do us.

SILVIA: So then, I'm no longer my own mistress!

ENZO: No. Not if you're not basically moral.

SILVIA: But my morality doesn't depend on what I'll have to tell my child.

ENZO: On that too.

FLORA: You won't be as untroubled about it as you think.

SILVIA: Well, so, up to now you've been talking to me about the child.

ENZO: Who is your destiny.

SILVIA: Must I sacrifice myself for the rest of my life?

ENZO: There's no other way.

FLORA: We're confident that you have the strength to do it.

ENZO: But I don't concede that you can love a man other than your husband.

SILVIA: Must I lie forever?

FLORA: If you're forced to lie, that's your fault. But you won't lie, because you will love Guido.

SILVIA: I've done everything. I've practiced self-denial day after day. I haven't been able to find any kind of relief. It's been such a struggle; it has taken all my strength. And I believed that, whatever might come of it, I still had a right to be honest.

ENZO (*derisively*): And how do you find it?

FLORA: Don't you realize that we can teach you things you don't know yet?

SILVIA: So then, it's no longer possible for me to start my life again?

ENZO: Only by embracing the happiness you'd like to reject. Everyone's destiny is predetermined.

FLORA: Every wife who loves her husband loves herself.

SILVIA: Can't there be an exception?

ENZO: Then every wife would believe she was that exception.

SILVIA: But I've done everything I can to believe otherwise.

ENZO: Then your trial must last longer.

FLORA: And you need more faith in those feelings that originally bound you to Guido.

SILVIA: My new feelings are stronger than those were.

ENZO: We bind ourselves only once.

SILVIA: But that can be dissolved.

ENZO: No, not even if your husband were to consent.

SILVIA: Who says that?

ENZO: I do; I'm teaching you. Because that's the way it was taught to me.

FLORA: And any other way is wrong. If you're experiencing motherhood, you must thank your husband. You can be a mother only because you've been a bride.

SILVIA: But shouldn't I tell Guido everything I've revealed to you? I don't want to deceive him.

ENZO: You're not driven by the desire to be honest, as you'd like us to believe, but by the desire to put an obstacle between you that will keep you divided. Instead, you should try, through tender devotion, to earn his pardon. He should know everything, but we don't want him to feel forced to reject you.

FLORA: We'll accept this deception for the sake of your happiness and take the responsibility for this suggestion ourselves.

ENZO: However, you do deserve to suffer the consequences of what you've done, even if it means paying with blood and tears. But your remorse over your deception will be more painful than any confession.

SILVIA: It's too hateful to go back to him, if I do go back, without his knowing everything.

FLORA: How stupid can you be! Every word you utter is self-destructive.

(**ENZO** *and* **FLORA** *exit through the door on the right.*)

Scene 5

SILVIA *walks back and forth nervously, uncertain of her decision.*

SILVIA: I must learn to make up my mind!

Scene 6

MARIO *enters from the door to the gardens, looking for Virgilio. Seeing* **SILVIA**, *he stops, at first surprised then completely confident, and walks toward her. They address each other formally.*

MARIO: Virgilio has been so kind!

SILVIA: It's no longer possible for you and me to speak to each other.

MARIO: He has told me everything.

SILVIA: Yes: I did love you perhaps.

MARIO (*still passionate*): Why don't you say you love me just as I say it to you?

SILVIA (*as if to herself*): I must suppress my feelings.

MARIO: In the name of our pure love, I beg you to tell me what is happening in your heart.

SILVIA: I don't know; don't ask me anything else, because my words are no longer expressing my thoughts.

MARIO: It's a moment of weakness! I understand! We must give our love its rightful place. Why have we been afraid for so long to even see each other?

SILVIA: It's all for the best. And it's all for the best that, in all this time, you've never so much as kissed my hands.

MARIO: But my longing, in the face of this rejection I cannot fathom, is more intense, and I'm asking you to be completely mine. It's no longer enough to entertain feelings that have led only to vain promises.

SILVIA: That's how things will remain.

MARIO: That is not what Virgilio told me.

SILVIA: I cannot be held accountable for what I am doing. Certainly, I wanted to have you reciprocate my feelings. But now everything strikes me as impossible, and I'm confused; so much so that I can't say anything that will satisfy you.

MARIO: Silvia! Today we are freer than ever. We can love each other without hiding anything from anybody.

SILVIA: Your voice is still so sweet to me, and I mustn't listen to it.

MARIO: If I could only tell you how your change of heart is tormenting me! Let me tell you.

SILVIA: I must come to a decision, but I still don't know what.

MARIO: You must love me as before. Let me persuade you.

SILVIA: I know, and I understand. But if you must, you will have to follow my example.

MARIO: Never. I will always love you.

SILVIA: Even if I don't love you?

MARIO: Yes, even then. But why don't you love me?

SILVIA: There are some things in life that are stronger than us.

MARIO: Don't talk that way! Speak to Virgilio.

SILVIA: We must not see each other any more.

MARIO: I cannot consent to that. I cannot resign myself to that. You've loved me till today, and, just like that, from one moment to the next can you really expect me to stop loving you!

SILVIA: I didn't say that. Let me be alone. I need to be alone. Go and find Virgilio.

MARIO: Is it possible that there's no longer anything I can say to you?

SILVIA: No. I have to find my way alone.

MARIO: I love you so much! I need only to speak to you to feel a tremor that makes my heart race. Oh, I will always love you so much!

SILVIA: You must content yourself with what I am about to tell you. Don't ask me to do anything that conflicts with my decision.

MARIO: If you promise not to let yourself be deceived and overpowered by others, that'll be enough.

SILVIA: I am still free.

MARIO: I'm afraid that's no longer true. You've spoken to your parents, and already you don't realize how you're making me suffer. Why?

SILVIA: Let me be alone.

MARIO: But we've planned everything, with Virgilio, too.

SILVIA: That's not my fault.

MARIO: Why are you talking this way today? What are you thinking? You haven't told me what you're really thinking.

SILVIA: If I told you, you would be more hurt. Don't be hurt. We must listen to the powers that are above us.

MARIO: You never gave them any thought until today.

SILVIA: I was wrong.

MARIO: So, you don't love me?

SILVIA: It's not up to me.

MARIO: Who is it up to then?

SILVIA: Don't ask me that.

MARIO (*warmly*): Can you really be feeling angry toward me?

SILVIA: I must suffer for myself as well as for you.

MARIO: That's not true; because I love you. Do you know how much I love you? Tell me you know. Save me from this anguish which you must feel too.

SILVIA: I can't say anything more.

MARIO: You don't love me!

Scene 7

Enter **FLORA**, *through the door on the left.*

FLORA (*to Mario*): I wasn't expecting to find you here. What do you want? Leave immediately. (*to* **SILVIA**) Your husband is here. What sixth sense made me come in before he did! (**MARIO** *exits through the door on the left, where he expects to find* **VIRGILIO**.)
What were you saying to him?

SILVIA: Mamma, it was absolutely essential that we speak to each other.

Scene 8

Enter **ENZO** *and* **GUIDO**.

ENZO: We give you back your wife.

FLORA: It was childish foolishness. She's very sorry.

GUIDO: That's not what Virgilio told me. But I'll be happy to hear what she has to say. I've been extremely unhappy.

ENZO: You will. We ask you to forgive her too. You must know how things are.

(ENZO and FLORA *exit through the door on the right.*)

Scene 9

GUIDO *and* SILVIA, *alone*

GUIDO: I wouldn't be here if your parents, whom I respect, hadn't sent for me.

SILVIA (*reproaching him passionately*): You should respect me.

GUIDO (*sincerely*): That's what I long to do.

SILVIA (*an even more anguished reproach*): But you said that if they hadn't sent for you, you wouldn't have come.

GUIDO (*sorrowfully*): Was I legally bound to come and find you then?

SILVIA: Legally bound, no; but because you love me, yes.

GUIDO: So then you're counting on the love I feel for you?

SILVIA: Only on that.

GUIDO: And was that the reason you behaved this way? Your brother, in defending you, has compromised you. You know what he told me? Did you hear him? I'm the one who loves you, not you me. And now you're crying! It's not the first time you've given me tears in exchange for all the love I give you. Why are you crying? Don't you want to tell me? Please, I'm running out of patience.

I may say things that will hurt us both.

SILVIA (*letting go*): Say what you want. You can say anything you want.

GUIDO: I won't say anything. I hope that we can understand each other. If you left, it means you thought that was the best thing to do. But now you must tell me everything. I'll accept any explanation, because you are a good person, and I believe in you, only in you. Raise your head. Look into my eyes the way I'm looking into yours. What do you have to reproach me for?

SILVIA: Nothing. That's why I'm crying.

GUIDO: Tell me if you aren't happy with me.

SILVIA: You're not to blame: I am.

GUIDO: What could you have possibly done to hurt me? Tell me.

SILVIA: It's my soul, which I don't understand any more.

GUIDO: Tell me, then, what is it in your soul? Won't you tell me?

SILVIA: But I love you!

GUIDO: Then you would not have left.

SILVIA (*in anguish*): You see, now you're doubting me! Don't doubt me. I need to have your trust.

GUIDO (*sorrowfully*): I want to trust you. But perhaps it's your words that are misleading.

You're talking to me in a strange way. You're not yourself any more. Why have you changed so much?

SILVIA: It's not up to me.

GUIDO: I don't understand you. (*still extremely sorrowful*) You should talk openly to me, as honestly as you can.

SILVIA: And then, I'll be afraid of telling you something that isn't true. Because I do love you.

GUIDO: Do you prefer not being near me?

SILVIA: No, not near myself.

GUIDO: Did you want to disappear from everybody?

SILVIA: I should have made myself disappear for ever.

GUIDO: But you never had such ideas before. Isn't it true that you never thought such things before?

SILVIA: I should have killed myself, but I wasn't able to.

GUIDO: And you would have left me all alone?

SILVIA: That's the only reason, perhaps, that I didn't kill myself, and now I've come back to you.

GUIDO: If you talk like that, it means you're hiding something from me.

SILVIA: I'm not hiding anything from you. You must believe me. That's what Mamma said too.

GUIDO (*on impulse*): I will believe you.

SILVIA (*testing him*): You're not upset?

GUIDO: I'd like to see you happier.

SILVIA: I'll do my best; I promise you. Sometimes you make a bigger mistake than you mean to. Sometimes you believe you're doing good, and instead the opposite happens.

GUIDO: I know, after you left yesterday, I wondered whether I would ever succeed in forgetting you. But that was absurd. I really feel that, now that I see you face to face. I will never forget you. Never! When I clasp you to me, your arms feel like the tips of two wings and your breath like the air they stir as they fly. But I cover them with my hands—I was about to say my fists.

SILVIA: So I'm not flying any more?

GUIDO: You are flying; but toward me. Always toward me, and it seems as if the flight is never ending. And your breast is full, made perfectly, just for me.

SILVIA (*with anguished gentleness*): Will you love me always? I thought that I could be loved even more. That was what I was longing for. And I was afraid that if I stayed with you, I would have to give that up.

GUIDO: And instead, don't you feel how much we love each other?

SILVIA: It's true.

GUIDO: And I will love you more and more.

SILVIA: Will you be able to forget what happened today?

GUIDO: I'll never think of it again. So long as I can always look into your eyes to find your soul.

SILVIA: If that is so, forgive me. I've acted badly. Very badly.

GUIDO: Perhaps this had to happen so that we could feel more for each other; as we have today.

Scene 10

VIRGILIO *enters from the gardens.*

VIRGILIO: Silvia!

SILVIA (*without leaving her husband, although full of feeling for her brother*): I'll speak to you later. Come to my house. I'm deliriously happy, I can't leave.

VIRGILIO (*sorrowfully*): You're happy?

SILVIA (*in bliss*): So happy! I've wanted this so much!

(**GUIDO** *takes her by the arm and leads her away, toward the door on the right.*)

Scene 11

VIRGILIO (*walks toward the sofa. He throws himself on it and sobs, covering his face*): But not me! I have only tears!

ACT 3

Five years have passed. **ENZO POGGI** *has died. The setting has changed from the ground floor of the villa to another room upstairs.*

Scene 1

VIRGILIO *and* **MARIO** *alone.*

VIRGILIO: I never imagined that I would get old too. In five years I've experienced nothing but bitterness. And I've done nothing. If I turn to look at my past, there is no trace of all those wasted seasons! And before, every morning would bring the feeling that I was entering a wood where sprouting trees reached straight upwards.

MARIO: I was wrong to leave you behind. I should have taken you with me.

VIRGILIO: I wouldn't have come. No one could have made me, not even you. But tell me, what have you learned from all your travels?

MARIO: Nothing. Absolutely nothing.

VIRGILIO: You mean your going away was useless, except for its helping you forget Silvia?

MARIO: I kept longing to come home, and the sweetest moments were when I remembered you and our friendship.

VIRGILIO: And I didn't even have that satisfaction. I haven't been able to think about anything. The greatest gift for me would have been if I had died. I feel, now, that my life is growing more and more useless and dull. You said that you want to be near me. What for? I would drag you with me into an abyss whose darkness is more horrible than anything you have experienced. You know the story: they say I'm a neurasthenic and there's nothing to be done, right?

MARIO: I will never resort to medical terminology.

VIRGILIO: Don't you feel that my words are ambiguous even when they're filled with violent feeling? Don't you sense that there is an unbridgeable gap between me and my words, a split that keeps on widening, cutting off my past?

MARIO: You're a better person than you were. These five years of solitude have brought you an understanding you didn't have before.

VIRGILIO: And what good does that do me? I've told you that I feel old and defenseless. I sometimes imagine that this villa with its gardens is a desert or some dead island. Doesn't it strike you that way?

MARIO: That's not true. I'm going to give you back twice what you once gave me. I'm not the same person I was. I'm clear about what I want and could almost draw you a picture. I've become a man of feeling and have tremendous energy to put back into life.

VIRGILIO: You'll do it all, and I'll listen to you the way you always listened to me. Do I deserve this kind of life?

MARIO: You will start a new life.

VIRGILIO: I don't believe it. And I'm overcome by remorse because my father died without knowing about my conversion and repentance. Poor old man! I keep seeing him during those last days when he was struggling to disguise his anger toward me. But he couldn't. We wanted to make peace, but it was impossible.

MARIO: Don't think about him any more. You're probably like him, although you're not old. You have another prime of life, the true one, which won't go awry.

VIRGILIO: And what about my real youth, five years ago, what was that?

MARIO: Only the seed, which still didn't know how to grow.

VIRGILIO: I hope that's true. Your words make me feel almost peaceful, at least for the moment. I've learned that each man's labor lies in the movement of his soul in accordance with reason, but a life needs to be whole; just because one branch flowers doesn't mean that spring has come.

Come and sit down, Mario. Perhaps we love each other more now, but not in the same naive way as before. We're more inside ourselves now, more closed off, but now that we're more rational, we'll be better friends without misleading one another.

Did you really just come back a few hours ago?

MARIO: One hour ago. And I came to see you immediately.

VIRGILIO: Didn't you run into anyone you know?

MARIO: No one.

VIRGILIO: That's too bad; I was curious to know the effect it would have on you to speak to someone besides me. Perhaps tomorrow you'll love me less because you'll be overwhelmed by all the other possibilities in the life you hope to pick up and start living again.

MARIO: Show some confidence!

VIRGILIO: I've also learned not to put too much faith in first impressions.

MARIO: How is your mother?

VIRGILIO: I don't think she loves me as she did before. She resents the fact that my father died without having seen me change. Her peace of mind would make me happy, because she's as essential to me as the foundations are to these walls. You will see her. But I'd better warn her first. She's one of those women who seem made only for family.

MARIO: It's best that I never see Silvia again.

VIRGILIO: Haven't you forgiven her yet? You wrote in several letters that you no longer loved her.

MARIO: That's true, but I haven't loved anyone else.

VIRGILIO: She did the right thing; believe me. She didn't need to change course too much before finding her path to happiness. You should see her. I want you to. You won't frighten her now. Her life is immaculate; she says that goodness and happiness come from honor. And you and I both wanted to betray her and cheat her of that!

What do you think of me, hearing me talk like this?

MARIO: It may seem strange to you, but I'm not drawing any comparisons between you then and you now. You have always been honest, and that is your salvation.

VIRGILIO: Honesty is not enough. We need to find a firm center within ourselves, but one not focused on ourselves alone.

MARIO: The goodness we seek is illusive.

VIRGILIO: Because we're not perfect. It depends on us. But goodness does exist, and we must respect it. I understand my father so well now; each of his words was more far-reaching than any moral discourse. He just didn't know how to express himself. His only mistake was in not sending me far away, because then I would have come back to him all the sooner.

Perhaps you're wondering why I attach so much importance to him, in my soul and conscience, now that he's no longer alive, and I no longer have to account to him. I'll tell you: my thoughts are more his than mine. And I take delight in this inexplicable likeness between us; it strikes me as beautiful.

Go and get some rest. I don't know when you can see me again.

MARIO (*surprised*): What have you got to do?

VIRGILIO: Nothing; but it's difficult for me to talk very much now, even with a friend like you. I need to be alone, most of all to feel I'm alone. Do you understand? When you reach a certain age, you withdraw from other people, not to avoid hypocrisy, but out of some instinct for self-preservation.

You've traveled too much to feel as secure with your thoughts as I do. You went away to forget the woman you loved.

As for me, I'm quite happy to be with my own thoughts, whatever they are.

(**MARIO** *bids him goodbye and exits through the door on the left.*)

Scene 2

VIRGILIO: I won't tolerate anyone coming to scrutinize me. I must be totally self-reliant.

Scene 3

FLORA enters

FLORA: What have you decided?

VIRGILIO: I'm staying here.

FLORA: You're tormenting your father's soul. Leave him alone, now that he's dead. Go away. You can come back when I'm dead too. Let me be alone with him.

VIRGILIO: I'll be your child again.

FLORA: You've never done anything with your life.

VIRGILIO: So I'll learn here with you.

FLORA: That's not true.

VIRGILIO: Mother, you always want to get even.

FLORA: You don't need me any more.

VIRGILIO: I do, more than ever before.

FLORA: Then are you weaker than I?

VIRGILIO: Perhaps I always was.

FLORA: Are you refusing to do what I ask?

VIRGILIO: I beg you not to insist. You make me feel so ashamed of myself. You're not acting like a mother should. I no longer feel capable of going into the real world. Men would realize that I once thought I could dominate them with my intelligence.

When I was young, I used to believe that my intelligence made me powerful. But it wasn't true. The only thing I had was an abstract perception of my own will, and then I discovered that no one would listen to me.

You don't realize how much you harmed me by not letting me leave back then. That was when I needed to be independent of you, to almost oppose you, to find a life that would allow me to discover truths unknown to anyone else. If I had believed in God, I would have been a saint. But I *was* a mystic and an ascetic. I was true to myself and I had my self-respect.

And now I'm just an ordinary man, mediocre, exhausted by merely trying to survive. And that terrifies me. If I were to go away now, I would kill myself a few steps down the road. I cling to you because I don't feel capable of loving.

Despite your white hair, you are younger than I.

FLORA: You've been consumed by some kind of hate since your adolescence. Leave this house. It's only if you make this sacrifice that I can give you your father's eternal blessing.

VIRGILIO: I'll hide in some part of this villa, and you'll never see me.

I'll never say a single word to you, even if you should happen to pass nearby.

I no longer hope for anything. But bit by bit you will see in my eyes that I am still your son.

FLORA: I promised your father I'd look after you. You are profoundly ill, and I no longer have the heart to send you away. But you'll never get well here. If you weren't ill, you would be evil.

VIRGILIO: What you're saying reminds me of smelling a new fragrance for the first time; how much sweeter it is if we don't open our eyes. Because my thoughts will make me die.

I know, in fact, that I shouldn't go on living.

FLORA: Five years ago, one could barely speak to you.

VIRGILIO: At that time—well, why not tell you?—I believed myself not mortal, but divine. As a mother, you may understand that.

I believed I could make myself immortal and escape death. And until now, I've wanted to escape it. But the greatest intoxication in life comes from some mysterious excitement about death.

It wasn't my youth that elated me, it was death, death, which no longer frightens me.

Why didn't we ever understand each other? It seemed useless to discuss anything with you then; I wanted to prove to you, by myself, that *I* had a strength that didn't come from *you*. And now, it doesn't seem important that I was born at all, as long as *you* can live forever.

FLORA: When you were a boy, you watched a swallow flying overhead and asked: Mamma, why are we human?

VIRGILIO: I've always been attracted to the infinite. I used to tell myself not to accept what was around me until I could find my own horizons. And that's why I wanted to leave your house.

My house was more invisible than pure air, but for me it was real, and I used to long to close myself in and stay there. Your warmth and closeness meant nothing to me. I wanted, first, to find that elusive answer, one that would keep forcing me, just like a bitter enemy, to follow it forever. Even when I no longer had the strength . . . If I *had* found it, I would have discovered an eternal truth, and I would have taught it to the rest of mankind.

FLORA: You must have suffered so much!

VIRGILIO: So much, Mamma! I turned away from you because I wanted an immortal mother.

FLORA: You are still not well; you're talking with your dreams again and not with me, and you're forcing me to tell you something that's so obvious I shouldn't even have to say it.

VIRGILIO: I only want kind words from you.

FLORA: Don't you realize that your father died of grief because you didn't love him? And you lived in the same house!

VIRGILIO: Am I the only one to blame? What you've just said would make me the worst son that ever lived.

FLORA: That's why you should get out.

VIRGILIO: I never knew that; I swear. I'm shocked; I can't believe it.

FLORA: It's just like when you were a little boy, you plucked the feathers off a live blackbird you kept in a cage.

VIRGILIO: I don't remember anything about that either. You mustn't remind me of it!

FLORA: But you're making me remind you of bad things.

VIRGILIO: I see: you've only stored up the bad things about me. Things I didn't know I was doing. But remember, you left my father once too. When *you* were young.

FLORA (*becoming violently agitated*): How dare you throw that in my face?

VIRGILIO: What's fair for me is fair for you.

FLORA (*beside herself*): Wait, just a moment! I'm no longer as strong as I used to be. One word is enough to destroy me!

VIRGILIO: So, even when we think we're following our conscience, we still do things that come back to torment us. You've almost accused me of killing my father. That might be true if I hadn't suffered as much as he did. And if I didn't wish I had died in his place!

FLORA: But one word from you might have been enough to save him. And now you've just said what I should never have heard! And your words cannot be taken back; I will have to atone for them myself.

VIRGILIO: I beg your pardon for having invaded the privacy of your youth. But I respect it, your youth that is, even if you've disowned it.

FLORA: You have no idea what I'm capable of doing. You have no idea what can happen! I'll never stand here again! You will always be a disgrace to me. There's no more Enzo! He was everything to me. Without him, the mold is broken. Oh, no! Before I become a witless old woman, I must do what I have to do. You will never see me again! Your words have made up my mind.

(*She exits through the door on the right.*)

Scene 4

VIRGILIO (*is distressed, and feels the onset of an attack similar to an epileptic seizure*): I don't want to dream! I don't want to have any more dreams! But I feel so weak. If I doze off, my dream will seem more real than anything else. It's stronger than I am. My head is bursting with light. It's worse than a nightmare, rising up from everywhere, as if I were being forced to feel a glimmer of the infinite on my face. My youth is taking its revenge and blinding me; I'm being possessed.

Scene 5

SILVIA *enters through the door on the right.*

SILVIA: Virgilio!

VIRGILIO (*in the grip of his nightmare*): Who told you to come in here just when I thought I was completely alone?

SILVIA: Why are you talking this way?

VIRGILIO (*hallucinating*): What was in your hands?

SILVIA (*frightened*): Nothing.

VIRGILIO (*goes to her and feels her hands*): You're right: there's nothing there. But where did you put what you were holding?

SILVIA (*trying to calm him*): I've come for a long visit, to keep you company. I've brought my daughter with me, to cheer you up. Come outside and see her. She's in the garden. Come and show her where the swallows nest.

VIRGILIO (*still delirious*): You'd hear me anyway, wouldn't you, even if you didn't make me go back to the stupid old habit of speaking? What a relief it is not to have to say anything! But, even though I know you exist and can't possibly mistake you for anyone else, I can't see you any more. I feel I'm your brother only because we used to be brother and sister. But now everything's changed, and all forms have crumbled. Only my ideas exist, and they are incapable of taking shape.

SILVIA: Perhaps you'll get better. You're going through the worst period of your life. You don't know how sad I am to see you like this.

VIRGILIO: You want to bring me back to life. But you won't succeed. You're still alive and you want me to be like you.

SILVIA: I will cure you!

VIRGILIO: I wouldn't obey under any circumstance. Please pray that I never wake up again.

SILVIA: I'll never leave you. I know my duty as a sister. (*to herself*) This is horrifying!

Scene 6

MARIO *returns through the door on the right. Seeing* **SILVIA**, *he turns to go.*

MARIO: Signora!

SILVIA: Please come in.

MARIO (*approaching and speaking in a hushed voice*): I'm afraid something terrible has happened.

SILVIA (*nodding toward* **VIRGILIO**, *who is on the sofa*): Can there be anything worse than this?

MARIO: Outside, in the garden . . . your mother has just drowned herself in the lake. I was walking by looking for Virgilio and saw them pulling her out. She's stopped breathing, and her body's cold.

SILVIA (*stunned and horrified, then indicates her brother*): At least he will be spared this blow!

(**SILVIA** *exits to the left with* **MARIO**. *There are several moments of silence;* **VIRGILIO** *remains prostrate on the sofa, still in the grip of his attack. Several* **SERVANTS** *and a* **GARDENER** *enter through the door on the right carrying* **FLORA'S** *body; they set it down gently on a large sofa far upstage.*)

Scene 7

VIRGILIO (*aroused by the noise the servants have made, he raises his head. He turns to looks upstage and slowly recognizes his mother's body. But he doesn't have the courage to approach her immediately. He is still half-dreaming and almost hallucinating*): My mother! They've brought her here to see if I recognize her! . . .

(*With a scream.*) I've killed her too! . . .

(*Kneels near her body, embraces it.*) If I press you to me now, it no longer does any good. I kiss you as I should have done before, just a moment ago. I kiss you to make you breathe again: I want to feel you breathe. If I can't make you breathe, it means that everything is dead for me!

Scene 8

SILVIA *and* **MARIO** *enter hurriedly from the left.* **SILVIA** *kneels next to her dead mother.* **MARIO** *embraces* **VIRGILIO**.

VIRGILIO: She died so that I could be well. I feel as normal as you. You don't believe it, but it's true. Have her laid out on her bed. It was an abomination to have her brought here.

(*The same* **SERVANTS** *reenter and carry* **FLORA'S** *body through the door on the right.* **SILVIA** *follows them, without leaving her mother's side.* **VIRGILIO** *wants to go too, but* **MARIO** *detains him.*)

Scene 9

MARIO: My friend! I'm so terribly sorry!

VIRGILIO (*still beside himself, but slowly returning to normal*): Words no longer make any sense. And she's in there. (*starts for the room where they carried* **FLORA'S** *body*) I barely embraced her!

MARIO: Stay with me. It's better if you don't see her again right away.

VIRGILIO: It's the most natural thing in the world for a person to die, but I pushed my mother into killing herself!

MARIO: Between the two of you, even the best intentions and the kindest feelings went wrong.

VIRGILIO: If only God would bring her back to life for an hour, so that she could relieve my conscience of this terrible guilt! Just one hour!

MARIO: You'll find a way to be forgiven.

VIRGILIO: I must obey her now more than ever: I cannot stay here. Every moment I delay, my profanation becomes more irreparable. I want to hold her once more, so that the chill of her cheeks will be imprinted on my flesh forever!

But I've made my decision. I'm leaving everything. I won't take anything that belongs to me. I'll borrow your clothes. But I'll have to change many other things about myself! Let me see her again.

MARIO: From all this confusion in your life you'll begin to have some understanding of who you are. And it is useless to fight who you are.

You're full of suffering. But it's true that sometimes we seem destined to descend into the depths of despair so that we can reach afterward for the greatest heights.

VIRGILIO: Where will I go to live?

MARIO: You will have to believe in God. You have no other choice! And faith, which is so essential, will come to you.

VIRGILIO: Without this faith I will never see my mother again.

MARIO: It will come to you. What is sown is not what grows; that dies beneath the ground. And then, when that's gone, there's a new plant in its place, which never existed before, pushing up through the earth.

VIRGILIO (*with guilty anguish and stirred by his newly found courage*): But why did I have to kill my mother? Doesn't that mean I'm undeserving, that I must refuse faith?

MARIO: No, because faith is the reality.

VIRGILIO (*still more invigorated by the strength that renews him after his attacks*): Sometimes I have it, then it goes, but I must follow it.

Scene 10

Enter SILVIA.

SILVIA (*seeing her brother near the door on the left*): Where are you going?

VIRGILIO (*turning around*): I'm leaving you another brother. He's worthy of you, because he learned how to give you up. Together you'll decide the right thing to do with mother's body. As for her soul, that's my concern, for as long as I feel its pain on my conscience!

(*Having said these words with complete tranquility, he leaves, in a disheveled state.*)

Scene 11

SILVIA: He's still beside himself. Don't let him out of your sight.

MARIO (*clearly and with complete faith in what he's saying*): He no longer needs us.

SILVIA (*apprehensive about what might happen to her brother*): Call him back. To go and see his mother, with me.

MARIO: That would be worse.

Let's pray for him, and for his long repentance.

SILVIA (*makes a gesture of distress, her eyes fixed on where her brother has exited. Then she rouses herself and, stunned by grief, moves quickly toward the room where* FLORA *is laid out. But as she is about to exit, she remembers her daughter whom she has left in the garden*): Mario! Go and find my daughter. Take her home, so that she doesn't cry. Tell her to wait for me there and not to cry, tell her I'll be home soon.

(MARIO *exits for the garden, and* SILVIA *enters the room where her dead mother is laid out.*)

CURTAIN

SEVEN

MASSIMO BONTEMPELLI

Introduction

Massimo Bontempelli was born in Como on May 12, 1878. He died in Rome in 1960, having survived two world wars, Mussolini's Fascist regime, and the postwar reconstruction. While a strong supporter of Mussolini and Fascism in the early 1920s, he later became disillusioned with Fascist policies, and in 1938 his open hostility at public meetings led to the revocation of his party membership. After the war, in 1949, he was elected senator for the Popular Front; he was unable to take his seat, however, because by law anyone who authored Fascist propaganda was ineligible, and in 1935 Bontempelli had edited an anthology intended for the schools.

Ranked among Italy's intelligentsia, Bontempelli was active as a playwright, critic, novelist, poet, and essayist, and as a composer and professor of literature; he also had an abiding interest in film. After much searching and experimenting, he began to find his own voice as a playwright in the 1920s in a style that he called *realismo magico.*

As a young high school professor Bontempelli wrote *Costanza* (Constance) (1905), a tragedy in verse about the Risorgimento rooted in romanticism. Ten years later, in 1915, having long since abandoned his teaching post for a career as a writer and having already published several collections of poetry, short stories, essays, and historical and literary monographs, two of his plays influenced by *verismo* reached the stage in significant productions in Milan: *La piccola* (The little girl), starring Maria Melato under Virgilio Talli's direction, and *Santa Teresa* (Saint Teresa), with Lyda Borelli in the title role.

At the same time Bontempelli was turning toward the newer avant-garde—the futurism of Enrico Cavacchioli, the fables of Luigi Antonelli, the *teatro grottesco* of Pier Maria Rosso Di San Secondo and Luigi Chiarelli—and also toward Luigi Pirandello. He published futurist poetry and wrote for futurist journals such as *Roma Futurista* and *Il Montello*. World War I, during which he served as an artillery officer, cut short his literary and theatrical activities for a time, although he acted as war correspondent for several newspapers.

By the end of the war, Bontempelli had undergone a transformation in his literary outlook and repudiated most of his earlier fiction, poetry, and drama. In a critical appraisal of his own play, *La guardia alla luna* (The watchman on the moon, 1916)[1] as produced by Talli's company in 1920, he wrote that it was a mixture of "sentimentalism, realism, colorism, aestheticism, folklorism, fragmentarism, impressionism," an outgrowth of the prewar experimental movement that had succeeded in breaking with the mediocrities of petit-bourgeois drama but had grown stale and morbid. Italian playwrights, he argued, now needed to rediscover the ideals, spirit, and clarity of great drama or great comedy.

Bontempelli felt it was one of the critics' duties to point the way into the twentieth century, into the art of the future.[2] To further that end, he founded the journal *900*. Between 1926 and 1928 this was the first journal to publish young Italian writers of the period, such as Corrado Alvaro and Alberto Moravio, and to introduce James Joyce and Virginia Woolf to Italian readers.

In other theater reviews of the 1920s Bontempelli expressed his dislike for the Italian theater's reliance on French bourgeois drama, and he encouraged the small Italian independent theaters then in vogue, which were experimenting with new dramatic forms, including some works by Bontempelli himself. Among these theaters were the Teatro Sperimentale in Bologna and Riccardo Gualino's private theater in Turin, which became the Teatro di Torino, one of the most successful little theaters in Italy. In 1928, two years before its demise, Teatro di Torino produced *La salamandra,* a mime piece by Pirandello with music by Bontempelli. Milan theaters included the Sala Azzurra, where Gualtieri and Beryl Tumiati experimented with puppets, the Piccola Canobbiana, and the Teatro del Convegno. In Rome, experimental theaters comprised the Villa Ferrari in Piemonte Street, Mario Cortesi's Teatro Moderno, and Gino Gori's Bottega del Diavolo (Devil's workshop), a futurist cabaret with interior design by Fortunato Depero. A puppet show written by Luciano Folgore and Massimo Bontempelli, and for which Enrico Prampolini designed the puppets and sets, was performed at the Bottega del Diavolo several times in 1923.[3]

The two most important experimental theaters in Rome, headed by Anton Giulio Bragaglia and Luigi Pirandello, produced in the mid-1920s two major Bontempelli plays written in the style of *realismo magico*. Bragaglia's Teatro degli Indipendenti, where many contemporary and classical pieces from throughout the world would be staged over the next fourteen years, opened its doors in January 1923 with a production of Bontempelli's *Siepe a nordovest* (Northwest barrier). Shortly thereafter, Pirandello and Bontempelli and others began to make plans for their own theater, and the Teatro d'Arte—also known as Teatro degli Undici—was formed in 1925. On April 22, 1925, at their Teatro Odeschalchi, which seated 348, the company produced *Nostra Dea (Dea by Dea)* directed by Pirandello.[4]

Minnie la candida, another important example of Bontempelli's *realismo magico,* was produced in Milan in 1927.[5]

Bontempelli's *realismo magico,*[6] while seeming to be an oxymoron, refers to the presence of an ideal world parallel to ours, a world of the imagination that coexists with the real world created for humanity by the positivists. Fifteenth-century painters, he argued, such as Masaccio, Mantegna, and Piero della Francesca, could create a precise real world, and yet their frescoes or canvasses reached for the world above and beyond that reality. In the same way, theater could reflect the *magico* behind the reality of every human being's daily life, but it had to use new forms to do so.

In the 1920s there was a serious crisis in the theater; box office millions were going to films rather than to theatrical performances.[7] Bontempelli believed that the *teatro di prosa* or traditional prose drama was essentially a dead form; it was impossible for audiences to believe in naturalism in the theater when films created reality so much more convincingly. On film, the actor's half-smile in close-up could have an effect unmatched on stage. Film used the cosmetic art to offer something new to the imagination. Even sport was better than the worn-out *teatro di prosa;* sport delighted with its rhythm and energy. The only way theater could compete with film and sport was by creating a *realismo magico* where the acting technique would not rely on psychological realism but on clowns and the commedia dell'arte; where new developments in lighting and stage machinery would be put to good use; where new rhythms and energy would be produced through all kinds of music, including jazz; and where the audience would learn to laugh at melodrama, bourgeois drama, psychological theater, and sentimentality.

Siepe a nordovest, Minnie la candida, and *Dea by Dea,* in which the fantastical coexists with the real, develop these theatrical ideas. The bourgeois characters are either bested by string- and hand-puppets with whom they share the stage, as in *Siepe,* or are puppetlike because they have no essence, as in *Dea,* or fearful of being automatons, are driven to suicide, as is the case with Minnie.

Bontempelli's other theatrical works include *La fame* (Hunger, 1935), which was censored by Mussolini, *Nembo* (Cloud) (1935), *Cenerentola* (Cinderella, 1942), *Venezia salva* (Venice saved, 1947), an adaptation of Thomas Otway's *Venice Preserved,* and *Innocenza di Camilla* (Camilla's innocence, 1948). An adaptation by Ivo Chiesa of Bontempelli's novel, *Gente nel tempo* (Period folk), was produced by Giorgio Strehler in 1949.

Strehler produced *Dea by Dea* in Milan and took the production to Buenos Aires in June 1954. A production directed by Mario Missiroli opened at the Teatro Argentina in Rome on January 30, 1992.

Bontempelli's own long "Note on *Dea by Dea* (*Nostra Dea*)" is printed here before the opening of the play. In this essay Bontempelli recalls productions of the play in Italy between 1925 and 1942, ponders the reasons for their success or lack thereof, and offers advice for future productions.

J. H.

Notes

1. He was a drama critic at the time. See M. Bontempelli, "Il teatro di prosa," *Il Primato* (Feb.–Mar. 1920), pp. 51–52. Reprinted in Alessandro Tinterri, ed., *Nostra Dea e altre commedie* (Turin: Einaudi, 1989), pp. 33–35.

2. Between 1920 and 1922 Bontempelli wrote for *Il Primato* in Milan and then for *Industrie Italiane Illustrate* in Rome. A selection of his theater criticism can be found in Ruggero Jacobbi, *Rivista italiana di drammaturgia*, vol. 2 (Rome: Bulzoni, 1976), pp. 123–78. For his ideas on the role of the critic, see the pages on theater in *Avventura novecentista* (Twentieth-century adventure) (1938; reprint, Florence: Vallecchi, 1974).

3. See the futurist review *Noi* (May 1923). Cited by Alessandro Tinterri, "Bontempelli e il teatro," in Alessandro Tinterri, ed., *Nostra Dea e altre commedie,* pp. 229–30.

4. See Bontempelli's own production notes that follow this essay.

5. The three plays, along with *Guardia alla luna,* are presented in the critical edition, *Nostra Dea e altre commedie,* edited by Alessandro Tinterri (Turin: Einaudi, 1989). These works originally appeared in vol. 1 of the two-volume *Teatro* (Milan: Mondadori, 1947).

6. See Massimo Bontempelli, "Spiegazione del realismo magico," (Explanation of magic realism) *Tempo* (June 24, 1943, and July 1, 1943). The basic ideas are also discussed by Paolo Pinto, "Prefazione," in Massimo Bontempelli, *Eva ultima* (The last Eve) (Rome: Lucarini, 1988), pp. vii–xiii.

7. For statistics, see Silvio d'Amico, *Il teatro non deve morire* (Theater must not die) (Rome: Eden, 1945), pp. 56–58.

A Note on Dea by Dea *(Nostra Dea)* (1947)

Pirandello used to say you should think about a play for a year and write it in a week.

I started thinking about *Dea by Dea (Nostra Dea)* in the summer of 1922, when I woke up one night in a little pensione at the foot of the Semmering Pass with the original idea in mind. When I got back to Rome, I was still thinking about it. I tried to sketch out the opening scenes, but I gave up on it right away. I wanted to graft the many complicated possibilities the notion was likely to give rise to onto a plot that was by contrast as simple and commonplace as possible (I have always been bothered and intimidated by the need for prior exposition, and I have almost always managed to do without it or reduce it to a bare minimum), and I was unable to come up with one. I decided to forget all about it. At about the same period, I went through—it wasn't the first, nor would it be the last—a kind of rejection crisis vis-à-vis the theater, any kind of theater, theater period. I was convinced I would never write another play. My new leaf and the birth of *Dea by Dea* are closely linked to the founding of the "Teatro degli Undici" (Theater of the Eleven) in Rome.

The idea for the company first occurred to Stefano Landi and Orio Vergani in the early months of 1924, and they immediately set about laying the practical foundations. The lifespan of the little theater was extremely brief, fertile, and very important. Today few people remember it, and their memories are confused. This is as good a moment as any for fixing the memory of it clearly.

Stefano and Orio, along with another nine (or was it ten?) of us, founded the Company of the Eleven in September of that year, with a capital of 150,000 lire. We rented the little theater in via Odescalchi that Vittorio Podrecca was leaving to take his glorious marionettes on a world tour. The task of remodeling the house and stage was assigned to the architect Virgilio Marchi.

We turned timidly to Pirandello for advice and help. He threw himself heart and soul into the venture, prepared a rich and varied repertory, egged on a number of playwrights (especially young playwrights) to write scripts, chose the actors, and directed (in those days the bureaucratic term in Italian was *direttore,* not *regista*) all the performances. Six plays were performed (in addition to the "Thursday matinees" devoted to musical comedies and ballets) between April and June of 1925: six of the most harmonious, mellifluous and perfect creations for the stage that our generation can remember.

I was one of the Eleven (some people said there were twelve, and the issue was never really settled), and Pirandello invited me to write a play for our repertory. For a while I managed to put him off, but one day I happened to tell him about the idea I had shelved. He liked it. He was so enthusiastic and imperious in urging me to take it up again that I promised I would, and a few months later, on the night between 1924 and 1925, after seeing in the New Year, I began writing. I realized that I must often have had the abandoned play on my mind for some time without being aware of it. I didn't leave the house again until I went out on the morning of January 16 with the completed script under my arm. (My work with that group of friends had cured me of my aversion to the theater.)

The company had been rehearsing for some time, on the stage of the little Metastasio Theater (now destroyed), Dunsany's *The Gods of the Mountain,* Pirandello's *Sagra del Signore della Nave,* Di Stefano's *Calzolaio di Messina:* all works that did not call for a leading lady. Once the script of *Nostra Dea* had been handed over, we began looking for an actress to play the title role. We were lucky. We had read an article by Marco Praga in the *Illustrazione Italiana* in which he sang the praises of a young debutante in the Talli company who had had great personal success in the role of Masha in Chekhov's *Seagull:* Marta Abba. We had a presentiment that this was the person we were looking for. Guido Salvini (who was beginning his career in the theater as one of the Eleven) went to Milan, saw Abba perform, and immediately signed her on as our leading lady. We sent her the script of *Nostra Dea.* A few weeks later, Marta Abba, having completed her tour with the Talli company in Bologna, arrived in Rome at the Metastasio, where we were anxiously awaiting her. We began the first rehearsal there and then; the other actors were reading their parts, but she already knew hers by heart. "I had given it a great deal of study," she would write in her memoirs ten years later, "and now in my dressing room I would try my voice out line by line with every conceivable intonation, in order to come up with the extremely varied accents and the different rhythms to give to every scene, so as to convey the innumerable facets of the protagonist, whose personality changes with the clothes she puts on. And quite spontaneously, along with the intonations and rhythms, the gestures and movements came to me." That first rehearsal was memorable. Every one of the ten or dozen persons present was filled with a sense of almost fearful expectancy. I think that even Pirandello's and Stefano's hearts were beating overtime. We had staked everything on an unknown card; for a few moments the card was face down, it was about to be turned over. Marta Abba on the other hand was as tranquil as a constellation.

From the very first lines, Pirandello and I turned to each other and exchanged glances of amazement. But at the end of the first scene—when Dea, suddenly vivacious because of the bold cut of the suit the maid Anna was going through the motions of helping her on with, quivered all over, her eyes flashing, and with the words "Yes, it suits me" sparked off a vortex, and, from a prenatal distance, in less than an instant conquered the third dimension, entering completely into the first of her many incarnations—a murmur went up all around, and Pirandello couldn't keep from bursting out and telling her there and then how delighted he was, we all were.

The rest of the winter and early spring were months of relentless work for Pirandello and the actors, who from dawn till dusk were now engaged in rehearsing four different plays, as well as for Stefano and Vergani and Salvini, who were battling against endless difficulties to decorate and equip the theater. In the meantime the public grew more and more impatient and excited. Politics had not yet invaded and shrunk every tissue of our national life, and the daily papers vied with one another for weeks and months with interviews, indiscretions, discussions, revelations. More than a theatrical success, the night of April 2—with Pirandello's *Sagra* and Dunsany's *Gods*—was a celebration brimful with joy and light. Marta Abba and *Dea* did not go on until the third performance, on the evening of April 22. I will let her do the talking: "It was a triumph. A triumph for Bontempelli, for Pirandello, for the Theater, for myself. I wept for joy and happiness. Never again, in the years that followed, was I to experience a joy so total and so pure." Our success with the press was also total: all the critics were in agreement in exalting the great new actress the Eleven had unexpectedly presented to the Italian theater.

The play was repeated for twenty-five nights. Pirandello's direction had also worked miracles. He had succeeded in creating the most harmonious unity between the play's burlesque aspects and its tragic roots, working up each and every one of the characters in depth. And each and every one of the actors—Picasso, Biliotti, Olivieri, Cervi, Gina Graziosi, Lia Di Lorenzo, Maria Morino (I could not be more mortified that I do not recall and have not been able to trace the names of the others)—gave it their all and acted like a well-rehearsed orchestra under the baton of a perfect conductor.

The play is printed here exactly as it was performed then, and as I would like it to be performed whenever anyone feels like reviving it. But the script I gave the Eleven had a different ending to act 1, which we were right to eliminate, if only after several rehearsals. After the words "My dear, my dearest, comma," Vulcan continued to dictate the letter, till Dea went through another change of clothes and another transformation. At the Odescalchi Theater we rehearsed for over a week with that ending, and we were never able to make it work satisfactorily. At length Pirandello realized that the problem was with the text and the fact that the ending was not really essential. We could in fact do perfectly well without it, ending with that "comma." I transcribe that ending here, as it was printed in a previous edition (and even performed by Tatiana Pavlova in her production of the play, as well as in some of the translations that were put on abroad).

VULCAN (*While he dictates,* **DEA**, *murmuring and cooing, repeats syllables and words as she writes*): "You have only just met me, and yet it seems as if we had been friends for years. I feel so lonely in the big city, where I have no real friends . . ." What am I supposed to be then? "and still less women friends. I am so fond of you. And I think I can sense that you will be fond of me too . . ."

COUNTESS ORSA: Yes, that's good.

DEA: Very good.

VULCAN: Thank you. "Will you do me an enormous favor? I don't think it would be much of an effort for you, on the contrary" . . .

COUNTESS ORSA: No, "on the contrary" won't do.

VULCAN: Take it out then. Let's proceed. "Unless you have a previous engagement . . ."

COUNTESS ORSA: Oh, for goodness sake. Dea is supposed to know already that I'm free. Otherwise he'll use it as an excuse. She should write as though everything were arranged.

VULCAN: But if we do that, Orso will take offense. And, in any case, you ought to have told him.

COUNTESS ORSA: That's true. But the letter must be carefully worded, in such a way as to give him no grounds for refusing. You know what I mean?

VULCAN: We must give it some thought. Let me reread it.

MADAME FIORA (*all at once, from beyond the screen*): Miss Dea, come here a moment, please.

DEA (*to* **MADAME FIORA**): Yes, dear. (*She gets up. To the other two.*) You think of the sentence, I'll be back to write it in a jiffy.

VULCAN (*immediately*): No, no.

DEA (*halfway across the room, turning to him with a smile*): My, aren't you impatient! I'll be right back. Here I am, Madame Fiora. (*She goes into the dressing room.*)

VULCAN (*getting up*): Oh no, excuse me, Miss Dea . . . (*He has a sense of foreboding and tries to cut her off.*)

(*The rest of the scene should be played in a crescendo of feverishness and foreboding.*)

COUNTESS ORSA (*to* **VULCAN**): Let her go, she'll be right back. Pay attention to me. (*Brandishing the letter.*)

MADAME FIORA (*as if possessed*): Here, here . . .

(**DEA** *is inside the dressing room.* **ORSA** *reads the letter over in a low voice.* **VULCAN** *is on tenterhooks.* **ORSA** *holds him back by the arm.*)

COUNTESS ORSA (*holding back* **VULCAN**, *her eyes on the letter*): What we need is "since you told me . . ." No, just a minute. (*She reads the letter over, her voice gradually getting louder.*)

MADAME FIORA (*on the other side of the screen, lifting up the white coat as she declaims, while*

VULCAN *on his feet strains to hear what she's saying, and* **DEA** *smiles beatifically*): It's an architectural monument, a Roman column. Truly imperial!

(*As she speaks* **MADAME FIORA** *puts the white coat over* **DEA** *and arranges it in a statuesque manner. It comes all the way down to her feet and has a hood that goes up over her head.*)

VULCAN (*to himself*): It's all over! (*imperiously, to* **DEA**) Madame Dea, don't come back over here, don't come back over here.

COUNTESS ORSA (*who has been reading, practically out loud, looks up, annoyed because* **VULCAN** *isn't listening*): Come on, come on, what's got into you? Pay attention to what I'm saying.

VULCAN: Give me the letter, and keep quiet (*He takes the letter.*)

MADAME FIORA (*to* **DEA**): Look at yourself in the mirror! (*pushing* **DEA** *in front of the mirror*) Agrippina! It's Agrippina! (*She is wild with enthusiasm.*)

(**DEA** *takes a few steps, still hidden by the screen, without showing the audience her face.*)

VULCAN: Agrippina!

COUNTESS ORSA (*to* **VULCAN**, *fatuous and dismayed*): Agrippina?

DEA (*stepping forward into the room, erect and statuesque, her face clenched and severe, like a character from one of Alfieri's tragedies*): Agrippina!

VULCAN (*still clutching the letter, flinging himself down in an armchair*): Good night!

And that was how the first act ended.

The scene was amusing, but I was happy to see it suppressed, since its suppression made for a closer connection between the first and the second acts, leaving Dea's less intimate and more disconcerting transformations for the third.

The same year, 1925, on November 9, *Nostra Dea* was performed at the Olympia Theater in Milan by Tatiana Pavlova, who gave the play a great deal of loving study (though she refused to listen to my explanations) and lavished on it an excessively elaborate mise-en-scène. The director, Strenkowski, had not taken the play's measure or foreseen its dangers. He overdid it. Above all they were determined at any cost to do something different from what Pirandello and his actors had done. Instead of presenting the action naturalistically, they insisted, in spite of my supplications, on every gesture and every intonation being totally portentous and on conveying the impression of God knows what metaphysical symbols and allusions: with the result that the whole thing turned out incredibly heavy-handed, and the play was as much of a disappointment in Milan as it had been a success in Rome in the spontaneous and in a sense traditional interpretation of the "old-fashioned" comic theater.

I have dwelt on this episode and on the contrast between the two interpretations as a warning to future directors, who might be tempted to philosophize at *Dea's* expense and at the expense of Vulcan, Marcolfo, and their author. The same lesson (which should in any case have been obvious, without further need for practical confirmation) is to be drawn from the discrepancy between the other two interpretations the play received outside of Italy two years later. In Warsaw, in February 1927, Maria Potocka, a fine actress, performed Sofia Chrzanowska's Polish translation as a grotesque piece full of hidden allusions and secret messages, which was not a success. On the other hand, in June of the same year, in Prague, the great Krombaurova, when she decided to stage the Czech translation by Wenseslas Jirina, called in Giulio Salvini to direct. He was able to elicit from the actors a lively, spontaneous acting style, in the Italian manner, which met with extraordinary acclaim.

The play (translated into Spanish by Vilaregut) was also performed with considerable success in Madrid by Margarita Xirgu, in December 1926. In March 1933, Piri Peéry put it on in the Hungarian translation by Bela E. Fray and under Anton Nemeth's direction at the Chamber Theater of Budapest, to the audience's considerable dismay. On the other hand, the play was positively received in 1942 in a Rumanian translation at the National Theater Studio in Bucharest. In Italy, after 1925, the year of its birth, it was never revived.[1]

PERFORMANCE NOTES

The misunderstandings to which the two antithetical ways of interpreting the play may give rise are what lead me to add one or two observations here concerning the only style of mise-en-scène I had in mind when I wrote it.

General Characteristics

The play must not be reduced either to a philosophical drama or a ballet. As I already mentioned, the entire performance (sets and acting) should be clear, natural, and innocent; in the first and third acts the pace should be rapid, even exuberant (discreetly pathetic in the second and fourth). To perform it as an authentic comedy of plot, in a pleasant, sunny atmosphere, is the only way to bring out certain meanings and get the audience to accept the air of paradox. In this kind of artistic composition you have to be able to say the most surprising and outlandish things in the most simple and ingenuous manner. It would be a serious mistake to attempt to endow them, by means of morbid sets or somnambulistic diction, with the colors of mystery or unrealistic fable.

Lighting

All changes of lighting must be soberly handled. In act 1, the first scene should take place with pale lighting; then, with Dea's first words after she has put on the red suit ("Yes, it suits me"), broad sunlight should flood the stage: a change realistically justified by the fact—mentioned in the stage directions—that Anna throws open the shutters. A bit later the lighting should be gradually reduced (without the audience noticing) so as to arrive at

---

1. Bontempelli wrote these "Notes" in 1947. [J. H., ed.]

a gentle bluish-tinted light when Dea appears wearing the doveneck-gray princesse dress. This lighting will remain unchanged to the end of the act. The second act should begin with bright but discreet lighting; it will fade gradually (as if twilight were coming on) when Dea and Marcolfo are left alone. What is left of the light will eventually be concentrated on them, while the rest of the stage will have become a great shadowy abyss. In act 3 full range can be given to the director's imagination: a carnival atmosphere. In the fourth act pale, washed-out lighting: the last sounds before the curtain falls (Dea's footsteps toward the sofa) in complete darkness.

Dance Music in Act 3 (see pp. 305–12) should be arranged for a small string orchestra with the addition of a saxophone and jazz percussion instruments, so as to give the music a jazz sound without its being really jazz.

Characters

Dea: All her changes of voice are dictated by the text. Her first words (all of her dialogue with Nina and part of that with Anna, until she gets dressed), and her very last words in the play, should be enunciated in the voice we might imagine coming from a dressmaker's dummy, but with something childlike about it too, being careful not to fall into the merely wooden and puppetlike.

As soon as she puts on the suit, the "Yes, it suits me" should be a fanfare of trumpets.

In the second act, the actress should be careful to ensure that the softness and sweetness of the doveneck-gray character nevertheless allows her an occasional note of seduction and female gratification, so as to obtain a scary effect when Marcolfo commits the error of covering her with an ash-gray shawl and her voice grows distant, as if it came from another dimension. And, after the effort it cost her to say "I, I" (that is, to create a personality for herself), the very last line of the act ("It doesn't mean anything") should be pronounced with something of a harsh inflection, bitter, definitive, dead.

Extreme rapidity is recommended in all changes of clothing. This recommendation is particularly addressed to the costume designer who should bear it in mind when designing all of Dea's dresses.

Vulcan: Confident, superior, at times mysterious (in act 1, for example, when Anna reveals Dea's secret). The monologue in the fourth act provides the opportunity for him to give vent to all the tragic and lyric qualities of his soul, contained till that moment by "decorum."

The actor must devote particular attention to studying the last line of act 1, so that in its tenuousness it can be given an air of "finality." The scene between the three actors should have an almost tender and idyllic ring. Vulcan should remember that the previous day he met Dea dressed in a pale color at Countess Orsa's and that he had found her "infinitely attractive." Coming upon her today wearing a suit and acting so vivacious, he found her considerably less so. The true mate for the intelligent and masculine Vulcan is a compassionate woman, not this female earthquake. She, on the other hand, is the perfect mate for Marcolfo, who in fact is in love with the Dea he met in the bar. But now Vulcan knows that Dea does not exist. As he begins to dictate, after the words "My dear, my dearest," he pauses for an instant, gives her a last admiring look, then, as if he were resigning himself to losing her, pronounces the word "comma," and the curtain falls.

Marcolfo: Very droll in act 1 and the first part of act 2, overcome by melancholy (a consequence of his intelligence, which even earlier should not be completely suffocated by his timidity) when he speaks the words "If everything you like, you like the way you like this tea," etc. This is the beginning of the dialogue of *sentimental and moral impotence,* the most important element in the whole play. It should be stressed that this dialogue could become prolix unless Marcolfo takes proper advantage of the moments that allow him to heighten and intensify the tone (the two occasions, that is, when, without looking at Dea, he reevokes the vision he had of her wearing her suit).

Other roles: Madame Fiora is a thoroughly comic figure, loud, fanatical, with a dialect accent.

Anna is extremely correct, ageless, attentive and at the same time distant; incapable of surprise; abstracted from the world.

The Doctor: pompous, deadpan comedy; his fanaticism is professorial in the first act, offended in the second, triumphant in the third.

End of Act 1:   I have already stated that I prefer the close of the first act without the scene cited in the Note, in which Dea is transformed into a classical character. In the event, however, that some company should someday decide, under exceptional circumstances, to attempt to perform the play with the original final scene restored, here are a few things to bear in mind. The restored final scene should be performed very briskly. The idyllic scene between the three is suddenly troubled, when Madame Fiora calls out to Dea, by a breath of anxiety, which continues to grow and precipitates everything toward the climax with extreme rapidity. Much is demanded of the spectators, when they are asked to accept this extreme conclusion from the paradoxical premise. They must therefore be made to accept it through the element of surprise, and the curtain must fall before they have had time to recover. The transformation of Dea into Agrippina appears to the audience in a flash of lightning and is gone in a flash. This conjuring trick needs all the help it can get from the fast pace and driving rhythm of the other actors, who, making the most of the comic aspects, will assume the same tone of voice and attitude they would have at the close of the act of a light comedy. Please note, the real visual focus of the scene is less the apparition of Agrippina than the comically desperate abandon of Vulcan when he flings himself down in the armchair with a resounding "Good night!"

■

DEA BY DEA

(Nostra Dea, 1925)

Translated by Anthony Oldcorn

■

Dramatis Personae

DEA

VULCAN

MARCOLFO

COUNTESS ORSA

DORANTE

DOCTOR

MADAME FIORA, artistic couturière

ANNA, Dea's first maid, an older woman

NINA, Dea's new maid, a young girl

EURIALUS, Marcolfo's manservant

ELDERLY WAITER at the "Polyhedric Palais"

HATCHECK GIRL

BELLBOY

SECOND BELLBOY, (nonspeaking part)

YOUNG WOMAN

EXTRAS FOR ACT 3

ACT 1

The bedroom, or, if you prefer, sitting room, of Dea, the protagonist. Couches, a sofa bed, pillows, small tables, drapes; a large table; and, dominating everything else, an enormous wardrobe upstage right. Main entrance upstage. Downstage left,[1] a small space is separated from the rest by a tall folding screen, which forms a partition on two sides: the space enclosed by the screen is furnished as a dressing room, with a vanity table, a tall three-leaved mirror, a hat rack festooned with women's hats in assorted colors and sizes. The time is late morning. The shutters are still closed.

DEA *is in her slip. She stands erect in the middle of the stage facing the audience, her arms hanging limp at her sides, motionless, her face absolutely without expression. There is something abandoned and at the same time rigid about her appearance, like a store window mannequin.* NINA *is addressing her.*

NINA (*stupidly*):   I think it's time for madam to go out. (*pause*) That's what Anna said.
DEA (*in a hollow, slightly falsetto voice, as though sounding out the syllables*):   I-think-so.
NINA (*seeing she doesn't move*):   Perhaps madam has changed her mind.
DEA: I-don't-think-so.

(*pause*)

NINA: Anna told me to come and help madam dress.
DEA (*still speaking in the same staccato way*):   Ve-ry well.
NINA (*going over to the huge wardrobe*):   Anna said all the dresses were in here. (*She throws open the doors of the capacious wardrobe, revealing a mass of dresses in a variety of colors, all on hangers.*) Oh, here they are. Which one would madam like to wear this morning?
DEA: Which one?
NINA (*continuing to inspect the dresses*):   It looks like the morning dresses are all together on this side. Yes, that's it. (*She turns toward* DEA *and waits for directions. Pause.*) If madam would just tell me . . .
DEA: I must tell you.
NINA: Madam must excuse me. This is my first day of service. I'm not sure . . .
DEA: I un-der-stand.
NINA: So if, for a day or two anyway, you could just tell me . . .
DEA: Pro-ba-bly.
NINA: If you could just show me . . .
DEA (*Pause. Without speaking, she takes three mechanical steps forward toward the audience, raises her arms symmetrically for a moment, lets them fall, stops*):   I don't know. No.
NINA: But if I don't dress you, you can't go out.
DEA: That's per-fect-ly true.
NINA: You can't even stay home.
DEA: Oh no, no.
NINA: Maybe you'd like me to choose?

---

1. Virgilio Marchi's set designs for the 1925 Rome production suggest that the stage directions are given from the audience's viewpoint. —Trans.

DEA: That is a good idea.

NINA: This white one?

DEA: White?

NINA (*bursting into tears*): I'm sorry, madam, but what do you want me to do, what do you want me to do?

(*Enter* **ANNA**.)

ANNA: You have visitors . . . (*She sees* **DEA** *still undressed and* **NINA** *in tears*). But it's already eleven, and madam still isn't dressed. Come along, Nina. It's late. The doctor came for his examination, but, when he heard she was still home, he went away again. He says he'll come back in fifteen minutes or so, but he asked that she not be at home, because he doesn't have much time.

NINA (*with her mouth wide open*): What?

ANNA: Never mind. Hurry up, Nina.

NINA: I can't figure out which dress . . .

ANNA: Run along then. Go and finish fixing her breakfast. Quickly. Then bring it here. Quickly. If anyone else should show up, let me know. I'll take care of things here for today. Quickly now. (*Exit* **NINA**.) Madam, a Mr. Vulcan came to see you too. (*As she speaks, she moves around the room putting things in order.* **DEA** *stands still where she was before, nodding her head every now and then, as expressionless as ever.*) I told him to wait, because he says you told him yesterday, at Countess Orsa's, that he could come round this morning . . . But if you want me to send him away . . . Alright, you can tell me later. Here I am then.

(*With a discreet touch of her hand, she heads* **DEA** *toward the screen. Once she reaches it,* **DEA** *enters the dressing room. While* **DEA** *is walking over to the screen,* **ANNA** *goes to the wardrobe, which has remained open, quickly chooses a dress, and closes the wardrobe doors. She hurries over to her mistress, who has come to a full stop on the other side of the screen in the same mechanical position as before. Now they are both on the left of the screen.*)

DEA: Here I am, Anna.

(**ANNA** *deftly helps her on with the outfit, bright red in color: a smart straight-cut tailor-made suit, very masculine and youthful. She takes a white carnation from a vase and puts it in Dea's buttonhole. She throws open the shutters. Bright sunlight floods the room.*)

DEA (*with a huge shudder, as if her whole body had been galvanized into life, she turns to the mirror and takes a rapid look at herself. Then in a warm vibrant voice*): Yes, it suits me. I look like a young man. (**ANNA** *in the meanwhile rapidly buttons up the outfit.*) I'd like to go out for a long walk. In fact I'm going to stay out for lunch. I know, I'll go to a bistro. (**ANNA** *in the meantime puts a red hat on her head that matches the dress, adding to the overall impression of vivacity, youth, and self-confidence.*) Capital!. You were saying that Mr. Vulcan . . .

ANNA: He's waiting outside. Oh, and Countess Orsa sent a message to say . . .

(*In the meantime both have emerged from the dressing area.*)

DEA (*interrupting*): Muddlers, meddlers. Tell them to go to hell. I feel like having a good time. They're nothing but a pair of meddlers. I feel like going riding. Oh, I wish I were a man, so I wouldn't have to take women seriously. And I'm hungry, very hungry. They're a pair of complicated melancholics. Yes, that's exactly what they are. Yes, show him in, show him in. I want to tell him to his face what he is. (*Exit* **ANNA**.) Then I'll send him packing. (*She lights up a cigarette. Enter* **NINA** *with breakfast.*) Good girl! Put it down there.

NINA (*surprised, cheerful*): Perhaps madam wasn't feeling well earlier?

DEA: Me, not feeling well? (*She sits down at the table and begins tucking in.*) Isn't there anything else to eat?

NINA: Oh yes. Right away, madam. (*Exits laughing.*)

(*Enter* **VULCAN**, *followed by* **ANNA**.)

VULCAN: I hope I'm not taking advantage . . . (*He stops short on the threshold in embarrassment.*) Oh, pardon me.

DEA: You are a complicated melancholic.

(**ANNA** *exits.*)

VULCAN: Thank you very much, and yourself?

DEA (*pointing to the tray*): Do you know what this is?

VULCAN (*stepping forward, peering cautiously at the tray*): A cup of hot chocolate. At first I didn't recognize . . .

DEA: The hot chocolate?

VULCAN: No, you. Because . . .

DEA: And what are these?

VULCAN: Rolls. You gave me permission to come round this morning, even before Countess Orsa got here, to give you a complete explanation . . .

DEA: Not on your life. I hate explanations. I'm eating. Can you ride?

VULCAN: Maybe you've changed your mind?

DEA: I never change my mind. I don't have a mind to change. What do I need one for? Anyway, if you're hungry . . . (*Reenter* **NINA**.) Oh, and here's the honey. Have breakfast with me at least.

(*Exit* **NINA**.)

VULCAN: That's not what I'm here for. When you're through eating, we can take up where we left off yesterday. By the way . . .

DEA: What's all this about yesterday? When I'm through eating, I'm going out. You couldn't direct me to a good place to buy doormats, could you?

VULCAN: What do doormats have to do with it?

DEA: Nothing. Why should they?

VULCAN: You see, I was right not to recognize you. Is it really you?

DEA: I believe so.

VULCAN: And now, when Countess Orsa gets here . . .

DEA: You know I can't stand women. If you're so keen on Countess Orsa, you stay here and meet her. See, now I'm through, and there's still lots of chocolate left, a clean cup, rolls, honey. All you need to stop being a . . . Oh, what did I call you?

VULCAN: I don't remember. I'm having trouble getting over my surprise.

DEA: You'll recover fine once you've eaten. It'll wipe that stunned look off your face. (**VULCAN** *sits down mechanically in front of the tray.*) This is not what you came for.

VULCAN: Oh, no.

DEA: So, thanks to me, the unexpected enters your life. There's cream here too.

VULCAN: Thank you.

DEA: What for?

VULCAN: I don't know. For the cream.

DEA: See how inept your answers are. You should have said, thanks for the unexpected. Goodbye, or au revoir, or . . .

VULCAN (*leaning toward her as if to detain her, almost beseeching*): But the meeting with Countess Orsa? You promised . . .

DEA: Let me go now.

VULCAN: Should I go with you?

DEA: No.

VULCAN: Should I go first? Should I follow?

DEA: I told you to stay here, and my mind is made up. Eat. That's your consolation prize. Then you can leave whenever you like. I intend to leave whenever I like, that is, right away.

VULCAN: This is a real mess. Because when she gets here, if I'm not here . . .

DEA: So stay then, you complicated man.

VULCAN: I can't. Marcolfo is expecting me.

DEA: Which Marcolfo would that be?

VULCAN: There's only one Marcolfo. He's a friend of mine.

DEA: You're a lucky man. I never met anyone called Marcolfo.

VULCAN: You don't know what you've been missing. He's waiting for me at the Looking Glass Bar.

DEA: Just a minute. Is he short, blond hair?

VULCAN (*testily*): Of course. Except, he's tall. Tall and dark.

DEA: Plump? Always wears dark blue.

VULCAN: Slim. Always wears light gray.

DEA: You see, we'll never agree. Is he smart?

VULCAN: A bit dim-witted actually.

DEA: I get the idea that you, me, and Marcolfo would make a fine bunch of friends.

(*Enter* **ANNA**.)

ANNA: Madam, the dressmaker sent to say she'll be here at noon.

DEA: Did you hear that?

VULCAN: Yes.

DEA: No. What this means is that a woman can never do what she feels like doing. Good bye, long walk; good bye, horseback riding; good bye, bistro. But not even the devil is going to stop me running one quick errand. (**VULCAN** *makes as if to get up.*) And where do you think you're going? What's the big idea? You can wait here. And Marcolfo is waiting there.

VULCAN: Who knows?

DEA: Of course he is. I can see him now. Poor chap. What an idea! Don't move a muscle. You'll see. I'll be back in no time. Keep your feet off the armchairs. (*she exits noisily, exclaiming*): Yes, that's it: a complicated melancholic.

(**VULCAN** *and* **ANNA** *are left on stage.*)

VULCAN (*after a pause during which he looks around the room*): So, you're the maid?

ANNA: The first maid.

VULCAN: I ask because I seem to have lost my bearings. The lady who just went out, who was she?

ANNA: You come to see her, and you don't know who she is?

VULCAN: Miss Dea. She was introduced to me yesterday, or rather, I was to her, at tea: a very elegant tea, at Countess Orsa's.

ANNA: I know. I dressed her for the occasion. A gray dress.

VULCAN: Yes. Very attractive! Dove gray, or no, doveneck-gray, when they move their necks like this, and coo. She was beautiful. I found her infinitely attractive. A veritable poem of softness, and she—she, Miss Dea, sweet as sweet could be, shy, a turtledove herself, she spoke in a very quiet voice, pitched very low, and when she looked at you her eyes were all liquid, and she said "yes," "yes." We asked her, Countess Orsa and I, in fact we agreed . . . no, I wouldn't go that far, but she said "yes" right away, "yes" to everything, gentle as an angel. This morning we were supposed to have the letter— but of course, you don't know what I'm talking about—a certain letter, very important. We said we would come here and discuss it, she said that all Orsa had to do was dictate it, you see, she said so herself, mind you, she did. I could see it was her, I didn't get the street wrong, the number, the floor. No, it's her alright, but . . .

ANNA: With a red suit, a white carnation, and a red hat.

VULCAN: Yes, very smart, but that's not what I meant: it's she who was changed. The way she acted, the way she talked, the way she moved. Her answers. Didn't you hear? Whatever happened to "yes, yes" and "just dictate the letter"? I can see now this is going to be more complicated than I thought. Anyway, it must be her; it is her, but my God, she's different; she's completely different from the way she was yesterday, timid and sweet . . .

ANNA: . . . dressed in dove gray, with a little hat with wings on it, two little wings.

VULCAN: That's right. And now . . .

ANNA (*interrupting*): You don't understand?

VULCAN: Me, understand? Not a thing.

ANNA: Madam is very sensitive.

VULCAN: What's that got to do with it? All women are very sensitive. More's the pity.

ANNA: Very sensitive to the clothes she wears. She's amazing! If she has on a bright-colored dress, she's bright, like today; if she has a timid dress on, she's timid, like yesterday: and she changes altogether, altogether. She talks differently. She's not the same person. One day I saw her in a Chinese outfit, and she began speaking perfect Chinese. If I were to put a black dress on her and a long black veil, she'd be off to the cemetery to blubber over one of the tombs.

VULCAN: Magnificent! Monstrous! But I still don't understand. Just a minute now. What about . . . ? (*He breaks off.*)

ANNA: Go on.

VULCAN: You must know. What I meant was, when she's all . . . You know. When she's taking a bath?

ANNA: Nothing.

VULCAN: What do you mean "nothing"?

ANNA: Like a baby. Just like a little baby. The well-behaved ones. The ones that don't cry, the ones that don't laugh, they just let you take care of them. Like I said, nothing. Then, no sooner do I slip on a dress than . . . well, all of a sudden she's just like the dress I put on her.

VULCAN: How extraordinary! It's so funny!

ANNA: Do you really think so? I'm used to it. I think it's like an illness.

VULCAN (*suddenly serious*): No, maybe it's not like an illness. And maybe it's not all that funny.

ANNA: Maybe not. But there's one thing for sure. That madam . . . that Miss Dea . . . that I create Miss Dea myself, two or three times a day.

VULCAN: But doesn't it ever happen, for instance, that when she's dressed one way she gives you an order, and when she changes, she contradicts herself.

ANNA: What difference would that make? I've been a lady's maid for twenty years, and none of them needed to change clothes to contradict themselves.

VULCAN (*after looking at her closely for a moment*): And what's your name?

ANNA: Anna.

VULCAN: Anna, you are an intelligent woman.

(*Enter* **NINA**.)

NINA (*a little scared*): There's a gentleman asking for another gentleman.

VULCAN: A fine state of affairs.

NINA: For another gentleman, whose name is Vulcan.

VULCAN: For me? What, is this where I live? Who knows I'm here? A creditor? An enemy?

ANNA: Please calm down. (*to* **NINA**) Ask him his name.

MARCOLFO (*from offstage*): It's me. Are you really there? It's me. Can I come in?

(**MARCOLFO** *sticks his head in at the door. Throughout the following scene,* **ANNA** *and* **NINA** *tidy up in the background, go offstage, come back on, etc.*)

VULCAN: Oh, it's you?

MARCOLFO (*from the doorway, relieved but embarrassed*): So it was true.

VULCAN: Where have you been?

MARCOLFO (*coming all the way in*): At the Looking Glass Bar. I was waiting for you.

VULCAN: Then what happened?

MARCOLFO: As a matter of fact, I blew a few curses in your direction.

VULCAN: They missed me.

MARCOLFO: I'll have to file a complaint. While I was waiting, I got a pain here . . . no, here; and I wanted to go look for a doctor, because one's health is not something to be taken lightly, but I had to wait there for you. So I started counting up to a hundred. I planned to leave when I got to a hundred-and-one. (*He starts counting rhythmically, beating time on his chest.*) One, two, three . . .

VULCAN: How far did you get?

MARCOLFO: To forty-five. When I got to forty-five—from now till the end of time, blessed be the number forty-five!—upon the stroke of forty-five there entered, like a breath of fresh air, no, like a ray of sunshine, no, more than that, like many, many, like a whole bunch of rays of sunlight borne on the South wind, like a sunlit garden, like a summer day, like . . .

VULCAN: I'm going out for a walk. I'll be back for the wrap-up.

MARCOLFO: A walk? You could take a round-the-world tour, before I got through delineating so much as a . . .

VULCAN: Okay, okay! Who was it came in? Only I think I already know.

MARCOLFO: I don't.

VULCAN: Who?

MARCOLFO: A woman. Fantastic. Beauty personified. Youth. Life itself. So there!

VULCAN: It was Miss Dea.

MARCOLFO: Dea? Is her name Dea? Yes, that's it. Dea.

ANNA: It was her for sure.

MARCOLFO: Her? Who is she?

VULCAN: Go on, you idiot.

MARCOLFO: You too!

VULCAN: What do you mean, "You too"?

MARCOLFO: Because she too.

VULCAN: What?

MARCOLFO: Let's proceed in an orderly fashion. She comes in, she takes one look at me, she starts laughing.

VULCAN: And what did you do?

MARCOLFO: I went like this. (*opening his mouth wide*)

VULCAN: Very impressive!

MARCOLFO: She was laughing, but with me not at me. Then she said, all in one breath: "You are tall, dark, slim, you are wearing a light gray suit. The only thing I need to know is whether your name is Marcolfo and whether you're a bit of an idiot."

VULCAN: And what did you say?

MARCOLFO: I said yes.

VULCAN: Two yesses, one on each count, or a single yes across the board?

MARCOLFO: I said "Yes, I'm Marcolfo," but, on the charge of being an idiot, I took the fifth.

VULCAN: You allowed her to judge for herself.

MARCOLFO: In any case, she did all the talking. What a voice! The voice of a hundred violas, the voice of the spirits of fire. She said: "So, it is you. Go to number such-and-such in so-and-so street"—here, in other words—"ring the bell, and have them give you a cup of hot chocolate . . ."

VULCAN: It's a mania of hers.

ANNA: Nina, bring some more chocolate.

(*Exit* NINA.)

MARCOLFO: At that point I interrupted: "You know, miss. I'm waiting for a fellow named Vulcan."

VULCAN: "A fellow"? How dare you call me a "fellow"!

MARCOLFO: She said: "Exactly. He's there, waiting for you." And I replied "Oh!"

VULCAN: Very impressive!

MARCOLFO: She had already gone, like . . . (*He pauses, seeing* NINA *come in with another tray. He sits down to eat without further ado.*) I accept, because it's good for the heart. How lovely she was! And I'm sure she still is. (*Exit* NINA.) The barman was laughing. But why did she send me here? The other customers were laughing too. Even the tropical fish in the fishtank were laughing. And what are you doing here? Does she live here? Is this her apartment? Did she sit in this armchair? Like this? Did she eat this roll? Like this? Oh! These are all her things . . .

(*A knock is heard at the door.*)

ANNA: Come in. (*The door opens gingerly.*) The doctor!

(*The* DOCTOR *enters slowly.*)

VULCAN (*aside*): Another visitor! Orsa will be here any moment. (*to the* DOCTOR) The lady's gone out. She's away. She's not here.

MARCOLFO (*with his mouth full*): She's not here. She's away. She's gone out.

DOCTOR: She's not here. Excellent. That way I can take my time examining her . . .

MARCOLFO: Examining her? So you're a real doctor?

DOCTOR (*to* MARCOLFO): And who might you be?

MARCOLFO: Marcolfo. I was just looking for a doctor. And here you are. Let me explain . . .

DOCTOR (*interrupting*):   Not so fast there, young man. I suppose you think . . . ?

MARCOLFO: I get it. Of course. I'll come to your office during . . .

DOCTOR: Oh no! You don't understand . . .

MARCOLFO: I get it. You only make house calls. Here's my card.

(*Hands him his visiting card.*)

DOCTOR: Very good. What time are you home?

MARCOLFO: Never. But . . .

DOCTOR: Perfect. So I can come anytime.

MARCOLFO: I don't get it.

DOCTOR: I have to come when you're not home. You don't understand what sort of a doctor I am. You consider me one of the usual necroscopes. No. Mine is a new specialty. It's all based on environmental semiotics. Normal medicine considers the body in isolation, as if it were a cadaver, albeit a living cadaver. Idiots! Then there are the metapsychiatrists, who treat the soul directly. Cretins! What is life? Body and soul together.

VULCAN (*aside*):   Orsa will be here any minute now!

DOCTOR: But where do they mingle? Where are the symptoms displayed, the residuals of life? Where do they show up? Where? (*menacingly to* **MARCOLFO**) I repeat, where?

MARCOLFO: Search me.

DOCTOR: In the environment! Idiot! Idiots!

VULCAN: In that case, allow me to introduce myself.

DOCTOR: Later. At the moment I'm talking. I'm not talking to you. I am talking to them. They're in the environment. Don't you see? And when can one diagnose the environment? When? (*threateningly to* **VULCAN**) When?

VULCAN (*terrified*):   On Mondays?

DOCTOR: It can be done when the patient is out. When the patient was there, but isn't there any longer. When the patient is present, his vital flux has a constant tendency to reabsorb some of the most valuable symptoms—those psycho-physical residues—from the environment, and to confuse them with kinetic pseudoresidues, with the plasmatic influences of the living being, etc. In that way the patient's presence disturbs the exophysical diagnosis—exophysical, mind you, not infrapsychical—of the residues. My own symptomology, mind you, is metacorporal, not metapsychical, as you imagine . . .

MARCOLFO: Who me? No, not me. Maybe he does. (*pointing to* **VULCAN**)

VULCAN: Who me? (*aside*) Any minute now Orsa will be here; Dea's out, it's all over.

DOCTOR: I don't examine patients: I examine patients' rooms. Miss Dea . . .

MARCOLFO: Miss Dea couldn't be healthier.

DOCTOR: You make me laugh. Nobody's healthy. What is an illness? It's a condition, which, spread over time and heightened in degree, leads to death. Therefore? Indeed, scientifically speaking, the healthier one feels, the sicker one is. But you could never understand.

MARCOLFO AND VULCAN (*both together*):   We understood perfectly.

DOCTOR: Let me get on with my examination. (*He goes over to the sofa bed.*) She slept here. (*He palpates the mattress.*) A trifle restless.

MARCOLFO: Her sleep!

DOCTOR (*bending to auscultate the pillows*): Faint residues of migraine. (*Holding up his watch, he takes the pulse of the arm of one of the chairs.*) Circulation regular. Heart strong.

MARCOLFO: Her heart!

DOCTOR (*shaking one of the drapes*): Stomach sound. (*Going over to the table, he runs his fingers along the rim of the tray, then, as if perplexed, glances in the direction of the other two, who are following his movements.*) Stand back! (*shouting*) Further back! (*The two of them are backed up into the two farthest corners of the proscenium arch.*) Further, further! What on earth? Here I can sense some kind of sexual disturbance of a strictly masculine type: maybe . . .

MARCOLFO: That's where I was eating.

DOCTOR (*with indifference*): In that case, everything's fine. (*As he speaks, he goes over to the screen, steps inside, and examines the mirror.*) I've told you before: too many sweets, Miss Dea: you must consider your intestines.

MARCOLFO: Her intestines!

DOCTOR (*emerging from the screened area*): All things considered, not bad. Reduce the morning medicine by two drops.

VULCAN: I beg your pardon. Who are you talking to? The environment?

DOCTOR: I'm talking to the maid. The maid is part of the environment. But she's an impure part. It takes a while to get through to the pure environment. A doctor must be able to communicate fully with his patient's environment, and not just to diagnose its symptoms, but to leave his prescriptions in it. I must be able to speak, so that the environment will be impregnated with my prescription; when the patient comes back, he or she senses what he or she has to do. Mark my words, gentlemen. The real authentic reform of medicine will come about when there are universities not only for doctors, but above all for patients. (*to* **VULCAN**) Do you imagine it's easy, being a patient? (*to* **MARCOLFO**) I will come, I will come to your house, maybe this very day. (*He studies the visiting card. With his back to* **MARCOLFO**, *walking away, he palpates the edges of the card, then he holds it to his ear.*) Yes, he has the makings of a reasonable patient, he's got the right stuff. (*He goes out, talking to himself, without saying goodbye.*) A bit of a dilettante for the moment, but with a dozen visits, I'll make him into a serious patient.

(*Exit* **DOCTOR**. **ANNA** *follows him off with the tray.* **VULCAN** *and* **MARCOLFO** *are left alone.*)

VULCAN: There's no time to lose. (*determined*) Listen, Marcolfo, we have important things to do here, secret things. You go away.

MARCOLFO: Away? But what will she say?

VULCAN: Nothing.

MARCOLFO (*practically in tears*): I shall never see her again!

VULCAN: Yes, you will. I promise we'll come round this very afternoon and visit you at your place.

MARCOLFO (*brightening up*):   Really! (*clouding over*) But I can't go home! What if the doctor comes?

VULCAN: If the worst comes to the worst, we'll go out as soon as he gets there. Go on. And then . . . then I'll leave you alone with her.

MARCOLFO: Alone? With her? I'll die before the afternoon comes.

(**ANNA** *comes back in.*)

VULCAN: I'll get you an invitation to the ball tonight at the "Polyhedric Palais." I know she's going. Now get out of here.

MARCOLFO: Oh my God! I'll die one more time before tonight.

VULCAN: Oh well, never mind. Get out of here.

(*He pushes him offstage.* **VULCAN** *is left alone with* **ANNA**.)

VULCAN: Anna, you're an intelligent woman.

ANNA: That's the second time you've said that.

VULCAN: I'm looking forward to telling you a third time. You've got to help me.

ANNA: How?

VULCAN: I'm thinking of that marvelous thing you told me about your mistress. When your mistress gets back, you must do me a favor, but she mustn't know why.

ANNA: I beg your pardon. In the first place, I have no earthly reason to do you a favor.

VULCAN: How severe you are, Miss Anna.

ANNA: Secondly, I could never do anything to harm my mistress.

VULCAN: I swear there's no harm.

ANNA: Or anything to displease her. You said: "Madam mustn't know why." And that's all I need to . . .

VULCAN: Let me explain. It's like this . . .

ANNA: It's none of my business, but go ahead. Make it brief.

VULCAN: Very brief. Countess Orsa has a lover. And as if that were not enough, this lover's name is Dorante. And as if that were not enough, this Dorante is a naval officer. The countess hasn't seen him for two years. He's arriving tonight, in the prince's entourage, and they'll be going to the ball at the "Polyhedric." Tomorrow morning he's leaving, shipping out on a long voyage. Count Orso is jealous, he's a tyrant; he can't go to the ball because he has a meeting of the Council of Twenty. It's no use at all the countess asking permission to go to the ball, either alone or in company, male or female. He's quite capable of locking her up in the house. Still . . .

(*Enter* **NINA**.)

NINA: Anna, can you come, there's a lady.

VULCAN: Oh my God! It's the countess.

ANNA: Coming.

(*The* **TWO MAIDS** *exit.*)

VULCAN (*left alone, he looks upstage toward the wardrobe*):   Maybe it's in there. (*He runs over,* *opens it rapidly, and spots a dove-gray dress.*) There it is. That's the dress she wore yesterday . . . But . . .

(*He closes the wardrobe quickly and moves away.*)

ANNA (*from offstage*):   Please come in then, you can wait for her here.

(*She shows* **COUNTESS ORSA** *in and leaves immediately.* **COUNTESS ORSA** *enters, out of breath.*)

COUNTESS ORSA: What are you doing here? Where's Dea? Did she give you the letter?
VULCAN: No. Let's wait for her. She'll be right back.
COUNTESS ORSA: Thank you very much! If she doesn't come back, if I don't see her right away, it'll be too late. (*anxiously*) Are you sure she'll be back?
VULCAN: Yes. But I'm afraid it looks as if she may not be willing to help you.
COUNTESS ORSA (*with a scream*):   No? Why not? What happened? Did somebody put her up to it? What shall I do, what shall I do?
VULCAN: It's a very weird thing . . . I hope . . .
DEA'S VOICE (*offstage*):   I'm hungry again.

(*Enter* **DEA**.)

COUNTESS ORSA: Dea, Dea my dearest! Here I am. I'm in your hands. I kneel before you.
DEA: No, no, get up, madam. What on earth are you doing?
COUNTESS ORSA: Oh, Dea. Yesterday you were the first to say: let's be friends. What's gotten into you now?
DEA: Sorry, I'd forgotten. Friend, friend, friend. Now that's settled. Oh, didn't that Marcolfo chap come?
VULCAN: Miss Dea . . .
COUNTESS ORSA: Dea, I don't recognize you. Don't you remember yesterday; don't you remember your promise?
DEA: Vaguely.
COUNTESS ORSA: The letter, the letter, Dea. My husband won't let me go if I ask him myself, not a chance; and still less if my other friends ask him: he hates all my women friends, he's suspicious of all of them. But now he trusts you, and only you, Dea; you charmed him with your winning ways. I believe he even fell in love with you a little yesterday. If you write me a letter like I told you, he'll let me come with you tonight. If you don't, he won't even let me look out the window, he's a monster . . .
DEA: So don't go. Why get all worked up about a ball at the Polyhedric anyway?
COUNTESS ORSA: But he'll be there. Him. To see him. To see Dorante. It's two years since I saw him. (**DEA** *is whistling through her teeth.*) Then he's going away, far, far away, for who knows how many years. I'm afraid that, if I don't see him tonight, I may never see him again. Oh, you don't understand.
DEA: No. To be perfectly frank, I'm not keen on this kind of thing. It's something I just can't get into. A lover. Two years? Two years. What's two years? Okay, I can almost

understand. But if you've gone without seeing him for two years, surely you can go without seeing him for another two. A lover. Find somebody else.

COUNTESS ORSA: It's terrible. But it's him, him, there's only him.

DEA: That's what I can't stand. I met your husband yesterday, I believe. Yes, I remember. Very well-mannered, couldn't have been nicer, and you want me to play a dirty trick like this on him as soon as I've met him. (*to* **VULCAN**, *who is sidling toward the door*) And where do you think you're going?

VULCAN: I was looking for Anna.

DEA: Just leave Anna be.

COUNTESS ORSA: You? So sweet and submissive . . .

DEA: Me sweet? Me submissive? Listen: it makes me sick to my stomach. Why should I do it? What's it got to do with me? Yesterday I didn't even know you, either of you; so when did I become so vitally important?

COUNTESS ORSA: That's just it. Fate sent you. It's destiny . . .

DEA: Destiny! Don't pester me. This fatal love stuff. It's a pest to me.

COUNTESS ORSA (*shrieking*): Murderess! Have you no feelings? Have you no heart? Oh, who ripped your heart out overnight? You wicked, wicked woman.

(*She flings herself to the ground sobbing uncontrollably. There is a loud knocking at the door. Then, without waiting to be let in, enter* **MADAME FIORA**, *the artistic dressmaker, along with* **ANNA**.)

DEA: Keep your voice down. (*to* **MADAME FIORA**) Come in, Madame Fiora. (*to* **ORSA**) It's my dressmaker, don't make a scene.

MADAME FIORA (*down-at-heel and fanatical*): A masterpiece! The masterpiece is ready at my shop. The masterpiece for you, for tonight.

DEA: Can you tell us what it's like?

MADAME FIORA: No. A great dramatist does not reveal the plot of his tragedy. The dress I have made for you is a tragedy. You come to my workshop at eight o'clock tonight, and we'll try it on. Between eight and midnight, we will make whatever alterations are necessary. But I already know it by heart.

DEA: What color is it? What's the style?

MADAME FIORA: I am telling you nothing. I came because I had an idea in the middle of the night for an addition to your white cape. I brought along everything I need, and I insist on fixing it right away. Mind you, the cape is not to wear with tonight's dress. Tonight, just a simple little fur.

VULCAN (*attempting to draw* **ANNA** *to one side*): Listen, Anna.

MADAME FIORA: I need Anna to help me. Bring me the white cape and come here and help me.

(**MADAME FIORA** *goes into the dressing room and unwraps a package she has brought with her.* **ANNA** *goes to the wardrobe, takes out the white cape, and goes to join* **MADAME FIORA**. *They set to work.* **ORSA** *is still on the ground sobbing from time to time.*)

DEA (*going over to* **ORSA**): Come on now, get up. Stop this nonsense. You start out thinking you're desperate, and before you know it you really are. Don't get me mixed up in these complicated muddles. Melancholical too. Yes, you and your muddles. Complicated and melancholical.

COUNTESS ORSA (*in tears*): But what about yesterday? Why, oh why were you ready to write yesterday? If my husband hadn't come back, you would have already written the letter yesterday, and . . .

DEA (*annoyed*): Always going on about yesterday! We seem to spend our entire lives listening to stuff about yesterday.

COUNTESS ORSA (*to* **VULCAN**): You tell her.

DEA: Precisely. Will you kindly explain to me what makes someone like you interested in this kind of scheming.

VULCAN (*an idea dawning on him*): Me? I'm not interested in anything. I was just admiring your beautiful dress.

MADAME FIORA (*from the other side of the screen*): Suit! Suit!

COUNTESS ORSA (*to* **VULCAN**): What's gotten into you? Don't tell me you're going to side with her too?

VULCAN (*signaling to* **ORSA** *to be quiet and speaking to* **DEA**): Your magnificent suit. Who made it for you?

DEA: Who do you think made it? Madame Fiora. Madame Fiora of the famous "Fiorà suits."

COUNTESS ORSA: Don't joke, my friend. Here I am dying.

VULCAN (*to* **DEA**): That princesse dress you had on yesterday though was ghastly.

(**MADAME FIORA** *stiffens and throws him a withering glance.*)

DEA: So, now you're a critic of the sartorial art?

(**MADAME FIORA** *is growling, so far under her breath.*)

COUNTESS ORSA: Oh, I beseech you . . . (*stretching her arms out imploringly*)

VULCAN: That gray thing. It was wrong from head to foot.

MADAME FIORA (*exploding in a shriek*): What is the matter with him? Is he crazy?

(*She rushes out of the dressing room, practically knocking the screen over.*)

VULCAN: Oh, forgive me. I had no idea . . .

MADAME FIORA (*speaking to* **DEA**): Stand up to him, say something.

DEA (*laughing*): I don't know. I didn't think it was all that bad.

MADAME FIORA: Not all that bad! Not all that bad!

(*Striding back and forth across the stage.*)

COUNTESS ORSA (*dramatically*): All of them, all ganging up on poor little me!

VULCAN: Forgive me, Madame Fiora, I was exaggerating. There was just one thing wrong with it. A little mistake, down at the flare . . .

MADAME FIORA: The flare? What flare are you talking about? The flare indeed! If you ask me you're the one that's flared. I'll give you flare! That's right, me, Madame Fiora! Where is it? Where is it? (*Rushing over to the wardrobe and throwing open the doors.*) Here it is. (*Grabbing the dress and closing the doors.*) Where is it, then, where's the mistake in the flare?

(*Shaking the dress in* **VULCAN'S** *face.*)

VULCAN: How should I know? Oh my God! There it is. I think. Yes, there it is.

(**DEA** *is laughing at both of them.* **ORSA** *is off in a corner weeping and wailing.*)

MADAME FIORA (*imperiously, to* **DEA**): Madam, come here at once. My honor's at stake.

(*Dragging her over to the screen.*)

DEA (*to* **VULCAN**): Tell her it's alright.

MADAME FIORA: No, no, no, no! It's too late for words . . . I refuse to put up with such a poisonous insinuation: I insist on clarification.

(*She has dragged* **DEA**, *who is laughing, behind the screen.* **VULCAN** *is very pleased with himself, and tries to make signs to* **ORSA**, *who doesn't see, fails to understand, and carries on weeping. Inside the dressing room, in a trice,* **MADAME FIORA**, *with* **ANNA'S** *help, takes off Dea's red outfit and puts on the gray one: the one previously described by* **VULCAN** *as "doveneck-gray": a princesse dress buttoned up to the chin with little buttons, which modestly but softly follows the lines of her body.*)

MADAME FIORA: Just a minute, just a minute, seeing we've come this far. (*She removes the red hat from* **DEA'S** *head, and, taking it from the hatrack, puts on the little gray hat with the two little wings.*) Out you go. (*Pushing* **DEA** *out onto the stage.*) Now where's that critic? Where's the flare? Where's the mistake?

(*A pause. Everyone looks at* **DEA**.)

DEA (*tenderly, sweetly, languidly, caressingly, softly, cooingly, fetchingly slow in her every glance, movement, word*): I think it's a really nice dress. Our Madame Fiora is so clever. (*She strokes* **MADAME FIORA** *on the cheek.*) Come on now, Vulcan dearest, be a good chap, you tell her. And where's Orsa? (*Seeing her in the corner in tears, she runs over to her.*) Oh, Orsa, what's the matter. Don't cry.

VULCAN: It's perfect. I was only joking. I just had to see it again. Forgive me. It's divine.

MADAME FIORA (*placated, but severe*): Jokes like that are in very bad taste.

DEA (*helping a stupefied* **ORSA** *to her feet*): Now, now. Come along. Tell us all about it. You too, Vulcan, come over here . . .

MADAME FIORA (*going back behind the screen, speaking to* **ANNA**): Just a few more stitches.

(*They go back to work.*)

DEA: . . . over here with us. We must do all we can to help this poor little thing. Was I a bit rude? Forgive me, I had something else on my mind. There are times when not even I can be sure what I'm doing or thinking. At times like that, just pay no attention.

Am I forgiven? Tell me, tell me we're friends. Give me a kiss. No, better than that. Like this. (*to* **VULCAN**, *who comes over beaming*) Yes, you too: but not like that. Like this. That's enough. Now then. So little Orsa wants to see her love. She wants to see him tonight. She wants Dea to help her. Is that it? What's he like, Dea's little friend's love? Tell me all about him. I love hearing about things like that.

COUNTESS ORSA (*still not believing her ears, with a trace of anxiety*): Will you write me the letter?

DEA: The letter? Oh yes, of course, I'll write you twenty letters. Tell me what I should say.

COUNTESS ORSA: Write it right away, right away. I have to have it when my husband comes home. Otherwise, he'll go out again without seeing it, and it'll be too late to do anything . . . Right away . . .

DEA: Yes, dear, right away. The wicked tyrant! I'll enjoy teaching him a lesson. Look, here's everything we need. Tell me exactly what you want me to say.

COUNTESS ORSA: You must say you'll come to pick me up tonight . . . No, that won't do . . . That you'll certainly . . .

VULCAN: Allow me. (*to* **DEA**) It would be better if you started off with a few friendly remarks: you know . . .

DEA: You're my friends. You tell me what to write. I'm so lazy when it comes to finding the right words. Here I am, ready and waiting. But, Vulcan, why should you get mixed up in something like this? It's because you're so kind. Other men are so naughty. For us women, it's a different story; it's something we do all the time.

VULCAN: Me? I'm an old friend of the countess . . . and then . . . and then, that's just the way I am, I can't help it. I just have to make myself useful to women, to women in love. It's like a mission. Once this case is over and done with, I'll find another. It's my fate. When I can lead an affectionate woman to the threshold of a faithful admirer, I'm happy. Do you need another explanation?

DEA: I understand. You revel in these things as much as I do. That's all there is to it.

(**COUNTESS ORSA** *is trembling with impatience.*)

VULCAN: So, if we revel in it so much, why don't you write, and as a reward I'll take you to tea this afternoon, guess where.

DEA: I have no idea.

VULCAN: To Marcolfo's.

DEA (*making a bit of an effort to remember, as she does every time she has to recall some detail connected with a previous personality*): Yes, that's right. Poor Marcolfo. Will we go? Will he be there?

VULCAN: He's expecting you, he's expecting you: I promised.

(*Meanwhile all three have sat down around a writing desk:* **VULCAN** *sits between the two women.*)

DEA: What a lot has happened today! At what time?

VULCAN: Whenever you like: at four o'clock.

COUNTESS ORSA: Let's get the thing written.

DEA: Yes, dear. Go ahead then.

VULCAN: Start like this: "My dear, my dearest" (*He stops for a moment, looking at* **DEA**.) Comma . . .

(*He looks blissfully, first at one and then the other, and prepares to continue.*)

CURTAIN

ACT 2

Marcolfo's place. Informal sitting room. Afternoon.

MARCOLFO *is discovered alone, in an informal smoking jacket, striking a Hamletic pose. He does not speak immediately.*

MARCOLFO: Will she come, or won't she come, that is the question. Or better: will they come? Will he come? (*with a voice full of dread*) Without her? Her? Them? And if she comes, if she really comes, oh then . . . then, maybe . . . Maybe I shouldn't be in my smoking jacket. (*calling*) Eurialus!

(*Enter Marcolfo's valet,* **EURIALUS**, *with an impassive expression.*)

MARCOLFO: Bring me my gray suit coat, please. (*Exit* **EURIALUS**.) These little everyday gestures do provide one with a salutary distraction from one's extreme mental anguish. (**EURIALUS** *returns with the suit coat and helps* **MARCOLFO** *on with it.*) There, that's better, isn't it? Now keep still and listen. Here are several hypotheses. First of all: There's a doctor coming, a new doctor.

EURIALUS: What doctor?

MARCOLFO: If he's new, you don't know him.

EURIALUS: Then how will I know he's the doctor you're waiting for?

MARCOLFO: You don't know him, but you'll know him. No doubt about it. A child would know him. He's the man people know, if ever there was one. If it's him, it can only be him; if it's somebody else, you'll know right away that it isn't him. That's all there is to it. Let me start again: if the doctor comes, and if nobody else has come before he comes, or, to be more precise, (*with a sigh*) no other woman . . . No, you're right, this way the whole thing's too formal; give me my smoking jacket again . . . (*He changes back, assisted by* **EURIALUS**, *who doesn't bat an eyelid.*) If the doctor comes, then, tell him I'm out.

EURIALUS: Yes, sir. I'll send him away.

MARCOLFO: Nooo. Let him in. You tell him: "My master's out," and he'll come in. He comes in here, and I stay out there; if he comes out there, I go round through the hall and come back in here. If you tell him I'm in, he'll go away. And that's that. Second hypothesis: if one or more persons should come, for example, a lady and gentleman, the gentleman being Vulcan, and you know him, or by herself, which is the same thing

. . . (*sighing*)—no, it's not the same thing, not for me; for you it's the same thing: in the line of duty, it's the same thing—in that case, be sure and tell her I'm in.

EURIALUS: And then the lady will go away.

MARCOLFO: No, no, no, no, no. She won't go away, she mustn't go away. If she goes away, hang on to her tight. She must come in.

EURIALUS: In that case, I'll tell her you're out.

MARCOLFO: No, no, no, no, no. Tell the lady I'm in, in, in, and she'll come in, in, in. That's all there is to it. Now I must make two supplementary hypotheses. First supplementary hypothesis: if the lady is already here when the doctor comes, then he can go away; just tell him I'm in, and he'll go away. Is that clear?

EURIALUS: Clear as a bell.

MARCOLFO: Second supplementary hypothesis. If the doctor is here, if he gets here first; in other words, if I'm in, but for him I'm out, which is why he's here, and she arrives in the meantime, then you must tell her . . . you must tell her . . . just wait a second, what should we do? (*The doorbell rings.*) The doorbell's ringing! Hurry up! Hurry up! Open the door! Did you get all that?

EURIALUS: Not a word!

MARCOLFO: Good. Go on then. No, the suit coat's better. Here. (*He takes off his smoking jacket and gives it to* **EURIALUS**. *The doorbell rings again.*) Hurry up now! (*Exit* **EURIALUS** *carrying both coats.*) Don't make any mistakes. (*He realizes he is in shirtsleeves.*) Oh God, I'm naked!

(**MARCOLFO** *scrunches himself up as if he were trying to be invisible. Enter the* **DOCTOR**, *followed by* **EURIALUS**, *carrying the two coats, one over each arm.*)

DOCTOR (*irritated at the sight of Marcolfo*): This is inconceivable! Your servant told me to come in. And here you are in. Is this any way to behave? Who do you take me for? You gave me an appointment this morning, and here we both are. I can't be expected to be at your beck and call. I'm not used to being kept waiting, to coming back some other time, to waiting on my clients' every whim. Either you leave at once . . .

MARCOLFO: Forgive me . . . An urgent matter . . . An unexpected commitment . . . Miss Dea . . .

DOCTOR: I don't want to know your business. I intend to abandon you to your fate. And a terrible fate it is! But all it takes is one look at that teapot handle to see you're cachectic. I tripped over the umbrella stand in the hall: an epileptoid umbrella stand if ever I saw one!

MARCOLFO: Listen, professor: Miss Dea . . .

DOCTOR: That's enough. You'd be well advised to stay away from that lady. If you only knew . . .

MARCOLFO: Oh, tell me about her . . .

DOCTOR (*supercilious*): Dyspepsia!

MARCOLFO: Well, at least that's something.

DOCTOR: And dysuria! And hereditary sterility! You'll be hearing from me. (*He stalks off* *in a fury. As he walks in front of* **EURIALUS***, he scornfully spits a word in his direction.*) Cyanotic! (*Exit.*)

(**MARCOLFO** *seems quite terrified and stands with his eyes fixed on the ground.* **EURIALUS** *stands behind him, impassive as ever. After a pause, he comes forward, holding out the two coats.*)

EURIALUS: Which one, sir?

MARCOLFO (*without turning to look at him, throwing out both hands at the same time, one with three fingers extended and one with two, as if he were playing odds and evens with himself. Then he silently adds up the fingers, and finally, all the time without turning round, says, with a disconsolate expression*): The one on the left.

(*He reaches his arms back for the coat to be put on.* **EURIALUS** *slips it on. It is the suit coat. Pause.*)

MARCOLFO: Did you hear what he said? What shall we do?

(*pause*)

EURIALUS: If you'll allow me, sir, I might make a suggestion.

MARCOLFO (*hopelessly*): Go ahead.

EURIALUS: Man is made up of body and soul. Place your body under the ascendancy of your soul. It's the only possible solution in calamitous times like these.

MARCOLFO (*turning to* **EURIALUS***, calm and consoled*): That sounds like a capital idea. Take that jacket away. Now my course is clear: whoever shows up, show them in. (*Exit* **EURIALUS**. **MARCOLFO** *returns to his Hamletic pose.*) She will come, she won't come. A daisy would be a godsend right now.

(*Pause. The doorbell rings.* **MARCOLFO'S** *face lights up. Enter* **DEA** *and* **VULCAN**.)

VULCAN (*gaily*): But of course. Marcolfo, I promised, and I'm a man of my word. (*He motions toward* **DEA**.)

DEA (*wearing her dove-gray dress*): Was I right to come?

MARCOLFO: Miss . . . Madam . . . Oh my God, please forgive me . . . I'm not sure . . .

VULCAN: Come along now. Miss Dea. The Looking Glass Bar. Hot chocolate.

MARCOLFO: Exactly. I'm at my wit's end.

DEA: Oh no. You're so cute. I wonder who you were expecting. I wonder what cute thoughts you were thinking, all alone here.

MARCOLFO: Exactly. No, no, absolutely not. I was thinking of you; no, of the lady in the Looking Glass Bar . . . Yes, that's it, you. You.

DEA: It's a funny thing about women. All it takes is a new hat to alter our features.

MARCOLFO: So, is it you? Are you here? Are you in my house?

VULCAN: Well, it certainly looks that way.

MARCOLFO: Oh God, here at my place, here with me, all alone.

VULCAN: And what about me?

MARCOLFO: You, yes, that's right, you, you, my only friend in the world. Forgive me if I'm in my smoking jacket.

VULCAN: You're not in your smoking jacket.

DEA: Oh, isn't he cute!

MARCOLFO: Exactly. But I was, I was earlier.

VULCAN: Me too. This morning.

MARCOLFO: No, not me. Later than that. A few minutes ago. It's unforgivable.

DEA: I forgive you. I forgive everything.

VULCAN: Consequently, we could even sit down.

MARCOLFO: Of course, of course. Here we are. There we are. Over there. Good. Now we can talk.

DEA: Let's talk.

MARCOLFO: Madam.

DEA: Sir.

VULCAN: A bit more variety. Please.

MARCOLFO: I must say, I'm a little confused. The pleasure . . . But is it really you?

DEA: There you go. You really are a singular chap.

MARCOLFO: That's all there is to it.

VULCAN: Listen. I shall have to go soon.

MARCOLFO (*immediately*): Oh, what a shame!

DEA: Now that wasn't nice.

MARCOLFO: Don't get me wrong. I'll let you into a secret: I'm shy.

VULCAN: But before I go now, pay attention. It's understood that tonight all four of us are going to the party at the "Polyhedric Palais."

MARCOLFO: All four of us. You, me, and her: all four of us.

VULCAN: And Orsa.

MARCOLFO: Oh my God, who's Orsa?

VULCAN: That's irrelevant. Just remember: at eight Dea's going to the dressmaker's, and she'll stay there. At about eleven, Count Orso will take Countess Orsa there.

MARCOLFO: You mean, to the dressmaker's.

VULCAN: And that, God willing, is where he'll leave her. I'll come and pick you up first, and we'll go keep a lookout from the café across the street. When the ladies come out, we'll be able to see them through the window. And we'll join them.

MARCOLFO: You've got the whole thing planned to a tee.

DEA: Count Orso won't change his mind?

VULCAN: Impossible.

DEA: The letter worked like a charm.

VULCAN (*smiling*): You really made me work for that letter! First yes, then no. Calming down Orsa, rushing off to look for you, who luckily have gone back to being . . . nice.

DEA: Really? You poor thing! You'll have to forgive me. Whoever thought I'd get the chance to do that darling woman a favor!

VULCAN: And what about me?

DEA: Yes, you too.

MARCOLFO: And what about me?

DEA: Everybody. Everybody's so nice. We must be as good as gold to everybody.

VULCAN (*getting to his feet*): Well, I must be off. (*to* **DEA**) You can stay.

MARCOLFO (*half rising*): I'll come with you. No, I'll stay. No . . .

DEA: But of course you must stay. You wouldn't want to leave me here alone? Can I offer you a cup of tea?

MARCOLFO: You? No, let me.

DEA: We have everything we need over there. Let me do it.

VULCAN: Goodbye, then. I'll come and pick you up. Be ready.

(*Exit* **VULCAN**, *leaving* **MARCOLFO** *and* **DEA** *alone. Pause.*)

MARCOLFO: There you are.

DEA: Really?

(*pause*)

MARCOLFO: Do you like that cushion?

DEA: Oh yes, very much.

(*pause*)

MARCOLFO: And do you like the curtains?

DEA: Oh yes, very much. And I like tea too.

MARCOLFO: Me too. (*They both look at the samovar.*) Should we make some?

DEA: Let's make some.

MARCOLFO: It won't make itself. We have to make it.

DEA: Us? We have everything we need. Oh, how nice.

MARCOLFO: How nice. You said you wanted to make it.

DEA: Of course. There's not a lot to it. All you have to do is light the flame. There.

MARCOLFO: Put a little tea there.

(*Meanwhile, neither one of them makes a move.*)

DEA: Wait for the water to boil.

MARCOLFO: Let's wait.

DEA: Then pour it over the tea.

MARCOLFO: And it's made.

DEA: And it's made.

MARCOLFO AND DEA (*both together*): So let's drink it.

(*They both laugh: then the laughter fades off into silence.*)

MARCOLFO: Do you like it?

DEA: Oh yes, very much.

MARCOLFO (*with infinite sadness*): If everything you like, you like the way you like this tea, I'm not sure I want you to like me.

DEA: That was a very nice thing for you to say.

MARCOLFO: Me? I didn't understand it.

DEA: I'm not very energetic.

MARCOLFO: Always?

DEA: Always? (*As though repeating the word to herself so as to understand it.*) Al-ways.

MARCOLFO: Me too, quite often.

DEA: Then we'll be friends.

MARCOLFO: Do you think so? And to think that yesterday, no, this very morning, I didn't even know you! And now, here you are, and here you'll be for hours. And then tonight.

DEA: Tonight.

MARCOLFO: This morning I go out all alone—I'm practically always alone—and I run into Vulcan, I meet you . . .

DEA: And tonight you'll meet Orsa. I didn't meet Vulcan and Orsa myself until yesterday.

MARCOLFO: And tonight we'll all be together at the ball, like characters in the third act of a play.

DEA: And we'll be friends.

MARCOLFO: Yes, that's the main thing. I have no friends. No lady friends either. This morning I liked you a lot.

DEA: Oh really! And what about now?

MARCOLFO: Excuse me. No. Yes.

DEA: I see. Not now. Not any more. (*sulking*)

MARCOLFO: That's not true, that's not true. I swear it's not true. How pretty you were, how vivacious! . . . Oh, excuse me again.

DEA: You excuse yourself quite a lot!

MARCOLFO: It's my fate. My friends . . .

DEA: You said you didn't have any.

MARCOLFO: The people who claim they're my friends. They treat me like an idiot, in a way. In fact I am an idiot. But, when you get right down to it, it's only because I let myself be treated like one. It's convenient for me. It's inertia. Like the tea. Intelligent things occur to me now and then, but I don't bother saying them. But the stupid things say themselves; they just come right out. People are happy being with idiots like me; they treat us nicely; we bring good luck. It's very relaxing to be an idiot.

DEA: You are a peculiar fellow.

MARCOLFO: When I saw you this morning, I felt really stupid. When you ran off, and I was supposed to see you again, all I could think of was showing you how smart I was. I should have known I was asking for trouble! When I rang your doorbell, I was still bowled over. (*Completely engrossed in the memory, he no longer looks at her.*) I saw all your things. It was as if I were seeing you everywhere, so glowing, so vibrant, so aggressive, oh! so magnificently aggressive . . .

DEA: Vibrant, me? Me, aggressive?

MARCOLFO: Yes, I . . . (*He looks at her and breaks off.*) It's true. Who knows. You? I'm a bit confused. Maybe your presence upsets me. Let me think. Who knows? It was this morning. And at a certain point I realized they had sent me away, God knows why. They told me you would come here, God knows why. Oh, what a time I had waiting! (*He has* *stopped looking at her again.*) I couldn't bring myself to believe it was true, I couldn't believe that here . . . here . . . this . . . (*gesture toward the room*) could ever hold all that light, all your gaiety. And I still had this enormous desire to be intelligent, incredibly intelligent, when I welcomed you here, to shower you with a flood of intelligence, to surround you with an air . . .

DEA: But you gave me a wonderful welcome, dear.

MARCOLFO (*looking at her again, still perplexed; then becoming calm and adapting almost unconsciously*): You are too kind. I feel that with you I can also be stupid.

DEA: You are a charming fellow, and the things you say are splendid.

MARCOLFO: I don't think that's the most precise description. But what does it matter? It's funny how pleasant it is to talk about oneself. I never noticed before. It never happened to me. Why don't you speak too, talk about yourself. What's made you become so calm?

DEA: I told you I'm lazy.

MARCOLFO: Maybe I understand. You must be someone who talks in the morning. Some people talk more at night. That must be it. I know that some people's intelligence comes out bit by bit as evening approaches, and for others it's the opposite.

DEA: Why do you think so much about intelligence?

MARCOLFO: Isn't it normal? Oh my God, I don't know. If I ask myself the question, I don't know any more. Please talk, talk about yourself.

DEA: What do you want me to say? About me? Here I am, you can see me. What more do you want?

MARCOLFO: I can't explain. Talking about yourself means talking about all sorts of things, from the inside; what you used to be like, yesterday, today; what you thought you'd find and what you found; what you hope for tomorrow; and then, bit by bit, you understand yourself, you make other people understand you.

DEA: I'm fine the way I am. Yesterday, I must have been the same as today, don't you think? What does "yesterday" mean? And "tomorrow"? (*sighing a sigh that rises up from unplumbed depths*) You make me work so hard!

MARCOLFO: You see? That's good. I really like you a lot. That's good too.

DEA: Yes, I think so.

MARCOLFO: Liking each other, it's like talking about yourself. That's when the real you comes out; you feel more you; you feel more sure of yourself . . . Maybe I'm not explaining myself clearly. Why are you shivering?

DEA: Perhaps I'm a bit cold.

MARCOLFO: Do you want me to . . . Wait. You stay still there, good, here we go. Look what a big shawl. (*As he speaks,* **MARCOLFO** *takes a large ash-colored shawl from one of the sofas.*) It hides you completely. Look. All the way down to your feet. All the way up to your chin. Dea's all gone!

DEA (*breathing out the words, as if from a sudden distance, and continuing the same way till the end of the act*): I'm still here, I'm still here.

MARCOLFO: You're almost gone. Lean your head back. Should I take your hat off? No, don't move. Let me do it. That's the way, gently does it. What beautiful hair you have! How lovely you are! You're more lovely than ever. How do you feel?

DEA: I feel fine. I'm so tired. I feel like I'm ebbing away. Come close to me. Closer.

MARCOLFO: Like this? At your feet.

DEA: Yes, say something else. Right away.

MARCOLFO: Don't talk like that, I get confused. What do you want me to say?

DEA: I don't know. Whatever. Just to hear your voice.

MARCOLFO: Do you want me to tell you a story.

DEA: Yes.

MARCOLFO: A story. I don't know any stories. (*desperately*) Not even one. Oh my God, oh my God. (*improvising*) There was once a cat, who was asleep by the fire. Wait. The fire was out. But the cat thought it was burning. That there were still some embers. Ehm . . . Yes, he thought there were two small embers at the back of the fireplace, because the fireplace was very big. What then? (*He thinks.*) Then, yes, then the cat came a bit closer, slowly—but not too close—and he realized that instead of the embers there was another cat, oh, it was the eyes of this other cat . . . Now it turns out that this other cat had also taken the eyes of the first cat for two embers. (*He sighs.*) So then what? Just a minute. Well, there are two possibilities: either they were happy with the situation or they weren't. That's the crux of the matter. Let's see . . . Are you asleep? Are you asleep?

DEA: No. Come closer.

MARCOLFO: Closer than this. How can I? Are you still cold? Let me feel your hand. Oh, how hard it is to find a hand under a shawl. Your hand's warm. It's not true, you know, that I'm such an idiot. What long nails you have! Just like that cat. I wonder what happened to it. Closer? Dea, Dea, let's be in love.

DEA: Yes? I think so. Maybe . . . What? Let's be in love?

MARCOLFO: Yes, yes, Dea.

DEA: How do you do it?

MARCOLFO: We put our faces together, like this. Then I say: "My dearest, I love you . . ." And then you say: "My dearest . . ."

DEA: "My dearest . . ." and then?

MARCOLFO: Then you say: "I"

DEA: "I" . . . "I" . . . (*completely exhausted*) It's so hard.

MARCOLFO: Can't you . . .

DEA: It doesn't mean anything. (*pause.*)

CURTAIN

ACT 3

A public room at the "Polyhedric Palais" communicating with other areas. Upstage right a balustrade overlooking a ballroom offstage below; next to the balustrade, a stairway leading down to the ballroom.

Upstage center, a doorway leading off toward other public rooms. Downstage left front, a doorway leading to the outside lobbies. Downstage right front, a smaller staircase leading up to the private rooms above. An open entrance without a door halfway down on the left. In the left-hand corner downstage front, a long buffet table with refreshments, almost completely cleared: all that remain are a few sandwiches and a bottle or two. Here and there, scattered armchairs and a sofa. It is night.

Before the curtain goes up, Music 1 begins and we hear a few musical phrases in a jazz style.[2] *Shortly after the curtain goes up, through the entrance halfway down on the left, four lines of alternating men and women, holding hands in a chain as in a quadrille, enter, circle the stage dancing and miming, and exit through the upstage center exit. They are preceded by a group of musicians playing as they go. As they stomp along, the members of the procession cry out, in an excited, childish, neurotic rhythm:* "Supper is served, supper is served." *Some of them are masked, or wearing dominos or other disguises, others are not. A number of the men and women in evening dress are also wearing painted cardboard masks. The procession goes out backstage headed to the right.*

A little to one side, a **STOUT LADY** *wearing a dilapidated domino and a silk eyemask and a* **YOUNG WOMAN** *also wearing a domino but without a mask stand watching. In another part of the stage, a group made up of the* **ELDERLY WAITER**, *the* **HATCHECK GIRL**, *and the* **BELLBOY**.

DILAPIDATED DOMINO (*observing the procession as it exits*):   The third from the last is one of ours. Not bad.

YOUNG WOMAN: I'd like to dance.

DILAPIDATED DOMINO: That's enough. We're not here to have fun. We're here for professional reasons.

YOUNG WOMAN: Should we go out there too?

DILAPIDATED DOMINO: First, let me take a look downstairs.

(*From offstage come the last faint echoes of the procession's chant.*)

ELDERLY WAITER (*imitating the chant*):   "Supper is served, supper is served." They'll be at it for an hour. We'll get an hour's rest.

HATCHECK GIRL (*looking down over the balustrade*):   And what about that lot? They must have had supper at home.

ELDERLY WAITER: Or else they're not having supper. (*imitating Mussolini*) "Supper is not a necessity."

HATCHECK GIRL (*motioning to the smaller staircase on the right*):   Are you here to keep an eye on the private rooms upstairs?

ELDERLY WAITER: All occupied. The prince makes merry. His entourage cools its heels.

HATCHECK GIRL: You are the only ones who can go up there. I'd love to take a peek.

ELDERLY WAITER: As for me, I couldn't care less. It's past my bedtime. Shut that door, young fellow, so there's less noise. (*The* **BELLBOY** *goes to close the door through which the*

---

2. Bontempelli composed his own music for act 3. It is reprinted here following the play. When it should be played is indicated in the text. —Trans.

procession exited. The noise that had faded is cut off completely. Music 1 stops. The **WAITER** *turns to the* **HATCHECK GIRL**.) Now you get back to your cloakroom. (*She exits through the door downstage left.*) Young fellow, you stay out there with her. (*contemptuously*) And here, here are the chips for the grand quadrille of the monks and the devils: the gray ones are the monks, the red ones the devils. (*As he is talking, he hands him the chips, along with the bags to put them in.*)

BELLBOY: Can I keep a red devil's chip for myself?

ELDERLY WAITER (*even more contemptuously than before*): What idiocy! Better leave that kind of thing to those numbskulls.

(*The* **BELLBOY** *goes off downstage left. The* **ELDERLY WAITER** *begins to snooze in an armchair in a corner near the smaller stairway on the right.* **VULCAN** *enters through the door on the left.*)

VULCAN: Over here, over here.

(**MARCOLFO** *follows through the same entrance.*)

MARCOLFO: What's your hurry?

DILAPIDATED DOMINO (*peering over the balustrade*): There! That's one of ours over there.

YOUNG WOMAN: The yellow? Yes, that's the actress.

DILAPIDATED DOMINO: Oh my God! What a disgusting corsage! She'll get a piece of my mind tomorrow.

VULCAN (*staring at the* **DILAPIDATED DOMINO**): I know that voice.

MARCOLFO: I don't.

VULCAN: Who on earth could it be?

(**COUNTESS ORSA** *rushes in through the entrance on the left.*)

COUNTESS ORSA (*agitated*): Is he through there? Or down there? Let's get a move on.

MARCOLFO: Where's Dea?

COUNTESS ORSA (*going over to look down from the balustrade*): Oh my God, Dea's stopped again, at the hatcheck. As if she hadn't held us up enough already! (*coming back over to the others*)

DILAPIDATED DOMINO (*to the Young Woman*): That's not one of ours. Let's go to the dining rooms.

(*They exit together upstage.*)

VULCAN: Whose voice is that? (*to* **ORSA**) You were saying?

COUNTESS ORSA: What time is it?

VULCAN: One o'clock. Dea's cost us an hour.

MARCOLFO: If she hadn't cost us an hour, it would still be midnight.

VULCAN: We thought we'd die in that café.

COUNTESS ORSA: And there I was, all by myself in that dressmaker's waiting room! She took forever to work on Dea!

MARCOLFO: So what's it look like, this famous dress? All the way over here, Dea never so much as opened her mouth, or her fur coat. With her head all muffled up too. What was the matter with her?

COUNTESS ORSA: I haven't seen it. I know as much about it as you do. Shall we go?

MARCOLFO: But what about Dea?

COUNTESS ORSA: Dea, Dea! You wait for her. And Vulcan, you come with me.

(*They are just about to leave, when* **DEA** *enters from the left. She is wearing a very tight-fitting dress of glittering green scales. The dress trails off in a long pointed tail. From the décolletage, some kind of serpent coils upward, spiraling a couple of times around her neck. The head of the serpent nestles in her hair, as part of her hairdo.*)

DEA (*her eyes darting, her voice sibilant*): Ssss. Aren't you waiting for me?

(*The three of them look at her for a moment in astonishment.*)

COUNTESS ORSA: Very nice! Shall we go in then?

VULCAN: A perfect cobra!

MARCOLFO (*extremely embarrassed*): I would never have recognized you.

DEA: Sssorry if I causssed a delay. Preciousss time wasssted. But maybe it was better for everyone.

MARCOLFO: Sybilline!

VULCAN: Serpentine!

COUNTESS ORSA (*on tenterhooks*): Let's go look for Dorante.

DEA: What's the use of looking? He could be anywhere, in any of the rooms.

COUNTESS ORSA: He isn't here, that's for sure. I'll go look in the others.

DEA: Yesss. You go with her. She's on her lassst legs. In the meantime, I'll stay here. I'll stay here, and if he should pass by, I'll stop him, and I'll send him to you. Yesss, my dear.

MARCOLFO: Good idea. I'll stay here too.

VULCAN: Whatever happens, this is our meeting point.

(**VULCAN** *and* **ORSA** *exit upstage center. Music 2 is heard briefly for the first time. The strains of this jazz music will be heard intermittently for the rest of the act, carried from rooms near and far, now from one side now from the other.* **DEA** *and* **MARCOLFO** *are left onstage.* **DEA** *takes a seat.* **MARCOLFO** *remains standing nearby.*)

MARCOLFO (*fumbling for a topic of conversation*): So, you . . . ah, so you know this Dorante.

DEA: No.

MARCOLFO: Me neither.

DEA: I know.

MARCOLFO: So how are we supposed to recognize him if he comes by?

DEA: What does it matter? You ssseem very concccerned.

MARCOLFO: You look very attractive. Earlier today you were even prettier. I mean, I don't know. And what about this morning? I'm totally confused.

DEA: You sound like your friend Vulcan.

MARCOLFO: Could be. Friends do end up imitating each other.

DEA: Friends? Are you good friends?

MARCOLFO: Yes, he's the only friend I have.

DEA: Oh, yesss? (*in a confidential whisper*) I wouldn't trust him.

MARCOLFO: Not trust him?

DEA: Don't trust anybody.

MARCOLFO: But not him!

DEA: Ssss . . . Darling, how can you be so naive.

MARCOLFO: I swear I don't understand you.

DEA: Don't tell him I told you that.

MARCOLFO (*with an effort*): No.

DEA: We two, we must be friends.

MARCOLFO: Oh yes, great friends. We said so earlier.

DEA: Really. Oh, yes. (*cajolingly*) Now listen here, if you really love me . . .

MARCOLFO: Oh, really, really I do . . . I think.

DEA: Go and catch up with Orsa and Vulcan in those rooms through there. Don't ask me to explain. But don't let them come back right away. Find a way to delay them . . .

MARCOLFO: How am I supposed to do that?

DEA: You'll find a way, if you really love me.

MARCOLFO: Yes. I'm still thinking about you, so sweet and angelic . . . I mean . . . (*He looks at her with a perplexed expression.*) Tomorrow I must see a doctor. (*putting a hand to his forehead*)

DEA: If they want to look around, have them look around downstairs, for a while at least . . . It's no good their looking for him here: all there are here (*motioning to the left*) are the anterooms.

MARCOLFO: And what then?

DEA: Then I'll join you, or after a while you can join me. Don't ask questions for now, if you really love me. And sssh, don't say anything, anything at all . . . to them, if you really love me. This is all because . . .

MARCOLFO (*anxiously*): Because of what?

DEA: Jussst becaussse. You'll understand later . . . Sssh . . . Go on now, it's a test. Get going. (*She pushes him off through the upstage center entrance. Pause.*)

DEA (*going over to the* **ELDERLY WAITER**): Ssss! (*He continues to sleep.*) Ssss! Ssss!

ELDERLY WAITER (*waking up and addressing her in French*): Oh, pardon, madame.

DEA: Ssss! Do you recognize me?

ELDERLY WAITER (*without looking at her*): No.

DEA (*handing him some money*): This is for you.

ELDERLY WAITER (*still without looking at her*): Oh yes, I believe I do recognize you.

DEA: Where's the prince?

ELDERLY WAITER: The prince?

DEA: Yes, with his adjutant. Lieutenant Dorante.

ELDERLY WAITER: If madam is already fully informed, there's no point in my being discreet.

DEA: Where are they?

ELDERLY WAITER: To tell you the truth, I don't know. (**DEA** *gives him more money.*) Oh yes, now I remember. They're up there. (*motioning to the private rooms upstairs*)

DEA: Is anyone with them?

ELDERLY WAITER: A few respectable gentlemen . . . a few melancholy ladies.

DEA: Will they be coming down? Will they pass by here?

ELDERLY WAITER: It's unlikely. They were dancing downstairs till a short while ago. Now they're dining . . . They'll make their own arrangements . . . I don't know, maybe they'll gamble.

DEA: Go and ask Lieutenant Dorante to come down here at once. Tell him that there's a lady waiting. He'll understand.

ELDERLY WAITER: You couldn't have put it more clearly. (*He starts on his way.*)

DEA: And mind you don't breathe a word!

ELDERLY WAITER (*pausing a moment, mustering all of his dignity*): Madam, I have been practicing this profession for forty years. (*Exit right.*)

(*Left on her own for a few moments,* **DEA** *slithers and hisses around the stage. Enter* **DORANTE**, *wearing tails, and the* **ELDERLY WAITER**, *by the staircase on the right.*)

DORANTE (*bounding in, animated and joyfully expectant, he suddenly stops and turns to the* **ELDERLY WAITER**): Where is she?

ELDERLY WAITER: There she is.

DORANTE: But . . .

ELDERLY WAITER: With your honor's permission (*pointing to the armchair*) I'll go back to sleep. (*He sits down and closes his eyes.*) I'm asleep.

DORANTE (*to* **DEA**, *who has come over to his side*): Excuse me, madam, but there must be some mistake.

DEA: I don't believe so. Are you Dorante?

DORANTE (*evasively*): I don't know . . .

DEA: You don't know who you are? Ssss!

DORANTE: I know who I am. I don't know if I'm the person you're looking for, because . . .

DEA (*interrupting*): Because you're not in uniform?

DORANTE: Oh!

DEA: You're not in uniform, because the prince is here incognito.

DORANTE: Go on.

DEA: But tomorrow you'll have to wear your uniform when you go away. And you'll be away for three years.

DORANTE: Well?

DEA: And just to show you I'm fully informed. Ssss. (*whispering*) Orsssa sssent me.

DORANTE: Orsa!

DEA: What fire! Are you very much in love?

DORANTE: Madam, I beseech you, explain yourself.

DEA: I'm a friend, Orsa's friend. I know everything, about her, about you.

DORANTE: Oh my God! Is she ill?

DEA: She couldn't be better.

DORANTE: She couldn't come?

DEA: That's it.

DORANTE: The Count wouldn't give her permission?

DEA: He gave her permission . . . but . . .

DORANTE: Oh, tell me.

DEA: I'm sorry to see you so passionate. How much in love you are! You're so young and naive. I suffer for you.

DORANTE: But it's I who am suffering. You're torturing me. If you don't tell me . . .

DEA: What do you want me to tell you, my poor friend?

DORANTE: Isn't she coming? Won't I see her? What happened?

DEA: Oh God, she may come . . . later . . . For the moment, she's making the most of it . . . Her husband's so jealous . . .

DORANTE: Making the most of it?

DEA: Count Orso's gone to a meeting of the Council of Twenty. He sent Orsa here with me . . . Orsa gets so little freedom. That's why I said she's making the most of it.

DORANTE: Doing what?

DEA: Oh. Ssss. My mission is very painful. It's distasteful, isn't it? But friendship demands it. On the other hand, when a woman hasn't seen her lover for years—two years—it's only human, come on, you can't really blame her . . .

DORANTE: What are you talking about?

DEA: Help me a little. What am I going to do?

DORANTE (*pacing, visibly upset, struggling to contain himself*): So that's it. Orsa sent you to give me a message . . .

DEA: Yesss. A message.

DORANTE: A message . . . saying she's no longer interested.

DEA: That's it.

DORANTE: So why did she write me yesterday and again today?

DEA: Ssss . . . She didn't have the courage. Knowing you were coming. She was so upset, poor Orsa. She had decided to come, to conquer her feelings.

DORANTE: Oh really! So what happened?

DEA: She didn't come.

DORANTE: She made the most of it.

DEA: Very good!

DORANTE: And she went . . .

DEA: Yes, that's it. With . . .

DORANTE: With someone else.

DEA: Yes.

DORANTE: Who?

DEA: Someone.

DORANTE: And later she'll come here, you said? But you must tell me . . . Why will she come here?

DEA: Oh my God. Because she has an appointment with me . . . The other man knows. Orsa couldn't tell him, the other man, that you were here!

DORANTE: Oh, splendid!.

DEA: What do you mean, splendid?

DORANTE: Splendid, splendid!.

DEA: What do you plan to do?

DORANTE: Me?

DEA: Yes, you.

DORANTE: Why should I tell you? Why should I do anything? And if I do do something, why should I plan to do it first? The things we do without planning to are the best. You know what I mean? On the spur of the moment.

DEA: Ssss . . . Oh my goodness.

DORANTE: Now listen. First of all, I must see her. Orsa.

DEA: Just a moment. May I make a request? I ask you to do one of the following.

DORANTE: Let's hear the choices.

DEA: Are you calm?

DORANTE: Yes.

DEA: One thing or the other: either you leave at once, like a sensible man, without seeing Orsa . . .

DORANTE (*without waiting for her to go on*): I'll take the other.

DEA: But you haven't heard it yet.

DORANTE: The other. I insist on seeing Orsa.

DEA: See her then. But in that case, I beseech you, don't even let on that you met me. Can I count on you?

DORANTE: Yes.

DEA: I prefer not to be there when you meet Orsa.

DORANTE: I can understand why.

DEA (*cocking an ear*): So, for the moment, go back upstairs. Come back down again later. I'll be gone shortly . . . maybe before Orsa gets here.

DORANTE: How will I know that you're gone?

(*The voices of* **VULCAN** *and* **MARCOLFO** *are heard offstage.*)

DEA (*hastily*): I'll let you know. (*indicating the* **ELDERLY WAITER** *who is snoring faintly*)

DORANTE: Very well.

DEA: Now get going.

(**DORANTE** *bows and retreats the way he came in. As he passes in front of the* **ELDERLY WAITER**, *the latter, continuing to snore and without opening his eyes, gets up and bows, then goes back to sleep.*

Some of the crowd who passed through at the start of the act come back onstage, making even more noise than before, and exit by the stairs leading down to the ballroom. Enter ORSA, VULCAN, *and* MARCOLFO *through one of the entrances.*)

COUNTESS ORSA (*tragic*):   He's not here!

MARCOLFO (*discouraged*):   He's not here!

VULCAN (*conclusive*):   He's not here!

COUNTESS ORSA: Nowhere. (*peering around*) Maybe? (*She runs toward the stairway leading up to the private rooms.*)

ELDERLY WAITER (*opening his eyes*):   Closed, madam. Closed for remodeling. (*Meanwhile,* DEA *takes* VULCAN *to one side.*)

DEA: Vulcan.

VULCAN: What is it?

DEA: I think I saw him.

COUNTESS ORSA (*comes over to them*):   What did you say?

DEA: Nothing.

COUNTESS ORSA: Yes, you did.

VULCAN: Come on now, don't make things any more complicated . . . (*to* ORSA) She thinks she saw him.

COUNTESS ORSA: Dorante?!

DEA: I think so. Why did you leave?

COUNTESS ORSA: But you don't know him.

DEA: A naval officer.

COUNTESS ORSA: Was he in uniform?

DEA: Yes, a naval lieutenant.

COUNTESS ORSA: Yes, yes. What did he look like?

DEA: A black moustache. Curled up at the ends.

COUNTESS ORSA: Oh my God!

DEA: Tall . . . The same height as him. (*pointing to* VULCAN[3])

COUNTESS ORSA: Where is he?

DEA: He left. (*pointing off to the left*)

COUNTESS ORSA: No!

VULCAN: Calm down. People come, and they go . . . Wait a minute . . .

DEA: Of course. I think he'll be back.

COUNTESS ORSA: How do you know? Where has he gone? Let's go . . .

VULCAN (*to* ORSA):   Please be still, and let her finish her story. (*to* DEA) And you, tell us all you know without our having to beg you.

DEA: As he was going out, someone said to him: "See you later, Dorante."

---

3. Or to Marcolfo, or saying "slightly taller than" or "slightly less tall," etc., depending on the relative height of the actors.—Bontempelli.

COUNTESS ORSA: So it was him!

DEA: And then the same person added: "Come back, if you can."

COUNTESS ORSA: Why "if you can"?

VULCAN: Quiet. (*to* DEA) And what did he say?

DEA: He didn't say anything. She answered . . .

COUNTESS ORSA: She!

DEA: I mean . . .

VULCAN: Forget the "I means." Out with it.

COUNTESS ORSA: He was with a woman!

DEA: Oh, now I've done it.

VULCAN: She said? . . .

DEA: She said: "I'll bring him back in an hour."

COUNTESS ORSA: Who was she? What did she look like?

DEA: I don't know. What does it matter? She was pretty, very pretty, tall, blonde. (*Or she could use other adjectives, as long as the person she describes is the opposite of the actress who plays* ORSA.)

COUNTESS ORSA (*practically choking*): Oh, oh, oh!

DEA: There, I've done it again. Listen, my dear. Sss.

COUNTESS ORSA (*shouting at the three of them*): Oh, why didn't you let me stay here?

DEA: I told you so.

COUNTESS ORSA (*shrieking*): Find them! (*shaking convulsively*) Oh, oh, oh, I think I'm going to die!

(*A trickle of people begins to come up the upstage staircase.*)

VULCAN: Let's go out there for a moment. (*He goes over to the entrance on the left, the closest to where they are standing, and peers out.*) Is there a maid or somebody? (*turning back toward them*) Marcolfo, help her over here. (*to* DEA) And you help him.

MARCOLFO: Come along now.

(*He leads* ORSA *on over, supporting her.* VULCAN, DEA, MARCOLFO, ORSA *go out by the entrance on the left. Meanwhile, people continue to come onstage via the upstage staircase. After a while, the* HATCHECK GIRL *looks in at the entrance they went through on the left.*)

HATCHECK GIRL (*holding a glass*): Is there a doctor in the house by any chance?

(*The people onstage, despite their disorder, happen to be in a line that crosses the stage diagonally from the upstage staircase to the entrance on the left.*)

THE MAN CLOSEST TO THE HATCHECK GIRL: What happened?

HATCHECK GIRL: Nothing serious. Someone almost fainted.

THE REST OF THOSE ONSTAGE (*passing on the message, in sequence, from the one near the door to the last one, at the top of the stairs*): Is there a doctor here? — Are you a doctor? — Not me. (*turning to someone else*) How about you? — No. (*turning around*) Is there a doctor here?

THE MAN NEAREST THE STAIRS (*leaning over the balustrade, addressing the people below*):   Hello down there. Is one of you a doctor by any chance? . . . What's that? . . . You're a doctor? . . . Could you come up here a minute? (*turning around to the others*) He's coming.

EVERYONE ONSTAGE (*in sequence as before, but in the opposite direction*):   Here he is. — He's coming. — He's on his way. — Here he comes.

THE MAN NEAREST THE STAIRS (*still addressing the people below*):   Can't he get through? Here, let me give him a hand up. You take his shoulders. That's it. Up we go.

NOISES FROM THE CROWD (*from below, out of sight*):   Ooops-a-daisy. There you go. (*And other lifting and carrying noises.*)

(*And, lo and behold, who should come into sight but the* **DOCTOR** *we met in the first two acts. The man closest to the stairs sits him astride his shoulders and carries him over to the* **HATCHECK GIRL**.)

DOCTOR: Who needs a doctor?

THE MAN CARRYING THE DOCTOR (*about to put him down*):   Here we go!

DOCTOR: No, no. Leave me up here. This is the ideal position for certain diagnoses.

HATCHECK GIRL: There's a lady fainted.

DOCTOR: Where is she?

HATCHECK GIRL: In here. Come on in.

(*The* **MAN** *carrying the* **DOCTOR** *prepares to follow her out the entrance.*)

DOCTOR: Whoa there! Are you insane? What's that? (*to the* **HATCHECK GIRL**, *pointing to the glass*)

HATCHECK GIRL: I gave her a drink of water.

DOCTOR: Hand it over. (*bending to take the glass*) Now you (*to the* **MAN CARRYING HIM** *on his shoulders, guiding him like a horse by tugging on his forelock*) take me over there, as far as you can, that'll do, whoa! (*They have arrived at the upstage right-hand corner. Everyone stops talking and stares at the* **DOCTOR** *without moving or speaking, open-mouthed. After emptying the last few drops of water on the head of someone standing nearby, he examines the glass, then he taps it.*) It's nothing. Just a moment. (*putting the glass to his ear*) There now, there now . . . She'll be better in no time . . . She's coming to . . . She's completely recovered. You didn't even need me.

(**ORSA** *in fact reappears in the doorway on the left. Behind her,* **VULCAN** *attempts to hold her back, but she drags* **VULCAN** *after her. After them come* **MARCOLFO**, *and, bringing up the rear,* **DEA**, *who remains in the doorway.*)

DOCTOR (*beginning to enjoy himself*):   Does anybody else feel ill?

CROWD (*in a frenzy*):   Bravo. Bravo. Who is he? (*They mill round the* **DOCTOR**.)

VULCAN (*insistently, to* **ORSA**):   It's no use. There are too many people. Let's go back. Take five minutes rest. Marcolfo, over here.

COUNTESS ORSA: It's all over. It's all over.

MARCOLFO: Let's go back, then.

(**MARCOLFO** *succeeds in turning her around.* **HE** *and* **VULCAN**, *one on either side, support her and lead her to the door on the left.* **DEA** *and the* **HATCHECK GIRL** *step out of the way to let them through. The* **HATCHECK GIRL** *exits upstage,* **DEA** *goes off by another exit looking to left and right as she goes. The crowd, spread out, continues to divide the stage diagonally in two, as they throng round the* **DOCTOR**. *The* **DOCTOR** *refuses to get down, though his* **BEARER** *is tired.* **DORANTE** *appears on the right.*)

DORANTE: I can't stand it any more. Oh! (*He glimpses* **ORSA** *from behind at the other side of the stage, with the two men holding her affectionately. He flings himself across the stage, but the crowd holds him back.*)

CROWD: Oh, look how upset he is! Doctor, examine him.

(*Meanwhile,* **ORSA** *and the* **OTHER TWO** *have exited to the left.*)

DOCTOR: Yes, take me away from him, if you want me to examine him. As far as you can . . . over here.

CROWD: Gangway, gangway!

(*They go boisterously off to one side carrying the* **DOCTOR**, *allowing* **DORANTE** *to come forward. At the same time,* **VULCAN** *and* **MARCOLFO** *come on from the left.* **MARCOLFO** *gives a huge sigh as if he were completely exhausted and flings himself into a chair.*)

DORANTE (*confronting them*):   My God, you'll pay for this!

MARCOLFO: You don't say.

DORANTE (*to* **MARCOLFO**):   Who are you? You'll have me to reckon with, unless you can come up with an explanation at once . . .

MARCOLFO (*exploding—the impetuousness of his speech contrasting with his immobility in the chair*):   Who am I? Let me tell you, sir. I am someone who has been searching for an hour, one whole hour, for someone to fight with, because I've had it up to here; and if I had anything to explain to you, I wouldn't explain anything, just to have an excuse for a fight; and I am delighted to have run into you, because you appear to be the very person I'm looking for. Come on then. Step forward. Put 'em up. (**DORANTE** *is momentarily at a loss for words.*)

VULCAN (*still standing, in a conciliatory tone*):   Now listen here . . .

DORANTE (*turning upon him*):   And who do you think you are? (*threateningly*) Are you aware that . . .

VULCAN (*seraphic*):   Who am I? Let me tell you, sir. I am someone who would do anything to avoid a fight or an argument; and therefore, though I haven't the faintest idea what you're getting at, I assure you, you are right, I am wrong, I didn't do it on purpose, I beg your pardon, and I won't do it again. Yes, yes, you couldn't be righter . . .

DORANTE: Abandon that woman, or else . . .

VULCAN: Yes, of course. I'll abandon her at once. What woman?

DORANTE (*turning to* **MARCOLFO**):   Or you abandon her, sir, if . . .

MARCOLFO: No, no. I'll never abandon her! Never! What woman?

DORANTE: You're making fun of me. Very well. I warn you I have to sail tomorrow morning in the line of duty (*doubletakes from the other two*), but we have the whole night before us. I am going back upstairs to the private rooms. I'll wait there for one hour. Lieutenant Dorante at your service.

VULCAN AND MARCOLFO: Dorante!

MARCOLFO (*getting to his feet*): Ah!

VULCAN: Oh!

DORANTE: Now what is it? (*about to fly off the handle again*)

VULCAN: Please, please. We've been looking for you all night.

MARCOLFO: Everywhere!

DORANTE (*to* **MARCOLFO**): Why?

MARCOLFO: Because . . . (*He falters and turns to* **VULCAN**.) Listen, it's not up to me, you tell him.

VULCAN: My God, what's all the to-do? . . . From one young chap to another . . . we're all gentlemen . . . Countess Orsa was with us; we came here together . . . We were looking for you . . .

MARCOLFO (*going over to the left to call her*): Countess!

DORANTE (*to* **VULCAN**): I don't understand . . . (**MARCOLFO** *has returned. Now* **VULCAN** *runs over to the door on the left.*)

VULCAN: Come on, Orsa.

DORANTE (*to* **MARCOLFO**): Maybe you can explain . . . (**ORSA** *rushes in from the left and finds herself face to face with* **DORANTE**.)

MARCOLFO: There you are. (*He stands looking at them, as if transfixed.*)

VULCAN (*in a whisper, tugging at* **MARCOLFO'S** *coat*): Let's get out of here. (*They back off to a distance.*)

MARCOLFO: Where's Dea?

VULCAN: That's it. Let's go and find Dea. (*They continue to back off.*) You were so happy keeping her company.

MARCOLFO: You think so? Maybe. I don't even know. I'm so confused!

(*They go off, leaving* **ORSA** *and* **DORANTE** *behind. Face to face, they stare at each other, full of contradictory feelings, without managing to speak. Finally:*)

COUNTESS ORSA: Go ahead, say it! Is it true? Confess!

DORANTE: You? Talking to me like that?

COUNTESS ORSA: Who was the woman you went outside with?

DORANTE: Went outside? I never moved from up there. I was waiting for you. But you, you've decided to leave me, you've already left me, and you send her to tell me so, just like that, with complete unconcern . . .

COUNTESS ORSA: Dorante, you're insane!

DORANTE: What? A few minutes ago, that friend of yours, on your behalf . . .

COUNTESS ORSA: A friend of mine? . . . On my behalf? . . . Oh no, you fibber, why don't you tell me . . . ?

DORANTE: Yes, a woman, dressed in green, with a serpent up here!

COUNTESS ORSA: Oh, the viper! That was Dea. It's not true, it's not true! For two years I've been waiting for you, every minute of every day; all night long I've been beside myself, searching for you high and low. Dorante, how can you believe it?

DORANTE: And you . . . Do you still love me?

COUNTESS ORSA: So it wasn't true that you were with someone else?! Oh my God, what have they done to us? Why?

(*Sounds of people approaching.*)

DORANTE: We can't stay here. Come on. I have so many things to tell you.

COUNTESS ORSA: So do I. Where shall we go?

DORANTE: It may be quieter over there . . . Before they come back . . . Oh my God, here she is.

(*The approaching sounds appear to have taken a different route and recede into the distance. Reenter* **DEA**.)

DEA: Ssss. My dear Orsa. So you've found him.

COUNTESS ORSA: What did you tell him, you fibber, you wicked girl!

DEA: Me?

DORANTE: Tell her it wasn't true, for heaven's sake.

COUNTESS ORSA: Dorante!

DEA: Ssss! I get it. Oh my goodness, my gracious, I was kidding. Yesss.

COUNTESS ORSA: You viper!

DORANTE: Come with me, come with me. (*They move away far upstage.* **DEA** *slinks along behind them.*)

DEA: Love each other, my dears. Very much. Yesss. (*The couple exits upstage center.* **DEA** *thinks for a moment, then quickly goes over to wake the* **ELDERLY WAITER**. *In a rapid whisper:*) Do you have something to write with? Quickly.

ELDERLY WAITER: Certainly. Being prepared for such eventualities is part of my profession. (*taking from his pockets a sheet of paper, an envelope, and a fountain pen*)

DEA (*writing on one knee, with one foot resting on the* **WAITER'S** *chair*): I need someone to take this note urgently, right now, double quick.

ELDERLY WAITER: I have just the person. Right away. I'll go get him.

DEA (*continuing to write*): As urgently as possible, to Count Orso, at the Council of Twenty . . . The building's next door . . . Ssss . . .

ELDERLY WAITER: I know. Let me have it.

DEA: No dawdling now. (*The* **ELDERLY WAITER** *goes off to the left. Reenter* **VULCAN** *and* **MARCOLFO**.)

MARCOLFO: But what happened? I don't understand a thing.

DEA: It must be hard for you to understand. (*Meanwhile, the* **ELDERLY WAITER** *returns, nods to* **DEA** *who is looking in his direction, returns to his seat and falls asleep again.*)

VULCAN: I didn't understand anything either . . . (*He catches the exchange.*) But something I do understand.

MARCOLFO: That must be even more difficult.

(*Enter* **BELLBOY** *from left.*)

BELLBOY (*in a monotone*): I have here the chips for the monks' and devils' quadrille . . . (*Crossing the stage. To* **VULCAN**.) Here are the chips for the quadrille . . .

VULCAN: Go away, go away.

BELLBOY (*to* **MARCOLFO**): Do you want to pick one?

MARCOLFO: I don't know.

VULCAN: No.

DEA: No.

BELLBOY: Why don't you want to pick a chip for the monks' and devils' quadrille?

VULCAN: Wait a minute . . . Take one. (*He takes one from the bag the* **BELLBOY** *is holding out and gives it to* **DEA**. *The* **BELLBOY** *goes off, repeating: "I have here the chips, etc."*) Dea, I have a vague suspicion that we ought to keep an eye on you. I have a feeling . . .

DEA: Have all the feelings you like, darling.

VULCAN: I have a feeling that you are about to unleash a tragedy. It's a good thing Vulcan's here.

DEA: Ssss. Aren't we lucky! (*She laughs and hisses; unable to contain herself she lets out a series of violent high-pitched hisses, rearing up and twisting from side to side. The last hiss is shrill and unnatural. It is interrupted by a voice from the back of the stage. It is the* **DILAPIDATED DOMINO** *who, all alone this time, has appeared at the top of the stairs and is admiring Dea.*)

DILAPIDATED DOMINO: Gorgeous! Absolutely gorgeous! (*All three turn toward her.*)

VULCAN: The voice I recognized! But who is it? Who are you, you in the mask?

DILAPIDATED DOMINO (*coming forward*): Well, look who's here. Our flare critic! (*She takes off her mask. It is* **MADAME FIORA**.) It's unbearable in here!

DEA: What are you doing here?

MADAME FIORA: Yes, it's me. I always come along, incognito, to check out the ladies who are wearing my dresses.

MARCOLFO: This one is magnificent. But I'm exhausted.

MADAME FIORA: I've seen four. Two were passable. One was horrible, and she's an actress to boot! Tomorrow I'll send round to get my dress back, on some pretext or other, and she'll never see it again, never, never, and this will be the last time she gets a dress from Madame Fiora.

VULCAN: Madame Fiora, couldn't you have worn a less down-at-heel domino? (**MADAME FIORA** *shrugs. A* **SECOND BELLBOY** *enters from the left and goes over to whisper in the* **ELDERLY WAITER's** *ear.* **DEA** *is watching. The* **SECOND BELLBOY** *exits.*)

ELDERLY WAITER (*to* **DEA**, *who has gone over to him*): He's on his way over.

DEA: Good.

VULCAN (*who has overheard*): Who's on his way over?

DEA: Ssss. I've ordered a vanilla and strawberry ice cream. Ssss.

VULCAN (*ironically*): Madame Fiora, this was a stroke of genius, dressing Dea up as a serpent.

MADAME FIORA (*simply*): I know. A brilliant idea. And just look how she wears it! And now come and take a look at the famous actress, and you tell me . . . (*She drags* **VULCAN** *over to the balustrade and makes him look down, then she leads him downstairs.*)

DEA: Marcolfo, don't you love me any more?

ELDERLY WAITER (*to himself*): They're beginning to get on my nerves. I'm not going to get any sleep here. (*He exits by the smaller staircase on the right.*)

MARCOLFO (*answering* **DEA**): I don't know. I'm tired. (*He flings himself down in a chair.*)

DEA: Tired of making love to me?

MARCOLFO (*looking at her*): I haven't a clue what's going on.

DEA: Am I pretty?

MARCOLFO: Oh, yes. Earlier today, you were so sweet . . .

DEA: What does that have to do with it? Will you do me a favor?

MARCOLFO: A favor moving, or a favor staying still?

DEA: A favor moving.

MARCOLFO (*with a sigh*): Oh, alright then.

DEA: I'm worried about Orsa. She went out that way (*motioning upstage center*) with Dorante, but who knows where they went from there. Go see where they've gotten to. Don't disturb her, she's with her true love, poor thing . . . Don't let them see you. Just come back and tell me where they are.

MARCOLFO: No sooner said than done. Why?

DEA: Just to be sure nothing bad happens to her.

MARCOLFO: What could happen?

DEA: Ssss. You ask too many questions. That's enough!

MARCOLFO: I'll be back in a jiffy. And then you . . .

DEA: And then . . .

MARCOLFO: Sweet.

DEA: Ssss . . . Sugar sweet. Get going. (**VULCAN** *comes back via the upstage staircase.*)

MARCOLFO (*on his way out*): We'll see. (*Exit upstage center.*)

VULCAN (*to* **DEA**): Did he get here?

DEA (*with a wriggle*): Who?

VULCAN: The waiter with the vanilla and raspberry ice cream.

DEA: Ssss, you silly. He's coming now. Yesss. He's coming. He's coming.

VULCAN: Before, you said a strawberry ice cream. This is serious, Dea, what are you plotting?

DEA: Nothing. Are you from the police?

VULCAN: Maybe.

DEA: Ssss . . . You won't want to miss this.

VOICE OF THE BELLBOY (*offstage*): All those with chips for the monks' and devils' quadrille, please come and pick up their costumes. And put them on when the gong sounds.

VULCAN: What are they shouting about? (*The* **BELLBOY** *comes onstage and repeats in a monotone: "All those with chips, . . .".*)

DEA (*malevolent, transported*):   Watch out! . . .

VULCAN: Dea, you're not yourself. Look at me.

BELLBOY (*pedantically*):   The lady here has a chip.

(*People hurry in via the other entrances and go out on the left, returning, some with red costumes, some with gray ones, and going back where they came from.*)

VULCAN (*to the* **BELLBOY**):   Don't bother us! (*The* **BELLBOY** *runs away, terrified, shouting: "Everyone put them on when the gong sounds."*)

VULCAN (*to* **DEA**):   Give it to me. I'll go get your costume.

(**DEA** *gives him her chip indifferently.*)

VULCAN (*aside*):   I have an idea! (*Rushing off to the left.*)

DEA: Good man! (*Reenter* **MARCOLFO** *out of breath.*)

MARCOLFO: I couldn't find them.

DEA: You fool!

MARCOLFO: First they were there. Then they weren't there. Then they were. Now they're gone again.

DEA: You idiot! You should have found them. Invented them.

MARCOLFO: Is it my fault if they went someplace else?

DEA: In any event, I insist on knowing where they are. Go and look for them!

MARCOLFO: What if they went out?

DEA: Look all over town.

MARCOLFO: What if they took the train?

DEA: Look all over Italy.

MARCOLFO: The boat?

DEA: Look all over the world. On the moon. In the Milky Way, imbecile. Now he's on his way over, and they're not here!

MARCOLFO: Who's on his way?

DEA: Ssss . . . The waiter with the strawberry ice cream. Ha! Ha! Ha! (*She bursts into a peal of spasmodic laughter, at the climax of which she slaps* **MARCOLFO'S** *face.*) You moron! (*At this point,* **VULCAN** *returns, carrying a monk's habit. He casts a rapid glance around the stage.*)

VULCAN: Don't dwell on it, Marcolfo. Here you are, Dea, the costume you picked for the quadrille. At the sound of the gong . . .

DEA: I don't give a damn about costumes. You're an idiot too.

(*The clang of the gong echoes in the depths of the building, and is repeated room by room, getting constantly nearer.*)

VULCAN: There you are. Put it on, Dea.

DEA: Have you gone out of your mind?

MARCOLFO: Go on, try it on. I want you to try it.

DEA (*cajolingly*):   Will you promise you'll go look for them right away . . .

MARCOLFO: Agreed. (*The gong sounds again. A few people dressed as monks and devils pass by at a distance.* **VULCAN** *helps* **DEA** *put on the hooded monk's habit as she wriggles into it.*)

MARCOLFO: Oh look, I want one too. I almost like you better like that. What a cute monk!

DEA (*immediately striking a preaching attitude and speaking with a nasal voice*): No, I'm a poor little nun, a humble sister, not a monk. God has sent me into these places of perdition to preach . . .

VULCAN (*speaking to her like a hypnotist*): What did you do to Orsa and Dorante?

DEA (*making an effort to remember*): Oh dear, I am a sinner. I tried to separate them from each other, to remove them from the occasion of sin! (*She goes over to the balustrade, and from there she preaches to the people below.*) Ladies and gentlemen, go back to your domestic hearths, to your peaceful firesides, and humble yourselves in prayer, be charitable, shun the maelstrom of concupiscence. Nay verily, I see arising from the depths of the waves . . . (*The people below heckle. Streamers and colored balls fly up and hit* **DEA**.)

DEA (*turning to the two men*): And as for you, my dearly beloved brethren . . .

MARCOLFO (*with conviction*): What an actress!

VULCAN (*anxiously*): Tell me. Do you know what happened to Orsa?

DEA: I don't know. But any moment now, as soon as her husband the count gets here . . .

VULCAN: The count's on his way here?!

DEA: . . . I will prevail upon his heart. That's why I sent for him . . .

MARCOLFO (*laughing*): Ha, ha, ha . . .

VULCAN (*aghast*): You sent for him!

DEA: . . . and I will persuade him to forgive and forget, to welcome back his adulterous wife under his dishonored roof, so that from their fruitful union . . .

VULCAN: Curses!

DEA: A reprehensible word, brother.

VULCAN: It mustn't happen! Run, Marcolfo . . .

MARCOLFO: Run? Again!

VULCAN: Quickly. Over there. (*pointing to the exit on the left*) Don't let Count Orso come in. Send him away. Find an excuse. Stop him. Tell him there's been some mistake. Insult him. Convince him. Kill him. But don't let him in. He must go away.

MARCOLFO: Kill him? What with?

VULCAN (*pushing him off to the left*): Whatever you do, don't let him into the public rooms. Now get going. (**MARCOLFO** *is shoved offstage. A scream is heard from the back of the stage. The scream comes from* **MADAME FIORA**, *who has appeared at the top of the stairs.*)

MADAME FIORA: What's this? What's this monstrosity? (*She comes up the last steps and runs toward* **DEA**. *Begin Music 3. From this point on, the rest of the act is accompanied by a continuous hubbub from the unseen crowd, accompanied by music offstage, the shouting increasing in volume at the points indicated.* **MARCOLFO** *reappears from the left and calls to* **VULCAN** *anxiously from the doorway.*)

MARCOLFO: Vulcan!

VULCAN (*running toward him*): Is he here? Did you send him away?

MARCOLFO: There's nobody here. (*practically sobbing*) But if he comes, I don't think I'll be able to convince him, or kill him, or send him away . . .

VULCAN: Why not?

MARCOLFO (*miserable*): Because it just occurred to me that I've never laid eyes on him in my life!

VULCAN: You idiot! Think of something. Ask everyone. Stop everyone.

MARCOLFO (*fiercely*): I'll kill everyone.

VULCAN: Get out of here! (MARCOLFO *rushes off to the left. Meanwhile* VULCAN *has returned to his former position. He sees* MADAME FIORA *strip the monk's habit off* DEA *with bellows of rage.* DEA *is now back in her serpent's outfit, her hair all disheveled.*)

MADAME FIORA: Shame on you! (*She rolls the monk's habit up into a ball and flings it angrily down into the crowd below. The crowd howls.* DEA *utters a long heart-rending hiss like a wounded serpent.*)

VULCAN: You devil! Oh no, whatever it takes, no!

(*He throws himself on* DEA, *putting one foot on the tail of her green dress.* DEA *whips round like a striking snake, and in so doing tears off the tail. She emits broken and spasmodic hisses.* VULCAN *grabs her and tears off the serpent's head. The coils that surround her neck also uncoil and come off, the top of the dress is torn and hanging limp.* VULCAN *throws the serpent's head violently across the stage, down among the crowd, which howls louder.*)

MADAME FIORA (*turning from the balustrade, and letting out a bloodcurdling yell*): Sacrilege! (*She flings herself upon* VULCAN, *foaming at the mouth, fetching him a haymaker punch that sends him reeling.*)

VULCAN: All we needed was this Valkyrie! (*He seizes* MADAME FIORA's *domino, tearing it. Then with a brainstorm he tears it off completely.*) Take that, then.

MADAME FIORA (*finding herself in her slip, rushes offstage to the left, screaming*): The coward! Attacking a woman!

(*Downstage front on the right,* DEA *is thrashing and writhing, her breath coming in short hisses, a wounded snake.*)

VULCAN: Now. May the devil help me. (*He seizes* DEA *by the shoulders and pulls the tattered domino forcibly over her head. He pulls it down over her body, tearing it still more in the process.* DEA's *head emerges even more disheveled than before.* VULCAN *accompanies his gestures with half-uttered inarticulate words.*)

DEA (*suddenly ceasing to hiss and throwing herself to the ground racked with pitiful sobs*): Oh my God, oh my God . . .

VULCAN: At least now . . . (*He stands there, looking down as she weeps, panting and still somewhat astonished.*)

DEA (*dragging herself off into a corner, still sobbing*): Oh my God, oh my God . . . (*She eventually stops moaning altogether.* MARCOLFO *reenters on the left.*)

MARCOLFO (*from the doorway, calling* VULCAN *in a hushed voice*): There's somebody out here who may be him. (*with an illustrative gesture*) A beard.

VULCAN (*realizing that it is indeed Count Orso, rapidly, briskly, almost under his breath*): I'll get him out of the way. You see that Dea gets home. We'll meet there, at her place. (*Exits quickly to the left.*)

MARCOLFO: This is easier. But where has Dea gotten to? They're not going to catch me again.

(*He staggers blindly off in some vague direction, in search of* **DEA**. *He fails to see her, crouched in the corner, like a bundle of rags. At this point the voices and the noises fade, then quit altogether. With the last of the racket, Music 3 stops also. Total silence.*

  DEA *is left alone on the stage. She stirs slightly and begins to moan again. She gets up onto her knees. She runs a hand over her disheveled hair and her face. She gives another painful moan, then gets to her feet, standing bowed and wretched. She looks down at herself and sees her clothes in tatters. She takes a mournful step or two across the stage.*)

DEA: All in rags . . . Poor little me . . . I'm poor and I'm hungry . . . (*She catches sight of a sandwich on the abandoned buffet table and snatches it, peering fearfully round her. She takes a ravenous bite, then hides it, clutching it to her bosom.*) Poor little me . . . (*She leans against a jutting corner near the entrance on the left and stretches out her hand like a beggar.*) A crust of bread . . . God bless you . . . A crust of bread . . . Can you spare a little change? For a poor little beggar girl . . .

CURTAIN

ACT 4

The scene is the same as in act 1. It is dawn. The stage is deserted, the wardrobe half open. Several dresses on hangers are scattered throughout the room. Which dresses they are will become apparent from **VULCAN'S** *monologue. A bell rings. Enter* **NINA**, *half-asleep, her hair uncombed.*

NINA: Madam, madam. (*She goes over to the sofa bed and sees there is no one there. The sofa bed is not even unmade.*) Oh dear, she's not here! How could madam have rung if she isn't here? (*The bell rings once again.*) Oh, it's somebody at the door; now I see how she did it.

(*She exits toward the door. For a moment the stage is again empty. Enter* **VULCAN**, *pursued by* **NINA**.)

NINA (*plaintively*): But sir, what do you think you're doing? At this hour!

VULCAN: What time is it?

NINA: I don't know.

VULCAN: So why did you say: "At this hour!"

NINA (*open-mouthed for a moment, then blurting out*): Madam isn't here.

VULCAN (*making fun of her*): What do you mean, Madam isn't here? At this hour!

NINA (*suddenly overcome with terror*): Oh my God, oh my God. What can have happened? She must be dead!

VULCAN: It's shocking what little fear women have of words! No, I don't believe your mistress is dead. On the contrary, I believe it would be very difficult for her to die.

NINA: Listen, I don't understand. I haven't done my hair yet.

VULCAN: You don't say!

NINA: In any case, you can see as well as I can. Madam's not here.

VULCAN: I think she is.

NINA: Oh well, in that case, make yourself at home, and have a nice chat.

(**NINA** *flounces off in a huff.*)

VULCAN (*alone*): Don't worry. I will. (*greeting some of the dresses*) My dear Dea, Miss Dea, Lady Dea! (*throwing open the wardrobe*) Dea, Dea, Dea, Dea. All these Deas! Take your pick. A bevy of Deas. All the Deas you could wish for. All you need is the cash to pay Madame Fiora the artistic dressmaker. Cynic! Who's a cynic? You call me a cynic? (*addressing the dove-gray dress*) You, who only yesterday—no, the day before yesterday; oh, was it only the day before yesterday that I first set eyes on you, at tea at the countess's? And now it's all over? Or will be—you, who the day before yesterday almost had me falling in love with you. You, my dear Dea, without knowing the meaning of the word, you call me a cynic. But you . . .

Now where is she? Ah, here she is! (*to the red suit*) You, Lady Dea, brought me straight to my senses next morning. My kind of woman—can I help it?—is the sweet, generous, submissive kind. You—let me give you a piece of advice—you should stick to men who are a trifle naive, a bit simple, like Marcolfo. Marcolfo. What's that you say? (*to the dove-gray dress*) That Marcolfo made all kinds of declarations to you too, that same afternoon, shall we say in act 2? That doesn't mean a thing. He was just making the best of a bad situation. You're not for him, my dear Dea. He's still thinking of Lady Dea . . . (*pointing to the red suit*) Lady Dea here, who—as I was saying—wouldn't call me a cynic simply because I said . . . I don't recall what I said: why should I remember? Why force me to be consistent? Here in the midst of your perfume, which is going to my head. Your perfume, yes, that's the one thing you have in common. Olympus, Mount Olympus of fair goddesses, before whom I am tempted to kneel, even though, yes, even though I know who you are (*to the dove-gray dress*), who you are (*to the red suit*), and who you are, my dear (*to a yellow dress with grape tendrils sewed onto the skirt*). Oh yes, with you, Dea, I can be frank and uninhibited from the start, seeing that you're a "creature of the night," as they put it in the dime romances. Go ahead, go about your business, do your thing, as long as you don't cause a scandal . . . (*breaking off to greet a little pink dress*) Oh, my dear little Dea, my how you've grown! And how's your papa? See you again soon. (*turning back to the yellow dress*) As long as you don't cause a scandal, I was saying, as long as you take the right precautions, Dea; don't go telling your secrets, for example, to Mrs. Dea here. (*to a very serious and prim-looking dark-colored dress*) Oh no, Mrs. Dea, that woman who just went by? (*motioning toward the yellow dress*) No, I don't know her, I only know her name's Dea. She asked me the way, and I told her. That's all there was to it. And how's your husband the judge? And your four children? Is your invalid aunt still living with you? Oh yes, don't I know it! Nowadays proper behavior's gone by the board, people seem to have lost that *savoir faire* . . . But, come now, you really are a bit of a busybody; yes, you; among all these ladies, you, Mrs. Dea, were the only one to ask me how things turned out last night. What makes you so eager to find out? Do you know Count Orso? He's a member of the Council of Twenty. No? And Countess Orsa? You barely know her? You read the tabloids, don't you? Why don't you fill in the grisly details yourself? Listen. I don't need a program. Do you want me to show you? Listen. Either Count Orso didn't catch them red-handed, and let himself be taken in by Vulcan—what? Yes, I'm Vulcan; I like to talk about myself in the third person when the occasion deserves it—in which case, no problem, the play has a happy ending. Or he had second thoughts and went back; and in that case, there are two further hypotheses, as we used to say in the trenches. Either they ended up dead—can't you just imagine it? Yes, just like Romeo and Juliet in that English anthology you studied in high school— in which case the comedy ended up as a tragedy. Or he went back alright, but decided to turn a blind eye. That would be a third "genre"—the "modern psychological drama." Whichever of the three possibilities it was, I assure you that I, that we (*indicating himself and the other dresses*), that they (*making a vague gesture in the direction of the audience*), all intelligent people, we couldn't care less. The important thing, whichever of the three scenarios it was, is that Marcolfo and Dea—yes, Dea—should come back onstage through that door. And do you know why? So that we can all go home and go to bed. (*While he is speaking, he puts the dresses away one by one into the closet, all except the yellow one.*) All except you. Oh, you're not one to spend your nights sleeping. So why don't you keep me company for a while. I adore them all, the whole Mount Olympus, but, when you get right down to it, the only one I really feel comfortable with is you. You're the most like myself, and that's why I want to kneel at your feet, like this, (*kneeling*) and reach out my arms, like this, in a Hellenic gesture, (*raising his arms*) and, if I wasn't wearing tails, I'd sing you a dithyramb, I would undo this grapevine—like this, (*undoing it*) because Madame Fiora the artistic dressmaker isn't here to see me anyway, Madame Fiora that great fabricator of divinities—and I would place it on my head like a crown (*twisting it into a crown and putting the crown on his head*), and I would get to my feet (*getting up*), and with a voice like a saxophone I would burst into song . . . But I'm in tails. Tails are our logic. Tails are a businessman's business. Tails make man man. Tails are a serious affair. Be off with you. (*He flings the dress into the wardrobe and shuts the door with a bang. Then all at once he stops short, as if stunned, staring at the closed wardrobe. And he suddenly shouts, but not loud:*) No! No! What shall I do now? Without you? Without you, without you, without you . . . (*in various directions, toward various points of the wardrobe*) Open up! (*He pushes feverishly against the door of the wardrobe: he thrusts and paws at it as if he were trying to break open a locked door.*) Come here; come back, come back to me. Why did you leave me? It's me. It's not true, it's not true, come back, I'll let you make game with my thoughts, if that's what you want, with my heart, it's yours, take it, but come back, my marvelous slave, Dea, come back, I can't live without you.

(*He collapses in an attitude of despair, half thrown forward, arms and hands upstretched, his chest against the wardrobe, as if lifeless. Pause. He suddenly raises his head, a sign that he has heard noises coming from the direction of the door. Then he quickly stands up straight, adjusts his clothes, puts a smile on his face, and turns toward the entrance.*

MARCOLFO *and* **DEA** *stick their heads in, then come forward.*)

DEA (*wearing a fur coat, with her head swathed in a white scarf, quite composed*): At least it's warm in here. (*She begins to unbutton her fur, starting at the top.*) I could really use a good rest.

MARCOLFO: It's very late.

VULCAN (*still worked up*): Or very early. We stand on the ambiguous boundary line between late and early. It's late, if you like; but give me a ray of sunlight, and it'll be early. (*Meanwhile* **DEA** *has unfastened her fur all the way down.*) Just as the clothes I see you have on under your coat, Dea, walk a fine line between the most abject debasement and the most triumphant Dionisiac ecstasy. (**DEA** *takes off her scarf.*) But, if I give you this crown . . . There! Now you're the perfect Bacchante.

(*He puts the crown on her head, at the precise moment she throws off the fur.*)

DEA (*with the picturesquely tattered domino she wore at the end of act 3, and the grape-leaf crown on her head, she bursts into peals of uncontrollable laughter, as if intoxicated*): Ha! Ha! ha! You silly, silly men! Always the same when we get back home. (*As she speaks, she spins round the room in a waltz.*) When we get back home early. Early from that place. Where the four of us went, and the three of us returned. Ha! ha! I know, you see, and you thought I didn't? Oooh, I can say it one time, two times, three times, two times, three times, four times (*stopping*) As long as you stop spinning. As long as you don't stare. As long as you don't open wide. As long as you don't talk to the driver. Noooooooooooo (*The note is held throughout the following dialogue.*)

MARCOLFO (*aghast, to Vulcan*): She never even so much as touched a glass of water!

(**VULCAN** *responds with a noncommittal shrug and a murmur of indifference.*

DEA *waltzes one more time all around the room, continuing her "oooooo," which turns into a high-pitched trill. Meanwhile* **ANNA** *enters.*)

ANNA (*carrying an elegant robe*): Here I am, madam. Nina didn't know what on earth was going on.

DEA (*extremely animated, singing the words out loud as she dances, followed by* **ANNA**): What on earth, what on earth, was going, ooon.

(**ANNA** *removes the crown and drapes the robe over her shoulders.*)

DEA (*suddenly very much a lady*): Thank you, my friends, for bringing me home. Forgive me if I don't ask you to stay. I'm so tired. We had a wonderful time. Good night, Vulcan, good night, Marcolfo . . . (*She holds out both hands for them to kiss. Not daring to say another word, they bow and withdraw.* **ANNA** *and* **DEA** *are left onstage.*)

ANNA: Sit down, madam, so I can begin . . .

(**DEA** *sits with her back to the audience.*)

ANNA (*kneeling, helps her off with her shoes, and maybe her stockings, as she talks*): Did you really have such a good time last night?

DEA: Oh my goodness, Anna, that's what people always say . . . (*As* DEA *speaks,* ANNA *puts on her slippers, helps her to her feet, and takes off in rapid succession, first the ladylike robe, then the torn domino, then what remains of the serpent's skin dress, so that finally Dea is left in her slip, as she was at the start of the play. The changes in Dea's words and intonation correspond to the various phases of her undressing.*) . . . that's what people say, but to tell you the truth, it's always the same old thing. Really, if I were to try and describe it to you, I couldn't. Very chic. (*in the tattered domino*) Oh, I'm so cold. Poor little me . . . (*in her serpent's skin dress*) Be careful, you idiot, ssss . . . (*In her slip, facing the audience, her arms still, a trifle raised, her movements mechanical: apathetic, she enunciates slowly, in the hollow, slightly falsetto voice she used in the opening scene.*) What-were-you-say-ing?

(*She takes three mechanical paces forward and stops. She lets her arms fall to her sides. Her gaze is blank.*)

ANNA: There you are. I'll turn back the sheets. (*Going over to the sofa bed.*)

DEA: Na-tur-al-ly.

ANNA (*turning back the sheets and signaling to* DEA *from the other side of the room to come over*): If you'd like to come over here.

DEA (*turning away from the audience*): I-think-that-I'm-ti-red.

(*She walks over to the bed. After she has taken two steps, the stage is thrown into total darkness. In the darkness, three more steps are heard distinctly. Then the curtain falls.*)

Dances for the Third Act of Dea by Dea

2) Slow Waltz

3) Fox Trot Tempo

Introduction

Achille Campanile was born in Rome on September 28, 1900, and died in Lariano (Rome) on January 3, 1977. He began his writing career at an early age; while still an adolescent, he wrote *Rosmunda*, a parody of a verse tragedy. In 1924, *Corriere Italiano* published *Le due locomotive* (The two locomotives), the first of a long series of miniature "tragedies." Between February 1924 and April 1925, Anton Giulio Bragaglia produced three of Campanile's one-act plays: *Centocinquanta la gallina canta,*[1] *Il ciambellone* (The large rubber-ring), and *L'inventore del cavallo* or *The Inventor of the Horse.*

His first novel, *Ma cos'è quest' amore* (But what is this love, 1927), was a great success. In 1930, however, the production of *L'amore fa fare questo e altro* (Love makes one do this and more) had a mixed reception. During the 1930s Campanile worked as a journalist for *La Tribuna* and *La Stampa.* In 1946 his revue, *Dietro quel palazzo* (Behind that palace) was staged, and in 1953 his *L'amore fa fare questo e altro* was televised. Beginning in 1959 he became a prominent television critic. His *Trattato delle barzellette* (Treatise on jokes), which appeared in 1961, formulated his theories on humor. In 1973 he was awarded the Viareggio prize.

Although Campanile described himself as the most booed author in Italy, the facts are otherwise. His plays achieved a certain success, although they were not as popular as his other literary works. Campanile lived during a historical period when comics were not highly valued. His texts openly and critically addressed the issues of the time. In the 1930s he wrote about Fascism and the bourgeoisie. In the postwar period, his themes were reconstruc-

EIGHT

ACHILLE
CAMPANILE

tion and its antithetical ideologies, consumerism, and the revolt of Italian youth. He was above all a satirist: he had an irresistible tendency to poke fun at events and people that present themselves in everyday life under a cloak of self-aggrandizing rhetoric.

After his death, a new wave of consumerism emerged, which provoked in Italy the posthumous "rediscovery" of his satirical treatment of the phenomenon. Indeed, the new appraisal of his work gave the public a standard by which to measure the worth of contemporary television comics. Certain critics emphasized the relationship between his work and aspects of the twentieth-century avant-garde, particularly futurism and the theater of the absurd. This comparison tends to minimize his originality. As in the case of Ettore Petrolini, humor in Campanile's plays is essentially verbal, based on quips and word play.

Campanile's most famous creations are his so-called *tragedie in due battute* (tragedies in two speeches). From 1924 until his death he wrote about five hundred of them. They have never been organized and published all together. The two exchanges that make up these "tragedies" create an unexpected new situation that does not build on the logical order the author established at the beginning in the stage directions.

In 1925 Campanile began to stage his farces, among them *L'inventore del cavallo*. Their novelty does not lie in their themes, which were already familiar to spectators, but in their mad energy, which reveals other dimensions of the characters. He creates humor without moralizing, without taking an ideological position. His is an anarchic stance. Campanile's more ambitious plays and his one-act plays were the least successful. For example, his one-act *Visita di condoglianze* (Condolence call, 1937) is too heavy to be amusing; the same theme was treated better by Alberto Savinio in *La famiglia Mastinu* (1940). Campanile's best longer works were his novels, such as *Cantilena all'angolo della strada* (Lullaby on the street corner, 1932) where he combines a melancholic tone with a prose that sings.

Campanile's wit is well represented in *L'inventore del cavallo*, written in 1925 and first presented at Anton Giulio Bragaglia's Teatro degli Indipendenti. He pulls no punches in parodying the pompous cultural institutions so admired by the Fascists. The critical and liberating aspects of comedy are revealed in his amusing presentation of everyone as immersed in a general stupidity that concludes with the suicide of Professor Bolibine.

A. A.

Trans. by J. H.

Notes

1. Literally "one hundred and fifty the hen sings," but this does not convey the nursery-rhyme, nonsense sounds of the title.

THE INVENTOR
OF THE HORSE

(*L'inventore del cavallo,* 1925)

Translated by Laurence Senelick

■

Characters:

PROFESSOR BOLIBINE (BOUNCIBAL), inventor
of the horse

THE PRESIDENT OF THE ACADEMY

THE PERMANENT SECRETARY

SIGNORINA YVONNE LA VALLIÈRE, a polyglot
and encyclopedic mind

**THE ILLUSTRIOUS, LATE LAMENTED
FRANCESCO ILARIO ROSSI,** clinician

THE ACCURSÈD POET

PROFESSOR POSIAKOFF, scientist

THE SERGEANT-AT-ARMS

THE PHOTOGRAPHER

THE MINISTER OF PUBLIC EDUCATION

THE MINISTER'S WIFE

OTHER ACADEMICIANS

Academy of Immortals, heavy tomes and dust. Upstage, a closed window. As the curtain rises the **PRES-IDENT**, *the* **ENCYCLOPEDIC MIND, F. I. ROSSI**, *the* **SCIENTIST**, *the* **POET**, *and* **OTHER ACA-DEMICIANS** *are taking their places in their high-backed chairs. Suddenly the* **PERMANENT SECRETARY** *enters supported by the* **SERGEANT AT ARMS** *who laboriously carries the minutes of the last meetings.*

PRESIDENT (*rings his bell loudly*): Permanent secretary, read the agenda for today.

SECRETARY (*takes his place and reads in an unearthly voice*): Today's agenda for the extraordinary session of the Academy of Sciences, Letters, and Arts: The reception for and nomination to academic honors of Professor Bolibine, inventor of the horse. Presentation to the members of the Academy and Professor Bolibine's illustrated lecture on the invention of the horse.

PRESIDENT (*ringing loudly*): Illustrious colleagues. Shortly we shall have in our midst the illustrious Professor Bolibine, who, by his invaluable invention, the horse, has shed new luster on the entire civilized world, rendering an inestimable service to the cause of progress which we all serve. (*murmurs of assent*) Just think: to have invented the horse. So useful and so noble a beast. We do not hesitate to proclaim Bolibine a benefactor of mankind. (*murmurs of assent*) I need not exhort you . . . (*He stops with his mouth agape and cannot go on.*)

(*Everyone crowds around him and pounds him on the back.*)

SECRETARY: What's the matter? Do you feel ill?

YVONNE: Don't alarm us like that, Mister President.

(*The* **PRESIDENT** *points to his mouth.*)

SERGEANT AT ARMS (*running up*): It's nothing. His dentures are stuck sideways again. All it takes to put them back in place is a punch in the jaw. (*He adjusts the dentures by punching the* **PRESIDENT** *in the jaw.*)

PRESIDENT (*continuing*): As I was saying, I need not exhort you to welcome the distinguished inventor of the horse in an appropriate manner. (*Pause. Takes a letter from the table.*) Meanwhile, I must inform the Academy that our illustrious colleague Professor Boltke, who has been ill for so long, is completely recovered and will return to us tomorrow.

(*Indications of general satisfaction.*)

POZIAKOFF (*extremely deaf, has followed the speech with a hand to his ear; speaks in a cavernous voice*): I request the floor.

PRESIDENT: Professor Poziakoff has the floor.

(*Indications of attention.*)

POZIAKOFF (*rises, pulls a notebook from his pocket, and reads*) The mournful notice of the death of our illustrious colleague Professor Boltke . . . (*His neighbors tug at his jacket, but he goes on.*) fills me with grief. With him there vanishes a figure . . .

YVONNE (*loudly into* **POZIAKOFF'S** *ear*): But he isn't dead!

POZIAKOFF: Eh?

YVONNE (*as before*): He's recovered; he isn't dead.

POZIAKOFF: Ah! (*calmly pockets the notebook and sits down again*)

(*Meanwhile the* SERGEANT AT ARMS *enters and hands a telegram or two to the* PRESIDENT.)

PRESIDENT (*ringing loudly*): The matter is closed. Congratulatory telegrams for the inventor of the horse continue to pour in. And since there is still some time before his arrival . . . (*looks at his watch and stops short*)

YVONNE: What's wrong? Are your dentures sideways again?

PRESIDENT: My watch has stopped.

(*Sensation. The* PRESIDENT *shakes the watch and holds it to his ear.*)

SECRETARY: Maybe the hairspring's broken. (*Takes the watch and examines it.*)

YVONNE (*taking the watch*): I think you have to change the balance-wheel.

POET (*takes the watch*): Or else the mainspring has to be fixed.

(*The watch passes from hand to hand amid pessimistic gestures.*)

SERGEANT AT ARMS (*timidly*): Maybe it needs winding.

PRESIDENT: Let's try it. (*He winds it. The watch begins to tick.*) It's ticking!

(*Sensation. The* SERGEANT AT ARMS *exits.*)

EVERYONE: Oh!

PRESIDENT: I have to reset it. What time is it?

POET (*takes out his watch; in a gloomy voice*): Midnight.

EVERYONE: Huh?!

POET (*as before*): Midnight. (*Shows his watch to his impressed colleagues.*)

PRESIDENT: And how did we get to that hour?

YVONNE: Goodness, how time flies!

POET (*who has stood staring at his watch, smacks his forehead*): What an idiot!

EVERYONE (*turning around offended*): Eh?

POET: I made a mistake. It isn't midnight, it's midday.

EVERYONE (*relieved*): Ah!

PRESIDENT (*ringing the bell*): The matter is closed. Please be noisy, illustrious colleagues! I beg your pardon, I mean: please be silent. And, since it is still early, we can put the time spent waiting for the distinguished inventor of the horse to good use. Frankie.

ROSSI: What?

PRESIDENT: Shall we exchange a few ideas?

ROSSI: With pleasure.

PRESIDENT: Then let's begin right away. Permanent secretary, take this down. (*thinks, then:*) Which do you prefer, summer or winter?

ROSSI (*silent, as if gathering his thoughts; then, slowly*): Whichever, cold is cold and hot is hot.

PRESIDENT (*as if speaking to himself*): How true that is!

ROSSI (*suddenly getting intense*):   After all, riches don't always bring happiness.

(*Murmurs of approbation.*)

PRESIDENT (*staring into space*):   That's the god's truth.

ROSSI: Do you know who's happy? (*The* **PRESIDENT** *looks at him with lifeless eyes.*) The man with nothing. So many millionaires commit suicide. Why?

PRESIDENT: If you don't know, why ask me?

ROSSI: Because, even though they may have riches and luxury, they don't have happiness, with a derry-down-derry, a derry-down-down.

(*Applause, congratulations.*)

VOICES: Great!

ROSSI (*to the* **PRESIDENT**):   And which do you prefer, summer or winter?

PRESIDENT: I don't complain about the heat because I am a thinker.

ROSSI: So thinkers don't suffer from heat?

PRESIDENT (*dryly*):   Will you please not interrupt me. You reprobate.

ROSSI: Reptile.

PRESIDENT: Vampire. As I was saying, I don't complain about the heat because I am a thinker. And what thoughts have I thought?

ROSSI: How the heck should I know?

PRESIDENT (*withering* **F. I. ROSSI** *with a glance; then continuing, intensifying and heightening the tone*):   And what thoughts have I thought? I thought that in winter we long for summer, and in summer we long for winter.

ROSSI: What a discovery!

PRESIDENT (*snapping*):   Oh, for heaven's sake, Frankie boy. You want to end up provoking me? (*Punches the* **CLINICIAN** *hard.*)

ROSSI: Sticks and stones may break my bones.

PRESIDENT: You were getting on my nerves. I won't say another word.

ROSSI: This time let's make up.

PRESIDENT (*calming down*):   Where was I? (*repeats hurriedly*) I don't complain about the heat because I am a thinker, and what I was thinking was, I thought that in winter you long for summer and in summer you long for winter. (*menacing gesture at the* **CLINICIAN**) Very well, in winter I pretend that it's summer, and in summer I make believe that it's winter. That way my summer is always extremely cool, and my winter not too severe.

(*Deafening applause.*)

VOICES: Print it and post it! Print it and post it!

PRESIDENT (*ringing loudly and mopping his brow; then makes a sign that he wants to speak*):   Frankie.

ROSSI: What?

PRESIDENT: I forgot to tell you that Indian Summer doesn't count.

(*Closes his eyes and leans back in his chair as if going to sleep. The* ACADEMICIANS *toss spitballs at one another.*)

YVONNE (*tugs at the* PRESIDENT'S *jacket*):   Mister President, what's up? You asleep?

PRESIDENT (*opens his eyes*):   I'm thinking, as usual.

YVONNE: And what were you thinking of, if it's not an indiscreet question?

PRESIDENT: I was just thinking that greed is very often connected with wealth.

YVONNE (*taking notes*):   That's good. (*Tugs the* PRESIDENT'S *sleeve, for he has closed his eyes again.*) Mister President. What are you thinking about now?

PRESIDENT (*gravely*):   Right now I'm thinking about my house.

(*The* POLYGLOT *takes notes.*)

POZIAKOFF: Mister President, did you see the Accursèd Poet? He threw a spitball at me!

PRESIDENT (*sternly*):   Ah, Accursèd Poet! (*rings loudly*) Frankie!

ROSSI: What?

PRESIDENT: Shall we exchange some more ideas?

ROSSI: If you like. You start.

PRESIDENT (*thinks, then, gravely*):   What a lovely day!

ROSSI: Yes, but a little hot, you've got to admit.

PRESIDENT: That's true, but that means the air'll get cooler toward evening.

ROSSI: Let's hope so.

SECRETARY (*who was recording this*):   What?

PRESIDENT (*prompting*):   Let's hope so. (*then to the* CLINICIAN) How long has it been since it rained?

ROSSI: Must be about a year.

PRESIDENT: Don't exaggerate! Can't be even three months.

ROSSI: You're right. Personally I feel the need of one of those downpours that goes on for a couple of hours, like the one yesterday.

PRESIDENT: The one the day before yesterday was much heavier and lasted six hours. Do you remember?

ROSSI: Do I remember! And the one the day before that . . .

(*Meanwhile the* ACADEMICIANS *are rioting like schoolboys.*)

USHER (*entering*):   Mister President is wanted on the telephone.

PRESIDENT: If you'll excuse me. (*Exits.*)

POZIAKOFF: Shall we take advantage of the President's absence to dance a tarantella?

POET: Great idea.

(*They pull out the necessary instruments: tambourines, accordions, Neapolitan drums, percussive mallets, etc. and, deserting their respective seats, they dance vigorously—beards and frock coats flying—a Neapolitan tarantella.*)

PRESIDENT (*reentering, at the very height of the dance*):   Bravi, bravissimi. (*They all return to* *their seats, embarrassed and ashamed.*) A lovely thing for me to have to see! Disgraceful! Men of science! Academics of world renown!

SERGEANT AT ARMS (*enters and announces*): Professor Bolibine, inventor of the horse!

(*All rise to welcome the illustrious guest. The* **SERGEANT AT ARMS** *stands aside to make way for the* **INVENTOR***, who enters followed by the* **PHOTOGRAPHER***, who carries a camera and a tripod.*)

BOLIBINE: Illustrious colleagues, great is my emotion on entering these precincts sacred to learning.

PRESIDENT: Welcome to our midst the illustrious scientist to whom we owe the invaluable invention of the horse.

(*Mutual bows.*)

SERGEANT AT ARMS (*announcing and showing in*): His Excellency the Minister of Public Education.

(*The* **MINISTER***, in a top hat, enters arm in arm with his* **WIFE***; hurries to shake everyone's hand.*)

MINISTER: Illustrious Mister President, we have met once before, but I don't recall the occasion.

PRESIDENT: Perhaps on the occasion of the Scientific Congress.

MINISTER: That may very well be. Except that I have never been to any Congress.

PRESIDENT: What am I talking about? Neither have I.

MINISTER: Then that explains it; we must have met because neither of us has ever been to a Congress.

PRESIDENT: In fact it's clear that, if either of us had been there, the other, who wasn't, couldn't have met him on that occasion.

PHOTOGRAPHER (*from under the black cloth*): Everybody freeze! (*They all stand in various attitudes, as if petrified.*) The pose will take a little time because there's not much light. You may speak, if you like. But please don't move.

PRESIDENT: Then let me make the official introductions. These are the Academicians. This is Professor Poziakoff, a benefactor of mankind. He invented the process for turning bowler hats into strawhats in the summer months.

POZIAKOFF (*to the* **INVENTOR** *who holds out his hand to him*): Not bad, thanks, and how about yourself?

PRESIDENT: He's a little hard of hearing. And this is the illustrious academician Signorina Yvonne La Vallière, historian, polyglot, encyclopedic mind: she knows all the dates in history, even the most remote and insignificant. Signorina, give us an extremely remote date.

YVONNE: April third, 2413 B.C.

BOLIBINE: Remarkable.

PRESIDENT: Unfortunately, she does not know the events that occurred on those dates, but she does know the dates. On the other hand, she knows English perfectly.

YVONNE: Impossible. The words I know in English nobody else knows.

MINISTER: The dickens you say. I possess an internal dictionary.

YVONNE: All right. Take the word "Ndrbl."

MINISTER: What?

YVONNE: "Ndrbl." Can you tell me what it means?

MINISTER (*annoyed*): As a matter of fact I don't know that word. What does it mean?

YVONNE (*laughs*): Aha! You think I'm going to tell you! I'm the only one who knows, and I know lots and lots of others like it that nobody else in the world knows. Just imagine, the English words I know are unknown even to the English!

MINISTER: Extraordinary!

PRESIDENT (*proceeding with the introductions*): Our Permanent Secretary, the great discoverer.

BOLIBINE: Oh really? What has he discovered, if it's not an indiscreet question?

PRESIDENT: He discovered a grammatical error in *The Divine Comedy*.

BOLIBINE: I would be glad to bow before such a discoverer, were I not afraid of breaking this pose.

PRESIDENT (*to the* **PHOTOGRAPHER**): Do we have to stand in these positions much longer? Photographer! Photographer! Are you dead?

SERGEANT AT ARMS: Photographer! (*tugs at his jacket*)

(*The* **PHOTOGRAPHER** *emerges from under the black cloth. He has a black beard, although he was clean-shaven before. General astonishment.*)

MINISTER: He's grown a beard!

ROSSI: It must be an advantage due to the long pose. (*Goes to examine it closely.*)

BOLIBINE: An advantage? Perhaps you mean a disadvantage.

PRESIDENT: No. This is the illustrious and late lamented Francesco Ilario Rossi, a clinical physician of world renown, to whom we owe the theory that illnesses represent an organism in a diseased state reaching its decisive crisis. Which is why he calls them "wellnesses" and not illnesses, since the individual is eventually cured, provided he hasn't died. If anyone asks news of a seriously ill patient, he answers: "He's doing very well, I believe he's just been given oxygen."

BOLIBINE: Splendid.

PRESIDENT: If the patient happens to be about to die, he says, "He seems to me to be very well indeed. Send for the priest." Go ahead and question him.

BOLIBINE: Glad to. (*To the* **CLINICIAN**.) How are you?

ROSSI: Not well, thanks. I have a bit of wellness in my head and wellness in my stomach; and then too a serious wellness in my teeth. My wellnesses are so many that I'll die of them. What can you expect? Things are going from good to worse!

BOLIBINE: Buck up. Not all wellnesses end fatally.

ROSSI: Oh, on the other hand, every man complains of his own wellness. Such is the wisdom of the tree of good and good.

BOLIBINE: Good. I mean: bad, in the sense . . .

PRESIDENT (*interrupting*):   And last, let me introduce you to our great Poet! The Accursèd Poet.

POET: Yes, I am an unhappy poet.

BOLIBINE: Unhappy? Why is that?

POET (*gloomily*):   Because I don't know how to make rhymes.

BOLIBINE: That's not such a disaster. Write free verse.

POET (*as before*):   I don't know how to write free verse either.

BOLIBINE: Never mind. As long as you've got poetic images, you can write prose poetry.

POET (*still gloomy*):   Unfortunately, I also don't have poetic images.

(*General shock, embarrassment.*)

BOLIBINE: If he doesn't mind, I should like to hear some little thing of his.

POET: Happy to oblige. I shall recite: *Love.* (*takes a pose and declaims expressively*)

> Tarazoon, tarazoon, teereetò
> eereepoccolo trallallà

BOLIBINE: Good.

PRESIDENT (*aside to the* **INVENTOR**):   He always recites the same poem.

POET:

> Teereetee, teereetee, beereebò
> parapà, parapà, parapà

BOLIBINE: Excellent. That's enough for now.

POET (*expressively*):

> Corocò, corocò, coccoday,
> Feereefeetzolee, keechkeereecà . . .

BOLIBINE: Keechkeereecà?

POET: Stands for keechkeereekee: poetic license. (*recites*)

> Corocò, corocò, coccoday
> Feereefeetzolee, keechkeerikà
> Prank of payraypaypay
> parapà, parapà, parapà.

EVERYONE: Good.

(*Applause.*)

PRESIDENT (*loudly ringing for silence*):   And now, illustrious Professor Bolibine, tell us a little bit about your invention.

MINISTER: How did you ever get the idea to invent such a strange animal?

BOLIBINE: If I may say so, I don't know myself. It just came to me, in the course of my studies.

PRESIDENT: It's a real find. But how exactly is it made?

BOLIBINE: I see you want a lecture good and proper. All right. (*pulls out a notebook*) I have here a few notes and illustrative charts. (*clears his throat*) Illustrious colleagues, my invention is simple, and if I may say so with pride, successful. Tall, noble, practical, and economical, such is the horse. (*unrolls the first chart with the picture of a horse which he strikes with a pointer*)

(*General admiration.*)

EVERYONE: Oh . . .

BOLIBINE: As the gentlemen may see from the illustrative chart I venture to submit to their attention, I have divided the horse into three parts: head, body, extremity. I made it with four legs, and I put a tail on it. (*points*) Legs, tail. From my first horse (*unrolls a second chart of a very hideous, deformed horse*)—still, as you see, in the rudimentary stage— to the latest (*points to the first*), I had a long row to hoe. But I am determined to keep on perfecting my invention, with appropriate modifications. So far, for instance, I am limited to producing horses in only white, black, gray, and tan. Later on I hope to be able to produce them in blue, green, and red as well. (*presents the third horse*) They will be highly effective on holidays. The many practical applications of my invention, as you can all imagine, are infinite. First of all, the horse can be harnessed to all sorts of carriages, carts, gigs. The horse can, in fact, pull. Nor is this all: a person can move atop them very nicely. Moreover, they can run races. Galloping races, trotting races. They can perform a number of graceful stunts in an equestrian circus. As you can see, infinite are the functions that can be served by the animal I have invented.

YVONNE: Excuse me, Professor. What is the tail used for?

BOLIBINE: I expected that question. The tail was given them a bit for ornament, a bit for shooing flies. But I intend to do away with it in the near future. My invention is capable of improvement destined to make it ever more useful. For instance, at present it kicks. I shall proceed to eliminate this defect. In short, I seek to achieve a type of horse that will be simpler, more economical, and within the range of everybody, as you may see from this rough outline on the fourth illustrative chart. (*unrolls the fourth chart on which is drawn a hideous horse with just two legs, no tail, no ears, etc.*)

EVERYONE: Great! Bravo!

(*Applause, acclamation, hand-shaking.*)

MINISTER (*affixes a medal to the* **INVENTOR'S** *chest*): In the name of the whole Nation and the Government, I am pleased to unite my own to the sentiments for which . . . this important assemblage . . . to the illustrious inventor of the horse . . . (*confused as to how to conclude*) auguring an era of fruitful labor, civilized conquest, glory, and freedom!

(*Applause. The* **SERGEANT AT ARMS** *enters with the insignia of the Academy on a cushion. The* **PRESIDENT** *solemnly invests the new* **ACADEMICIAN** *and then embraces him, according to the rite. A* **UNIFORMED ATTENDANT** *brings a big laurel wreath, which is offered to the* **INVENTOR**. *Meanwhile* **THE ACADEMICIANS**, *here and there, examine the charts and discuss them heatedly.*)

YVONNE: What a great invention!

ROSSI: What a brain!

PHOTOGRAPHER (*who has continued to appear and disappear under the black cloth, his beard ever longer and now white*): Everybody freeze.

(*Everyone forms a group with the* **INVENTOR** *in the middle. In the distance can be heard the march of the light infantry, first quietly, then growing in intensity. The group of Academicians fidgets.*)

SECRETARY: Oh, the soldiers are passing by, let's go look.

PRESIDENT: Open the window to the Academy.

(*The* **SERGEANT AT ARMS** *opens it with difficulty; sounds of rusty chains. Everyone, except for the* **MINISTER** *and the* **INVENTOR**, *presses forward.*)

Oh, the light infantry . . . Here come the foot-soldiers . . . hey, . . . hey . . . , what's that over there?

(*The music gets louder.*)

YVONNE: A cavalry regiment!

(*Sensation. The* **INVENTOR** *grows increasingly alarmed on the other side of the stage.*)

POZIAKOFF: A regiment . . . ?

POET: Of cavalry.

PRESIDENT: But that means the horse already existed!? (*The* **INVENTOR** *is deflated. Everyone looks at him in indignation.*) Swindler!

YVONNE: Impostor!

PRESIDENT: Give me back the insignia.

POET: Liar!

MINISTER: Hand over that medal. (*to his* **WIFE**) Let's get out of here.

(*They leave.*)

MINISTER'S WIFE: Give me back my flowers.

SECRETARY: Let's get out of here too.

PRESIDENT (*strips the insignia off the* **INVENTOR** *who is more dead than alive*): Shameless creature!

(*Everyone leaves, scandalized. The military music is now heard fortissimo under the window, along with the noise of the horses' hooves. Slowly the* **INVENTOR** *pulls out a revolver and prepares to commit suicide.*)

PHOTOGRAPHER: Freeze a minute, please. (*The* **INVENTOR** *freezes, with the revolver to his temple.*) Smile! (*The* **INVENTOR** *smiles.*) All done.

BOLIBINE: May I, now?

PHOTOGRAPHER: Sure.

BOLIBINE: Thanks. (*shoots and dies*)

CURTAIN

Introduction

By any standards, Italo Svevo, whose real name was Aron Ettore Schmitz, is one of Italy's major twentieth-century authors. He was born on December 19, 1861, in Trieste. He died, the victim of an automobile accident, on September 13, 1928, at the height of his long overdue success. Svevo spent most of his life as a businessman and satisfied his literary passion occasionally by writing theater reviews and other critical pieces in local Triestine newspapers such as *L'Indipendente* and *Il Piccolo*. A number of his short stories and his first two novels were serialized in *L'Indipendente*. However, he had to pay for the publication of his three novels: *Una vita*, *Senilità*, and *La coscienza di Zeno*.[1] Each book was met with silence on the part of Italian critics. That he continued to write in the face of these rebuffs must be attributed to his passion for writing. It gave his life spiritual meaning and helped him define himself and the world. Recognition of the value of his novels came only in the mid-1920s, and then only through the efforts of such literary figures as James Joyce, Eugenio Montale, Benjamin Crémieux, and Valéry Larbaud.

His thirteen plays did not fare so well. During his lifetime only one, the monologue *Prima del ballo* (Before the ball, 1891), was published, and only one, the one-act play *Terzetto spezzato* (Broken triangle, c. 1912), reached the stage. It was performed in 1927 at Bragaglia's Teatro degli Indipendenti. However, theater was Svevo's first and enduring love. Although the teenage Svevo wrote only seventy lines of *Ariosto governatore* (Ariosto, the governor, 1880), a very early effort at playwriting, those lines were in the fourteen-

■

NINE

ITALO SVEVO

■

syllable Martelliano meter; this was to be his sole attempt at writing in verse, no doubt under the influence of the nineteenth-century literary tradition.

The pseudonym by which he is remembered, Italo Svevo—he used a number of others—refers to his divided Italian and German background. "Svevo" is the Italian adjective derived from the German duchy of Swabia. As his pen name suggests, Svevo was conscious of a dual heritage in Italian and German language and culture. Indeed, his birthplace and home, Trieste, had a double identity. A major port on the Adriatic, it was part of Austria until World War I, but the people of Trieste, including the Schmitz family, spoke an Italian dialect. There was no doubt where Svevo's loyalties lay. During the war he supported the struggle to Italianize Trieste and in 1918 joined *La Nazione*, a new Italian newspaper published there.

As the son of a Jewish businessman who expected him to follow in his footsteps, Svevo was encouraged to develop his linguistic skills. He was sent to a business school in Germany between 1874 and 1877; at seventeen, he was enrolled in an Italian business institute in Trieste. Despite this emphasis on business schooling, Svevo remained an avid student of literature throughout his life. By age sixteen he was reading Schiller, Heine, Goethe, and, in German translation, Shakespeare and Ivan Turgenev. He moved on to Italian writers like Boccaccio, Machiavelli, and Francesco De Sanctis, and the French naturalists: Flaubert, Daudet, Zola, and Balzac, as well as Stendhal and Renan. Any dream he might have had of furthering his formal education was thwarted in the early 1880s when his father encountered financial difficulties. From that time forward Svevo made his living as a businessman. He was a banker until 1898, when he joined his father-in-law's Veneziani paint factory, which specialized in protective paints for ships' hulls. The Veneziani association brought him prosperity and took him all over Europe, including England. He opened a branch of the firm near London in 1901. During his free time in England, he attended the theater and recorded his experiences in a diary, "Soggiorno londinese" (London sojourn).[2]

There were three major figures in his life, people he felt close to with whom he could discuss his writing. The first was his younger brother, Elio, who died prematurely in 1886. The same year, he struck up a friendship with the Triestine impressionist painter Umberto Veruda, which lasted until Veruda's death in 1904. In 1905 he met James Joyce who was his English teacher at the Berlitz School in Trieste, and the two spent many hours discussing literature and their own efforts to enlarge the boundaries of naturalism. Joyce read to Svevo the poems of *Chamber Music*, as well as stories from *The Dubliners* and parts of *A Portrait of an Artist*, and insisted on Svevo's showing him *Una vita* and *Senilità*, of which he preferred the latter. Their relationship encouraged Svevo to continue his literary efforts despite lack of recognition.

Between 1905 and the publication of his third novel in 1923, Svevo became familiar with Freud's work.[3] The Freudian influence can be seen in *La coscienza di Zeno*, which is considered the first Italian psychoanalytic novel. By 1923 Italo Svevo had come a long way from his early efforts in the naturalistic tradition.

Svevo's extant plays, many of them difficult to date precisely, number thirteen. They often have an ironic or cynical edge. Beginning as an ardent admirer of Zola, Svevo saw the bourgeois society around him as hypocritical, lacking in morality, and subservient to money and social position. His plays seldom have heroes or heroines; his characters reveal inner voids beneath their social masks. In the short four-act play *Il ladro in casa* (The thief in the house, c. 1892), a swindler exposes the mercenary drive of his bourgeois in-laws. In the dramatic monologue *Prima del ballo*, a debutante tells the audience about the dreadful society surrounding her but then resolves to use people to get ahead. Svevo could be critical of the excesses of naturalism. In his two-act thesis play *Le teorie del Conte Alberto* (Count Alberto's theories, c. 1885), the scientist Count Alberto decides that faulty heredity can be ameliorated by love.

Other works from Svevo's early period, 1885–1892, besides the three mentioned above, are the sketch *Le ire de Giuliano* (Guiliano's anger) and the one-act *Una commedia inedita* (An unpublished play). While the theme of adultery runs through his early plays, he made his first attempt at treating it seriously in the three-act drama *Un marito* (*A Husband*) of 1903. Through the characters of the lawyer, Federico Arcetri, who killed his first wife because she committed adultery, her bereaved mother, and his unloved second wife, whom Arcetri also suspects of adultery, Svevo exposes the emptiness within the bourgeois Italian male who holds on to concepts of family pride and honor above all else. In the one-act *La verità* (The truth, 1921–26), Svevo, in tackling the theme of adultery, plays with the idea that truth is always relative.

In 1913 he wrote the farce *Atto unico* (One-act play), the only play he wrote in his Triestine dialect. In this social satire, Svevo exploits the master-servant theme, but this time the mistress outwits her thieving servants, who decide they prefer jail to being black-mailed into good service. Svevo's strongest dramatic works, besides *Un marito*, are considered to be the one-acts *Terzetto spezzato* and *Inferiorità* (c. 1921) and the three full-length plays, *L'avventura di Maria* (c. 1892–1901), *La rigenerazione* (1926–28) and *Con la penna d'oro*, translated here as *With Gilded Pen* (1926).

With the exception of *Terzetto spezzato*, it was not until the late 1950s, thirty years after his death, that Svevo's plays began to reach the stage, thanks particularly to the Teatro Stabile di Trieste and to Milan's Teatro Filodrammatici. Some noteworthy adaptations, primarily of his stories and novels, by Tullio Kezich and Aldo Nicolaj reached both stage and television in the 1960s and 1970s.[4] Svevo's plays have also been produced in German, French, and English, but they have remained relatively unknown in English-speaking countries despite the existence of a number of English translations.[5]

In a perspicacious essay on *Con la penna d'oro*,[6] Olga Ragusa emphasized that Svevo's dramatic output has been neglected by his critics, that scholars disagree widely on which is his best drama, and that Svevo himself was unsure about the stageworthiness of his plays and had no opportunity to see how they worked in production. She stressed that, although *Con la penna d'oro* has structural problems (particularly a lack of focus and resolution), because of its thematic richness, it invites a closer look than do some of Svevo's finished plays.[7]

Con la penna d'oro seems to be what is called today a woman's play. One of the major themes concerns the power of charity to spiritually enslave as it materially liberates. In this case the benefactress is a woman and the object of her bounty her cousin. A crippled aunt and a lively maid become unwittingly enmeshed in the cousins' machinations. The men only serve as a backdrop to the action; it's the women, their jealousies, passions, and insecurities, that are the focus of the drama. As Anthony Oldcorn has noted, "The play as a whole could be read as an illustration of Machiavelli's 'It is human nature for people to oblige themselves as much for the benefits they give as for those they get,' or, better yet, Hobbes's 'Acts of kindness imply obligation, and obligation is slavery.'"

Its focus on women might explain why there has been renewed interest in this work. After the first staging of the play in Trieste in 1976 under the title *Le cugine* (Female cousins), it was produced at the Pompidou Center in Paris as *Les Deux Cousines* in the late 1970s. More recently, in 1988, it was a critical success in the production by Milan's Teatro Filodrammatici, in which the cousins were played by twins.

The text of *Con la penna d'oro* that appeared in Svevo's collected works[8] was edited by Umbro Apollonio from several extant manuscripts. As a number of scholars have pointed out, this reconstruction by Apollonio is suspect.[9] We are following Apollonio's version, however, since at present no scholarly edition of this play exists, including Apollonio's, which adequately explains the state of Svevo's manuscript.

Two major problems present themselves in a discussion of *Con la penna d'oro*. The first is that the drama is in an unfinished state. Svevo died while he was still experimenting with the structure of the play and rewriting large portions of it. That the text is far from having been given the finishing touches may be discerned by the attentive reader in a number of repetitions and inconsistencies, in the existence of alternative versions of several scenes, and both in the fact that some characters appear with different names in the alternative versions—the maid Clelia, for instance, was called Maria in early drafts—and that a number of scenes have no closure. We are not even certain that Svevo gave the play its present title, which appears, according to Apollonio, only once, as a heading to one of the fragments he relegates to his appendix.

The second problem centers on Apollonio's reconstruction of the play. Since Svevo's manuscript or manuscripts are chronologically layered and contain more than one version of a number of scenes, Apollonio was forced to choose between these alternative versions in preparing his reconstruction. Unfortunately Apollonio's description of the state of Svevo's manuscript, which was obviously a work still in progress, and his justification of the choices he made as editor are vague and inadequate. Those portions of the manuscript or manuscripts he did not use, he placed in an appendix with very little explanation. In the interest of completeness, the translator, Anthony Oldcorn, has included, in a section entitled "Alternative Versions and Dialogue Fragments," all of Apollonio's appendix materials.

Clearly, a new and critical edition of the text that will clarify these matters is called for. In the meantime, though the precise status of the miscellaneous materials is moot, the play will give the interested reader a fascinating insight into the author's workshop; much as studies of a great painter, like Michelangelo or Degas, for a larger masterpiece will intrigue a student of art. And, since the interest of the play lies not so much in its plot as in its whimsical and paradoxical dialogues, the dialogue fragments frequently prove as intriguing as the reconstructed text itself.

J. H.

Notes

1. *Una vita* (Trieste: Ettore Vram, 1893); *Senilità* (Trieste: Ettore Vram, 1898); and *La coscienza di Zeno* (Bologna: Cappelli, 1923). The three novels have been published in English, respectively, as *A Life*, *As a Man Grows Older*, and *Confessions of Zeno*. See the bibliography of this volume.

2. Italo Svevo, *Opera omnia: 3—Racconti, saggi, pagine sparse*, ed. Bruno Maier (Milan: Dall'Oglio, 1968), pp. 685–705.

3. With the help of Aurelio Finzi, his nephew, Svevo undertook the translation of one of Freud's works. It is unclear whether this was *On Dreams* or *The Interpretation of Dreams*. See Naomi Lebowitz, *Italo Svevo* (New Brunswick: Rutgers University Press, 1978), p. 29; F. N. Furbank, *Italo Svevo: The Man and the Writer* (London: Secker & Warburg, 1966), p. 107; and "Soggiorno londinese" in *Opera omnia: 3* (Milan: Dall'Oglio, 1968), pp. 686, 807.

4. Among these are *Il ladro in casa*, *La coscienza di Zeno*, and *Una burla riuscita* in their adaptations by Tullio Kuzich for television in 1962, 1966, and 1978, respectively, and Aldo Nicolaj's 1972 stage adaptation of *Senilità*.

5. See bibliography.

6. Olga Ragusa, "'The Light is Split in the Prism . . .': Svevo's Unfinished Play, *Con la penna d'oro*," in *Narrative and Drama: Essays in Modern Italian Literature from Verga to Pasolini*, pp. 109–21 (Paris: Mouton, 1976).

7. Ibid., p. 109.

8. *Opera omnia: 4. Commedie*, ed. with an introduction and notes by Umbro Apllonio (Milan: Mondadori, 1960; repr. Milan: Dall'Oglio, 1969), pp. 351–440, 641–55.

9. See, for example, Ruggero Rimini, *La Morte nel salotto: Guida al teatro d'Italo Svevo* (Florence: Vallecchi, 1974), pp. 172–79; and Ragusa, "'The Light is Split . . .,'" p. 109.

■

WITH GILDED PEN

(Con la penna d'oro, 1926)

Translated by Anthony Oldcorn

■

Dramatis Personae

CARLO BEZZI
ALBERTA, his wife
ALICE, Alberta's cousin
TERESINA, Alberta's and Alice's aunt
CLELIA GOSTINI
DONATO SERENI
ROBERTO TELVI
DR. PAOLI
CHERMIS
MAID

ACT 1

Scene 1

A room adjoining the dining room, visible in the background, where the **MAID** *is busy preparing for dinner. Evening.* **ALBERTA BEZZI** *and* **CLELIA GOSTINI**.

ALBERTA: Of course, it's a plus that you have a nursing diploma, but it really wasn't essential. My aunt is a chronic invalid by now. To tell you the truth, she's perfectly healthy, apart from her legs. She spends her entire day in a wheelchair, but she has no problem eating or sleeping. In other words, your job won't be difficult.

CLELIA: I can see that. Still, my salary should be more or less in line with my qualifications.

ALBERTA (*hesitating*): Of course, it's better for my aunt to have a companion who can talk to her, keep her amused, read to her. The point here, however, is what's best for me. I'm the one paying, my aunt can't afford it, all I have to pay for are her basic needs, no extras. I'm not paying for her amusements as well.

CLELIA: Madam! I can see where sombody handing out charity would prefer to keep it down to a minimum. (**ALBERTA** *laughs.*) But you're well known for your generosity. I plan to devote myself entirely to your aunt. Entirely! Aren't I entitled to a little charity too from someone like you?

ALBERTA (*laughing.* **CLELIA** *laughs too.*): You mean I can afford to spend a bit more because, instead of having only one charity case on my hands, I have two?

CLELIA (*no longer laughing*): I also have to dress in a way that reflects credit on my employers and on my position and on the people who gave me such glowing recommendations.

ALBERTA (*somewhat irritated*): This is a nuisance . . . But alright then. I'm going to have to go over my figures again to see what my aunt's going to cost me. That's the thing that annoys me.

CLELIA: Do you need any help? I'm good at figures. I was training for an office job till I realized my poor family's predicament meant I'd have to go out and find work. (*wiping away her ready and abundant tears*) Excuse me . . . I'm so sorry . . .

ALBERTA (*very kindly*): I'm sorry I upset you. I didn't mean to. You're the one who should excuse me. Alright then, as far as the salary goes that's settled. I also realize that you can't afford to wait till my aunt gets here to start working. You can come and start working for me right away, as of tomorrow. I'll give you some sewing to do. If I can make time, I'll spend an hour or two with you and explain how I want my aunt to be treated. It'll be your responsibility to bring a little order into the household of that untidy cousin of mine, Alice.

CLELIA: Who?

ALBERTA: Didn't I tell you already? My aunt won't be staying here but at Alice's.

CLELIA (*anxiously*): And me with your aunt?

ALBERTA: Yes, of course. Didn't you know?

CLELIA: No.

ALBERTA (*curtly*): Well, you know now. It's up to you; you can take it or leave it. Alice's house isn't my house, but there's no shortage of food even there, and the heating is perfectly adequate. Otherwise, you understand, I wouldn't be sending my aunt to live there. Are you willing to give it a try? It's not as if we were getting married. With the proper notice I expect from a well-brought-up girl like yourself, you can stay or you can leave.

CLELIA: I accept, I accept. You see, madam, I thought you were going to let me stay here with you. That was my comfort in my time of trial. I'd heard how kind you were, and I felt so safe with you! I know you'd have gotten to like me.

ALBERTA: Don't worry. Even though you're staying at Alice's, I'll be with you often enough. We'll see a lot of each other. I intend to look after my aunt as if she were staying here with me.

Scene 2

Enter **CARLO BEZZI**.

CARLO: Hasn't Donato shown up yet?

ALBERTA: No.

CARLO: When he gets here, send him in, so I can show him the prints I've been offered. I have to make up my mind tomorrow. I asked him to get here early. There's nothing worse than having to deal with an artist. (*about to leave*)

ALBERTA: Just a second. I have something to say to you. (*to* **CLELIA**) Goodbye then, young lady. Be here tomorrow morning without fail.

CLELIA: At what time?

ALBERTA (*hesitating*): Between nine and eleven.

CLELIA (*a bit surprised*): I'll come at ten then.

ALBERTA: Yes. Ten or ten thirty. (*Exit* **CLELIA**.)

CARLO: Who was that?

ALBERTA: The nurse for Aunt Teresina. I took my time choosing her. She's very nice, and I hope she'll make my aunt's life less of a burden. And it's not going to cost me much either, because I found the right kind of young lady at the right price. And the job I'm offering is a godsend for her too. This is all very good. It makes three of us happy: me, her, and my aunt. She'll be good company for Alice too.

CARLO: You, her, your aunt, and Alice too! I'm happy to see you happy. (*about to leave*) If Donato shows up, send him in.

ALBERTA (*irritated*): Carlo, please, stay here and listen to me for a minute. It isn't often I drag you away from your business and your prints.

CARLO (*affectionately*): You drag me away more often than you think. Aren't I always thinking about you?

ALBERTA: Even when your mind's on your prints?

CARLO (*hesitating*): Even then. Even then I have the feeling that my collection is here in this house, and that this house with its order and its peace is all your work.

ALBERTA (*lightly*): You always come up with something nice to say. But it's not going to work this time. Now I want you to think about me and forget your business and those prints of yours. Listen! Alice says she needs at least another thousand lire a month.

CARLO: Yes, I can see why! The cost of living's going up every day.

ALBERTA: That's a good reason for us to spend less! We don't have to raise Alice's allowance just because the cost of living's going up!

CARLO: I can't argue with that. If that's what you've decided, it's alright by me. After all, she's *your* cousin.

ALBERTA: The fact that she is my cousin puts me in a somewhat more awkward position than you. I'm going to tell her I have to talk to you, because I can't give her anything without your authorization. Proud as she is, there's no way she'd approach you directly, but you never know, and I want to be quite sure you're prepared.

CARLO: It's simple. I'll tell her you're against it.

ALBERTA: No way! That's exactly what I'm trying to avoid. You must tell her you can't afford to give her any more. Business is bad, times are hard. Stuff like that. Whenever I talk to you, I find it hard to believe you're the shrewd, canny businessman people say you are. To me you're just an average dope, and I don't understand why somebody doesn't take you for everything you own.

CARLO: My business is simpler than yours. Don't forget, I do almost all my business by cablegram. And cables cost money. I'm only allowed a certain number of words. So I leave out all the unnecessary ones, and that makes me very clever. But where women are concerned, words are not at a premium, and it's harder to be clever. That time with Alice, you wanted me to tell her you'd gone out. So I told her, but then we went on chatting, I can't remember what about, and I blurted out: Alberta told me something or other just a second ago.

ALBERTA: It was obvious: "just a second ago"!

CARLO: It would have been less obvious if you hadn't admitted you'd been home all along the minute she asked you.

ALBERTA: Knowing you, I figured you'd made it even more obvious than it was.

CARLO: You've only got your own suspicious nature to blame. I'm a bit absentminded now and then. My mind's on those cablegrams. Only a few words, but every one has to be carefully weighed. But I get it now: I'm supposed to make Alice believe it's me who's forbidding you to give her any more money. You're not doing much for my image, because I happen to think it's not right to let such a pretty lady and her two children suffer.

ALBERTA: But if we give her everything she asks for, she'll end up asking for the moon. She'll be spending as much as we spend! I'm thinking of giving her half of what she wants.

CARLO (*chuckling*): In business we bid down by ten or twenty percent, never fifty!

ALBERTA: How much would twenty percent come to?

CARLO: You'd have to give her eight hundred instead of a thousand.

ALBERTA: Not a chance! It'd be like giving her the whole thing. Alice spends too much.

On the children and on herself. She gets herself up like a princess, and she dresses the children in white. She says white will wash. But other colors wash too, and they don't need washing so often.

CARLO: I see! It's really bad of her to spend so much. But doesn't she usually wear your hand-me-downs? The other day I ran into her on the stairs and I thought: Now there's a dress I once had my arms around!

ALBERTA: Don't let the cover fool you! But I trust you, because, while you were busy thinking up those little tiny words for your cables, you'd give yourself away. And I trust Alice too. (*with feeling*) That poor girl is the pride of our family. When she was left a widow so young, she could easily have gotten her hands on the money I refuse her. (*tenderly*) You know, I really don't think I'm being so cruel to her. I just think it's wise for the moment not to give her everything she asks for. We'll see later. I certainly won't let her suffer.

CARLO (*bending to give her a fatherly kiss*): That's my girl! That's the way I love you.

Scene 3

Enter **MAID**.

MAID: Mrs. Peretti.

ALBERTA: Alice! Show her in, show her in.

CARLO: I'm off. If Donato shows up, send him in right away. (*Exit* **CARLO**.)

Scene 4

Enter **ALICE**. **ALICE** *is about the same age as Alberta: twenty-five. She is blond, whereas* **ALBERTA** *is dark. Slenderer than Alberta and less robust.*

ALBERTA (*after kissing and hugging her*): Are the children well?

ALICE (*smiling*): I left them in tears. Emilio because today was his first day at school, and little Helen because she can't go to school yet. In other words, tears that are no cause for concern. Are we going to be here late?

ALBERTA: No. You'll be able to leave at ten or ten thirty. The only people we've invited to dinner are you, Sereni, Telvi, and the doctor. Your two admirers and the doctor to calm them! We didn't do it on purpose. Carlo needs Sereni's advice about some prints he's thinking of buying. As for Telvi, he's so out of it that when we don't invite him, he ends up spending the night at the office. My husband says he keeps the night watchman and the cleaning people from their rest.

ALICE (*sympathetically*): Poor fellow!

ALBERTA: I agree. Poor fellow! Whenever I set eyes on him though, he makes me feel like laughing. I can't help it. (*laughing*) Remember? He comes home, he tells the maid he doesn't want to eat dinner till his wife gets back, and he waits for her. When he finally decides to sit down and have dinner, he finds his wife's letter. Well, it's like seeing somebody slip in the street. They could break an arm, but you laugh anyway.

ALICE (*laughing too*):   Did he end up eating alone?

ALBERTA: I don't know if he ate at all. He studied the letter. His wife didn't ask for forgiveness. She blamed him. He had bored her. He'd bored her by being so pedantic, which is understandable, but he'd also bored her with his affection—always the same! so monotonous!—with his company, his business, his attentions. It was crushing. I still don't know how he survived it. The next day he was very depressed, but two days later he was mad, and then furious. Now that he's had all this time to think about it, he's convinced it was just his bad luck that the woman he met was a monster . . . And he's looking for another who isn't.

ALICE (*smiling*):   And you'd like to propose me as a candidate?

ALBERTA: It did occur to me for a minute. That is, I was going to do my best to bring the two of you together, hoping you'd get the idea of proposing yourself. It would have been a very good deal all around, except maybe for you. If you could only get used to the idea of putting up with *a good man,* a bit of an antique maybe, a little gouty; *a good man,* but as precise as clockwork; *a good man,* but—as Emma told me the day before she ran off—a man who keeps talking about business even after he gets home. Except when his jaw is stretched open in a yawn, or slackened in the silence that has given his mouth its normal expression, because in back of it there's a cerebral cavity stuffed with powerful gray cells, but with a vitamin deficiency. Nobody would have had a word to say against it. But you can't, because it can't be done. He's married for good, and, now that Italy's lost Fiume, there's no way out.

ALICE: Thank goodness, that way I'm safe.

ALBERTA (*waxing eloquent*):   Oh yes, you're safe. If that's how you describe missing out on a golden opportunity to make yourself and your children rich. I gave it a lot of study. It wasn't hard, because in the beginning he needed somebody to confide in—or, to be more precise, a woman to confide in—and when he sighed that he'd lost his home and his peace of mind along with his wife, it was easy for me to say: "Come on now, it's not as if every woman in the world had run away. All we have to do is put another woman in her place, and you'll get your home and peace of mind back." But he's a loser. He has no choice but to stay Italian till the day he dies. He has business interests that prevent him from changing his nationality. Therefore there's no way he can get a divorce. So he's out of the running. I know you, and I know how your mind works.

ALICE: You're right! (*laughing briefly, then explaining herself*) What with divorce being out of the question and that vitamin deficiency, there are no two ways about it. Let's forget about him. I'm sorry I laughed at him, since he's such a loser. Believe me, if I could . . . I'd get him his Emma back so he could enjoy her with the full blessing of the law. She lived with him for two years. A little while longer and she would have gotten used to it.

ALBERTA: And I had to put Sereni next to you tonight too, but it won't happen again. Put up with him again this one time.

ALICE: What do you mean? Sereni is delightful company. He makes me laugh, and he makes me think. And he's not short of vitamins!

ALBERTA: That's true. On the other hand, he's a lot like Telvi. He's married to his art, and he can't or he won't get a divorce. In other words, he wants his women for nothing too.

ALICE: That sounds like the right price for a woman to me.

ALBERTA (*sharply*): Then what would we women have left? Love?

ALICE: It's something. If we give it, we get it back in return.

ALBERTA: How young you've stayed! Life goes on, you make the best of it, and you know it, because you're smart, but you don't change your outlook, the attitude you were born with. When I talk about you to my husband, I say: Alice is stubborn. You just shut your eyes and act as if nothing had happened.

ALICE: It beats me what I could possibly have learned from. The worst thing that happened in my life was the death of my husband. A stupid, pointless case of pneumonia. He came home, went to bed with a chill, and died. It was a mystery to me.

ALBERTA: But there was more to it than that. Before and after. All I know is what you told me.

ALICE: Oh, I haven't forgotten! That bout of pneumonia brought me to tears, but then there was Mrs. Romeri on the second floor, and the concierge's daughter upstairs in the attic. The whole house was swimming in tears. (*suddenly moved to tears*) Death came in the door and showed me what my life had been like. But the pneumonia was the worst of my troubles. Yes! His worst crime was leaving me like that . . . without any warning . . . all by myself. And without any money. Maybe because he'd been spending so much on the home front!

ALBERTA: I'm really sorry I reminded you of all this. (*hugging her*) There now! Let's dry those pretty little eyes. Those eyes full of wonder. Those eyes whose natural expression is wonder, like the Mona Lisa with her naturally ironical smile. Something totally uncontrived, created by chance—a wide-open wondrous wonderful wonderment!

ALICE (*smiling*): The Sereni routine!

ALBERTA: He tried them out on you too? What a nerve!

ALICE: Yes, a number of times. But what does it matter? . . . I don't care.

ALBERTA (*tenderly*): I know! The fellow is carrying a new torch every six months! He says you can't paint without women. Though it's hard to see why. He paints such monstrosities, with their legs in the wrong place, swollen hips, contorted arms, you'd think his models were hippos. He needs love, poor thing! And not just one love, but one love after the other. When he was courting me, he painted a woman with no head. That's when I broke it off and told him I was insulted he should be looking at me and painting something like that!

ALICE (*her curiosity aroused*): He courted you too?

ALBERTA: Yes. I never told you before because I can't stand thinking about it. What bad taste! To get into my good graces, he started running down my husband, his best friend! He made me sick. I like to make fun of my husband. He's so absentminded, he can't keep his mind on my business for a moment, he's so concerned with his own. But when all's said and done, I am his wife. Sereni is bound to put his foot in it with you too, if he hasn't already.

ALICE: Not that I'm aware of. I hardly ever see him, except here at your place.

ALBERTA: He lives practically next door to you on Via Battisti, on the other side of the street, a few doors up.

ALICE: I know, but I never see him.

ALBERTA (*after a short pause*): I've spoken to Carlo and I managed to get him to increase your monthly allowance by five hundred lire, though it wasn't easy. You've no idea how I had to beat about the bush. He says these are hard times, he has a lot on his mind, and so on and so forth.

ALICE (*hugging her*): Thank you, my dear Alberta. I'll try to get by, I'll cut down on my expenses.

ALBERTA (*touched*): Forgive me. It's the best I can do for now. We'll have to see later. We haven't heard the last word yet. I'll keep working on Carlo. In the meantime, here's your money in this envelope.

ALICE: Thank you! Oh, thank you! You've already done so much for me, I don't dare ask for anything more. If it hadn't been for you, the children's inheritance would have gone up in smoke long ago. Thanks to you and you alone, when they grow up, I'll be able to pass on to them the little my poor husband Silvio was able to leave his family.

ALBERTA (*hesitating*): I'd prefer it too if you could arrange it so you didn't even touch the interest on your capital. It's a small sacrifice now, but it would be a real godsend for the children in the future. Carlo explained to me how interest accumulates.

ALICE: At the moment I simply can't. I'll see about it . . . later . . .

ALBERTA (*put out*): Of course, it's none of my business.

ALICE: Of course it is! You have a right to be involved in everything that concerns me. Aren't you the one who supports me and the children? But you must understand too. I showed you my budget yesterday. I can't do it right now. It may be a small amount, but I need it.

ALBERTA: In your shoes, I'd do anything to avoid touching that money. I'd like to be able to say to Carlo: see how important our help is to that little family? They're getting richer and richer.

ALICE (*going over the figures in her head*): It can't be done! It's really impossible.

ALBERTA: Then let's forget about it for now.

ALICE: I'll see. I'll think about it. You know how strong I am. I'll try, I'll do whatever I can.

ALBERTA: Good. And if you can't, just forget it. (*She laughs.*)

ALICE: Why are you laughing?

ALBERTA: I'm laughing because you say you're strong. You've never been strong, little Goldilocks, dear little Goldilocks!

ALICE: It's easier to be strong in some positions than in others.

ALBERTA: You're kind, and you're plucky, but you'd never be strong in any position.

(*laughing*) Look, I can remember the very first time I realized I was stronger than you, and I've thought so ever since. It's ancient history, in fact, because I was about eight, and you were nine and a few months. One day a boy our own age chased me, threatening to hit me. At first I was scared stiff—at that age boys make a big impression—and I ran away. He was just about to catch me when you stepped in determinedly, hollering and crying. The little boy was really furious—apparently it was his first run-in with women, and he still had to learn the difficult rules of chivalry—he knocked you down with one blow, and you were about to get your licks for sure, because to my amazement I saw that all you were doing was protecting yourself. At that point I stepped in, and in the end you had to drag the boy away from me; otherwise, I would have given him a real hiding. And I also remember that, as I was hitting him, I wasn't blinded by anger. Every one of my punches was carefully aimed and powerful, just to show you how you were supposed to use your hands.

ALICE: It's funny how each of us only remembers what we want to remember from the distant past. I don't remember a thing about this scuffle in which I played such a generous role . . .

ALBERTA: Generous, but weak.

ALICE: What I remember is something that happened a lot more recently, something so painful for you, you can't have forgotten it, in which I played the stronger role. Do you remember? You were already thirteen, so I must have been fourteen and a few months. You'd just lost your mother, and I came to stay with you because your father didn't know what to do to comfort you. I think I stayed with you for about two months at the time. But I never forgot them. Day after day, you would spend hour after hour with your curly head in my lap, you said you were keeping your eyes shut to forget that it wasn't your mother's lap. You were so weak and sick with grief that I thought: Here I am being a mother! And I want to be a mother, I want to love her and protect my little baby, just a tiny bit younger than I am. Then fate decided I would be the one to need you.

ALBERTA: But I do remember! Of course, I remember, Alice dear. It's just that I also remember what I was thinking while I was in that position. I was thinking: Sweet and kind and weak like my mother. And if a bad boy attacked her, I'd step in and protect her.

ALICE (*hesitantly*): Nowadays the bad boys leave me alone.

ALBERTA: Is Sereni painting your portrait?

ALICE (*flushing*): What's wrong with that? In my own home.

ALBERTA: The only thing wrong will be the portrait itself.

ALICE: I think it's coming along fine. He's going to give it to me as a present. He's painting me in that Friulan peasant costume you and I used to wear when we were kids at Tricesimo.

ALBERTA: What a lovely idea! Remind him not to put your mouth where your ear is. You don't even have to be a painter to see where the ears go. It's harder to paint a woman naked, to get the color of the flesh right. But Sereni gets out of it by painting her all green or all blue. Does he look through a piece of colored glass when he's painting? If not, I don't see how he does it. It's just as well he isn't thinking of getting married, because all he'd have to feed his family on would be paints. There would be one advantage to that though—once they'd been eaten, we wouldn't have to look at them any more. As long as he's single, he can get by on the rent from that apartment building in Via Battista he owns. The one he lives in.

ALICE (*slightly annoyed*): I haven't the slightest intention of either eating his paints or sharing his measly income.

ALBERTA: I know, I know! And, if you're wearing a Friulan costume, maybe it'll be a good likeness. Those peasant outfits cover a lot, and, when he's painting clothes, a painter's at liberty to choose his own colors. Oh, and while we're on the subject of clothes, your dress—my dress, that is, up till now—is laid out waiting for you in the bedroom. I'd like you to wear it to supper. You'll see how nicely it's been altered by our seamstress. Come on. (*They prepare to leave.*)

Scene 5

Enter **MAID**.

MAID: Signor Telvi!

ALBERTA: Here already? He's a bit early. Okay, listen, Alice. Help yourself. You'll find everything ready. Make yourself beautiful, just for me. You'll see how nicely it suits you! In the meantime, I'll have to put up with this charming company!

ALICE: You're complaining about having to put up with him for ten minutes, and, if things had worked out, you were ready to inflict him on me for a lifetime!

ALBERTA: But he and I are going to be completely alone for ten whole minutes! He's very intense company. In a lifetime, there are times when you sleep, times when you eat, and times you go out for a walk. You don't have to spend a lifetime in somebody's company!

(**ALICE** *exits left, and* **ROBERTO TELVI** *enters.*)

TELVI (*giving her his hand*): How do you do?

ALBERTA: Fine, thanks. How are you, Signor Telvi? Carlo is busy with some prints. He'll be here any minute now. Won't you sit down while you're waiting?

TELVI: Him and his prints! I could understand if they were paintings. But, black and white, a drawing with nothing to it. Of course, I'm no expert. And buried away in those boxes, where you have to take them out if you want to look at them! But to each his own, it's not for me to judge. Who knows how many questionable ideas I have in *my* head?

ALBERTA: Right! Sometimes I even suspect there are questionable ideas in *my* head as well.

TELVI: But nobody tells a woman that, and rightly so, because we need women. Nowadays, especially with their hair cut short, women have been given an external appearance of order. But inside the confusion must be even worse. I'm not referring to you of course, Alberta. Present company excepted.

ALBERTA: I'm excepted as long as I'm present. But, as soon as we separate, I'm included again.

TELVI: You're right. If I were to deny it, you wouldn't believe me. So I'll let it go. Anyway, I am one of those men who can do without women. That's no excuse to be rude, but it's an excellent excuse to be honest. I think they're right to show their legs and cover their heads with hats pulled down over their ears.

ALBERTA: Careful now, Telvi, there've been lots of men before you who thought they could do without women. I seem to remember something. Was it in history or mythology? Help me out, Signor Telvi.

TELVI: No need to go so far afield. Just go out into the street. Among all those men that walk around constantly accompanied by women, there are some who once thought they were capable of walking all by themselves. (*thoughtfully*) I know! It could happen to me. But is that any reason for me to think and act as if I was already accompanied by a woman? Alberta, you know my story. I'm not in the least offended if you want to talk openly about it. I don't expect that kind of consideration.

ALBERTA (*suppressing a yawn*): Have you had any news?

TELVI (*offended*): Me? News? I don't go looking for news, and nobody bothers to send me any. How could I have news?

ALBERTA: I see, I see. I only asked because other times you've talked about news you'd received.

TELVI: Yes, once. Someone came to see me once who'd been to their place. In fact, he'd just come from their place. At that point, short of running away, I had no choice but to listen to his news. It really is a small world. I had no excuse to run away. Not that he had much to tell. She's living in somewhat reduced circumstances. I expect she's regretting it a bit by now. If not, so much the better. What's in it for me knowing she's unhappy?

ALBERTA: And there's no chance of a real divorce?

TELVI: No! At this point, everything's settled. I could have harassed her; I could have made her life miserable. But I didn't. What's the use? You have to be prepared to take things in stride in this world. (*bitterly*) Even something like this. (*pause*) I've already stopped thinking about it. I have so much work to do I wouldn't have time to think about it anyway. Divorce is out of the question. My lawyer went into it in depth. (*anxiously*) I thought Signora Peretti was going to be here.

ALBERTA: She's in there. She'll be right back.

TELVI: Don't get me wrong. I just feel comfortable with that lady. What life took from me, death stole from her. The result's practically the same. (*shrugging his shoulders*) Who's to say which way is better? Still, she has her regrets. I can't afford any. Maybe she's even more unlucky than me.

ALBERTA (*feelingly*): Yes, she does have her regrets, poor thing! (*pause*) But she shouldn't have. He was disgustingly unfaithful.

TELVI (*cheering up*): And she knows? I'm only asking because that ought to lessen her sorrow. That's all.

ALBERTA: It seems nothing in this life serves to lessen our sorrows, and for Alice that's just one sorrow more.

TELVI (*with feeling*): I'm sorry.

ALBERTA (*playfully threatening*): Telvi! Telvi! It sounds like you're sorry that Alice can't bring herself to hate her late husband's memory!

TELVI: How could you think such a thing? What would be the point? For my own sake? (*shrugging*) As if a man my age and in my situation could think about Signora Alice.

ALBERTA: Why not? All I have to do is to look around me to see that harsh laws just don't work.

TELVI (*depressed*): Oh, they work alright! They work! From where I'm standing they work perfectly. I'm not complaining. It wouldn't do any good. And anyway, I'm not a man who could inspire the kind of love in a woman that would make her go against these absurd conventions. I've lived long enough to know what I'm like. I'm not attractive to women. I used to think, once they'd had a chance to live with me, to get to know the depth of my feelings, and the respect I can show for a person in love . . . But I'm a bit rough around the edges. I'm not a clever talker. A lifetime in business doesn't make a man more sensitive. It's not art, it's not painting.

ALBERTA: Are you alluding to Donato Sereni?

TELVI: Not to him precisely, but to him among others. I've watched him. He's sensitive, he's interesting. When he picks something up, it's like he was caressing it with his hands and his eyes. Women must like that.

ALBERTA: What a funny idea!

TELVI: I was thinking that the other day, when you were showing him that Chinese ivory. I, on the other hand, look as if I'm about to smash things. Would you believe it? Last night I picked up a Ginori vase of mine, and I was turning it over in my hands imitating Sereni's gestures. Would you believe it? I had to stop because I was sure the vase was going to slip out of my fingers and fall down and break. It's a good thing to know yourself and your limitations. That way they're less painful.

Scene 6

Enter **MAID**.

MAID: Signor Sereni!

ALBERTA: Come on in. Lupo . . .

TELVI: Lupo! Wolf! But a gentle wolf when it comes to objects. I don't like to think less of a man because he's better at some things than I am. And anyway, there are some things I'm better at.

ALBERTA: But some things are less important.

TELVI: Why? Even money has its importance.

SERENI: Good evening, signora. (*He kisses her hand and shakes hands with* **TELVI**, *to whom the* *following remarks are addressed.*) Do you plan to be more cheerful tonight? The other night you were nothing like the portrait I did of you. I still consider it my finest statement of health and strength.

TELVI: Those days are over. I'm not saying that my health and strength won't come back. I await them serenely.

SERENI: The ability to wait is a strength in itself. There are lots of things I can do in this world, but waiting isn't one of them.

ALBERTA: What do you do then? If what you're waiting for doesn't show up, do you run away and miss the opportunity of letting it catch up with you?

SERENI: I wait and I suffer and I howl. I have no alternative. To tell the truth, I'm always waiting. Take just now for instance. Carlo told me to come early. I got dressed, and then I thought she'd come back . . .

TELVI: Who?

SERENI: My inspiration! I didn't want to waste the opportunity, so I started drawing a head. I kept drawing till I managed to give it an expression. But it was a mocking expression right from the start, so I tore it up. Imagine my surprise when a face I'd created, no sooner does it see the light of day, thanks to my efforts, than it starts to mock me, the one who created it? I tore it up in a rage.

ALBERTA: Too bad, if it really was capable of mockery!

SERENI: There was no way it could have been beautiful. I drew it from memory, the head of a beggar I had given a few lire to a few minutes earlier and who had given me a look of gratitude and happiness—an expression you don't encounter too often in this harsh world we live in.

TELVI: Maybe he had a look of veiled scorn on his face. So many people you do favors for have that expression.

SERENI: No, no! The scorn was in my own fingers. I drew it with an incredible feeling of boredom. It couldn't have come out any other way. I'm through. Inspiration will never visit me again.

ALBERTA: I get along fine without it.

TELVI: So do I. But I can see why you feel bad. When something you're used to is no longer there, it's like a wound, it's painful.

ALBERTA: I can imagine what it must be like too. I remember how you were when you were painting that picture that got accepted in the Biennale. You didn't talk about it, but you were a changed man. Much more vibrant than you are now, more absorbed and more concentrated. Yes, that's for sure. Inspiration was written all over your face.

SERENI: And when the painting left, I got back to work right away. I worked so hard that when I saw a copy of my painting in a satirical magazine, where my nymph had been given crutches and a hunchback, I was almost ready to agree with the caricaturist. Now I'm happy just to get away from my studio. When you throw me out tonight, I intend to wander around town and not go to bed until dawn, so I'll be so tired during the daylight hours tomorrow I can avoid them by sleeping.

ALBERTA: I suppose I'm bourgeois, but my advice to you would be to go straight to bed. What if inspiration were to come back tomorrow, what would you make of it if you were tired? A beautiful dream, gone without a trace.

SERENI: My inspiration is not about to come back tomorrow. I know that for sure! It's not coming back tomorrow or in the foreseeable future. Maybe never again.

ALBERTA: So you have plenty of time to kill. Go look for Carlo then, he's waiting for you; you can look at his prints together. He thinks he's got a real bargain. It's terribly important to him to look clever. He's delighted with those prints because he thinks he got them cheap. If he'd paid a lot for them—even if they were better—they wouldn't mean so much to him.

SERENI: A man like him, who has everything, is easily satisfied.

ALBERTA: Does Carlo have such a lot? To tell the truth, it doesn't seem like so much to me. A woman, his business, and those poor old prints! *You* need a woman a month!

SERENI: I've never had a woman, not a real woman, one of those women who are good for a lifetime.

ALBERTA: I'll get you one, if you like. But you have to take a real woman in front of a Justice of the Peace.

SERENI: And if she turned out not to be real? I mean, what if she wasn't the right one?

ALBERTA: You're supposed to buy women the way you buy prints. Carlo bought his first, and only now, after he bought them, he's asking for your professional advice. If they're not worth as much as he thought, that's just too bad.

SERENI (*hesitating*): Oh, is that how you do it? You take a woman first and then wait to see if she actually lives up to what you saw in her?

ALBERTA: Exactly!

TELVI (*with a sigh*): Unfortunately, that's how it is.

SERENI: But can't you keep on trying, especially after all the disappointments I've had?

ALBERTA: If there were a trial period, there'd be no more marriages. Look. There's always the possibility that the woman won't like the man or the man won't like her. In addition to that, there are other negative possibilities. That either one, he or she, may only like the other for a limited time—a week, say, or a day. Or that either one may be attractive to the other only at night, say, or only in the day time, or only when he or she is speaking or—even worse—when they're not speaking. There'd be no more marriages.

SERENI: So what's wrong with that? We'd do without them.

ALBERTA: Go, go to Carlo. He's waiting for you. For tonight, tell him his prints are Piranesi originals. That way he'll be in a good mood at supper.

SERENI: He should be, he has everything!

ALBERTA: He doesn't have inspiration, but he doesn't notice.

SERENI: Maybe he's not without it. It's a kind of inspiration that leads us to happiness.

ALBERTA: Thank you. You're too kind. (*Exit* **SERENI**.)

Scene 7

ALBERTA: Inspiration? There goes another man who needs women.

TELVI: But I don't! The opposite is true in my case. I should never have had even one.

ALBERTA: I wasn't thinking of you, my dear friend. I was thinking of five hundred thousand others, but not you.

TELVI: And anyway, who can say if it's really a woman he needs. He kept on about inspiration. Who said it has to be a woman?

ALBERTA: Yes. It doesn't have to be *one* woman. It could be any number of women. It's so obvious that any man who goes around proclaiming his need for women strikes me as ridiculous. What happened to discretion, for goodness sake? That's the best way to get women to avoid you, beating your drum to attract them. It's all this hollering out of place that makes him put everything else out of place—legs, thighs, colors . . .

TELVI: I don't like it either, but maybe that's because I don't understand it. It was Emma who wanted him to paint a portrait of me. I keep it as a souvenir, but I can't stand it. Another souvenir of my own stupidity. It's very instructive. Ugly, serious, and sad as I am, I stare at that sad, ugly face, and it stares right back at me. It's as if I were looking in a mirror. A mirror daubed with colors that have nothing to do with anything. Like chocolate-coated carnations.

ALBERTA: And he calls it painting! He probably calls his need for inspiration love!

TELVI: But that's the kind of man women fall for. Not that I've anything against it. Let them fall for him. But they're making a mistake. Take it from me . . . now I'm out of the running.

Scene 8

Enter **ALICE**.

ALICE: There you are! Good evening, Mr. Telvi.

TELVI (*kissing her hand enthusiastically*): Good evening, madam. How are you?

ALBERTA (*examining* **ALICE**, *who is still holding the envelope with the money*): Very nice, very nice, but too low-cut. Much too low-cut! What on earth has that idiot done to this dress? I'm sure it wasn't like that when I wore it. I was never so naked.

ALICE (*laughing*): Oh, but I bet you were. People have quite a different impression of their own nudity compared with other people's. A bit of a draft like I'm feeling right now is nowhere near as noticeable as the sight of so much bare flesh, or—as Mr. Telvi is probably thinking—of so much barefaced impudence!

TELVI (*embarrassed*): Me, madam? That's not what I'm thinking at all. Everyone has the right to dress as they see fit. And in any case, you, madam, could never dress badly.

ALBERTA (*emphatically*): Well, you can't stay like that. Listen! I have a shawl in the other room that will keep off the draft. Come. Or stay here. I'll be right back. (*Exits left.*)

Scene 9

ALICE (*looking in the mirror at a distance, so she can see herself full-length*):   How decisive Alberta is! She knows what she wants. I like that. I wish I knew what I wanted. Listen, Mr. Telvi. They say you have studied a number of languages in depth. Is there a language in which you can say the opposite of "I want"? "I'm wanted," or "People want me," for instance.

TELVI: Oh yes! In a lot of languages you could say a lot of people would want you.

ALICE (*looking at him with surprise for a moment, then going back to the mirror*):   The really big problem, the only problem, is the skirt. It's too plain. They got it wrong last year. What idiots! If the dressmakers back then had had the same bright idea they had this year, I'd be much happier with it. Fashion is so cruel. If it didn't exist, there'd be less difference between the rich and the poor. What a shame! It would be so nice to be poor and still dress in fashion.

TELVI: I like fashion. When I still had my wife . . . Oh, you don't have to pretend you didn't know. I'm talking about the wife who ran away one night because she couldn't stand it anymore. I don't think I need to have any secrets from you, madam, I admire you so much. In any case, I can only converse with people who know what happened to me. I feel embarrassed and annoyed with the others. So, when my wife was still with me, and when all those accessories and outfits that fashion dictates would arrive, the cluttered house would seem more and more like a home, more and more like *my* home . . . like *our* home, I mean, and I used to greet those useless objects littered about— objects I couldn't care less about really, because I can't see what makes them attractive or useful—like so many friends and allies.

ALICE (*touched*):   Because they belonged to your wife!

TELVI: To the woman who now belongs to somebody else. Who is now decorating another home. I shouldn't think she's on such intimate terms with fashion anymore. She's probably condemned to wearing last year's fashions too.

ALICE: Poor thing! (*on second thought*) Oh, I'm sorry.

TELVI: Go ahead, say what you like. I don't feel any hatred. What would be the point of hating her?.

ALICE: Forgive me. I let that word of sympathy slip out because I was thinking in part of myself. You see how I expose myself to get you to forgive me? You might even say I bare myself. Do you forgive me?

TELVI: Do I forgive you? Just wait and see. I'm going to expose myself to you too. Are you ready to look? (**ALICE** *is scared.*) Listen! I couldn't care less about my wife. I don't know what people told you about me, but I think I can say I'm no fool. I know five languages. Lots of people know languages, but there aren't many people like me who've done business successfully in five different languages. So you can believe me when I say I'd suspected what was going on in Emma's head for some time. Not that I thought it would end the way it did. I was so considerate myself I thought she might have had a little consideration in her heart for me too. But she wasn't in love with me; I'd been certain of that for over a year. But what did it matter? Time went by pleasantly in that house full of our things. The hours at home were short, because business took up most of my time, but so pleasant! I'd tell her all about my day, then I'd watch how she arranged and kept an eye on things, I was full of gratitude because she was working for me. It's not the woman I miss, but now she's gone, everything's fallen apart. My house is still full of stuff, but it's a warehouse. I only go there when I go groping around looking for my bed among all that clutter.

ALICE: I'm so sorry to hear you're unhappy. What a pity you don't have a child. It would make such a difference.

TELVI: A child without a mother. I couldn't imagine such a thing.

ALICE: That's true. But with money you can provide for a child's welfare. I have two children. They are my consolation and my sorrow, because the poor things don't have a father.

TELVI: That's why I feel so much at home in your company. The difference between us is that you regret the loss of your husband whereas it's my duty not to regret the loss of my wife.

ALICE: You're right! My husband, poor thing, isn't to blame if he had to leave me.

TELVI (*who had been expecting her to confide in him is visibly disappointed*): Poor thing! That's what I say too.

Scene 10

Enter **CARLO**.

CARLO: Miss Alice and Telvi! (*shaking hands*) I didn't know you were here. Where's Alberta?

ALICE (*covering her décolletage with her hands*): I don't know what's keeping her. She went to look for a shawl to cover my décolletage. She thought it was too much.

CARLO (*confidentially to* **ALICE**, *with a laugh*): And yet, if I'm not mistaken, she used to wear this very same dress herself without any extenuating circumstances!

ALICE: You can speak out loud. Mr. Telvi knows about the dress and the need for the shawl. He also heard me discover that one's own nudity is always more chaste than other people's.

CARLO: Being a man, I'm only familiar with other people's décolletages. (*Considering* **ALICE**, *who has let her arms fall to her side.*) There is a difference certainly between one's wife's décolletage and that of other women. The former arouses less curiosity.

ALICE: Don't be naughty, Carlo.

CARLO: Excuse me, Miss Alice. Would you like to come and see my new prints? Sereni is examining them.

ALICE: I should wait here for Alberta. If I let everyone see me like this, then the shawl will be superfluous, at least for tonight. Why don't you go, Mr. Telvi? If Alberta takes much longer, I'll go look for her in her room.

(**TELVI** *bows and withdraws.* **CARLO** *is about to follow him.*)

ALICE: Carlo! (*hesitating*) I just wanted to thank you. (*She holds up the envelope.*) You've been so kind. I'm really sorry to be such a bother. I had no other choice. The trustee who handles the children's inheritance is so strict.

CARLO: But, Alice, what are you talking about? You know how happy it makes me to please Alberta. Because of business and hard times and so on I had to refuse you part of what you needed. But where you needed a thousand, eight hundred is bound to be enough.

ALICE (*hesitant but happy*): It's enough. It's certainly enough.

CARLO: I'm delighted to see you happy. For Alberta's sake as well as your own. So let's leave it at that. (*shaking her hand*) Now I'm off to enjoy my Piranesis. It seems they really are Piranesi originals. (*Exit* **CARLO**.)

ALICE (*taking the money out and counting it*): One, two, three, four, five. (*She counts it over a second time, then puts it back in the envelope.*)

Scene 11

Enter **ALBERTA**.

ALBERTA: Sorry to take so long. It needed a few stitches. It's real lace. I'll lend it to you for tonight. This antique lace is so delicate. Look! It'll look great on you.

ALICE (*laughing*): You mean, I'll look better than before? That depends on your point of view. You should ask your guests—Telvi and Sereni.

ALBERTA: Those animals, they want to see women naked without having to marry them.

ALICE: The painter must have seen plenty of nudes in his day. I shouldn't think he's interested in seeing any more.

ALBERTA: If you look at his paintings, you'd think he'd never seen real flesh in his life.

ALICE: Not everybody thinks so. It seems a nude can be any color.

ALBERTA: Seen through colored glass.

ALICE: He says it's like the sea, it depends on the position of the sun; in other words, on the painter's desire.

ALBERTA: He's very good at pretending to be a painter so he can talk about his desire!

ALICE (*laughing*): Don't get the idea he has to pretend much to proclaim his desires.

ALBERTA: I know, I know that from my own experience.

ALICE: When did you acquire this experience?

ALBERTA: Six months ago, I think. Or was it a year? Or a year and a half? I don't remember anymore. I didn't write it down on my calendar!

ALICE: And how did it end?

ALBERTA: I got mad when I saw one of his paintings. Or rather I got mad after seeing one of his paintings, when he had the nerve to tell me *I* was his muse. You know how blunt I can be.

Scene 12

Enter **DR. PAOLI**.

PAOLI (*greeting the two ladies*): You can't say I always get here late. For once I'm here before you even start thinking of sitting down to dinner.

ALBERTA: We're about to sit down very soon, doctor. Another fifteen minutes at most.

PAOLI: I'm in no hurry. Nobody knows I'm here, so I can be sure of enjoying a few hours respite. (*to* **ALICE**) Are the children well?

ALICE: Very well, thank you, doctor.

PAOLI (*relieved*): How pleasant it is to be with people who don't need me!

ALICE: I think people who don't need us are always our favorites.

ALBERTA (*almost angrily*): Why? I prefer people who need me.

ALICE (*laughing*): Thank you, Alberta.

ALBERTA (*sincerely studying her feelings*): I think they make me more aware of myself, of my life and my strength.

ALICE (*warmly*): And then there's their gratitude.

ALBERTA (*absently, continuing her confession*): Everybody knows you should never count on gratitude. I'm not referring to you of course. You don't owe me a thing.

PAOLI: But we're getting away from my point. When my patients need me, I examine them, they pay me, and we're even. Only there's a difference. If the illness is minor or nonexistent—that can happen too—then it's all very pleasant. But today was hell. First call, a case of pneumonia in a decrepit organism, second call, cardiac angina, third call, a unique case, a disaster, something obscure and uncertain, but so far gone already that even through the fog the signs of death were unmistakable. At that point I got mad. It was too much.

ALICE: It's your compassion that makes you suffer, doctor.

PAOLI: If there were anyone else here besides Miss Alberta, I'd have to whisper in your ear what it is that makes me suffer. But with you two I can be frank. You're both so healthy, you have no need to depend on my services. Though it wouldn't hurt to touch wood! What makes me suffer is my own impotence. Out of the three cases, I was able to deal with the first: I diagnosed him as hopeless; the second died without further ado before my very eyes. As for the third, he'll be some consolation. Tomorrow we have a diagnostic conference, and my ignorance will be abundantly excused by that of my colleagues. I've come to the conclusion that the medical profession is not meant for people. A good doctor would have to be a superman, no, that's not it, a completely different kind of animal, with far more senses than a man, and all super powerful.

ALICE: But I think that if you were to put this super-powered animal any place in the world he'd do a better job than a poor little man. It doesn't just apply to doctors.

PAOLI (*eying her with interest*): Good point. Yes, it's clear that a shopkeeper too, a porter or a sailor could all be better than they are. What you say is a consolation to me.

ALBERTA: But even the poor beggar who holds out his hand on the street corner would be better off if he had a larger and more generous heart. No rage, all gratitude.

PAOLI: In that case he wouldn't hold his hand out anymore.

ALICE: And even the person who puts money in his hand . . .

PAOLI: We're getting terribly deep. We've reached the conclusion that for life in general what we need is something that isn't a man but a being superior to a man. If a patient wasn't a man, he wouldn't be a patient. The wards would be empty. How marvelous! We'd all be superior, so there'd be no more doctors or patients, bums or benefactors. I could come here to dinner from morning till night.

Scene 13

Enter **CARLO**, **SERENI**, *and* **TELVI**.

CARLO (*shaking hands*): Greetings, doctor.

SERENI (*going over to* **ALICE** *and kissing her hand, then shaking the* **DOCTOR'S** *hand*): Lucky fellow, that Carlo! Ten Piranesis for a crust of dry bread.

CARLO (*to* **ALICE**, *with a smile*): You're not feeling the draft anymore. (*indicating* **TELVI** *who is standing next to* **PAOLI**) I wonder if the others have cooled off.

ALICE: You're being very shocking, Carlo. But you're very kind.

PAOLI (*to* **SERENI**): Are they real Piranesis?

SERENI (*confidentially to* **PAOLI**): I'm not really an expert. But it makes him so happy. And anyway, he showed them to me after he'd already bought them, so I'm not going out on a limb. (*out loud*) When I look at a print I bathe it in color. Nobody looks at a print like I do. (*confidentially*) There, I made my confession.

ALBERTA: That's right. Unless you're a painter, you don't even know how to look at a woman. I'm quoting Sereni. It's funny so many men who weren't painters, from Adam on down, should have looked at them.

SERENI: But only a painter can look at them with a pure mind, admiring the lines and the colors.

ALBERTA (*with a burst of laughter*): That's a good one! So is a priest less pure than a painter?

SERENI: A priest doesn't look at women, or at least he doesn't see them. I'm talking about the people who look at them.

PAOLI: In some instances one may suppose that even a doctor could look at a woman with a pure mind.

SERENI: When she's sick.

PAOLI: Not necessarily. With a few exceptions a doctor tends to see everyone as a patient.

SERENI: Especially as he gets older.

PAOLI: There are certainly cases in which age is an advantage. No one can deny that. But even young doctors get to be like painters, though what they see in women, instead of lines and colors, which are always seductive, is sickness and suffering, which are abominable. A young friend of mine was about to kiss a woman for the first time when he noticed that the shadow his head cast on the lady's eyes was not producing any reaction from her pupils. The doctor in him revived, and he was saved.

SERENI: A pupil that doesn't react! For a painter that's an interesting eye.

PAOLI: A horror! A man with a pupil that doesn't react is as inferior as a body that stinks. It's a stench, like the stench of a cadaver.

ALICE: Steer clear of doctors! Now I know, I'd never have one for a husband. During the engagement—or, worse still, afterward—he might just screw up his nose and make a negative prognosis.

SERENI (*moving over to the table where* **ALICE** *is sitting*): Don't you believe it. A doctor's a man like anyone else. There's a little bit of the painter in him too that medicine hasn't managed to kill off, and he can kiss the flush of tuberculosis convinced it's the bloom of health in its purest form.

TELVI: Even those of us who aren't doctors sometimes suspect disease. You soon know if it's incurable. At that point you make the best of it, you protect the invalid, you love her more. Later on you realize you were wrong. Wrong? I mean: you thought you'd solved everything by not seeing anything and not saying anything. Then what happens? The sick person can't stand the healthy person and . . . leaves. (*an embarrassed pause*) Okay, okay. I've embarrassed you by bringing up my private affairs. But it can be discussed openly. I don't mind talking about it. And anyway, I'm not good at expressing myself, so I took advantage of the example in front of me. (*shrugging his shoulders.*)

PAOLI (*getting up and going over to* **TELVI**): You were right to bring it up. It's interesting to hear you say that, in relationships between sick people and healthy people, the sick person may take the initiative. (*reflectively*) The sick person may in fact be more decisive than the healthy person. Indeed, it's often that way. (**ALBERTA** *wants to say something but can't.* **CARLO** *shakes* **TELVI**'s *hand.*)

SERENI (*confidentially, to* **ALICE**): I wouldn't dare make a pass at you here. Miss Alberta would never stand for it.

ALICE (*suddenly flaring up*): She wouldn't dare stick her nose into something that's none of her business.

CARLO: If you ask me, it's always the weaker ones who rule the world.

ALBERTA: Are you talking about women? (*Everyone laughs.*)

CARLO: No, by God. I'm talking about men.

ALBERTA (*getting up and going over to the table where* **SERENI** *and* **ALICE** *are talking together*): In fact the world is ruled by men. Not all of it. A teeny-weeny part is set aside for women.

CARLO: Teeny-weeny! The man makes the business, and the woman makes the businessman; the man is up front, like the horse pulling the carriage, but the woman does the driving; men make the arts and the sciences, and women decree what will be successful.

ALBERTA: If that's how you see things, I'm done for.

CARLO: Why? I'm not done for myself.

ALBERTA (*with a hearty laugh*): You hypocrite! He knows what he wants when he wants it.

CARLO: That's right! What you really mean is: If I should happen to want something, I'd want it.

ALBERTA: Who knows where you'd be if it weren't for me?

CARLO: But, little kitten—excuse me—I'm not saying I'd be better off without you.

ALBERTA: And I say you would be better off, but things would be too quiet. You'd send off a couple of cablegrams a day, you'd buy a few prints, and you'd ask Sereni over to give you his opinion. But Sereni might not come. Mind you, Sereni, I'm not saying you only come around because of me. But you're glad to come around because Telvi and Paoli and Alice are coming. An opportunity for inspiration! And if I weren't here, who'd come?

TELVI: I would, for sure. Especially if you'd run away. Carlo and I could cheer each other up. (*He looks round, expecting everybody to laugh. Everyone looks bored.*) Alright, I know you think I talk too much about Emma.

CARLO: Not at all, my dear Telvi. We're just afraid it's unpleasant for you.

TELVI: If it were unpleasant, I'd keep my mouth shut. (*He shrugs.*)

ALBERTA (*softly, to* **ALICE** *and* **SERENI**): Poor fellow!

ALICE (*with deep feeling*): He's really suffering!

SERENI: He'll get over it. The wound is still too recent.

TELVI: But we can talk about something else if you like. I'll help you, I'll take care not to interrupt you again. (*He slumps back miserably against the back of the chair. Silence.*)

PAOLI: I don't know much about what goes on between a husband and wife. Only what my patients have taught me. By the time I get involved, one or the other is sick, so they're both being as nice as can be. That's why I always say marriage is a good thing.

TELVI: Even if you see them when they're healthy, they can seem sweet and loving and tender. And even when they're talking to one another all alone together, it can be really nice. Then one of them runs away. The other is left all alone and . . .

SERENI (*coming over to him*): . . . curses!

TELVI: Oh, no! He doesn't curse. He's just a bit dazzled by all the light . . . and he talks about it all the time, trying to understand. (*pause*) Forgive me. There I go again.

ALBERTA (*to* **ALICE**, *who has gotten up from her chair*): I must speak to you Alice. I was so busy I forgot to tell you something very important.

ALICE: What's it about?

ALBERTA: Aunt Teresina. Take a look. I got this letter from her a short time ago. (*Handing* **ALICE** *a letter.*)

ALICE: Can't it wait till tomorrow?

Scene 14

Enter **MAID.**

MAID (*going up to* **ALBERTA**): Everything's ready, ma'am.

ALBERTA: Very well, let's go in. Alice, read that letter, then you come too. It'll only take a minute.

SERENI: Can't we wait for the lady?

ALICE: I'll be right there. I'll just be a second.

(*All leave except* **ALICE**. **ALBERTA** *comes back right away.*)

ALBERTA (*speaking rapidly*): Perhaps it'll be quicker if I tell you what it's all about. Aunt Teresina is coming to Trieste. We couldn't leave her all by herself at Tricesimo.

ALICE: Of course not. It's the right thing to do. (*Attempting to give back the letter.*)

ALBERTA: She's agreed to come and stay with you.

ALICE: But that's impossible! I'd have to rent another apartment to make room for her. How do you expect me to do that?

ALBERTA: Your apartment is big enough. The two boys have that big front room they could sleep and study and play in. Why do they need a special room to study in?

ALICE: Convenience is an incentive to study, whereas if it's inconvenient . . .

ALBERTA: As long as the convenience doesn't cost too much. You have to consider that too. Your boys are both good boys, they'll study just the same whether they have that expensive convenience or not.

ALICE (*quivering with agitation*): Listen, Alberta. I'd give anything to make you happy, but I don't want Aunt Teresina in my house. She's a malicious old woman, she's constantly complaining, and she's so sick these days she would rob me of what little peace and quiet I have.

ALBERTA: But we have a responsibility toward our mother's sister.

ALICE (*hesitating on account of all the things she would like to say*): We! did you say we?

ALBERTA (*also hesitating*): Yes, we! (*pause*) It's just that I'm not free in my own home, because I have a husband who would never allow a third party to come between us, though she's nowhere near as bad as you make her out to be. But I'm willing to take care of the nurse and all the other expenses. You're going to have to keep careful accounts.

ALICE (*bitterly*): There'll be account books to pay for!

ALBERTA: What do you suggest we do? Do you want to put our aunt in a nursing home?

ALICE: I don't want anything. My life is difficult and complicated enough as it is . . .

ALBERTA (*emphatically*): I hate to be the one to bring it up, but you can't say I'm not doing my best to lighten your load. You must admit that. (*continuing, in a milder tone*) Poor Alice! I know you can't afford it. But you must see what a difficult position I'm in. We haven't heard the last word yet. I'll do all I can—if not today, in a month or two—to make sure you have everything you want . . . well, almost everything you want.

ALICE (*in a murmur, unconvinced*): Thank you.

ALBERTA: My position is not all that simple either. (*pause*) Take a look at our aunt's letter. She doesn't seem as nasty as you said she was. Look at the nice things she says thanking you for your invitation.

ALICE (*astonished*): My invitation? (*skimming quickly through the letter*) You wrote her without consulting me to say she could come and stay with me?

ALBERTA: Of course! You'd already agreed, hadn't you?

Scene 15

CARLO *enters from the left.* **SERENI** *and* **TELVI**, *after peeking in at the door, enter also.*

ALICE: Me? Agreed?

ALBERTA: Certainly. Sereni was there. We can ask him. I said right away: I can't assume any responsibility for our aunt. You on the other hand shouted, there's no other word for it, I can hear you now (*imitating somebody shouting*): I owe so much to my aunt I could never refuse her a place in my house. (*pause*) Wasn't I supposed to consider myself authorized to pass on what you'd said?

ALICE: What are you talking about? I never said anything of the kind. Oh, yes, I may have said I felt sorry for my aunt, that I'd cry for her or cry with her, but take her in and never have another moment's peace . . . Never!

CARLO: Hadn't we better go in to dinner now and leave this discussion for later?

ALBERTA (*paying no attention to him*): If I were to swear that that's what you said, would you believe me?

ALICE (*laughing scornfully*): If I were going to believe you, I'd have to admit I didn't know what I was doing, that I was out of my mind. You're making it up now, just to get out of it.

CARLO (*extremely embarrassed, looking in the direction of the door, where* **SERENI** *and* **TELVI** *are standing*): Come now, ladies. After all you're cousins. You can settle this in no time when you're all by yourselves.

ALICE: I now know what I must do. I can't stand being in a position like this for another minute. I'd sooner starve, starve to death, me and my children. The help you provide doesn't give you the right to treat me like you owned me. Nobody's coming to stay at my house unless I invite them.

ALBERTA: I have no desire to lay down the law in someone else's household. I'd prefer to have nothing to do with other people's households.

ALICE: You are hereby exonerated from having anything to do with mine!

ALBERTA (*pretending to be disgusted*): I'll have nothing to do with it, then, I'll have nothing further to do with it anymore. I'll write auntie to tell her that, since you don't want her in your home, I'm going to take a room for her in a nursing home.

ALICE: You're wicked! Wicked! So now you're going to tell auntie I'm putting her out on the street. I don't want that either. Now you've invited her, let her come. I insist! I want her in my house, so she can poison my every minute, and so I can remember every minute what you did to me.

ALBERTA (*as if terrified by a sudden revelation*): I can see your hatred, Alice, your terrible hatred.

ALICE: *My* hatred? What scares you is the sight of your own hatred, the hatred you've felt for me all along. I don't want anything else from you. You've been good to me, but now I've had enough. Here, take your money. Take your shawl. (*tearing it off*) Tomorrow I'll send you this dress. The one I just took off in there is yours too. I don't want anything else from you. (*making for the door*)

CARLO: Alice, are you sure you're not being unfair to Alberta. She was always so fond of you.

ALICE (*in tears*): Oh, Carlo. You're too kind to understand . . . Let me go. (*Exit.*)

Scene 16

CARLO: She shouldn't be left alone in that state.

SERENI: You're right. I'll go with her. (*rushing off*)

ALBERTA: She'll calm down; she'll calm down. When she finds herself alone in that miserable little house, it won't take her long to realize the harm she's done herself and me. Where's Sereni? He'll remember . . .

CARLO: I asked him to go with Alice. We couldn't leave her alone in that state.

ALBERTA: I see. (*pause*) But why Sereni? Wouldn't it have been better if you'd gone with her?

CARLO: Do you want me to go and take his place? Maybe I can catch them. I thought I should stay with you. I've never seen you so upset.

ALBERTA (*on the verge of tears*): It's too late now. I wouldn't want it to look like I was meddling in her business again. (*becoming aware of* PAOLI *and* TELVI) Did you hear that? A fine scene I invited you here for! Forgive me. Why did you let Sereni go with her? He was a witness to what Alice said the other day. All I'm interested in is making sure I'm right.

PAOLI: The poor lady was so upset she didn't know what she was saying. I know how these things go. One person says one thing, the other denies it, they argue, they get away from the point, and finally, without anyone knowing why, they start lashing out at each other. If they were to allow for a little pause for the doctor to step in with a sedative, nothing would come of it.

ALBERTA: She said things I shall never forget. (*preoccupied*) What does she think of me? If she were right, I'd be desperate. But she isn't right. I was always so fond of her. (*pause*) Listen. Excuse me. I can't stay and have dinner with you. Let me go to my room. Call me if Sereni comes back. (*making for the door*)

CARLO: Alberta, I beg you to stay. How can you leave us three men alone?

ALBERTA (*bursting into tears*): Let me go, Carlo. I need to be alone. (*repeating Alice's words*) You've been good to me, but now I've had enough. Did I hate her then? Did I hate her? How could she think such a thing? And it didn't occur to her just now, she was too upset. She must have been thinking it for a long time, and she blurted it out when she was angry.

PAOLI (*affably*): No, that's not it, that's not it at all. She said the first thing that came to her in the heat of the argument, to put herself in the right. The words are irrelevant. Where you women are concerned words are always irrelevant.

ALBERTA: Oh, doctor. You don't know what words are. The terrible thing is, it's as if I had guessed the words she was going to say before she said them. I believe I read them in her heart yesterday, maybe before. But it's only now that I know what they were. It hurts so much! (*She weeps.*)

CARLO: Calm down and stay here with us.

ALBERTA: I can't, I can't. Excuse me. (*Exit* **ALBERTA**.)

CARLO (*following her offstage*): Come on now, little kitten. (*Exit* **CARLO**.)

Scene 17

PAOLI: And to think I didn't tell anybody at home where I was going, for fear of being disturbed by my patients! It never occurred to me I might need protection from people who are supposed to be healthy. A fine scene we've been subjected to!

TELVI (*staring into space*): We witnessed a great event. A scene I shall never forget!

PAOLI: What are you talking about?

TELVI: How marvelous she was, how marvelous!

PAOLI: Miss Alice? (**TELVI** *nods without speaking.*) When she took off her shawl?

TELVI: When she bared her great and noble soul. My wife ran away too against her every interest. And I suffered because I felt I should have admired her. Now I'm not suffering anymore. This woman is pure and noble. She throws away everything for the sake of preserving her freedom. My wife preferred my rival to me. But I know, if the same thing had happened to Miss Alice, she would have thought of how much I would suffer and stayed with me. That's how someone capable of giving up everything like that would have behaved. Oh! How marvelous she was!

PAOLI: She'll be back tomorrow, and everything will be as right as rain.

TELVI: Oh! You don't know Miss Alice.

PAOLI: How long have you known her?

TELVI: I just met her.

PAOLI: I say we go out to dinner in a local restaurant.

Scene 18

Enter **CARLO**.

CARLO: She wouldn't be convinced. We'll have to have dinner by ourselves. If you ask me, Miss Alice could have waited till tomorrow to make a scene. Come! Come! I'll see if everything's ready. (*Exiting ahead of the others.*)

PAOLI: Or even till tonight. She could have waited until after we'd gone.

TELVI: Why? If she'd been able to wait, she'd have been less heroic. Just like the other one. She waited until I'd gone out—and for my longest absence of the day!

PAOLI: My poor friend, you've fallen in love!

TELVI: If this is love, it's the first time in my life I've felt it! Heaven be praised! Is it true then—I never loved the one who ran away?

CURTAIN

ACT 2

A room in Alice's house. One entrance at the back of the stage, another on the right.

Scene 1

TERESINA *is onstage in her wheelchair.* **CLELIA** *enters in answer to her call.*

CLELIA: She's getting dressed to go out. She'll come through here, and then you can speak to her.

TERESINA: Maybe it's just as well you didn't say anything. That way I can see . . . I can think about it. It's easy enough to say what's on your mind. But then you have to live with the consequences. It's very hard to say to somebody: I'm really, really comfortable being in your house, but I'd like to leave. How do you go about it?

CLELIA: Nothing to it! All you do is say: What a dear pretty comfortable house this is! Just right for me. I wouldn't want it any bigger or fancier. I like it just the way it is. I'd like to leave though, because I'm a bit strange, and when I like something too much, I don't want it.

TERESINA: All you do is make wisecracks instead of giving me sensible advice.

CLELIA: You've already had my advice. I think this is a very nice place to be. There's the painter, I really enjoy seeing him.

TERESINA: Have you fallen in love with him?

CLELIA: In love, no. I'm just a poor girl, I could never aim so high. It's enough for me to watch how other people make love. I made that peephole in the door, and I watch them getting closer and closer and closer.

TERESINA: It's not nice to spy on people like that. What do you see?

CLELIA: So far he paints, and she sits still. But they're getting closer. He's been working on that painting for a month, and he still hasn't decided on the proper distance from the model. He always thinks she's too far away. They started out like this: him over there, and her over here in the corner near the window. Then he began to get closer and closer, and they drew a curtain over the window. So now he's practically in the corner as well. But it's gotten so dark I had to make the hole bigger if I wanted to see anything. How can he see to paint? In fact, it doesn't look to me as if the picture's making much progress. Every day I look at it, and I can't spot anything new. (*She picks up the picture and studies it closely.*) He did more work than usual yesterday. He put his signature on it. See there: Sereni! But I don't think he did anything else.

TERESINA: Put that picture down. Alice is coming. (*pause*) I thought I heard a noise.

CLELIA: What harm would there be if she found me holding the picture? (*putting it back in its place*) I also like that plump old gentleman down in the street who walks up and down with the patience of a saint looking up at the window. I have fun going to the window and making signals to him. He can't see me, only my handkerchief. But I can see him. When I wave my handkerchief, he stops and leans up against the lamppost, as if he was afraid the sudden rush of hope might knock him over.

TERESINA: You're being bad, very bad. Please stop sticking your nose in other people's business. If Alice finds out, she's sure to think it was me who put you up to spying on her.

CLELIA: What's to stop me saying I enjoy seeing love out in the street as well as in here?

TERESINA: They'll never believe you. What sense is there in enjoying watching other people make love? They'll think it's an old woman who wants to watch people make love, because young people don't watch, they do it themselves. They'll think it's Aunt Teresina who wants to know, just like she wanted to know everything that went on in the house she lived in while her legs and her eyes were still good. I kept an eye on everything. This house would be a very different place if I wasn't sick. That servant who steals the choice tidbits, those children with nobody to bring them up properly. They're so badly behaved! When I could get about in the world, you wouldn't find children like that!

CLELIA: Lucky for me I didn't run into you sooner!

TERESINA: Why? I was kind, very kind, but very active too. I was never lucky. I was the eldest of three sisters. They got married, and I stayed on at home with our parents. We couldn't all get married. I turned down lots of good prospects! If I'd had half a mind . . . But the most sensible person had to stay home. That was me . . . naturally. Alice's mother was too stubborn, and they didn't want her. Stubborn like her daughter. Alberta's mother was too vain. She would have pulled up all the flowers in the garden just to make herself look pretty. Alberta is vain too, but it's not so obvious, because she lives in the big city and she has her hairdressers and dressmakers. She's a fine lady. So I stayed at home, and my mother sat here in this hard chair, and I was where you are. But I was more careful. You're too young. When you push this chair, you bump it so much it's as painful as if I was being forced to run myself.

CLELIA: But it's hard to make a wheelchair go the way you want it to go.

TERESINA: When my mother was in this chair, I pushed it with more love.

CLELIA: So what did she say about the chair?

TERESINA: Poor thing, her personality was ruined by old age and sickness. No matter how gently and carefully you went, she still complained. The chair could go as smoothly as if it was running on tracks, she'd still feel bumps and jolts. I'm happy, I'm really happy with you, Clelia dear, I'm not saying this to complain. In fact, just ask Alice or Alberta, they'll tell you, I'm always singing your praises. I never finish a sentence without saying how lost I'd be without you. You're my one consolation in life. (*pause*) You're a bit of a heavy sleeper though. Last night I started calling you at five and you didn't answer till seven. That was a long two hours. When my mother used to call me, I'd be out of bed and by her side in one bound.

CLELIA: Did you ever ask your mother if you really did wake up that fast when she called you?

TERESINA: She never accused me of being a heavy sleeper.

CLELIA: Being your mother, she was obviously pleased to see you sleeping so soundly.

TERESINA: Nobody ever showed me that much consideration.

Scene 2

Enter **ALICE.**

ALICE: I have to go out now, auntie dear. I know Alberta is supposed to be coming to see you in half an hour. Do me a favor and tell her I'm very, very sorry I couldn't wait for her. I have so many things to do while I'm out, I can't be back for another two hours. I think she wants to talk to me about you. Maybe you don't feel at home here? (*coldly*) I'd be so disappointed.

TERESINA: Whoever told you anything like that? Me, not at home here? Me? I just dote on you and the children. I'd be heartbroken if I had to leave. The thought of leaving never entered my mind. To go to Alberta's? That posh house where there couldn't possibly be room for me? Never. I'd rather stay here.

ALICE (*brusquely*): Listen, Clelia. Go in there for a moment. I have something to say to my aunt.

CLELIA: I'll go right away, madam. (*Dragging* **TERESINA** *along with her by mistake.*)

ALICE: What are you doing? I told you to go by yourself. Leave my aunt here.

CLELIA (*embarrassed*): Oh, so sorry! I forgot to take my other hand off the chair. (*Exit* **CLELIA**.)

Scene 3

ALICE: Listen, auntie. I'm not going to tell you who told me . . . I must tell you, however, that I know you're not happy here, because it upsets me. So why beat about the bush? Just tell me, tell Alberta, and let's get it over with. I'm doing my best to make sure you have everything you need, but more I can't do.

TERESINA (*having difficulty breathing*): But whoever could have said such a thing? Who?

ALICE (*more gently*): Calm down, auntie dear. It isn't a problem. Whoever told me is only interested in your welfare. They want to be sure you don't have to suffer anymore.

TERESINA: Anyone who would say a thing like that is a scoundrel, that's what he is. Because I never, never said anything of the kind. If I wasn't happy, I'd come right up to you—or at least, I'd have myself brought—and I'd say: Niece, my dear niece, I don't feel good here. You are doing all you can for me, but it isn't enough. What would be the harm in that? I'd leave, but I'd love you just the same . . . But, in fact, I'm perfectly happy here, and I wouldn't go away unless you sent me away.

ALICE: Come now, aunt. How can you say such a thing? Me, send you away? Never! I'm your niece, I'd do anything to make you happy.

TERESINA (*doubtfully*):   Are you sure?

ALICE: So, are you unhappy with Clelia? Because there's certainly something here that's bothering you. You complained to somebody. Perhaps you didn't make yourself clear.

TERESINA (*obstinately*):   I never complained to anybody about anything.

ALICE (*eying her indecisively*):   Then I don't know what to do. (*sighing*) Let's make a deal: the minute you're not happy here, you tell me, and we'll go our separate ways in peace.

TERESINA: Maybe yesterday, in a moment of pique, I did complain to your neighbor, Mrs. Albi. Was it her who told you?

ALICE: I've never spoken to Mrs. Albi.

TERESINA: Well! I never said anything to anybody else. Who else do I see around here? I may have complained about Clelia. (*with a suspicious look in the direction of the door*) But it's nothing important. She's a bit of a heavy sleeper. But I'm not even complaining about that. It's such a treat to see someone in this world sleep soundly. I assure you, Alice, I would never even dream of leaving this house. And by now I'm so fond of the children. What little darlings! I'm especially fond of little Emilio, though he's a bit precocious for his age. Somebody should tell him not to read so much.

ALICE (*testily*):   I will, I will, auntie. So, goodbye for now. You won't forget to tell Alberta how sorry I was I couldn't wait for her. (*heading for the door.*)

Scene 4

Enter **TELVI**.

TELVI: May I?

ALICE (*surprised*):   Mr. Telvi! Please come in. How can I help you?

TELVI: Help me? That's not exactly the right word. I just need to talk to you.

ALICE: Do you know my Aunt Teresina?

TELVI: Only by name.

ALICE (*introducing them*):   Mr. Telvi, Mrs. Baretti.

TELVI (*shaking hands*):   A real pleasure. Are you well?

TERESINA: Very, very well. I couldn't be better. In this house. I couldn't be better.

TELVI: Since I've already been so bold, I'm going to be even bolder, I'm going to go all the way. I'd like to speak to you alone.

TERESINA: I'm going, I'm going right away. (*without budging*)

ALICE: My aunt can't get around on her own. But, if Alberta has given you a message for me, my aunt—I mean, Alberta's and my aunt—can hear anything you have to say.

TERESINA: Oh, no, Alice. I don't want to hear any secrets. I'm much better off not knowing them. I assure you.

TELVI: I just have a few words to say to the lady of the house. It'll only take a few minutes.

ALICE (*going to the door*):   Clelia!

Scene 5

Enter **CLELIA**.

CLELIA (*staring at* **TELVI** *with unabashed curiosity*):   Did you want me for something?

ALICE: Please take my aunt in there for a few minutes.

TELVI (*as* **CLELIA** *pulls the wheelchair toward the door*):   Madam, I hope to have the pleasure of seeing you again soon.

TERESINA: Me too, me too. (**CLELIA** *and* **TERESINA** *exit.*)

Scene 6

TELVI: Yes! There's no time like the present. (*addressing* **ALICE** *who motions him to sit down*) I have no messages for you from Miss Alberta. Last evening she said she was anxious to make peace with you. I pretended I hadn't heard. But I thought to myself that this peace would never come to pass.

ALICE (*smiling*):   How can you know that? Did Alberta tell you everything?

TELVI: She didn't tell me a thing. It's my own idea. I saw how sweet you were and how proud, so terribly proud I thought no one could ever put you down. That's the way I see you. I thought so as soon as I laid eyes on you. I first saw you when I was still with my wife. Then, when my wife ran away, all I could think about was you, and I thought of you as heroic and proud. (*timidly*) Yes! All I could think about was you. There, that's all I wanted to say. (*almost happy.*)

ALICE (*astonished and embarrassed*):   All? I don't understand.

TELVI: Let me explain. I've been walking up and down this street for a month. I look up at that window . . . I think that's the one. Every now and then, I can't figure out how, but the sun's rays strike it so you think the person you're dreaming about is there at the window. I rub my eyes . . . but it's no use. You must realize that for a respectable person like me standing sentry duty outside somebody's window is not a very nice position to be in. But then it occurred to me, I might as well risk everything, because I had nothing to lose, nothing, nothing at all. Looking silly? There are lots of people who think I look silly already.

ALICE (*protesting*):   Oh no!

TELVI: Thank you. But you did know my wife.

ALICE: I knew her very well. I was very fond of her. I considered her a model wife . . .

TELVI: So did I. That's something I can never forgive her. At twelve noon she plants a kiss on this cheek—right here, I can still feel it burning—and at five, or a few minutes past five, she runs away. Afterward she said living with me was impossible. Did she tell you that too?

ALICE: Oh no. Otherwise I certainly couldn't have considered her a model wife.

TELVI: That's true, that's true. You could never tell a lie. That's what won me over. But let's not talk about my wife anymore.

ALICE: Listen, Mr. Telvi. I think I know what you're trying to tell me.

TELVI (*quite relieved*): Thank goodness. You've caught on, and I don't have to say anything else. I'd just like to ask you something.

ALICE: What I mean is, I feel very flattered . . .

TELVI: Forgive me for interrupting. That's just what I wanted to ask you. I don't expect an answer right away. In fact, I don't expect an answer at all . . . if it's not the answer I want. For you it should be simple to humor me. To act as if I hadn't said anything. Isn't it simple? Though in point of fact I've said everything. That's the only way I can stop traipsing up and down Via Battisti umpteen times a day. Now I've seen that window from the other side. It's empty . . . for the time being.

ALICE (*smiling*): Why should I be silent? I have lots of nice things to say to you. You have my complete sympathy. I know what you've been through, and I sympathize with you heart and soul.

TELVI: In that case, I have good news for you. It will make you happy if you've been telling the truth. I'm not suffering any more. Or, to be more precise, I'm suffering for different reasons. You're the reason I'm not suffering anymore, and you're also the reason I'm suffering again. Be so kind as to act as if I hadn't said anything . . . That way I've said all I had to say, and no harm has come of it. (*smiling*) Aren't we businessmen practical people? As a matter of fact it's on account of my business I'm doing this. I haven't been able to give it my full attention lately. First of all on account of my wife and then on account of the person who made me forget her. But now I'll be less uptight. I've done everything I had to do. It would be childish to keep thinking about it. My love is the love of a grown-up. I'm thinking of myself, but I'm thinking also and especially of the other person. I'd like her to have everything. Every comfort, every pleasure. If she had children, I'd adopt them.

ALICE (*embarrassed*): I don't know how to thank you.

TELVI: There's nothing at all to thank me for. And nothing to reproach me with either. (*eying her anxiously*) That's true, isn't it? I'm doing what I have to do, so there can't be any blame. Now let's get to the other part. I want to talk about the other part. Some people who know me say I'm a very boring person. Were you told that? (**ALICE** *nods.*) Thank you for being honest. It's true, I'm a bit boring. If I see that the house is a mess, I can't help saying so. That's understandable and excusable in a businessman. In my business dealings I leave nothing to chance. I anticipate everything that can be antici-pated, and I insist on order. But this aspect of my personality ends up being a plus for whoever has to put up with me . . . I'm talking about the one who ran away. That was why, whenever she wanted a piece of jewelry or an expensive outfit, she always got what she wanted. It's true I sometimes got angry if she mislaid the jewelry or left the expensive outfits lying about on the floor. (*angrily*) On the floor, under a chair even! (*continuing*) I am a bore. And it's only now I see how wrong I was. Who knows if I could be any different? But it's too risky to try, isn't it? If it were just me, I'd try, but I can't very well advise other people to try. People have their own lives, and they should be free to do what they like with them. (*pause*) And another thing, I'm a bore at the table. My doctor told me not to eat meat, because otherwise I might have a heart attack. In a household like ours, it should have been easy to cater to my needs. No such luck! And do you know why? Because sometimes, when I'm through eating that tasteless stuff I'm condemned to eat, I end up eating the other stuff on the table. So then she'd say there was no point going out of her way to fix my special diet. I got mad. It's two different things if I get a heart attack by my own choice, or if I get it because of the person who's supposed to stick by me and keep an eye on my health. You may say that a heart attack is a heart attack, and that one heart attack's as good as another. But that's not how I feel. I'm probably being unfair and a bore in this too. Right now it doesn't seem possible to bother someone over something like that, but the time may come when it no longer seems so impossible. You see how sincere I'm trying to be? I do my best not to deceive people. It's true that when business is involved, I behave differently, and business is the only thing in my life that I'm good at. Wouldn't I do better to treat the whole of life as if it were business?

ALICE (*continuing to be embarrassed*):   I do appreciate sincerity. However . . .

TELVI: I know you appreciate sincerity, I'm sure of it. Let me say one more thing . . . That business of the divorce. It's not an insoluble problem. All you have to do is change nationalities and give up your religion. It's no big deal to give up one's religion. On the other hand, with things the way they are, giving up one's nationality could turn out to be expensive. I'd lose a lot of money and most of my social position. That doesn't matter. If it must be done, why not get used to the idea? I can hardly ask someone to marry me without a marriage ceremony. Only someone who expects love and passion can do that. A man more attractive than me, and less tiresome.

ALICE (*gently*):   Don't say things like that, Mr. Telvi. I won't have it. I refuse to admit that you're tiresome, or that there's any reason why you shouldn't be treated with respect and consideration. There's no way I can . . . But you ask me not to say anything that could be interpreted as an answer. Why should I say anything? Perhaps you were right to speak out as you did. (**TELVI** *listens anxiously.*) If it brings you a little peace of mind. (**TELVI'S** *anxiety recedes.*) I'd like to see you more cheerful. Unfortunately, there's nothing I can do to help.

TELVI: And can I see you again, not often, just once in a while?

ALICE (*after a slight hesitation*):   I'd be delighted to see you in the company of our mutual friends.

TELVI: I'm afraid we don't have any mutual friends anymore.

ALICE: That's true. But you never know. Alberta seems to be changing her mind. For the moment she persists in thinking it's up to me to make the first move. But she could change. I'm sure she'll come to her senses and see what she can't see now.

TELVI: So I should get back into the habit of going to Carlo's?

ALICE (*laughing*):   Had you stopped?

TELVI: As a matter of fact I had. Not deliberately, mind you. It's not my style to assume rights I don't have, so I really couldn't take your side openly. But Carlo got on my nerves. He didn't even seem to remember there had been a pretty lively exchange in his house between two of his female relatives. It's all very well taking your wife's part— (*laughing*) otherwise she may run away!—but not to that point!

ALICE: Did he blame me?

TELVI: No, no. He never said a thing to me. Not a word. For him, the scene never took place.

ALICE: He always has his head in the clouds; he never knows what's going on. I went a bit too far. What do you think?

TELVI: I don't think so.

ALICE: Go on, admit it! I went too far. But what does it matter? I'm glad I went too far; I thrive on it. It's a tremendous satisfaction, saying exactly what's on your mind. Going too far means doing something you regret, not something it's so much fun to remember.

TELVI (*murmuring the words*): I thrive on your going too far as well.

ALICE (*interrupting what she was saying with a smile*): We agreed I wouldn't respond to remarks of that sort, so I'm not going to say anything. Listen, Mr. Telvi. Your visit was a very great honor. In addition, I'm flattered by certain things you said, even those I don't have to respond to. I'm also gratified that you realized who was in the right in my quarrel with Alberta. That speaks well for you. That shows you're a gentleman, and I'm very grateful. A number of people, who were better informed, were not as perceptive as you are. Carlo, for example. But now I must go. I have an errand to run, and besides, I don't want to be home when Alberta gets here.

TELVI: Alberta? Here?

ALICE: Yes, she's coming to see our aunt. I don't think the time has come for me to meet her just yet. I'm still quite ready to say the same things I said a month ago. And I'm afraid she hasn't changed her way of seeing things either. So I'd better go.

TELVI: I have a couple more things to say, and then I'll let you go. If we businessmen can't agree on a deal, when we part company we say: There's always the next time. That's not the right thing to say here. But do we really have to say, goodbye forever? Goodbye forever is almost a silly thing to say. Who knows how things will turn out in the end? Then again, do things end? Isn't there always hope?

ALICE: Sometimes there just isn't. Really, I know of lots of cases where there isn't. But you asked me not to give you an answer.

TELVI: And in fact, you haven't. If you said something, I didn't hear it. And if you had said something, I wouldn't believe it, and, at the risk of displeasing you, I'd keep saying there's still hope.

ALICE (*offering him her hand*): Keep on saying it. Maybe it'll bring me luck too.

TELVI (*a little upset*): If it was just for you, I wouldn't say it. (*then making the best of it*) Alright, I'd say it for you too, just for you. (*He kisses her hand and exits.*)

Scene 7

ALICE (*going over to the upstage entrance*): Clelia! You can bring my aunt back in here. (*Putting on her hat in front of the mirror.*)

(*Enter* **CLELIA**, *dragging* **TERESINA** *onstage in her wheelchair.*)

TERESINA (*shouting*): But why, why? I was perfectly fine out there where I was.

ALICE: But that's not what I meant. If my aunt wanted to stay out there, she was perfectly entitled. Go ahead. Take her back.

TERESINA (*screaming at* **CLELIA**, *who has started to drag her out*): No, no! Now I'm here, leave me here.

ALICE: Clelia! Can't you hear her?

CLELIA (*confused*): Excuse me, madam, I didn't hear her.

ALICE: Forgive me, auntie, if those of us who are around you are sometimes a bit slow in interpreting your wishes. As long as you're living in my house, I fully intend for you to have free run of it and stay in any part you see fit. I only asked you to go out because that gentleman wanted to speak to me in private. (*with some effort*) If I did anything to upset you, please forgive me.

TERESINA: You're asking me to forgive you? What for? You sent me out because you had things to say to that gentleman that were not meant for everybody's ears. What's wrong with that? Aren't you the mistress in your own home?

ALICE: No, I'm not, and I refuse to be the mistress, not when you're here, my mother's sister. (*She hesitates, as if she were thinking of embracing her aunt before she went out.*) While I was talking to that other person, I still kept thinking about you. It really does look as if somebody told me a lie. I'm delighted to hear that you're happy here with me. Excuse me if I was rude.

TERESINA (*uneasily*): You've never been rude to me, I assure you. I never noticed.

ALICE: Goodbye, aunt. (*to* **CLELIA**) And you, try to pay closer attention to my aunt's wishes.

TERESINA: But she's already extremely attentive. I was just telling you how pleased I am with her.

ALICE (*giving her a surprised look, then continuing*): Yes, auntie, you're always pleased with everything and everybody.

TERESINA: Are you blaming me for that?

ALICE: No, auntie. I'm beginning to understand a lot of things. Goodbye, auntie. I don't want to be too late. I'll go out by the other door. (*Exit upstage.*)

Scene 8

CLELIA: It's pretty clear that, the way you talk about me, it's only out of the goodness of their hearts they don't fire me.

TERESINA: But didn't you hear what she said? They complain that I'm too pleased with everybody. That's something I'll never understand. They're unhappy because I'm happy. She's "beginning to understand a lot of things!" (*terrified*) She doesn't like me.

CLELIA (*trying to reassure her*): What makes you think she doesn't like you? She's in a hurry. She wants to avoid Miss Alberta, who was supposed to be here already, it's gone three. Or maybe she wants to catch up with that stout gentleman who walks so slowly and heavily but who left such a long time before she did. Who knows? It looks as if she's getting ready to cheat on the painter even before she becomes his lover. That really upsets me. For his sake as well as hers.

TERESINA: What are you saying? How dare you talk about lovers? (*pause*) And how do you know they're not lovers already?

CLELIA: It's obvious. If they were lovers, they wouldn't pretend to be painting.

TERESINA: But what do you know about love? You're not even married?

CLELIA: I know very little about it in fact. I've only been able to study it in my free time, and you know how little I have of that!

TERESINA: You were free twenty-four hours a day before you came here.

CLELIA: Not on your life! I was working for my mother, and when you're working for family is when you really work.

TERESINA: Yes, that's true.

CLELIA: And working for you is like working for family.

TERESINA: You don't have to do much for me.

CLELIA: People who give money think they're giving a lot, and people who give work think they're not giving much. I'd like to put an odometer on this wheelchair just to see how many miles a day I have to push you.

TERESINA: At times I wish you'd leave my wheelchair alone. But you're so young . . . Have you already had a lover?

CLELIA (*astonished at the question*): Me? Never. What about you?

TERESINA: Me? Never. Never never never.

CLELIA: Go on! You've probably forgotten. Try to remember, please. A lover's a man. He walks, sometimes he climbs, he hollers, he talks, and sometimes, quite often, in fact, he doesn't say a word.

TERESINA (*going over her memories*): Never. Never. Really. You see, our destinies are practically identical.

CLELIA: Yes, it looks that way. (*then continuing, with a laugh*) But I'm younger than you are, and I still have time to make up for all this . . . neglect.

TERESINA: Be careful what you do. A girl's honor is soon lost.

CLELIA: On the other hand, some people manage to live a long time without losing it!

TERESINA: That's something to be proud of. Staying pure for a lifetime . . .

CLELIA: What's the point?

TERESINA: What's the point? Honor's not supposed to have a point. Or . . . Yes! For one thing it can be used to blame those who no longer have it.

Scene 9

Enter **ALBERTA**.

ALBERTA: Good morning, auntie. You look well this morning. (*giving her a kiss*) I'm so pleased.

TERESINA (*eying her*): Do I really look well?

ALBERTA: And where's Alice? Is she in there? Shouldn't someone tell her I'm here?

TERESINA: Alice went out a few minutes ago.

CLELIA: And she also said she wouldn't be back for a while.

ALBERTA (*addressing her aunt, with some irritation*): Did you tell her I was expected?

TERESINA: Of course, I told her right away yesterday.

CLELIA: I was there too when your aunt told her.

ALBERTA (*angrily*): Who asked you to make corroborating statements my aunt doesn't need?

CLELIA: I thought you'd asked me. Excuse me.

ALBERTA: Very well. Now leave me alone with my aunt.

(*Exit* **CLELIA**.)

Scene 10

ALBERTA: What cheek!

TERESINA: She's a good girl . . . with plenty of faults. If you like, we can fire her. But, if she has to be fired, I'd like her to be given her notice just before she has to leave. Please. I'm completely at her mercy, if she got upset, she could smash me and the wheelchair up against the wall. She's very strong.

ALBERTA: I would never think of depriving you of someone you're fond of.

TERESINA: Fond? That's not exactly the word. It's no fun being pushed around all over the place. But if it has to be done, I might as well have somebody around to do it.

ALBERTA: And yesterday, when you told Alice I'd be coming to see you, did she say right off she was planning to go out?

TERESINA: No! No! She didn't say anything. It was only today she said she was going out, and in fact she did go out.

ALBERTA (*quite disappointed*): She's so stubborn!

TERESINA: Her mother was just the same. She insisted on marrying whenever and whomever she liked. She insisted . . . she insisted . . . she was always insisting.

ALBERTA (*taking off her hat*): Very well! I shall wait here for Alice. You see, auntie, there are two of us quarreling, and this stupid quarrel looks like it might go on forever. It's obviously up to me to be flexible. I have nothing to gain by making up. Quite the opposite in fact. But if we continue to quarrel, she'll be completely ruined. That's why I have to be the one to give in.

TERESINA: And she still bears you a grudge, even though she has so much to lose? In that case, you must have given her good reason to take offense.

ALBERTA: No, auntie! No! I don't even know how it happened. I had written to you to come to Trieste, and I forgot to tell Alice I'd decided you should stay at her place. After all, what was the inconvenience to her? I was paying all the expenses. I insisted on paying for everything.

TERESINA (*deeply hurt*): So it was because of me you fell out! That's all I needed! Oh, if I'd only known, I'd never have accepted your invitation. So that's why Alice welcomed me the way she did.

ALBERTA: I don't understand, auntie. What do you have to do with it?

TERESINA: You're asking me what I have to do with it, when here I am caught in the middle, between your two hatreds! Oh! Oh! My whole body's aching. It's like I was being ground between two millstones!

ALBERTA: But, auntie! Two hatreds has nothing to do with it! It's exactly the opposite. I love Alice. For the last three or four years she's all I've been thinking about. I've given her money, clothes, furniture. She spends the summers at my villa in Tricesimo, where I'd like to be staying myself if I didn't have to go along with my husband, who refuses to take more than one month's holiday and insists on spending it curing his liver at a spa. But did Alice really talk about hatred?

TERESINA (*emphatically*): No, she didn't say anything. I never heard her say anything.

ALBERTA (*looking at her undecided*): I really don't think the argument began over you. (*pause*) But in that case I'd have to conclude there was some deeper resentment behind it. But how could I have given her cause for resentment? Envy? For a month I've gone over every single word of the argument, and I still don't understand it. Well! Today I want to get things out in the open. Even if I have to stay here till nightfall, I intend to talk to Alice. (*She takes off her hat and puts it down.*)

TERESINA (*preoccupied*): Well, it's nothing to do with me, is it? If you're determined to stay, there's nothing I can do to stop you.

ALBERTA: Of course, it's nothing to do with you. But what are we going to do to make all this time pass? By the way, auntie, why did you send word you were so impatient to see me?

TERESINA: Did they say impatient? I don't think that's the word I used. I just wanted to see you, that's all.

ALBERTA (*coldly*): Thank you.

TERESINA: All things considered, I'm comfortable here. Still, I think it would be good for me to get back to the country. How can I stay here knowing my arrival led to such a falling-out between you. Poor little me, caught in the middle! (*She weeps.*)

ALBERTA: But, auntie, as far as I know, neither of us has done you any harm.

TERESINA: But neither of you loves me. Don't you know that when people are ailing and feeble, they need help and support. Neither of you loves me. (*She continues to weep.*)

ALBERTA: But I am very fond of you.

TERESINA: Alice says the same thing, the exact same thing. (*pause*) And people like me who were born in the country can only be happy in the country. If I were there, I couldn't go hiking in the hills anymore, but at least I could breathe the air from the hills. And I could stretch my feet out of my wheelchair and feel the grass, cool and damp and softer than any pillow, feel it, and maybe get some strength from it. (*pause*) Why couldn't you put me up in your villa at Tricesimo? I can't go back and stay with my cousin. He wanted me out of the way.

ALBERTA: Alice usually goes to the villa with her children in summer.

TERESINA: Even now you're no longer talking to each other?

ALBERTA: It's up to her. Of course, I'll make it available, as if nothing had happened.

TERESINA: If you two don't make up, she's not about to accept.

ALBERTA: Is that what you think? I don't believe she'll give up her children's health for the sake of a silly stubborn whim.

TERESINA (*bitterly*): Those kids are strong and healthy and want for nothing. You should hear their voices! Like a herd of trombones! And even if they do come, there's room enough for everybody. I could stay in that little tiny room through the little door next to the barn. And I could lend Alice a hand, because I know the ins and outs of living in the country. I wouldn't be much help, of course, but a bit more than here. And if you want to be happy in this world, you have to feel a little bit useful. If you're no use for anything, good for nothing, everybody looks at you with those eyes like you weren't even there.

ALBERTA: Auntie, if that's all you want, you'll go to Tricesimo.

TERESINA (*touched, kissing her hands*): Oh, thank you, thank you.

ALBERTA: But, auntie, (*snatching her hands away and bending down to kiss* **TERESINA** *on the forehead*) tell me something, auntie: how is it you got so much nicer as you got older? And yet everybody says people get more and more bitter as they get older. Remember? When we used to come in the summers to stay in poor old grandfather's house, our mothers would give us to you to take care of. All it took was one look from you to make us behave, and, (*with a smile*) if my memory serves me, even our mothers were a little bit afraid of you.

TERESINA: Those days, I was useful to everybody . . . things were different then. Our mother, your grandmother, died when I was seventeen, and I was left in charge of all those younger children. I realized right off that in the interests of the family I was going to have to raise my voice. The more I hollered, the better everything ran. The herds multiplied, the wine yield increased by the gallon, and the potatoes grew to unheard-of sizes. And I hollered and hollered. My father praised me for hollering. So I hollered louder. Your mother married very young. She was sweet pretty and kind, and she never hollered, because I was doing the hollering. Alice's mother was pretty and kind too. But stubborn! I hollered and she wept; then she did as she pleased without saying a word. The man who married her must not have noticed her beforehand! But you didn't have to marry me to hear me. And I waited in vain for a husband because—it's strange—men marry the woman they choose, then insist straightaway she should become the woman they need. That's why Alice's mother's marriage didn't work out too well. I was stupid, but so was she.

ALBERTA: It's fate.

TERESINA: My fate was hollering. Then, as he got older, your grandpa got soft in the head and signed some promissory notes, so we had to sell everything to pay them off. Daddy died shortly after, and I went to work for Uncle Enrico. I hollered a lot there too. I hollered on my uncle's behalf. I hollered less though, because he hollered more. As soon as he saw me, he'd start yelling. I quit hollering when they put me in this chair. Ask Alice and Clelia. I never raise my voice. I could still make myself useful, but they won't let me. I could help Alice raise her children. But I don't get involved in anything anymore. I need other people so much.

ALBERTA: But if that's how it is, you could even come and stay at my place.

TERESINA: Were you afraid of me? Is that why you stuck me here?

ALBERTA (*embarrassed*): No! No! I couldn't at the time. I had another house guest, there was no room.

TERESINA (*not especially convinced*): Oh, so that's it. (*pause*) You can imagine how happy I'd be to come and stay in your beautiful building. But still, I'd prefer to go stay in Tricesimo. I'm dying to see the country again.

ALBERTA: Look, auntie, the spring hasn't made up its mind yet. It still rains every day. The Tricesimo house is quite old. It's one of those houses in which the weather indoors is exactly the same as the weather outdoors. It must be very damp now.

TERESINA: But I don't want to come to your place, because I don't want to offend Alice. You're like cat and dog. I don't want to be caught in the middle, even when you're only looking at each other. Hatred's a terrible thing for sick people.

ALBERTA: But what do you care about Alice? She couldn't even show you enough affection to make your stay in this house bearable.

TERESINA: But that's not what I said. If that's what you thought I said, there's been some misunderstanding. She's always been kind to me, very kind. It's just that, a few minutes ago, when she thought I'd been complaining about her, she gave me such a look! Red and yellow, terrible!

ALBERTA: But you don't have to see Alice anymore if you don't want to. What's she to you?

TERESINA (*hesitantly*): You two are all I have in the world. Two people for an old woman like me may seem like a lot. But if I were to lose one of you, I'd only have one left, and one isn't many, not many at all. *You* might get tired of me too, and what then? It wouldn't be my fault, because I spend my days in this chair trying to figure out what to do so as not to be at fault. But the rich and the powerful get sick of seeing the same pathetic face all the time. I'm not talking about you, because you're so kind. I'm talking about people in general. Myself first and foremost. Do you remember old Anastasia? I brought her her bowl of soup every day for six whole months. But when she asked for something else to eat I got mad. I figured that somebody·who'd been saying how grateful she was for so long had no right getting mad at somebody else who was refusing her her one-hundred-and-eighty-first bowl of soup. But she went right ahead and cursed me anyway, with every curse she could think of; so I got mad too and kicked her workbasket. Maybe that's why I was punished by not being able to kick anymore. (*with a sigh*) The old witch! (*pause*) I know you don't kick, but, even though I may not have too long to live, I could still need everyone I can get, even Alice.

ALBERTA (*laughing*): What a strange one you are, auntie dear. Don't you know that what I do for you I also do for strangers? You'll never need Alice. You don't even need her now. And, in any case, sooner or later Alice will give in, and the two of us will take care of our dear auntie together. You'll see, you'll see. I know more about life than you do. Necessity knows no law. Did the doctor come today?

TERESINA (*curtly*): Yes, thanks. (*pause*) Does he come just for me?

ALBERTA: Of course, auntie dear.

TERESINA: He spends five minutes with me, then a whole lot longer with Alice.

ALBERTA: I asked him myself to have a word with her. You see, auntie, how I'm doing my best to achieve the goal I've set myself. When Alice recognizes the error of her ways, all three of us will be better off, especially Alice. I intend to be very generous with her. Obviously, our relations will never be what they once were. There are words that can never be forgotten.

TERESINA: Yes, words are even harder to take than looks. Don't I know it! These are all things I've learned since I've been in this chair. (*pause*) I knew the doctor wasn't coming just for me.

ALBERTA: But of course he comes here for you. Nobody else in the house is sick.

TERESINA: If you ask me, he pays me so little attention, he still doesn't know that my legs are the sick part. He examined my eyes, my back, and my chest. What did he say about Alice?

ALBERTA: He's supposed to come round tonight. I'll find out then.

TERESINA (*thoughtfully*): If you make up with Alice, I'll have to be that much more careful not to offend her. I'm sure she'll be more important to you than I could ever be. That's why I'm begging you to send me to Tricesimo. Not that I've anything against Trieste. I like your city too, a lot. It's so full of stones. But in Tricesimo I'd be less of a nuisance.

ALBERTA (*quite harshly—enough to shock* **TERESINA**): Don't keep insisting, aunt. You're making me mad. (*as before*) But auntie! You'll see how happy we'll be together. You can tell me all about the older generation, and my mother, and me too when I was a child.

TERESINA: And when I'm through?

ALBERTA: You're so suspicious! When you're through we'll talk about something else. What have we been talking about until now? And yet we've spent a very pleasant half hour together.

TERESINA (*opening her eyes wide in surprise*): Really? But if I come to stay at your place, I don't want Alice to know till it's time for me to leave here.

ALBERTA: Are you really scared of Alice?

TERESINA: I've no reason to be, because she's never said a harsh word. But from this chair I hear things that never get said. I must have picked it up from Uncle Enrico.

ALBERTA: Were Uncle Enrico's ears so sensitive?

TERESINA: No! He couldn't hear a thing. But when he was mad he had a special way of moving, so that everyone could tell what he was thinking. So, bit by bit, I learned to interpret the same movements, even when they're less noticeable, in everybody.

ALBERTA: I'll do it the way you want then. I'll send the car around to pick you up this afternoon, and I'll send Alice a note.

TERESINA: No! No! First send the car, then write the note later. That way I can leave, and I won't see her again until after you two have made up. In other words, not for a very long time, if you ask me.

ALBERTA (*speechless*): Do you really think so, auntie?

TERESINA (*hesitating*): I don't know. I get a lot of ideas sitting here all alone, and they could be wrong. If you ask me . . . I figure if she were so anxious to make up, she would at least have mentioned your name. She knows I see you every now and then, never for as long as today, mind you—though she wouldn't know that, because she's always out when you come. She's never mentioned your name in my presence, except to ask me to tell you that she wouldn't be home to see you.

ALBERTA (*disheartened*): Yes, it's obvious.

TERESINA: But what do you care? If you want to know the truth, I think this quarrel is to your advantage. It's different for her. But what makes her so proud? I happen to know, but you mustn't tell anyone, mind, that the children's trustee ended up advancing her considerable sums of money. I don't know what she does with it. Just after I got here I know she hired a governess to take the children out for walks. (*incensed*) She doesn't take care of the children herself, even when they're not in school. Or the house either. Out there in the kitchen, there's a cook who keeps the choicest tidbits for herself—that is, when she's not taking them home to her lover.

ALBERTA: Still, Alice was always a good mother. (*discouraged*) She must really hate me if she's willing to use up the children's measly inheritance.

TERESINA: I don't know what mothers are like in town. Where I come from, in the country, things are different. If you like, you can talk to Clelia. She knows everything, everything. (*laughing hysterically*) She doesn't miss a trick. She knows what the painter says and what she says and how that portrait's going that will never be finished. Ask her, ask Clelia. That's what she does for entertainment. She loves this house because there's the painter, and because down there in the street there's an elderly gentleman who looks up longingly at that window. He was here a few minutes ago, maybe Clelia knows what he said.

ALBERTA: Does she spy on people then?

TERESINA (*terrified*): Naturally, I tell her off; I try to prevent her eavesdropping. If you want, we can fire her. I end up having to listen to her because I can't get away.

ALBERTA (*after hesitating for a moment, going over to the door and calling*):   Clelia![1]

Scene 11

Enter **CLELIA.**

CLELIA: What's all the shouting about? Is the house on fire?

TERESINA (*meek and mild*):   Listen, Clelia, why don't you tell my niece what you know about this household?

CLELIA: About Miss Alice's lover? I don't know much. They kiss so it's a pleasure to hear them.

TERESINA (*pretending to be annoyed*):   What are you saying? I wanted you to talk about all the confusion.

CLELIA: Oh, that! You can see that anywhere. But a pretty lady like that getting kissed by such a worthy lover, now that's something you don't see just anywhere. What would we do without it! In this house, if it was just you and me, we'd be in danger of dying of boredom.

ALBERTA (*indignant*):   You've got to be lying!

CLELIA: So why ask, if you don't intend to believe me? Do you want me to show you the house where Miss Alice's lover lives? (*taking* **ALBERTA** *over to the window*) Over there, the last house on the right.

ALBERTA (*murmurs*):   Sereni!

CLELIA (*laughing*):   Would you like to see him in person? Watch this! I hang the hem of this curtain out of the window, and in ten minutes you'll see him appear on the door-step. I've been dying to have him come over when Miss Alice wasn't here for ages!

ALBERTA: I don't follow!

CLELIA: That's the signal! If you'll just be a little patient, you'll see him in person.

ALBERTA (*quickly pulling in the curtain*):   Don't do that! I forbid you!

CLELIA (*as above*):   One of these days I'm going to have the satisfaction of giving a hand-some man like that the runaround!

ALBERTA: You are not to permit yourself to play tricks like that on your employers.

TERESINA (*laughing*):   I tell her it's wrong to talk that way too. And remember, it wasn't me who brought all this up. I just wanted to tell you about the confusion there is here. Tell the truth, Clelia. Didn't we have to go without bread at lunch yesterday?

CLELIA: You bet! Yesterday the hem of the curtain was out taking the air, and at times like that there's always something missing in the house.

ALBERTA (*curious*):   You're something else!

---

1. Another version of act 2, scenes 11–14, as well as an alternative ending for act 2, scene 10, and an alternative beginning for act 3, will be found in "Alternative Versions and Dialogue Fragments."—Trans.

CLELIA: Believe me, if you saw everything that goes on here, you'd find plenty to amuse you as well. Here people don't make love like they do in other houses—at night. Here they do it during the day. The kids are in school. Berta's practicing petty larceny in the kitchen, and I am in exile with Miss Teresina at the far end of the hall. What could be more convenient? The middle of the house is completely free. But I can get to the keyhole from the far end of the hall in no time. I take a peek, then I go brighten Miss Teresina's solitude and report on what stage things have gotten to. She acts like she doesn't want to know, but . . . she enjoys it.

TERESINA: You saucebox!

CLELIA: And it's good for her legs. Just imagine, yesterday she made it halfway down the hall leaning on my arm. The only reason she went back to her chair was because she couldn't walk on tiptoe. Otherwise she could have gotten all the way to the keyhole like me. See what love can do!

TERESINA: I only wanted to see if I knew him.

ALBERTA: But you don't know anybody in Trieste!

TERESINA: It could have been somebody from back home.

CLELIA (*pleading*): Let me hang the hem of the curtain out the window. It would be wonderful to see the expression on his face when he found us standing around here waiting for him.

ALBERTA: I absolutely forbid it! Leave me alone with my aunt.

CLELIA (*dangling the curtain out of the window*): Oh, please! Leave the curtain where it is!

ALBERTA: Will you stop putting your nose in other people's business? What cheek! (*pulling in the curtain*)

CLELIA: It's business you'd never have known about if it wasn't for me.

ALBERTA: Get out! And remember you're going to have to behave more discreetly at my house and not tittle-tattle.

CLELIA (*inquiringly*): Are we coming to stay at your house?

ALBERTA: This very day!

TERESINA (*smiling*): You'll see, we'll be better off, much better off.

CLELIA: Yes! But why so soon? Aren't you even going to let Miss Alice know?

TERESINA: Of course! Everything will be handled properly. Alberta, you will tell Alice, won't you, that it wasn't us who asked to leave?

CLELIA (*shrugging*): I certainly didn't want to leave!

ALBERTA: That's enough out of you! Go get my aunt's things ready! (*She turns to face* **TERESINA**. *Meanwhile,* **CLELIA** *tiptoes over to the window, hangs out the hem of the curtain, then exits.*)

Scene 12

ALBERTA: My God! That Alice! No sooner is she through quarreling with me . . .

TERESINA: But who knows if it's true. I can't believe it. I never saw anything. What Clelia says is not necessarily gospel.

ALBERTA: Oh, it's a fact! Now I understand everything! And maybe she quarreled with me on purpose, just to get away from me and my surveillance.

TERESINA: I don't believe it! She must really have it in for you.

ALBERTA: How do you know?

TERESINA: Ever since I've been obliged to stay still, I've gotten used to studying people's faces. Whenever we talk about you, it's like a cloud of resentment passes over her eyes. If she can, she avoids even mentioning your name.

ALBERTA: And yet, believe me, I never did her any harm. Do you want to know why we quarreled? You won't believe it. We were having a conversation about your future! I couldn't take you in because my husband . . . I mean . . . I'm so busy I'd have had trouble finding time for you. Alice on the other hand said right out she felt responsible for taking you in.

TERESINA (*mortified*): She's fonder of me than I thought.

ALBERTA: Less than you think. Because naturally, when I heard that Alice considered it her duty to take you into her home, I wrote to tell you about it. These women who have nothing to do take forever just to write a letter, so I thought I was doing her a favor by writing it for her. She took it as an excuse to quarrel with me (*becoming upset*) in a way beyond belief.

TERESINA: I'm sorry I was the cause of your quarrel.

ALBERTA: You had nothing to do with it. Nothing whatsoever. If she'd criticized me, I wouldn't have been in the least offended. First she wanted Aunt Teresina, then she didn't want her. It's simple!

TERESINA (*with an effort*): Of course! It's simple!

ALBERTA: It was something that could have been patched up so easily! Now, for instance, you want to leave Alice's house, don't you? And should Alice feel offended?

TERESINA: Certainly not! But please remember you promised not to tell Alice I want to leave her house.

ALBERTA: Don't worry, auntie. I even offered to correct my mistake if I'd made one and write you another letter, whereupon she flew off the handle and said things I will never forget.

TERESINA: So it's true, it's all my fault. Now I understand why Alice gives me those dirty looks.

ALBERTA: Don't you believe it, auntie! It was just an excuse! She wanted to get rid of me! And now she has a lover, she doesn't need my help anymore! And to show her gratitude, she gives me one last kick!

TERESINA: Shush, for heaven's sake. (*cocking an ear*) She's coming! I recognize her foot-steps. (*After a brief pause,* **ALICE** *enters.*)

Scene 13

ALICE (*hesitating briefly on the threshold*): Good morning!

ALBERTA: Good morning, Alice! I'm running late. But since I've caught you, I can tell you I've decided to take Aunt Teresina in with me!

ALICE (*eying* **TERESINA**): I hope I didn't give auntie any cause for complaint.

TERESINA (*lowering her eyes*): No! Alberta will tell you in fact how sorry I am to have to leave.

ALICE: So who's forcing you?

ALBERTA: Auntie would like the use of a garden, and you don't have one.

ALICE: Seeing how I live on the fourth floor, all I could have would be a hanging garden.

ALBERTA: And naturally nobody's blaming you for not having one. But since I have one, it's only natural that I should let our aunt use it.

TERESINA (*stammering*): Maybe I could even do without the garden until summer, when I go to Tricesimo.

ALICE: But no, auntie, you don't have to be polite. I'm sure you'll be better off at Alberta's. In fact I'll come round and see you . . . like Alberta comes to see you here.

TERESINA (*sincerely affected*): Thank you, Alice dear. I'm so grateful you let me stay at your house.

ALICE: Why thank me? I didn't do anything special for you! (*sincerely*) There was nothing I could do, I'm so poor.

TERESINA: I'm so grateful to you because I know you had to make sacrifices to make room for me.

ALICE: I was glad to do it, auntie!

ALBERTA: So, auntie, I'll come for you in the early afternoon. Goodbye for now! (*She gives* **ALICE** *her hand, but avoids meeting her eyes, gives her aunt a kiss, and prepares to leave.*)

Scene 14

SERENI *comes in practically at a run and is surprised to see* **ALBERTA** *and* **TERESINA**. **ALBERTA**, *astonished, notices immediately that the hem of the curtain is hanging out of the window. She stands there speechless.*

TERESINA (*to herself, after looking first at* **SERENI**, *then at the curtain*): That Clelia!

SERENI: Mrs. Bezzi!

ALBERTA (*hesitantly*): How are you?

SERENI: I'm glad to see we've made up . . . How's Carlo?

ALBERTA: He's very well. He was asking about you in fact and why we never see you anymore.

SERENI (*still embarrassed*): Well, if I'm expected, I'll be sure to come round.

ALBERTA: What made you think you weren't expected? A word here or there isn't going to spoil an old friendship like ours.

SERENI: Thank you! And to show you I was only waiting for a word from you to go see my old friend Carlo, if you can hold on a second, I just have something to ask Miss Alice, and then I'll be right with you. Mrs. Carsti called me on the phone and asked me to come and make inquiries about a maid who worked for you for a while. She

knows we're next-door neighbors, and I was happy to oblige. The maid's name was . . .
Mrs. Carsti is not even sure she ever worked for you!

ALICE (*after a moment's reflection, striding over to* **ALBERTA** *with her cheeks aflame*): That's al-right, Sereni, don't try too hard! (*quietly but between clenched teeth to* **ALBERTA**) How dare you do such a thing?

ALBERTA (*quietly to* **ALICE**): I assure you I am perfectly innocent in all this.

ALICE: I don't believe you! Even now that I'm not taking money from you anymore, you still think you have rights in this household.

ALBERTA: I have nothing to do with it, I tell you. It must have been that nasty little maid you hired to take care of Aunt Teresina. Get a hold of yourself now!

ALICE (*out loud*): For whose sake? For you, who already know, for our aunt, who already knows, or for us two, who already know?

ALBERTA: For my sake. I don't want to know. Sereni, I'll be expecting you this evening. I must run. Goodbye. (*Exit* **ALBERTA**.)

ALICE (*going over to her aunt*): You really paid me back for the kindness I showed you! The kindness you were always talking about! Spying on me in my own house!

TERESINA: Oh! I swear it's not true. I swear! It must have been that girl Clelia! (*terrified*) Alice, I beg you, don't look at me like that, you're hurting me. Now you hate me! I didn't do anything, I swear! (*She hides her face and sobs.*)

ALICE (*going over to the door and calling*): Clelia!

TERESINA (*weeping*): You won't tell Clelia I accused her!

ALICE: I don't argue with servants!

Scene 15

Enter **CLELIA**.

ALICE: My aunt wants to go back to her room. (**CLELIA** *stares at* **SERENI** *inquisitively and then drags the weeping* **TERESINA** *offstage.*)

SERENI: I don't know what's going on. Who could have let the cat out of the bag by hanging out that curtain?

ALICE (*abandoning herself on his shoulder*): I don't care who did it. They sent you to me, and they were right to do so. Now stay here!

SERENI: And why didn't you let me go through with my act?

ALICE: I could see it was pointless! Nobody believed you! Couldn't you see they were all in cahoots? As a rule Alberta only stays for a few minutes. When the maid or my aunt showed her that by hanging out the hem of the curtain they could make my lover appear, she decided to satisfy her curiosity and find out who it was. She was the one who gave you the signal before I came home. It was a coincidence I happened to be here.

SERENI: I think that she guessed it was me as soon as she heard you had a lover. She knew I was in love with you.

ALICE: But she also knew you were in love with her. (*in response to a gesture of* **SERENI'S**)

I mean in the old days. Oh! What really riles me is that I was too surprised when you appeared out of the blue to say right out: Here he is! Have you met my lover?

SERENI: I'm sorry to see you found out like this. Our little secret meant a lot to me!

ALICE: The only thing that means anything to me is you. Secret or out in the open, my love is no different.

SERENI: It was bound to end up like this! It all began when we both stopped going to their house the same day . . . the same evening.

ALICE: You stopped because she was pressuring you to marry me. That's how she brought things to a head in exactly the opposite direction from what she wanted.

SERENI: Really? Do you think if she hadn't said what she did, I'd still be off on my own waiting for you?

ALICE: Maybe I shouldn't say that. I always loved you, from the very first day you said you loved me, and sooner or later I would have come to you, but . . . if you think back, even you couldn't get over how quickly things went. Everyone says you're a playboy, but you can't hide your surprise, it couldn't be more obvious. Well. It was my anger that made things move along so fast.

SERENI: So, I owe my happiness to Alberta?

ALICE: I loved you before, and I still love you now! It's hard to say what makes a woman give in. All I know is I was seething with jealousy. (*full of feeling*) Good God! I thought of her as so powerful! You didn't deny you'd been flirting with both of us!

SERENI (*taking her in his arms*): Well, you know how it is! Flirting . . . Still, I can't say I feel sorry for the way I acted if I got to you more quickly. It was obviously the right thing to do. But you're full of remorse because we became lovers!

ALICE: No! No! Though I was certainly a better mother before!

SERENI: Why? Have I come between you and your children? I never even see them.

ALICE: If you only knew how distant I feel from them. You and I see each other for an hour a day, but that one little hour invades all the rest.

SERENI: If we'd gotten married it would have been even worse!

ALICE (*doubtfully*): Do you think so?

SERENI: Did I let you down? Is that why you're sorry?

ALICE: No! I'm not sorry! Tell me the truth! If I hadn't given in, would you still think of me as an easy conquest just because I'm hard up?

SERENI: Heavens, no!

ALICE: Yes! Yes! That's what you'd think. Didn't you offer me money right off? And it was Alberta who made you think I was like that!

SERENI: No! I swear! I made inquiries, I discovered Alberta was giving you money and that she was about to stop . . .

ALICE: How quickly you spring to her defense! You know she was giving me money, and you also know that she's not giving me any anymore . . . and you guessed all that through some kind of magic. How discreet she's been! I bet there are lots of people who know she was giving me money and that she's not giving me any anymore.

SERENI: You can't believe that! Alberta's a good woman! Admittedly, the business she's in is not conducive to ennobling the soul. She spends her time doing charity work! Still, she's a good woman! She may make an occasional mistake . . .

ALICE: If you only knew how much you were hurting me by taking her part . . .

SERENI: Anyway, if I offered you money, I was well within my rights. It upset me to think that, while I was so happy, you might be struggling to cope with all kinds of hardships and worries. It was my right and my duty. Now I know you don't need it, my only regret is that you're depriving me of one of love's pleasures: the pleasure of giving!

ALICE: Darling! That was a nice thing to say and I'm grateful. (*with violent energy*) But even if I needed help, I would never accept it, never! Not even from you!

SERENI: I find this fixation of yours insulting! Aren't I practically your husband?

ALICE (*sharply*): No! Not from that point of view! And please, don't let's talk about it anymore.

SERENI (*taking her in his arms*): Whatever you say. I certainly didn't come here to quarrel. But listen! Lies—as I see it—are a necessary evil, even when nobody believes them. With Alberta, I have no alternative but to lie. How am I going to explain today's weird scene?

ALICE: You still plan to go to Alberta's? Never! Never! You must never see Alberta again.

SERENI: But that will confirm all her suspicions . . .

ALICE: So be it. What do I care? I'm sure she'll give me a bad name with everybody. I can't wait! It will give me another reason to hate her—my benefactress!

SERENI (*indignantly*): But she wouldn't do a thing like that.

ALICE: Oh! She'll do it! She'll do it alright! Today she's taking in that nasty old woman who spied on me, so she can get the whole story. That's why she's doing it!

SERENI: Oh! You're seeing conspiracies where . . .

ALICE: Wasn't that business about the curtain enough to show you what she's capable of?

SERENI: You've no proof she had anything to do with it!

ALICE: How naive you can be . . . when you want to be.

SERENI: Shoo, you little serpent! (*checking himself*) That's one of my friend Carlo's expressions.

ALICE (*staring him down*): Because you're thinking of Alberta!

SERENI (*irritated*): No! I was thinking of Carlo, just Carlo. How can I turn down an invitation from Carlo? We were childhood friends, you know.

ALICE (*with extreme violence*): You're lying! You want to go to Alberta's! Do you think I don't know you despise Carlo? Didn't you tell me yourself you were glad you didn't have to see him anymore? So! Go then!

SERENI: But Alice! I'll never set eyes on Alberta again if that's what you want. You can count on it.

ALICE (*weeping*): You've hurt me!

SERENI: You're in a frame of mind . . . I don't like. You know how I like it when you're sweet.

ALICE: I'll be as sweet as can be, all the time, if you'll just stop talking to me about Alberta.

SERENI: Why all this hatred? And for somebody who thought of herself as your sister, somebody who may have said something that offended you without meaning to.

ALICE: Oh! You'll never understand! Day in, day out with a person who never does anything to harm you, a person who's convinced in fact that they're being good to you. They humiliate you, they take away your freedom, while you lower yourself more and more every day. You smile when you feel like crying, you say thanks when deep down inside you don't feel any gratitude, you go out when you'd rather stay put, you stay put when you'd rather go out . . . All insignifcant little things in themselves, but taken all together big enough to fill up a lifetime! And you're not even aware of who it is that's making you do it. And then, one fine day, that person puts on a little more pressure than usual, and you're finally driven to rebel. And you finally know why your life— month after month, year after year—has not been worth living. You can breathe! You're finally free, and you know who's been humiliating and demeaning you. And you hate her!

SERENI: I don't understand!

ALICE: Living the way we do, the two of us, there are plenty of things you don't understand. But I want to tell you something. Of course, you're not married to me, but now hear this: I'm married to you. You remember, when you were waiting for me the first time, how I was late for our appointment? On my way over to meet you, I went into a church. There was no minister around to officiate, but I bound myself to you just the same. What does God expect of us if He's not going to punish us, what do men expect if they are not going to despise a union like ours? That it be a lifetime commitment! So I committed myself to you for a lifetime! I can't take it back now, but you could still forbid me to be yours, yes, that could still happen.

SERENI (*extremely irritated*): What are you talking about?

ALICE (*upset*): If you did, there'd only be one way for me to avoid the shame of having people consider our union just an ordinary affair! This is it! (*taking a little bottle on a chain from her bosom.*)

SERENI (*horrified*): A skull and crossbones! It's poison!

ALICE: Yes! I got it before I made up my mind to become your lover.

SERENI: I hope the bottle isn't easy to open.

ALICE: All you have to do is put your fingernail there! See! Right there! And press a little. But just a minute! If you were to go to see Alberta, that would be the time when I knew the time had come to use this bottle. I wouldn't hesitate, not even for an instant! Now go ahead. Accept her invitation, go to her!

SERENI: So, if I were to go to Carlo's . . .

ALICE: Come off it! To Carlo's! Do you think I couldn't read what you wanted in your eyes? Her invitation was shameless! It was more insulting to me than hanging out that curtain. It was an invitation made to *my* lover, with the added satisfaction of being able to make it in *my* presence. And why not? She owns me! Why should she care about me? And you, you accepted in a flash . . . in a flash, with your eyes all shining!

SERENI: But my only thought was to save your reputation. How could I refuse if I was supposed to be pretending there was nothing between us?

ALICE: That's true! That's true! Oh, darling! Forgive me! But promise me you'll never ever go to Alberta's.

SERENI: I'd like to see you calm down and show more confidence in my affection.

ALICE: If you'll help me get rid of Alberta, throw out the intruder, then you'll see me calm again. Listen! Listen! We've only been lovers for a few days, I don't think you feel desire for other women just yet! But that day will come, and the day will also come when you'll think of other women when you're with me, and I'll know right away. Well, that won't be the time to make use of this vial. No! I'll put up with the fate of so many wives! As long as you'll have me by your side—as long as I'm yours!—I'll put up with it. But woe betide you if Alberta is one of those women! You must forget you ever knew her, you must forget Carlo who belongs to her and her house and the things she says and the things people say to her. Everything about her offends me. You must never call me serpent again! Call me by the name of some other animal if you like, even more repulsive, but not by the one given to his wife by Carlo, who knows what he's talking about.

SERENI: You're going too far!

ALICE: I don't expect you to approve! But I've given you so much, you must grant me this. Swear you'll never see Alberta again. Swear!

SERENI: But it's my responsibility not to act as if I were your lover, even with her. What excuse can I give for refusing to pay her an innocent visit?

ALICE: I'll give you an excuse: you can tell her you're my lover and that I won't allow the person I love most to have anything to do with the person I hate most.

SERENI: I think you're being very unfair!

ALICE: Oh! I beg you! Promise me you'll never see her again! Save my life!

SERENI: She means nothing to me! Still . . .

ALICE: Swear! Don't argue! It's useless!

SERENI: Very well! I swear! But now you'll allow me to say . . .

ALICE: No! No! Now you've sworn, let's say no more about it! Now I'm calm, now I'm happy, now I'm in love! (*She flings her arms around his neck, then has second thoughts and tiptoes over to the door on the right and flings it open.* **CLELIA** *has been listening outside.*)

Scene 16

ALICE (*to* **CLELIA**): What are you doing there?

CLELIA (*half embarrassed, half smiling*): I was just looking . . . I was looking to see if Miss Teresina had left her handkerchief in here.

ALICE (*calmly*): Look then. Were you afraid to knock?

CLELIA: I had time to wait; I didn't want to disturb you.

ALICE: Now you've seen that the handkerchief isn't here, you can go! (*throwing the door open*)

(**CLELIA** *exits after giving* **SERENI** *a searching look.*)

ALICE (*slamming the door behind Clelia and drawing the curtain across it*): Her spy is out there! Oh, it makes me so happy! I love you so much! It's like I was kissing you in front of her!

CURTAIN

ACT 3 [2]

Summer. The same drawing room as in act 1.

Scene 1

AUNT TERESINA *and* **CLELIA.**

CLELIA: All Miss Alberta said was: "I'll have a word with my aunt today."

TERESINA: Did she seem angry?

CLELIA: No. Just a bit put out.

TERESINA: But I told you to tell her I was very happy here. The only reason I wanted to leave was to go stay in the other house in Tricesimo—that belongs to her too—because I was dying for a little greenery and fresh air.

CLELIA: As far as I know, that's what I told her, but she was put out all the same.

TERESINA: Still, I don't think I said anything out of place.

CLELIA: I think we've both been using the wrong tack with Miss Alberta. It's completely different with Miss Alice. You could win her over with a little buttering up. But with the other one, you've got to come right to the point. Miss Alberta doesn't have time. I mean she doesn't have time for us. I was in the middle of explaining to her how you have no desire to leave this house . . . no desire whatsoever . . . You couldn't imagine having to give up all these conveniences. On the other hand, seeing how she does have the house in Tricesimo too . . . and so on and so forth. She started stamping her feet on the floor with impatience, then thumping her fists on the table. She knew right away what I was leading up to, and she repeated two or three times: "I'll have a word with my aunt myself!" So in the end I had to shut up.

TERESINA (*terrified*): Did she seem that angry?

CLELIA: Don't let me scare you! Can't you see I'm exaggerating to make you laugh? Of

---

2. Parts 3 and 4 of the section "Alternative Versions and Dialogue Fragments" contain fragments of what Apollonio identifies as earlier drafts of act 3, in which Clelia was named Maria.—Trans.

course, I'm not too crazy about being interrupted by somebody who couldn't listen to me enough as long as I was living at Alice's!

TERESINA (*looking round*): To tell you the truth, I always liked Alice better than Alberta. Poor Alice, she's unhappy. She was fond of me, but she was always so distracted by her own hard luck . . .

CLELIA: You call that hard luck!

TERESINA: Of course! You wouldn't understand, but it's hard luck for Alice. Oh, the poor thing! Couldn't you see she was suffering?

CLELIA: Now and then, but there were times when I saw she was anything but unhappy. Sure, I liked her better too than this one with all her airs. But you have to admit Miss Alberta knows how to run a house a bit better than Miss Alice. Here everything runs by the book! It's like living inside a clock!

TERESINA: Big deal, with all the money she's got! Sure, Alberta is generous, I've heard she gives plenty to charity. But, in terms of real caring, all her charity is not worth the tears Alice cries over her children. Poor unhappy little mother! I don't lack for anything in this house, but it's two whole days since I last set eyes on Alberta. Don't go telling her, but, if you ask me, with an aunt in the house, she could take a bit better care of her. It all started when she suggested I eat my meals in my room. Okay, it suited me too. It bothered me eating in front of that Carlo, always on about business, and not very polite. Another thing. In this house they talk a lot about money. The subject doesn't interest me much because I don't have any. They went on about a hundred thousand lire, two hundred thousand, even three hundred thousand. All the same, it wasn't very nice of her to forbid me to sit at their table. Alice didn't talk to me much, but when she looked at me through her tears, all I could see in her eyes was affection.

Scene 2

CARLO *enters by the upstage door.*

CARLO: Isn't Alberta here?

TERESINA: Good morning, Carlo, sir.

CARLO: Good morning, madam. How are you? You're looking well today. I'm delighted to see it. Goodbye. (*He hurries off to the right.*)

Scene 3

CLELIA (*laughing*): He's really curious to know how you are!

TERESINA: He never once stayed to hear my answer. Every day he repeats the same sentence. If I had the nerve, I'd say right away, as soon as I saw him: "I'm fine, thanks, I'm fine." That way I'd save him the bother of asking! But I'd never dare do such a thing.

CLELIA: I'll do it then! The next time he sails into sight, I'll holler: "Madam's fine, she couldn't be better. So don't bother asking."

TERESINA: Oh, you wouldn't do a thing like that! Promise me now! Swear it!

CLELIA: Don't panic! I'll swear if you like. But that Mr. Carlo, I can't stand him! I don't know anything about Alberta, but him, with all his business and all, it would serve him right if his wife was two-timing him.

TERESINA: Will you be quiet!

CLELIA (*dancing and prancing around*): Two-timing! Two-timing!

TERESINA: You're crazy. Will you shut up? You're making me die of fright.

Scene 4

Enter **ALICE**.

ALICE (*obviously very upset, to* **CLELIA**): So where's Alberta?

TERESINA: Not even you bother to notice me, Alice.

ALICE: Sorry, auntie, I didn't see you. I came to see Alberta.

TERESINA: It's been a month since I left your house, and you haven't found a minute yet to come say hello?

ALICE: You know how it is. I didn't want to run into Alberta.

TERESINA: And now you want Alberta, and you still don't want me? (*weeping*) And I was always so fond of you!

ALICE: But you didn't want to stay on at my house.

TERESINA: I didn't want to! Good heavens! That's exactly what I did want. Tell her, Clelia. Was I the one who wanted to leave? You tell her!

CLELIA: It's no use. She wouldn't believe me.

ALICE (*rather indifferently*): Why not?

CLELIA: In that case, I can say it. Your aunt was put up to it by Alberta.

TERESINA (*terrified*): But keep your voice down, keep your voice down. (*lowering her own voice to a whisper*) And in any case, you know, I wasn't glad to be leaving your house. That's the truth.

ALICE: Believe me, auntie, all that's beside the point. I love you just the same. Isn't Alberta home?

TERESINA: Clelia, please go and tidy my room.

CLELIA: It's already tidy.

TERESINA: Then, go away anyway, please. I want to be alone with my niece.

CLELIA (*annoyed, getting ready to leave*): Very well! If you don't want me around!

TERESINA: Please, Clelia, don't get mad. I'll call you as soon as we're through.

(*Exit* **CLELIA** *with a shrug.*)

Scene 5

TERESINA: I'm so sorry she got mad. I'll tell her everything later. But I couldn't talk in front of other people. (*unusually lively*) Come over here, Alice. Sit down, please. Sit closer to me.

ALICE (*intrigued, doing as she's told*): Do you have something to tell me?

TERESINA (*after a moment's hesitation*): Yes! (*suddenly kissing* **ALICE'S** *hands*) I wanted to tell you I love you. That's what I wanted to tell you. That's all. If you only knew how much! I think of you a lot. You're all I think about. You bad girl! A whole month and you never came to see me a single time! And I was burning up with desire to see you. But that doesn't matter! Still, when I wake up at night, I feel a warm glow around my heart: I love somebody too. After all these years.

ALICE (*trying to pull her hands away*): But, auntie dear . . .

TERESINA: Now don't you say a thing, because you can't possibly love me like I love you. But that doesn't matter. When did children ever love their parents as much as their parents love them? I'm the mother, and I must love you without asking for anything in return. Look, since I started loving you, a new warmth has stolen back into my old limbs! (*She attempts to get up, but immediately falls back down into her chair.*) It's not much. But I know that, if you were in any kind of danger, I'd even be able to get up and come running to help you.

ALICE: Poor auntie! (*giving her a kiss*) Calm down! It could be bad for you to get worked up like this. But didn't you love me as much before?

TERESINA: Always! I always loved you! When you were a child, I felt I should be strict with you because you seemed so stubborn. But I remember how fond I was of you even then! After I was done scolding you, I couldn't help but smile when I remembered how cute and rebellious you'd been. You'd plant yourself there on your two little legs and stare at me with those big blue eyes to see if I really meant it. When I came to stay with you, I was obsessed with the idea of being a nuisance. But when I came here, (*lowering her voice*) the only good thing I discovered was how fond I was of you, all my affection for you. (*Her tone changes.*) Poor little mother, how come you love your children so much, and you still haven't learned how to set them straight and scold them? Is crying for them all you can do? How can this be? Your home is the last thing you think of. You're headed for ruin. Can't you see that, Alice dear?

(**ALICE** *looks at her hesitantly for a moment, then abandons herself to sobbing in her lap.*)

TERESINA (*profoundly moved and happy*): That's right! Stay like that! Nobody can do anything to you here! Make yourself more comfortable! There! There!

ALICE (*her voice broken by sobs*): Alberta told you that, but she only told you just now . . .

TERESINA: I never talked to Alberta. I saw everything, Alice dear, my own little girl. (*kissing her*) Because you are my little girl! The only daughter I have! And I feel myself getting so strong because I'm your mother! And what I'm telling you is the truth. I can tell you this: you're failing in your duty—to your children, your home, and yourself.

ALICE: It's true! It's true! But I'm so unlucky!

TERESINA: I know! I know! But help me think of a way for us to be less unlucky. (*timidly*) Couldn't you leave that man who's making you lose your head?

ALICE (*attempting to get up*): Never! Never!

TERESINA: Stay there! Don't get up! I'll never force you to do anything that would make you want to leave me. Do you love him?

ALICE: Yes! I couldn't live without him.

TERESINA: In that case why doesn't he marry you?

ALICE: Let me get up, auntie. What if Alberta saw us like this! She'd think we were plotting against her.

TERESINA: Let me hold your hand at least!

ALICE: There you are. But, auntie, you don't understand. Of course, I always thought he'd marry me eventually. That's how it looked. He can tell I'm restless and unhappy, and I think he loves me sincerely. A few weeks ago I thought he was ready to make the sacrifice for me.

TERESINA: Sacrifice!

ALICE: Well, yes, auntie. These days it's not much fun marrying a widow with two children.

TERESINA: But if he loves you . . .

ALICE: He loves me alright, but after all . . . I'm already his lover, and he might not see the point of marrying me.

TERESINA: And you were saying you've been finding him less affectionate lately.

ALICE: Yes, and it's all her fault!

TERESINA: Whose? Alberta's?

ALICE: Yes, hers. You ought to know that at one time Donato made advances to Alberta. Being an honest woman, she let him know in no uncertain terms that he was wasting his time. But now, just to spite me, she flirts with him and gets his hopes up, and he feels his old desire coming back, and it bothers him.

TERESINA: He loves you, and he wants her?

ALICE: I know nothing for certain about him. But I do about her. Here, take a look! (*She takes a letter from her bosom.*) I found this in Donato's pocket. (*desperately*) It's already bad enough that he didn't show it to me. (*She reads.*) "My dear Sereni, when are you going to keep your promise and come and see me? Let me know when you plan to come, so I can be sure to be at home. Alberta." Everything about this note shows her evil intentions. Does she mean she needs the advance warning to be sure to be alone when he comes? Just imagine what he must have thought of a note like this if he was once in love with her.

TERESINA (*thinking it over*): I don't believe he ever took her up on the invitation.

ALICE: How would you know?

TERESINA: I wouldn't. But Clelia would. She knows everything! I think she can see through walls.

ALICE: Oh sure! In my house it was easy! But in an enormous place like this it's another story.

TERESINA: Believe me, even if it were twice the size, she'd have the whole place under observation.

ALICE: Couldn't we question her?

TERESINA: Why not? (*then, with ill-concealed satisfaction*) She can't stand Alberta. It's instinctive. So she'd never tell her we'd been questioning her.

ALICE: Even if she told her, I wouldn't care. (*running over to the door on the left*) Clelia! Clelia!

Scene 6

Enter **CLELIA**.

CLELIA: Do you need me?

TERESINA: Yes, Clelia dear.

CLELIA: I'll say you need me! Now it's "dear"!

TERESINA: How can you say a thing like that? Don't I always call you "dear"?

CLELIA: Sure, when we're alone. But when there's anyone else around, you'd be too embarrassed.

TERESINA: How can you say such a thing? Isn't Alice here now?

CLELIA: You mean you both need me!

ALICE (*angrily*): Very well. Let's leave it at that. You were quicker to answer when Alberta wanted you to tell tales on me.

CLELIA (*laughing*): So that's what you want me for. My goodness! If I can be of any help . . . Though I don't see what good it'll do you to know what's going on in the kitchen or the hall or out in the garden.

TERESINA: What we would really like to know is what's going on in all the other places.

CLELIA: I'm no help there. I'm not allowed in the other places.

TERESINA (*thinking it over*): Listen. Haven't you ever seen anyone here you used to see at Alice's?

CLELIA: Lots of people! You and me to begin with.

TERESINA: And nobody else. Think about it, Clelia.

CLELIA: Oh, yes! This morning for the first time I saw that nice-looking young fellow, the one with the profile like a statue, and the little black moustache . . . Donato Sereni.

TERESINA: And you didn't tell me?

ALICE: But are you sure?

CLELIA: Oh, I like that! It was here I found out what his name was. Because here it was spelled out when he was announced: Donato Sereni.

ALICE (*extremely upset*): Goodbye, aunt. I'm going to get to the bottom of this right away. (*making for the door*)

Scene 7

Enter **CARLO**.

CARLO (*coming in and seeing Alice*): Good morning, Alice! How are you?

ALICE (*stopping*): I'm very well!

CARLO: This is the first time I've seen you here in ages!

ALICE: Well, all your friends come back here sooner or later.

CARLO (*a bit taken aback by her answer, after a slight hesitation*): That's because Alberta and I are very attached to our friends.

ALICE: Yes! Very attached! Donato Sereni has been back here too.

CARLO: Back here?

ALICE (*watching his face*): You didn't know?

CARLO (*mumbling*): Alberta must have forgotten to tell me.

Scene 8

Enter ALBERTA.

ALBERTA (*sweetly*): Alice!

ALICE (*drawing away in disgust*): I came to see auntie.

ALBERTA: That's good! (*turning to* CARLO) And you were in such a hurry . . .

CARLO (*hesitantly*): Alberta, I'd like you to have a few words with your cousin. From certain things she said I gather she's making insinuations about you that you've done nothing to deserve—I'm quite sure of that. (*more forthright*) Your relations can stay as they are, but that's no excuse for somebody on whom you've lavished your affection to think things like that about you. If you like I can leave, and you can have it out between yourselves.

ALICE: I don't feel the need for any explanations. You understood perfectly well, Carlo, what I meant to say. You can tell her yourself. That's all I want. (*preparing to leave*)

ALBERTA: Please, Alice. Wait a minute. I have something to say to you too. I still can't resign myself to the idea that—on account of that little misunderstanding we had because of that business about auntie—we have to be enemies for the rest of our lives. Do you want to talk about it?

ALICE: Who remembers *that*? This is about something altogether different.

ALBERTA: I know! I know what it's about, but I'm sure that when you find out how things really stand you'll change your opinion of me.

ALICE: I was just on my way out to find out how things stand.

ALBERTA (*calmly*): Fine! You can check later if what I say is true. But can't you listen to my side of the story? (*to* TERESINA) Auntie! Don't you usually go out in the garden about now?

CLELIA: It looks like rain.

ALICE: As far as I'm concerned, auntie can stay here for any explanations there may be.

TERESINA: I'd like to go out in the garden. If it rains, I'll take shelter in my room. My being here won't do you any good. What could I have to say? Who would listen?

ALICE (*angrily*): We should all listen to you. You're our mother's sister!

ALBERTA: Go ahead and stay, auntie. I've always honored you as my mother's sister, and I don't think I have anything to be embarrassed about in front of you. (*to* CLELIA) When I need you, I'll call you. (*Exit* CLELIA.)

TERESINA (*who has been thinking*): But, Alberta dear, I never said you had failed to show me affection and respect.

ALBERTA (*shrugging*): It's not important, auntie dear. (*to* **ALICE** *and* **CARLO**) It's true! Donato Sereni has been here to see me. I didn't tell you because he made me promise not to say anything, not even to you. And would you like to know why? Because Alice swore that if she ever found out he'd set foot over that threshold she'd kill herself! Do you hear? That's what things have come to!

ALICE (*calmly*): I wonder if Carlo knows that Donato Sereni and I are lovers.

ALBERTA: He knows! He knows! Who doesn't! But come here, Alice, come here, you poor thing! You changed your personality from one minute to the next! You used to be the soul of discretion, or better yet innocence. All you could think of was respect for society and its laws. And now you've suddenly thrown all that out the window and are affecting these rebellious attitudes that will be your downfall. There's just one thing I want you to tell me: Am I to blame for all this? Am I the one who drove you to despise everything you once looked up to, am I the one who drove you to abandon the path that was supposed to be leading to your happiness and that of your children? I don't know, but my conscience cries out when I think that one fine day you turned your back on me, and at the same time you started behaving as if life didn't mean a thing to you anymore! Am I the one to blame for all that? (**ALICE** *looks at her hesitantly.*) How come I do harm when all I want to do is do good? You can confirm that. I'm not talking about the pocket money I gave you, but I helped you most of all with advice, and I gave you all, all my affection. (*moved to tears*) I certainly got what I deserved!

ALICE (*once more insulted and determined*): We're not talking about the way things used to be. What I want to know now is why you insisted on Donato coming to see you.

ALBERTA (*pale*): I didn't have to insist! All I had to do was open the door, and he walked right in.

ALICE: You opened it more than once. I was there once when you invited him, and he didn't come. I don't know how many more times you had to open this door to get him to come in. I'm sorry to have to talk like this in front of your husband . . . But in any case everybody here knows you didn't send for him out of love. You sent for him out of hatred, to humiliate me.

TERESINA (*taking the hand of* **ALBERTA**, *who happens to be standing near her chair*): Be kind, Alberta. If you only knew how unhappy she is!

ALICE: Auntie! Let me make it clear that I don't need anyone here.

TERESINA: Excuse me, Alice! Forgive me! I was only trying to help.

ALBERTA: You were the one who said we should listen to our aunt, our mother's sister.

TERESINA: No! No! I'm not asking to be listened to. I don't know, I don't understand. All I can say is this: I'd like you to make up. I don't understand anything, and what I'm saying is foolish, but I'd like you to kiss and make up without any more fuss.

ALBERTA: Be still, aunt! You'll see, it'll all be settled in no time.

ALICE (*in a challenging tone*): Really?

ALBERTA: All I want is for you to hear me out. Like I told you: I was distressed to see you embarked on a path which—if I you'll permit me to say so—was never meant for you, and I was distressed to think that maybe—without intending to, without even suspecting I was offending you—I swear I never offended you on purpose—you'd been driven off the right track by me, by your hatred for me.

ALICE: You're not as important in my life as you seem to think.

ALBERTA: So be it! If I could have gotten you to admit that earlier, I would never have sent for Sereni. Instead I thought: maybe, without knowing, in all innocence, I had a share in Alice's downfall. So I had a responsibility to set things to rights. That's why I called Sereni.

ALICE: To set things to rights! That's a good one!

ALBERTA: Yes, to set things to rights! So here I am. Sereni has authorized me to ask for your hand. Do you hear?

ALICE: And I refuse! Do *you* hear? I refuse! But it is a bit weird! He feels the need to ask for my hand using you as a go-between! It's incredible! He sees me every day, and he feels the need to come looking for you to ask you for my hand! Out with it! Did you have your work cut out persuading Sereni to marry me?

TERESINA: But Alice! Can't you see she's doing it for your own good?

ALICE: Auntie! You don't know Alberta like I know her. Look! Even if I thought it was true that Sereni was marrying me as a favor to her, I'd still refuse the favor. I don't want to be beholden to her for anything! But I've known for some time that Sereni intended to marry me. There was no need for her to stick her nose in and cast a pall over our happiness. Oh yes! Her conscience told her to help me! What rubbish! Her conscience! She wanted to reduce me to slavery again! That's what she wanted.

CARLO: Good heavens! Alice, I think you're being unfair to Alberta.

ALICE (*she would clearly like to say something to* **CARLO** *but checks herself*): Forget it!

Scene 9

Enter **MAID.**

MAID (*going over to* **ALBERTA**): Mr. Chermis has been waiting for some time. He wants to know if you can see him this morning.

ALBERTA (*very violently*): Tell him not to bother me. Let him wait. (*Exit* **MAID.**)

ALICE: Goodbye, auntie. As long as you stay in this house, I won't be seeing you again. (*to* **CARLO** *and* **ALBERTA**) What's the point of all these explanations? You always end up saying something you never intended to say. But I did want to say this. It will give you some satisfaction! You said you were afraid your getting involved in my life had done nothing but harm me. There's something to what you say, though perhaps not as much as you think. I ran into Donato (*continuing to hesitate slightly*) when I was feeling humiliated by you, by your gifts, and also by my own rebellion. You won't believe this, but I have a conscience too, and my rebellion bothered me. Someone who didn't know you and me, might have found it unfair. And it happened just like that, just the way you imagined. He was the only one who could cleanse me of your charity and my own ingratitude. I guessed as much, and it turned out to be true, because I never gave you another thought until you came back into my life as an enemy.

ALBERTA (*flabbergasted*):   As an enemy?

ALICE: That's right, as an enemy. Excuse us, Carlo. (*She goes over to* **ALBERTA** *and speaks to her in a low voice, practically whispering in her ear, separating each syllable.*) Because now I know that he wants to marry me, but I don't know whether he loves me anymore. Do you know what made him accept your invitation and come to your house? Do you know? Did you say you wanted to talk to him about me from the very beginning? Tell me! Is that what you wrote to him?

ALBERTA (*haughtily*):   Yes, that's what I wrote.

ALICE: But he didn't believe you! He came here hoping you wanted to talk to him . . . about yourself! And you know it! Don't try to deny it! Didn't we talk about him together all those times? You knew him then, and now you've forgotten him?

ALBERTA: That's a lie.

ALICE (*with a sneer*):   Ha! Ha! (*She gives her a triumphant look, then continues.*) And now, to cleanse myself of your latest good deeds, all I have to do is give up my love affair? This I cannot do, but surely you must have understood at long last that the only good deed I will accept from you is for you to leave me in peace. Goodbye. (*Exit* **ALICE**.)

Scene 10

ALBERTA (*extremely agitated*):   Did you hear that?

CARLO: I didn't hear what she whispered in your ear. What did she say?

TERESINA: Show her you're superior, Alberta. She's so unhappy!

ALBERTA (*ringing the bell angrily and going over to the door and calling*):   Clelia!

Scene 11

Enter **CLELIA**.

ALBERTA: Take my aunt out of here!

TERESINA (*whimpering, as she is wheeled toward the door*):   You're angry with me!

ALBERTA: No, auntie! I assure you I'm not angry with you. (*running after her and giving her a kiss*) Forgive me for sending you away, but I have to talk to my husband. Afterward, I'll come straight to your room to talk about that trip to Tricesimo you're so set on. (*Exeunt* **CLELIA** *and* **TERESINA**.)

Scene 12

ALBERTA: You have a right to know what it was she whispered in my ear. I want to get it right. She said that now she knows Donato wants to marry her, but she doesn't know if he still loves her. Because she knows—she knows, you hear?—that the reason he came running when I invited him was because he hoped to find *me*—you hear?—*me*, ready to entertain his love.

CARLO: So what did you answer?

ALBERTA: Me? Nothing! What was there to answer? Am I supposed to know what goes on in Donato's mind?

CARLO: Don't you know?

ALBERTA: It was months since I'd seen him.

CARLO: I don't want to upset you by criticizing you too, but it strikes me you were wrong to get mixed up again in Alice's business.

ALBERTA: That's easy to say for somebody like you who never gets involved in other people's business. But how could I put up with all that contempt, after all I'd done for her? How can Alice not realize that it's nothing short of abject on her part to treat me like this, now that she no longer needs me?

CARLO: Donato made passes at you before! You used to make so much fun of him I never thought of barring him from my house! You know I'm not jealous, but I think you were wrong to receive him in secret like that.

ALBERTA: In secret! I saw him just a few minutes ago in this very room in broad daylight.

CARLO (*embracing her*): I'm asking you never to see him again.

ALBERTA: Of course, I'll never see him or Alice again. I see even you think I'm to blame. And yet I never meant any harm. I thought I'd found the best way to make up with Alice. That's all! (*She bursts into tears and abandons herself in* **CARLO'S** *arms.*)

CARLO: Nevertheless, you did do harm, my poor little wife! You're crying because you know you did.

ALBERTA (*weeping*): No! I'm crying because there's no justice.

Scene 13

Enter **MAID.**

MAID: Excuse me, madam. Miss Alice has fainted out in the hall.

ALBERTA: Miss Alice? What? Is she still here? Did she stop in the hall?

MAID (*discreetly*): Mr. Chermis was talking to her, and then I saw her fall down.

ALBERTA (*making for the door*): Chermis? I don't understand. (*pause*) Please, Carlo! It's better if you go. (*to the* **MAID**) Send Chermis in right away. (**CARLO** *and the* **MAID** *exit,* **ALBERTA** *goes to the door and calls*) Chermis!

Scene 14

Enter **CHERMIS.**

CHERMIS: It's nothing! She's already come round. I always said it was easier to deal with a thousand men than with one woman.

ALBERTA: In other words, you made her faint? What did you say to her?

CHERMIS (*hesitating*): Me? Nothing! Do you want to know why she fainted? I said: I'm going to have to tell Miss Alberta. And crash-bang-wham! down she went.

ALBERTA: But what was it you wanted to tell me?

CHERMIS: Can I tell you now? Just the threat of telling you made her faint. If I really do tell you, she'll die.

ALBERTA: This is no time for wisecracks. Tell me what this is all about, right now.

CHERMIS: You know me, madam, thrifty, close to my money . . .

ALBERTA (*stamping her foot*): What does that have to do with anything?

CHERMIS: Well, I'd saved up 2,000 lire, and I lent it to Miss Alice . . .

Scene 15

Two servants help **ALICE** *in, set her down in an armchair, and leave.* **CARLO** *enters with them.*

ALBERTA (*to the servants*): Call a doctor.

CARLO: Perhaps that won't be necessary. She only fainted.

ALICE (*opening her eyes*): Alberta! (*She closes them again.*)

ALBERTA (*all upset*): Oh, Alice! How do you feel? Open your eyes again.

ALICE (*weeping*): Oh, Alberta! Help me! I can't take it anymore!

ALBERTA: Sister of mine! You don't have to beg me.

CARLO (*to* **CHERMIS**):[3]

CURTAIN

ACT 4

Scene 1

CHERMIS *and* **ALBERTA**.

ALBERTA: Here's your money—2,100 lire.

CHERMIS: And here are your IOU's. But you're going to need a receipt.

ALBERTA: That won't be necessary! (*tearing up the IOU's*)

CHERMIS: You act like you had it in for me. Do you think I stole this money from you?

ALBERTA: I'm just disappointed to see you in the role of usurer.

CHERMIS (*incensed*): Usurer! Me!

ALBERTA: I'll say! Thirty percent interest . . .

---

3. Act 3 is incomplete and ends with Carlo's cue. All the remaining notes and fragments for act 3 are contained in the section "Alternative Versions and Dialogue Fragments."—Trans.

CHERMIS: What do you mean, thirty percent? It says two and a half percent a month.

ALBERTA: That makes thirty percent a year.

CHERMIS (*half embarrassed, half petulant*): What are you talking about? This kind of business is done by the month.

ALBERTA: You'd better watch out. Otherwise, hearing you talk like that, I'm going to lose all confidence in my expert business agent. Do you really not realize you asked for too much?

CHERMIS (*slyly, finding the right approach*): No! I didn't ask for too much. You know, ma'am, there are two kinds of money. The money you earn, dressed up like that and living in this fancy place, and the money I earn, dressed like this and living in a hovel. Sure, you can give away yours for a bow and a curtsy, or two bows, or ten bows. But not mine! My money has to be paid for! I wouldn't know what to do with a bow.

ALBERTA (*irritated*): I'm not trying to make you give your money away. But you should ask the kind of interest an honest lender would ask for.

CHERMIS (*exploding*): And what if there were people who prefer to borrow money at the interest I give rather than pay the interest you ask?

ALBERTA: Come on now!

CHERMIS: Oh, you don't have to look far to find people like that. Take Miss Alice for instance!

ALBERTA: You'll notice she took the money from me in the end.

CHERMIS: Because I wanted mine back! I'm not surprised! She was left with no alternative. She wasn't even paying me the interest. And she won't pay you either. There's a woman who pays neither principal nor interest.

ALBERTA (*rather violently*): But I'm not asking her for anything.

CHERMIS: In that case, you'll get exactly what you're asking for. But you're not going to be satisfied! I'm nobody special, but there are some things where I know what I'm talking about. You're not going to be satisfied!

Scene 2

Enter **CARLO**.

CARLO: Good morning. How is she?

ALBERTA: She had a good sleep, and she seems to be completely recovered.

CHERMIS: Is Miss Alice still not well?

ALBERTA: No. She's very well now. You can go now, Chermis. Come back tomorrow. I've heard as much as I care to for today.

CHERMIS: Good day! (*laughingly to* **CARLO**) A nice lady, Mrs. Alberta. But not with everybody! She really has it in for me.

ALBERTA: Don't talk silly and leave us alone, please.

CHERMIS: I'm going, I'm going. What's all the rush? Goodbye, sir. (*Exit.*)

Scene 3

CARLO: Donato will be here shortly.

ALBERTA (*observing him closely*): You! My dear friend, you're jealous! You've abandoned your business to come here and keep an eye on me!

CARLO: What? To keep an eye on you? You can't say that.

ALBERTA: Well, something like that.

CARLO (*smiling*): Yes. To keep an eye on Donato. It's not you I'm afraid of, it's him! (*drawing her toward him*) You see! He's a well-known ladies' man, but I was never so afraid of him as I am now. Everybody knew he flirted with you. But he didn't make an impression until now.

ALBERTA: Now that he's about to get married?

CARLO: Yes, but it seems he's getting married in order to please you.

ALBERTA: But didn't you hear Alice say that even if I hadn't stepped in, he would have married her anyway?

CARLO (*thoughtfully*): And is that true?

ALBERTA: You know, I had to promise Sereni I would foot the bill for Alice's children's education. It was the least I could do. (*putting her arms around him*) Please, don't torment me. Today, when I'm so happy to have won back Alice's trust and affection. What I've told you till now wasn't the whole truth! I had my share of guilt, and I'm ready to admit it. With all my charity I ended up creating a bit of a mess. I should have treated Alice more like a sister and not like some poor creature who only needed charity and not, first and foremost, affection.

CARLO: But you claimed you had given her your affection.

ALBERTA: Yes, that's what I said, and that's what I thought, too. But apparently that's not the way it was. She felt I wanted to lord it over her, and she rebelled. Maybe she was wrong, because I was hurt, very hurt. But it only made me think more highly of her. She wouldn't accept anything from him. She would sooner have gone into debt. She was so strong! He told me himself he'd never given her a penny, but I wouldn't believe him. That's how I knew I was wrong.

CARLO: Believe me, if you want to preserve your cousin's affection, you better be careful how you handle Sereni. She's jealous of you.

ALBERTA (*laughing*): You too! How come Sereni's the only one you're afraid of, and how come only now?

CARLO: Do you want to know the truth? Even though it may upset you? Alright then. I saw you were so eager to have Alice at your feet that I thought you might be capable of getting involved with Sereni in order to get what you wanted.

ALBERTA: Oh my God! How could you and Alice have thought such a thing? You see, I must have done something wrong to acquire such a bad reputation in your eyes and hers. But don't worry about Sereni! If you like, I'll only see him for as long as it takes to be there for Alice when she needs me.

CARLO: I have no intention of worrying, but I don't want Alice to worry either. You notice I didn't say anything till she came to me and accused you.

Scene 4

Enter **ALICE**.

ALICE (*leaning against the doorpost*): See, I can stand up pretty well on my own. Now I can go home.

ALBERTA: But what for? What's your hurry?

ALICE: Let me go. I have so much to do.

ALBERTA: You plan to work, the state you're in?

ALICE: I don't mean work. I have a lot of things to see to. Auntie told me I've been neglecting my children. Neither you nor I would have thought she had it in her. I don't want to neglect them any more. Now my affairs have been settled, thanks to you, I don't want to give people an excuse to say things like that about me again. My first thought must be for my children. (*choking up, then continuing*) I'm sorry for my husband . . . We agreed to call him that right away, didn't we?

ALBERTA (*going over and helping her across to the table*): He'll be here any minute. The two of us are going to leave you alone, you'll have your little talk, and then you'll be completely at ease again. It's that simple!

ALICE (*looking at her curiously*): Do you really think so? At one time I thought so too, . . . After all, what responsibilities did I have? Responsibilities toward myself? But I didn't care about myself! All in all, I must admit, I've been lucky, very lucky. (*completely dispirited*)

ALBERTA: You don't seem too happy.

ALICE: The fact is I'm not well. And anyway, the way things have turned out, I feel a bit ashamed having to face the two of you.

CARLO: Even for a businessman like me, a love like yours is nothing to be ashamed of.

ALICE: Thank you, Carlo. But that's not what I'm ashamed of. It's looking like a naughty, weak, little girl. Yes. Naughty! And weak! A rebellious child! Who rebels . . . Then gives in . . . ! And what do I find? You two, like good parents. You welcome me like . . . like . . . the prodigal son. (*confidentially to* **ALBERTA**) Did you give that man his money?

ALBERTA: Yes.

ALICE: But did you give it all, everything I promised to pay? You thought it was too much.

ALBERTA: Of course, everything.

ALICE: And how much do I owe you?

ALBERTA (*taken aback for a moment*): There's no hurry. I'll let you know later.

CARLO: I know you two have a lot to talk about, so I'll be going. I hope this heart-to-heart will be good for both of you. I'll see you later. I'll be back in half an hour, and I hope you'll still be here, Alice. (*kissing her hand*)

ALBERTA (*going with him to the door*):   Have you gotten over your sulks?

CARLO: If you ask me, it's that lady who looks a bit gloomy. She's the one you have to cheer up. (*He gives her a kiss on the forehead and exits.*)

Scene 5

ALBERTA (*coming back over to* **ALICE** *and giving her a searching look*):   Tell me, Alice. Have you forgiven me? Completely?

ALICE: What a question! (*with a forced laugh*) That's exactly what I wanted to ask you.

ALBERTA: You wouldn't have had to wait so long for an answer. Can't you see I'm studying your face, trying to figure out what you expect from me? *You* tell me. How can we be like good sisters again, like we were when we were little?

ALICE: Is that what you want? Do you really want that? Listen. If you want to be good, you must help me. But don't offer me charity.

ALBERTA: How can you use that ugly word, when I'm ready to give you everything, everything? Charity means something small, insignificant. Whereas I'm saying I'll give you everything you could possibly need, everything I can give. I don't think you can call that charity.

ALICE: It's charity with no strings attached, but it's still charity, and I don't want it. Right now I need a lot of money, and if I didn't have you, I'd be desperate, but I don't want it as a gift. Why don't you lend it to me? I'll be pretty well off before long. Couldn't I pay you your money back?

ALBERTA (*icily*):   In that case we'd have to agree on a suitable rate of interest, like Chermis.

ALICE: You're offended? (*suddenly decisive*) If that's how it is, I don't want your money. I'll do what I didn't want to do for the world. I'll ask him for it.

ALBERTA: No! I never said I didn't want to give it to you. How much do you need?

ALICE: In addition to what you gave Chermis, I need about 3,000 lire . . . Maybe 2,500 would do.

ALBERTA: Do you need it right away?

ALICE: No. There's no hurry. (*after a slight hesitation*) Tomorrow's soon enough. (*rather anxiously*) Can you give it to me?

ALBERTA: How can you doubt it?

ALICE (*gratefully*):   Thank you, thank you. A thousand times thank you. You are saving me from a very nasty situation. Because . . . I must tell you . . . Chermis was not the only one I owed money to.

ALBERTA: And you preferred all this worrying and scheming to coming and giving me a kiss, when that was the one thing I wanted!

ALICE: Yes. That's the way I was . . . then! And I needed such a lot of money. After all, I had to look pretty . . . for him.

ALBERTA: But, how did you think this was all going to turn out?

ALICE: My God! Everything in the world ends sooner or later. I'd gotten hold of a little bottle of poison.

ALBERTA (*covering her face with her hands*): Oh, how could you? How could you? What about your children?

ALICE: My children? They were my only regret. But I knew you. The minute you heard I was dead, you'd have come running. And, still being so small, they could have been brought up to show the gratitude you wanted.

ALBERTA: So you think people have to show themselves very grateful to preserve my friendship?

ALICE: Not *very* grateful, only what you're entitled to. I was ungrateful. I know, I know. But I don't know how else to behave. The only thing that could change me was that little bottle . . .

ALBERTA: Don't talk about it!

Scene 6

The **MAID** *enters and hands* **ALBERTA** *a visiting card.*

ALBERTA: Sereni! Show him in, show him in.

ALICE (*annoyed*): I could have seen him at my place without bothering you here.

ALBERTA: Please, Alice. See him here and not someplace else. That's all I'm asking. Not gratitude, for instance. I'll spare you that. You don't owe me a thing. I'll proclaim it out loud: I'll be grateful to you forever if you let me handle this solution in the most seemly fashion.

ALICE (*with a grim look*): The family reputation's at stake. I get it!

(*Enter* **SERENI**.)

SERENI (*happily, pausing to take* **ALBERTA's** *hand*): Thank you, thank you. (*hurrying over to* **ALICE** *and kissing her hand*) Do you feel well?

ALICE (*offering him her lips*): Why so formal? I understand why you're doing it, and I'm grateful. But, in front of Alberta . . . Do you think she doesn't know?

SERENI: My plucky wife! You're right. No hypocrisy in front of the lady of the house. We owe her so much. She understood better than I did what we both needed.

ALBERTA: Come on now, don't thank me. I didn't do a thing. (*signaling to* **SERENI** *to keep silent*) The thing I have to do now—and I'm sure you'll be grateful for that if nothing else—is to leave you alone. Then Alice wants to go home. I would have liked to keep Alice here as long as she's so weak, but she tells me she's expected, and she has lots of things to do.

SERENI: Wouldn't you be better off here than at your house where you have nobody to help you?

ALICE (*a bit on edge*): No. Please. Don't make me argue about something that isn't worth arguing about. I want to go home! Excuse me, Alberta, but I can't stay here.

ALBERTA: But who's trying to stop you doing what you want? The carriage will be ready right away. You can call me as soon as you're through talking.

SERENI: Can't we talk just as well in front of Alberta? After all, what secrets are there between us? She knows I love you!

ALICE: Exactly! We can talk at my house.

ALBERTA: No. Talk here. I beg you. And another thing, until you get married, I'd like you to see each other only in this house. Will you do that for me?

SERENI: Perhaps it would be better. (*He looks toward* **ALICE**, *who shrugs.*)

ALBERTA: I'll make sure nobody disturbs you. (*Exit.*)

Scene 8

SERENI (*kneeling next to the chair where* **ALICE** *is sitting*): If you only knew how much I've suffered since I heard you were ill! You already knew about the arrangements that had been made with Alberta, didn't you?

ALICE:

[*The manuscript breaks off at this point.*]

ALTERNATIVE VERSIONS AND DIALOGUE FRAGMENTS

1. Alternative Version of Act 2, Scenes 11–14

Scene 11

Enter **CLELIA**.

CLELIA: Did you call me, madam?

ALBERTA (*very circumspect*): That gentleman who was here a short while ago to see Miss Alice, what did he look like? I'm only asking . . . to pass the time of day. I'll be seeing my cousin soon, and I can ask her.

CLELIA: He's a gentleman with glasses, rather heavyset; he walks slowly, at least when he's walking in front of this house. (*thinking*) A bit balding . . . a little moustache . . . and when he talks he waves his arms a lot.

ALBERTA: Mr. Telvi?

CLELIA: I don't know. I only heard his voice for a second. Miss Teresina was looking for her handkerchief. I wanted to see if she'd left it here, and I'd gotten as far as the door when Miss Teresina stopped me.

TERESINA (*pleased with herself*): You hear that?

CLELIA: I heard his voice. He was saying something strange. I remember now! "And yet you did know my wife."

ALBERTA: She knew her very well. That much I know. What else?

CLELIA: If Miss Teresina hadn't stopped me I would have heard more. But under the circumstances . . . that's all.

ALBERTA: Miss Teresina did the right thing to call you back. It's not nice to eavesdrop.

CLELIA: In a little apartment like this you can hear everything whether you want to or not.

ALBERTA: That's true.

CLELIA: Yesterday I was going around collecting Miss Teresina's things, and I was so embarrassed when I happened to go into Miss Alice's room while she was in there with a gentleman.

ALBERTA: The painter?

CLELIA: No, no! This room's as far as he gets. It was a gentleman who was giving her some money, a lot of money, and she signed an IOU.

ALBERTA: Are you sure? Oh, the poor thing!

CLELIA: I'm quite sure, because Miss Alice didn't notice I was there till they were all done. Then she told me to leave, very rudely.

ALBERTA (*very upset, thinking of Alice*): Oh, the poor thing!

CLELIA (*smiling*): It certainly isn't nice being mistreated.

ALBERTA: I wasn't referring to you. You deserved to be told off for entering a room where you didn't belong.

CLELIA: I made a mistake, and I was sorry. I was still there, though I didn't want to be, when the gentleman left saying: "Goodbye. I'll be back in a month."

ALBERTA: Promising her more money?

CLELIA: Do you think so, madam? I think he was talking about coming back to collect the money he'd given her. He was the ugliest-looking gentleman I've ever seen here, or anywhere else for that matter. Completely bald, with a lot of hair where it didn't belong, on his throat for example . . . a real ape.

ALBERTA (*hesitating again*): And the painter?

CLELIA: Mr. Sereni?

ALBERTA: You know his name too?

CLELIA: It's the only thing finished in the picture. Look. (*She runs over to the painting and holds it up to show it.*) The name's not all that clear. It looks more like Pirini, but I was told his name is Sereni.

ALBERTA (*looking at the painting*): As far as I can recall, Alice doesn't have a gold and blue dress. Did she just have one made?

CLELIA: She always sits in that white dress of hers.

ALBERTA: I wonder how Sereni imagines a dress. Put that picture back where it was. My aunt will soon be coming to stay at my house, and you too. You're going to have to behave differently once you're in my house.

CLELIA: But I didn't do anything wrong. You can't help seeing everything here, unless you go around with your eyes closed.

TERESINA: Listen, Clelia, you mustn't say that I'm leaving. Alice will be informed in due time.

CLELIA: I understand, I understand. I know how to keep my mouth shut.

ALBERTA: And the painter, does he come every day?

CLELIA: Practically. But not always at the same time. He lives just across the street. It's very easy to call him. Look! Would you like to see him? (*She takes the hem of the curtain and hangs it out the window.*) If he's at home, he'll be here in ten minutes.

ALBERTA: What did you do?

CLELIA (*laughing and going over to her*): You want to see? Just wait and see.

Scene 12

Enter **ALICE**. *She enters briskly and stops dead in her tracks when she sees* **ALBERTA**.

ALBERTA (*going over to her*): Oh, Alice. Here we are together at last!

ALICE: How are you?

ALBERTA: I'm well. And you?

ALICE: Very well, thanks. (*A strained silence. In the meantime* **CLELIA** *tries to get over to the window to put the curtain back in its place.*)

ALBERTA (*firmly*): Listen, Clelia. Do me a favor and take my aunt out of the room for a moment. Do you hear? (**CLELIA** *tries to signal her intentions to* **ALBERTA**.)

CLELIA (*frustrated*): At your service, madam. (*carrying out Alberta's orders*)

TERESINA (*who has also been trying unsuccessfully to signal to* **ALBERTA**, *when* **CLELIA** *gives the chair a good push*): Gently now. Please! (**CLELIA** *and* **TERESINA** *exit.*)

Scene 13

ALICE (*after another pause*): I had a few more visits to make. But then I got fed up. It's raining, so I came home earlier than I'd expected.

ALBERTA: I'm grateful to you for coming. At least that way I get to see you again finally.

ALICE: Did you really want to? Me too. But the person I wanted to see was my old childhood friend, not the other one.

ALBERTA (*offended*): What other one?

ALICE: I know what I'm talking about. (*pause*) The other one, the one who sent the doctor over to tell me that if things were ever going to be the way they once were between us, I'd better apologize.

ALBERTA: Apologize? The doctor can't have chosen his words very carefully. I asked for a word, one word, of explanation. You said some terrible things. I was very upset.

ALICE: I was upset too because I believed them. I mean I believed them at the time. And I kept on believing them for a long time after. Until now.

ALBERTA: And now?

ALICE (*hesitantly*): I don't believe them anymore, if you really suffered as much as you say.

ALBERTA (*touched*): Will you give me your hand, my dear cousin? (**ALICE** *does so.*) Will you give me a kiss? (*They kiss.*) I'm so happy.

ALICE: I think I am too.

ALBERTA: What do you mean you just think so?

ALICE: Because, while I may not have to apologize, like the doctor said, it's still true I owe you a great deal. A great deal. I owe it to you to be completely honest. I must be honest, because it makes me unhappy, very unhappy, if I'm not honest. And after all, we're cousins, aren't we? The first duty of cousins is to be honest with each other.

ALBERTA: Alright then. Let's sit down side by side and you tell me everything as honestly as you can. Come and sit here. Here.

ALICE: I didn't love you anymore, and I was deeply ashamed. That made me sad.

ALBERTA: And now? Now?

ALICE: Now I want to love you, and I hope I can love you. But, cousin, you've got to collaborate, you've got to help me. I can't control my emotions, and it shocks me: I don't love when I should, and at times I even hate when I shouldn't.

ALBERTA: Just tell me what you want me to do. I'm ready to do anything you like to hold on to your affection. I'm willing to spare no expense just to give you peace of mind and security and happiness.

ALICE (*in a low voice, but feelingly*): You mustn't give me anything anymore. Nothing. Ever again. That's what I discovered when I studied my sickness. Nothing. Ever again. Listen, Alberta, if you want me to love you, you mustn't give me money.

ALBERTA: I'll give you things I buy myself, so they'll be beautiful and worthy of my cousin.

ALICE: You're a better person than I am. I'm grateful. (*kissing her with deliberate effusiveness*) But I don't want anything. I can't accept.

ALBERTA: Ours is going to be a strange relationship. Me rich, with everything I could possibly want. And you poor, underprivileged.

ALICE: I'm not as poor as all that. There's the children's little inheritance. That will have to go for their education.

ALBERTA: It's not going to be enough.

ALICE: How do you know?

ALBERTA: It's a matter of accounting. Poor thing, you've never been very good with figures.

ALICE: But I can also get a job. I've imagined all kinds of things. First I thought I'd get a job in an office. They told me it was so easy to learn to type. Then I discovered it would be easier for a mother to get housework. And I thought of designing clothes for boutiques, or working in one.

ALBERTA: Have you tried?

ALICE: The only thing I've made so far is this hat I'm wearing. It's nice, isn't it?

ALBERTA (*not very convinced*): Very nice. But have you tried selling anything?

ALICE: No, not yet! You know, I haven't gotten things organized here yet as I'd like them.

I'm going to have to start pinching pennies. That way I'll look even poorer, and it'll be easier to sell my work.

ALBERTA (*laughing*):   Poor Alice! It's easier to sell if you look rich. Looking poor is bad for business.

ALICE: Thank you, thank you. Give me advice. That's what I need. You're such a practical person, and you have no need to be practical!

ALBERTA: I am a practical person. Certainly. That's why, if I were in my little cousin Alice's shoes, and had an active brain full of daydreams but without much experience, I'd go to the practical person, my cousin Alberta, and I'd say: You guide me.

ALICE: And if I did that, how would you guide me?

ALBERTA: Alright. This is what I'd say to my cousin Alberta: You weren't as good as you might have been, and I was a very bad girl for a moment. But nothing terrible happened, and now we can go back to the way our lives were before.

ALICE: You weren't as good as you might have been, were you.

ALBERTA (*hugging her*):   No, I wasn't. But you were very naughty. Like a peevish child.

ALICE (*laughing*):   Exactly!

ALBERTA: So now let's go back to being the way we always were. And I'll do the right thing to make amends and take Aunt Teresina in with me.

ALICE (*unconvinced*):   Why? Why put yourself out? You realize the real issue had nothing to do with Aunt Teresina.

ALBERTA (*laughing*):   I seem to recall that Aunt Teresina had a little bit to do with it.

ALICE: Yes, a little bit. (*pause*) Well, if that's what Aunt Teresina wants, I'm not going to stand in the way of her coming to stay with you. But she was telling me a few minutes ago how happy she was here.

ALBERTA: You know, you can't believe what Aunt Teresina says. She's so scared she'd say anything she thought you wanted to hear as long as you were there. (*after a moment's reflection*) As long as I was there too, probably.

ALICE: Scared of me? Maybe it's my fault. Oh, the poor thing! But I was so unhappy. I'll try to explain to her. She is our mothers' sister. We owe her respect.

ALBERTA: And, to my great surprise, I also discovered our aunt isn't boring at all. It's funny to hear her recount her experiences when she was at Uncle Enrico's. And at your house as well.

ALICE: At my house?

ALBERTA: Yes! She described a look of hatred you gave her. She saw all kinds of colors in it. Quite a rainbow!

ALICE: Hatred? Me? For our aunt? Never! Oh, now I remember: anger, yes, anger. I couldn't get it across that she could stay here or leave without me feeling resentful. (*thinking about it*) But it was even worse than hatred. Tremendous indifference. Total unwarranted contempt. (*still mulling*) Did she really say that?

ALBERTA: To be truthful, I don't really know, because she never told me. She just mentioned that look you gave her. Like thunder and lightning.

ALICE: What a bad girl I've been! I remember looking at her like this. It was just a look of impatience. I wanted to go out as quickly as I could, so as not to run into you, and I just couldn't figure out what she wanted. You see how bad we are?

ALBERTA: What does it have to do with me? (*laughing*) I don't know how to give people technicolor looks. Since when did I ever look at someone like that?

ALICE (*resigned*): You're right. (*pause*) Couldn't auntie's departure be postponed a bit? I'd really like to make peace before we split up. I'd also like to get used to seeing her as my mother's sister, a living memory of her.

ALBERTA: It can't be done, Alice dear. Today's the only day I have the car free. I'll send it over, it'll only take a minute. But you can come and see her whenever you like, and we'll both keep auntie company.

ALICE (*giving in reluctantly*): Alright then. It would have been better . . . But what the heck, it doesn't really make any difference.

ALBERTA: And what did Telvi have to say when he showed up uninvited?

ALICE: How did you know he'd been here?

ALBERTA: Clelia told me. That is, she described him to me, and there couldn't be any mistake. Rather old, rather ugly, and extremely boring. She had a hunch he must be boring. That's a smart girl. I'm really glad I chose her as auntie's companion.

ALICE: Telvi, poor thing, is in love with me. Do you remember when I told you the nicest thing about him was his love for his wife and his sorrow at being abandoned? Well now, poor thing, he doesn't have his love or his sorrow anymore. He's naked and alone, just like Mother Nature made him.

ALBERTA: So what did he say?

ALICE: He'd like to get a divorce, even if it means losing lots of money, and marry me.

ALBERTA: And you?

ALICE: I couldn't say no, because he wouldn't let me. I wasn't allowed to say either yes or no. I did my best to make him understand no. But he wasn't having any of it, and he left. I'm afraid he'll come back, and I don't have a doorman I can give instructions to not to let him in.

ALBERTA (*as if she had decided to make the best of it*): Well, if that's what you've decided. I hope you've given it plenty of thought, and considered your future and that of your children.

ALICE: *My* future certainly. And theirs too. It couldn't possibly be good for them to be around such a bore. And anyway, if he's going to lose all that money by marrying me, it would end up being a bad deal for both of us.

ALBERTA: But you mustn't take what businessmen say literally. When they make money they underestimate their profits, and they exaggerate their losses when they lose. Believe me: Telvi is a safe that can't be cracked.

ALICE: I see! But he's too heavy even for a safe.

ALBERTA: But he's kind, generous, and, basically, intelligent.

ALICE (*shortly*): Don't insist, for goodness sake. I'm still young, but I've given up on love. I'll never get to the point where I'd be willing to pretend a love I don't feel.

ALBERTA: What a child you are.

ALICE: Oh, I'm not such a child: after all, I've managed—or been forced—to forget about love.

ALBERTA: You been forced?

ALICE: What I mean is: love has abandoned me. You know, the pleasure of having someone admire and desire you. Oh, *you* still feel it. It's part of life, and not the least significant part. It's stupid, but that's how it is. Well, I don't. For me, love is off limits. When it's offered, it disgusts me. It's as if my whole mind were concentrated on something else, but I don't know what it is. It can't be money, can it? Because then all I'd have to do would be to marry Telvi. But I have no time for love. It makes me laugh. It doesn't seem important.

ALBERTA: In that case, you're ripe for marrying Telvi.

ALICE: No fear! I still respect love too much. You must have met totally unreligious people who had nothing but reverence for the religion of their forefathers or their childhood? They're really the most religious people of all. They can't pray, and they suffer because of it. They look up to heaven with sorrow and regret. That's how it is with me and love. It should be there in my heart, but instead there's just a hole, dug by God knows whom. And it aches, like a wound.

ALBERTA: But, after your husband died, you never had a chance to fall in love. You were always so concerned with the thought of your children and your . . . problems.

ALICE: Oh yes, I had problems alright. But when I fell out with you a month ago, I had every intention of forgetting my problems and . . . and . . . making love.

ALBERTA (*rather violently*): Are you talking about Sereni?

ALICE: Exactly. He's the one I'm talking about.

ALBERTA: A man who needs to change women every time he paints a new picture. Now I see why you can't enjoy love.

ALICE: Why? Even that kind of love is understandable. It's total! It may end sooner or later, but it can still be enjoyed, even if you don't share it. What could be nobler than helping inspiration along? When Sereni says that our early painters had life—art, that is—easier because women were different then, I think he may be right. Unfortunately this is the way I am, and I can't help him. That picture there will never be finished.

ALBERTA: A good thing too.

ALICE: You and I are in no position to judge. And it would take so little for me to tell him I love him . . . But I can't. My children, and, as you put it, my problems, are too important. When he offers me love, I feel like someone thirsty being offered something to eat.

ALBERTA: And if I knew it was your problems that were stopping you doing such a thing, I'd make them worse; I'd make them worse because they're what's saving you.

ALICE: What does it matter to you?

ALBERTA (*shocked*): Don't you see why it matters to me?

ALICE: No, I don't.

ALBERTA: If you don't see why I'm concerned, it's not for me to explain.

ALICE: How would I change by becoming Sereni's lover? I mean, for you, you're my cousin, how would I change for you?

ALBERTA (*shocked*): I love you, but I also love your purity, your innocence. (*pause*) But what are we doing talking about something that doesn't exist, when you tell me yourself there's no way it will ever exist?

ALICE: Because it's important to me. I was telling you just now how painful it is for me not to be able to live and to love, and all you do is yell: Thou shalt not live, thou shalt not love. I hate the part of myself that tells me that. Whereas I'd like to be able to love you, I'd like to love you with all my heart.

ALBERTA: But Alice, the part of yourself you hate is the best part, the noblest part.

ALICE: I'm not at all sure of that.

ALBERTA: Cousin of mine, let's talk about more important things. How much money do you need?

ALICE: Me? I don't need money.

ALBERTA: I thought you promised to be honest with me. How can you say such a thing? Do you think I don't know you borrowed money from a loan shark?

ALICE (*taken aback*): You know that too?

ALBERTA: Clelia told me.

ALICE: Clelia, the girl you're so pleased with . . . I borrowed that money just for a month. I couldn't wait for the legal transactions that will give me access to my money to be over. But by the end of this month, I'll be in a position to pay back my debt to that gentleman, who is not a loan shark but a decent person. He only asked for five percent interest.

ALBERTA: Per month?

ALICE: Seeing I'm only keeping the money for a month, it doesn't much matter whether it's per month or per year.

ALBERTA: You're so innocent it's impossible to be angry with you. Tell me how much you need, and you can have it right away. I've convinced Carlo that in matters where you are concerned, I'm not going to let him tell me what to do. So tell me. Quickly. Your refusal pains and offends me. You can't get by without my help, and I insist you inform me of all your expenses before you end up ruining yourself.

ALICE: But if I want to try and live on my own resources, wouldn't it be better for you too?

ALBERTA: It would only be better if I knew you could get by without me. The way things are now is unbearable. Just think: if you had to pay all your bills yourself, you'd end up needing more than I could afford to give you. This way, I wouldn't even notice the little advances I'd give you every day.

ALICE: Every day! Not several times a day?

Scene 14

SERENI *enters confidently. When he sees* **ALBERTA**, *he can scarcely conceal his surprise.*

SERENI: Alberta! What a pleasant surprise! Have you two made up?

ALBERTA: Of course we have! You know how much I was counting on it.

SERENI: I was counting on it too. Alice can tell you. I see her often. She was kind enough to take on the task of sitting for that portrait.

2. Alternative Ending to Act 2, Scene 10

ALBERTA: Still, she's always been a good mother. And she always dressed simply . . .

TERESINA: In that case, I haven't the slightest idea what I'm talking about, and you have to promise not to tell anyone I said anything of the sort. I thought you felt the same way I did, and I thought that's what you wanted to hear. If we don't agree, then I'm certainly the one in the wrong.

ALBERTA: But auntie! You've nothing to be afraid of! Aren't you about to leave this house this very day and forever? I want you to speak frankly; I want to hear the truth. I haven't seen Alice for ages! She must have changed!

TERESINA: A good mother? I'm sure she still is! Like rabbits who eat their litters, they love them so much! As soon as she sets eyes on her children, she bursts into tears! She bathes them in tears. One of these days, they'll catch pneumonia!

ALBERTA (*touched*): The poor thing!

TERESINA: What's that you said: The poor thing? In other words, this is normal behavior in town, and I don't understand a thing!

ALBERTA: I said: The poor things! I meant the children.

TERESINA (*distrustful*): Did you really mean the children? (*reassured*) Just think: Ottavio, the older boy, refuses to study. They sent for her to go to his school. She soaked the child's curls with her tears, but she couldn't find a single free minute all week to go talk to the teacher.

ALBERTA: She never was a very energetic person.

TERESINA (*distrustful*): And you make excuses for her?

ALBERTA: Excuses? Not at all! I'm the first to criticize her lack of energy. Poor children!

TERESINA: There are times I have to take care of them myself from this wheelchair. That was when she too gave me one of those looks of cold hatred people in my position have to put up with so often. But I can't shirk my duty. Aren't I partly to blame for things being in such a state of disorder in the house I live in? There's just one maid in the kitchen, and would you like to know her chief occupation? Stealing! She takes the best tidbits home with her. Even this wheelchair can see it, but Alice can't!

ALBERTA: Auntie, all this you're saying comes as news to me, you know. Alice was never a model of order, but I didn't think it had gone this far. Neglecting her children! She used to live for her children!

TERESINA: Well! If you want to hear some stories that'll make your hair stand on end, call Maria!⁴

ALBERTA (*hesitantly*): Maria?

TERESINA (*shouting*): Maria! Maria!

3. Alternative Opening of Act 3

ACT 3

A drawing room in **ALBERTA'S** *house, as in act 1. Evening. The room is poorly lit. The table is more brightly illuminated than the rest.*

Scene 1

CHERMIS *and* **ALBERTA**, *as in act 1.* **ALBERTA** *is wearing an evening gown.*

ALBERTA (*closing a ledger*): You can go now. I'm expecting guests. Goodbye! (*She is nervous.*)

CHERMIS: Excuse me, madam, but I'd like to talk to you about some business of my own.

ALBERTA (*looking at her watch*): It's already seven thirty. If it won't take long, speak up, but make it snappy.

CHERMIS (*embarrassed*): It's not something that can be . . .

4. Fragment, considered by Apollonio to be the first draft of Act 3, Scenes 1–5

ACT 3

Scene 1

TERESINA *and* **MARIA**.

MARIA: I told you once and I'll tell you again: she wasn't angry, just irritated. If anybody was being sent to the devil, it was me, not you. She interrupted me, shouting: "I'll have a word with my aunt later today." And then: "I understand. Do you understand? I understand."

TERESINA: I thought I told you to tell her I was happy here, and the only reason I wanted

---

4. An earlier name for Clelia.—Trans.

to leave was to go stay in that other house—it's her property too—at Tricesimo, because I was dying for a little greenery and fresh air. You didn't tell her all that.

MARIA: You can tell her yourself, if you can get a word in edgewise. Miss Alberta doesn't have time; I mean she doesn't have time for us. I was explaining to her that you didn't want to leave here . . . that that was the last thing you wanted . . . because you couldn't imagine having to get by without all these modern conveniences . . . but that . . . and I was about to bring up the subject of Tricesimo. As I was speaking, I heard someone beating time to my words. It was Miss Alberta's impatient and nervous foot. I pretended not to notice, but I had to stop when she began thumping the table with her hands as well. Dainty feet and hands. But so rude! I was a bit surprised to be cut off short by someone who was only too happy to hear me out as long as I was living with Alice.

TERESINA (*in a low, contrite voice*): We treated her badly, the poor thing.

MARIA: Why? What harm did we do her?

TERESINA: I hope we didn't do her any harm. If we did, I could never forgive myself.

MARIA: And yet you couldn't wait to get out of her house.

TERESINA: That house was in such a mess . . . and my heart was in such a mess too. There was nothing I could do to help her. That's why I thought I ought to turn my back on her as soon as I could, as soon as I could . . . (*weeping*) She was always my favorite. I don't know how I could have held back my affection for so long.

MARIA: Don't cry, you have good reasons of your own for crying.

TERESINA: But these tears, shed for love, are sweet tears. The tears I shed for myself and for my poor legs and for this wheelchair choke me. These are a comfort. Without needing anyone to push me or carry me, I cross the miles that lie between us in thought, and there I am at her side, the poor thing. I live again because I love again. I'm no longer just the same old Teresina, scared of everyone her fate depends on. I am something else too . . . (*secretly pleased with herself*)

MARIA (*smiling*): What else are you? Tell me so I can see if I can be this something else too.

TERESINA: No! Not you! Look, for Alice's sake I could forget all my afflictions. If Alice needed me . . . I think I could even walk. Yes! I know I could! I'm a mother too!

MARIA: I wouldn't want to be a mother . . . At least, not until I get married.

TERESINA (*with a forced laugh*): Ha, ha! That was a good one! Very funny!

MARIA: When all's said and done, Miss Alice is better off than you seem to think. If we were having such a good time ourselves, just think what a good time she must have had.

TERESINA: I know you can't be serious. Even you could tell how unhappy she was. Admit it.

MARIA: I saw she was always crying, but that didn't stop me envying her. It's true, even I liked her better than this lady with all her airs. On the other hand, it's true this house is better run than the other. It's like living inside a watch, it's so well run.

TERESINA: What's so clever about that, with all that money! I'm not saying Alberta isn't generous. They say she gives a lot away to charity. But in terms of genuine affection all her charity is nothing compared with the tears Alice sheds over her children. Poor, unhappy little mother! And what if Alice didn't take good care of me? She had an excuse because she was so worried. Alberta, on the other hand . . . Of course! She's so busy. It's two days since I saw her. She won't let me eat with them . . . I'm not saying it wasn't the right thing to do. I felt uncomfortable around Carlo, always wrapped up in his business. They talked a lot about money: a hundred thousand, two hundred thousand, even more. For me that's a sore subject. I used to think: all I'd need is ten thousand and I'd leave for Friuli . . . with you, naturally.

MARIA: But I wouldn't come. What would you do with ten thousand lire? You'd have to live on polenta!

TERESINA: You don't know how good polenta can be when you're hungry. And it's healthy, you know? I think this fancy food makes me sick to my stomach.

MARIA: Why don't you tell Miss Alberta?

TERESINA: I already told her. She called the doctor and had him examine me, and now she gives me what the doctor said to give me.

MARIA: Now there's a no-nonsense woman. At Miss Alice's house she made a completely different impression.

TERESINA: What do you expect? She wasn't at Alice's house to bring order.

Scene 2

Enter **ALBERTA** *and* **CHERMIS**.

ALBERTA: Here I am, auntie. Are you well? I brought Chermis along because he knows how you'd find things right now at the Tricesimo house. You tell her, Chermis. Can she go to Tricesimo now?

CHERMIS (*as if he were reciting a lesson he's learned by heart*): Impossible! We're expecting the right moment for sowing any day now. So, as soon as the rain stops, every available person is going to be busy, even the children. You'd be left all by yourself in the house . . . unless you wanted to give a hand with the sowing. (*He laughs.*)

TERESINA: Yes, I know. I know how these things are . . . I know all about the country.

ALBERTA: That's why you're going to have to postpone your trip to Tricesimo. The bad weather's another good reason for not going to stay in that damp house. It's uninhabitable except at the height of summer.

TERESINA: I know . . . I know . . . I told you so, didn't I, Maria?

MARIA: Me?

TERESINA: Yes! Remember? You! I admit I also said, speaking as someone who's lived in the country all her life, in those houses with the flimsy walls and the unprotected windows, that the dampness of the bracing open air wouldn't do me any harm. But then there's that other business. When the weather's like it's been this year, and the sun finally comes out and manages to dry the ground out, everybody has to be out in the fields. That's what I told Maria. Although, when everybody else went out in the fields, Maria could stay home with me.

ALBERTA: But who'd do the cooking? Who'd clean up your rooms?

TERESINA: Do you know, you're right! There'd be nobody . . . nobody.

ALBERTA: So let's leave it like this, auntie dear. I'll tell you when you can leave. Don't be impatient. Then you can stay at Tricesimo for as long as it's sunny. Goodbye, aunt. Now I must get back to my accounts.

TERESINA: Please, Alberta, there's something I want to say to you. (*joining her hands*)

ALBERTA: Right now? Right now I can't. I'll be with you in half an hour. Come along, Chermis. (**ALBERTA** *exits with* **CHERMIS**.)

Scene 3

TERESINA *stares after* **ALBERTA** *for a long time.*

MARIA: What did you want to say to her?

TERESINA: I wanted to ask her if she had any news about Alice. It's been a week since she was here, and I never managed to get a minute alone with her. I have so much to say to her. Oh! I wish I could go back to Alice's, at least until it's time to go to Tricesimo.

MARIA: I'm afraid that if you were to go back to Alice's, in a few days you'd want to leave again and come back here. I'd like to see how things are going there too. But I'd still like to come back here for lunch and dinner. The stuff they used to serve up at Alice's was always either uncooked or burnt!

TERESINA: There you go again. For you eating is something essential. As far as I'm concerned, considering what little I eat . . .

MARIA: But you like that little well-cooked.

TERESINA: I'd have given anything to talk to her about Alice. Since I can't talk to Alice directly, I could have talked about her and taken her part. I was all ready to tell her, without beating about the bush: You take the first step, you're the richer one, you certainly don't need Alice. If you're the benefactress you think you are, you be the first to hold your hand out.

MARIA: You'd never have had the courage to say all that.

TERESINA: Oh, yes, I would! I was all ready. Maybe I wouldn't have said that bit about the benefactress. It would have been bad policy. But the rest . . . There was no harm in it anyway.

Scene 4

Enter **CARLO**.

CARLO: Isn't Alberta here?

TERESINA: Good morning, Mr. Carlo.

CARLO: Good morning, madam! How are you? You look well today. I'm delighted. Goodbye. (*He exits hurriedly to the left.*)

Scene 5

MARIA: He's so curious to know how you are!

TERESINA: He all wrapped up in his business. Every day he says the same thing and then rushes off.

MARIA: I'll tell you what. Tomorrow I'm going to go up to him as soon as I see him and holler: Madam is well! Don't bother to put yourself out!

5. Svevo's Working Notes for Part of an Earlier Version[5]

A breakfast room next to the dining room, which can be seen in the background. Six P.M. Alice and Paola. The dress. It's ready. She can go try it on in the bedroom. As for the increase in her allowance, she has not gotten Carlo's approval yet. It's not as easy as it looks to get him to part with his money. But she'll see. She'll get it.

Chermis. It's September, and they need money for the grape harvest. Chermis would like to rent the land to sharecroppers. That way there wouldn't be any additional expenses. Paola disagrees. Her husband doesn't interfere, and here he is trying to interfere! She needs something to keep her busy. Sure!! Don't you have all your charity cases to think of? The maid announces a girl who's come about a position. Berta, a rather cheeky girl, enters. Chermis leaves. Paola and Berta reach an agreement. Carlo arrives and Paola leaves him alone to go and get dressed. Alice and Carlo. Alice is dressed differently. Looking at herself in a mirror, she tells Carlo that she regrets that this year's fashions are not the same as last year's. She asks Carlo to raise her allowance. It becomes evident that he knows nothing about it. The painter Clessi enters. He makes rather reckless advances to Alice. Mr. Debiasi enters. He too is obviously enamored of Alice.

6. An Early Fragment of Act 1, Scene 1

Scene 1

It is clearly spring from the sunlight pouring in through a big window on the right. Drawing room in the Berri's house. Eleven A.M. **ALBERTA**, *still dressed in an elegant negligee, is sitting at a table in front of a sheaf of papers on which she is making notes with a pencil. She is a handsome and elegant lady going on for thirty. Despite her elegance, she is not dressed in the very latest fashion, which gives her a rather serious look.* **CARLO BERRI** *is lying back in an armchair yawning. He is over fifty. He is dressed casually like an artist.*

ALBERTA (*scrawling something energetically on one of the papers and then putting it on one side*): There, that's taken care of.

---

5. Several of the characters have different names. —Trans.

CARLO: Can I go now?

ALBERTA: A fine one you are! Don't you realize that if things go on this way, if I were to lose my mind, I could send this property of yours that was saved so miraculously during the war up in smoke?

CARLO: I think it's indestructible. The Austrians used it for their maneuvers, and it looks like all they did was fertilize it. You couldn't be worse than the Austrians.

ALBERTA: How do you know? Here I am managing a country property, and yesterday Chermis burst out laughing because we were standing in front of a barley field and I called it wheat!

CARLO: You'll make a fortune.

7. Fragment of Dialogue, Possibly for Act 3, Scene 5

TERESINA: You remember why you love your mother. You remember why you hate Alberta. Would you still remember your mother if she were alive? No! People only think of their loved ones who are alive as long as they're talking to them. But they think of the dead all the time. People think of the living all the time only when they hate them. There's a big, big difference between the dead and the living.

ALICE: But I don't hate Alberta. I'm mad at her because she could have been kinder to me and more affectionate. If I were rich, I'd give her everything I had, everything, just so she'd love me. So I don't hate her. I've no desire to see her, and I'd like to get her out of my mind. But I don't hate her.

TERESINA: I don't hate her either. If she were sick, I'd run to her side to take care of her. No! I couldn't run . . .

Introduction

Luigi Pirandello was born on June 28, 1867, in the place known as *il Caos*, in the vicinity of Girgenti (now Agrigento), Sicily. In 1887 he moved to Rome, enrolling in the Faculty of Letters. A few years later in 1889 his first collection of poems, *Mal giocondo* (Joyful sorrow), was published. Having decided to continue his studies in Bonn, in April 1891 he received his degree in Romance languages and returned to Rome where the writer and philosopher Luigi Capuana introduced him to the capital's cultural world. His first novel, *L'esclusa* (*The Outcast*), written in 1893, came out in installments in 1901. In 1894 he married Maria Antonietta Portulano, who bore him three children: Stefano, Lietta, and Fausto. His first drama, *Perché?* (*Why?*), which we are presenting here, was published in 1892 in *L'O di Giotto*,[1] a weekly journal connected with the Roman *La Tribuna*, and reveals his early preoccupation with the relativity of truth. It has been produced only once, in 1986, in Rome. His next drama to be published, *L'epilogo* (The epilogue), appeared in *Ariel* in 1898.[2] *Il fu Mattia Pascal* (*The Late Mattia Pascal*), the novel that became his first great international success, came out in 1904. His critical essays, *Arte e scienza* (Art and science) and *L'umorismo* (*On Humor*), are from 1908. The following year he began to work with the foremost Italian daily, *Il Corriere della sera*.

Actual production of Pirandello's plays began in December 1910 when *Lumie di Sicilia* (*Sicilian Limes*) and *La morsa* (*The Vise*), the new title given to *L'epilogo*, opened in Rome at Teatro Metastasio under Nino Martoglio's direction. Beginning in 1916, his theatrical activity came to the fore, and his plays were staged by various Italian companies. The first version of *Six Charac-*

■

TEN

LUIGI

PIRANDELLO

■

ters in Search of an Author was produced in Rome in 1921 by Dario Niccodemi and met with criticism from both public and critics. In 1922 the collection of his short stories entitled *Novelle per un anno* (Short stories for a year) came out. By the early 1920s his plays were being produced abroad. In France Aleksander Pitoëff presented *Six Characters in Search of an Author* (1923), *Henry IV* (1925), and *Each in His Own Way* (1926), and Charles Dullin produced *The Pleasure of Honesty* (1922) with Antonin Artaud in a small part, as well as *It Is So (If You Think So)* (1924) and *All for the Best* (1926).

In 1924, after the murder of Giacomo Matteotti, the leader of the opposition—a murder ordered by Mussolini—Pirandello wrote a public letter to Mussolini asking to join the Fascist party. Soon thereafter, in 1924, he helped found the Teatro d'Arte[3] in Rome and applied to Mussolini for a subvention. It was at the Teatro d'Arte that he gained important experience as a company manager, playwright, and director. However, the art theater was rejected by the Italian theater circuit; within a few seasons and after tours through Europe and South America the company was on the edge of bankruptcy and had to close in 1928 at a great financial cost to Pirandello personally. In 1934 Pirandello was awarded the Nobel prize for literature. He died of pneumonia on December 10, 1936, leaving his last work, *I giganti della montagna* (*The Mountain Giants*), unfinished.

Pirandello's relationship with the theater took various forms. At the beginning his plays were characteristically adaptations of his short stories, the setting was Sicily, and the tone was tragicomic. These were the years of his bitter "comedies," culminating in *The Rules of the Game* (1918), a marvelous reversal of the love triangle. The subject of these plays is primarily the couple, while the favorite setting is "the room" inside the petit bourgeois household. In this first phase, Pirandello appeared to adhere only to the idea of theater as a conflict between truth and fiction; in reality, he demonstrated how impossible it was to establish what truth is. This new vision separated him from the bourgeois theater, which assumed that one could find truth beyond culture, in a "natural condition."

Knowing that realism was the language his audience and readers, the middle or bourgeois class, would understand, Pirandello used realism as a guise. However, one should look for the inspiration and inner content of all his plays on other planes. For example, the sacred scriptures are the more or less hidden underpinnings of many texts, among them *To Clothe the Naked* (1922) and *The Life I Gave You* (1923). This is because, influenced first by silent film and then the talkies, over the years Pirandello formed a particular idea about theater and conceived of the stage as a place that called for magical evocations rather than photographic realism, that acted on the audience's imagination and resisted fulfilling its expectation to see an everyday reality. The importance of the imaginative element for Pirandello is amply demonstrated by his "theater within theater" trilogy—*Six Characters in Search of an Author*, *Each in His Own Way* (1924), and *Tonight We Improvise* (1930). In this trilogy, imagination is fundamental to the reality of the play. As a consequence the artifice of theater (for instance, an actor's lack of naturalness) need not be a limitation but can be an opportunity to demonstrate to the public that ghostly creations—for example, the Six Characters—and their stories, represent something real in our own lives or in the realm of factual news. In the late 1920s, Pirandello felt desperate about the materialism and lack of spirituality in his contemporaries, but he reacted with optimism, introducing real metaphysical shocks into his apparently realistic plays, and implanting in his texts some positive characters or symbols of hope. For instance, in several plays Pirandello creates the vision of the *lux* of salvation. But this *lux* remains outside the world of the human beings or characters, who only see its reflection (*lumen*) on the stained-glass window that separates the two realms.

Up to the end of the 1920s, one gathers from Pirandello's scripts that he was also interested in psychoanalysis, particularly in the idea of the subconscious as a motivating force underlying human behavior. Furthermore, some critics today, such as Claudio Vicentini,[4] show that Pirandello reworked with great originality the aesthetics of futurism (exposing the mechanics of the theater, for instance) and of surrealism (the reality of dreams, the oneiric aspect of so many everyday situations). He did this without giving up his own metaphysical search, a penchant shown by his interest in spiritualism and theosophy at the beginning of the century as well as by his study of medieval mysticism—Umberto Artioli has indicated how the structure of *I quaderni di Serafino Gubbio operatore* (*The Notebooks of Serafino Gubbio; or, Shoot!*) is based on *Itinerarium mentis in Deum*, written in 1259 by the Franciscan mystic, Bonaventura da Bagnoregio[5]—and finally by his use of mythic and occult symbols (for instance, the conflict between the Giants and artists in his final work, *Mountain Giants*). Studies such as those cited by Vicentini and Artioli allow one to assign to Pirandello a conscious twentieth-century gnosticism, but the complex nature of his "secret office" has not yet been comprehensively examined by scholars.

From the *realismo magico* (a term devised in the 1920s by Massimo Bontempelli) of his most creative period, which also coincided with his commitments as a director and manager of a theater company, Pirandello moved on to an original kind of classicism in his last works, where he tried to create modern myths. In *The New Colony* (1928), *Lazarus* (1928), *When One Is Somebody* (1933), *La favola del figlio cambiato* (The fable of the changed child, 1934) and *The Mountain Giants* (1936), the setting has shifted from the family to a larger social group, while next to the symbol there appears, with greater and greater frequency, the archetype, and Pirandello's meditation has shifted from the individual's problem to the impasse of an entire civilization. In this last vision, he seems to have lost any sense of art's potential usefulness to society. A memorable production of *The Mountain Giants*, directed by Giorgio Strehler in 1966, ended with the image of a steel curtain, the symbol of spectacular and inhuman power, crushing the cart belonging to the actors, the last exponents of humanism; Strehler's 1994 production had the same finale. Despite some moments of bombastic rhetoric, it is not surprising that this is the Pirandellian text-testament favored today by actors and directors. It asks questions about the meaning of art today—to which each performing artist gives different answers.

An important interview containing Pirandello's last statements was published in the journal *Termini*[6] in October 1936. Without mincing words, the playwright states that his theater is "difficult and dangerous" because it puts humanity in front of the abyss; he defines it as a "modern mystery play," adding, "In times of action and of revolutions this theater is a theater of revolutions and of firing squads" and also that, in the "absolute freedom" of art, the theater should be a spiritual exercise for the spectator. At the end of the interview,

Pirandello refers to the absolutely orthodox nature of his theater "with regard to its position vis-à-vis problems (. . .) that involve a Christian solution." But this emphasis should be interpreted in light of his fear at that time that the Roman Catholic church might ban his work, something that was averted only because of the mediation of Silvio d'Amico with Cardinal Montini, the future pope.

Tonight We Improvise was written at the height of Pirandello's maturity as a man of the theater. If Dr. Hinkfuss is the caricature of a director, he also voices Pirandello's ideas on the life of a work of art, and the author advised that any cuts in his opening speeches be made carefully.[7] The story that serves as Dr. Hinkfuss's experiment is Pirandello's own "Leonora, Addio!" a tale of jealousy set in Sicily.[8] The world premiere took place in Königsburg, Germany, in January 1930, (in a German translation) and was followed by a Berlin production that opened on May 31. Pirandello was present at all rehearsals for the Berlin production, but the results disappointed him. He thought the director, Hans Karl Müller, neglected the question of tempo and got lost in too much detail.[9] The Italian premiere in Turin in April 1930 was directed by Guido Salvini in consultation with Pirandello.[10]

A. A.

Trans. by J. H.

Notes

1. 3:25 (June 12, 1892). Reprinted in Edoardo Villa, ed., *Dinamica narrativa di Luigi Pirandello* (Padova: Liviana Editrice, 1976), pp. 173–80.

2. *L'epilogo* was included in a definitive collection of his dramatic works entitled *Maschere nude* (Naked masks) (Milan: Mondadori, 1956). This collection is considered the most accurate edition of Pirandello's dramatic texts and, with the commentary by Alessandro d'Amico, an in-depth critical study of the Sicilian author. In 1910 *L'epilogo* was produced as *La morsa* (*The Vise*).

3. It was also known as Teatro Odescalchi, which was the name of the theater where the Teatro d'Arte company performed for a time, and Teatro degli Undici, after the eleven founders.

4. *Pirandello: Il disagio del teatro* (Pirandello: The discomfort of theater) (Venice: Marsilio, 1993).

5. Umberto Artioli, *L'officina segreta di Pirandello* (The secret office of Pirandello) (Rome-Bari: Laterza, 1989).

6. Giovanni Cavicchioli, "Intervista a Luigi Pirandello," *Termini*, Fiume (October 1936), pp. 5–6.

7. Letters to his assistant, Guido Salvini, cited by A. Richard Sogliuzzo, *Luigi Pirandello, Director: The Playwright in the Theatre* (Metuchen, N.J. and London: Scarecrow Press, 1982), pp. 29–32.

8. See Luigi Pirandello, *Tonight We Improvise and "Leonora, Addio!,"* trans. with an introduction and notes by J. Douglas Campbell and Leonard G. Sbrocchi (Ottawa: The Canadian Society for Italian Studies, 1987).

9. Letter to Marta Abba, cited in Marta Abba "Introduction," in Luigi Pirandello, *The Mountain Giants and Other Plays* (New York: Crown, 1958), p. 24.

10. A promptbook exists for this production in the Guido Salvini Collection at the Actors' Museum of Genoa.

■

WHY?

(Perché?, 1892)

Translated by Jane House

■

Characters:

GIULIA, (25 years old) wife of
ENRICO, (28 years old)
A SERVANT

Setting:

An elegantly furnished drawing room. Side entrances on the right and on the left, with ornate drapes. Door with glass panes at the rear.

ENRICO *is sunk into a little settee, his body completely stretched out in gloomy indolence. After a pause* **GIULIA** *enters through the rear door, wearing a hat and carrying an umbrella. She has run upstairs in a hurry. She sees her husband, plants herself in front of him and says flirtatiously:*

GIULIA: Where have I been? Go on, ask me!

ENRICO (*gestures vaguely with his hand, as if to say:* "Why should I care?")

GIULIA: You're not feeling inquisitive today?

ENRICO (*indifferent, to make her happy*):   Where have you been?

GIULIA: What's the matter?

ENRICO: Nothing.

GIULIA: Not true. Tell me what's the matter?

ENRICO: Nothing! (*continues*) I'd say you were the inquisitive one.

GIULIA (*looking at him*):   Yes . . . right . . . (*preoccupied, but eager to change the subject and talk about something else*) Any letters? Nothing for me? (*then rousing herself*) Oh, I'm so tired!

(*She takes off her hat, sticks the hatpin in it, and goes over to put it on the table with the umbrella.*)

ENRICO (*after a pause*):   You know? I've been thinking . . . (*He breaks off.*)

GIULIA: What about?

ENRICO: About you.

GIULIA: About me? What?

ENRICO (*doesn't reply, sad, preoccupied.*)

GIULIA (*observes him, then heaving a big sigh*):   Ah! so it's the same old story . . . (*goes over to the table to sit down and, resting her elbows on the table, she puts her head in her hands*)

ENRICO (*getting up from his seat and speaking as if to himself*):   Madness! Madness!

GIULIA (*turns to give him a rueful look of reproach.*)

ENRICO: Enjoy yourselves. A great piece of advice! What are you doing to keep me entertained?

GIULIA: It's completely wasted on you. You're not interested!

ENRICO: Yes, yes, I am! I don't ask for anything more!

GIULIA: There, you see how you are? What can I do for you? I try to say something, and you won't let me finish . . .

ENRICO: That's not true.

GIULIA: Not true! You stand there, not saying a word, continually obsessed with that same thought . . . If you never pay attention to anything I say! How many offers do I have to come up with? All you say is no, no, no! every single time . . .

ENRICO: There was a time when you were always cheerful—but now . . . (*He breaks off.*)

GIULIA: Ah, and now?

ENRICO: Now you've forgotten how to laugh, you never say anything anymore. But this is me! Right here, look—did someone die on you? (*bursting out*) Oh, what have you done? What have you done? It's impossible! Things can't go on this way! (*goes back to the settee and sits down, with his elbows on his knees and his head in his hands*)

GIULIA: And he expects me to be cheerful! I like that . . .

ENRICO: Who reduced me to this state? You just don't know, you don't know how much I suffer.

GIULIA: You want to suffer . . .

ENRICO: Oh yes? So to top it all, it's my fault.

GIULIA: No. It's no one's fault. It's fate! Is it my fault that I didn't meet him sooner? That I met him too late? Would you look at this!

ENRICO: I know that.

GIULIA: So?

ENRICO: So nothing! I'm not accusing you, if you don't understand . . . I am-not-ac-cu-sing-you!

GIULIA: Why do we have to live like this, then? Unhappy for no reason!

ENRICO: For no reason . . .

GIULIA: Why did you marry me, if you seriously believe you have a reason for living like this? Why?

ENRICO: It's useless explaining it to you. You see me like this—you don't believe me! You think I don't love you and that I have no respect for you . . . Wrong! It's exactly the opposite. I suffer because I love you and respect you. Alright, so it's crazy, alright, yes! Who's denying it? But, you see, if I ask myself: why did you give yourself to me, the last comer? I think you were capable of loving . . .

GIULIA: Of loving . . .

ENRICO: Of loving, yes—don't deny it now!

GIULIA: But no one like I love you!

ENRICO: I know! But, someone, yes, you did love someone . . . at least maybe not the other imbeciles. There I believe you. But why it didn't burn your tongue to say "I love you" to some of those idiots I'll never know! And to think you could expect one of them to be a potential life partner . . . that naval officer cousin of yours, for instance, that tall what's-his-name character who was so vacant and insipid, the one who left you in the lurch afterward, like all the others, you, who are now my wife, the woman I love. . . . Weren't you ever ashamed! . . . Am I making you suffer? Yes, I can see that I am, and it gives me such satisfaction . . . Oh I'm going mad, mad, I really am . . . (*Overcome by emotion, he kneels at her feet and hides his face in her lap.*)

GIULIA (*stroking his hair*): It's the bad luck that's dogged me since childhood, I know it is! I told you: "Be careful what you're doing! There's still time—I bring on bad luck . . ." But you wouldn't listen! I resigned myself . . . Remember? I was always laughing back then . . .

ENRICO (*without lifting his head*): A beautiful laugh!

GIULIA: Nothing mattered to me anymore. You're the one who changed me. Better to have left me as I was—at least I used to laugh.

ENRICO: I taught you how to love.

GIULIA: That's true, but the pupil surpassed the master.

ENRICO: The crazy things I did for you!

GIULIA: It all seemed so unreal to me . . .

ENRICO (*irritated, looking up*): Why? What do you mean, unreal? You see? It's you, it's your fault, yours. You always have to humble yourself in my eyes. But don't you see? It seemed unreal to you! Why? Because those other men left you? While I . . . You see how it is? That's what's tormenting me! I don't know what I feel anymore: irritation? rage? love?—yes! love—but, see: all those other men, I'd like to walk all over them for leaving you . . .

GIULIA: Oh, you're so proud! . . . (*getting up*) Do you think I must have less respect for you than for the others just because you married me and they didn't?

ENRICO: No—that's not what I said!

GIULIA: Oh, you're all so . . .—listen, shall I tell you what you men are like, my friend?

ENRICO: Mad!

GIULIA: No, please! — ri-di . . .

ENRICO: Ridiculous.

GIULIA: Right, you said it!

(*A long pause. She goes over to a mirror, looks at herself, rearranging her hair here and there on her forehead. Confused, he watches her every move closely, then goes to sit in the rocking chair and speaks, enunciating expressively.*)

ENRICO: You didn't un-der-stand me.

GIULIA (*sharply*): Didn't I?

ENRICO: No, you didn't, you never do, you never did, and you never will.

GIULIA: If that's the way you want it, so be it! (*changing her tone, sadly*) I do understand one thing though, my dear—you should have done what the others did.

ENRICO: Should I?

GIULIA: Yes, it would have been much better for you.

ENRICO: And for you, too.

GIULIA: Oh, for me, what does it matter? I am accustomed to suffering . . . The point is, I should never have said yes. Because you were like a little boy, you still are, but I knew it would end like this . . .

ENRICO: Idiots!

GIULIA: Do they really upset you? But what do they matter? Aren't I yours, completely and forever? Suppose someone else had taken me?

ENRICO: I wouldn't be suffering like this today!

GIULIA: And you love me?

ENRICO (*looks at her in indignation, as if to say: How can you ask me that?*)

GIULIA: You're too difficult to read, I really don't understand you.

ENRICO: No, it's I who will never be able to tell you what I feel: it's so strange! If only I could find some peace of mind! I don't know how to ease the pain, you understand? It's over, it's all over—it's all in the past, in your past! Which I would like, how can I put it, I would like to fill it up with myself, I don't know . . . Don't laugh, don't laugh like that!

GIULIA (*laughing loudly*): But it's so laughable! *With yourself, with yourself* . . . *my past* . . . —was mine really any different from that of nine out of ten women who take a husband? There's no trace of that past left in my heart. Wait a minute, one trace, just one, to be honest, a memory so faint and so far away . . . just think, I was seven . . .

ENRICO: You started early, didn't you! . . .

GIULIA: It was innocent! He was a boy of eight. His name was Attilio. We used to walk to school together. If you'd only seen how sweet he was! He brought me a flower every morning. He was blond, with long hair, cut in a fringe on his forehead. He was the son of a major in the bersaglieri.[1] Wait, I'd like to . . . (*She searches in her pocket for the keys.*) I still have a picture of him, but it's all crumpled, I think. He gave it to me back then. I came across it again much later—he had already gone away by then. Can you imagine, I didn't even recognize him anymore. I want to show it to you. (*She goes to open a little cupboard on the wall, above the table, pulls out a box made of black wood, opens it, and begins to rummage inside.*) You're not jealous of Attilio now, are you?

ENRICO: All those papers . . . You still have them?

GIULIA: What? You see? Look! I must have asked you a hundred times whether you want me to burn them. I'll burn them right now, if you want. But you always told me not to!

ENRICO: Yes, yes, what do I care about them, really? (*picking out a photograph from among the papers*) Wait a minute, who's this one?

GIULIA: Let me see. But you know him! Carlo. (*resumes her search*)

ENRICO: The naval officer?

GIULIA (*searching*): In civilian clothes. Didn't you ever see him? He didn't have a beard then. But I can't find . . .

ENRICO (*turns over the portrait and reads*): "To my Giugiù!"

GIULIA: Revolting! That's what he used to call me!

ENRICO: Giugiù? I like it. I'm going to call you that too.

GIULIA: I absolutely forbid it.

ENRICO: Why, Giugiù?

GIULIA (*emptying the box onto the table and crossing in annoyance to sit on the settee*): Och! I should have known . . .

ENRICO: What? Why? I've cheered up. I'm having a good time, I really am. Come on, Giugiù! Come on . . . show me little Attilio! . . . No? Then shall I look? May I? (*He picks out a letter.*) "Giulia, my dear!" This one doesn't use a pet name. Oooh! Look: *college* written with one l! "Who is it whom . . ." and *tribulation* with two ls! . . . (*turns the paper and reads the signature*) Filippo; clever Filippo! Well, *this* cousin obviously wasn't much of a speller. Curious! You specialized in cousins. Be honest now: I think you led

---

1. A special unit of sharpshooters in the Italian army.—Trans.

them all on for fun, on both sides of the family! What idiots! Not one of them married you . . .

GIULIA (*her head resting on the back of the settee*):   Oh, please! Will this go on forever?

(*Someone knocks at the glass door.*)

ENRICO: Come in!

SERVANT (*carrying a letter*):   A letter has . . . (*hands it to Enrico and exits*)

GIULIA (*anxiously*):   Isn't it for me?

ENRICO (*reading the address, indifferently*):   For you.

GIULIA: Open it!

ENRICO (*handing her the letter with a meaningful smile*):   Oh please, be so kind . . .

(*Goes back near the table to look among the papers, unfolds one of them. Meanwhile GIULIA reads the letter and from time to time bursts out laughing; he turns, looks at her, but refusing to pay attention to her, returns to his search.*)

GIULIA (*laughing, when she's finished reading*):   Guess who wrote me?

ENRICO: Your mother.

GIULIA: Yes, and who else? She encloses a letter from . . . guess who!

ENRICO: From her business manager, her usual nonsense. Your mother always loves to joke around . . .

GIULIA: You're right, it is a joke, actually. But this time it's not from . . . Look! (*shows him the letter*) Carlo!

ENRICO: The officer? He wrote? To you?

GIULIA: Poor man; he obviously never got our wedding announcement.

ENRICO: What does he say?

GIULIA: You read it. He's asking my mother to help him. Look. It's funny! (*hands him the letter*)

ENRICO (*opens the letter and reads*):   "Giulia! I've traveled all over the world and I haven't found one woman who compares with you." Cute!

GIULIA: "In body and soul."

ENRICO: What?

GIULIA: Doesn't he say that? I thought . . . It was one of his favorite expressions.

ENRICO (*continues to read*):   "I'm not just being complimentary: What I mean is that I was an idiot not to appreciate you earlier."—That's for sure!—"Can you forgive me? Your mother will speak for me. I'll be there in two months. Carlo." (*He stands there with the letter in his hands, smiling, looking at GIULIA.*)

GIULIA (*on the settee, her head resting on the back, looking at the ceiling, lets these words drop*):   So, here we have another man who would have married me! You hear, my love? You're not alone any longer now! Are you happy? But the thing is that if I were free, with what I know now, I wouldn't marry anyone. (*gets up from her seat*)

ENRICO: Not even . . . me?

GIULIA: You? (*Looks at him a moment, then takes her hat and umbrella from the table and walks toward the door on the right.*) Who knows! You . . . yes, maybe! (*moving aside the drapes that hang over the door and turning*) You are a bit silly, very silly . . . but you really do love me! (*without letting go of the drapes she kisses him on the lips*)

CURTAIN

■

TONIGHT WE IMPROVISE

(Questa sera si recita a soggetto, 1930)

Translated with notes by
J. Douglas Campbell and
Leonard G. Sbrocchi

■

PROLOGUE

*The announcement of the play in newspapers and on
posters must appear without the name of the author, thus:*

The . . . . THEATER presents
TONIGHT WE IMPROVISE
under the direction of
Doctor Hinkfuss (. . . . . .) and with the
kind participation and assistance of the
audience and of . . .

. . . .
. . . .
. . . .

Fill in the blanks with names of the main actresses
and actors.
It's more than you need; but it'll do.

The theater is filled tonight with the people one always sees at the premiere of a new play.

The announcement of an improvised play in the newspapers and on the posters has aroused much curiosity. It is only the drama critics of the city newspapers who try not to show it. They think that they will have no trouble pointing out tomorrow what a mess it was. ("Oh Lord, they'll probably try for something like the old commedia dell'arte. But where are you going to find modern actors who can improvise like that? They were inspired, those commedia actors! It was easier for them, though—much easier: they had their old scenarios, their traditional masks—a whole bag of tricks.") The critics are rather annoyed because the name of the writer—the one who must have given this evening's actors and their director some kind of scenario—is not known; it does not appear on the posters. They have no clues to help them fall back on ready-made judgments, and they are afraid of getting caught contradicting themselves.

At the precise moment the play is scheduled to begin, the houselights dim and the footlights come up.

In the sudden darkness the audience at first pays attention, then, not hearing the bell that usually signals the opening of the curtain, they begin to fidget a little, particularly when through the closed curtain they hear muffled, excited voices, as though the actors are protesting, and someone is asserting his authority over them to silence their protests.

A GENTLEMAN IN THE STALLS[1] (*looking around and asking loudly*): What's happening?
ANOTHER IN THE BALCONY: Sounds like an argument backstage.
A THIRD IN THE ORCHESTRA: Maybe it's part of the show.

(*Someone laughs.*)

AN OLDER GENTLEMAN IN A BOX (*as if, being a fastidious playgoer, his sense of propriety is offended by these noises*): But this is outrageous! Who ever heard of such a thing!
AN OLD LADY (*jumping up from her seat in the back of the stalls, with the face of a frightened chicken*): It's not a fire, is it? God forbid!
HER HUSBAND (*immediately holding her back*): Fire? Are you crazy? Sit down and be quiet.
A YOUNG SPECTATOR NEARBY (*with a sad, indulgent smile*): Don't say that even as a joke, madam. They'd have lowered the safety curtain by now!

(*Finally the stage bell rings.*)

SOME SPECTATORS: Ah, there we are now!
OTHERS: Quiet! Quiet!

———

1. There seem to be no exact correspondences between Italian practices and English ones with respect to the terminology describing the parts of a theater auditorium. We have translated *platea* as stalls, *galleria* as balcony, *poltrone* as orchestra, and *palco* as box. See Ingrid Luterkort et al., eds., *Theater Words* (Stockholm: Nordic Theater Union, 1980).

(*But the curtain does not open. Instead, the bell is heard again, and from the back of the hall can be heard the irritated voice of the director,* DOCTOR HINKFUSS, *as he bangs the door open and advances angrily down the aisle that divides the orchestra in two.*)

DOCTOR HINKFUSS: The bell! The bell! Who said to ring the bell? I'm the one to say when it's time to ring the bell!

(DOCTOR HINKFUSS *shouts these words as he goes down the aisle and climbs the three steps that lead from the auditorium to the stage. Then he turns to the audience, bringing his nervous excitement under control with amazing promptness.*

Dressed in a frock-coat, with a small roll of paper under his arm, DOCTOR HINKFUSS *has been condemned—and a terrible and unjust punishment it is—to be a little fellow, not much more than a yard tall. But he has taken his revenge—he sports a huge head of hair out to here. First he looks at his tiny hands; maybe he finds them repulsive himself, they are so thin, and the pale little fingers are as hairy as caterpillars. After a moment, without giving much weight to his words, he says:*)

DOCTOR HINKFUSS: I'm sorry about the moment of confusion you probably noticed behind the curtains. I beg your pardon. Although . . . perhaps if we were to think of it as an involuntary prologue—

THE GENTLEMAN IN THE ORCHESTRA (*interrupting, extremely pleased with himself*): See? Just what I said!

DOCTOR HINKFUSS (*with cold severity*): You have something to say, sir?

THE GENTLEMAN IN THE ORCHESTRA: No. I'm just pleased to have guessed right.

DOCTOR HINKFUSS: Guessed what?

THE GENTLEMAN IN THE ORCHESTRA: That those noises were part of the show.

DOCTOR HINKFUSS: Oh? Really? You thought we were playing games with you? And to think that tonight I had decided to lay my cards on the table! No, don't flatter yourself, sir. I said an *involuntary* prologue. And I might add it wouldn't be entirely inappropriate, considering the unusual nature of the performance you're about to see. But please don't interrupt.

Here it is, ladies and gentlemen. (*He takes the little roll from under his arm.*) In this little roll of paper, only a few pages, I have all I need. Hardly anything. Just a little story, not much more, turned into dialogue here and there by a writer whose name will not be entirely unfamiliar to you.

SOME SPECTATORS: What is it? What's his name?

SOMEONE IN THE BALCONY: Who is he?

DOCTOR HINKFUSS: Please, gentlemen, please. I didn't intend to hold a public meeting. Certainly I'm willing to answer for what I've done, but I can't allow you to call me to account during the performance.

THE GENTLEMAN IN THE ORCHESTRA: It hasn't started yet.

DOCTOR HINKFUSS: Yes, it has started, sir. You're the last one who should question that, you're the one who thought that those noises in the beginning were the start of the performance. The performance has begun, in that I am standing here before you.

THE OLDER GENTLEMAN IN THE BOX (*flushed with anger*): I thought you were here to apologize for that disgraceful uproar! It's scandalous! And I tell you this: I didn't come here to listen to you give a lecture.

DOCTOR HINKFUSS: Lecture? How dare you? What are you shouting about? Do you think I would bring you here to listen to a lecture?

(*The* **OLDER GENTLEMAN**, *very angry at this outburst, jumps to his feet and leaves his box, grumbling.*)

You're quite free to leave, you know. No one is keeping you here. Ladies and gentlemen, the only reason I'm here is to prepare you for the unusual things you'll see tonight. Surely I deserve your attention. You wanted to know who the author of this little story is? I suppose I could tell you . . .

SOME SPECTATORS: Well then, tell us! Tell us!

DOCTOR HINKFUSS: All right, I will: Luigi Pirandello.

EXCLAMATIONS IN THE HOUSE: Ohhhh . . .

THE MAN IN THE BALCONY (*loudly, over the noise of the crowd*): And who is he?

(*Many in the stalls, in the orchestra, and in the boxes laugh.*)

DOCTOR HINKFUSS (*also laughing a little*): Oh yes, it's him all right! He's incorrigible, isn't he! Always the same! You remember what he did to a couple of my colleagues? First he sent one of them six lost characters looking for an author; they turned the stage upside-down and drove everyone crazy Then another time, some people in the audience recognized themselves in the characters on stage; the audience was all up in arms and the performance was ruined.[2] Well, there's no danger that he'll put one over on me this time. Don't worry: I've eliminated him. His name doesn't even appear in the posters. In any case, it wouldn't be right to hold him responsible for tonight's performance, no, not even for a small part of it.

The only one responsible is me.

I've taken one of his stories. I could have taken someone else's, but I preferred one of his, because he is the only theater writer I know who has shown some understanding of the fact that the work of a writer ends the moment he puts his last word down on paper. He has his audience—the readers, the literary critics—and he'll answer to them for what he has written. As for those who sit here in the theater and judge—the spectators, the drama critics—he cannot answer to them, nor is he obliged to.

VOICES FROM THE HOUSE: Oh no? That's a good one!

DOCTOR HINKFUSS: No, ladies and gentlemen, because in the theater the writer's work ceases to exist.

---

2. Doctor Hinkfuss is referring to *Six Characters in Search of an Author* (1921), and *Each in His Own Way* (1925). According to Pirandello, these two works together with *Tonight We Improvise* constitute "a trilogy about the theater within theater." (Prefatory note to volume 1 of the first collected edition of his plays. [Milan: Mondadori, 1930]; reprinted in *Maschere nude* [Milan: Mondadori, 1958], 1:51.

THE MAN IN THE BALCONY: What's left, then?

DOCTOR HINKFUSS: The theatrical work that I have made of it, and that is mine alone.

But again I'd like to ask you not to interrupt me. I can see that some of you critics are smiling, but I assure you that this is a firm conviction of mine. You're free to reject it and continue to direct your criticisms, unjustly, at the writer. Of course, you must allow him the right to smile at your criticisms, just as you are smiling at the principle I've just presented. Mind you, I'm assuming that your criticisms are unfavorable. On the other hand, if there's praise to be given, it would be just as unfair for the writer to take any that belongs to me.

I have some sound reasons for my beliefs.

The work of the writer? Here it is. (*He holds up the little roll of paper.*) What do I do with it? I take it as the raw material for my theatrical work; I use it, just as I use the skills of the actors I've chosen to act the parts according to my interpretation. It's the same with the scenographers—I tell them how to build and paint the sets—the stage crew that puts them up, the lighting technicians who light them—everyone directed by the plans, the procedures, the instructions that come, in every detail, from me.

Now you'll grant me this: that in another theater, with other actors and other sets, with different blocking and different lighting, the theatrical work will be entirely different. You can see then, that what one judges in the theater is never the work of the writer (that unique text of his), but this or that theatrical creation that was made of it, each one different from the others, and that they are many, while this is one. To judge a text one must know it. It can't be known through its theatrical interpretation; when certain actors do it, it's one thing, and when others do it, it will necessarily become something else. If only the work could stage itself, not with actors, but with its own characters, who, by some miracle, could acquire a body and a voice, then it could be judged directly in the theater. But can such a miracle ever happen? No one's ever seen it yet. What's left then, ladies and gentlemen? The miracle the Stage Director tries—with more or less conviction—to accomplish every night with his actors. That's the only miracle that's possible.

In order to remove any suggestion of paradox from what I say, I'd like you to consider the notion that a work of art is fixed forever in an immutable form, and that that form represents the liberation of the poet from his creative labor, the state of perfect peace after all the tumult of that labor is done.

Well then . . .

Would you say, ladies and gentlemen, that there is life where nothing moves, where everything rests in perfect peace?

Life must obey two necessities that, because they are opposed to one another, prevent life from either staying always the same or constantly changing. If life were always changing it would never endure; if it always remained the same it would never change. Life needs both fixity and movement.

The artist[3] is deceived if he thinks that he has freed himself, that he has reached peace when he fixes his work of art forever in an immutable form. It's only that particular work that he has finished living. You can only have freedom and tranquillity if you pay the price: you must stop living.

Anyone who has found this freedom and tranquillity lives in a lamentable state of illusion in which he thinks he's still alive, but he's not; he's so dead he doesn't even smell the stench of his own corpse.

If a work of art survives, it is only because we can still free it from the fixity of its form. We can release this form within us by means of an impulse of vital energy. We are the ones who give it its life; it is different for each one of us, and it changes every time. Not one life, but many. Look at the constant discussions we have about it. They arise from our reluctance to believe this very fact: that we are the ones who give it its life. But the life I give it cannot possibly be the same as the one someone else gives it. Please forgive me, ladies and gentlemen, for the roundabout way I came to it, but this is the point I wanted to make.

Now someone might ask me: "But who said that art must be life? It's true that life must obey the two opposite necessities you spoke about—but that's why life is not art. Just as art is not life precisely because it is able to free itself from those contradictory necessities; it consists forever in the immutability of its form. That's why art is the kingdom of completed creation, whereas life is, as it should be, an infinitely varied and constantly changing process. Each one of us, as he tries to create a self and a life, uses the same faculties of the spirit[4] as those with which an artist creates a work of art. In fact, a person who is better endowed with those faculties, and knows better how to use them, is able to reach a higher state and to sustain it for a longer time. But it will never be true creation. First of all, it is destined to decay and die with us in time; then, since it is directed toward a particular objective, it can never be free; finally, it is subject to unforeseen and unforeseeable circumstances, to all the obstacles that others set against it; it risks being constantly thwarted, deflected, deformed. In a certain sense art vindicates life. It is truly created, because it is free from time, from circumstance, from any other end but itself."

And I answer, "Yes, ladies and gentlemen, you're right." But I'll go even further than that: many a time I've found myself thinking, with painful bewilderment, of the eternal existence of a work of art; it's like an unreachable, divine solitude, from which even

---

3. Text has *poeta,* poet. By "poet" Pirandello means an individual endowed with great sensitivity who is the "instrument" in the creation of a work of art. The medium in which this work is produced, whether it be poetry, drama, novel, painting, sculpture, or music, is not important; they are all the work of a "poet." See Pirandello's Preface to *Six Characters in Search of an Author.*

4. For an analysis of the process Doctor Hinkfuss is referring to, see Pirandello's Preface to *Six Characters in Search of an Author.*

the poet himself, the moment he has created it, is excluded: he is mortal, the work is immortal.

It's terrible, the immobility of the gesture of a statue, the eternal solitude of immutable forms outside of time.

Every sculptor (I don't know this, but I assume it's true) after he has created a statue, if he really believes he has given it eternal life, must wish that, as a living being, it could free itself from its pose, and move about, and speak. It would cease being a statue; it would become a living person.

There's only one way, ladies and gentlemen, in which something that art has fixed in the immutability of a form can come back to life and move about again. It must take back its life from us, a life that is various, diverse, and momentary; the life that each one of us is able to give it.

Nowadays, people are quite willing to leave works of art in that divine solitude of theirs, outside of time. After a long day of hard work and tiresome duties, with all its annoyances and anxieties, when an audience comes to the theater in the evening it wants to be amused.

THE GENTLEMAN IN THE ORCHESTRA: With Pirandello? That'll be the day! (*They laugh.*)

DOCTOR HINKFUSS: Don't worry. Everything's under control. (*Again he holds up the little roll of paper.*)

Nothing much to this. It's what I'll do on my own that counts.

If the scenes and the dramatic action follow along just as I've prepared them—not just the overall flow, but the details as well—and if my actors justify the faith I've placed in them, I'm sure you'll find it will be a pleasant show I've arranged for you. Besides, I'll be there among you, ready to step in if necessary, to get the show going if things go wrong, to clarify or explain to make up for any shortcomings. If I may say so, this will make the novelty of this experiment in improvisation more pleasing to you. I've divided the performance into several scenes—there will be short pauses between them. Occasionally there will be a moment of darkness from which a new scene will suddenly emerge, either here on the stage, or even down there among you. Yes, that's right, in the auditorium. (I have purposely left a box empty. When the time comes, it will be occupied by the actors; then, all of you will participate in the action.) There will also be a longer pause so that you can leave the auditorium, but—I'm warning you now— it won't be to take a break. I've prepared another surprise for you, there in the foyer.

One last very brief note, to help you find your bearings.

The action takes place in a city in the interior of Sicily, where (as you know) passions are strong; they smolder inside, then burst out violently. And the fiercest of them is jealousy. It's a case of jealousy that this story presents, and it's the most terrible kind of jealousy, because it allows for no remedy: jealousy of the past. And it happens in the very family it should have stayed away from. This family lives in almost hermetic seclusion from all others, because it is the only house in the city open to outsiders. It practices this excessive hospitality deliberately, to defy slander, and to challenge the scandal that others make of it.

The La Croce family.

As you'll see it is made up of the father, Signor Palmiro, a mining engineer: "Sampognetta," everyone calls him, because he's like a little reed pipe, always whistling absentmindedly; the mother, Signora Ignazia, of Neapolitan origin, known in town as "La Generala"; and four pretty daughters, rather plump and sentimental, lively and passionate:

MOMMINA,

TOTINA,

DORINA,

NENÈ.

And now with your permission.

(*He claps his hands as a signal, and, drawing one end of the curtain aside a little, gives an order.*) The bell! (*The bell rings.*)

I'm going to call on the actors to introduce their characters.

(*The curtain opens.*)

ACT 1

A light curtain, green in color, that can be opened in the middle, can be seen downstage.

DOCTOR HINKFUSS (*drawing the curtain aside a little and calling*): Please, Mr. ___.[5]

(*He says the name of the* **LEADING ACTOR**, *who is playing the role of* **RICCO VERRI**. *But the* **LEADING ACTOR**, *although he is there behind the curtain, won't come out.* **DOCTOR HINKFUSS** *repeats:*)

Please, please, come out here, Mr. ___. I hope you won't insist on having your say in front of the audience as well.

THE LEADING ACTOR (*coming out from behind the curtain, dressed and made up as Rico Verri, in an air force officer's uniform; extremely agitated*): Yes I do insist! Especially if you have the nerve to call me by my real name in front of the audience.

DOCTOR HINKFUSS: Does that offend you?

THE LEADING ACTOR: Yes, it does. And you don't seem to realize it, but you're making it worse by keeping me here arguing with you after forcing me to come out here.

DOCTOR HINKFUSS: Who asked you to argue? You're the one who's arguing! I'm asking you to do your job.

THE LEADING ACTOR: I am ready. When I hear my cue.

(*He withdraws, moving the curtain with an angry gesture.*)

----

5. Wherever the formula "Miss" or "Mr." appears, the name of the actor playing the appropriate role should be inserted. In the text Pirandello usually uses the formula: a *signor . . . (dirà il suo nome),* "Mr. . . . (he or she will say his / her name.)."

DOCTOR HINKFUSS (*disappointed*): I wanted to introduce you . . .

THE LEADING ACTOR (*coming back*): No! You will not introduce me! The audience knows me. I am not a puppet for you to show to the public like that box you have left empty, or some chair that you put in a particular place to create some magical effect.

DOCTOR HINKFUSS (*tight-lipped, fuming*): You're taking advantage of the fact that out here I have to put up with . . .

THE LEADING ACTOR (*interrupting immediately*): No, my dear sir: it's not a matter of putting up with anything. You've got to understand: there is no more Mr. __ here under this costume. He's committed himself to this evening of improvisation of yours, but if I'm to have words ready—words that come from the flesh and blood of my character— and if I'm to keep the action flowing naturally, and every gesture spontaneous, Mr. __ must *live* the character of *Rico Verri*, he must *be Rico Verri*. And he is: he already is. So much so that, as I was telling you before, I don't know if he'll be able to adapt himself to all those coincidences and surprises, all those plays of light and shadow you've planned so as to amuse the audience. Do you understand?

(*At this point a resounding slap is heard from behind the curtain, and immediately after, the protests of the* **OLD COMIC ACTOR**, *who is playing Sampognetta.*)

THE OLD COMIC ACTOR: Ouch! Why are you doing that? Don't ever slap me like that again! My God, that one was real!

(*There is laughter behind the curtain at this outburst.*)

DOCTOR HINKFUSS (*looking through the curtain at the stage*): But what the devil is going on? What is it?

THE OLD COMIC ACTOR (*coming outside the curtain with his hand on his cheek, dressed and made up as Sampognetta*): I will not put up with Miss __ slapping me the way she did. Did you hear it? Improvisation is no excuse. Among other things (*showing his slapped cheek*), she's ruined my makeup. See?

THE CHARACTER ACTRESS (*coming out, dressed and made up as Signora Ignazia*): But good heavens, you should protect yourself! It takes so little to protect yourself! It's instinctive and natural.

THE OLD COMIC ACTOR: How can I protect myself if you slap me without warning?

THE CHARACTER ACTRESS: It's only when you deserve it, dear.

THE OLD COMIC ACTOR: Of course! But I don't know when I deserve it, dear!

THE CHARACTER ACTRESS: Well then, always protect yourself, because as far as I'm concerned you always deserve it. And if we're improvising, I can't wait for some particular moment to slap you!

THE OLD COMIC ACTOR: But there's no need for you to give me a real slap anyway!

THE CHARACTER ACTRESS: What do you mean? Pretend? I don't have any lines memorized! Don't you see? It must come from here (*making a gesture from the stomach upward*), and everything must move along quickly, you see? You ask for a slap, and I give it to you.

DOCTOR HINKFUSS: Please, please, there's an audience out there!

THE CHARACTER ACTRESS: But Doctor Hinkfuss, we're already in character.

THE OLD COMIC ACTOR (*again putting his hand on his cheek*):   Are we ever!

DOCTOR HINKFUSS: Oh! Is this what you mean by . . .

THE CHARACTER ACTRESS: Excuse me, you wanted to introduce us? Well, here we are introducing ourselves. A slap, and this husband of mine, this imbecile, is already introduced. (*The* **OLD COMIC ACTOR**, *as* **SAMPOGNETTA**, *starts to whistle.*) There he is, you see. He's whistling. He's completely in character.

DOCTOR HINKFUSS: But do you think it's right to do it this way—in front of the curtain, without a set, just like that?

THE CHARACTER ACTRESS: It doesn't matter! It doesn't matter!

DOCTOR HINKFUSS: What do you mean it doesn't matter? How can the audience understand?

THE LEADING ACTOR: Of course it will understand! It will understand better this way! Leave it to us. We've all taken on our characters.

THE CHARACTER ACTRESS: Believe me, it'll be easier and more natural for us to play without the limitations of a particular place or a prearranged action. And we'll do everything you've prepared, too. Don't worry! But meantime, wait. Please, let me introduce my daughters too. (*She moves the curtain and calls:*) Here, girls! Girls! Come here! (*She takes the first one by the arm and pulls her out:*) Mommina. (*Then the second:*) Totina. (*Then the third:*) Dorina. (*Then the fourth:*) Nenè.

(*Each one except the first makes a beautiful curtsy as she comes out.*)

Would you look at them! My Lord! They should be queens, all four of them! Who'd have thought they'd be born of a man like that?

(**SIGNOR PALMIRO**, *seeing himself pointed at, immediately averts his face and begins to whistle.*)

Whistle! Go on! Whistle! Oh, my dear, if only a bit of gas[6] from that sulfur mine of yours would find its way up your nostrils—just a little sniff, the way I take a pinch of snuff—and then, that'd be it for you my dear, stone dead and out of my sight for good!

TOTINA (*rushing with* **DORINA** *to hold her back*):   Please, Mama, don't start that!

DORINA (*at the same time*):   Leave him alone, Mama, please leave him alone!

THE CHARACTER ACTRESS: Look at him! He whistles! That's all he does! He whistles! (*then, out of character, to* **DOCTOR HINKFUSS**) It's going as smooth as silk, don't you think?

DOCTOR HINKFUSS (*with a flash of artfulness, realizing that this is the way to save his prestige*):   As you'll have guessed by now, the actors' refusal to do what I say is part of the performance; we planned it together, to make the presentation more lively and spontaneous.

---

6. Text has *grisou*, fire-damp, an explosive mixture of methane gas and air, found especially in coal mines.

(At this treacherous, underhanded remark, the actors freeze in gestures of astonishment, like so many puppets. **DOCTOR HINKFUSS** *immediately realizes what has happened; he turns to look at them and points them out to the audience.)*

Even this astonishment is a pretense.

THE LEADING ACTOR *(shaking himself, indignant)*: What a circus! Please believe me, ladies and gentlemen: my objections were in no way a pretense. *(As before, he moves the curtain and goes away in a fury.)*

DOCTOR HINKFUSS *(immediately, to the audience, as if in confidence)*: It's all invented, even this last outburst. The pride of an actor like Mr. __, one of the finest on our stage, demanded some satisfaction, and I was glad to concede it to him. But you understand that anything that happens up here must necessarily be a fiction. *(turning to the* **CHARAC-TER ACTRESS)** Continue, continue, Miss __. You're doing fine! I wouldn't have expected less from you.

THE CHARACTER ACTRESS *(disconcerted, almost shocked by such effrontery, no longer knowing what to do)*: Uh, you want . . . you want me to continue? Now? And . . . and . . . excuse me, to do what?

DOCTOR HINKFUSS: The introduction, of course. It started so well, just as we planned it.

THE CHARACTER ACTRESS: No, please, please, don't say planned, Doctor Hinkfuss, unless you want me to stand here unable to say a word.

DOCTOR HINKFUSS *(again to the audience, as if in confidence)*: She's magnificent!

THE CHARACTER ACTRESS: Excuse me. Do you really want people to think there was an agreement among us to start out the way we did?

DOCTOR HINKFUSS: Ask the audience if it doesn't think we're improvising right now.

(THE GENTLEMAN IN THE ORCHESTRA, *the* **FOUR IN THE STALLS,** *and the* **ONE IN THE BALCONY** *begin to clap their hands; they will stop immediately if the real audience does not catch on and follow their example.)*

THE CHARACTER ACTRESS: Ah, well, yes! This? Yes! Truly improvised! We came out improvising, and we're improvising now, both you and I.

DOCTOR HINKFUSS: Then let's carry on . . . Carry on! Call the other actors in and introduce them!

THE CHARACTER ACTRESS: Yes! Right away! *(calling from the curtain)* Hey, young men, come here, come here, everybody!

DOCTOR HINKFUSS: Back in character, of course.

THE CHARACTER ACTRESS: Don't worry, they are. Here! Here, dear friends!

(Five young air force officers in uniform come out noisily. First they enthusiastically greet **SIGNORA IGNAZIA:)**

— Dear, dear Signora!
— Hail to our great Generala!
— To our patron saint!

(And other similar exclamations. Then they greet the four girls, who answer joyfully. Someone even

greets **SIGNOR PALMIRO**. **SIGNORA IGNAZIA** *tries to interrupt all these noisy greetings, which are genuinely improvised.*)

THE CHARACTER ACTRESS: Easy, easy, my dears. Let's not all talk at once. Wait, wait! You, here, Pomàrici, what a dream for Totina! Here, take her arm—that's it! And you Sarelli, here, with Dorina!

THE THIRD OFFICER: No, no! Dorina is with me (*holding her by the arm*) let's not joke about it!

SARELLI (*pulling her by the other arm*): Give her to me; her own mother assigned her to me!

THE THIRD OFFICER: Oh, no! No! The young lady and I have an agreement.

SARELLI (*to* **DORINA**): Ah, an agreement! Congratulations! (*denouncing them*) Signora Ignazia, did you hear them?

THE CHARACTER ACTRESS: What do you mean, an agreement?

DORINA (*annoyed*): Yes, but . . . excuse me, Miss __. We've agreed to play our roles.

THE THIRD OFFICER: Miss __, please don't confuse things. We've already worked it out.

THE CHARACTER ACTRESS: Oh yes, excuse me, I remember now! Sarelli, you are with Nenè.

NENÈ (*to Sarelli, opening her arms*): With me, don't you remember? That's what we agreed on!

SARELLI: Well after all, we're only here to make a little noise.

DOCTOR HINKFUSS (*to the* **CHARACTER ACTRESS**): Please, Miss __, take care!

THE CHARACTER ACTRESS: Yes, yes, excuse me. Be patient. There are so many of them I got a little confused. (*turning to look around*) But Verri! Where is Verri? He should be here with his friends.

THE LEADING ACTOR (*immediately, sticking his head through the curtain*): Oh yes, fine friends, aren't they! Just the ones to teach your dear daughters lessons in modesty!

THE CHARACTER ACTRESS: Would you like me to keep them with the nuns learning the catechism and embroidery? "Those times have gone, Aeneas . . ."[7]

(*Going to get him and bringing him out by the hand.*)

Come on now, come here, be nice! Look at them. They may not look it, but they do have them, you know? Those fine old housewifely virtues. There aren't many like them today! Talk about modesty! Mommina can cook —

MOMMINA (*in a reproachful tone, as though her mother were revealing a shameful secret*): Mama!

SIGNORA IGNAZIA: — and Totina mends —

TOTINA (*as above*): What are you talking about!

SIGNORA IGNAZIA: — and Nenè —

NENÈ (*immediately and aggressively, threatening to silence her*): Will you be quiet, Mama?

---

7. There is an old proverb, *Passo quel tempo che Berta filava,* "The time has gone when Berta used to spin"; the Character Actress may also be misquoting or paraphrasing a line from a melodrama, possibly *Didone abbandonata*.

SIGNORA IGNAZIA: — you won't find many like her: she'll take a suit, and make it look as good as new —

NENÈ (*as above*): Please! That's enough!

SIGNORA IGNAZIA: — she takes out the stains —

NENÈ (*stopping her mother's mouth*): Enough, Mama!

SIGNORA IGNAZIA (*freeing herself from Nenè's hand*): — and turns it inside out—and Dorina: she can keep the accounts!

DORINA: Have you finished spilling the beans?

SIGNORA IGNAZIA: What's the world coming to! They're ashamed —

SAMPOGNETTA: —as though they were secret vices!

SIGNORA IGNAZIA: On top of that, they're unpretentious; they don't ask for much. Why they'd even do without food, so long as they could have the theater. Ah, there's nothing like the old melodramas! I'm very fond of them myself!

NENÈ (*who has come out with a rose in her hand*): But Mama, don't forget *Carmen!*[8]

(*She puts the rose in her mouth and sings, twisting her hips provocatively.*)

> "*È l'amore uno strano augello*
> *che non si può domesticar . . .*"[9]

THE CHARACTER ACTRESS: Oh yes, all right, *Carmen* too. But it doesn't have the passion of the old melodramas, that set your heart apounding—Innocence that cries out but is not believed; and the Lover's Despair: "Ah quell'infame l'onore ha venduto . . ."[10] Ask Mommina! But enough of that. (*turning to* **VERRI**) Remember the first time you came to our house? It was these young men who introduced you —

THE THIRD OFFICER: We should never have done it!

CHARACTER ACTRESS: — the supply officer at our airport —

THE LEADING ACTOR: — Please, *reserve* officer—but only for six months—then, God willing, that's it for these fellows, no more fun and games at my expense!

POMÀRICI: Us? At your expense?

SARELLI: Would you listen to him!

THE CHARACTER ACTRESS: That's not the point. What I wanted to say is that neither myself, nor my daughters, nor that . . . (*Again* **SIGNOR PALMIRO**, *the moment he is pointed*

---

8. An opera by Georges Bizet (1838–75) based on a story by Prosper Merimée (1803–70), first performed in Paris, March 3, 1875. Signora Ignazia's grudging acceptance of *Carmen* suggests that even after fifty years, respectable provincial audiences were still resistant to this opera because of its violence and frank sensuality.

9. "Love is a strange bird that cannot be tamed . . ." (*Carmen,* I:5). This is the "Habanera," sung by Carmen and the chorus. She has a flower in her mouth. As she sings, she flirts with the soldiers, and at the end she throws the flower to José, who will later become her lover.

10. "Ah, the scoundrel has sold the honor . . ." This line could come from a number of melodramas, but we have not been able to find it.

at, averts his face and begins to whistle.) Stop it, or I'll throw my purse at you! (*It is a large purse, and* **SIGNOR PALMIRO** *stops immediately.*) Not one of us realized at first that you had that cursed Sicilian blood in your veins —

THE LEADING ACTOR: — I'm proud of it! —

THE CHARACTER ACTRESS: — Ah, I know that now! (I know it too well!)

DOCTOR HINKFUSS: Don't anticipate, Miss __; for heaven's sake, let's not anticipate!

THE CHARACTER ACTRESS: No, no. Don't worry, I won't anticipate anything.

DOCTOR HINKFUSS: Just the introduction, as clearly as possible. That's all.

THE CHARACTER ACTRESS: As clearly as possible: yes, yes, don't worry. I must say, though, the truth is that at first he didn't boast about it. On the contrary, he went along with us when we argued with the savages of this island. They thought it shameful, our living—quite innocently—the way they do on the Continent, welcoming young men into the house and encouraging them to have a good time—as young people should— my God, there's nothing shameful about it! And he himself had his fun with my Mommina . . . (*She looks around for her.*) Where is she? Ah, there she is! Come, come here, my poor unfortunate daughter; it's not time yet for you to be like that. (*The* **LEADING ACTRESS**, *who is acting the role of* **MOMMINA**, *is pulled by the hand, but resists.*) Come, come along.

THE LEADING ACTRESS: No, let me go, let me go, Miss_____.

(*Resolutely, coming forward to* **DOCTOR HINKFUSS**.)

I can't do this, Doctor Hinkfuss! I'm telling you straight. I can't do it! You've made a scenario; you've set up a scene outline! Well then, follow it! I have to sing. I must feel secure. I have to know my place in the action as it was assigned to me. I can't perform like this, fluttering in the wind.

THE LEADING ACTOR: I see! The young lady must have some speeches all written and memorized according to the outline.

THE LEADING ACTRESS: Of course, I prepared myself. Didn't you?

THE LEADING ACTOR: Yes, I did too, but not the actual words. Look, let's be clear about this, Miss __. Let's understand each other: don't expect me to say what you want me to according to the lines you've prepared for yourself, all right? I'll say what I have to say.

(*This squabble is followed by a muttering of simultaneous comments by the other actors.*)

THE ACTORS: — That would really be something!

— If each of us were to make the others say what we want them to!

— So much for improvisation then!

— In that case, she might as well have written the other parts!

DOCTOR HINKFUSS (*cutting the comments short*): Ladies, gentlemen, not so much talking! Say as little as possible! I told you that before. But let's stop there. The introduction is over. Let your gestures speak for you—keep the words to a minimum. Listen: trust me—the words will come by themselves, spontaneously, when you adopt a set of gestures that arise from the action as I outlined it for you. Follow it and you won't go wrong. Put yourselves in my hands: follow the blocking that we'd agreed upon . . . Come on now, come on. Off the stage. Let's have the curtains closed.

(*The main curtain is lowered.*)

DOCTOR HINKFUSS (*remaining on the stage, turns to the audience and adds*): I beg your pardon, ladies and gentlemen. The performance is now going to start. The real one. Five minutes, only five minutes, if you don't mind, so that I can see that everything is in order.

(*He withdraws, moving the curtain aside. A five minute pause.*)

ACT 2

The curtain rises.

DOCTOR HINKFUSS *begins to fritter away some time. He had thought to himself, "Wouldn't it be a good idea to bring together a few representative images of Sicily in a little religious procession! It will add color."*

And he has set things up so that the procession moves from the entrance door of the auditorium toward the stage, down the aisle between the two halves of the orchestra, in the following order:

1. *four altar boys, dressed in black cassocks and white albs with lace trim, two ahead and two behind: they carry four small lighted torches;*
2. *four girls, called* verginelle, *or "little virgins," dressed in white and enveloped in white veils. They have been deliberately dressed in white crocheted gloves that are too big for them, so that they will appear a little awkward: two in front, two behind, they carry the four supports of a small baldachin of sky-blue silk;*
3. *under the baldachin, the holy family, that is, an old man made up and dressed as St. Joseph, as seen in sacred paintings of the Nativity, with a red band around his head and in one hand a long crosier, flowering at the end, and beside him, a lovely blonde girl, with her eyes lowered and a sweet, modest smile on her lips, made up and dressed as the Virgin Mary, also with a band around her head, and a beautiful big wax doll in her arms representing baby Jesus; one can still see them today in Sicily at Christmas time in primitive mystery plays that are performed to the accompaniment of bands and choirs;*
4. *a shepherd with a fur hat and an* albagio[11] *coat, his legs wrapped in goat skin, with another young shepherd; one plays the bagpipe, the other an* acciarino.[12]
5. *a group of simple men and women of every age, the women with long pleated skirts puffed at the sides and mantillas on their heads, the men with short jackets tight at the waist and bell-bottom*

---

11. *Albagio,* al-baz. From Arabic *al-bazz,* a kind of rough cloth, usually white in color, used for garments, curtains, and the like.

12. *Acciarino,* a rhythm instrument made of metal, used to beat time. The triangle is a form of *acciarino.*

trousers held up by wide colored silk sashes: in their hands they carry their black knit stockinglike caps with little tufts at the ends. Accompanied by the music of the bagpipe and the acciarino, they enter the hall singing this little tune:

> Oggi e sempre sia lodato
> nostro Dio sacramentato:
> e lodata sempre sia
> nostra Vergine Maria.[13]

Meanwhile on the stage one can see a city street and the rough white wall of a building that runs from left to right for almost three-quarters of the stage, to the point where, at the back of the stage, there is a streetcorner. At the streetcorner there is a lantern in its sconce. Beyond the corner, on the other wall of the building, which is at an obtuse angle, one can see the door of a cabaret lit by colored lights, and almost across from it, a little further back, at an angle, the doorway of an old church, with three steps up to it.

A little before the rise of the curtain and the entrance of the procession into the auditorium, the sound of church bells is heard on the stage, and the barely perceptible rumble of an organ being played inside the church. As the curtain rises and the procession comes in, some men and women (no more than eight or nine) who happen to be passing along the road are seen kneeling along the right wall. The women make the sign of the cross; the men take their hats off. As the procession climbs onto the stage and enters the church, these men and women join it and enter the church as well. When the last one has entered the bells stop ringing. In the silence the sound of the organ is heard more distinctly: it will slowly die out as the stage lights are gradually dimmed.

The moment this sacred music ends, the sound of jazz suddenly bursts out from the cabaret in violent contrast, and at the same time the long white wall that takes up three-quarters of the stage becomes transparent. The interior of the cabaret can be seen, glowing with colored lights. At the right, almost up to the entrance door, is the bar, and behind it three luridly painted girls with low-necked dresses. At the back next to the bar is a wall-hanging of flaming red velvet, and in front of it, looking like a bas-relief, is a strange singer dressed in black veils. Pale, her head bent backward and her eyes closed, she is mournfully singing her song. In the cramped space between the bar and the first row of round tables where the customers (not many) are sitting with their drinks, three mediocre blonde dancers, their backs to the bar, are moving their arms and legs in unison.

Among the customers is **SAMPOGNETTA**, with his little hat on his head and a long cigar in his mouth. A customer sitting behind him in the second row of tables, seeing him absorbed in the movements of the three dancers, is preparing to play a vicious joke on him: two long horns have been cut out of the cardboard of the cabaret's program and wine list. The other customers, noticing what is happening, are enjoying it thoroughly and making gestures urging him to hurry up. When the two horns have been cut out—they are beautifully long and straight upon their cardboard base—the customer gets up and very cautiously places them on **SAMPOGNETTA'S** little hat. Everybody starts to laugh and clap their hands. **SAMPOGNETTA**, believing that the laughter and applause are for the three dancers, who have

---

13. "Today and always our Lord be praised, in the most holy Sacrament of the Altar, and always praised be our Virgin Mary."

just finished, joins in. This makes everyone roar even louder, and the applause becomes noisier. He cannot understand why everybody is looking at him, even the women at the bar, even the three little dancers, who are splitting their sides with laughter. He is bewildered; his laughter dies on his lips; his applause fades in his hands. At that moment, the strange singer explodes in indignation; she leaves her velvet backdrop and reaches out to pluck the mocking trophy from **SAMPOGNETTA'S** *head, shouting:*

THE SINGER: No! The poor old man! Come on, shame on you!

(*The customers stop her, all shouting at the same time in great confusion.*)

THE CUSTOMERS: — Stay there, stupid!
— Shut up, go back to your place!
— What poor old man?
— Who asked you?
— Leave us alone!
— He deserves it!
— He deserves it!

(*During this confused shouting, the* **SINGER** *keeps protesting and struggling with those who are keeping her back.*)

THE SINGER: You cowards, let go of me! How does he deserve it? What's he done to you?

SAMPOGNETTA (*getting up, more bewildered than ever*): What do I deserve? What do I deserve?

THE CUSTOMER WHO PLAYED THE JOKE: Nothing, Signor Palmiro, don't listen to her!

A SECOND CUSTOMER: She's drunk, as usual!

THE CUSTOMER WHO PLAYED THE JOKE: Go on, get out of here, this is no place for you! (*With the others, he pushes him toward the door.*)

THIRD CUSTOMER: We know very well what you deserve, Signor Palmiro!

(**SAMPOGNETTA** *is led outside with his fine horns on his head. The scene behind the wall disappears. The shouts of those who are holding the singer back can still be heard; there is a big laugh, and the jazz begins again.*)

SAMPOGNETTA (*to the two or three customers who have pushed him out; they are now enjoying the sight of his crown under the lighted street lamp*): But I'd like to know what happened.

SECOND CUSTOMER: Nothing. It's because of what happened the other night.

THIRD CUSTOMER: Everyone knows you're fond of this singer . . .

SECOND CUSTOMER: Just as a joke they wanted her to give you a slap, just like the other evening—

THIRD CUSTOMER: That's right—that's why they were saying that you deserve it!

SAMPOGNETTA: I see! I see!

FIRST CUSTOMER: Oh, oh! Look! Look! There, in the sky! The stars!

SECOND CUSTOMER: The stars?

FIRST CUSTOMER: They're moving! They're moving!

SECOND CUSTOMER: Come on!

SAMPOGNETTA: Really?

FIRST CUSTOMER: Yes, yes, look! As if someone were touching them with a couple of poles. (*He raises his arms to make horns.*)

SECOND CUSTOMER: Come on, be quiet! You can't see straight.

THIRD CUSTOMER: Do the stars look like little street lamps to you?

SECOND CUSTOMER: What were you saying, Signor Palmiro?

SAMPOGNETTA: Oh, oh, yes . . . well, I . . . tonight—I don't know if you noticed it— I deliberately watched the dancers: I kept my head turned away from her. She has such a strong effect on me, the poor thing, the way she sings, her eyes closed and the tears running down her cheeks!

SECOND CUSTOMER: That's her job, Signor Palmiro! Those tears don't mean a thing.

SAMPOGNETTA (*protesting earnestly, wagging his finger*): No, no! Oh, no, no! Job? What do you mean, job? I swear it, on my word of honor, that woman suffers, really suffers. And not only that, but she has the same voice as my eldest daughter, exactly the same! Exactly the same! And she comes from a good family, too: she told me in confidence.

THIRD CUSTOMER: Oh, yes? Really? She's an engineer's daughter too, is she?

SAMPOGNETTA: That I don't know. But one thing I do know: there are some troubles that can happen to anybody. And whenever I hear her sing, it takes hold of me . . . so sad, and bitter, and hopeless . . .

(*At that moment,* **TOTINA** *appears, marching in from the left, on* **POMÀRICI'S** *arm,* **NENÈ** *on* **SA-RELLI'S**, **DORINA** *on the* **THIRD OFFICER'S**; **MOMMINA** *is at* **RICO VERRI'S** *side, and* **SI-GNORA IGNAZIA** *on the arms of the other two young officers.* **POMÀRICI** *marks the time for everyone, even before the group enters the scene. The three customers, now four or more, withdraw toward the door of the cabaret when they hear the voices, leaving* **SIGNOR PALMIRO** *alone under the street lamp, with the horns still on his head.*)

POMÀRICI: Left, right — Left, right —

(*They are going to the theater: the* **FOUR GIRLS** *and* **SIGNORA IGNAZIA** *are in gaudy evening dresses.*)

TOTINA (*seeing her father with the horns on his head*): Oh, my God! Father, what did they do to you?

POMÀRICI: Filthy cowards!

SAMPOGNETTA: Me? What?

NENÈ: Take that thing off your head! Please!

SIGNORA IGNAZIA (*while her husband fumbles with his hat*): The horns?

DORINA: The scum! Who did it?

TOTINA: Look over there!

SAMPOGNETTA (*taking them off*): The horns, for me? So that was why . . . ? What despicable . . .

SIGNORA IGNAZIA: And he's still holding them in his hands! Throw them away, you imbecile! That's all you're good for, a clown for all the lowlife to laugh at!

MOMMINA (*to her mother*): Now you're starting on him too —

TOTINA: — it was those swine there who did it.

VERRI (*going toward the door of the cabaret where the customers are watching and laughing*): Who did that? Who did it? Was it you? (*grabs one of them by the shirt*) Was it you?

NENÈ: They're laughing . . .

THE CUSTOMER (*trying to free himself*): Let go of me! I didn't do it! Get your hands off me!

VERRI: Then tell me who did it!

POMÀRICI: Hey Verri, forget it!

SARELLI: There's no use staying here and making a row!

SIGNORA IGNAZIA: No! no! I want satisfaction from the owner of this rats' nest!

TOTINA: Forget it, Mama!

SECOND CUSTOMER (*coming forward*): Watch what you say, Signora. Some of us here are gentlemen.

MOMMINA: Do gentlemen do things like this?

DORINA: Savages! Animals!

THIRD OFFICER: Forget it, Signorina, forget it.

FOURTH CUSTOMER: It was just a couple of young fellows having a joke . . .

POMÀRICI: You call it a joke?

SECOND CUSTOMER: We all respect Signor Palmiro —

THIRD CUSTOMER (*to* **SIGNORA IGNAZIA**): — but as for you—we don't think very highly of you, my dear lady!

SECOND CUSTOMER: You're the talk of the town!

VERRI (*on the attack, his arms up*): You keep your tongue to yourself if you know what's good for you.

FOURTH CUSTOMER: We'll report you to the Colonel!

THIRD CUSTOMER: Shame on you, in officers' uniforms!

VERRI: Who's going to report us?

THE CUSTOMERS (*even those inside the cabaret*): All of us! Everybody!

POMÀRICI: You insult ladies who are in our company, and it's our duty to come to their defense.

FOURTH CUSTOMER: Nobody's insulted anyone.

THIRD CUSTOMER: She's the one who did the insulting, the signora!

SIGNORA IGNAZIA: Me? No, I didn't insult anyone! I told you to your face what you are! Hoodlums! Louts! Good-for-nothings! You deserve to be in cages like wild animals! That's what you are! (*and when all the patrons laugh mockingly:*) Go ahead, laugh, sure, laugh, you ruffians, you savages!

POMÀRICI (*with the other officers and her daughters, trying to calm her down*): Let's go, let's go, Signora!

SARELLI: That's enough now!

THIRD OFFICER: Let's go to the theater!

NENÈ: Don't dirty your mouth by answering them!

FOURTH OFFICER: Let's go! Let's go! It's late!

TOTINA: The first act will be over by now.

MOMMINA: Yes, please, let's go, Mama! Forget them!

POMÀRICI: Come along, Signor Palmiro, come to the theater with us!

SIGNORA IGNAZIA: The theater? Him? No! Go home! Go on home! Right now! He has to get up early tomorrow to go to the sulfur mine! Home! Home!

(*The customers laugh again to hear how sternly the wife orders her husband around.*)

SARELLI: Let's go to the theater! Let's not waste time!

SIGNORA IGNAZIA: Imbeciles! Fools! You're laughing at your own ignorance!

POMÀRICI: That's enough! That's enough!

THE OTHER OFFICERS: Let's go to the theater! The theater!

(*At this point* **DOCTOR HINKFUSS**, *who had returned to the auditorium at the end of the procession and who has been sitting in a seat reserved for him in the first row, keeping an eye on the performance, gets up and shouts:*)

DOCTOR HINKFUSS: Yes, that's enough! That's enough! You go to the theater! Go on! To the theater! Everybody exit! The customers go back into the cabaret! Everyone else exit right! And close the curtains a little on both sides.

(*The actors do as they are told. The curtain is drawn in a little from either side so as to leave a part of the white wall visible in the middle, which will serve as a screen for the film projection of the opera performance. After everyone has disappeared only the* **OLD COMIC ACTOR** *remains on the stage.*

THE OLD COMIC ACTOR (*to* **DOCTOR HINKFUSS**):   If I don't go to the theater with them, I must exit left, right?

DOCTOR HINKFUSS: Of course, exit left! Go on, go on! What a question!

THE OLD COMIC ACTOR: No, no! But I wanted to point something out to you: they didn't let me get a word in edgewise. There's too much confusion, Doctor Hinkfuss!

DOCTOR HINKFUSS: Not at all! It went very well! Go on, go away!

THE OLD COMIC ACTOR: But I didn't have my chance to say that I'm the one who always pays for everything!

DOCTOR HINKFUSS: All right, now you've made your point! Go away! It's time for the theater scene!

(*The* **OLD COMIC ACTOR** *exits left.*)

Is the sound ready? The projector set up? All right: Go![14]

(**DOCTOR HINKFUSS** *returns to his seat. Meanwhile, the stage hands have placed a gramophone at the right, behind the curtain that has been closed far enough to hide the corner of the wall with the*

---

14. Text has *Tonfilm*, a German word meaning sound film.

street light. A record is playing the end of the first act of some old Italian opera, something like "La forza del destino" or "Un ballo in maschera,"[15] *and it is synchronized with the projection on the white wall that acts as a screen. As soon as the sound from the gramophone is heard and the projection starts, the box in the auditorium that has been left empty is lit with a special warm light from an invisible source.* **SIGNORA IGNAZIA,** *her* **FOUR DAUGHTERS, RICCO VERRI,** *and the* **OTHER YOUNG OFFICERS** *are seen entering it. Their noisy entrance provokes immediate protests from the audience.*)

SIGNORA IGNAZIA: There, I was right! It's already the end of the first act.

TOTINA: That was quite a race! Oof! (*She sits in the first seat of the box, opposite her mother.*) My God, it's hot! We're all out of breath!

POMÀRICI (*cooling her with a little fan*): Here I am, ready to serve you!

DORINA: No wonder! Marching so fast! Left, right, left, right . . .

VOICES IN THE HALL: — Will you stop it!

— Quiet!

— Is this the way to come into a theater?

MOMMINA (*to* **TOTINA**): You took my place! Get up!

TOTINA: Well, Dorina and Nenè are sitting in the middle . . .

DORINA: We thought Mommina wanted to stay in the back with Verri like last time.

VOICES IN THE HALL: — Quiet! Quiet!

— It's always them!

— It's disgusting!

— And they're supposed to be officers!

— Can't they be made to behave properly?

(*Meanwhile there is a great to-do in the box as they change their seats:* **TOTINA** *gives up her place to* **MOMMINA** *and takes that of* **DORINA,** *who takes the chair emptied by* **NENÈ,** *who goes to sit on the couch next to her* **MOTHER. RICCO VERRI** *sits next to* **MOMMINA** *on the opposite couch: behind* **TOTINA** *is* **POMÀRICI;** *behind* **DORINA** *is the* **THIRD OFFICER;** *in the back,* **SARELLI** *and the other two officers.*)

MOMMINA: Quiet, please! Quiet!

NENÈ: Yes, quiet! First you make a big fuss —

MOMMINA: — Me? —

NENÈ: — I'll say! All these changes!

DORINA: Let them say what they want!

TOTINA: As though they'd never heard (*She says the name of the opera.*)

POMÀRICI: They should have some consideration for the ladies!

VOICES IN THE HALL: — Be quiet!

— Disgraceful!

---

15. Operas by Giuseppe Verdi (1813–1901). *La forza del destino* was first produced in St. Petersburg in 1862, and *Un ballo in maschera* in Rome in 1859.

— People who cause a disturbance should be kicked out!

— Throw them out!

— And in the officers' box! It's scandalous! Really!

— Out! Out!

SIGNORA IGNAZIA: Cannibals! It's not our fault we got here so late! Look at that! Can you call this a civilized town? First they assault us in the street, and now in the theater! Cannibals!

TOTINA: This is the way they act on the Continent!

DORINA: You get to the theater when you want to!

NENÈ: There are people here who know how to behave, how they do things on the Continent!

VOICES IN THE HALL: Stop it! Shut up!

DOCTOR HINKFUSS (*getting up, turning to the actors' box*): Yes, that's enough! That's enough! Don't go overboard, please. Don't overdo it!

SIGNORA IGNAZIA: Come on now, what do you mean, overdo it? We're just defending ourselves![16] They're the ones to blame! See how unbearable it is, the way we're persecuted just because we made a little noise coming in!

DOCTOR HINKFUSS: All right! All right! But that's enough for now. You can see the act is over!

VERRI: It's over? Thank God! Let's go, let's get out of here!

DOCTOR HINKFUSS: Fine—away you go—go ahead.

TOTINA: I'm so thirsty!

(*Leaves the box.*)

NENÈ: Let's hope we can find some ice cream!

(*As above.*)

SIGNORA IGNAZIA: Come on, let's go. Let's get out of here, or I'll burst.

(*The film is over and the gramophone stops. The curtains close completely.* **DOCTOR HINKFUSS** *climbs up on the stage and turns to the audience while the houselights come up.*)

DOCTOR HINKFUSS: Those of you who usually leave the auditorium during the intermission can go if you want, and watch these fine people continue to make a scandal out in the foyer. It's not because they want to, but because by now everything they do, people notice it. Everybody points at them and makes them pay for all the malicious rumors that are flying about. Go ahead, go ahead . . . No—oh—not everybody, please! Besides, you might find it too crowded out there, with so many wanting to see—and it'll be more or less what you've already seen here.

I can guarantee you that the ones who stay will miss nothing of importance. Those

---

16. Text has *il coraggio lo pigliamo da giù,* "we get our courage from below," i.e., from the people in the auditorium.

same people you saw leaving their box will spend the interval mingling with the audience!

I'll take advantage of this break for a set change. And I'll do it right here in front of you, as a demonstration, to give you the opportunity too, those of you who stay here in the auditorium, to see a show that's somewhat out of the ordinary.

(*He claps his hands as a signal, and orders:*) Open the curtains!

(*The curtains are opened.*)

Interlude

The performance proceeds simultaneously in the foyer and on the stage. During the interval, the actors and actresses act in the foyer as spectators among spectators, as freely and as naturally as they can (each in character, of course). They gather in four different places in the foyer, and each group acts its scene independently of the others and at the same time: **RICCO VERRI** *is with* **MOMMINA**; **SIGNORA IGNAZIA** *sits on a bench, talking with the two officers,* **POMETTI** *and* **MANGINI**; **DORINA** *strolls along talking to the* **THIRD OFFICER, NARDI**; **NENÈ** *and* **TOTINA** *go with* **POMÀRICI** *and* **SA-RELLI** *to the back, where there is a sales counter with drinks, coffee, beer, liquor, candies, and other tidbits.*

These scattered and simultaneous little scenes are transcribed here in sequence, because of the demands of space.

1

NENÈ, TOTINA, SARELLI, *and* **POMÀRICI** *at the counter at the end of the foyer.*

NENÈ: No ice cream left? What a shame! Give me a soft drink then. Make sure it's cold! A mint, yes.

TOTINA: Lemonade for me.

POMÀRICI: A bag of chocolates and some candies.

NENÈ: No, don't bother, Pomàrici! Thanks anyway.

TOTINA: They're probably not very good. Are they? Well, in that case, then, buy some! Buy some! There's no greater pleasure —

POMÀRICI: — than chocolates? —

TOTINA: — no—than for us women to make their men spend money on them!

POMÀRICI: It's nothing much! Too bad we didn't have time to stop at the cafe on our way to the theater —

SARELLI: — all because of that damned row . . .

TOTINA: Good Lord! It's Papa's fault! He seems to go out of his way to give people an excuse to pester us! Imagine, hanging around a place like that!

POMÀRICI (*putting a chocolate in her mouth*): Don't worry. Don't worry.

NENÈ (*opening her mouth like a little bird*): What about me?

POMÀRICI (*popping a candy in her mouth*): Right away, but you get a candy!

NENÈ: Are you really sure this is the way it's done on the Continent?

POMÀRICI: Of course! Popping candies into pretty young ladies' mouths? No question about it!

SARELLI: And that's only the beginning!

NENÈ: What else is there?

POMÀRICI: Well, if we wanted to do everything the way they do it on the Continent . . .

TOTINA (*coyly*): Like what?

SARELLI: We can't do it here.

NENÈ: All right then, tomorrow the four of us will come and take over the airfield!

TOTINA: And if you don't take us for a plane ride, you'd better watch out!

POMÀRICI: We'd love you to visit us, but I am afraid a plane ride is . . .

SARELLI: It's not allowed!

POMÀRICI: And with the Commander we have now . . .

TOTINA: Didn't you say that monster was going to leave soon?

NENÈ: I don't want to hear any excuses: I want to fly over the city and have the pleasure of spitting on it. Can't I?

SARELLI: But that's impossible!

NENÈ: No, but just spit on it, that's all, like this: ptuh! Well then, you'll have to do it for me!

2

DORINA *and* **NARDI**, *walking.*

NARDI: Did you know that your papa is madly in love with the singer at that cabaret?

DORINA: Papa? What are you talking about?

NARDI: Your papa, your papa. No kidding, the whole town knows about it.

DORINA: Are you sure? Papa, in love? (*A hearty laugh that makes all the nearby spectators turn.*)

NARDI: Didn't you see him there?

DORINA: Don't say a word to my mother about it, please! She'd skin him alive! But who is this singer? Do you know her?

NARDI: Yes, I saw her once. She's just a pathetic old fool.

DORINA: What do you mean?

NARDI: Well, they say she always shuts her eyes when she sings, and she cries, really cries. Sometimes it gets too much for her—whatever hopelessness it is that gets her going—and she passes out right there, dead drunk.

DORINA: Must be the wine that does it!

NARDI: On the other hand, it's probably the hopelessness that makes her drink.

DORINA: Oh God, and Papa . . . ? Oh, the poor thing! Really, what an awful life he has, poor Papa! No, I don't believe it.

NARDI: You don't believe it? How about this, then? One night, he was probably a little drunk himself, he made a fool of himself in front of the whole cabaret. He took a handkerchief—he was crying a bit himself—went over to her while she was singing, her eyes closed as usual, and he tried to dry her tears.

DORINA: No! Is that true?

NARDI: And do you know what she did? She gave him a terrific slap in the face!

DORINA: Oh no! Her too? As if Mama didn't give him enough of them! Poor Papa!

NARDI: That's just what he said, right there, in front of the whole crowd—they were in stitches, of course—"You too? That's the thanks I get? I get plenty of those at home!"

(*By now they are close to the counter.* DORINA *sees her sisters* TOTINA *and* NENÈ *and runs to them with* NARDI.)

3

In front of the counter, NENÈ, TOTINA, DORINA, POMÀRICI, SARELLI, *and* NARDI.

DORINA: Do you know what Nardi's telling me? Papa is in love with that singer at the cabaret.

TOTINA: What?

NENÈ: You believe that? It's some kind of joke!

DORINA: No, no, it's true! It's true!

NARDI: I can guarantee it.

SARELLI: It's true, I heard it myself.

DORINA: If you only knew what he did!

NENÈ: What?

DORINA: He got himself slapped by that woman, right there in public.

NENÈ: Slapped?

TOTINA: Why?

DORINA: He wanted to dry her tears!

TOTINA: Her tears?

DORINA: Yes, because he says this woman is always crying . . .

TOTINA: You see! Wasn't I right? It's his own fault! How can you expect people not to make fun of him?

SARELLI: If you don't believe me, look in his jacket pocket, next to his heart . . . You'll probably find a picture of the singer there: he showed it to me once and made a few comments that were . . . well . . . poor Signor Palmiro!

4

RICCO VERRI *and* MOMMINA, *apart.*

MOMMINA (*a little frightened by the gloomy look on Verri's face when he came out of the auditorium*): What is it?

VERRI (*in a bad temper*): What? Me? Nothing.

MOMMINA: Then why are you like that?

VERRI: I don't know. I only know that if I'd stayed in that box a little longer I'd have ended up doing something foolish.

MOMMINA: This is no way to live: we can't go on like this!

VERRI (*loudly, harshly*): So now you realize it!

MOMMINA: Please be quiet! Everyone's looking at us.

VERRI: That's just it! Exactly!

MOMMINA: I've got to the point where I hardly know how to move or speak.

VERRI: I'd like to know why they have to keep looking at us and listening to our private conversations.

MOMMINA: Control yourself. Please, for my sake, don't provoke them!

VERRI: Aren't we here like everyone else? What's so strange about us that they stare at us like that? I ask you, is it possible . . .

MOMMINA: — I know—to live—as I said—to make the slightest gesture, to raise your eyes, like this, with everyone watching. Look over there, around my sisters, and around my mother over there.

VERRI: As if we were here to put on a show!

MOMMINA: I know!

VERRI: Unfortunately though, your sisters there . . . excuse me, but . . .

MOMMINA: What are they doing?

VERRI: Nothing. I wish I didn't see it, but they seem to enjoy it . . .

MOMMINA: What?

VERRI: Being noticed!

MOMMINA: But they're not doing anything wrong; they're just laughing, and chattering . . .

VERRI: That defiant attitude of theirs is a deliberate challenge . . .

MOMMINA: Come on, now, your friends, as well . . .

VERRI: I know, they put them up to it. They're really beginning to bother me, especially that Sarelli, and even Pomàrici and Nardi.

MOMMINA: They're just having a little fun . . .

VERRI: They might consider that they're having their fun at the expense of three respectable girls; they might at least refrain from certain gestures, certain familiarities.

MOMMINA: Yes, I know, that's true.

VERRI: For instance, as far as you're concerned, I simply will not stand any of them presuming to —

MOMMINA: Well, in the first place, I wouldn't allow it myself, you know that!

VERRI: Oh, let's just forget about it; please, let's just forget about it. But even you, you allowed it too . . . before.

MOMMINA: Not any more, not for a long time. Surely you know that!

VERRI: It's not enough for me to know it; they should know it too!

MOMMINA: They know! They know!

VERRI: They don't know! In fact, they've made it a point more than once to make it clear to me that they didn't want to know. It was almost as if they wanted to provoke me.

MOMMINA: Surely not! When? Please don't let yourself think like that!

VERRI: They should understand that I'm not a man to fool around with!

MOMMINA: They understand, don't worry! But the more you show that you can't take an innocent joke, the more they keep it up, partly to show you they didn't mean any harm.

VERRI: You're making excuses for them?

MOMMINA: No, no, I'm saying this for you, to calm you down. I'm saying it for my own sake; I live in a constant state of nerves, knowing the way you are. Come on, let's go. Mama's just got up. It looks as if she wants to go back inside.

5

SIGNORA IGNAZIA, *on a bench, with* POMETTI *and* MANGINI *on either side.*

SIGNORA IGNAZIA: You should gain a bit of credit for yourselves, my dear friends, in the great march toward civilization!

MANGINI: Us? How is that, Signora Ignazia?

SIGNORA IGNAZIA: By giving lessons at your club!

POMETTI: Lessons? Who to?

SIGNORA IGNAZIA: To these boorish peasants here in town! An hour or so a day, at least.

MANGINI: Lessons in what?

POMETTI: Manners?

SIGNORA IGNAZIA: No, no, no! A lesson a day, for an hour, showing them how they live in the big cities of the Continent. My dear Mangini, where are you from?

MANGINI: Me? From Venice, Signora.

SIGNORA IGNAZIA: Venice? Oh God, Venice, my dream! And you, Pometti?

POMETTO: I'm from Milan.

SIGNORA IGNAZIA: Oh, Milan! *Milano . . .* imagine! *El nost Milan . . .* And I am from Naples! Naples—and I say this without offense to Milan—and putting aside the beauties of Venice—as far as nature is concerned, it's paradise! Chiaja! Posillipo! I feel like crying when I think about it! Oh, such beauty! Vesuvius! Capri! . . . and you have the Duomo, the Galleria, La Scala! . . . And you, of course, the Piazza San Marco, the Grand Canal . . . How marvelous! How beautiful! . . . While here . . . nothing but *fetenzieríe,*[17] filth everywhere. If only it were just outside, in the streets!

MANGINI: Please, not so loud, right in front of them!

SIGNORA IGNAZIA: No, no, I'll say it out loud! Santa Chiara di Napoli, my dears, they even have it inside, this *fetenzieria.* They have it in their hearts, in their blood. They're always in a rage, all of them. Don't they give you that impression—that they're always in a rage?

MANGINI: To tell you the truth, I . . .

---

17. *Fetenziería* is a Neapolitan word meaning filth, a filthy thing or action (pl. *fetenzieríe*).

SIGNORA IGNAZIA: Don't they seem that way to you? Oh yes, everybody is always burning with . . . how shall I say it? Yes, it's an instinctive rage that always keeps them in a
fury with one another. All it takes is for someone, let's say, to look here instead of there,
or to blow his nose a little harder than usual, or to smile at something that happens to
pass through his head—God forbid!—He smiled because of me; he blew his nose like
that on purpose just to insult me; he wanted to spite me, so he looked here instead of
there! You can't do anything without their suspecting some hidden malice. It's because
there's a spirit of evil in all of them. Just look in their eyes. They're frightening. Eyes
like wolves . . . Come along now. It's time to go back inside. Let's get back to those
poor daughters of mine.

*(The time it takes for all those groups to play their scenes simultaneously will have been worked out; it
may be necessary to add or cut a line or two, but it is essential that they all move at the same time so
that they leave the foyer together. This simultaneous move must also be regulated according to the time*
DOCTOR HINKFUSS *needs to complete his miracles on the stage.*

These miracles could be left up to **DOCTOR HINKFUSS** *and his bizarre whims. But since he himself, and not the author of the story, wanted* **RICCO VERRI** *and the other young officers to be aviators,
it was probably because he wanted to have the pleasure of preparing a beautiful scene for the spectators
who have stayed in the hall. It represents an airfield which, as if by magic, gives the effect of perspective.
At night under a marvelous starry sky, with a few lightly sketched elements: everything on the ground
is made small in order to give the sensation of the vast space of the sky dotted with stars; in the back,
the small white quarters of the officers, with small lighted windows; two or three small airplanes scattered on the field here and there; a general impression of many dim lights; and the humming of an
invisible plane, flying in the calmness of the night.* **DOCTOR HINKFUSS** *may be allowed this pleasure, even if not a single spectator has stayed in the auditorium. Should this happen (this should also
be anticipated), the interlude cannot be performed simultaneously in the foyer and on the stage. But
this problem can easily be corrected. When* **DOCTOR HINKFUSS** *sees that his exhortation does not
succeed in keeping even a small portion of the audience in the auditorium, even after he has raised the
curtain, he'll be a little upset, and he'll withdraw behind the scenes. But when the performance in the
foyer has ended, and the spectators called by the ringing of the bells have come back to the auditorium
to take their places, he will relieve his feelings by giving a display of his skills.*

*It is most important that the audience bear with all this, which, if not really superfluous, is certainly
peripheral. But since there are many indications that the audience enjoys them, and indeed that it seeks
out these side dishes greedily, even voraciously, much more than it does plain, honest main courses, let
it do so.* **DOCTOR HINKFUSS** *is right: so let him give them something new after the airfield scene,
let him declare, with the studied carelessness of a great gentleman who can allow himself certain luxu-
ries, that really the first scene can be dispensed with after all, because it is not strictly necessary. It may
seem that a bit of time has been lost just for the sake of a fine effect. But the audience must be made to
understand that the opposite is the case: wasting time is the last thing we want to do. In fact we were
able to skip a whole scene without doing any damage to the play. We also omit the instructions for
setting up the airfield.* **DOCTOR HINKFUSS** *can easily work them out between himself and the stage
manager, the electricians, and the stage hands. As soon as everything is ready, he comes down from the*

stage into the auditorium, stands in the middle of the aisle to give the necessary instructions to adjust the lighting, and once he has made it perfect, climbs up onto the stage again.

DOCTOR HINKFUSS: No, no! Take it all away! Cut the sound! Take the lights out! I think we can do without this scene. Yes, I know it's a nice effect, but we have ways of getting effects just as nice as that that will do more to advance the action. Luckily I am free tonight. I hope you don't mind my showing you how a performance is set up, not only before your very eyes, but with your collaboration as well—why not? You see, ladies and gentlemen, the theater is the gaping mouth of a huge machine. The machine is hungry, but the gentlemen who write[18] . . .

A POET IN THE ORCHESTRA: Please don't patronize writers; we writers are not gentlemen!

DOCTOR HINKFUSS (*immediately*): In that sense, not even critics are gentlemen. But still, I spoke that way as a kind of polemical affectation—with all due respect, I'd have thought you'd allow me that much license. As I was saying, the machine is hungry, but the gentlemen who write don't know how to satisfy it, at least not with enough of the right kind of nourishment. It is deplorable how their imaginations have failed to keep pace! It's the same with all those other wonderful machines that have grown and developed so tremendously. Now I'm not saying that theater is more than anything else simply a spectacle. It is an art, yes; but it's life too. It is a genuine creation, but it doesn't last; it's a thing of the moment. It's a miracle: form and movement in one. A miracle, ladies and gentlemen, can only be a thing of the moment. In one moment, right before your eyes, to create a scene; and within that, another; and yet another. A moment of darkness, a quick rearrangement, a dazzling play of lights. Here, I'll show you. (*He claps his hands and orders:*) Blackout!

(*It is dark; the curtain is silently closed behind* DOCTOR HINKFUSS. *The houselights come on, while the bells ring to call the spectators back to their places. In the event that the entire audience has left the auditorium, the simultaneous performance in the foyer and on the stage will not have happened, and* DR. HINKFUSS *will have been forced to wait in the auditorium for the audience to return before he can set up the airfield scene and have his little chat with them. In that case, of course, the curtains will not be opened. After he has ordered the blackout he will continue to give the other orders so that the performance can continue in front of the whole audience in the auditorium. Here we assume that the simultaneity we hope for has succeeded. Indeed a way should be found to ensure that it does. Then, when the curtain is closed and the lights in the hall have come on,* DOCTOR HINKFUSS *will go on to say:*)

DOCTOR HINKFUSS: Let's wait for the audience to come back. Besides, we've got to give Signora Ignazia and the La Croce girls time to get back home after the theater, arm in arm with their young officer friends. (*turning to the* GENTLEMAN IN THE ORCHES-TRA *who is just now returning to the auditorium*) But meantime if you, sir, my relentless

---

18. Text has *poeti,* poets. See note 3.

interrupter, could tell the people who stayed in here, did anything new happen out there in the foyer?

THE GENTLEMAN IN THE ORCHESTRA: Are you talking to me?

DOCTOR HINKFUSS: Yes, you. Would you be so kind as to . . .

THE GENTLEMAN IN THE ORCHESTRA: No, nothing new . . . Just a nice break. They chatted. The only thing we found out is that that funny Signor Palmiro, "Sampognetta," is in love with the cabaret singer.

DOCTOR HINKFUSS: Yes, yes, but you could have figured that out already. Anyway, it's not very important.

THE YOUNG SPECTATOR FROM THE STALLS: No, excuse me, we've also found out that Officer Rico Verri . . .

THE LEADING ACTOR (*putting his head out between the curtains behind* **DOCTOR HINKFUSS**): Enough of that "officer" business! It won't be long before I'll be getting myself out of this uniform!

DOCTOR HINKFUSS (*turning to the* **LEADING ACTOR**, *who has already withdrawn his head*): Excuse me, but what are you butting in for?

THE LEADING ACTOR (*putting his head out again*): Because it irritates me! I just want to keep things straight: I am not a career officer. (*He withdraws his head again.*)

DOCTOR HINKFUSS: You told us that from the start. That's enough! (*turning to the* **YOUNG SPECTATOR**) Excuse me, sir, you were saying?

THE YOUNG SPECTATOR (*intimidated and embarrassed*): But . . . nothing . . . I was saying that . . . out there in the foyer Signor Verri showed more of his bad temper and that . . . and that he is beginning to get more than a little fed up with the scandalous behavior of those young ladies and . . . their . . . mother . . .

DOCTOR HINKFUSS: Oh, yes, yes, all right; but that was obvious from the beginning too. Thanks anyway.

(*The piano can be heard playing the aria of Siebel from Gounod's "Faust" from behind the curtain.*)

"*Le parlate d'amor . . . . o cari fior . .*,"[19]

Ah! There's the piano: everything is ready. (*Moves the curtains a little and calls backstage:*) The bell!

(*At the sound of the bell he goes to his seat, and the curtain rises.*)

ACT 3

Upstage right, the skeleton of a glass wall; there is a door in the middle so that you can just barely glimpse the waiting room, with its appropriate touches of color and lighted lamps. Halfway downstage

---

19. "You speak to her of love . . . oh dear flowers" (III:1). *Faust,* by Charles Gounod (1813–93), was first produced March 19, 1859.

there is another skeleton wall, this one also with an open door in the center, which leads from the drawing room on the right into the roughly sketched dining room with its pretentious sideboard and its table covered with a red cloth. There is a lamp with an enormous ball-shaped orange and green shade hanging from the ceiling. The lamp is turned off now. Among other things on the sideboard there is a metal candlestick with a candle in it, a matchbox, and a cork from a bottle. In the drawing room, besides the piano, there is a sofa, some little tables, some chairs.

When the curtain is raised **POMÀRICI** *is seated at the piano playing a waltz.* **NENÈ** *is dancing with* **SARELLI**, *and* **DORINA** *with Nardi. They have just returned from the theater.* **SIGNORA IGNAZIA** *has a black silk kerchief tied around her face because of a sudden toothache.* **RICCO VERRI** *has dashed to an all-night pharmacy seeking some medicine to make it go away.* **MOMMINA** *is seated next to her mother on the sofa, and* **POMETTI** *is standing nearby.* **TOTINA** *is in the other room (off-stage) with* **MANGINI**.

MOMMINA (*to her mother, while* **POMÀRICI** *plays and the two couples dance*):   Does it hurt a lot? (*reaching out with her hand to her mother's cheek*)

SIGNORA IGNAZIA: It's driving me crazy! Don't touch me!

POMETTI: Verri's just run down to the pharmacy. He should be back any minute.

SIGNORA IGNAZIA: They won't open up for him! You'll see!

MOMMINA: But they have to: it's an all-night pharmacy!

SIGNORA IGNAZIA: As if I didn't know what town we're living in! Oh! Oh! Don't make me talk! I'm going crazy! They're capable of refusing to open when they find out it's for me!

POMETTI: You'll see! Verri will get it open! Why he'd tear the door off its hinges!

NENÈ (*calm, continuing to dance*):   Yes, Mama, don't worry.

DORINA (*as above*):   Of course they'll open for him! Once he puts his mind to something, he's worse than they are!

SIGNORA IGNAZIA: No, no, poor thing, don't say that. He's such a good boy! He ran off right away.

MOMMINA: Yes! All by himself, while the rest of you stay here and dance.

SIGNORA IGNAZIA: Oh, let them dance, let them dance! After all, it won't help the pain if they just stand around asking me how I feel. (*to* **POMETTI**) The rage, the fury these people provoke in me! That's the cause of all my troubles!

NENÈ (*stops dancing and runs to her mother, glowing with the excitement of the proposal she is about to make*):   Mama, what if you said the *Ave Maria*, like last time?

POMETTI: Yes, that's it! Good idea!

NENÈ (*continuing*):   Remember? As you were saying it, the pain just disappeared!

POMETTI: Try it, Signora! Try it!

DORINA (*as she continues to dance*):   Yes, yes, say it, say it, Mama! It'll go away! You'll see!

NENÈ: Yes, but you have to stop dancing!

POMETTI: And you stop playing too, Pomàrici, OK?

NENÈ: Mama's going to say the *Ave Maria*, like the last time!

POMÀRICI (*getting up from the piano and running over*):   Yes! Great idea! Let's see if the miracle repeats itself.

SARELLI: And in Latin, you've got to say it in Latin, Signora Ignazia!

NARDI: Yes! It's more likely to work that way!

SIGNORA IGNAZIA: No, no, leave me alone! What do you want me to say?

NENÈ: You've got proof from last time, haven't you? It went away!

DORINA: But it's got to be dark!

NENÈ: Quiet! Quiet! Pomàrici, turn the light off!

POMÀRICI: But where's Totina?

DORINA: She's in the other room with Mangini. Don't worry about Totina: just turn the light off!

SIGNORA IGNAZIA: No, no, no! We'll need a candle at least. And keep your hands to yourselves! And Totina has to come here.

MOMMINA (*calling*):   Totina! Totina!

DORINA: The candle is in the other room!

NENÈ: You go get it; I'm going to get the little statue of the Virgin!

(*She runs out through the back, and* **DORINA** *goes into the dining room with* **NARDI** *to get the candle from the sideboard. Before they light it,* **NARDI** *embraces* **DORINA** *very tightly and kisses her on the mouth.*)

SIGNORA IGNAZIA (*shouting after* **NENÈ**, *who has run off*):   No, forget it! It doesn't matter! What little statue? We can do without that!

POMÀRICI (*as above*):   But make sure Totina comes back here!

SIGNORA IGNAZIA: Yes, yes, get Totina in here! Right now!

POMETTI: A little table for an altar! (*goes to get it*)

DORINA (*returning with the lighted candle while* **POMÀRICI** *turns the light off*):   Here's the candle!

POMETTI: Here on the table!

NENÈ (*from the back, with the statue of the Virgin*):   And here's the Virgin!

POMÀRICI: And Totina?

NENÈ: She's coming, she's coming! Will you stop bothering about Totina!

SIGNORA IGNAZIA: But what on earth is she doing in the other room?

NENÈ: Nothing! She's getting a surprise ready, you'll see! (*then, summoning everybody with a gesture:*) Come over here, gather around, everybody! Concentrate, Mama!

(*Tableau: In the darkness slightly broken by that flickering candlelight,* **DOCTOR HINKFUSS** *has prepared an exquisite effect: the trancelike glow of a very soft green "miracle light," almost a manifestation of the hope that the miracle will take place. This happens at the moment that* **SIGNORA IGNAZIA**, *kneeling before the Virgin placed on the table with the candle, her hands together, begins reciting, slowly and in a low voice, the words of the prayer, almost expecting after each word that her pain will disappear.*)

SIGNORA IGNAZIA: Ave Maria, gratia plena, Dominus tecum . . .

(*Suddenly the whole effect is shattered by a crash of thunder and a violent, even diabolical flash of red lightning.* TOTINA, *dressed in Mangini's uniform, comes in singing, followed by* MANGINI, *who is wearing a long dressing gown belonging to Signor Palmiro. The thunder immediately becomes the voice of* TOTINA *singing, and the red lightning, the light* MANGINI *turns on in the drawing room as he enters.*)

TOTINA:

> "Le parlate d'amor—o cari fior . . . ,"[20]

(*A loud shout of protest from everyone.*)

NENÈ: Shut up, stupid!

MOMMINA: She's ruined everything!

TOTINA (*stunned*): What is it?

DORINA: Mama was reciting the *Ave Maria.*

TOTINA (*to* NENÈ): You could have told me!

NENÈ: Oh yes! I should have guessed you'd pick just this moment to pounce on us!

TOTINA: I was already in my costume when you came in.

NENÈ: You should have realized!

DORINA: All right! That's enough! What shall we do now?

POMÀRICI: We'll start all over! Right from the beginning!

SIGNORA IGNAZIA (*speechless, waiting, as though the miracle had already taken place there in her mouth*): No . . . Wait . . . I don't know . . .

MOMMINA (*happy*): Did it go away?

SIGNORA IGNAZIA (*as above*): I don't know . . . it must have been the devil . . . or maybe the Virgin . . . (*She grimaces with another sharp pain.*) Oh no . . . oh! . . . again . . . it didn't go away at all! Aaah! . . . God, what agony . . . (*Suddenly controlling herself, she stamps her foot and tells herself:*) No! I won't give up! Sing, girls! Sing! Sing, my children! Please, please, sing! Sing! I can't let this pig of a toothache get me down! Come on, come on Mommina: "*Stride la vampa!*"[21]

MOMMINA (*while everybody applauds, shouting:* "Yes, yes! Bravo! The gypsy chorus from "Trovatore"!) No, no, Mama, I don't feel like it! No!

SIGNORA IGNAZIA (*pleading angrily*): Do me this favor, Mommina! It's because of the pain!

MOMMINA: But I'm telling you—I don't feel like it!

NENÈ: Go on! Just this once. Make her happy!

TOTINA: You heard what she said! She doesn't want the pain to bring her down!

SARELLI AND NARDI: — Yes, yes, come on!

> — Make her happy, please, Signorina!

---

20. See note 19.

21. "The flames are roaring," Verdi's *Il Trovatore* (II:1). *Il Trovatore* was first performed in Rome, January 19, 1853.

DORINA: God! You really want to be coaxed, don't you!

NENÈ: Do you think we don't know why you don't want to sing any more?

POMÀRICI: Of course the signorina will sing!

SARELLI: If it's because of Verri, don't worry about it. We'll take care of him!

POMÀRICI: I swear it: singing is a charm against pain!

SIGNORA IGNAZIA: Yes, please sing! Do it for your mother!

POMETTI: The courage she has, this Generala of ours!

SIGNORA IGNAZIA: Totina, you play Manrico, all right?

TOTINA: Of course. I'm already dressed for it.

SIGNORA IGNAZIA: Someone draw some whiskers on her!

MANGINI: Here, yes, I'll do it!

POMÀRICI: No, I'll do it, if you don't mind!

NENÈ: Here's the cork, Pomàrici. I'll go get the big feathered hat! And a yellow kerchief and a red shawl for Azucena!

(She runs out through the back; she will return a little later with the items she mentioned.)

POMÀRICI (*to* **TOTINA**, *as he is drawing the whiskers*): Please stand still a little!

SIGNORA IGNAZIA: Fine! Mommina, Azucena . . .

MOMMINA (*almost to herself now, lacking the strength to resist*): No, I, no . . .

SIGNORA IGNAZIA (*continuing*): . . . Totina, Manrico . . .

SARELLI: — and all of us, the gypsy chorus!

SIGNORA IGNAZIA (*humming it*):
>"All'opra, all'opra! Dàgli. Martella.
> Chi del gitano la vita abbella?"

(She directs the question to some of them; they stare at her, not knowing whether she's really asking or just joking: then, turning to the others, she asks again:)

>"Chi del gitano la vita abbella?"

(But they look at her as the first ones did. She cannot stand the pain any more, and asks everyone again. She's really angry by now, because she really wants them to answer:)

>"Chi del gitano la vita abbella?"

EVERYBODY (*finally understanding, they start singing the answer*):
>"La zingareeee-eeeella!"[22]

SIGNORA IGNAZIA (*She sighs, because she has finally been understood*): Ahhhh! (*then, while the others hold the note, to herself, writhing in pain:*) Damn! Damn! I can't bear it any longer! — Come on! Come on, children, sing! Hurry!

---

22. See below, note 23.

POMÀRICI: No, damn it, wait till I've finished.

DORINA: Aren't you finished? That's good enough!

SARELLI: She looks fine!

NENÈ: She's a beauty! Now the hat! The hat! (*She gives it to her and turns to* **MOMMINA**.) And you, no more fuss! Put on the kerchief! (*to* **SARELLI**) Tie it behind her neck! **SARELLI** *does so.*) And the shawl around her shoulders, like this!

DORINA (*shoving* **MOMMINA**, *who remains still*): Come on, hurry up!

POMÀRICI: We need something to beat on!

NENÈ: Oh, I know! The brass basins!

(*Goes to get them from the sideboard in the dining room: returns and passes them around.*)

POMÀRICI (*going to the piano*): Now pay attention! Let's start from the beginning!
"*Vedi le fosche notturne spoglie . . .*"

(*He begins to play the gypsy chorus from the beginning of act 2 of "*Il Trovatore.*"*)

CHORUS (*starting*):
"*Vedi le fosche notturne spoglie
de' cieli sveste l'immensa volta:
sembra una vedova che alfin si toglie
i bruni panni ond'era involta*"

(*Then banging on the basins:*)

"*All'opra, all'opra! Dàgli. Martella.
Chi del gitano la vita abbella?
La zingarella!*" (*Repeated three times.*)[23]

POMÀRICI (*to* **MOMMINA**): Now get ready, Signorina: it's your cue! And gather round, all of you!

MOMMINA (*coming forward*):
"*Stride la vampa! La folla indomita
corre a quel foco lieta in sembianza!*

23.　　"*See the somber hues of night
From the face of heaven depart:
Thus the widow casts away
The tokens of her bereavement.
To our work—each to his hammer!
Who is it that makes the gypsy life so gay?
'Tis the gypsy girl!*" (See note 21.)

> *Urli di gioja intorno echeggiano:*
> *cinta di sgherri donna s'avanza."*[24]

(*While the others sing, first in chorus and then* **MOMMINA** *by herself,* **SIGNORA IGNAZIA** *sits on a chair, restless as a bear, stamping her feet one after the other. She mutters in rhythm, as if she were reciting a litany or prayer:*)

SIGNORA IGNAZIA: Oh God, I'm dying! Oh God, I'm dying! It's penance for my sins! God, God, what pain! Come on, Lord, strike me! And let me be the only one to pay: God let me be the one to pay for my daughters' pleasures! Sing, sing, yes, yes, enjoy yourselves, my children! Let me be the one to go mad with pain, the penance for all my sins! I want you to be happy, happy! — that's it! Yes, "dàgli," "martella," hammer me! hammer me, Lord! Let my girls enjoy themselves! Ah God, the pleasures that I never had — never, never! Oh God, never, never — I want my daughters to have them! — They must! They must! I'll pay for it, I'll pay for it in their place, Lord, even if they disobey your holy commands.

(*And she starts to sing with the others, while tears trickle from her eyes:* "La zingareeee-eeeellaaa! . . .")

Quiet! Now sing, Mommina. She has the voice of a diva. *La vampa,* yes! Ah . . . The flame, I feel it in my mouth. *Lieta,* yes, *lieta in sembianza . . .*

(*At this point* **RICCO VERRI** *enters from the back. At first he stops in his tracks; it's as if a deep gulf of astonishment has opened up before his anger. He leaps forward and throws himself on* **POMÀRICI***: he tears him from the piano bench and throws him to the ground, shouting:*)

VERRI: God damn you! Make a fool of me, would you!

(*At first everyone is bewildered; there is a general babble of confusion.*)

NENÈ: What a way to behave!
DORINA: Is he crazy?

(*Then, an explosion:* **POMÀRICI** *springs up and throws himself on* **VERRI***, while the others try to separate them and stop them. There is great confusion, with everyone speaking at once.*)

POMÀRICI: I'll see that you answer for that!
VERRI (*pushing him away violently*): I haven't finished yet!
SARELLI AND NARDI: — Don't forget us! — You'll have to answer to all of us!

---

24.   "*The flames are roaring!*
     The merciless crowd runs toward the fire,
glee on their faces; shouts of joy sound round about
          as the woman comes forward,
     surrounded by ruffians." (See note 21.)

VERRI: Everyone, everyone! I'll smash your faces, all of you!

TOTINA: Who asked you to take charge here?

VERRI: First you send me out to get the medicine . . .

SIGNORA IGNAZIA: . . . the medicine? Yes? And then?

VERRI (*pointing at* **MOMMINA**): — and then I find her, dressed for a masquerade!

SIGNORA IGNAZIA: You get out of my house right now!

MOMMINA: I didn't want to do it, I didn't want to! I told everyone I didn't want to!

DORINA: Look what we have to listen to now! The little fool makes excuses!

NENÈ: He takes advantage of the fact that we don't have a man in the house who could kick him out as he deserves!

SIGNORA IGNAZIA (*to* **NENÈ**): Go call your father right now! Tell him to get out of bed and come here this minute!

SARELLI: For that matter, we can throw him out ourselves!

NENÈ (*rushing to call her father*): Papa! Papa!

(*Goes out.*)

VERRI (*to* **SARELLI**): You? I'd like to see that! Throw me out! (*to* **NENÈ**, *who is rushing out*) Go ahead, call your father, call him: I'll answer to the head of the house for what I do! I only demand that they all treat you with respect.

SIGNORA IGNAZIA: Who asked you to do that? What right have you to make demands?

VERRI: What right? The signorina knows how I feel! (*points to* **MOMMINA**)

MOMMINA: But not this way, not violently like this!

VERRI: Am I the violent one? What the others do to you, that's not violent?

SIGNORA IGNAZIA: As I said before, I don't want to know anything about it. There's the door: go!

VERRI: No. Not unless she tells me to.

SIGNORA IGNAZIA: My daughter will tell you the same thing! In any case, I am mistress in my own house!

DORINA: It's the same with all of us!

VERRI: That's not enough if the signorina supports me! I'm the only one here whose motives are honorable!

SARELLI: Honorable! Listen to that!

NARDI: There's nothing dishonorable about what we do here!

VERRI: The signorina knows it!

POMÀRICI: You clown!

VERRI: You're the clowns! (*brandishing a chair:*) You'd better not get in my way again, or I'll settle it right now!

POMETTI (*to his friends*): Come on, come on, let's go. Let's go home.

DORINA: No, no! Why?

TOTINA: You're not going to leave us alone! He's not in charge here!

VERRI: Nardi, don't call in sick tomorrow! We'll be seeing each other!

NENÈ (*returning, greatly distressed*): Papa—he's not in the house!

SIGNORA IGNAZIA: Not in the house?

NENÈ: I looked everywhere for him! I can't find him!

DORINA: What do you mean? Hasn't he come home?

NENÈ: No he hasn't!

MOMMINA: Where can he be?

SIGNORA IGNAZIA: Still out, at this hour?

SARELLI: Maybe he went back to the cabaret.

POMÀRICI: We're going home, Signora.

SIGNORA IGNAZIA: No, no, wait . . .

MANGINI: No, no! Wait! I can't go home like this!

TOTINA: Oh yes! Sorry! I forgot. I'm still wearing your uniform. I'll take it off right away. (*rushes off*)

POMÀRICI (*to* **MANGINI**): You can wait to get it back from her, but we're going.

SIGNORA IGNAZIA: But please, I don't see . . .

VERRI: They do, though; you may not want to, but they can see!

SIGNORA IGNAZIA: I'm telling you again, you're the one who has to go away, not them! Do you understand?

VERRI: No, Signora: they're the ones! Because when they're face to face with a man who takes things seriously, they know there's no more room for their contemptible jokes.

POMÀRICI: Oh sure! You'll find out tomorrow whether we're joking!

VERRI: I can't wait!

MOMMINA: Please, Verri, please!

VERRI (*quivering*): You must not beg!

MOMMINA: I'm not begging! I simply want to say it was my fault, because I gave in! I shouldn't have, knowing that you . . .

NARDI: . . . as a true Sicilian, you're well past the point where you can take a joke.

SARELLI: But now it's beyond a joke for us too!

VERRI (*to* **MOMMINA** *as* **LEADING ACTRESS**, *dropping out of character without warning; his anger is that of the* **LEADING ACTOR**, *forced to say what he doesn't want to*): Well. Are you happy?

MOMMINA (*as* **LEADING ACTRESS**, *disconcerted*): About what?

VERRI (*as above*): You shouldn't have said that! Why did you have to blame yourself there at the end?

MOMMINA (*as above*): It came to me spontaneously.

VERRI: But you let them off the hook. I've got to have the last word: I've got to shout that they'll all have to deal with me, all of them!

MANGINI: Me too, in a dressing gown? (*And he awkwardly takes the* en garde *position.*) Ready! En garde!

NENÈ AND DORINA (*laughing and clapping their hands*): Bravo, bravo!

VERRI (*as above, angry*): What do you mean "bravo"? Don't be stupid! The whole scene is ruined! And we'll never finish!

DOCTOR HINKFUSS (*rising from his seat*): No, no! Why? Everything was going so well! Go on, go on!

(*A knocking is heard from offstage, louder and louder, as though at the front door.*)

MANGINI (*excusing himself*): Now I'm in this dressing-gown, maybe I could do a little song and dance!

NENÈ: Why not!

VERRI (*scornfully to* **MANGINI**): Go somewhere and play cards![25] Don't come here to act!

MOMMINA: If Mr. __ wants to perform by himself, without us, why doesn't he say so, and we'll all go away.

VERRI: No—if you all just want to do what you please, as you please, whether it's right or not, I'll go myself.

SIGNORA IGNAZIA: But for heaven's sake, it was so well done, so natural—the signorina pleading, "It was my fault, because I gave in!"

POMÀRICI (*to* **VERRI**): After all, we're here too, you know!

SARELLI: We have to live our parts too!

NARDI: He wants to show off all by himself! Everyone has to play his own part!

DOCTOR HINKFUSS (*shouting*): That's enough! Stop! Keep the scene going! It seems to me that it's you, Mr. __, who's ruining everything now . . .

VERRI: No, it's not me—please! On the contrary, if anyone feels he has something to say he should say it, but it has to fit! (*refers to the* **LEADING ACTRESS**) For three hours I've been saying to myself, "The signorina knows how I feel; the signorina knows!" But Miss __ can't find a word to support me! She always takes on this pose of The Victim!

MOMMINA (*exasperated, almost ready to cry*): But I am, I am a victim, the victim of my sisters, the victim of the house I live in, your victim, everybody's victim . . .

(*At this point, while the actors on stage are talking to* **DOCTOR HINKFUSS**, *the* **OLD COMIC ACTOR**, **SAMPOGNETTA**, *makes his way through them. He has the face of a dead man and his bloodied hands are clutching his stomach, where he has been wounded with a knife: his vest and trousers are also stained with blood.*)

SAMPOGNETTA: To make a long story short, Doctor Hinkfuss, I knock, knock, knock, all covered with blood like this; I have my guts in my hands, I've got to come on stage to die—and that's not easy for an old comedian—and no one lets me in. And what do I find here? Confusion. The actors are all out of character. And the effect of my entrance was lost, because you see I'm not only bleeding and dying, but I'm drunk as well. So tell me, what are we going to do about this?

DOCTOR HINKFUSS: We'll fix it up right away. Lean on your singer . . . Where is she?

---

25. Text has *morra*. This is a gambling game in which two players call out a guess as to the total number of fingers the two of them put forth at the same time.

SINGER: Here I am.

A CUSTOMER FROM THE CABARET: I'm here to help too.

DOCTOR HINKFUSS: Well, hold him up then.

SAMPOGNETTA: And I had the stairs to climb, with the both of them carrying me . . .

DOCTOR HINKFUSS: Let's say you've already done that! Good God! And you, all of you, to your places! And let yourselves feel it—the grief, the sorrow . . . I can't believe it! To drown yourself in a glass of water! (*returns to his seat, muttering:*) All because of a stupid point of principle! It makes no sense!

(*The scene starts again.* **SIGNOR PALMIRO** *appears from the back, supported on either side by the* **SINGER** *and the* **CUSTOMER FROM THE CABARET**.

As soon as his wife and daughters see him they start screaming. But the **OLD COMIC ACTOR** *stays out of character and lets them vent their feelings for a while. He has a tolerant smile on his face and an air that says, "When you're finished, I'll begin." As for the hysterical questions that swirl around him, he lets the singer answer some, and the customer others, although he wishes they would be quiet so that the others would be forced to wait for the real answer, which he is going to give at the end. The others are puzzled by his nonchalance, but they continue the play as best they can.*)

SIGNORA IGNAZIA: Oh, God! What happened?

MOMMINA: Papa, oh Papa!

NENÈ: You're hurt?

VERRI: Who did it?

DORINA: Where is he hurt? Where?

THE CUSTOMER: In the belly.

SARELLI: A knife wound?

THE SINGER: Yes, a big gash! He's lost a lot of blood along the way.

NARDI: But who did it? Who did it?

POMETTI: Did it happen in the cabaret?

MANGINI: Lay him down, for heaven's sake!

POMÀRICI: Here, here, on the sofa!

SIGNORA IGNAZIA (*while the* **SINGER** *and the* **CUSTOMER** *lay* **SIGNOR PALMIRO** *down on the sofa*): Did he go back to the cabaret?

NENÈ: Don't worry about the cabaret now, Mama! Don't you see how he is?

SIGNORA IGNAZIA: Well, when I see, coming into my house . . . Look! Look at him with his arm around her! Who are you?

SINGER: Well, Signora, at least I'm a woman with more heart than you!

THE CUSTOMER: Signora, can't you see? Your husband is dying!

MOMMINA: How did it happen? How did it happen?

THE CUSTOMER: He started to defend her . . . (*indicates the singer*)

SIGNORA IGNAZIA (*with a sneer*): Oh, I see! A knight in shining armor!

CUSTOMER (*continuing*): — a fight started —

SINGER: — and that murderer —

CUSTOMER: — he let go of her and turned against him!

VERRI: Did they catch him?

CUSTOMER: No, he ran away, threatening everybody with a knife.

NARDI: But do they know who he is?

CUSTOMER (*pointing at the* **SINGER**): She knows all right . . .

SARELLI: Her lover?

SINGER: My tormentor! My tormentor!

CUSTOMER: He threatened to kill everybody!

NENÈ: We've got to send for a doctor right away!

(**TOTINA** *arrives still half undressed.*)

TOTINA: What happened? What happened? Oh God, Papa? Who hurt him?

MOMMINA: Say something, say something at least, Papa!

DORINA: Why do you stare at us like that?

NENÈ: He just stares and smiles.

TOTINA: But where did it happen? How did it happen?

SIGNORA IGNAZIA (*to* **TOTINA**): At the cabaret! Don't you see? (*indicating the singer*) What can you expect?

NENÈ: A doctor! a doctor! We're not going to let him die like that.

MOMMINA: Who's going to call him?

MANGINI: I would if I weren't dressed like this . . . (*indicates his dressing gown*)

TOTINA: Oh, that's right. Go get your uniform; it's in the other room.

NENÈ: Sarelli, you go, please!

SARELLI: Yes, yes, I'll go.

(*Exits upstage with* **MANGINI**.)

VERRI: Why isn't he saying anything? (*refers to* **SIGNOR PALMIRO**) He should say something . . .

TOTINA: Papa! Papa!

NENÈ: He keeps staring and smiling.

MOMMINA: We're all here with you, Papa!

VERRI: Surely he wouldn't want to die without saying anything?

POMÀRICI: That's a fine thing! He's lying there, neither dead nor alive. What is he waiting for?

NARDI: I can't think of anything else to say! Lucky Sarelli—he went for the doctor, and Mangini went to put on his uniform . . .

SIGNORA IGNAZIA (*to her husband*): Speak up! Speak up! Can't you say anything? If you'd done what I told you! If you'd thought of your four daughters: they'll have nobody to provide for them!

NENÈ (*having waited a while, like everyone else*): Nothing. He just lies there, smiling.

MOMMINA: It's not natural.

DORINA: You can't just look at us and smile like that, Papa. We're here too!

THE CUSTOMER FROM THE CABARET: Maybe he had a little too much to drink.

MOMMINA: It's not natural. When someone drinks a lot, if it makes him sad, he keeps quiet; but if it makes him laugh, then he talks. He shouldn't be laughing!

SIGNORA IGNAZIA: Could you at least tell us why you're smiling like that?

(*Once again there is a brief pause; they all remain out of character.*)

SAMPOGNETTA: Because I'm pleased to see how much better you all are at this than I am.

VERRI (*while the others look at each other, suddenly caught at their own game*): What are you talking about?

SAMPOGNETTA (*sitting on the sofa*): I'm simply saying this: if I don't know how I got into the house, since no one came to open the door, even after I'd knocked at it for so long, I —

DOCTOR HINKFUSS (*getting up from his seat, extremely angry*): What, again? Are you starting all over?

SAMPOGNETTA: I can't die, Doctor Hinkfuss. When I see how well everyone is doing, I feel like laughing, and I can't die. The maid (*Looks around.*) — where is she? I don't see her—she should have cried out: "Oh God, the master! Oh God, the master! They're bringing him up! He's wounded!"

DOCTOR HINKFUSS: What are you talking about now? Hadn't we agreed you're already in the house?

SAMPOGNETTA: In that case I might as well just consider myself dead and forget the whole thing!

DOCTOR HINKFUSS: Not at all! You've got to speak, play the scene, die!

SAMPOGNETTA: All right! Here's the scene: (*He lies on the sofa.*) I'm dead!

DOCTOR HINKFUSS: Not like that!

SAMPOGNETTA (*getting up and coming forward*): My dear Doctor Hinkfuss, come up here and finish killing me yourself. What else can I say? I repeat, I cannot die just like that, on my own. I'm not like an accordion that you can squeeze and pull, and make a song come out just by pressing the keys.

DOCTOR HINKFUSS: But your colleagues —

SAMPOGNETTA (*immediately*): — are much more skillful than I am; I've said so, and I congratulate them. I can't do it. For me everything depended on the entrance. You wanted to skip it . . . In order to get into character I needed that shout of the maid. And Death had to come in with me, make its appearance here, in the shameless gaiety of this house of mine: Death, the drunkard, as we had agreed: drunk with wine, which had now become blood. And I had to speak, yes, I know; I had to begin my speech in the midst of everyone's horror—finding my courage in the wine and the blood, leaning on this woman (*He draws the **SINGER** to him and leans on her with an arm around her neck.*)— like this—and say senseless, wandering, terrible words to my wife, my daughters, even to these young men. I had to show them that if I had appeared to be a fool it was because they were wicked: my wife, too, and my daughters, and my friends, wicked, all of them; it was not because I was stupid, but because I alone was good, and they are evil.

I was the intelligent one, it was they who were stupid; I was naïve, but they were brutally wicked; yes, yes; (*getting angry, as though he was being contradicted:*) yes, intelligent, intelligent as children are (not all of them, only those who grow up joyless amid the stupidity of their elders). But I had to say these things as a drunkard, in a delirium; and pass my bloodied hands across my face—like this—and smear it with blood (*asks his companions:*) — is it smeared? (*and as they motion yes:*) — good (*he continues:*) and terrify you and make you cry—really cry—and I can't find the breath any more, as I try to shape my lips — (*he tries to whistle, but he can't: "fhhh, fhhh"*) — to whistle my last song; and then, there — (*to the* **CUSTOMER FROM THE CABARET**.) — come here, you too — (*he places his other arm around the* **CUSTOMER'S** *neck*) — like that — between the two of you—but closer to you, my dear—bow my head—and—quickly, as little birds do—die.

(*His head drops onto the* **SINGER'S** *breast; then he relaxes his arms, and falls to the ground, dead.*)

THE SINGER: Oh God, (*tries to hold him, but then lets go*) he's dead, he's dead!

MOMMINA (*throwing herself on him*): Papa! Papa! Papa!

(*And she bursts into tears. At this outburst of true emotion on the part of the* **LEADING ACTRESS**, *the other actresses also break into real tears. At this point* **DOCTOR HINKFUSS** *gets up and shouts:*)

DOCTOR HINKFUSS: That's very good! Cut the lights! Cut the lights! Blackout! (*It becomes dark.*) Everybody out! — The four sisters and the mother, around the table in the dining room—six days later—the light in the drawing room is off; turn on the lamp in the dining room.

MOMMINA (*in the darkness*): But Doctor Hinkfuss, we have to go and dress ourselves in black.

DOCTOR HINKFUSS: Oh, of course! In black. The curtain should have been closed after the death scene. Doesn't matter. Go dress yourselves in black. Close the curtains. Houselights, please!

(*The curtain is closed. The houselights are turned on.* **DOCTOR HINKFUSS** *smiles dolefully.*)

That effect didn't quite come off. But we'll have it tomorrow night, I promise you; it'll be very powerful. Even in life, ladies and gentlemen, it sometimes happens that a carefully prepared effect, something that we've counted on, doesn't materialize when it's supposed to, and naturally we reproach our wives, our daughters: "You should have done this," or "You should have said that." It's true that here it was a question of a death scene. Too bad that Mr. __, fine actor though he is, was so stubborn about his entrance! But he is a good actor. Tomorrow night he'll do this scene marvelously, no doubt about it! It's a very important scene, ladies and gentlemen, because of its consequences. It's my invention; it's not in the story. But I'm sure the author would never have put it in anyway, even if it weren't for a scruple of his that I had no reason to respect: you see, he did not wish to reinforce the widespread belief that they're so free with the knife in Sicily. If it had occurred to him to have his character die, perhaps he would have let him die of a heart attack or some other accident. But you can see that you get a different theatrical effect by having him die as I've imagined it, with the wine and the blood and one arm around the neck of that singer.

The character must die; as a result the family must plunge into poverty. If that doesn't happen, it doesn't seem natural to me that the daughter Mommina would consent to marry that savage, Rico Verri, and resist all her mother's and sisters' arguments to the contrary. They've made enquiries already in the neighboring town on the southern coast of the island, and they've found out that, true, he comes from a well-to-do family, but not only is his father a well-known money-lender, but he has such a jealous nature that his wife died of a broken heart after only a few years of marriage. How can this girl see the fate that awaits her? What conditions did Rico Verri have to agree to with his jealous father, the money-lender, so that he could marry her to spite his officer friends? What conditions did he have to agree to with himself, not only to compensate himself for the sacrifice his stubbornness cost him, but even to show his face again before his fellow villagers, who are well aware of the reputation of his wife's family? Who knows how he'll make her pay for the pleasure she has already enjoyed, living at home with her mother and sisters! As you can see, these are very powerful arguments.

Miss ___, my excellent leading lady, doesn't really agree with me. For her Mommina is the wisest of the four sisters, the one who sacrifices herself, the one who has always set up entertainments for others, but who has never enjoyed any of them herself without paying the price, in hard work, sleepless nights, and troubled thoughts. The whole weight of the family is on her shoulders. And there are so many things she is conscious of: first of all, that the years are passing by; that her father, with all that disorder at home, hadn't been able to put anything aside; that there isn't a young man in town who'd marry any one of them; but Verri . . . Verri will fight not one but three duels with the officers, who all disappeared at the first sign of misfortune. After all, like her sisters, Mommina has a passion for melodrama: Raul, Ernani, Don Alvaro . . .

> "né toglier mi potrò
> l'immagin sua dal cuor . . ."[26]

She holds firm, and she marries him.

(**DOCTOR HINKFUSS** *has spoken at length in order to give the actresses time to dress in black; now, however, he has had enough. He has a fit of temper. He draws the curtain a little to one side and shouts backstage:*)

Well, what about the bell? Aren't the ladies ready yet?

———

26. "Nor am I able to tear / His image from my heart" *La forza del destino* (IV:2). The three characters Doctor Hinkfuss names are the heroes of their respective operas: Ernani is from Verdi's opera of the same name (1844); Don Alvaro is from *La forza del destino* (1862); there is an opera named *Raoul,* to which Doctor Hinkfuss may be referring.

(*And he adds to someone behind the curtain:*)

No? — What's the matter? — What? They don't want to act any more? Why? There's an audience out there waiting! Come out here, come on!

(**DOCTOR HINKFUSS'S SECRETARY** *comes forward, embarrassed and dismayed.*)

SECRETARY: Well . . . I don't know . . . they say . . .

DOCTOR HINKFUSS: What?

THE LEADING ACTOR (*behind the curtain, to the* **SECRETARY**): Speak up, loud and clear. Tell him why!

DOCTOR HINKFUSS: Oh, it's Mr. __ again . . .

(*The* **LEADING ACTOR** *and all the other actors and actresses come out from behind the curtain, beginning with the* **CHARACTER ACTRESS**, *who takes off her wig in front of the audience, and the* **COMIC ACTOR**. *The* **LEADING ACTOR** *has taken off his military uniform.*)

THE CHARACTER ACTRESS: No, no, it's everybody. Everybody, Doctor Hinkfuss!

THE LEADING ACTRESS: We can't go on like this!

THE OTHERS: It's impossible! Impossible!

THE COMIC ACTOR: I've finished my part, but I'm here too —

DOCTOR HINKFUSS: In the name of God, will somebody tell me what more has happened?

(*The end of the* **COMIC ACTOR'S** *sentence, spoken so calmly, has the effect of a cold shower:*)

THE COMIC ACTOR: — and I agree with my colleagues!

DOCTOR HINKFUSS: Agree? Agree with what?

THE COMIC ACTOR: We're all leaving, my dear Director!

DOCTOR HINKFUSS: Leaving? Where are you going?

SOME: Just away!

THE LEADING ACTOR: Unless you leave yourself!

OTHERS: Either you leave or we do!

DOCTOR HINKFUSS: Me leave? How dare you suggest such a thing!

THE ACTORS: — Then we'll leave!

— Yes, yes. Let's go! Let's go!

— We're not going to be puppets any more!

— Let's go, let's go away!

(*And they move about excitedly.*)

DOCTOR HINKFUSS (*stopping them*): Where? Are you crazy? There's an audience here that's paid its money! What are you going to do about the audience?

THE COMIC ACTOR: That's up to you! We're telling you: either you go, or we go!

DOCTOR HINKFUSS: I'm asking you again! Has something else happened?

THE LEADING ACTOR: Something else? Don't you think what's already happened is enough?

DOCTOR HINKFUSS: But I thought we'd fixed everything!

THE COMIC ACTOR: What do you mean, fixed everything?

THE CHARACTER ACTRESS: You asked us to improvise —

DOCTOR HINKFUSS: And you'd agreed to do it!

THE COMIC ACTOR: Oh, but please, not like this, skipping scenes, telling me—"die!"— just like that!

THE CHARACTER ACTRESS: Picking up a scene right in the middle—cold!

THE LEADING ACTRESS: We can't find our words any more —

THE LEADING ACTOR: There! It's just as I said at the beginning! The words must be born of flesh and blood!

THE LEADING ACTRESS: Excuse me! You were the first one to object when I spoke out spontaneously!

THE LEADING ACTOR: Yes, you're right! But it's not my fault!

POMÀRICI: Oh, of course, he only started it!

THE LEADING ACTOR: Let me speak! It's not my fault! It's his fault! (*points at* **DOCTOR HINKFUSS**)

DOCTOR HINKFUSS: My fault? What do you mean? Why?

THE LEADING ACTOR: Because! Here you are! Right in the midst of us! Keeping us in this cursed theater of yours, God damn it to hell!

DOCTOR HINKFUSS: Theater of mine? Have you gone crazy? Where are we? Isn't this a theater?

THE LEADING ACTOR: Is this a theater? Fine! Then give us the parts to play —

THE LEADING ACTRESS: — act by act, scene by scene —

NENÈ: — the lines written down, word for word —

THE COMIC ACTOR: — yes, then you can cut as much as you like. You can make us skip around as you please—but at a point that you've marked and that we've all agreed upon beforehand!

THE LEADING ACTOR: First you bring out the life from within us —

THE LEADING ACTRESS: — with such a storm of passions —

THE CHARACTER ACTRESS: — you see, the more we speak, the more we get into character —

NENÈ: — we're all in a turmoil . . .

THE LEADING ACTRESS: — we're all shaking!

TOTINA (*pointing at the* **LEADING ACTOR**): — I could kill him! —

DORINA: — that bully, who comes to our house and lays down the law!

DOCTOR HINKFUSS: But it's better, it's better that way!

THE LEADING ACTOR: You can't say "it's better," and then ask us to pay attention to the staging as well —

THE COMIC ACTOR: — so that we don't miss some particular effect —

THE LEADING ACTOR: — because we are in the theater! How do you expect us to think about your theater, if we have to live? Don't you see what's happened? I've been thinking about that scene you wanted to end with me having the last word; well I was wrong to get angry with Miss __ (*indicates the* **LEADING ACTRESS**). She was quite right to be begging at that moment, no question about it—

THE LEADING ACTRESS: — I was begging for you! —

THE LEADING ACTOR: — of course, exactly — (*to the actor who played* **MANGINI**) just as you were right to clown around with that dressing gown—I beg your pardon: I was a fool to listen to him (*points at* **DOCTOR HINKFUSS**).

DOCTOR HINKFUSS: Watch what you're saying!

THE LEADING ACTOR (*dismisses him, and again impetuously turns to the* **LEADING ACTRESS**): Don't interrupt me now! You really are the victim; I can see it, I can feel it: you're living fully in your role, just as I am in mine. When I see you there, (*he takes her face in his hands*) with those eyes, those lips, I suffer all the pains of hell. You're trembling! You're dying of fear in my hands. There is an audience here that we cannot send away. Theater? No, neither of us can act in the normal way any more. But just as you must cry out your desperation and your suffering, I must shout out my passion, the one that drives me to commit the crime. Well then, let this be a tribunal that hears us and judges us! (*Suddenly, turning to* **DOCTOR HINKFUSS***:*) But you must go away!

DOCTOR HINKFUSS (*amazed*): I?

THE LEADING ACTOR: Yes—and you must leave us alone! Just the two of us!

NENÈ: That's right!

THE CHARACTER ACTRESS: To perform it as they feel it!

THE COMIC ACTOR: What is born within them—exactly!

ALL THE OTHERS (*pushing* **DOCTOR HINKFUSS** *down from the stage*): Yes, go away! Go away!

DOCTOR HINKFUSS: You're throwing me out of my own theater?

THE COMIC ACTOR: There's no need for you any more!

ALL THE OTHERS (*now pushing him away through the corridor*): Go away! Go away!

DOCTOR HINKFUSS: This is unheard of! It's an outrage! You want to make this into a tribunal?

THE LEADING ACTOR: Theater! Real theater!

THE COMIC ACTOR: The theater you toss aside every night so as to turn each scene into a mere spectacle for the eyes!

THE CHARACTER ACTRESS: To live a passion, that's true theater! Then a simple placard is all you need!

THE LEADING ACTRESS: You can't play with passions!

THE LEADING ACTOR: And manipulate everything just to get an effect. It's only in cheap farces you can do that!

ALL THE OTHERS: Go on! Get out!

DOCTOR HINKFUSS: I am your director!

THE LEADING ACTOR: Nobody can direct life as it's coming into being!

THE CHARACTER ACTRESS: Even the writer himself has to do what it tells him!

THE LEADING ACTRESS: That's right! You've got to obey its commands!

THE COMIC ACTOR: Away with everyone who wants to command!

ALL THE OTHERS: Go on! Away with you!

DOCTOR HINKFUSS (*with his back to the entrance door to the auditorium*): I'll protest! It's a scandal! I am your direct— . . .

(*He is pushed out of the auditorium. Meanwhile, on the stage, which is empty and dark, the curtain has been opened.* **DOCTOR HINKFUSS'S SECRETARY**, *the* **PAINTERS**, *the* **ELECTRICIANS**, *the entire stage crew has come to watch this extraordinary spectacle: a theater director thrown out by his actors.*)

THE LEADING ACTOR (*to the* **LEADING ACTRESS**, *inviting her to return to the stage*): Come on, come on! Let's get right back to work!

THE CHARACTER ACTRESS: We'll do everything ourselves!

THE LEADING ACTOR: We won't need anything!

POMÀRICI: We'll put up the sets ourselves —

THE COMIC ACTOR: Fine! And I'll take care of the lights!

THE CHARACTER ACTRESS: No, it's better like this, all empty and dark! It's better this way.

THE LEADING ACTOR: Just enough light to isolate the figures in the darkness!

THE LEADING ACTRESS: Without the set?

THE CHARACTER ACTRESS: The set doesn't matter!

THE LEADING ACTRESS: Not even the walls of my cell?

THE LEADING ACTOR: Yes, but barely visible—there—for a moment, when you touch them . . . nothing else: darkness; we want people to understand, you see, that it's not the setting that controls us!

THE CHARACTER ACTRESS: All it needs is for you to feel that you're inside your jail, child; then it will appear. Everyone will see it just as though it were there around you!

THE LEADING ACTRESS: But I must put on some makeup . . . at least a little . . .

THE CHARACTER ACTRESS: Wait! I have an idea! (*to a* **STAGE HAND**:) Here, a chair, right away!

THE LEADING ACTRESS: What's your idea?

THE CHARACTER ACTRESS: You'll see!

   (*to the actors:*) Meanwhile set things up, but only the little that we can't do without. The small chairs for the two little girls. Check to see if they're there, and ready. (*A* **STAGE HAND** *brings the chair.*)

THE LEADING ACTRESS: . . . but I thought . . . a little makeup . . .

THE CHARACTER ACTRESS (*handing her the chair*): Yes, of course; sit here, my dear.

THE LEADING ACTRESS (*perplexed, almost dismayed*): Here?

THE CHARACTER ACTRESS: Yes, here, here! And you will feel the pain — Quick, Nenè, go get me the makeup box, a towel — Oh, and make sure the little girls wear their nightgowns!

THE LEADING ACTRESS: But what do you want to do? What do you mean?

THE CHARACTER ACTRESS: Leave it to us, to me, your mother, and your sisters. We'll do your face for you! Go on, Nenè!

TOTINA: Bring a mirror too!

THE LEADING ACTRESS: And my costume too then!

DORINA (*to* NENÈ, *who is already rushing toward the dressing rooms*): Yes, her costume! Her costume!

THE LEADING ACTRESS: My gown and my cloak; they're in my dressing room!

(NENÈ *nods and exits left.*)

THE CHARACTER ACTRESS: It must be our torture too, do you understand? For me, your mother, who knows what it is to be old—to make you old before your time, my child —

TOTINA: — and for us, who used to help you look pretty—now to make you look ugly —

DORINA: — so that you waste away —

THE LEADING ACTRESS: — to punish me for wanting that man?

THE CHARACTER ACTRESS: — yes, there's punishment, but there's pain, too: the punishment —

TOTINA: — for having broken away from us —

THE LEADING ACTRESS: — but please believe me: I didn't do it out of fear of the poverty that was waiting for us when our father died—no! —

DORINA: Then why? Because of love? Could you really have fallen in love with a monster like him?

THE LEADING ACTRESS: No: because of gratitude —

TOTINA: — for what? —

THE LEADING ACTRESS: — because I believed he was the only one — after all the scandal we caused . . .

TOTINA: — to prove that one of us could still get married?

DORINA: A lot you gained by marrying him!

THE CHARACTER ACTRESS: What did you gain? — Now — now, you'll find out!

NENÈ (*returning with the makeup box, a mirror, a towel, the gown, and the cloak*): Here's everything! I couldn't find . . .

THE CHARACTER ACTRESS: Give it to me! Give it to me! (*She opens the box and begins to put makeup on* MOMMINA.) Lift your face. Oh my dear, dear child, do you know how many people in town still say, as though they were speaking about a dead person, "She was a fine young lady! and what a heart she had!" — Your face is white now, like this, there . . . and this, and this, . . . like someone who never goes out or sees the sun —

TOTINA: — with bags under her eyes, she's got bags under her eyes now —

THE CHARACTER ACTRESS: — yes — there — that's it —

DORINA: — not too much! —

NENÈ: — no, no! A lot! —

TOTINA: — the eyes of someone who'll die of a broken heart —

NENÈ: — and now, here, on her temples, her hair —

THE CHARACTER ACTRESS: — yes, yes —

DORINA: — not white! not white! —

NENÈ: — no, not white —

THE LEADING ACTRESS: — dear Dorina . . .

TOTINA: — there — that's fine — like that . . . just a little over thirty —

THE CHARACTER ACTRESS: — already dusty with age! —

THE LEADING ACTRESS: He doesn't even want me to comb my hair.

THE CHARACTER ACTRESS (*messing it up*):   — in that case, wait: there . . . there . . . that's it . . .

NENÈ (*handing her the mirror*):   And now look at yourself!

THE LEADING ACTRESS (*immediately pushing the mirror away with both hands*):   No! He's taken them away, he's taken all the mirrors from the house. Do you know the only way I could still see myself? A shadow in the windowpanes, or all distorted in the tremor of the water in my basin—and I was terrified!

THE CHARACTER ACTRESS: Wait, your mouth! your mouth!

THE LEADING ACTRESS: Yes! — take away all the red: I have no more blood in my veins . . .

TOTINA: And wrinkles, wrinkles at the corner . . .

THE LEADING ACTRESS: At thirty, I could even have lost some teeth.

DORINA (*in a burst of emotion, embracing her*):   No, no, my Mommina, no, no!

NENÈ (*almost angry, also deeply moved, moving* **DORINA** *aside*):   Her corset! Take off her corset! Let's undress her!

THE CHARACTER ACTRESS: No, the gown and the cloak will go on top!

TOTINA: Yes, good, she'll look more clumsy that way!

THE CHARACTER ACTRESS: Your shoulders will sag like an old lady's, like mine . . .

DORINA: — You'll walk through the house, short of breath —

THE LEADING ACTRESS: — numb with grief —

THE CHARACTER ACTRESS: — dragging your feet —

NENÈ: — your listless flesh —

(*As she says her last line, each actress withdraws to the right into the darkness. The* **LEADING ACTRESS** *is now alone within the three naked walls of her cell, which have been set up in the darkness while she was being made up and dressed. She strikes her forehead first against the right wall, then against the back wall, and finally against the left. As her forehead touches it, each wall becomes visible for a moment in a flash of light from above, like cold lightning, and then disappears again in the darkness.*)

THE LEADING ACTRESS (*in a mournful cadence, increasing in depth and intensity, hitting her forehead on the three walls like a crazed beast in a cage*): This is a wall! — This is a wall! — This is a wall!

(*She goes to sit on the chair; she looks and behaves like a madwoman. She remains motionless for some moments. From the right, where her mother and sisters have withdrawn into the darkness, a voice arises, the voice of her mother; it is as though she were reading a story from a book:*)

THE CHARACTER ACTRESS: " — She was imprisoned in the highest house in the town. The door was locked: the house was all closed up, both the windows and the shutters: only one window was open, a small one that looked out on the faraway fields and the faraway sea. All she could see of the town on the top of the hill was the roofs of houses, the bell towers of churches: roofs, roofs, dripping—some more, some less— stretching away in so many terraces—tiles, tiles, nothing but tiles. But it was only in the evening that she could look out of that window and take a breath of fresh air."

(*In the back wall a little window becomes transparent, but veiled and far away, and pale moonlight can be seen through it.*)

NENÈ (*in the darkness, softly, happily, in the voice of a wondering child, while from far, far away one can hear the faint sound of a distant serenade*): Oh look, the window, a real window . . .

THE COMIC ACTOR (*softly, also from the darkness*): Yes, it was there, but who lit it?

DORINA: Quiet!

(*The prisoner has remained motionless. The mother continues, still as though she is reading:*)

THE CHARACTER ACTRESS: "All the roofs of the town, aslant upon the hill, were like so many little black blocks shimmering below her, in the light drifting up from the lamps in the narrow streets. From the deep silence of nearby alleys she could hear the echo of footsteps, the voice of some woman who was, perhaps, waiting as she was, the barking of a dog, and even more sadly, the ringing of the hour from the bell tower of the nearest church. Why does that clock continue to measure time?

> For whom does it count the hours?
> All is death and vanity."

(*After a pause, five strokes of a bell are heard, veiled, far away. Five o'clock.* RICCO VERRI *appears, gloomy and sullen. He is just getting home. He has a hat on his head; the collar of his overcoat is raised; a scarf is around his neck. He looks at his wife, still motionless in the chair; then he looks suspiciously at the window.*)

VERRI: What are you doing there?

MOMMINA: Nothing, I was waiting for you.

VERRI: Were you at the window?

MOMMINA: No.

VERRI: You are there every night.

MOMMINA: Not tonight.

VERRI (*after throwing his overcoat, his hat, and his scarf on a chair*): Don't you ever get tired of thinking?

MOMMINA: I'm not thinking anything.

VERRI: Are the girls in bed?

MOMMINA: Where do you expect them to be at this hour?

VERRI: I'm simply asking you so as to remind you that they are the only thing you should be thinking about.

MOMMINA: I've been thinking about them all day.

VERRI: And what are you thinking about now?

MOMMINA (*realizing why he is asking so insistently, she first looks at him disdainfully, then, falling back into her attitude of listless immobility, answers him*): About throwing this flabby, useless body of mine into bed.

VERRI: That's not true! I want to know what you're thinking about! What have you been thinking about all this time while you were waiting for me? (*A pause. She does not answer.*) You don't answer? Huh! Of course! You can't tell me! (*another pause*) You confess then, do you?

MOMMINA: What should I confess?

VERRI: That you think about things you can't tell me!

MOMMINA: I told you what I'm thinking about: about going to sleep!

VERRI: To sleep? With eyes like that? With a voice like that . . . ? To dream, you mean!

MOMMINA: I don't dream.

VERRI: It's not true! We all dream! No one can sleep without dreaming!

MOMMINA: I don't dream.

VERRI: That's a lie! It's not possible, I tell you!

MOMMINA: All right, I dream: as you wish.

VERRI: You dream, eh? . . . You dream . . . You dream, and you get your revenge! — You think, and you get your revenge! — What do you dream? Tell me what you dream!

MOMMINA: I don't know.

VERRI: What do you mean, you don't know?

MOMMINA: I don't know. You're the one who says I dream. My body's so heavy, I feel so tired that the moment I get into bed I fall into a dead sleep. I don't know what it means to dream any more. If I do have any dreams, when I wake up, I don't remember them. It's as if I didn't dream at all. Perhaps that's God's way of helping me.

VERRI: God? God helps you?

MOMMINA: Yes, to get through this life of mine. If a dream were to make me think I had another life, then when I opened my eyes this one would seem even more terrible. But you know all this; you understand it. What do you want from me? You want me dead; dead; so that I can't think any more, can't dream any more . . . And yet, and yet, thinking—that depends on the will; but dreaming (if I were to dream)—that would happen without my willing it, while I was asleep: how could you prevent me from doing that?

VERRI (*tormented, trembling now, like a wild beast in a cage*): That's it! That's it! That's it! I lock the doors and windows, I bar them and bolt them, but what's the use, if the betrayal happens here inside the jail itself? Here, in her, inside her, in this dead flesh of hers— alive—alive—the betrayal—if she thinks, if she dreams, if she remembers? She's here right in front of me: she looks at me—can I crack her head open to see what's inside, what she thinks? I ask her: she answers me, "nothing"; and at the same time she's think-ing, she's dreaming, she's remembering, right under my eyes, looking at me, but maybe she's seeing someone else, inside, in her memory. How can I know? How can I see?

MOMMINA: But how can you expect me to have anything inside me when there's nothing left of me? Don't you see me? I hardly exist, there is nothing left! My mind is almost dead. What do you expect me to remember?

VERRI: Don't say that! Don't say that! You know it's worse when you say that!

MOMMINA: Oh well then, I won't say it. I won't say it. Don't worry.

VERRI: Even if I blinded you, what your eyes have seen—your memories, your memo-ries—you have them here in your eyes—they'd stay in your mind; and if I tore your lips—these lips that have kissed—the pleasures, the pleasures, what they've felt and tasted when they kissed, you'd still be able to feel it inside, remembering it, even to the point of dying of it! The joy of it! You can't deny it; if you deny it, you're lying; how can you do anything but weep, terrified by the suffering I share with you, because of the wrongs you've committed, that your mother and your sisters drove you to; you can't deny it, you did it, you did it, this wickedness. You know it, and you can see that I suffer because of it. I suffer almost to the point of madness: not through any fault of mine, but because of that one act of madness I committed when I married you.

MOMMINA: Madness, yes, madness: you knew what you were like! You shouldn't have done it . . .

VERRI: What I was like? What I was like, you say? Knowing what you were like, you should say: the life you'd led with your mother and your sisters!

MOMMINA: Oh, yes, yes, that too! But you knew that I didn't approve of the life we lived in that house —

VERRI: — but you lived it too!

MOMMINA: — I had no choice! I was there —

VERRI: — and it was only after you got to know me: it was only then that you started to disapprove —

MOMMINA: No, before that, too, before that!—in fact you yourself thought I was better than the others—I don't say it for my own sake, to accuse the others and excuse myself: no, I say it for you, so that you'll have pity—not for me, not for me, if you find some kind of satisfaction in not having any, or even in showing other people that you don't have any. Be cruel to me: but at least have pity on yourself by remembering that you thought I was better than the others: that even seeing us living the way we did, you thought that you could love me—

VERRI: — So much so that I married you! — of course I thought you were better! — and what about it? — pity for myself? — when I think that I loved you, that I could love you there, even the way you were living . . . — pity?

MOMMINA: — yes — when you recognized that there was something in me, something that might partly excuse that act of madness you committed when you married me. There — I'm saying it for you!

VERRI: And isn't this worse? Do you think I can erase the life you led before I fell in love with you? The simple fact that I married you because you were better doesn't excuse my madness. Doesn't this make it worse? The better you were, the worse that life of yours seems by comparison. I took you out of that wickedness, but when I took you, I took the whole thing and brought it home, here to this prison, to pay for it along with you, as though I had committed it too. And I feel it swallowing me up—it's always alive, kept alive by what I know about your mother and your sisters!

MOMMINA: I don't know anything about them any more!

NENÈ (*from the darkness, protesting*): The coward! Now he's talking to her about us!

VERRI (*shouting, frightful*): Quiet! You are not here!

SIGNORA IGNAZIA (*coming toward the wall, from the dark*): You animal! You wild beast! There you are in your cage, and you have her between your jaws, tearing her apart!

VERRI (*touches the wall twice with his hand, making it visible each time*): This is a wall! This is a wall! You are not here!

TOTINA (*also coming toward the wall, with the others, aggressively*): And you take advantage of it, do you, you coward, to tell her shameful things about us?

DORINA: We were starving, Mommina!

NENÈ: We had touched bottom!

VERRI: And how did you get back on your feet?

SIGNORA IGNAZIA: You scoundrel! You dare throw it in our faces, while you're driving her to despair!

NENÈ: We're having a good life!

VERRI: You sold yourselves! You're dishonored!

TOTINA: You've preserved her honor, but how are you making her pay for it?

DORINA: Mother is fine now, Mommina! You should see how well she is! How well she dresses! What a beautiful beaver coat she has!

SIGNORA IGNAZIA: It's Totina's doing, you know! She's become a great singer!

DORINA: Totina La Croce!

NENÈ: All the theaters want her!

SIGNORA IGNAZIA: Feasts! Triumphs!

VERRI: And dishonor!

NENÈ: Well, if what you're doing to your wife is honorable, then hurrah for dishonor!

MOMMINA (*immediately, with a burst of affection and compassion for her husband, who has broken down, clutching his head*): No, no! I'm not saying this! I'm not saying this: I don't regret anything . . .

VERRI: They want me condemned to . . .

MOMMINA: No, no, I can understand: you must cry out your suffering: shout it out, all of it, rid yourself of it!

VERRI: They keep it burning! If you only knew how scandalously they behave—even now! Everybody in town talks about it—you can imagine my face . . . Their success has set them free, made them completely shameless . . .

MOMMINA: Even Dorina?

VERRI: Everyone, even Dorina; but especially Nenè. She is a whore — (**MOMMINA** *covers her face.*) — Yes, yes—for anyone who comes along!

MOMMINA: And Totina has started to sing?

VERRI: Yes, in the theater—the opera houses of the small towns, where the scandal gets worse and worse, what with that mother, those sisters —

MOMMINA: Does she take them with her?

VERRI: Yes, all of them—it's just one long party! What's the matter? Does this excite you?

MOMMINA: No . . . I'm just finding this out . . . I didn't know anything about it . . .

VERRI: And you feel all upset? The theater, eh? And the time when you used to sing too? . . . With your beautiful voice! You had the best voice, didn't you! Imagine that other life! To sing, in a big theater . . . Singing was your great passion! . . . The glittering lights, the glamour, the thrill . . .

MOMMINA: No, no . . .

VERRI: Don't say no! You're thinking about it!

MOMMINA: I tell you, no!

VERRI: What do you mean, no? If you were still with them . . . away from here . . . you'd have a very different life from this one.

MOMMINA: But you're the one who makes me think about it! How do you expect me to think about it any more, now, in this state?

VERRI: Are you having an attack?

MOMMINA: My heart is in my throat . . .

VERRI: No wonder! There it is, that gasping for breath . . .

MOMMINA: You want me to die!

VERRI: Me? It's your sisters, what you once were, your past, pulsing inside you and making your heart jump into your throat!

MOMMINA (*panting, her hands on her chest*): Please . . . I beg you . . . I can't breathe . . .

VERRI: But can you see it's true, it's true what I'm telling you?

MOMMINA: Have pity . . .

VERRI: What you once were—the very thoughts, the very feelings—did you think they'd been erased in you, that they were dead? It's not true! The slightest hint, and there they are, still there, alive, the very same!

MOMMINA: It's you who's calling them back . . .

VERRI: No, the slightest hint recalls them, because they're always alive—you don't know it, but they're always alive in you—just below your consciousness! It's always alive, within you, all the life you've lived! All it needs is the tiniest thing— a word, a sound— the smallest sensation—Listen: for me it's the smell of sage, and I see myself in the country, in August, a boy of eight, behind the servant's house, in the shade of a big olive tree, frightened by a big blue hornet, dark blue, buzzing greedily in the white cup of a flower. I see that ravished flower, trembling on its stalk, under the savage, gluttonous assault of the beast—that terrifying beast! And I still feel the fear—here, in the pit of my stomach! Think of what you must feel—that exciting life you led, the things that happened between you girls and all those young men about the house, locked up alone in one room or another . . . — Don't deny it! — I saw — things . . . Nenè, she was with Sarelli . . . — They thought they were alone, they'd left the door ajar—I could see them—Nenè pretended to run away from him toward the other door at the back— there were curtains, green—she went out, but came right back in between the curtains—she had opened her blouse — it was pink . . . silk . . . and she uncovered a breast . . . she offered it to him with a gesture of her hand, but then at the same moment she covered it up again . . . I saw her. What a lovely breast! Small, small enough to hold in your hand! You were free to do anything, you and Pomàrici, before I came . . . — Yes, I found out! — But who knows how many others before Pomàrici! For years you lived like that, with your house open to anybody . . . (*He approaches her, trembling, demented.*) You . . . there were certain things . . . certain things . . . that first time, with me . . . If you'd really been ignorant of them, as you said you were . . . You'd not have been able to do them . . .

MOMMINA: No, no, I swear, never, never until you, never!

VERRI: But fondling, embracing, that Pomàrici, yes — your arms, your arms, how did he squeeze them? Like this? Like this?

MOMMINA: Oh! You're hurting me!

VERRI: But he gave you pleasure, didn't he? And your waist, how did he hold your waist? Like this? Like this?

MOMMINA: Please, let me go! I'm dying!

VERRI (*grabbing her by the neck with one hand, furious*): And your mouth, your mouth . . . how did he kiss your mouth? Like this? . . . Like this? . . . Like this?

(*And he kisses her, bites her, tears her hair, laughs scornfully as though he has gone mad; while* **MOMMINA**, *trying to free herself, cries desperately:*)

MOMMINA: Help! Help!

(*The* **TWO FRIGHTENED LITTLE GIRLS**, *in their nightgowns, run in and clasp their mother, while* **VERRI** *runs away, taking only his hat from the chair, and shouting:*)

VERRI: I'm going mad! I'm going mad! I'm going mad!

MOMMINA (*covering herself, using the two girls as shields*): Get out! Get out! Go away, you monster! Go away! Leave me alone with my babies!

(*Exhausted, she drops down into the chair: the two little girls are beside her, and she embraces them tightly, one on each side.*)

Oh my dear, dear children, the things you have to see! Locked in here with me, with your little waxen faces and your big eyes wide with fear! He's gone, he's gone away. Don't tremble. Stay here with me a little . . . You're not cold, are you? . . . The window is closed. It's already late. You're always hanging there at the window, like two little paupers begging for a glimpse of the world . . . You count the white sails of the fishing boats in the sea, and the little white villas in the countryside, but you have never been there! And you want me to tell you what the sea and the countryside are like. Oh, children, my dear children, what a fate you've had! Worse than mine! But at least you don't know it! Your mama has such a pain, here in the chest. My heart is pounding: it's galloping in my chest, like a runaway horse. Here, here, give me your hands. Listen, listen . . . — I pray God doesn't make him pay for this, for your sake, my darlings! But he'll torture you too, because he can't help himself; it's his nature. He does the same thing to himself, he tortures himself too! But you are innocent . . . you are innocent . . .

(*She presses the little girls' heads to her cheeks and stays that way for a moment. As though they were conjured up from the night, her mother and sisters, gorgeously dressed, approach the wall out of the darkness; they make a vividly colored picture, suitably lit from above.*)

SIGNORA IGNAZIA (*calling, softly*): Mommina . . . Mommina . . .

MOMMINA: Who's that?

DORINA: It's us, Mommina!

NENÈ: We're here! All of us!

MOMMINA: Here? Where?

TOTINA: Here in town. I came to sing here!

MOMMINA: Totina? You? To sing here?

NENÈ: Yes, here: at the theater!

MOMMINA: Oh God! Here? When? When?

NENÈ: Tonight. Tonight!

SIGNORA IGNAZIA: My dear girls, let me say something too! Listen, Mommina . . . look . . . — what did I want to say? Oh, yes . . . look, do you want proof? Your husband has left his overcoat over there on the chair.

MOMMINA (*turning to look*): Yes, I see.

SIGNORA IGNAZIA: Look inside one of the pockets and see what you find! (*aside, to the girls:*) (We must help her set the scene now; we're getting to the end!)

MOMMINA (*getting up and going to look feverishly in the pockets of the overcoat*): What? What?

NENÈ (*aside, to the* CHARACTER ACTRESS): . . . (Are you going to answer?)

THE CHARACTER ACTRESS (*aside*): (No, you do . . . go ahead!)

NENÈ (*aloud, to* MOMMINA): The theater playbill . . . one of those little yellow notices— you know—in small towns like this they distribute them in the cafés . . .

SIGNORA IGNAZIA: You'll find Totina's name, printed in big letters . . . the name of the prima donna!

(*They disappear.*)

MOMMINA (*finding it*): Here it is! Here it is . . . (*She opens it and reads:*) "IL TROVATORE . . . IL TROVATORE . . . *Leonora (soprano)*, Totina La Croce!" . . . Tonight . . . — Your aunt, your aunt, my dear little girls, your aunt singing . . . and your grandmother and your other aunties . . . they're here! You don't know them, you've never seen them . . . neither have I, for so many years . . . They're here!

(thinking about her husband's fits of rage:) (Ah, that's why . . . — They're here, in town — Totina singing at the theater, here . . .) So there's a theater here too? . . . I didn't know that . . . Aunt Totina . . . then it's true! Perhaps after some training, her voice . . . Well, if she can sing in the theater . . . — But you don't even know what a theater is, my poor little girls . . . The theater, the theater, I'll tell you what it's like . . . Aunt Totina is singing there tonight . . . How beautiful she'll look, dressed as *Leonora* . . .
(She tries to sing:)

> *"Tacea la notte placida*
> *e bella in ciel sereno*
> *la luna il viso argenteo*
> *mostrava lieto e pieno . . ."*[27]

You see? I can sing too. Yes, yes, I can sing too, I can sing too! I used to sing all the time! I know *Il Trovatore* by heart, all of it; I'll sing it for you! I'll do the whole thing for you, the theater and all! You've never seen it, my poor little darlings, locked up here with me! Sit down side by side in your little chairs, right in front of me! I'm going to do a play for you! But first I'll tell you what it's like:

(She sits before her astonished girls; she is trembling, and as she goes on she gets more and more excited, until eventually her heart will fail her and she will fall dead with a crash:)

A hall, a big, big hall, with many tiers of boxes all the way round, five, six tiers, filled with beautiful, elegant ladies, with feathers, and jewels, and fans, and flowers; and the gentlemen in formal dress with little pearls in their shirtfronts for buttons, and white ties; and many, many people down below, in the red seats of the stalls; and in the pit, a sea of heads; and the lights, lights everywhere; a chandelier in the middle that looks as if it's hanging from the blue sky, and it seems to be all diamonds; a dazzling light, it makes your head spin—you can't imagine it; and a whispering, a movement; the ladies speak to their escorts, they greet each other from one box to the other; some of them sit down in the stalls, some look around with their opera glasses—remember the ones we looked at the countryside with—they're made of mother-of-pearl—your mother used to bring them to the theater with her, and she looked through them, and . . . — Suddenly the lights go off; the only ones that stay on are the green lamps on the music-stands of the orchestra, down at the front of the stalls, below the curtain. The musicians are already there—oh so many of them!—and they're tuning their instruments. The curtain is just like ours, but very big and heavy, all red velvet with golden trim: it's so

---

27.   *"The peaceful night lay silent*
        And lovely in the quiet sky;
     The silver moon showed its joyous face. . ."
             (Il Trovatore, [I:2]).

beautiful! When it opens (after the maestro has come in to lead the musicians with his baton) the opera begins. And there on the stage there's a forest, or a square, or a royal palace; and Aunt Totina comes in and sings with the others while the orchestra plays. That's what the theater is like. Back then, before, I was the one with the prettiest voice; it wasn't aunt Totina, it was me, a much better voice; everybody used to say that I should have gone to sing in the theater, I, your mother. Instead it was Aunt Totina who went . . . Ah, well! She's had the courage . . . — The curtain opens—listen—they pull it from both sides—it opens and there on the stage you can see an entrance hall, the entrance hall of a big palace, soldiers in armor strolling about in the background, and lots of cavaliers, and a certain Ferrando, all waiting for their leader, Conte di Luna. They're all dressed in old-fashioned clothes, with velvet capes, and feathered hats, and swords, and leggings. It's nighttime; they're tired of waiting for the Count. He's in love with Leonora, a great lady of the Spanish court, and he's waiting under her balcony in the gardens of the royal palace. He's jealous, because he knows that every night a troubadour (that's a man who sings, but who's a warrior as well) comes and sings this song to her:

(She sings:)

> "*Deserto sulla terra . . .*"

(She stops for a moment to say, almost to herself:)

Oh God, my heart . . .

(And immediately begins to sing again, but with difficulty now, fighting against her shortness of breath, which attacks her partly as a result of the emotions she feels when she hears herself sing:)

> "*Col rio destino in guerra,*
> *È sola speme un cor* (Repeated three times.)
> —*un cor—al Trovator . . .*"[28]

I can't sing any more . . . I . . . I can't breathe . . . my heart . . . my heart stops my breath . . . It's so many years since I've sung . . . — But perhaps little by little my breath, my voice will come back . . . — Now I should tell you that this troubadour is the brother of Conte di Luna—yes—but the Count doesn't know it, and the troubadour doesn't know it either, because he was stolen by a gypsy when he was a child. It's a terrible story — listen! In the second act it's narrated by the gypsy herself, whose name is Azucena. Yes, that was my part, Azucena, it was mine. This Azucena stole the child to avenge her mother, who had been burned alive by the father of Conte di Luna.

28.　　"*Alone upon the earth,*
　　At war with his wicked destiny,
　The only hope for the troubadour is love . . ."
　　　(*Il Trovatore,* [II:2])

Gypsies are vagabonds who read people's fortunes—you can still see them—they say that they really steal children, so much so that every mother is very careful. But as I said, this Azucena steals the son of the Count to avenge her mother. She wants to give him the same death as her innocent mother had suffered. She lights the fire, but in the fury of her vengeance she mistakes her own son for the son of the Count, and burns her own son—do you understand? — her own son! . . .

> "Il figlio mio . . . Il figlio mio."[29]

I can't. I can't sing it for you . . . You don't know what it means to me tonight . . . My dear little girls . . . It was *Il Trovatore,* this aria of the gypsy—one night while I was singing it—everyone was there— (*She sings through her tears:*)

> "Chi del gitano la vita abbella?
> La zingarella!"[30]

My father . . . that was the night my father . . . your grandpa . . . he was brought home all covered with blood . . . and he had a sort of gypsy with him . . . and that was the night, my darlings, that my destiny was fulfilled . . . my destiny . . . was fulfilled . . . (*She gets up, desperate, and sings in full voice:*)

> "Ah! che la morte ognora
> è tarda nel venir
> a chi desia
> a chi desia morir!
> Addio,
> addio, Leonora, addio . . ."[31]

(*Suddenly she falls dead. The two little girls, more bewildered than ever, do not have the least suspicion. They think it is the performance their mother is putting on for them, and they remain there, motionless in their little chairs, waiting.*

The silence in that stillness becomes the silence of death. Finally, in the darkness, from upstage left come the anxious voices of RICCO VERRI, SIGNORA IGNAZIA, TOTINA, DORINA, *and* NENÈ.)

VERRI: She was singing: did you hear? It was her voice . . .

SIGNORA IGNAZIA: Yes, like a bird in a cage!

TOTINA: Mommina! Mommina!

DORINA: Here we are! We're here with him! He gave in . . .

------

29. "*My son, my son,*" (*Il Trovatore,* [II:2]).
30. See note 23.
31.   "*Ah, death is always slow in coming*
         To one who wishes to die!
      Farewell, Leonora!" (*Il Trovatore,* [IV:1]).

NENÈ: With Totina's triumph . . . You should have heard it! . . . The town in del . . .

(*She wants to say "in delirium," but she stops short, terrified with all the others at the sight of the lifeless body there on the floor, and of the two little girls, still waiting, motionless.*)

VERRI: What is it?

SIGNORA IGNAZIA: Is she dead?

DORINA: She was performing for the girls!

TOTINA: Mommina!

NENÈ: Mommina!

(*Tableau: From the entrance to the auditorium* **DOCTOR HINKFUSS** *comes running down the aisle to the stage.*)

DOCTOR HINKFUSS (*enthusiastically*): Fantastic! A fantastic scene! You've done just what I told you to! This wasn't in the story!

THE CHARACTER ACTRESS: Here he is again!

THE COMIC ACTOR (*coming from the left*): But he was always here, hiding up there with the electricians, directing all the lighting effects!

NENÈ: Ah, that's why they were so beautiful . . .

TOTINA: I suspected it when we came on stage as a group . . . (*She points to the other side, to the right, behind the wall.*) . . . what a lovely effect it must have been from the house!

DORINA (*indicating the* **COMIC ACTOR**): I thought it was a lot better than he could have done.

THE CHARACTER ACTRESS (*indicating the* **LEADING ACTRESS** *still lying on the floor*): But why doesn't Miss __ get up? Why is she still lying there . . .

THE COMIC ACTOR: Oh! I hope she's not really dead!

(*Everybody crowds solicitously around the* **LEADING ACTRESS**.)

THE LEADING ACTOR (*calling her and shaking her*): Miss __! Miss __!

THE CHARACTER ACTRESS: Is she really feeling ill?

NENÈ: Oh, my God, she's fainted! Let's lift her up!

THE LEADING ACTRESS (*half raising herself*): No . . . thank you. It really was my heart, though . . . Just let me, please, let me get my breath . . .

THE COMIC ACTOR: I'm not surprised. If he wants us to live . . . look what happens! But that isn't what we're here for, you know! We're here to perform written parts, as we've memorized them. You can't expect one of us to drop dead here every night!

THE LEADING ACTOR: We have to have an author!

DOCTOR HINKFUSS: No, not an author, no! The written parts, maybe, yes, if you must, so that they can come to life for a moment through us, but (*turning to the audience*) without any more of this evening's irregularities, for which the audience may wish to forgive us.

(*Bows.*)

CURTAIN

Introduction

PAOLA QUARENGHI

Eduardo De Filippo, born in Naples on May 24, 1900, is often referred to quite simply as Eduardo even today. He had a wealth of talent that has been practically unsurpassed in twentieth-century Italy. Actor, playwright, director, company manager, and owner of a theater (as well as writer, poet, man of the theater and film), he combined in one person roles that have usually been spread among many in the theater of our time.

He was the second of three illegitimate children (Titina, 1898 and Peppino, 1903) born from the union between Luisa De Filippo and Eduardo Scarpetta, the famous Neapolitan actor and playwright. Eduardo De Filippo made his stage debut with his father's company when he was six years old and, when he was twelve, joined the company of his brother, Vincenzo Scarpetta, where he remained until 1930. He wrote his first works for this troupe: *Farmacia di turno* (Pharmacy on call, 1920), *Uomo e galantuomo* (Man and gentleman, 1922) and *Ditegli sempre di sì* (Always tell him yes, 1927). During the same period he also worked with other traditional theater companies and in revues. One of his first big successes was *Sik-Sik, l'artefice magico* (*Sik-Sik, the Masterful Magician*, 1930), a sketch written for a revue.

In 1931 Eduardo and his two siblings, Titina and Peppino, formed the company Il Teatro Umoristico I De Filippo. Their success at Naple's Kursaal cinema-theater turned a week's engagement into a stay of many months and opened doors for them to major Italian theaters. At the beginning the company's repertory consisted almost

ELEVEN

EDUARDO DE FILIPPO

exclusively of sketches and one-acts and then two- and three-act plays were added, among them: *Chi è cchiù felice 'e me?* (Who is happier than me?, 1929) *Natale in casa Cupiello* (*The Nativity Scene*, 1931–34), *Gennareniello* (Little Gennaro, 1932), *Uno coi capelli bianchi* (A man with white hair, 1935), *Non ti pago* (I won't pay you, 1940), *Io, l'erede* (I, the heir, 1942). They also collaborated with other writers, above all with Pirandello, whose works the De Filippos would stage—among them *Liolà* (*Liolà*) and *Il berretto a sonagli* (*Cap and Bells*)—and with whom Eduardo would write the play *L'abito nuovo* (The new suit).

The De Filippo company ran successfully until 1944, when a serious falling-out between Eduardo and Peppino led to the company's dissolution; from then on, the two brothers followed separate artistic paths. Eduardo created the Teatro di Eduardo in which Titina took part. This new company debuted at the San Carlo theater in Naples in 1945 with *Napoli milionaria!* (*Napoli Millionaria!*), which marked a change of course in Eduardo's repertory. Many other plays would follow and have enormous success in Italy and abroad, among them *Questi fantasmi!* (*Oh, These Ghosts!*, 1946), *Filumena Marturano* (1946), *Le voci di dentro* (*Inner Voices*, 1948), *Sabato, domenica e lunedì* (*Saturday, Sunday, Monday*, 1959), *Il sindaco del Rione Sanità* (*The Local Authority*, 1960), *Il contratto* (The contract, 1967), ending with his last comedy, *Gli esami non finiscono mai* (Examinations never end, 1973). Among his other important memorable productions are those for La Scarpettiana, a permanent company he founded in Naples at the San Ferdinando theater (which he owned), those for the Piccolo Teatro in Milan, those for the company of his son, Luca, who inherited Eduardo's repertory when he retired from the stage in 1980–81, and numerous operatic works in Italy and abroad.

In addition to his multiple theatrical activities, Eduardo had many film engagements (as actor, director, and writer) beginning in 1932, and worked extensively in television, for which he directed a great many of his plays.

In 1972 he received the Feltrinelli Prize for theater from the Accademia dei Lincei, the most prestigious cultural institution in Italy, and the degree in letters *honoris causa* from Birmingham in 1977 and Rome in 1980. In his last years, he dedicated himself, first in Florence, then at the University of Rome, to teaching playwriting.

In 1981 he was nominated senator for life by President Pertini and began his work with imprisoned juveniles. Eduardo De Filippo died in Rome on October 31, 1984. His last work, published and taperecorded a few weeks before his death, was a translation of Shakespeare's *The Tempest* into old Neapolitan.

THE NATIVITY SCENE: THE PLAY'S EVOLUTION

The three-act version of *The Nativity Scene* had a singular genesis. The author called it "triplets with an incubation period of four years."[1] It began as a one-act play on the stage of the Kursaal, an elegant cinema-theater in Naples, when the Teatro Umoristico company made its debut on a Christmas evening in 1931. Intended for a film-going audience who were treated to sketches or variety acts between each film projection, the play was comic in nature and made few scenic demands.

The plot of this one-act (which became the second act of the three-act version) involves a Neapolitan family who gather to share the Christmas meal. But the feast is irremediably spoilt by the head of the family, Luca Cupiello, who invites a friend of his son's to eat with them, unaware that he is also the lover of his unhappily married daughter. A painfully funny dramatic tension was created by the contrast between characters who knew the truth (the mother Concetta, the daughter Ninuccia, her lover, and her husband) and those who did not (Luca, above all). The audience waited expectantly for the moment when the latter would have to open their eyes to the truth. The curtain fell, providentially, just as the action came to a head.

The action, by itself very thin in this first version, was stuffed with a whole series of farcical situations not directly linked to the central theme, such as the leitmotif of Tommasino quarreling with his uncle, Pasqualino, and the gags over Tommasino's Christmas letter to his mother and the escaped eels—both gags were added to the first script with the note "improvisation." Thus, characters such as Tommasino and Pasqualino, who had little to do with the main event, became theatrically very prominent. In the first version these roles were assigned to Peppino De Filippo and Agostino Salvietti, the most important actors in the company after Eduardo, who played the protagonist.

While this little one-act was already much more than a scenario, it was not yet a proper text. The actors embellished it with speeches and situations. The author-director then reworked the material, set it during the course of rehearsals and performances, and wrote it into succeeding versions of the script.

As a consequence of their unexpected success at the Kursaal, the Teatro Umoristico signed a contract with Naples' fashionable Sannazaro theater for the 1932–33 season and Eduardo added one more act to the play, the first act. This additional act served as a prologue and also gave the spectator a more detailed view of domestic life in the Cupiello family, as well as time to see how much damage was inflicted by an overly indulgent mother and an inattentive and inept father. This new script was really a montage of the new first act typescript and the old one-act handwritten script, on which only a few changes were marked in pencil. Neither the one-act nor the new script have many stage directions. Much of the action is summarily indicated with the initials "c.a.c.," meaning *come a concerto* or "as rehearsed." The subsequent addition of the notation *"soggetto"* or "improvisation" at various points in the script shows that it was Eduardo's practice to derive the final form of a script from working with the actors on stage.

Even with the insertion of the first act, the play retained its eminently comic and at times farcical tone in, for example Tommasino's refrain of "I don't like the crib!" and the scene in which Tommasino confesses to having sold Pasqualino's shoes, overcoat, and suspenders when the latter was sick in bed. This two-act version of *The Nativity Scene* was presented in Rome during the 1933–34 season. A journalist described the play as "a series of very funny scenes, where various Neapolitan types get upset, scream, swoon, or break plates."[2] None of the Roman critics I have been able to trace saw any value in the text. One reviewer called it "an insubstantial excuse to display the expert skill of two actors."[3]

On April 9, 1934, *The Nativity Scene* was staged in Milan at the Olimpia theater. Eduardo wrote a third act for the occasion. The tone of it was bitter in contrast to the first two acts and the full weight of the action shifted to Luca Cupiello. This defective paterfamilias, faced with the revelation of his own failure and that of his family (a revelation the spectators do not see but which is related in the third act), falls prey to an illness from which he will never recover.

Renato Simoni, an outstanding critic of the day, was possibly the first to give the text some attention. "Its traditional roots," he wrote,[4] "are obvious, especially in Nennillo [Tommasino]. The character is still enveloped in the shell of a fixed type and is trying to fight free, but the mixture in him of the old and the new, of the clumsily conventional and foolishly realistic, is very interesting." Of Luca he wrote that he possessed a kind of "gaiety [. . .] which swings between the farcical and the grotesque, but is grounded in excellent comic insights." He observed, however, that the play "in the first part, is broken into too many details," and that the transition from a farcical tone to the third act's "painfully realistic gestures, phrases, and performances" was too audacious.

The play was not presented in three acts again until the 1936–37 season, although the company did perform it in the two-act and one-act versions during those two years. Eduardo may have given a clue as to why this was so in a manuscript dating back to the summer of 1936, "Primo . . . secondo. (Aspetto il segnale)" (One . . . two. [I'm waiting for the go]). Here he indicates why he had never been able to produce the three-act version of the play in Naples. "I haven't ever had the courage to present the last [version]," he wrote, "because it's painful, full of bitterness, and particularly wrenching for me because I knew that family. They weren't called Cupiello, but I knew them. . . ."[5]

Despite his misgivings, it was in Naples, at the Mercadante theater, on December 20, 1936, that Eduardo presented a newly revised three-act version of *The Nativity Scene*. The reviews in the Neapolitan press indicate that the tone of the work had completely changed from the time the two acts were presented in Rome three years earlier, and that it had also changed somewhat from the three-act version seen in Milan in 1934. With the Neapolitan production of the play in view, Eduardo had reworked the script, attempting to soften the lines between its two opposing tendencies—the farcical and the painfully realistic. While he made the latter more terse by eliminating mawkish and quasi-melodramatic speeches, he brought down the comic level by cutting some speeches or situations that were too farcical, such as those that played up the illicit dealings of Tommasino and Pasqualino.

It was the 1936 production at the Mercadante that ratified the three-act form of the play. From then on, until the break-up of the Teatro Umoristico in 1944, it would be presented every season in this form, and as such, it was published in *Il Dramma* in 1943.[6] This is not to say that there were no further changes. If we compare the play as it appeared in the first edition of *Il teatro di Eduardo: Cantata dei giorni pari*[7] with the revised edition of the same collection dated 1979, we can find a number of differences between them as well as between them and the 1943 text published in *Il Dramma*. The number of characters also changed substantially. The neighbors who come to visit Luca, for example, change from being one (only Carmela) in the *Il Dramma* text, to thirteen in the 1959 radio version, and seven in the last Einaudi revised edition.

For Eduardo the play never ceased to be in flux. Perhaps this was the secret to its success over so many years. As Ennio Flaiano wrote,[8] by 1941 the play was a classic of the dialect theater. Audiences knew the text and delighted in each production's "intimate minutiae." This enjoyment of "minutiae" that Flaiano talked about suggests that by 1941 *The Nativity Scene* had traveled far from the smashing farce it must have been at first and had become a "copy" of life. There is no longer any sense of clamorous fighting between uncle and nephew, or the pyrotechnics of their interpreters. The emphasis is on the daily routine of Luca, the man of habit, and the domestic rhythms and situations that, far from being theatrically archaic, could be those of every spectator in the audience.

In October 1944, after the painful break between Eduardo and Peppino, *The Nativity Scene* was shelved for twelve years; for Eduardo and for the public, it may have been too searing a reminder of the magical and harmonious partnership that was now gone forever.[9]

When it was revived by the Teatro di Eduardo company in the 1956–57 season—from that time on it would figure in the company's repertory several times until 1977—it could be said that the play had reached full maturity. Now the center definitely belonged to Luca, the character, but also to Eduardo, the actor. The character was like an old suit of clothes to him, as natural and comfortable as his own skin.

The action, even more than the dialogue, had been enriched over time by a hundred barely perceptible nuances that, taken all together, heightened the sense of truth. In the course of time performances were filled with special details: symbolic objects, silences, repetitions, gestures, stage business such as the action of Luca at the beginning of the first act when he wakes up and unwraps the scarves and shawls that protect his head from the night cold. There was no trace of this business in the early versions, but since having appeared, it grew more and more complicated, developing from one wool shawl to a kind of multilayered shroud. The actor unwrapped his head very, very slowly delighting the public by mischievously delaying the moment when he would effectively make his stage entrance by unwinding the last shawl.

The text, in the last revised Einaudi edition, is the account, the written record, the echo of the stage production. The stage directions, almost nonexistent in the early versions, are lengthy, and describe actions, objects, behavior, with almost dogged care. The Cupiello family and the text of *Nativity Scene* have gone through all sorts of experiences. Some have had a lasting effect, others have just grazed the surface. Luca's death caused a great deal of controversy. Critics disagreed about whether it was useless, efficacious, poetic, cruel, moving, necessary, or mistaken. Consequently Luca came close to living on; the doctor's speeches once held out hope that he would survive. Over the years Tommasino has gone through youthful protests and has been transformed from a caricature into a realistic young man, and Ninuccia and Concetta have been interpreted through the feminist experience.

And then there are the performers who have taken turns in giving life to the characters in this play. They all have left behind them in the text, if not a word, then a gesture, a thought, a character trait, which the author, a perceptive observer, has recorded. The text Eduardo has left us—and which has been rendered the definitive version only by the fact of his death—is a condensation and refinement of many previous versions produced during the almost half century of life the play and its author-interpreter spent together in front of generations of spectators. Certainly, therefore, the text of *The Nativity Scene* is like a house inhabited by many ghosts.

P. Q.

Trans. J. H.

Notes

1. Eduardo De Filippo, "Primo . . . secondo (Aspetto il segnale)," (One . . . two [I'm waiting for the go]), *Il Dramma* 240 (1936); also reprinted in Isabella Q. De Filippo, ed., *Eduardo: Polemiche, pensieri, pagine inedite* (Controversies, thoughts, unpublished writings) (Milan: Bompiani, 1985), p. 121.

2. Hermes, review of the play, *La Scena Italiana*, no. 15, (November 10, 1933).

3. Vice, review of the play, *La Tribuna*, November 5, 1933.

4. Renato Simoni, review of the play, *Corriere della sera* April 10, 1934.

5. Cited in Isabella Q. De Filippo, ed., *Eduardo: Polemiche*, p. 125. It is not inconceivable that he was referring to the De Filippo family of his maternal grandparents, Luca and Concetta to be exact, who had three girls, one of them named Ninuccia.

6. *Il Dramma* 397–98 (March 1–15, 1943).

7. Eduardo subdivided his dramatic works into two collections: *Cantata dei giorni pari* (Turin: Einaudi, 1959, with new and revised editions in 1962, 1971, 1979), which comprises the plays up to 1942, and *Cantata dei giorni dispari* (Turin: Einaudi, three volumes, 1951, 1958, 1966 respectively, with new and revised editions in 1971 and 1979), which contains the texts written from 1945 on.

8. Ennio Flaiano, "Le minuzie," *Oggi*, May 17, 1941.

9. The alternation of comic and tragic elements in the play, its double-sidedness, which is one of its merits, can be read as a happy marriage between traditional farce and modern realism; it can also be seen as the contrast or even the collision between two actors' temperaments: Eduardo's sad realism and Peppino's comically artless and almost Pulcinellesque character.

■

THE NATIVITY
SCENE

(*Natale in casa Cupiello,* 1931)

Translated from the Neapolitan-Italian by
Anthony Molino, with Paul N. Feinberg

■

Characters

LUCA CUPIELLO
CONCETTA, his wife
TOMMASINO, their son
NINUCCIA, their daughter
NICOLA, Ninuccia's husband
PASQUALE, Luca's brother
RAFFAELE, the doorman
VITTORIO ELIA
THE DOCTOR
THE NEIGHBORS:
CARMELA
OLGA PASTORELLI
LUIGI PASTORELLI
ALBERTO
ARMIDA ROMANEILLO
RITA
MARIA

ACT 1: Naples, Dec. 23, 9 A.M. The Cupiello bedroom.
ACT 2: Christmas Eve. The Cupiello dining room.
ACT 3: Three days later. Again the Cupiello bedroom.

ACT 1

Naples. The Cupiello household. A double bed and a single bed. Hall door up right, a balcony on left. On a table in front of the balcony there is a Nativity scene in construction, together with all the necessary construction materials: papier-mâché, brushes, strips of cork, a can of glue. Between the balcony and the single bed there is a small folding screen with a washstand and basin in front of it. Next to the screen is a white enamel bucket; a towel is hanging on the screen. On right, next to the wall, is a dresser with holy pictures and figurines, with unlit candles and small oil lamps in front of them.

Nine a.m., December 23d. **LUCA** *is sleeping in the double bed. His wife's side of the bed is rumpled as if she had just gotten up. Son* **TOMMASINO** *is sleeping in the single bed.*

CONCETTA (*Enters right, carefully carrying a steaming cup of coffee in one hand, in the other a pitcher of water. She is wearing a white cotton nightgown with a woolen shawl around her shoulders. Her slippers are an old pair of her husband's shoes. Half-asleep she sets the coffee on the dresser, then sets the pitcher next to the washstand. She opens the balcony shutters then returns to the dresser, where she takes the cup and places it on the night table. In a monotone voice, she then tries to wake up her husband*): Luca, Luca . . . it's nine o'clock. (*A short pause then she tries again.*) Luca, wake up. (**LUCA** *grunts and turns over; she continues.*) Luca . . . it's nine o'clock!

LUCA (*starts, wakes*): Uhh . . . (*mumbles*) nine o'clock . . .

CONCETTA: Drink your coffee. (**LUCA**, *lazy and sleepy, gestures as if to take the cup only to fall back asleep. Undaunted,* **CONCETTA** *intensifies her lament while she continues to dress in front of the chest.*) Luca, get up . . . Will you please! It's nine o'clock!

LUCA: (*sitting in the middle of the bed, he unwraps two small woolen shawls and a scarf from around his head; then, looking at his wife out of the corner of his eye, he grumbles*): Huh? Nine o'clock!? Already? A man barely falls asleep and already the world's pestering him to wake up . . . Is it cold outside?

CONCETTA: Cold? It's freezing.

LUCA: Last night, too. I couldn't sleep. Two woolen undershirts, a scarf, my shawl, I

A Note by the Translator, Anthony Molino

This translation is derived primarily from the version of *Natale in casa Cupiello* that appears in Einaudi's first edition of *Cantata dei giorni pari* (1959). In light of the play's history as a work forever-in-process (as described by Paola Quarenghi in the introductory comments to this play), I have also availed myself of the 1973 version appearing in volume 1 of Einaudi's *I capolavori di Eduardo* (Eduardo's masterpieces). The main differences between these two texts involve the quicker pace and more effective use of slapstick elements in the later version, especially in act 1 where Luca's character is also more fully developed. I have integrated some of Eduardo's later revisions in an attempt to lend greater economy to the comical slant of the earlier version. It is this result, in fact, that Eduardo himself achieved in his staging of the play for television in the mid-1970s.

even had stockings on. You remember those slipper socks you bought? The ones that were "a real bargain, one hundred per cent wool." Do you remember? (**CONCETTA** *continues to dress, ignoring her husband's insinuations.* **LUCA** *picks up his glasses from the night table and starts to clean them meticulously.*) Do you Concetta? Concetta? (*She doesn't answer.*) Concetta, are you there?

CONCETTA (*annoyed*):   Here, Luca, I'm here.

LUCA: Well answer then, show some life.

CONCETTA: Talk, talk, I hear you.

LUCA: Those slipper socks you bought, the ones you said were "pure wool." Concetta, that wasn't wool. Whatever wool was in those socks they pulled over your eyes. My feet are frozen. See, pure wool shrinks when you wash it. These things stretch. They're more like longjohns! . . . Concetta, where's my coffee?

CONCETTA: It's on the night table.

LUCA: Oh . . . (*He puts on his glasses, takes the cup, yawns.*) Concetta, is it cold out?

CONCETTA: Yes Luca, (*impatiently*) it *is* cold out! Now that's enough!

LUCA (*rubbing his hands*):   Ahh, a Christmas God made to order. The spirit's everywhere! (*He sips the coffee and immediately spits it out.*) What is this slush?!

CONCETTA (*resentfully*):   Excuse me, but I guess you expected a cappuccino straight from the café. (*referring to the coffee*) OK, so it's watery, but it's still coffee.

LUCA: Coffee!? When was there ever any coffee in this cup?!

CONCETTA (*rummaging through her drawer: pulls out hairpins, a comb, a spool of white thread*): Aren't you funny this morning? Instead of being grateful . . .

LUCA (*sarcastically*):   Grateful? For what? Coffee that's got more bedbugs than coffee grains?!

CONCETTA (*angry*):   So don't drink it . . . and go crucify someone else.

LUCA: You're just such a penny-pincher. Trying to save on coffee all the time . . . (*sets the cup on the night table*) Concetta, is it cold out?

CONCETTA (*extremely annoyed*):   Yes, Luca it's cold, very cold! Are you deaf?

LUCA: You'd think I'd whacked you with a broom or something.

CONCETTA: You asked me three times. It's cold!

LUCA: This is a Christmas God . . .

CONCETTA: . . . made to order. You said that too.

LUCA: I did, didn't I . . . (*Yawns, looks about as if searching for something, without knowing what. Suddenly it dawns on him, and he asks in trepidation, as if expecting the worst.*) The Crib, where's my Crib?

CONCETTA (*exasperated*):   Over there, where nobody'll touch it.

LUCA (*admiring his own work*):   This year's will be the best ever. Pastorelli, from the third floor, he's making one too. But there's no comparison . . . (*to his wife*) Concetta, is the glue ready yet?

CONCETTA (*rudely*):   Listen, Luca, I just got up. With your permission I'd like to get dressed and go to market; or if you like I can sit here and wait for further orders from Your Majesty. (*She sits and folds her arms.*)

LUCA (*aggressively*):   You didn't melt it, did you?

CONCETTA: No, I didn't.

LUCA: What did I tell you last night? "Tomorrow morning, as soon as you get up, even before you make coffee, melt the glue. That way I can get an early start." Now how am I ever going to finish the Crib by tomorrow?

CONCETTA (*rises suddenly, grabs the can of glue and moves to exit left*):   Yessir, let's melt the glue, that way we can all have glue for breakfast this morning. Christmas comes, and it's hell on earth. Shepherds, paints, glue, and garbage!

LUCA (*shouting as if to drown out his wife*):   Have you gotten old! I mean old!

(*He finally decides to get up, and approaches the dresser and holy pictures. Passing in front of them, he half genuflects, crossing himself as he gazes at the pictures. He turns toward the bed and sits in the chair at its foot, struggling to slip on his worn trousers. Then, turning toward the night table, he puts on a beret that was hanging on the headboard. He tries again to drink his coffee, but the bad taste forces him to spit it out. Still trembling from the cold, he rubs his hands together to stay warm, then rolls up his shirt sleeves, yawns, and moves toward the wash basin, picking up on the same refrain Concetta had used to wake him.*)

Tommasino, get up! It's nine o'clock. (*no answer*) I know you're awake, stop pretending you're asleep. (*Filling the basin with water he soaps his hands, continuing every now and then to prod Tommasino.*) Come on, get up! What is it with you? It's nine o'clock! At your age I was at work by the crack of dawn. (*Now he soaps his face and washes with gusto. He can't find the towel and twists himself inside-out to prevent water from dripping down his back. Finally, he finds the towel and dries his face. Annoyed, he shouts again, this time at* **TOMMASINO**.) Did you hear me? Wake up! (*Seeing that* **TOMMASINO** *doesn't answer, he opts not to make a fuss.*) I'd do better to ignore you, or I'll be doing penance instead of celebrating Christmas.

TOMMASINO (*whining, curled up and buried under the covers*):   Where's my bread and milk?!

LUCA: Is that all you ever think of? Get up and fetch your own! There's no maids in this house.

TOMMASINO: Either you bring it here or I don't budge.

LUCA: You'll budge alright, or you'll be curling up in a hospital bed.

CONCETTA (*returning with the steaming can of glue*):   Here's your glue . . . (*putting it down on the table where the pieces of the Nativity scene are laid out*) I can't understand all this fuss for a Crib. The family's a mess, there's no money . . . At least if it turned out good for once!

TOMMASINO (*still lying down, in all comfort, hands behind his head*):   You can say that again . . . You'd think he'd get it right at least once!

LUCA: What do you know? It was me who started the tradition . . . they came to me for advice, from all over . . . How can you say you don't like it?

TOMMASINO (*stubbornly*):   Personally, I don't like it.

LUCA: That's 'cause you want to be fancy, and the Christmas Crib isn't modern enough for you. Of all people . . . There's not a soul in the world who doesn't adore it.

TOMMASINO (*as above*):   I don't like it! Is there a law that says I have to?

LUCA (*out of spite, he shakes the headboard of the bed, demanding*):   Will you get out of bed!

TOMMASINO (*spitefully*):   I want my bread and milk!

CONCETTA (*ignoring her husband, lovingly to her son*):   Come on, sweetie, get up. You make yourself handsome, and I'll make a special breakfast just for you.

LUCA (*to* **CONCETTA**):   You bring him breakfast and I'll have both your heads! (*referring to the bad job his wife has done bringing up their son*) You've brought him up to be a jailbird!

CONCETTA (*in a conciliatory tone*):   He'll be up in a minute. (*Unseen by* **LUCA**, *she gestures toward* **TOMMASINO**, *prompting him to get up; it's not long, however, before* **LUCA** *catches on.*)

LUCA: So what's this, a wireless telegraph?

TOMMASINO (*shamelessly*):   I want my bread and milk! . . .

LUCA (*peeved*):   And I'll glue your face to the wall. Since when is your mother your servant anyway? (*He's put on his vest, a jacket, and a woolen scarf, and now begins work on the Crib, gluing cork and tacking together bits of wood. After a short silence he turns to his wife.*) Is Pasquale up?

CONCETTA: Yeah, he's up. The pain! A little sore throat and he's in bed for a week.

TOMMASINO (*alarmed*):   He's up? Is he going out?

CONCETTA: He said he wanted to take a walk, that after the fever he needed a breath of fresh air before going back to bed.

TOMMASINO: Do you know if he plans to get dressed?

LUCA: No, he's going to bare his ass to the wind . . .

TOMMASINO: No, I mean . . . is he going to wear his coat?

LUCA: Of course, what do you expect in December?

CONCETTA (*getting a bit suspicious at the odd questions*):   What's with the questions?

TOMMASINO (*evasive*):   No, nothing. I thought it'd be better if he didn't go. He could have a relapse.

PASQUALE (*outside the door, knocking lightly he asks courteously*):   Luca, can I come in?

LUCA: The door's open, Pasquale.

PASQUALE (*opens and enters. He is dressed to a tee, except that he is wearing slippers.* **TOMMASINO** *dives under the covers.*) Good morning, Concetta.

CONCETTA: 'Morning.

LUCA (*approaches his brother with concern*):   How are you?

PASQUALE: Better . . . still a little weak, but I'm better . . .

LUCA (*taking his pulse*):   I was afraid you'd be in bed for Christmas. At least your pulse is good . . .

PASQUALE: My tongue, it's my tongue you have to check. (*He sticks out his tongue.*)

LUCA (*after examining it closely*):   Don't worry, it's clean. Now listen to your brother. You have to eat red meat and drink red wine; take long walks by the sea, so your room can be cleaned too. You were in there for seven days you know . . . (*to his wife*) Concetta, did you hear me, nice and clean.

CONCETTA: Yeessss, Luca, I heard you.

PASQUALE: I am ready for a walk. I'll go play the lottery and come back. (*to* **CONCETTA**, *with badly hidden suspicion*) My dear, I haven't been able to find my shoes.

CONCETTA: So?

PASQUALE (*patiently*): Not that you have them, but I did spend seven days in bed . . . I simply asked if you'd seen them.

LUCA: Where was it you put them before you got sick?

PASQUALE: Where do you think, under the bed!

CONCETTA: Then that's where you'll find them.

PASQUALE: Concetta, they're not there; they're gone. (*pointing at* **TOMMASINO'S** *bed*) Ask little Tommasino there.

TOMMASINO (*springs upright, sitting in the middle of the bed. He confronts everyone with shameless arrogance, as if to head off his uncle's charges, which he knows are well-founded*): Let's not start! Am I the kind who would sell his shoes?!

LUCA (*with an air of certainty, knowing how his son reacts when guilty*): He sold 'em alright.

PASQUALE (*bitterly*): So he did, didn't he?! So now what do I do?

CONCETTA (*wanting her son off the hook*): No, he didn't!

LUCA (*convinced*): He's a thief, that's what he is! A hardened criminal!

TOMMASINO: I didn't sell a thing!

LUCA: Don't lie!

PASQUALE: Confess!

LUCA: Confess!

TOMMASINO (*spitefully*): I don't like the Crib! So what of it? I get blamed for everything in this house!

CONCETTA: We've been at this all morning!

TOMMASINO: I want my bread and milk!

LUCA (*fed up, hammer in hand*): I'm going to put you in traction! (*accusing* **CONCETTA**) A jailbird, you've raised a jailbird!

PASQUALE: Now how am I to go out?! Seven days in bed with a fever . . . and he sells my shoes.

LUCA: Pasquale, you have to find yourself a furnished room . . .

PASQUALE: I hear you, I'm leaving.

LUCA: There's just no way we can live together. I can't be responsible for this thief. Here, wear these . . . (*takes a pair of shoes from under the bed and hands them to* **PASQUALE**) Then buy yourself a new pair after the holidays, and I'll pay for them.

PASQUALE: Hallelujah . . . Why don't you put him away? Lock him up even. He's a menace. God knows what he might do next. A man gets laid up with a fever, then wakes up with no shoes! Why'd you sell my shoes?! Why?!

LUCA: Why in the world did you sell his shoes?

TOMMASINO: I had my reasons.

PASQUALE: What, you sell my shoes and you got reasons?

TOMMASINO: You bet, I had plenty of reasons . . . I sold the shoes . . . 'cause I thought you'd never get up again. The doctor was very clear when he came.

PASQUALE: The doctor? Clear? (*speaking to everyone*) What are you all hiding?

LUCA: Don't pay any attention to him!

TOMMASINO: Sure, why would anyone listen to me! The doctor said he was in danger. Hell . . . I even sold his coat!

PASQUALE: Luca, can you believe this? He even sold my coat . . . my tan coat . . .

LUCA (*to* **CONCETTA**): The tan coat.

PASQUALE: The one with the fur collar.

LUCA (*to* **CONCETTA**): The one with the fuzzy collar . . . (*to* **PASQUALE**) You mean your coat.

PASQUALE: The one with the plaid lining.

LUCA: Yeah, your coat.

PASQUALE: The one with the half-belt.

LUCA: Pasquale, you've only got one coat! (*fed up*) And he sold it!

PASQUALE (*violently throwing the shoes to the ground*): And I'm not going out! He's made a pauper of me! (*He sits down.*)

LUCA: Pasquale . . . you should get a place of your own.

PASQUALE: But do you realize what he did, selling everything I own before I even died! Give me a chance to croak at least!

LUCA: Pasqua', it's only child's play. OK, so he sold your coat and shoes . . . (*to* **TOMMASINO**) Not to mention that, as his brother, I inherit his belongings here.

PASQUALE (*sickened*): Well then, make up your minds. Who *is* going to peddle it all? . . . God forbid! Cannibals, all of you! And you—you're my brother? You're worse than Cain! Don't kid yourselves! Me, I haven't got a penny. Nice family you are! Waiting for me to kick the bucket . . . (*reflecting on the lack of hospitality.*) Then people say . . . "Lucky you, living under your brother's roof, with *family*." If they only knew . . . You make me sick.

LUCA (*somewhat offended*): Pasquale, how dare you complain? Just for once let's set the record straight: morning coffee, breakfast, lunch, dinner . . . all for a scudo[1] a day? Not to mention that poor wife of mine, washing, ironing, cleaning your chamber pot, mending socks with more holes in them than Swiss cheese . . . now just because the boy was playing around . . .

PASQUALE: Playing around!!! Playing around . . .

LUCA (*at a loss as what to do with his rebellious son*): So tell me Pasquale, what should I do? Kill him? Enough's enough. (*exaggerating, out of impotent rage*) But perhaps I'd best invoke your forgiveness for the boy's abuse of your precious wardrobe.

---

1. A gold or silver coin of Italy and Sicily, no longer in use today. —Trans.

PASQUALE (*also exaggerating*):   No, please, I'm the one who ought to apologize, for even asking about my shoes in the first place.

LUCA (*bowing, brushing the floor with his cap*):   I beg your forgiveness, Pasquale.

PASQUALE (*imitating his brother's gesture*):   No, Luca, please. I humbly regret this most unfortunate inconvenience.

LUCA (*carried away by the ironic tone of the exchange*):   I am at your command, Pasquale. (*kneels*)

PASQUALE (*kneels also*):   I will kiss the ground you walk on, Luca.

LUCA (*exasperated, he bolts up to put an end to the charade, tipping his cap as if to signify "farewell"*):   Ciao Pasquale, *ti saluto!*

PASQUALE (*also vexed, imitating the gesture*):   Yeah ciao, and I salute you too. (*As* **LUCA** *turns to work on his Nativity scene,* **PASQUALE** *leaves the room, exclaiming*) Family . . . phooey! God help us all. (*offstage*) You're all leeches, that's what you are! Leeches!

CONCETTA: What a pain in the ass.

LUCA: He does have a point. (*adamantly, to* **TOMMASINO**) Will you get out of bed! (*He whips the covers off his son's bed.*)

CONCETTA (*promptly*):   Luca, you want him to catch a cold?

LUCA: I'd rather he catch a bullet . . .

CONCETTA (*to* **TOMMASINO**, *sweetly*):   Come on in the kitchen and I'll make your breakfast. (*Exits left, gesturing to* **TOMMASINO** *to get up.*)

LUCA (*catching her gestures*):   You'll ruin us yet, won't you, woman? (*He goes back to work on the Crib, addressing* **TOMMASINO** *who has finally gotten out of bed and is slipping on his pants.*) You're impossible. I love you, but sometimes you're just too thickheaded. (**TOMMASINO** *goes to the washstand and empties the basin full of dirty water into the bucket. Then he fills it with clean water, and dabs his face with soap and water.*) Deep down, you're a good boy. Your heart's in the right place, but you belong in a cage. You never listen to anybody. (**TOMMASINO** *dries himself.*) Where's your common sense? Selling your uncle's coat in December! What's the world coming to anyway? You're a man now, not a baby. You didn't want to study, so you got kicked out of every school in Naples. "I want to work," you said. Third grade. So what are you waiting for? It's the early bird that catches the worm. Go check the stores with "Help Wanted" signs. That's how you start out. A man needs to learn a trade, to make something of himself. I won't be here forever, you know. (*shifts emphasis, endearingly*) But how about that new suit you need? The tailor will be here after Christmas with his samples, so I thought I'd get you one. That thing you've got on is all worn. And I'll even have him cut you two shirts. Your mother says she can't salvage the two you have. Just think: a new suit and two shirts! (*pointing to the Nativity scene*) Now, here's where the snow-capped mountains will go. With tiny houses because of the distance. I'll put the washer-woman here, the inn over here, and over here the stable where the Babe is born. (*fishing for a compliment*) You do like it, don't you?

TOMMASINO (*tying his tie*):   No.

LUCA: Well, I can understand. It is still unfinished. Too early to express an opinion. I'll even buy you two ties: the one you have on is a rag. Tell you what: for Christmas, I'll even give you ten scudi, so when you go out with your friends, you can treat like the rest of them. That way you'll make a good impression. (*pointing to another part of the Crib*) Then this is where the pond and the fisherman go, with the waterfall here, off the mountain. Using real water, too!

TOMMASINO (*skeptically*):   Real water, huh.

LUCA: Uhm hmm. I'm going to use an enema pump in back, and just open the valve. Good idea, huh?

TOMMASINO: No.

LUCA: I can't believe you! We're talking about something sacred!

TOMMASINO (*adamant*):   An enema pump?! Sacred?!! . . . Be serious!

LUCA: There you go wanting to be modern again, thinking you're better than everybody else. How can anybody say: "I don't like it," when the thing isn't even finished?

TOMMASINO: What is it you want from me? Is it my fault if I don't like it? (*walks over to the Crib, scrutinizes it, and exclaims*) There . . . And I won't like it when it's done either!

LUCA (*angered*):   Then leave! I want you out! I'm tired of loafers in my house. Find yourself a job, and don't you ever set foot here again.

TOMMASINO: Don't worry, I'm leaving. I'm leaving alright. (*referring to the Crib*) This is ridiculous! Why do I have to like it if I don't?

LUCA: I want you out of here anyway.

TOMMASINO: And I still don't like the Crib.

LUCA (*infuriated*):   And you'll still leave, 'cause the Crib's not going anywhere.

TOMMASINO: I'm leaving, I said. But first I'll eat my bread and milk; then I'll leave.

CONCETTA (*she enters, placing a bowl of milk and some bread on the night table.* **TOMMASINO,** *already dressed, begins to eat, while* **CONCETTA** *walks toward the dresser and rummages through a drawer.*) Luca, what do you want eat today?

LUCA: Here we go again. Every morning, "Luca what do you want to eat?" It's pure torture. Why do you even ask me? I tell you one thing, you do another . . . Know what? Tomorrow's Christmas Eve, then come all the other holidays when we eat a lot. We'd better take it easy. Just make some vegetable broth, and throw in three-hundred grams of tubetti.

TOMMASINO (*immediately*):   I don't like tubetti . . .

LUCA: You're on your way out. Tubetti are none of your business.

CONCETTA (*having taken some money from the drawer and divided it up: part of it in her worn leather bag, and a five-scudo bill clasped tightly in her right fist; she is putting on an old coat and a makeshift hat*):   And no fruit either! And tomorrow's Christmas . . . If you only knew the kind of money that goes into Christmas. I'll take twenty scudi for shopping and leave you five, in case you need it for a shepherd, or some nails . . . (*She leaves the bill next to the Crib.*)

TOMMASINO (*having devoured his breakfast*):   My last breakfast with the patriarch! I'll be going now—banished by a heartless father, in the very midst of Christmas. The gall of the man! But I'll do what I must . . . find work, and never return here again.

CONCETTA: What are you saying?

TOMMASINO: What am I saying? (*He approaches his father's worktable and stealthily pockets the five-scudo bill.*) You wait and see. (*ambiguously*) You'll never see your baby boy again! (*He moves toward the exit.*) Forget he ever existed! He's gone, mother, forever! (*He exits.*)

CONCETTA: Tommasino, come back here . . .

LUCA (*finally catches on to* **TOMMASINO'S** *intentions as he notices that the five-scudo bill is missing. In a matter-of-fact way, he says*): He snatched the five scudi . . . (*yelling after* **TOMMASINO**) Keep the money, and my blessing with it! But don't ever show your face in this house again!

CONCETTA: Tommasino . . . sweetheart, come back . . . (*then, rudely to* **LUCA**) What happened?

LUCA (*returning to work*): Don't worry, he'll be back for lunch.

CONCETTA: Your son said he's leaving home.

LUCA: It's about time! He's got to find his way in the world, and learn to work. In my house he's no longer welcome.

CONCETTA (*pushing her husband in the back, wanting to know the reason for the argument*): Will you tell me what happened?

LUCA (*rocked by the push, he nearly falls on the Nativity Scene. Luckily he catches himself in time, but loses all patience*): I kicked him out, that's what happened! Now will you please leave me alone! You almost made me break the Crib. (*infuriated*) I can't be distracted. I have to work on the Crib. Alone!

CONCETTA (*ironically, surprised by the unusual tone of his reply*): You'd think you were putting the dome on Saint Peter's! (*doorbell rings*) And while you're at it, why don't you stick two shepherds on the tip . . . (**CONCETTA** *exits by the upstage door; offstage, she exclaims:*) What are you doing here at this hour?

(*Enter* **NINUCCIA**, *followed by* **CONCETTA** *who stops and looks at her with concern. Ninuccia is the couple's older child. She is dressed in an elegant winter outfit of hat, gloves, and handbag, and flaunts several heavy gold bracelets. She is still raging and heated from yet another fight with her husband.*)

LUCA: Nina, is that you?

NINUCCIA: Good morning, father.

(*She takes a chair and brusquely sets it in the center of the room between* **LUCA** *and* **CONCETTA**, *where she sits and sulks morosely.*)

(*The two parents exchange meaningful glances, each one communicating what he/she thinks of the other.* **CONCETTA'S** *look is a puzzled one, whereas* **LUCA'S** *is accusing. After they've both mimed their feelings,* **LUCA** *addresses his daughter tenderly, affecting the patience of a saint.*)

LUCA: What happened? (**NINUCCIA** *doesn't answer.*) Did you fight with your husband again? (**NINUCCIA** *still doesn't answer.*) I just don't understand . . . The man adores you. He gives you everything. Look at you, you're a lady . . . not to mention the apartment he bought. The man has to work for a living, he needs his peace and quiet. Ninuccia, the man's got problems, what with hundreds of workers under him . . . Why did you argue? (**NINUCCIA** *stays stubbornly silent.*) Why did you argue? (*Since his daughter doesn't answer, he raises his voice, repeating the same question as if offended.*) Why did you argue? (*The outcome is the same, prompting* **LUCA** *to chastise* **CONCETTA** *while pointing a finger at his daughter.*) Here's another one of your masterpieces!

(**CONCETTA** *dismisses the remark, takes a chair, and sits down next to her daughter for a mother-daughter talk carried out in mumbled whispers.* **LUCA**, *anxious to understand what's going on, perks his ears. Failing in his attempt, he exclaims indignantly:*)

LUCA: Keeping me in the dark, eh!

CONCETTA (*practically pitying him*): What is it you want? There's nothing to know . . . Go worry about your Crib.

LUCA: You're my ruination! I've said so for years. Worry about the Crib? I'll worry about it alright! My God, what people . . . I can't understand it. But don't come running to me when there's trouble. If there's trouble, I'll be busy with the Crib. (*picks up the glue can*) I'm going to heat the glue. But you'll regret this when you burn in hell! What people! Enemies of their own blood! (*The two women start to whisper again, heedless of his words.* **LUCA** *again perks his ears but finally gives up when he sees it's to no avail.*) Nothing, not a word. Between mother and daughter it's another language. (*Exits grumbling.*)

CONCETTA (*rid of her husband, asks* **NINUCCIA** *to finish her story*): And then what?

NINUCCIA: I turned my back and left.

CONCETTA (*alarmed*): My God in heaven! Are you crazy? He's on his way here for sure.

NINUCCIA: I can't bear it any more. His jealousy is killing me.

CONCETTA: But you, my dear, would do well to toe the line. I am your mother, I can tell you so.

NINUCCIA: But why, what have I done? What have I done? (*disrespectful toward her mother*) Don't make me laugh! The real problem is that I'm a fool. That's it! All I do is yap instead of getting down to business. Well, now it's time. (*takes a letter from her purse and shows it to her mother*) Here! I'm done with him. (*reading what's on the envelope*) "To Mr. Nicola Percuoco, Urgent." (*She extracts the letter and reads aloud.*) "Our marriage was a mistake. Forgive me. I am in love with Vittorio Elia and will elope with him this evening. Goodbye forever, Ninuccia."

CONCETTA (*terrified*): Are you crazy? The poor man'll die . . . (*driven to maternal rage*) You're shameless! Give me that letter . . . (*She grapples with her daughter for the letter.*) I said give me that letter!

NINUCCIA: No, Mother, no!

CONCETTA (*finally wresting the letter from her daughter*): Give it to me!

NINUCCIA (*vexed*): Go on, take it! (*sits angrily*)

CONCETTA (*approaches the dresser where, nearly in tears, she pleads with the image of the Blessed Mother. In Italian:*) Madonna, madonna, madonna mia! (*Her tone is decisive as she turns to* **NINUCCIA**.) And if you repeat what you said again, you can forget you have a mother! The man's not just anybody, he's your husband. And if you didn't love him you should have thought of it before!

NINUCCIA: I didn't want him! It was you two that forced me!

CONCETTA: Well, now it's done, and there's no going back.

NINUCCIA: And I'm leaving.

CONCETTA: And I'll crack your face!

NINUCCIA (*enraged*): Go ahead! What are you waiting for? Kill me . . . (*cursing her fate*) What did I ever do to deserve this? But I'm not as stupid as I used to be . . . Now you can't push me around anymore. I'm at my wits' ends, and I'll wreck everything in my way.

CONCETTA (*dumbfounded by her daughter's unusual rebellious behavior*): Uhh, what . . . !!

NINUCCIA: Yes, I'll wreck everything!

(*Like a madwoman she circles the room, breaking anything she can lay her hands on: Tommasino's bowl, the dish that covered it, objects on the night table, even three or four ceramic and plaster knickknacks that decorated the dresser. Still not satisfied, she halts before the Nativity scene, then tears it furiously to pieces.* CONCETTA, *angered and disheartened, sits at the foot of the double bed. As* NINUCCIA'S *fury is placated, she bursts into tears and sits back down, hiding her face in her hands.*)

NINUCCIA: Are you happy now?

LUCA (*enters right, totally absorbed in slowly mixing the melted glue. Two steps beyond the doorway he stops, having kicked by chance a broken plate. He looks around at the damage wrought by* NINUCCIA, *sees his wife sobbing, and asks with concern*): What happened?

CONCETTA: Nothing, nothing . . .

LUCA: Nothing?! It looks like Hannibal's elephants were here! (*Only now does he realize the fate of his Nativity Scene. He totters; wide-eyed and with a voice cracking with rage he demands:*) The Crib?! Who broke the Crib?! I do all this work, and for what? For this madness . . . I said who broke it?!

CONCETTA (*weary and disheartened*): Your daughter there. Take it up with her.

LUCA: With her? No, it's with Donna Concetta that I'll take it up! With you, understand?

CONCETTA: With me? . . .

LUCA: Yes, you. You! This is all your fault. I've always said you're my ruin! Look at how you raised your kids, just look at the results. (*ranting and raving*) Spoiled rotten! Then you complain when I take it out on you . . .

CONCETTA (*feeling victimized and abused*): Me . . . so it's all my fault then . . . and why not? . . . it's always me getting stuck in the middle. That one with her husband, you with your asinine Crib! (*Suddenly, she starts screaming and gesticulating like a woman possessed: pounding the bed with her fists.*) I'm sick and tired of all of you! I can't take this anymore! I can't take it! You've crushed me! All of you . . . (*Finally, delirious, she crumples at the foot of the bed, her head pressing against the mattress. As she collapses, she inadvertently drops the letter amid the debris on the floor.*) Help me . . .

NINUCCIA: Mamma, mamma! (*running toward her mother*)

LUCA: Concetta's dead! My wife's dead . . . (*Together with* NINUCCIA *he lifts* CONCETTA *onto the bed.*) Concetta, I beg you, for the love of God, talk to me! (*He runs upstage, yelling.*) Pasquale, quick, my wife is dying! (*Returns to* CONCETTA'S *side.*) My wife, she's dead! . . . (*Turning toward the dresser, he takes off his beret as he implores the Virgin.*) Maria Santissima, have mercy on us, please! (*heading upstage again*) Hurry up with the vinegar!

PASQUALE (*from upstage*): Luca, what happened?!

LUCA: My wife, she's dying . . .

PASQUALE: What?!!

LUCA: Go get the vinegar.

PASQUALE: Let's not worry now, it's nothing serious. (*exits right*)

LUCA: Concetta, it's me, Luca . . . Talk to me, Concetta! (*He shakes her.*) Concetta . . .

NINUCCIA: Easy, easy . . .

PASQUALE (*returns with the vinegar and gives it to* **LUCA**): Here's the vinegar.

LUCA (*waving the bottle under* **CONCETTA'S** *nose, he says to his brother*): Light the candles! (**PASQUALE** *takes a box of matches out of his pocket, strikes one, and gets ready to light the closest candle.*) Concetta, open your eyes.

CONCETTA (*reacting to the smell of the vinegar, opens her eyes and mumbles*): What . . .

LUCA (*making* **PASQUALE** *stop*): Pasquale, wait . . . blow it out, her eyes are open. Concetta, talk to me . . .

(**PASQUALE** *puts the candle back and approaches the bed.*)

NINUCCIA: Mamma, are you alright?

CONCETTA (*with a weak voice*): Help me . . .

PASQUALE: Will you tell me what happened?

CONCETTA (*evasive*): Nothing, nothing . . .

LUCA: Don't even bother to ask. You know a person can't know anything in this house.

PASQUALE (*having a hard time holding up his pants, ever since he entered the scene*): Hey Luca, your son even stole my suspenders . . .

LUCA (*whips out his belt and hands it to his brother as if to shut him up*): Pasquale, what is it you want from me? Here, take this.

PASQUALE (*willingly accepting the offer*): What can we do about him?

LUCA: He's a bum, Pasquale. That's all there is to it. Just go find yourself a room of your own . . .

PASQUALE: I will, I will . . . I can't live with that nightmare. (*Grumbling, he heads for his room, convinced more than ever there's no room for him in the household.*) I've got to get out of here. I just have to go. What am I waiting for anyway? My bed could even disappear— with me in it! (*exits*)

LUCA (*nearing the bed, he asks his wife tenderly*): How do you feel now?

CONCETTA (*with a more reassuring tone of voice*): Uhm . . . a little better.

LUCA: You shouldn't scare me like that . . . (*touched*) You had me terrified . . . Concetta, we only have each other . . . The children, they are what they are. Forget them. We need to think of ourselves. (*genuinely bitter*) So you sacrifice yourself for them . . . And for what? Concetta, if you die, we both might as well be dead. (*Choked up, he takes off his glasses and dries a tear.*) How do you feel?

CONCETTA: Better.

LUCA (*to* **NINUCCIA**): She is better: her color's back.

NINUCCIA: I can tell.

LUCA (*focusing on the destroyed Crib, he stops for a moment and mumbles*): Now to start the Crib all over again . . .

NINUCCIA (*in disbelief*): How can you be thinking about the Crib?

(*The doorbell rings.*)

LUCA: I'll go, you stay with your mother. (*As he heads toward the door, passing the dresser, he tips his beret to thank his holy intercessors, and exits.*) Grazie . . .

NINUCCIA (*as if to beg forgiveness for her earlier outburst*): Mamma . . . !

CONCETTA: You want me dead. You do. How could you write that letter? You know your husband's a serious man. If he ever knew for certain . . . he'd kill you! Listen to me: swear you won't send the letter. That you'll make peace and put an end to this mess. Swear it!

NINUCCIA (*unconvincingly*): I swear, mother.

LUCA (*enters with* **NICOLINO**): Nicola, my wife was dying . . .

NICOLINO (*forty-five years old, he is shrewd rather than intelligent. He dresses with exaggerated elegance, wearing several rings and flaunting a gold tie pin. His bearing is very deliberate and controlled. He has come directly from home, running after his wife with whom he'd fought. For that reason he appears dishevelled: his vest is buttoned crookedly, his tie haphazardly knotted, and his shirttail sticks out from under his jacket.*): What are you saying?

LUCA: All of a sudden, she just collapsed. We practically saw her slipping away.

NICOLINO (*approaching the bed, affectionately*): Ma', what happened?

CONCETTA: Nothing, my head was spinning . . .

LUCA: She doesn't eat enough, she eats like a bird. Not to mention her worries . . . Ninuccia was all upset when she arrived . . . I knew you two had fought, but I still don't know why. Why did you fight?

NICOLINO: It was nothing . . .

LUCA (*to the two women*): Excuse us. (*pulling his son-in-law aside*) Nicola, you know what it is? That woman keeps me in the dark so as not to trouble me . . . She means well. But just between us men: what did you fight about?

NICOLINO: No, it was nothing . . .

LUCA (*exasperated by the same answer all the time*): This is a conspiracy!

NICOLINO (*conciliatory, to his wife*): Why are we doing this? (*As* **NICOLA** *turns toward his wife*, **LUCA** *notices his shirttail. Amazed, he doesn't dare bring it to the others' attention.*) Fighting like teenage lovers . . . (*making sure he's overheard*) You know I'm a man who takes things seriously.

LUCA (*looking at the shirttail*): Exactly what I say.

CONCETTA (*eyeing Ninuccia*): So you had a misunderstanding: now go ahead and make up.

NICOLINO (*cordially*): For my part, I'm ready. She's the one who's impossible to figure out.

LUCA: It takes patience, Nicola. (**TOMMASINO** *enters. Sulking grimly, he sits by himself on the bed.*) So you're back, eh? Swallowed your pride?

TOMMASINO: I've decided to spend Christmas here. Then I'll leave.

LUCA: I knew it! (*to* **NICOLINO**) Nicola, what can I do? I was unlucky with my kids. And he's worse than the female. You're the one to blame, Concetta . . . and don't go getting angry or start fainting on me either. You just weren't strong enough. (*referring to* **NINUCCIA**) I admit, the girl was partly my fault. You know how it is, how a father feels for his baby girl . . . Only I know the sadness it cost me, the sorrow . . . (*to* **CONCETTA**) You remember when she was sick? With the *typhoon* fever? And the vow we made to the Virgin? (*He takes off his beret.*) You never know with children . . . sorrow, joy . . . Then there was school: she'd read all the time . . . Our house was full of books. She studied hard. That one, (*pointing to* **TOMMASINO**) he's totally *illegible,* not her though, when she opens her mouth, boy, can she talk. It would be two, three-thirty in the morning, and she'd still be reading. "Nina, put the light out," I'd say. And she'd answer: "It's only a little light." As if I was worried about saving . . . It's that a child needs a good night's sleep . . . Like I said: sorrow and joy. Then you showed up asking to marry her. That was the icing on the cake.

NICOLINO: Let's not exaggerate now!

LUCA: Nicola, until your wedding day, all we did was cry in this house.

NICOLINO: You'd think she was marrying a scoundrel!

LUCA: God forbid, Nicola! I love you. You're the crown prince of this family. It's just that, you know, a man's only daughter, leaving home . . . When you said you'd be moving into your own apartment, Concetta and I just cried for days . . . We couldn't even sleep at night, losing our baby girl . . . (*hinting at* **TOMMASINO**) Now, if you had married him . . . For that I'd have built you a monument! (*laughs with the others*)

TOMMASINO: Right, as if I'd marry him.

LUCA: No, I mean if you were a girl.

TOMMASINO: I wouldn't marry him.

NICOLINO (*jokingly*): As if I'd marry you.

TOMMASINO: You two are crazy.

LUCA: What do you mean crazy? I said if you were a girl.

TOMMASINO: And I say I wouldn't marry him.

LUCA: Don't be such a fool. Nico, do excuse us. (*to* **TOMMASINO**) I said *if* you were a girl . . . Are you a girl by any chance?

TOMMASINO: No.

LUCA: Now, *if* you were a girl, being that children must obey their father, and I ordered "You're to marry Nicolino," you would have to marry him.

TOMMASINO: And *if* I were a girl, my answer would still be: "I don't like him."

LUCA: It's useless. The dunce was born to contradict me!

NICOLINO (*disdainfully*): That's just his way, Papa.

LUCA (*changing the subject, picking up where they'd left off earlier*): Now you two make up. And no more fussing, either.

(**CONCETTA** *pushes* **NINUCCIA** *toward* **NICOLINO**, *and* **LUCA** *pushes* **NICOLINO** *toward* **NINUCCIA**.)

TOMMASINO (*upon noticing Nicolino's shirttail, he singsongs*):   Nico's got his shirttail out!

(**NICOLINO** *runs into the kitchen to tuck his shirt in.*)

LUCA (*to* **NINUCCIA**):   You're driving the man crazy. Did you see the state he was in, from running after you? (*to* **TOMMASINO**) I noticed it too, but I was waiting for the proper time to tell him. Since when do you say: "Nico's got his shirttail out?"

TOMMASINO: What was I supposed to say?

LUCA: You pull him aside and whisper: "*Scusate,* but your shirttail is out of place." (**NI-COLINO** *returns and* **LUCA** *pushes him toward* **NINUCCIA**.) Now stop acting like fools. Tomorrow's Christmas, and there should be peace between you. You'll eat here. Concetta's prepared a magnificent dinner.

NICOLINO: I've ordered four lobsters. I'll send them over this evening.

CONCETTA: I'm going out a minute. There's still some shopping to do.

LUCA: Are you crazy? You were just on your deathbed, do you want to head for the grave? I'll do the shopping.

NICOLINO: By no means. I'll see to it . . . I'll have one of my boys deliver whatever you need.

LUCA: OK, but don't overdo it. We want to eat lightly. Just a bit of vegetable broth . . . Ninuccia knows what to buy . . . along with five-hundred grams of tubetti.

NICOLINO: Vegetable broth? Come now, I'll send you a nice soup chicken!

LUCA: You're right, chicken soup is hearty . . . but we want a light meal, and I'd been wanting vegetable broth for some time. Vegetable broth and five-hundred grams of tubetti.

NICOLINO: No sir, you have to eat well. I'm sending you a nice chicken.

LUCA (*stubbornly*):   You send the chicken. I'm making vegetable broth. (**CONCETTA** *and* **NINUCCIA** *leave the room whispering to each other.*) (*to* **NINUCCIA**) And you be good to your husband!

NICOLINO: You take care of yourself, Papa.

LUCA (*alluding to his daughter*):   Nicolino, be patient with her, please . . . I don't know why you fought, but . . . just be patient.

NICOLINO: Rest assured, Papa . . .

LUCA: Nicola, I know Ninuccia's not easy to put up with. (*with passion*) But promise me you'll love her! I'm getting old, and God knows so is Concetta . . . Nina's the apple of my eye. And I need to know that when I'm gone, there'll be a man like you to understand and care for her. If not, I'll never have any peace.

NICOLINO (*sincerely*):   Papa, please don't worry. You've no idea how much I love her . . . (*wipes away a tear*)

LUCA: Thank you, my son. Thank you. (*After clasping* **NICOLINO'S** *hand, he raises it to his lips and kisses it.*)

NICOLINO (*unable to pull his hand away in time, he is mortified*):   What are you doing? I should be kissing your hand. (*He kisses it.*)

LUCA (*tries to pull his hand away but can't, since* **NICOLINO** *refuses to let go believing that* **LUCA** *will want to kiss his hand again. Excitedly*):   Nico, let me go. Let go of my hand!

NICOLINO: I will not! (*He holds on.*)

LUCA (*emphatically*):   Nicola, let go! (*He pulls his right hand away, pointing to his pants, which he's barely been able to hold up with his left hand.*) My pants are falling!

NICOLINO: I'm sorry. But why aren't you wearing a belt? Anyway, take care of yourself.

LUCA (*as he walks* **NICO** *to the door, he smiles and points out the plate shards*):   Look at this, she wrecked everything in sight. Even the flower vase . . .

NICOLINO (*walking toward the door*):   Add everything up, then let me know.

LUCA: It was all junk. Don't even give it a second thought.

NICOLINO: We'll see you tomorrow. (*exits*)

LUCA (*while picking up the shards he comes across Ninuccia's letter, which Concetta had dropped. Out of curiosity he picks it up; seeing that it's addressed to his son-in-law,* **LUCA** *calls him back before he reaches the stairs*):   Nicolino!

NICOLINO (*returning to the door*):   What is it, Papa?

LUCA: Here. This is yours.

NICOLINO (*thinking he'd lost a letter, he tucks it away in his pocket*):   Thank you. I'll see you to-morrow.

LUCA: I'm sure we'll have a wonderful and blessed Christmas Eve. (**NICOLINO** *exits, as* **LUCA** *goes directly to the damaged Nativity scene. Meanwhile* **TOMMASINO**, *oblivious to every-thing that has happened in the room, has built and is having a world of a time with a paper puppet of Pulcinella.* **LUCA** *begins to repair the Nativity scene.*)

LUCA: Now to start the Crib again . . .

ACT 2

The Cupiello dining room. Hall door upstage; kitchen door at left; on right, a door to the rest of the apartment. Up left, on a cupboard, homemade Christmas pastries are on display. At center stage is the dining room table, duly set for the Christmas Eve feast. Up right, in the corner, the completed Nativity scene stands out, commanding attention. A chandelier in the middle of the ceiling is decorated with silver stars and other Christmas ornaments. Four crepe paper streamers run from the chandelier to the four corners of the ceiling. The time is approximately 9 P.M. The family is waiting for Ninuccia and Nicolino to begin the holiday dinner and go to Midnight Mass. **CONCETTA** *sits at the table breaking up broccoli, collecting the florets in a big salad bowl. She is talking to* **RAFFAELE** *the doorman, who feigns interest in a story he's heard a hundred times before.*

CONCETTA: Believe me, Raffaele, it's too much to bear.

RAFFAELE: I know, I know . . .

CONCETTA: No, Raffaele, you can't possibly know. I'm a martyr. Heaven chose to punish me with a husband who's good for nothing. In twenty-five years of marriage he's used me up, made a rag out of me. You think I'm the woman I used to be? And if it wasn't for me, God knows how many times this house would have fallen apart.

RAFFAELE: My wife and me always said you wear the pants in this house!

CONCETTA: That's the gospel truth! (*pointing to the Nativity scene*) Can you believe it: a man, at that age, building a Crib? I actually came close to telling him: "Why? Why are you doing it?". . . Raffaele, you can understand, the children are grown now: it seems such a waste of time and money . . . you know what he said? "I do it for me, it's my fun!" You have no idea . . . He just left the house.

RAFFAELE: I saw him, he was running like mad!

CONCETTA: He was off to San Biagio to buy some more shepherds.

RAFFAELE: And to think you could be living in heavenly peace. Your daughter's nicely set. Tommasino . . . he's a bit of a headache, but . . . by the way, where is he?

CONCETTA: I wish he was my only worry! Granted he's a bit wild, but he's young, and that I can forgive. It's my husband who's the real problem!

RAFFAELE (*grinning*): Signora mia, you just have to be patient. Is Ninuccia coming to-night?

CONCETTA: Of course. She'll be here later with her husband.

RAFFAELE (*toasting*): Here's to them! Were you happy with the eels?

CONCETTA: They were splendid! . . . even though personally I find them a bit disgusting . . . Luca, though, he's crazy about them.

RAFFAELE: Well, enjoy your dinner. And if you need anything, call me.

CONCETTA: We will. Thank you.

(**RAFFAELE** *exits.*)

PASQUALE (*ranting offstage*): Now enough's enough! This has got to end! I'm tired of it all!

CONCETTA (*screaming*): What now?!

PASQUALE (*enters in a frenzy*): And what else could it be, my dear Concetta? Another five scudi! Missing! Soon he'll have me stealing for a living! To earn that much takes a week of research into the Lottery! This is sickening! But I'll catch the bum this time. Because all my money's marked with a cross. And if I ever find that bill, you'll need a straitjacket to keep me off him!

CONCETTA (*defensively*): Who in the world would take your money?

PASQUALE: Concetta dear, this is typical Tommasino.

CONCETTA: My dear Pasquale, you watch your mouth. My son touches nobody's money in this house.

PASQUALE: My dear Concetta, the boy is a crook! And you still insist on defending him! Don't get me wrong: I'm his uncle, he's my brother's son. I can't help but love him. But I've nabbed him with his hand in my pocket one too many times!

CONCETTA: You know he's always looking for a pencil . . .

PASQUALE: What pencil and pencil! He confessed it himself yesterday that he stole my shoes and coat.

CONCETTA (*playing down the incident*): That was all a coincidence . . .

PASQUALE: A coincidence? . . . You call that a coincidence?

CONCETTA: Whatever you say, Pasquale . . .

TOMMASINO (*offstage*): After you, Vittorio.

PASQUALE: Here he is now, our prize package. (*preparing to confront his nephew*)

TOMMASINO (*entering*): Come on, stay awhile, then you can leave.

VITTORIO (*A young man of twenty-five with a serious, melancholy air about him, Vittorio dresses with discreet elegance, wearing a winter coat and gloves. Upon entering, he sights* **CONCETTA**, *which puts him ill at ease; lowering his eyes he can barely utter a nondescript*): Buonasera.

CONCETTA (*with death in her eyes and clenched teeth, she answers*): Good evening to you . . .

TOMMASINO: Mamma, this is my friend Vittorio.

CONCETTA (*evasive*): I'm glad to meet him.

TOMMASINO (*suspicious of* **PASQUALE'S** *pacing—who in the meantime has been casting menacing glances his way—he tests the waters*): Buonasera, Uncle Pasquale.

PASQUALE (*with emphasis*): Hello Tommasino. (*He continues pacing, then suddenly confronts his nephew, wagging his finger in* **TOMMASINO'S** *face.*) Don't deny it! You took my five scudi off the night table!

TOMMASINO: Me? When?!

PASQUALE: Either hand over the money, or I'll hand you over—even if it is Christmas!

TOMMASINO: I didn't take anything . . . You must be crazy! Insulting me like this, in front of my friends no less! (*He breaks down in an unbelievably exaggerated display of tears.*)

PASQUALE: You can cry all you want: just give me the money.

CONCETTA (*offended and moved to pity*) Pasquale, don't you think that's enough? You're being downright cruel. (*She brings* **TOMMASINO** *to her breast, caressing his head.*) Come here to mamma . . .

PASQUALE: You little snot . . . Only a mother could fall for those tears.

TOMMASINO (*grimly threatening his uncle*): Just one more time . . .

PASQUALE: He's even threatening me! Don't you forget I'm your father's brother. And when he comes, he'll hear about this. Cough up the money!

CONCETTA: Look again. Maybe it fell on the floor.

PASQUALE: My dear Concetta, I've combed that entire room. But still I'll give him the benefit of the doubt. I'll look again. But if I don't find the five scudi, you'll need a straitjacket to keep me off him!

TOMMASINO: Not by yourself you're not! This time we're going together.

PASQUALE: Why? Do you think I'd lie to you if I found it?

TOMMASINO: I don't know. I just want to be there. And if we find the money, I swear on my mother's . . .

PASQUALE: My God, she's alive and he's swearing on his mother!

TOMMASINO: Since when do you swear only on the dead? I swear on the living soul of my living mother: you'll hear from my lawyer.

PASQUALE: And this is my sacred vow, one I've never made before: I swear on the soul of the Executive Director of the Lottery of Naples that if I don't find the five scudi, you'll be spending Christmas in a wheelchair.

TOMMASINO: We'll see.

PASQUALE: We will indeed.

(*They exit.*)

VITTORIO (*commenting on* **CONCETTA'S** *coldness*): Signora Cupiello, was I wrong in coming?

CONCETTA: Get out of here. My daughter is coming with her husband tonight, and we don't want our Christmas ruined.

VITTORIO: What do you mean?

CONCETTA: Don't you play the fool. And be careful: her husband knows everything.

VITTORIO: He knows?

CONCETTA: Thanks to a letter my husband gave him, without knowing what it was. If you only knew what it took me to get them together again. (*almost crying*) I shed more tears . . .

VITTORIO (*after a brief pause, passionately*): Signora, I love your daughter.

CONCETTA (*shocked by* **VITTORIO'S** *audacity*): And you say it to my face! My daughter's a married woman. She's married, can't you understand?! Why do you keep playing with our lives? You can thank God I'm alone, you know . . . My husband . . . I can hardly say I have one. And my son is just a boy . . . With a man beside me, this would have ended long ago.

VITTORIO (*sincerely*): Please. There's no need for concern. I'm leaving. (*pauses briefly*) But you've no idea of the pain we're suffering. She doesn't love her husband! She doesn't love him!

CONCETTA (*knowing her words aren't true*): She does too! She loves him, I tell you! Now leave. Please. Immediately. (*She exits quickly, leading the way.*)

(**VITTORIO** *does an about-face and slowly follows* **CONCETTA**; *he stops, however, when a frantic* **CONCETTA** *returns gesticulating wildly and blocks his way. Shortly thereafter* **LUCA** *appears, without even noticing Vittorio. He takes off his hat, puts it on a chair, then enters.*)

LUCA (*to* **CONCETTA**): Were you going out?

CONCETTA (*muddled*): No.

LUCA: Then why did you open the door?

CONCETTA: I thought you had knocked.

LUCA: No, I didn't knock. Why did you open the door?

CONCETTA: I thought you were coming; so I opened the door.

LUCA: You thought I was coming so you opened the door . . . and then I really came.

CONCETTA: Huh-uh.

LUCA: Telepathy.

CONCETTA (*not understanding what the word means*): I guess . . .

LUCA: Do you know what telepathy is?

CONCETTA: No.

LUCA: It's when I don't knock and you open the door. (*As he turns around, he sees* **VITTORIO** *and asks* **CONCETTA**.) Who's that?

CONCETTA: He's a friend of Tommasino. He was just leaving. (*trying to dismiss* **VITTORIO** *in a hurry*) Goodbye now.

LUCA: Wait a minute. (*speaking to* **VITTORIO**) So you're a friend of my son's?

VITTORIO: I do see him often.

LUCA (*introducing himself*): Luca Cupiello, Tommasino's father.

VITTORIO: Vittorio Elia.

LUCA: Elia . . . I'm glad my son has friends who are . . . how can I say, so . . . distinguished. I can tell by the way you're dressed. Gloves too, very nice. I always tell my son to choose his friends carefully; the wrong company could deform someone so young.

VITTORIO: That's true . . .

CONCETTA: Shouldn't you be going? It is getting late.

LUCA: Why the rush? Can't you see we're talking?

CONCETTA: But he's got things to do . . .

LUCA: It looks like you want to kick him out! Did you offer him something? (*to* **VITTORIO**) A liqueur, or a cup of coffee maybe?

CONCETTA: He didn't want anything.

LUCA: A pastry perhaps . . . homemade.

VITTORIO: No, I'd better not.

LUCA: As you wish. (*suddenly shifting topics*) Have you seen the Crib?

VITTORIO: No, I haven't.

LUCA (*to* **CONCETTA**): You didn't show it to him, did you?

CONCETTA (*gritting her teeth*): Lucaaa . . .

LUCA: Then why did I build it? (*showing the Crib to* **VITTORIO**) Here it is. Step back, that way you get a *bull's-eye* view. (*Leaving* **VITTORIO** *where he is,* **LUCA** *goes to the Crib and switches on a myriad of tiny Christmas lights that decorate the holy scene. With pride, he exclaims:*) How's that?!

VITTORIO: Very nice.

LUCA: I built it all myself.

VITTORIO (*with good-natured irony*): Really? Without any help?

LUCA (*seriously*): Not only: with my whole family against me!

VITTORIO: I'm impressed.

LUCA: Come take a closer look. You know, it's my passion. If Christmas comes and I don't build one, it's like a bad omen. My father, God rest his soul, used to make the Crib for me and my brother when we were little . . . We'd be so happy! So I started doing the same for my children. Even now that they're grown . . . There's still something . . . holy, something sacred about it.

VITTORIO: This grass . . . was that your idea too?

LUCA: Yessir!

VITTORIO: Nice, very nice. (**LUCA** *nods, uncertain of Vittorio's sincerity.*) And the snow . . . it's all so even . . . Did you sprinkle that all by yourself?

LUCA: Well, yes, I did. (*skeptically, aside to* **CONCETTA**) Why do I feel he's making an ass of me? . . .

CONCETTA: Because he is!

LUCA: What do you mean he is? (*waving a dish*) I'll crack his skull, the smart aleck . . . (*to* **VITTORIO**) Is there something about it you don't like? You don't have to like it you know . . . Then again, it's not the only one in Naples, every family builds one . . . Perhaps you don't care for it . . .

VITTORIO: Oh no, of course I do!

LUCA (*showing him a package*): I just went to buy three new Wise Men. I found one with its head broken off from last year . . . and ended up buying all three, so that the old ones wouldn't look so ugly compared to the new one. (*He very carefully unwraps the three figurines.*) These are the three I chose . . . out of hundreds! And was it cold! But I must say, I did choose well. All three: Gaspar, Melchior, and Balthasar, who brought their gifts to the Baby Jesus. Just look at their faces: look how lovely!

VITTORIO: Gorgeous! And you chose them yourself?

LUCA: All by myself. Out of hundreds. Some were chipped, some were scratched, but these, these are simply perfect!

VITTORIO: My compliments!

LUCA (*certain by now that Vittorio is making fun of him, he wraps the Wise Men up again*): You are a friend of my son's, aren't you . . . I should have known . . . (*He goes to put out the decorative lights, then turns to* **CONCETTA**.) Did Ninuccia and Nicolino come yet?

CONCETTA: Not yet.

LUCA: Ninuccia's my married daughter. She and her husband will be here for dinner. Christmas, Easter, the commemorable holidays . . . like New Year's . . . that's when we *congress,* . . . when we *regress,* I mean . . . when we all . . . *relate* . . . (*Huffs and puffs out of frustration, not being able to pronounce the word "congregate".*) I mean, my daughter no longer lives here.

VITTORIO: She doesn't?

LUCA: Not anymore! She married the well-to-do Mr. Nicola Percuoco, of Percuoco Inc. Perhaps you've seen his commercials on the walls: Percuoco, Inc. The man employs hundreds of workers. He's got responsibilities, you know. Manufactures all sorts of gift items . . . but the real money's in the buttons! You should see their apartment! It's magnificent! Isn't that right, Concetta dear?

CONCETTA (*nodding*): Certainly is . . .

LUCA: When I go visit my daughter, since she's always inviting me there to eat, I say: "Nina, if you want to make me happy, just let me eat in the kitchen." You can breathe there, plus it's big and modern, all white tiles, with a big window overlooking the sea. I eat by that window, and I'm in heaven . . . Concetta, and what about the parlor? Isn't the parlor beautiful?

CONCETTA: It's lovely.

LUCA: Paintings, tapestries, silver plates . . . I tell you, every piece of furniture in that house is a work of art. There's even a piano. It's a shame they don't know how to play it . . . But it's important to have a piano in the house. They're always entertaining, you know, dinner parties, baptisms . . . A maestro comes, he plays, people sing and dance . . . then sometimes months go by without us seeing each other. Because I work too, you know. All day. With the holidays now it's different, but otherwise I'm out of bed at 7:30, and set at the typographer's by 8:15.

VITTORIO: So you're a typesetter?

LUCA: No, gofer. I took my father's place. They trust me with large sums of money, and I pay the bills . . . I have the keys too, keep them safe. That's a big responsibility . . . Concetta, show him the keys.

CONCETTA: What for? All they are is big door keys.

LUCA: I close up at night, open up in the morning . . . how else would they get in? But as I was saying: sometimes I don't see my daughter for months. That's why when Christmas and the other commemorable holidays come, we all . . . *con-flate,* . . . we (*making a silent mental effort to get the word right, counting syllables with his fingers*) we *con-cen-trate,* . . . we . . . (*still frustrated at not being able to pronounce the word "congregate," he decides to clarify what he means.*) Basically, they come over and we eat together. (*After a brief pause, he asks* CONCETTA.) Where's Tommasino?

CONCETTA: He's in the other room, with your brother, who insists that our son filched his five scudi . . .

LUCA: That's nothing new. Money really does disappear around here. Mr. Vittorio, what if you talked to him? Where he won't respect us, you he might, since you're a friend. But this time I took my precautions, and laid a little trap . . . And if I nab him, I'll put him out to sea, where he can't steal anymore!

(*Offstage one hears the ongoing heated argument between* PASQUALE *and* TOMMASINO.)

PASQUALE: As you can see, we've yet to find it.

TOMMASINO: And I'm innocent, I tell you.

PASQUALE (*enters and sees* LUCA, *by whose presence he's reassured. He walks toward his brother.*) He took five scudi!

TOMMASINO: It's a lie!

LUCA: Calm down, let's get to the facts.

TOMMASINO: I don't know any facts.

LUCA: You shut up! (*to* PASQUALE) Pasquale, you're in the wrong.

PASQUALE: I'm wrong?!

LUCA: You can't accuse anybody without some *unrefusable* proof. You should first come to me, let me investigate, then if he's the culprit, you'll have your satisfaction. Mr. Vittorio, please stay. I want to see him humiliated in front of his friends. (*to* TOMMASINO) You, come here, and empty your pockets.

TOMMASINO (*indignantly*): Is it possible I always get treated like a thief?

LUCA: I'm your father. Now show me what's in your pockets. (*He grabs* TOMMASINO *and goes through his pockets.*) If I find those five scudi . . . (*He pulls out a tie from one pocket, a top and its string from the other; then, finally, he finds the five scudi. He then addresses* **TOMMAS-INO** *on the side.*) So there! But why are you such an embarrassment? (*He shows the bill to his son, taking care that no one else sees it.* **TOMMASINO** *doesn't react at all, only he looks his father straight in the eyes, shamelessly, as if it were his right to have taken the bill.* **LUCA** *then gets an idea, and asks* **TOMMASINO** *brusquely, in a whisper.*) Do you like the Crib?

TOMMASINO (*quickly catching on to his father's ulterior motive for asking the question, he realizes that to consent would mean gaining his father's support—and the bill. Struggling with himself, he hesitates for a moment, then proudly affirms his decision*):   No.

LUCA (*showing the bill*):   Here it is! (*giving it to* **PASQUALE**)

PASQUALE (*exulting*):   I knew so all the time!

LUCA: For shame . . . You thief!

TOMMASINO (*allusively*):   I still don't like it!

PASQUALE (*after looking closely at both sides of the bill, he finally identifies the mark he'd made on it, thus proving what he'd suspected from the start. He then taps the bill with his index finger.*) Here's the cross . . .

LUCA: Let me see that. (*takes the bill from* **PASQUALE** *and looks at it closely*) You couldn't be a bigger embarrassment! He marked the bill, now you can't deny it. (*He notices another mark on the bill, the one he himself had made in order to catch his son. For a moment, he is somewhat perplexed. Then he pulls his brother aside and informs him of what he's just discovered.*) Pasquale, this here is the star I had marked.

PASQUALE: Where?

LUCA: Right here. Since my money would often disappear, I marked it.

PASQUALE: It must have been . . .

LUCA: That way you steal from me, and he steals from you . . .

PASQUALE: Now wait a minute . . .

LUCA: Pasquale, leave my money alone. With God as my witness, I . . .

PASQUALE: A pure coincidence. You used a star? And I used a . . .

LUCA: A lowdown trick is what you used. I turn my head, and the five scudi are gone. (*Trapped by the truth,* **PASQUALE** *remains silent.*) Now, how can I say anything to the boy? You know his answer: "Look at my uncle". . . But now that's enough. It's Christmas, so let's just forget the whole thing.

PASQUALE (*to his nephew*):   Don't you do it again.

LUCA: No one here will do it again.

VITTORIO: Well, I'd best be on my way.

LUCA: Already?

CONCETTA: Yes, it's time for him to leave.

TOMMASINO: Why don't you stay awhile?

VITTORIO: I'm sorry, but I really must go.

LUCA: Where will you spend Christmas?

VITTORIO: I'm by myself here in Naples. My family's in Milan. I'll probably eat out and retire early.

LUCA: Why not eat here?

CONCETTA (*out of an instinctive protest she punches her husband in the back*): You can't do anything right . . .

LUCA (*resentfully*): Concetta, will you calm down?! (*rubbing his lower back*) I've got a bad back. (*aside to his wife*) What's with that face? You'd think we were starving! Dinner's ready, and there's plenty of food. How much can he eat anyway? Gentlemen like him don't eat a lot. (*with determination, to* VITTORIO) I insist that you be our guest. The thought of you eating out, alone, on Christmas Eve, that saddens me . . . (*With the help of* TOMMASINO *and* PASQUALE, LUCA *removes* VITTORIO'S *coat, while* VITTORIO *makes only a weak show of resistance.*)

PASQUALE: Please, do make yourself at home. My brother really means what he says.

VITTORIO: I know he does, but . . .

LUCA: I'll take offense if you leave. You're my son's friend, and I just won't allow you to spend Christmas Eve alone. (*doorbell offstage*) That's my daughter with her husband! Tommasino, the door!

(TOMMASINO *exits quickly.*)

CONCETTA (*pulling* VITTORIO *aside*): You snake!

VITTORIO: You know I couldn't refuse.

NINUCCIA (*dressed elegantly, she carries a gift-wrapped box of pastries, which she hands to her mother*): Merry Christmas! (*embraces her mother*)

NICOLINO (*giving another box of pastries to Luca*): Merry Christmas, everybody! (*approaching* CONCETTA *and* NINUCCIA)

LUCA (*after helping his son-in-law off with his coat, he folds it and hands it to* PASQUALE): Pasquale, put it in the other room, on the couch.

PASQUALE: I'll take care of it. (*He starts off, then, taking advantage of the general confusion, he runs his hand through the coat's pockets.*)

(*The move does not escape* LUCA'S *attention. In angry disbelief he wrenches the coat from his brother, whose venturesome hand remains stuck in a pocket.*)

LUCA: Since when does family have to go through customs?!

PASQUALE (*confused*): I was only sticking his gloves in the pocket.

LUCA: I'm sure you were! (*In the meantime,* LUCA *notices* TOMMASINO *obsequiously approaching his sister, whom he helps with her hat and pocketbook. Having taken them, he artfully fingers the pocketbook as he exits right, hurriedly.* LUCA *follows him. Shortly thereafter,* TOMMASINO *returns to the dining room and takes cover behind his mother.* LUCA *is at his heels, carrying the pocketbook, which he hands over to* CONCETTA.) You hold on to this!

NICOLINO (*moving away from the women and closer to* PASQUALE): Pasquale, how's the lottery these days?

PASQUALE: Things are so good that my head's even spinning with numbers! It's the holidays, and there's people lining up everywhere. (*The two continue to talk.*)

(*Meanwhile, the two women are off by themselves.* **LUCA** *is busy giving his son another lecture.* **VITTORIO**, *who has remained unnoticed since the couple's arrival, is looking at the Crib.*)

NICOLINO (*having exhausted the conversation with* **PASQUALE**):   Are we all here?

LUCA (*joyfully*):   Sure are! Nicolino, by the way, there's even a friend of my son. His family is up in Milan, so I told him to stay and eat with us . . . Is that alright?

NICOLINO: Of course it is. Why not?

LUCA: I'll introduce you . . . (*The women's dismay is obvious.*) Vittorio, I want to *represent* you to my son-in-law. (**VITTORIO** *approaches with downcast eyes.*) Nicolino, this is Mr. Vittorio Elia, who'll be spending Christmas Eve with us. (*proudly, pointing to his son-in-law*) Nicola Percuoco, button manufacturer. (*Upon seeing* **VITTORIO**, **NICOLINO** *is petrified. His face betrays a surge of boundless scorn, as* **VITTORIO** *hints at a nod of acknowledgment.* **LUCA** *and* **PASQUALE** *look at each other, surprised by the coldness between the two.* **CONCETTA**, *with dread in her heart, rearranges something on the cupboard, in order to look busy while whispering to* **TOMMASINO**. *A disoriented* **LUCA** *asks his brother*):   What happened?

(**PASQUALE** *shrugs his shoulders.*)

NICOLINO (*pulling a devastated* **NINUCCIA** *aside, he asks with repressed rage*):   Did you know about this? (*Fist trembling, he clutches* **NINA'S** *hand.*)

NINUCCIA (*screaming, out of pain*):   Aahhhh! (*She frees her hand, and while massaging it with the other says through clenched teeth.*) Stop it, you're hurting me!

LUCA (*after seeking an answer from the others with his eyes*):   What happened?

NINUCCIA: Nothing . . .

LUCA: Concetta, what happened?

CONCETTA: Nothing, nothing . . .

LUCA (*he picks up a soup bowl and rattles it threateningly against the underlying plate*): What happened?

CONCETTA: Nothing, Luca, nothing.

LUCA (*vexed*):   As if I can ever know anything!

TOMMASINO (*aping his father, he asks* **CONCETTA**):   What happened?

CONCETTA: Nothing, sweetheart, nothing.

TOMMASINO (*more forcefully*) What happened?! (*He bangs the bowl against the plate, smashing both.*)

CONCETTA: My God, what madness! Nina, come give me a hand in the kitchen.

(*The two women exit left.*)

NICOLINO (*having succeeded in pulling* **VITTORIO** *aside, he addresses him in a low voice*):   You owe me an explanation.

VITTORIO: What do you mean?

NICOLINO: You know what I mean.

VITTORIO: I'm not the diviner you think I am.

NICOLINO: This won't end here, you can be sure.

VITTORIO: As you wish.

LUCA (*interrupting the hushed conversation, he proudly shows* **NICOLINO** *the Three Wise Men that Vittorio has already seen*):   These here are the Three Wise Men: Gaspar, Melchior, and Balthasar . . .

NICOLINO (*distracted by his own thoughts*):   Are they eating with us too?

LUCA (*amused*):   Are you ever in a daze! You fought with Ninuccia again, didn't you? . . . Ah, always making fools of yourselves . . . Vittorio, just look: husband and wife, and they're always at it. (*to* **NICOLINO**.) It was over food, wasn't it? (*laughs in a good-hearted way*) My daughter there, she tortures the man . . . Doesn't want him eating pasta, says he gets fat . . . But he doesn't want to eat vegetables . . . Can you blame him? Tell me the truth, you had pasta, didn't you? (*Annoyed,* **NICOLINO** *nods in assent, with a bitter smile.*) So what if you did! As if a working man should worry about the size of his belly . . . Is that what you fought about? Was that it?

NICOLINO (*haphazardly toying with a knife, feigning indifference*):   No, no, you're wrong. Never before has there been such . . . unity. (*As he speaks, he points at everyone in the room with the knife, tracing a semicircle in the air, then stretches his arm toward the kitchen, to include even* **CONCETTA** *and* **NINUCCIA** *in the lot.*)

LUCA (*sensing that something is troubling his son-in-law, he remains tentative*):   That's good to hear . . . Then you and Ninuccia must have worked things out . . . I'm always fighting with my wife, too . . . People in the alley even hear us yelling sometimes . . . But we still love each other. Just try badmouthing me to Concetta! She'll have none of it! There's a real bond between us, between all of us . . . Right, Tommasino? (*He has barely uttered the sentence when everyone is startled by a thud:* **TOMMASINO**, *overcome by an irresistible urge, has just thrown the core of an apple he'd been eating at the Crib.* **LUCA**, *realizing what has happened, pounces on his son for an explanation.*) What happened? Why, I'll break every bone in your body!

TOMMASINO: There was a fly on top of St. Joseph's head.

LUCA: A fly . . . whoever heard of flies in December?! I don't understand you, you say you don't like the Crib, but then you're always around it. (*to* **NICOLINO**) It's just that he's a bit spiteful; deep down he really loves the family. Even though he's a big boy and not a baby anymore, every year he still writes his mother a Christmas letter. As well he should. I don't care how old they are, but children should always respect their mother. (*turning proudly to his son*) Tommasino, let's hear the letter you wrote.

TOMMASINO (*reluctantly*):   What's to hear? It's like every other year's.

LUCA: So what if it is? Nicolino wants to hear you read it.

PASQUALE: Here we go again . . . Every year, the same story . . .

LUCA: You can go to your room if you don't want to hear it. (*to his son*) Go on, read . . . (*alluding to* **CONCETTA**) Go on: she can't hear you, she's in the kitchen. (*to* **NICOLINO**) Listen, just listen to the passion in the boy.

(*He sits next to* **NICOLINO**, *getting ready to listen with attention. A hostile* **PASQUALE** *sits across the room, skeptical about Tommasino's show of filial piety.*)

TOMMASINO (*sitting in the middle of the group he takes the letter out of his pocket. After lowering* *his eyes toward* **PASQUALE***, he reads*): "Dear mother, Merry Christmas to you. Dear mother . . ."

PASQUALE: Again?!

LUCA: Pasquale, shut up. You know the boy was sick with his nerves, what it took to *restore* him . . . I refuse to assume any responsibility: what if he smashes a plate on your head? . . . You know he's nervous. Look at his leg.

(**TOMMASINO** *twitches his leg in the way of a threat.*)

PASQUALE: I see it. I see it . . .

LUCA (*to* **TOMMASINO**): Continue.

TOMMASINO: "Dear mother, starting today I want to be a good son. I promise to respect you always. I've made up my mind, and want to change. Please prepare . . ."

PASQUALE (*quickly, ironically*): . . . my socks, shirt, and underwear. (**TOMMASINO** *responds by hurling a plate at Pasquale's feet. Aghast,* **PASQUALE** *jumps out of his seat and looks in disbelief at the scattered shards, frightened at the thought of what might have happened had the plate hit him.*) Luca, he threw a dish at me!

LUCA: I warned you about his nervous condition, how we had to restore him . . . He's nervous!

TOMMASINO: You see my leg? Look at my leg.

LUCA: Pasquale, just be quiet. We have to eat, and there aren't many dishes left!

PASQUALE: OK, I'll keep quiet. I'll shut up. You louse! (*Mumbling,* **PASQUALE** *turns his chair around and his back to* **TOMMASINO**.) Read, read . . . I could care less.

LUCA: Continue.

TOMMASINO (*gloating over his "heroics," he gets ready to read again*): "Dear mother, I've decided: I want to change. Please prepare me a nice present. I told you so last year, and I'll tell you again."

LUCA: That line is the same every year.

TOMMASINO (*reading*): "Dear mother, may the good Lord grant you a long life, together with Papa, Ninuccia, Nicolino, and me . . . Dear mother . . ."

PASQUALE: I'm not on there, am I?

LUCA (*to* **TOMMASINO**): Continue.

PASQUALE: Wait a minute, I want to clear this up.

LUCA: I know you do, but it's best that we continue.

PASQUALE: Wait a minute. (*to* **TOMMASINO**) Why wasn't I on the list?

LUCA: Pasquale, forget it.

PASQUALE: What do you mean forget it? I'm his uncle, and he should have me on the list.

TOMMASINO: I can't.

PASQUALE: Why not?

TOMMASINO: Because I can't. There's not enough room.

PASQUALE: No room? That paper's the size of a billboard. You put me on the list. (*becoming enraged beyond all reason*) You hear? You put me on there: if not, this'll be one Christmas you'll never forget! (*He takes a fork and threatens to stick it right in the middle of his nephew's head.*) You put me on that list, you hear, or I'll stick this fork in your head! (*He then throws the fork violently onto the table, hollering as he moves away.*) His number's up, and they'll soon be playing it in the alley . . . This time I want more than just his head!

LUCA (*terrified*): Pasquale, you wouldn't!

PASQUALE: I would, too!

LUCA (*mocking his brother's gestures*): Pasquale, what is this? Father was right to call you a "hothead"!

PASQUALE: Damn right I'm a hothead! Just watch I don't set fire to your son . . .

LUCA: Now tell me: if he puts you on the list, you really think you'll live to be a hundred?

PASQUALE: No.

LUCA: So then . . .

PASQUALE: It's the principle of it all!

LUCA: All right, all right. (*addressing his son with an air of indisputable authority*) Put him down for a long life as well.

TOMMASINO: But how?

LUCA: I said put him down for a long life too. The rest is God's business.

PASQUALE (*exasperated*): Pharisees, that's what you are, pharisees! (*to **TOMMASINO**, with an air of superiority*) See if I care, don't put me down.

TOMMASINO (*having amended the list, he starts reading again*): Cara mamma, "may the good Lord grant you a long life, together with Papa, Ninuccia, Nicolino and me, and to Uncle Pasquale too, but not without being sick now and then . . ."

PASQUALE (*fuming, pacing around the room*): You bastard, you! . . .

LUCA (*amused by his son's wit, to **PASQUALE***): Come on, can't you tell it's all in fun . . . (*turning to **VITTORIO***) We may make a fuss, but there's no bad feelings. We're all family, and there's nothing more important than family. You know, we even exchange gifts almost every holiday. Me, I buy my wife a present every year. Two years ago I gave her some fabric to make a coat for herself. Last year I *redempted* her earrings from the pawn shop . . . I left them on the table for her . . . she was so happy . . . This year I pawned the earrings and bought something else. Wait, I'll show you. (*exits right*)

PASQUALE: I want to get my present too. (*exits up left*)

LUCA (*enters right, carrying a wrapped woman's umbrella. He goes to **VITTORIO***): Look here. (*showing the umbrella*) She lost her umbrella, and I bought her one that's even more beautiful. I got a good deal on it from a shop owner friend of mine. The frame's really strong and the fabric is good for rain, wind, and sun. Especially in winter, with all the wet weather.

VITTORIO: Truly lovely.

PASQUALE (*returning, he approaches the two and shows them a purse of fake leather*): And this is my gift.

LUCA: I've even thought of how we'll give them . . . Nico, you watch for my wife, I want to arrange a little surprise. (*He pulls **TOMMASINO** and **PASQUALE** aside.*) When we sit down to eat . . . after Concetta sits down, we'll come out just like the Three Wise Men carrying their gifts: Gaspar, Melchior, and Balthasar . . . I even thought of what to say. I'll sing: (*to the tune of "Little Drummer Boy"*)

> *My dear Concetta*, pa-ra-pa-pum-pum . . .
> *I bear a gift for you*, pa-ra-pa-pum-pum . . .
> *take this umbrella*, pa-ra-pa-pum-pum . . .
> *Concetta bella . .* '

PASQUALE: And I'll sing:

> *My dear Concetta*, pa-ra-pa-pum-pum,
> *I bear a gift for you*, pa-ra-pa-pum-pum,
> *accept this purse from me*, pa-ra-pa-pum-pum,
> *to hold your money* . . .

TOMMASINO (*interrupting, disappointed*): And what do I sing?

LUCA: Nothing . . . You follow along and go: *"Pa-ra-pa-pum-pum!"*

TOMMASINO: I want to carry the purse!

LUCA: You can't, that's Uncle Pasquale's gift. You bring your letter in a dish.

(*Offstage: the sound of a flurry of excited footsteps, a dull thud, the crash of kitchenware and rolling pots.* **CONCETTA** *is heard shrieking.*)

CONCETTA (*offstage, crying for help*): Luca, Luca!

LUCA (*alarmed*): What happened?

NINUCCIA (*entering, hysterically, on the verge of despair*) We were cutting the eels when one escaped!!

LUCA: So?! All that ruckus for an eel . . .

NINUCCIA: Mamma was trying to catch it when she banged her head against the stove.

LUCA (*alarmed*): Is she hurt? (*exits left, running*)

PASQUALE: You two . . . (*exits after* **LUCA**)

TOMMASINO: Mother, are you hurt? (*runs to help his mother*)

(*Offstage the four voices are heard. While* **CONCETTA** *moans and* **LUCA** *chastises her,* **TOMMAS-INO** *and* **PASQUALE** *are busy helping* **CONCETTA** *to get up. Shortly thereafter, she appears supported by* **LUCA**. **PASQUALE** *and* **TOMMASINO** *are anxious to find out the seriousness of the injury.*)

LUCA (*he enters holding up* **CONCETTA**, *whom he sits down in a chair in the middle of the room.*) Sit here. Does it hurt bad? (**CONCETTA** *is a bit dazed: she answers absentmindedly, talking to everyone indistinctly as she rubs the bump on her forehead.* **LUCA**, *pointing to the bump, continues.*) Look at that! You could have lost an eye! And a little more to the side and you'd be dead . . . When will you learn you're not a spring chicken anymore? Will you get it through your skull that you've gotten old!

(**NINUCCIA**, *in the meantime, has folded a napkin in the form of a triangle, and wraps it around her mother's head.*)

LUCA: Where'd the eel end up?

CONCETTA: Under the stove, with the kindling.

LUCA: Let's see if we can get it. (*exits left with* **PASQUALE** *and* **TOMMASINO**)

(*Shortly thereafter, the clatter of pots, pans, and broken dishes can be heard as the three battle the stubborn eel. Then there follows the tumbling, crashing sound of furniture. The women are aghast.*)

TOMMASINO (*enters running*):   The cupboard fell! (*runs back to the kitchen*)

(*Other sounds follow. The three men finally return, disheveled and out of breath.* **LUCA** *is limping;* **PASQUALE** *is rubbing his back. Only* **TOMMASINO** *comes out unscathed, having also managed in the scuffle to sneak some food which he stealthily eats.*)

LUCA: You can forget that eel! . . . He jumped right out the window and into the courtyard.

CONCETTA: Alright now, let's eat. I'm going into the kitchen. (*exits left*)

NICOLINO: I'd like to wash my hands. (*He follows* **CONCETTA**.)

LUCA: Let's all go wash our hands. Pasquale, do you have a pumice stone and some soap?

PASQUALE: In my room. (*exits up left*)

LUCA (*to* **TOMMASINO**):   You come too. You should wash your hands before you eat. (**TOMMASINO** *exits up left.*) Mr. Vittorio, we'll be right back. Nina, you keep Mr. Vittorio company. (**LUCA** *also exits up left.*)

VITTORIO (*after a brief pause, in which he takes note of Ninuccia's coldness*):   I didn't want to stay . . . Your father insisted. But I can still leave.

NINUCCIA: Now it'd be worse. But I know why you're doing this: you've decided to make happen what never should happen.

VITTORIO (*bitterly*):   You're right. (*He shows her a letter from his pocket.*) It's from my mother. She wants to know why I'm not spending Christmas with her . . .

NINUCCIA (*with intended indifference*):   So why aren't you?

VITTORIO: When you talk like that God knows what I'd do . . . (*passionately*) I don't mean a thing to you anymore, do I?

NINUCCIA (*breaking down*):   Vittorio, I don't know what to say anymore . . .

(**VITTORIO** *pulls her to himself, ardently embracing and kissing her.*)

NICOLINO (*having entered a few seconds earlier, he now approaches the two and separates them violently. He slaps* **VITTORIO** *across the face, choking as he yells*):   You son of a bitch!

VITTORIO: You swine!

NICOLINO (*after brandishing a knife, he is now on the defensive, backing into the china closet*):   I want you downstairs! Now!

VITTORIO (*accepting the challenge, he threatens in turn*):   So let's go!

NINUCCIA (*taking sides with* **VITTORIO** *against her husband*):   Vittorio, no, don't! (*She throws herself between the two men to defend* **VITTORIO**.)

VITTORIO: Your wife doesn't love you! You hear! She doesn't love you!

CONCETTA (*ignorant of what has transpired, she brings in a steaming bowl of broccoli*):   Let's all enjoy God's favor and eat! (*Upon seeing the three she immediately realizes what's happened and remains transfixed.*)

NICOLINO (*his teeth clenched, he points out to* **CONCETTA** *the appalling sight of the two lovers and says*):   This is your daughter. Look at her, defending her lover! (*meaning to insult* **CONCETTA**) And you, Madam, knew all the time!

CONCETTA: How dare you . . . !

VITTORIO (*threateningly, to* **NICOLINO**):   Let's go. (*quickly exits up*)

NICOLINO (*threateningly, to* **NINUCCIA**):   I'll see to you later. (*exits after* **VITTORIO**)

NINUCCIA (*distraught, to her mother*):   Mamma, they'll kill each other! (**CONCETTA**, *stunned, has fallen into a chair by the table. All she can do is communicate to* **NINUCCIA** *that her legs are as if paralyzed.*) Mother, mother! (*having made up her mind*) By the time you move . . . (*exits running upstage, yelling after* **VITTORIO**) Vittorio, Vitto' . . .

(*After a brief pause,* **LUCA**, **TOMMASINO**, *and* **PASQUALE** *enter upstage. Using multicolored throw rugs and paper crowns, they are dressed in makeshift costumes like the Three Wise Men.* **LUCA** *carries the umbrella,* **PASQUALE** *the change purse, and* **TOMMASINO** *the dish with the letter. Each of them whirls a sparkler, as together they sing their Christmas song.*)

THE THREE:
> My dear Concetta, pa-ra-pa-pum-pum.
> I bear a gift for you, pa-ra-pa-pum-pum.
> Take this umbrella, pa-ra-pa-pum-pum.
> Concetta bella .

(**PASQUALE** *follows with his version for the change purse, with* **TOMMASINO'S** *accompaniment. After going halfway around the table, they stop, kneel, and lay their gifts at* **CONCETTA'S** *feet, who stares at them in crazed disbelief.*)

ACT 3

Once more Luca Cupiello's bedroom, three days after that disastrous Christmas Eve. **LUCA** *is bedridden, practically unconscious. Reality has broken the tried and tired body of a man who for years had lived in naive and ignorant bliss. His back supported by four or five cushions, his chin pressed against his chest,* **LUCA CUPIELLO** *has just dozed off after a long and sleepless night.* **CONCETTA** *is sitting in an armchair to his right surrounded by* **CARMELA**, **OLGA**, *and* **MRS. ARMIDA ROMANIELLO**. *The latter are all friends from the building, who apparently have been comforting* **CONCETTA** *all night long. To* **LUCA'S** *left are* **RITA**, **MARIA**, *and* **ALBERTO**, *another group of concerned friends from the building sitting on Tommasino's bed. While the group of women to his right talk in hushed and commiserating tones about the incident, the younger group to his left is busy whispering about superficial matters of concern to them alone. After a brief pause, the upstage door opens and* **RAFFAELE**, *the doorman, enters. He is carrying a tray with six mismatched coffee cups, teaspoons, and saucers. He comes forward cautiously as he carries a brimming coffee pot in the other hand, using a small rag as a potholder. He approaches the group of women on Luca's right to begin pouring the coffee.*

RAFFAELE: I just made it fresh.

CARMELA: We're living on coffee.

RAFFAELE (*to* **OLGA**): Your husband called me from the kitchen window.

OLGA: What did he want?

RAFFAELE: I really didn't hear him since just then I was busy with the coffee. He did say he's on his way down. (*offering a cup to* **CONCETTA**) Concetta, here, have a sip.

CONCETTA (*worn ragged*): I can't. I just can't.

CARMELA: But you must. How else will you hold up?

(**CONCETTA** *barely sips the coffee and immediately pushes the cup away.*)

ARMIDA (*softly addressing the group on the left*): Children, have some coffee.

(**RAFFAELE** *moves toward the younger group and serves them.*)

ALBERTO: If I don't have my coffee, I fall asleep standing up.

(*There are two cups on the tray:* **RITA** *takes one,* **MARIA** *is about to take the second.*)

RAFFAELE: Wait, we'll give this one to Pasqualino. (*He approaches* **PASQUALE**, *who is standing by himself looking out the balcony doors.*) Pasquale, have some coffee.

(**PASQUALE** *takes the cup from* **RAFFAELE** *and sips it as he continues to stare out the window.*)

ALBERTO (*to Raffaele*): Bring two more cups.

RAFFAELE: From where? There were only four in the kitchen . . . I brought two, which are all I have . . .

RITA (*lifting her cup*): Here, use this. I'm finished.

(**RAFFAELE** *fills Rita's cup again.*)

MARIA: Wait, me first. (*She drinks.*)

LUIGI (*he is a well-to-do older businessman, the husband of* **OLGA PASTORELLI**. *He enters quickly, being in a hurry to get to the office.*) Buongiorno. (*He approaches the group of women; to* **CONCETTA**, *with deference.*) Buongiorno, Concetta.

(**CONCETTA** *acknowledges him with a nod.*)

OLGA (*alluding to what* **RAFFAELE** *had said earlier concerning her husband*): What is it you wanted?

LUIGI: I wanted to know if you were staying here, or if you were going back up . . . I have to run. (*handing a key to his wife*) Here's the house key. I didn't even have coffee.

RAFFAELE (*showing the coffee pot to* **LUIGI**, *he leaves* **ALBERTO** *dumbfounded, who just then was extending the cup that Maria had used to have it refilled*): Here you go . . . (*Approaching the group on the right, he takes Olga's cup and refills it.*) Your wife drank out of this cup.

(**LUIGI** *drinks.*)

ALBERTO (*claiming his share of the coffee*): Raffaele . . . ?

RAFFAELE: It's all gone. (*turns over the coffee pot to show* **ALBERTO**) I'll go make you a small pot.

(**ALBERTO** *resigns himself to waiting and starts talking again with the girls.* **RAFFAELE** *exits upstage.*)

LUIGI (*to* **CONCETTA**):   Signora, how goes your husband?

CONCETTA: The doctor came last night. He frowned at what he saw.

LUIGI: Did he sleep well?

CONCETTA: Sleep? Who slept? He kept calling Nicolino, he wanted Nicolino . . . He wouldn't stop!

CARMELA: I have a feeling things are going to turn out. Last night he was bad, really bad . . . but now he's resting well.

CONCETTA: No, there's something not right with my Luca. His left arm, it doesn't move, his tongue is stiff, he talks funny . . . I don't know what's going on . . .

LUIGI: Does he recognize anybody?

CONCETTA: Sometimes yes, sometimes no. Last night I was by his side trying to talk to him: "Luca, it's me. It's me, Concetta." Do you know who he thought I was? He looked at me and said: "Basilio!" He was still thinking of the *Barber of Seville;* we saw it three weeks ago at the Opera House together. (*The group on Luca's left laughs at Concetta's words.*) We got the tickets free. You should have seen our seats . . .

ALBERTO (*quietly, to the girls*):   She's the spitting image of Basilio . . .

(*The* **GIRLS** *laugh the hardest; the group to Luca's right picks up on the inopportune laughter, emphasizing its displeasure with gestures.*)

ARMIDA: Did we miss something?

MARIA (*covering up as best she can*):   No, it's . . . uhh . . . just that Alberto doesn't have any coffee.

NINUCCIA (*enters left carrying a steaming bowl of broth. Her face betrays her intense suffering*):   Mamma, should we give him some chicken broth? It's nice and hot.

CONCETTA: Let's leave him be: he just dozed off . . . Carmela, what do you think?

CARMELA: It's better that he rest.

OLGA: You can always heat it again for him when he wakes up.

(**NINUCCIA** *covers the bowl with a plate and puts it aside.*)

CONCETTA: When's the doctor coming?

NINUCCIA: He should have been here by now.

CONCETTA: Where's Tommasino?

NINUCCIA: He went to send another telegram to Nicolino. He'll be here soon.

LUIGI (*looking at his watch*):   I should run, but then, I would like to wait for Luca to wake up. In fact, I will wait. Then I'll leave.

CONCETTA (*to* **NINUCCIA**, *chastising her*):   Are you happy now? . . . We were standing right here when I told you: "Swear to me that you'll make peace with your husband and put an end to all this" . . . Now look what you've done!

(*A dejected* **NINUCCIA** *hangs her head.*)

CARMELA: Concetta, leave the girl be . . . How could she have known it would come to this?

CONCETTA: She was stubborn. And since I never told Luca anything, what happened three nights ago was too much for him . . . He took sick, and now he's in bed, closer to the next world than to this one. All he does is call for Nicolino. He wants to see Nicolino, and meanwhile we've sent three telegrams, and Nicolino still hasn't shown up . . .

CARMELA: Why? Did her husband leave her?

CONCETTA: Right away. He went to stay with some relatives in Rome, said he doesn't want to see her again. (*whimpering*) We're finished . . .

CARMELA: Concetta, come now . . .

LUIGI: I really should run.

OLGA: So what are you waiting for? If you have to leave, leave. Can't you ever make up your mind?

LUIGI: I thought I had something else to tell you . . . Oh yes: should I come home to eat?

OLGA: If you want to come home, come home. I'll make some pasta with butter.

LUIGI: Concetta, I would stay . . . but I have to show some samples to a customer from Milan.

TOMMASINO (*enters quickly up right and heads straight toward his mother*): I sent the telegram . . . (*He gives* **CONCETTA** *the receipt and some change.*) Here's the change. How's Papa?

CONCETTA: He's resting, don't make any noise. (*praising her son's closeness to his father under such tragic circumstances*) My son . . . He's all I have left! Look at that face of his. It's three nights he's watched by his father's bedside. As if he had nothing else to do . . . Running up and down the building twenty, thirty times a day . . . to the pharmacist, the doctor . . . My poor son! And to think they used to say he was no good.

(*Meanwhile,* **TOMMASINO** *is sitting at the foot of the bed, next to his father.*)

LUIGI: I really do have to run.

LUCA (*he awakens with a jolt, stuttering*): Did Nicolino come?

(*Everyone immediately shows great concern and moves toward the bed as if to surround him.*)

CONCETTA: He's awake. What'd he say?

CARMELA: He wants to know if Nicolino came.

CONCETTA: Nicolino, he's always mumbling about Nicolino . . . (*sweetly, to* **LUCA**) Nicolino's coming, he'll be here later.

NINUCCIA: Papa, have some broth.

CONCETTA: Go warm it first.

(**NINUCCIA** *takes the bowl and exits left.*)

TOMMASINO (*concerned, glass in hand*): Father, your medicine . . .

CONCETTA: Later, the doctor said every hour.

TOMMASINO: Well, the hour's up.

PASQUALE (*with an air of superiority*):   No sir, it's not. There's still time.

TOMMASINO (*hostile as always toward his uncle*):   You shut up.

PASQUALE: I'm his brother, and I'll talk when I want.

TOMMASINO (*threateningly*):   We'll see about that.

PASQUALE (*in the same threatening tone*):   I'm sure we will.

CARMELA: This is no time to pick a fight.

RAFFAELE (*enters upstage, carrying a tray with two cups and a small coffee pot*):   Concetta, the doctor's here.

DOCTOR (*entering*):   Good morning everyone. How is everything?

CONCETTA: We've been on edge waiting for you. (*Meanwhile* **RAFFAELE** *has filled a cup with coffee and is handing it to* **ALBERTO**.) Raffaele, coffee for the doctor.

(**RAFFAELE** *takes the cup out of Alberto's hands, walks toward the* **DOCTOR** *and offers him the cup.*)

DOCTOR: Thank you. I left home in a hurry. I'll gladly have some. (*He drinks.*)

(**RAFFAELE** *moves toward* **ALBERTO** *but is stopped by* **TOMMASINO**, *who gestures with a cup to have it filled.*)

CONCETTA: Tommasino, have some, it'll do you good.

ALBERTO (*to the two girls*):   I'm going down to the cafe . . .

DOCTOR (*handing the empty cup to* **CONCETTA**):   Did he rest last night?

CONCETTA: He kept every one of us up . . . (*She takes a slip of paper from the night table and hands it to the* **DOCTOR**.) That's his temperature.

DOCTOR (*glancing at the sheet, he asks* **LUCA**):   Signor Cupiello, and how are we today? You look splendid . . .

LUCA (*ironically, pronouncing his words with difficulty*):   I wish I could say the same for you. (*He stares at* **LUIGI** *and happily exclaims.*) Nico! . . .

CONCETTA: It's not Nicolino, dear, it's Mr. Pastorelli. Luigi Pastorelli . . . Carmela's here too, and so is Armida and her daughter, and Mrs. Olga, Mr. Alberto, Maria, Miss Rita . . . They're all here to see you!

(*Everyone approaches the bed.*)

ALBERTO: Mr. Cupiello, we all want you up and out of bed!

LUIGI: We'll go and spend a day in the country.

MARIA: I'm coming too. Me too, me too!

RITA: We'll all be there together.

CARMELA: We'll have a party.

OLGA: A great big party to celebrate Mr. Luca!

ARMIDA: Hear, hear.

(*As the show of affection becomes deafening the* **DOCTOR** *intervenes.*)

DOCTOR (*clapping his hands*):   Enough, that's enough! (*to* **CONCETTA**) I told you yesterday, there are too many people in here.

CARMELA: But Doctor, these ladies just got here. It was only me keeping her company last night.

ARMIDA: We'd better leave. Let's go.

DOCTOR: Yes, that would be better.

(All the neighbors head for the door.)

ALBERTO: I'm going out for a cup of coffee.

RITA: Wait, give me a cigarette.

MARIA: Give me one too.

(ALBERTO hands out the cigarettes and exits, followed by the girls.)

LUIGI *(heading for the door with his wife)* I want to hear what the doctor says, then I'll run.

(They exit together.)

NINUCCIA *(enters left, carrying the bowl of broth)*: Mamma . . .

CONCETTA *(asking the DOCTOR for permission)*: Can he have some chicken broth? . . .

DOCTOR: Wait, I want to examine him first. *(Examines Luca's pupils, then raises the sheets to continue the routine examination. Amazed, he stops when he touches something unusual under the sheets. At first he relies on his sense of touch to figure out what it is; finally, he pulls out a pair of shoes. He then holds them up, as if to ask for an explanation.)*

CONCETTA *(deeply ashamed)*: Uhm . . . uhm . . . I'm so sorry, Doctor.

PASQUALE: If he didn't hide them, his son would sell them.

DOCTOR: Are you serious?!

TOMMASINO: As if I'd sell my father's shoes . . .

PASQUALE: Why not? Don't tell me you'd be afraid to.

(This time they limit themselves to miming their disagreement.)

DOCTOR *(after having listened to Luca's heart, he addresses everyone less than wholeheartedly)* Good. I'd say we're doing better.

CONCETTA: Our Lady is with us! *(With new vigor, she turns to LUCA.)* Luca, what's with you? Say something! Last time you were sick you never shut up. *(bringing CARMELA to his attention)* Carmela's here, tell her the story about the beans.

CARMELA *(playing up the part of the gossip)*: The beans? What about the beans? I'm dying to hear . . .

LUCA: Now there's a story for you . . . *(Amused by the memory, LUCA wants to tell the story, but his thought process is impaired as he constantly returns to the one idea that occupies his mind. In fact, out of the clear blue, he asks:)* Did Nicolino come?

CONCETTA: Not yet.

CARMELA: Tell us about the beans.

LUCA *(he tries to smile, but only manages a tragic grimace with his contorted mouth)*: One morning I woke up with a touch of fever. Right away Concetta said: "Call the doctor." Then I said: "Concetta, don't worry, it's nothing. Tomorrow I'll be fine." "No Sir," she says, "you're calling the doctor. Before you know there'll be complications and it'll be worse." "Alright, alright," I said: when that woman puts something in her head . . . So the doctor came, examined me, and said . . . Concetta, what did he say?

CONCETTA: He said it's intestinal.

LUCA: Intestinal, that's it. Can't eat. You eat and the fever stays with you . . . When is Nicolino coming?

CONCETTA: He's coming, Luca, he's coming.

LUCA: But did you send the telegram?

CONCETTA: Yes, yes. Tell Carmela about the beans. What did I do that day?

LUCA: That day Concetta had made pasta and beans. The aroma filled the whole house . . . I said: "Concetta, just today that I'm sick you go make pasta and beans? You know how much I like them!" "What pasta and beans?," she says, "I made soup." You see, Concetta knows soup's not my favorite . . . "Oh! Then where's that scent coming from?" "The lady across the way made them," she says. "Well then tell the lady across the way to send me some." "Nossiree," says Concetta, "you have to keep an empty stomach, or your fever won't go down. Then what will the doctor say?" "OK," I said, "we'll talk this over tonight." I am one of a kind! Right, Concetta?

CONCETTA: My Luca? There's only one . . .

LUCA: Concetta had fallen asleep. Then I got up and went into the kitchen, because I know when Concetta makes beans there's always enough for three days, 'cause we like to eat them cold the next day, or heated up at night . . . even for a late morning snack . . . So I sat down . . . there was already a spoon in the pot . . . and . . . (LUCA *makes a long series of smacking, slurping sounds while repeating a spooning motion with his hand.*) I ate all the beans! Wiped that pot clean. Then I came back here, slipped under the covers, and said: "There's always tomorrow." Concetta, aren't I something else? Next day I woke up with no fever at all. You tell her, Concetta: how was I the next day?

CONCETTA: Better, much better.

LUCA: I was all better. Then Dr. Know-It-All arrived: "You see? If you'd eaten you'd still have a fever." The jackass!

DOCTOR: I'll be leaving now, since I do have important calls to make.

(*The* DOCTOR *gets up while* CONCETTA, *with Carmela's help, fixes her husband's bed.*)

CONCETTA: Doctor, do excuse him . . .

DOCTOR: It's nothing, really.

NINUCCIA (*pulling the* DOCTOR *aside*): How is he, Doctor?

DOCTOR: There's no reason to lose hope. He's been hit hard, but I've seen worse cases turn out for the better.

NINUCCIA: Let's hope so . . . (*She then goes to her mother to share the doctor's words with her.*)

PASQUALE (*who's been listening to the doctor as well*): Won't you be calling tomorrow?

DOCTOR: What for? Pasquale, be strong, and keep the ladies' spirits up.

PASQUALE: What do you mean?

DOCTOR: Only a miracle, Pasquale . . . but he won't make it. In any case, if there's a change, send for me. (*to everyone*) Good day.

(*They all bid farewell to the* DOCTOR *as he takes his leave, and accompany him to the upstage door.*)

CONCETTA: Nina, let's get these cups out of the way. (NINUCCIA *does so.*) Now watch them all come back.

CARMELA: I'll give you a hand.

CONCETTA: In three days three pounds of coffee.

TOMMASINO: That's why they came in the first place.

PASQUALE: But they'll hear from me yet . . .

CARMELA: They deserve it. The way they were smothering the poor thing . . .

PASQUALE: I'm going to tell them right now. (*He makes for the door, but stops as he runs into* VITTORIO, *who is just arriving.*)

CONCETTA (*speechless at the sight of* VITTORIO; *after a brief pause she confronts him*): What are you doing here?

VITTORIO (*stricken with grief*): Signora Cupiello, don't chase me away. You have no idea how I've suffered these past three days. I know, it's all my fault . . . But believe me, I wish I were dead. I've been pacing outside for three nights now . . . I just saw the doctor leave . . . I wanted to kiss Signor Luca's hand. Please, don't deny me!

LUCA (*delirious, he thinks* VITTORIO *is* NICOLINO. *With a flash of joy in his eyes, he exclaims*): Nico! (*He leans over the side of the bed and grabs* VITTORIO'S *arm.*) Nicolino's here! Nico, you don't know how happy I am. They all said you weren't coming . . . (*No one dares to intervene. Even* VITTORIO, *eyes downcast, is frozen.* LUCA *pulls him close, and speaks to him tenderly.*) Nicolino does love me, doesn't he? (NINUCCIA *crumples onto the bed, as if in a daze.* TOMMASINO *is the only one to grasp the full impact of the tragedy: his face is alternately streaked with despair and rage.*) Where is Ninuccia?

NINUCCIA (*in tears*): I'm here, Father . . .

LUCA: Give me your hand . . . (*He manages to take* NINUCCIA'S *hand, and joins it with* VITTORIO'S. *His face brightens, and he speaks with greater clarity and strength.*) I want you to make peace right here before me and swear you'll never leave each other again. (*As the two don't speak, he insists.*) Swear it! You hear me? Swear it!

(*Offstage, the sounds of muffled excitement, from which the voice of* NICOLINO *emerges.*)

NEIGHBORS (*offstage voices*): Good day, signor Nicola.

NICOLINO: Where is he?

(CONCETTA *is the first to run in a frenzy toward the door; the others follow, similarly aghast.*)

RAFFAELE (*sticking his head in the doorway, he solemnly announces*): Signor Nicola.

(NICOLINO *appears, and heads directly for Luca's bed. Upon sighting his wife and* VITTORIO *before* LUCA, *the blood rushes to his head. He starts to lunge at them, but is forcibly held back by the other members of the family. Meanwhile, the group of neighbors has gathered behind* NICOLINO, *urging* him in hushed tones to have pity for the others consumed by the tragedy. Together, they manage to remove **NICOLINO** from the scene, who is alternately acquiescent and rebellious.)

LUCA (happy to have made peace between Ninuccia and her husband, he laughs out of satisfaction): They made up! I finally got them to make up! . . . Concetta, look! (to **NINUCCIA** and **VITTORIO**) You two were made for one another. So love each other. Concetta's suffered a lot, don't cause her any more grief . . . (**NINUCCIA** and **VITTORIO** slowly let go of each other's hands. **LUCA**, now totally delirious, mumbles something incomprehensible, waving his right arm as if to clutch something out of the air. His look is one of complacence, as his eyes wander and he asks:) Tommasino, Tommasino . . .

TOMMASINO (engulfed in despair, he moves toward his father, and murmurs): I'm here.

LUCA (shows his son his paralyzed arm: lifting it up with his other hand, he lets it drop, as if to prove its uselessness. He then entreats his son): Tommasino, do you like the Crib?

TOMMASINO (overcome with choking tears, can only say): Yes.

(Having heard his son's long-desired "yes," **LUCA** gazes off into the distance, as if following a magical vision. He sees a Nativity scene as big as the world, where festive swarms of tiny people are bustling toward the stable, and a tiny real donkey and a tiny real cow are warming a gigantic Baby Jesus with their breath: the Babe is stirring and crying, much like any tiny newborn would . . .)

LUCA (to himself, lost in his vision): What a lovely Crib! What a pretty, pretty Crib!

CURTAIN

ALTERNATE VERSION OF ACT 3

Translated by Anthony Molino from "*Natale in casa Cupiello*," *Il Dramma* 397–98 (March 1–15, 1943), pp. 72–86.

Translator's Note: From a practical standpoint, the entrance of only one neighbor in act 3 of this first printed version of the play will facilitate productions where cast size is a concern. This version can, in fact, be easily adapted to the first two acts presented in this anthology. The reader will note the playwright's changes in character depiction, especially of Concetta and Ninuccia; his description, through Luca's and Concetta's words, of the details of the confrontation between Nicola and Vittorio; and, perhaps most importantly, the doctor's appraisal of Luca's condition (and of Luca's character) in a conversation with Ninuccia that is not in the later revised version.

ACT 3

The scene is the same as in act 1. **LUCA**, *however, is ill; everything around him denotes a sense of an anguished bedside vigil. On the night table by the bed are several bottles of medicine. Candles are lit before the holy pictures on the dresser.* **PASQUALE**, *arms crossed, head hanging, is wearing a flimsy shawl and has his back turned.* **CONCETTA** *is seated stage left and is talking to* **CARMELA**. *The* *effects of watching over Luca all night are visible: her voice is tired; her eyes are red from crying bitterly; her gestures, slow and desolate.*

CONCETTA: Just like that, Donna Carmela . . . just like that: a house in ruins.

CARMELA (*a good neighbor, she tries to console* **CONCETTA**): Come now, don't be senseless. I have a feeling things are going to turn out . . . He's better than yesterday, and even you said he rested well last night. If it's God's will . . .

CONCETTA (*gesturing wearily*): Carmela, I no longer have the strength to go on . . . I've struggled all my life, and now I just can't anymore. (*She pauses.*) Poor Luca! Look at what's left of him . . .

CARMELA (*again trying to console her*): He'll recover, you listen to me.

CONCETTA (*disconsolate, shaking her head*): No, Carmela, no . . . When the doctor came yesterday, I looked at him, and his face said it all. I knew right away, but I didn't want to worry the children and Pasquale . . . Luca's only pretending he's okay . . . But I know there's something not right with him. His left arm doesn't move, his tongue is stiff, he talks funny . . . And you think something's not wrong? . . . (*She wipes away her tears.*)

CARMELA (*concerned*): Does he recognize anybody?

CONCETTA: Sometimes yes, sometimes no. Last night I was by his side trying to talk to him: "Luca, it's me. It's me, Concetta." You know who he thought I was? He looked at me and said: "Basilio! Don Basilio!" (*She explains.*) He was thinking of the *Barber of Seville;* we'd seen it at the Opera House together . . . You know, where there's the actor with the funny hat . . .

NINUCCIA (*enters left carrying a steaming bowl of broth*): Mamma, should we give him some chicken broth? It's nice and hot.

CONCETTA: Let's leave him be: he just dozed off . . . Carmela, what do you think?

CARMELA (*approvingly*): It's better he rests.

CONCETTA (*to* **NINUCCIA**): You can always heat it again for him when he wakes up.

(**NINUCCIA** *covers the bowl with a plate and places it on the night table.*)

CONCETTA: When's the doctor coming?

NINUCCIA: He should have been here by now.

CONCETTA: Where's Tommasino?

NINUCCIA: He went to send another telegram to Nicolino. He'll be here soon.

CONCETTA (*to* **NINUCCIA**, *chastising her*): Are you happy now? Are you? . . . We were standing right here when I told you: "Swear to me that you'll make peace with your husband and put an end to all this" . . . Now look what you've done!

NINUCCIA (*out of despair, eyes filled with tears*): Stop reminding me, will you! . . . Isn't there any pity in your heart? . . . (*moves toward Luca's bed, where he remains motionless*)

CARMELA: Concetta, please, leave the girl be . . . How could she have known it would come to this?

CONCETTA (*shaking her head*): Carmela, she was stubborn. You I can tell what happened: on Christmas Eve, the husband found them in the dining room, in each other's arms.

And when they went downstairs, ready to kill each other, Luca ran to separate them. That's when he found out. And since I never told him anything, what happened three nights ago was too much for him . . . He took sick, and now he's in bed, closer to the next world than to this one. All he does is call for Nicolino. He wants to see Nicolino, and meanwhile we've sent three telegrams, and Nicolino still hasn't shown up . . .

CARMELA (*after a pause*):   Why? Did her husband leave her?

CONCETTA: Immediately. He went to stay with some relatives in Rome, said he doesn't want to see her again. (*in an outburst of pain*) We're finished, Carmela, we're finished . . .

CARMELA (*with genuine regret*):   Now I see why . . .

TOMMASINO (*enters quickly up right and heads straight toward his mother*):   I sent the telegram . . . (*He gives* CONCETTA *the receipt and some change.*) Here's the change. (*looking toward his father*) How's Papa?

CONCETTA: He's resting, don't make any noise.

(TOMMASINO *sits at the foot of the bed, contemplating his father with sad, gloomy eyes.*)

CONCETTA (*to* CARMELA, *praising her son*):   My son . . . He's all I have left! Look at that face of his. It's three nights he's watched by his father's bedside. As if he had nothing else to do . . . Running up and down the building twenty, thirty times a day . . . to the pharmacist, the doctor . . . (*moved*) My poor son! And to think they used to say he was no good.

(LUCA *mumbles something.*)

CONCETTA (*she runs to the bed, followed by* CARMELA, *and places her finger on his lips to quiet him*):   He's awake.

(*All hold their breath, trying to make out Luca's drooled words.*)

LUCA (*whispering at first, then with greater strength*):   Nicolino! . . . Where's Nicolino?! . . . (*forcefully*) Nicolino!

(*Everyone is taken aback by his sudden show of energy.*)

CONCETTA: What did he say?

NINUCCIA: He wants to know if Nicolino's come.

CONCETTA: Your husband's all he thinks about . . . (*to* LUCA, *as if talking to a child*) Nicolino's on his way, he's on his way. We sent him a telegram. He'll be here soon.

TOMMASINO: Papa, have some broth.

CONCETTA (*to* NINUCCIA):   Go warm it first. It's gotten cold by now.

(NINUCCIA *takes the bowl and exits left.*)

TOMMASINO (*concerned, glass in hand*):   Father, your medicine . . .

CONCETTA: Later, the doctor said every hour.

TOMMASINO: But the hour's up . . .

PASQUALE (*matter-of-fact*):   No sir, it's not. There's still time.

TOMMASINO (*hostile as always toward his uncle*):   You shut up.

PASQUALE: I'm his brother, and I'll talk when I want, you hear . . .

TOMMASINO: We'll see about that, won't we? (*The brief altercation is different than usual. Caught in a routine, it's clear they now take no pleasure in arguing.*)

CARMELA: Now is this the time to pick a fight?

RAFFAELE (*enters upstage. With a subdued voice, he says*): Concetta, the doctor's here.

CONCETTA: Come in, please, do come in . . . Finally!

DOCTOR (*entering*): Good morning everyone. (*pulls up a chair and sits next to* **LUCA**) How is everything?

CONCETTA: Doctor, we've been so restless waiting for you.

DOCTOR: Did he sleep last night?

CONCETTA: He woke up a few times . . . then calmed down. (*She takes a slip of paper from the night table and hands it to the* **DOCTOR**.) That's his temperature.

DOCTOR (*he glances at the sheet and, with the hint of a frown, gives it back to* **CONCETTA**): Well then, that's fine . . . (*to* **LUCA**, *upbeat*) Signor Cupiello, and how are we today? You look splendid . . .

LUCA (*ironically, pronouncing his words with difficulty*): I wish I could say the same for you. (*His thought process impaired, he returns to the one idea that occupies his mind.*) Nico! . . .

CONCETTA: It's not Nicolino, dear, it's the doctor . . .

NINUCCIA (*enters left, carrying the bowl of broth*): Mamma . . .

CONCETTA (*asking the* **DOCTOR** *for permission*): Can he have some chicken broth? . . .

DOCTOR: Wait, I want to examine him first. (*Examines Luca's pupils, then raises the sheets to continue the routine examination. Amazed, he stops when he touches something unusual under the sheets. At first he relies on his sense of touch to figure out what it is; finally, he pulls out a pair of men's shoes. He then holds them up, as if to ask for an explanation.*)

CONCETTA (*deeply ashamed, she takes them and puts them away*): Uhm . . . uhm . . . I'm so sorry, Doctor. I guess he felt he had to hide them . . .

PASQUALE (*again, matter-of-fact*): His son would sell them if he didn't.

TOMMASINO (*again with hostility*): As if I'd sell my father's shoes . . .

CONCETTA (*signaling to the two men*): Stop it, both of you!

DOCTOR (*after having listened to Luca's heart, unconvincingly*): Good. I'd say we're doing better. Much better. (*He fixes Luca's bed and helps him get comfortable again before sitting back down.*)

CONCETTA (*flustered, but with sadness in her heart.*) Luca, what's with you? Say something! Last time you were sick in bed, you never shut up. (*suffering at the sight of his silence*) Donna Carmela's here, tell her the story about the beans.

CARMELA (*playing up the part of the gossip*): The beans? What about the beans? I'm dying to hear . . .

LUCA (*Luca's eyes are half-closed as the memory brings a smile to his face—a smile his contorted mouth can only turn into a tragic grimace. He tries to talk, but his tongue refuses to obey his thoughts. Finally, he strings together a story that, meant to entertain his family and friends, only intensifies their sadness and grief.*) When I was sick, last time . . . (*he chuckles*), the doctor said I shouldn't eat . . . (*He imitates the doctor.*) "He's not to eat anything, understood?"

(*chuckles again*) Well, that day Concetta had made pasta and beans. I love pasta and beans. Their scent filled the whole house, they were so good . . . And she cooked them just the way I like them too, a little on the hard side . . . So, anyway, Concetta wasn't around, so I got out of bed, headed for the kitchen, and licked the whole pot clean. Next day I woke up with no fever at all. And to think Dr. Know-It-All had said . . . The jackass!

CONCETTA: Doctor, do excuse him . . .

LUCA (*he continues*): So then . . . Nicolino . . . the crowd . . . Nicolino had a gun in his hand, and my daughter, Ninuccia . . . (*Luca's mind is tormented by the vision of the two men fighting on Christmas Eve. Fearful, with his paralyzed arm across his chest, he gesticulates frantically, out of anguish, with his good arm, mumbling the only name that still means something to him.*) Nicolino! . . . Go call Nicolino! . . .

(*With a show of affection, everyone tries to calm him down while again fixing his bed and propping him up against the pillows.*)

DOCTOR (*getting up from his chair*): I'll be leaving now, since I do have other calls to make. But send for me tomorrow, if there is any change.

CONCETTA: You mean you're not coming tomorrow?

DOCTOR: There's no need to . . . He's doing much better . . .

(CONCETTA *heaves a sigh of relief as she looks gratefully at the statue of the Madonna on the dresser.*)

NINUCCIA (*pulling the* DOCTOR *aside before he leaves*): Doctor, it's been three days you've been mincing your words. How is he, Doctor, the truth?

DOCTOR (*he looks at her seriously*): How is he? (*paternally*) Nina, I've known you since you were a little girl, so we can be frank. Your mother told me everything the other day.

NINUCCIA: (*hangs her head.*)

DOCTOR: When he found out you'd betrayed your husband, it was as if lightning hit him. (*Wanting to make sure* NINA *understands what he's about to say, as she continues to stare at him silently.*) Your father, Nina, Luca Cupiello, was an overgrown child: the world for him was one big toy . . . But when he realized it was time to play with that toy like a man, and not like a child . . . he simply couldn't. There is no man in Luca Cupiello . . . and the child had already lived too long.

NINUCCIA: (*continues to stare at him, without understanding.*)

DOCTOR (*commiserating with her, lovingly*): Ninuccia, Ninuccia . . . Like father, like daughter . . . (*softly, deciding to reassure her*) But he is doing better now.

NINUCCIA (*reassured, she lets out a sigh of relief as she settles in with the delusion*) Oh, Thank God! Let me walk you to the door . . .

DOCTOR: Why, thank you . . . (*While* NINUCCIA *goes to share the good news with her mother, he pulls* PASQUALE *aside and tells him in no uncertain terms.*) Pasquale, your brother's ill. Be strong, and keep the ladies' spirits up.

PASQUALE (*shrinking at the doctor's words, his voice trembling*): What do you mean?

DOCTOR: It'll take a miracle . . . Again, good day everyone!

CONCETTA (*happy at what Ninuccia's told her*):   Arrivederci! And thank you!

(*The* **DOCTOR** *exits through the upstage door. Suddenly, by the doorway,* **VITTORIO** *appears. He is extremely pale, and carries his hat in his hand.*)

CONCETTA (*she turns around and, at the sight of* **VITTORIO**, *confronts him contemptuously.*) What are you doing here?

VITTORIO (*grief-stricken*):   Signora Cupiello, don't chase me away. You have no idea how I've suffered these past three days. I know it's all my fault . . . But believe me, I wish I were dead and buried. I've been pacing outside for three nights now . . . when I just saw the doctor leave, and talked to him . . . (*His voice cracks.*) Donna Concetta, please, allow me to see him, to kiss his hand. Please, don't deny me!

LUCA (*delirious, he thinks* **VITTORIO** *is* **NICOLINO**. *With a flash of joy in his eyes, he exclaims with difficulty*):   Nicolino! You're here! Finally! I didn't think you'd make it in time! Nico! (*Everybody is shocked and left speechless.* **VITTORIO** *can only approach the bed, as* **LUCA** *grabs and pulls his hand.*) Nicolino's here! He's back! He came back! (*Crying,* **LUCA** *takes Vittorio's hand and brings it to his face, as if to ask Nicolino's forgiveness.*)

(*Dazed,* **NINUCCIA** *sits on the bed next to her father.* **TOMMASINO**, *meanwhile, eyes everyone with hostility, and* **VITTORIO** *with hatred. For him the deception has gone too far, and now borders on sacrilege.*)

LUCA (*still clutching at Vittorio's hand*):   Nicolino . . . (*looks about, straining his eyes to see*) Where's Ninuccia?

NINUCCIA (*gets closer*):   I'm here, Father . . .

LUCA: Give me your hand . . . (*He snatches Ninuccia's hand, and joins it with Vittorio's. His pitiful face brightens; surprisingly, he speaks with greater clarity and strength while everyone else looks on aghast.*) I want you to make peace right here before me, and swear you'll never leave each other again.

(*A bewildered* **NINUCCIA** *lowers her head. She doesn't dare lift her eyes to look at Vittorio.*)

LUCA (*insisting*):   Swear it! You hear me? Swear it!

NINUCCIA (*whispers*):   I swear, Father . . .

NICOLINO (*offstage*):   Where's Papa? . . . Where is he?

(*Everyone except* **VITTORIO** *and* **NINUCCIA**, *who continue to be held together by* **LUCA**, *runs toward* **NICOLINO**, *who appears upstage together with* **RAFFAELE** *the doorman, who is carrying his suitcase.*)

NICOLA: Papa! . . . (*He is taken aback: first at the sight of Vittorio, then of Vittorio and Ninuccia holding hands. Ready to lunge at them, he is held back and pulled away by* **CONCETTA, PASQUALE, CARMELA**, *and* **RAFFAELE**. *Together, they cover his mouth to smother his outrage, while gesturing desperately to communicate to him that Luca is dying. They finally manage to drag him outside while* **LUCA**, *delirious and about to expire, mutters.*)

LUCA: You two were made for one another, and must love each other until you die . . .

Concetta's suffered a lot, don't cause her any more grief . . . Please . . . The poor woman, she's been a martyr all her life!

(**VITTORIO** *slowly pulls away and hides his face in his hands, while* **NINUCCIA** *stays crumpled on her father's bed.*)

LUCA (*his fading voice more and more feeble*): Tommasino . . . Tommasì . . .

TOMMASINO (*choked and unable to speak, he looks at his father with desperate love.*)

LUCA (*shows his son his paralyzed arm: he lifts it up two or three times with his other hand, and each time lets it drop, as if to prove its uselessness*): Tommasino . . . (*His mind wanders back to his life's tender passion.*) Do you like the Crib? (*as if imploring his son to make him happy this one last time*) Do you like it, Tommasì?

TOMMASINO (*overcome by choking tears, he manages to whisper the one word* **LUCA** *had always hoped to hear, and to make him happy*): Yes, papa . . . yes.

LUCA (*in his childlike delirium, a vision of a myriad of Nativity scenes, of all sizes, dances in his head. In his imagination he is running after them, wanting to touch and embrace them. Bright candles, tinsel, and little stars swirl around him, lulling him into his final sleep. As the curtain drops,* **LUCA** *continues to swing his arm in the air as he exclaims*) So many Cribs . . . Look at all the pretty Cribs!

CURTAIN

Introduction

Ugo Betti was born in Camerino, in the Marches region, on February 4, 1892. His *Le nozze di Teti e Peleo* (Marriage of Thetis and Peleus), a blank verse translation of Catullus' *Epithalamium*, was published in 1910. He studied law at the University of Parma. During World War I, he served in the artillery from 1915 to the defeat at Caporetto in October 1917; until the end of 1918, he remained in a German prison camp, where he met Bonaventura Tecchi and Carlo Emilio Gadda. After the war, in 1919, he returned to Parma, entering the magistrature in 1921, and becoming a judge in 1923. His first play, *La padrona* (The mistress of the house, 1925), premiered in Leghorn and won a prize from the theater journal *La Scimmia e lo Specchio*. In 1930 he married Andreina Frosini. He was a judge in Rome between 1930 and 1943 when he retired to Camerino until after the liberation. After the war he worked as librarian for the Justice Department in Rome and served as a legal consultant to Coordinamento Spettacolo, the national association of writers and publishers. He died of cancer on June 9, 1953.

Ugo Betti is widely considered one of the most important Italian dramatists of the twentieth century, second only to Pirandello. Like other writers, he was strongly affected by the experience of World War I. In his 1914 university thesis, "Revolution and the Law," he argued that human nature is essentially egotistical and that violent revolution is a necessary prerequisite for progress. These views reflected the general outlook of Italian youth in the period preceding World War I, an outlook closely associated with the Futurist movement, which was then exploding in Italy. His war experiences from 1915–

■

TWELVE

UGO

BETTI

■

18, however, made him reappraise his ideas. The influence of the "twilight" poets and the symbolist movement can be seen in *Il Re pensieroso* (The pensive king),[1] a collection of poetry written in prison camp. In these early works Betti juxtaposes the fabulous world of childhood innocence and the adult world where death, disease, corruption, and poverty are components of reality. This became a recurring theme in his work.

While Betti continued to write in other modes throughout his career, it was as a play-wright that he made his major contribution to world literature. He wrote twenty-six plays, of which the majority are tragedies. In his first eight plays, Betti experimented with various styles: fairy-tales in the ballet-drama *L'isola meravigliosa* (The marvelous island, 1929) and the verse play *La donna sullo scudo* (The lady on the shield, 1927), written with Osvaldo Gibertini; symbolic realism in *La casa sull'acqua* (The house on the water, 1928); naturalism in *Albergo sul porto* (An inn on the harbor, 1930); and surrealist farce in *Il diluvio* (The flood, 1931). It was not until *Frana allo Scalo Nord* (*Landslide*, 1932), his first masterpiece, that his vision came into focus and critics recognized in him a powerful dramatic talent.

In the mid- to late 1930s, one of the most escapist periods in Italian drama, Betti wrote four charming and diverting comedies peopled with stock characters: *I nostri sogni* (Our dreams, 1936), *Una bella domenica di settembre* (A beautiful Sunday in September, 1936), *Favola di Natale* (Christmas fable, 1940), and *Paese delle vacanze* (Summertime, 1937). The latter is an idyllic love story full of jovial warmth, but even here, Betti contrasts innocence with corruption. Alberto, a country boy, finds he is more deeply attached to his poor, sweet childhood girlfriend than to the rich girl who has been tainted by the urban world of power and money. It is the best known of Betti's comedies to English readers and has had the most success in Italy. Betti has been accused of writing these comedies in order to sidestep important political issues, such as the invasion of Ethiopia and Spain by Fascist Italy, which occurred during that period.

The fourteen plays Betti wrote between 1940 and 1953 have been described by Henry Reed as one of "the greatest outbursts in dramatic literature." With the exception of his early masterpiece, *Landslide*, his best work belongs to this period: *Corruzione al Palazzo di Giustizia* (*Corruption in the Palace of Justice*, 1944–45), *Delitto all'isola delle capre* (*Crime on Goat Island*, 1946), which we are presenting here, *La regina e gli insorti* (*The Queen and the Rebels*, 1949) and *Il giocatore* (*The Gambler*, 1950).

Betti's drama reflects his concern with human motivations, the nature of evil, justice, and the law, a career to which he devoted himself for over twenty years. These preoccupations carried Betti into an existential realm where he examined the spiritual aspirations of human beings and the incongruity between those aspirations and the actuality of human existence. Any attempt to place his drama exclusively in a socioeconomic framework trivializes it. He is not as concerned with a scientific investigation of reality or with the influence of environment and heredity on people's lives as the nineteenth-century realists were but rather focuses on mankind's neverending quest for meaning. This is true even in his two plays that are explicitly concerned with politics—*The Queen and the Rebels* and *L'aiuola bruciata* (*The Burnt Flower-bed*, 1951–52).

Some critics have tried to link his drama with the tenets of Fascism. Betti's work, however, transcends any particular political period. Moreover, the Fascist authorities often censored his plays, and in 1938 he was charged with being both a Jew, which he was not, and anti-Fascist. After the war there was an investigation into Betti's Fascist alliance, but he was cleared of all charges.

While none of his plays adopt orthodox Roman Catholic tenets, they are metaphysical in nature, and the later plays are increasingly Christian in outlook. In the essay *Religione e teatro*,[2] written in 1953, the year of his death, Betti states that important contemporary theater draws breath from needs that are essentially religious and expresses them in a variety of ways. For him, religion is not a palliative to ease the human conscience but the fulfillment of human beings' spiritual needs, which include mercy, harmony, communality, immortality, trust, forgiveness, and above all, love. It is not surprising that at the time he wrote this essay, he himself had returned to Catholicism.

Betti seems to blend realistic and symbolic dimensions in his plays. His settings have no geographical specificity, and time is vaguely contemporary. As for the characters, their names often do not sound Italian, but the bureaucratic procedures, the familial relation-ships, the subordinate social position of women, the descriptions of city and country life, are all recognizably Italian.

Betti reveals the shadowy side of the human condition. He plumbs the depths of human behavior and brings his characters to the edge of nightmare. The stage atmosphere is often one of a dark dream. He has been called the Kafka of drama. Some of his favorite theatrical devices are the arrival of a stranger, as in *Crime on Goat Island* and *La casa sull'acqua*, the return to the scene of action of a known person, as in *La padrona*, *Lotto fino all'alba* (*Struggle Till Dawn*, 1947), *Fuggitiva* (*The Fugitive*, 1952–53), and the trial or investigation, as in *Landslide*, *Corruption in the Palace of Justice*, *Ispezione* (*The Inquiry*, 1945–46), *The Gambler*, and *Irene innocente* (Innocent Irene, 1947).[3] One might say that Betti returns to a subject that concerned Sophocles in his Theban trilogy: an investigation of the relationship between human beings and the gods. Betti's main characters often come to an acceptance of the demands of justice and to a realization of the presence of a supernatural force or God. In *Landslide*, the whole society realizes it is responsible for an accident that killed three work-ers. In *Corruption in the Palace of Justice*, Cust, obsessed by guilt, longs for atonement, and submits to a higher spiritual power. In *Crime on Goat Island*, a chilling investigation of the boundaries of sexual relationships, a family splits apart, and Agata must live alone with her guilt in the face of eternity.

J. H.

Notes

1. Naples: Treves, 1922.

2. *Religione e teatro.* Foreword by Andreina Frosini Betti. (Brescia: Morcelliana, 1957). Also in English as "Religion and the Theater," trans. Gino Rizzo and William Meriwether, in *The Tulane Drama Review* 5 (Dec. 1960): 3–12.

3. The 1960 London production was entitled *Time of Vengeance*.

■

CRIME ON GOAT ISLAND

(Delitto all'isola delle capre, 1946)

Translated by Henry Reed

■

Characters

AGATA
SILVIA
PIA
ANGELO
EDOARDO

The time is the present.

ACT 1

The action of the play takes place in a lonely house, surrounded by a barren, sun-baked tract of heath land. The scene throughout is a room on the ground floor—almost a basement—used as a kitchen. A shaft of sunlight strikes in through the bars of a window. Beyond the open door at the back of the stage, the parched, arid countryside can be seen. Other doors lead to the inner apartments of the house. Against one of the walls, in a recess, is a well.

As the curtain rises, EDOARDO, *a dull, stupid-looking old man, is drinking a glass of water.* PIA *is seated at some distance from him. He is seeking an opportunity to linger; but she gives him none.*

EDOARDO: Good water, this is, very good . . . It's nice and cool in here: wish I didn't have to get up. I'm getting a bit too old, you know, now, to drive that broken-down truck all over the place. And in this heat as well. (*after a pause*) You won't forget to tell your sister-in-law I'll be back this way on Monday, will you? And every Monday from now on. If any of you want anything, just come out and wave, will you? (*He waits for a reply; there is none.*) Has your sister-in-law gone to the post office?

PIA: Yes.

EDOARDO: I wanted to ask her about the things I brought her last week. Were they all right? Was she satisfied?

PIA: Yes.

EDOARDO: Ah. Has your niece gone to the post office with her?

PIA: No.

EDOARDO: Your niece is quite well again by now. I suppose?

PIA: Very well, thank you.

EDOARDO: Ah, good. That's good. (*He tops his glass.*) Do you think I might have another glass, please?

(PIA *gets up, takes his glass, and fills it from a jug. He drinks; then he rises, still reluctant to go.*)

EDOARDO: You say you won't need any flour next time?

PIA: I've given you the list, haven't I?

EDOARDO: Yes, yes, yes, all right, never mind. (*He takes it out, and looks at it.*) Yes . . . Very well, then: till next Monday, then, eh? (*He moves toward the door.*) It's not only the sun, it's the air as well. (*At the door he turns back to her.*) It's the wind: it burns: it burns right into you . . . Well, I'm off now . . . Give my respects to your niece and sister-in-law, won't you?

PIA: Good-bye.

(EDOARDO *goes.* PIA *wanders idly over to the window and watches the truck depart. Silence falls over the place once more, and she goes over to the well. She takes a rope with a little hook on the end, and lets it dangle into the well, patiently maneuvering it about. A shadow falls across the shaft of sunlight.* A MAN *outside stands looking in through the window, unobserved, watching her. After a few moments, he addresses her, politely.*)

THE MAN: Have you dropped something down the well?

PIA (*starts, sharply*):   What do you want?

THE MAN: I wanted to ask if this is the way to Goat Island?

PIA: This is Goat Island. This is it, here. Where do you have to get to? (*then, as he fails to reply*) Which way did you come?

THE MAN (*vaguely*):   Oh . . . from over there, along the road.

PIA: There's nothing else along this way: this is the only house. If you want the post office, you'll have to go back the way you came.

THE MAN: Oh. Is that very far?

PIA: Are you walking?

THE MAN: Yes.

PIA: A couple of hours then.

THE MAN (*appears to ponder this for a moment*):   Thank you. Good day.

PIA: Good day.

(*He disappears.* **PIA** *goes over to the window to watch him go. Then she returns to the well, and resumes her task.* **THE MAN** *reappears, this time at the door.*

He comes in soundlessly. He is a robust, healthy-looking young man with fair hair and complexion. He stands a moment, looking at **PIA**, *and then raps with his knuckles at the doorpost.* **PIA** *turns around with a start, and says with a mixture of fear and harshness.*)

PIA: Who told you you could come in here?

THE MAN (*politely*):   Forgive me: but I've just realized this is the house I was looking for.

PIA: What do you want? (*She calls:*) Silvia! Silvia!

THE MAN: There's no need to be frightened. I'm sorry to come here looking so dirty and untidy. It's the road: it's thick with dust. (*His voice is very courteous and pleasant.*) This is the house that used to belong to Professor Enrico Ishi, isn't it?

PIA: The Professor died several months ago.

THE MAN: I know. Are you his widow?

PIA: No.

THE MAN: You must be his sister, then: Pia.

PIA: Yes.

THE MAN: You're young. Is his widow not in?

PIA: She'll be back shortly.

THE MAN: Ah, then I'll wait for her. And the daughter: Miss Silvia, how is she? Is she getting on well at the university? Is she at home?

PIA: I don't know. I think she is.

THE MAN: Do you mind if I sit down? (*At a vague shrug from* **PIA** *he does so.*) Thank you. It's very beautiful round here. Lonely: but very attractive, somehow. Don't you think so?

PIA: No. Nor would you if you had to stay here long. We don't come from these parts.

THE MAN: Why doesn't anything seem to grow round here?

PIA: It's because of the goats. They eat everything up.

THE MAN: Goats? Have you a lot of them?

PIA: We make our living from them.

THE MAN: Who do you have to look after them?

PIA: We look after them ourselves. Myself, and my sister-in-law, and the girl.

THE MAN: Haven't you a herdsman?

PIA: No.

THE MAN: You'd find a herdsman very useful. It's much better for the animals. They get used to obeying him. Haven't you any servants, either?

PIA: We used to have a peasant woman who came in. We manage by ourselves now.

THE MAN: Will you excuse me a moment, please? I've left some of my things outside.

(He goes out, returning immediately with a suitcase and a sack. He sits down again.)

THE MAN: I think this is a very pleasant house, whatever you say. You can see it sticking up from the distance, like a tower.

PIA: It's not a house, it's a hovel. Did you notice the balcony, upstairs?

THE MAN: What about it?

PIA: You can't go out on to it; it's crumbling to pieces. At night, whenever there's a wind, the shutters start to rattle: whang-whang, all night long. You can't sleep for it. It drives my niece almost crazy.

THE MAN: Whang-whang. But surely all you have to do is to go up and tie the shutters back . . . or else pull them down? I . . . could do that for you.

PIA: Yes; and you and the balcony and everything else would all come down together. If it weren't dangerous, we'd have fixed it ourselves, long ago.

THE MAN: Have you and the widow and the girl been here a long time without a man in the place?

PIA: Five years: ever since my brother went away.

THE MAN: I suppose your sister-in-law doesn't ever think of getting married again?

PIA: I don't suppose the idea's ever entered her head. *(a pause)* What is it you've come for?

THE MAN: Me? Oh, I was a friend of your brother's. I was with him when he died, as it happened. I heard what must have been his very last words. It all happened out there . . . in that hellhole in Africa they shut us all up in.

PIA: Were you taken prisoner with my brother? *(He nods.)* Did you get on well with him?

THE MAN: Your brother had other companions who'd been taken prisoner with him: men from his own country, who spoke the same language. Yet, gradually, somehow he singled me out for his own special friend. I was the only one he ever talked to. We were together the whole time.

PIA: Are you a foreigner?

THE MAN: Yes. I'm not really supposed to be staying in this country. I haven't got a permit to settle here.

PIA: You speak the language perfectly.

THE MAN: Yes. *(with a smile)* I'm so fond of talking: perhaps that's why.

PIA: Where do you come from?

THE MAN *(with a laugh, and a vague wave of the hand)*: Miles away . . . it's very hot in my country: as hot as it is here. But it can be cold as well. In winter we have to wall up the windows with bricks and plaster, and keep great big stoves burning the whole time. It's not so bad then. (*He laughs again.*)

PIA: What do you work at there?

THE MAN: I used to study. I studied a great deal. And I thought a great deal too. My name's Angelo. Angelo Useim.

PIA: Why ever haven't you gone back home?

THE MAN: I didn't want to. (*He speaks with frankness and dignity.*) I wanted to come to this country; to come to this house.

(*There is a pause.*)

PIA (*her curiosity aroused*): Did my brother ask you to do anything for him . . . ? Is that the reason you've come here? Did he ask you to bring us some message or other?

ANGELO: Yes, that was the reason.

PIA: A message for me?

(ANGELO *vaguely indicates no.*)

For the girl?

(ANGELO *again, vaguely indicates no.*)

Ah, then it must be for his wife . . . his widow. I don't think she'll be long. You don't know her, of course?

ANGELO: No.

PIA (*a note of hostility in her voice*): My sister-in-law is a woman we . . . all admire very much. I have always felt very small beside her. (*She laughs.*) When the shutter bangs at midnight, it says: Agata! Agata!

ANGELO: Is that your sister-in-law's name?

PIA: Yes. The whole place is called Agata. We owe her the privilege of being allowed to rot away here. Do you know what the trouble with this place is? (*He looks inquiringly at her.*) Loneliness: day after day after day of loneliness. It could drive anyone mad . . . I'm hoping to get away before very long . . . fortunately. Were you an officer?

ANGELO: Yes.

PIA: I'm a schoolteacher. I teach languages. I've been abroad a great deal . . . Sprechen Sie Deutsch? . . . Vous le trouvez joli, cet endroit?

ANGELO (*haltingly tries to repeat the last words, but gives up with a laugh*): No, it's no use: I don't understand.

PIA: I once spent a whole year in Vienna. Have you ever been there?

ANGELO: No.

PIA: Lovely . . . lovely city! I used to stay with very important people there. Every night we went to theaters or parties . . . in evening clothes. Every day was full of excitement. Can you dance?

ANGELO: Yes.

PIA: I can't believe I'm the same woman here as I was there. I seem to have become almost a savage. I've neglected myself; I'm only a bundle of rags now. Horrible.

ANGELO (*smiles*):   Don't you think a man has eyes and can see with them? You're not horrible. Did you have love affairs in Vienna?

PIA (*laughs*):   Ah, love affairs . . . ! You men are the same everywhere, aren't you? I was going to ask you if you'd like a drink of water? It's very cool. And you must be thirsty.

ANGELO: Yes, I would; thank you very much.

(*He comes to the table; she brings the water to him. He drinks.*)

ANGELO: It's very pleasant in here.

PIA: It's the only cool spot there is.

ANGELO: Do you know? I've been in exactly the same state as you. You've been here a long time without a man. I was a long time out there without a woman.

PIA: Ah, yes. In the prison camp. You must all have been very bored.

ANGELO: Well, it was not so pleasant as Vienna . . . A man wants a woman. He needs a woman.

PIA (*maliciously*):   Still . . . they did let you out in the end.

ANGELO: Certainly, they did . . . It's an unfortunate thing, but men are full of . . . sin. It is the way they are made. (*calmly, almost sadly*) And the way I am made perhaps makes me even more addicted to that sort of thing than most men. I am driven to it: driven to sin. Aren't you?

PIA (*with an embarrassed laugh*):   Oh, dear . . . Surely . . . you must know that those things aren't half so important to a woman as they are to a man. We . . . don't think about such things as much as you do.

ANGELO: A man is always a man, and a woman is always a woman. What are men and women bound to think about when they're alone together?

PIA (*laughs*):   I'm sure they can find many other things to think about . . .

ANGELO (*still serious and amiable*):   Have you a husband? Or some man or other . . . ?

PIA (*expostulating*):   Please . . . I must ask you . . .

ANGELO (*courteously; he does not move toward her*):   Are we alone in the house?

PIA: Whatever do you mean? My niece is in there, and I shall most certainly call her if you go on . . . talking like that. My sister-in-law will be back at any moment.

ANGELO (*as before*):   If your sister-in-law lets me stay here tonight, will you be nice to me?

PIA: Are you crazy? Really, I don't know whether to be angry with you or to laugh at you. It's easy to see you're a foreigner. You'll have to learn to think very differently about things like that if you're going to stay in this country.

ANGELO (*as before*):   You won't?

PIA: I've told you not to talk like that! We've hardly known each other for ten minutes, and you think you can . . . Good heavens, don't you see how silly it is?

ANGELO: I see. (*then, as if he had completely forgotten the matter*) Look: when I came in, weren't you trying to get something out of the well? Have you dropped something down it?

PIA: Down the well? Yes. (*She returns to the former subject.*) Please, you mustn't think I meant to offend you. But you must realize that you can't make the same kind of . . . approaches to women everywhere you go. Women aren't all like the kind of women you've probably been used to since you came back from the prison camp. Perhaps that's what's given you such silly ideas.

ANGELO: Yes. What was it that fell in?

PIA: Where?

ANGELO: Into the well.

PIA: A goatskin. We've a lot of them.

(*She points to a pile of goat skins. They form a sort of couch.*)

ANGELO: You didn't manage to fish it out?

PIA: It must have got caught. There are hooks on the inside down there.

ANGELO: What will you do, then?

PIA: Go down and fetch it up. Why do you ask?

ANGELO: I'd like to make myself useful, that's all. I'm very obliging; I'm always anxious to be of use to people. Besides I must make people . . . like me, mustn't I? . . . especially as I haven't a penny to my name. You say someone will have to go down the well?

PIA: Yes.

ANGELO: How?

PIA: We have a ladder.

ANGELO: What about the water?

PIA: It's only a few feet deep.

ANGELO: Isn't it dangerous?

PIA: No.

ANGELO: I can do it for you. I'll get the skin back for you right away.

PIA (*laughing*): Do you really want to?

ANGELO: Certainly.

(PIA *takes a rope-ladder from a corner and lowers it down the well, fixing it to a hook.* ANGELO *leans over the parapet, and calls down.*)

ANGELO: Hi, there! Look out! I'm coming down! (*He turns to* PIA, *laughs and begins to take off his shoes, and turn up his trousers.*)

PIA: You men are extraordinary creatures aren't you? (*He looks at her inquiringly.*) I . . . was thinking about what you said a few moments ago; I just don't know how a man can want such a thing of a woman, before he can even so much as tell whether they—well—like or understand each other even. It's like . . . it's the way animals behave. (*Her embarrassment causes her to laugh again.*)

(*A few moments before this, another woman—*AGATA—*has appeared in the outer doorway. She stands watching them, unnoticed, though in no way furtively.* ANGELO *is still preparing to descend the well.*)

ANGELO You are sure it isn't dangerous?

PIA: No, no, don't worry . . . I was saying that you men think all women are exactly the same. You can't really have meant you liked me. Why should you? I think it must be the hot weather: it's given you a touch of the sun.

(**ANGELO** *has taken off his jacket, and is preparing to clamber over the parapet of the well.*)

PIA: I think you probably behave in just the same way to every woman you meet. It doesn't mean a thing; it's just a form of greeting with you; it doesn't mean anything at all.

(**ANGELO** *disappears over the side of the well as she speaks. She leans over and calls down.*)

PIA: Is it cold down there?

ANGELO (*a hollow echo*): Cold . . .

PIA: Are you right at the bottom?

ANGELO: Yes.

PIA: Have you found it?

ANGELO: Not yet.

PIA: I expect you'll find a lot of other things down there as well: clothes, probably . . . Wait, I'll go and get the lamp.

(*She runs away from the well, and almost bumps into* **AGATA**. *The two women whisper together for a moment or two, and then go off together. The stage remains empty. The voice of* **ANGELO** *comes up from the well. He is singing: a kind of dirge.*)

ANGELO:

> *Esevi—uttu—sehe*
> *Bi—be—ba*
> *Esevi—uttu—sehe*
> *Bi—be—ba.*
> *Agliela cicha*
> *Falhu manà.*
> *Bibete bibete*
> *Bibete bà.*
> *Agliela cicha*
> *Falhu manà*
> *Bibete bibete*
> *Bibete bà.*

(*During this,* **AGATA** *has returned, and sits waiting at the table.*)

ANGELO: I'm bringing up a whole pile of stuff from down here.

(*He is coming up the well again; he throws up from the inside a goatskin, and a bundle of rags, dripping with water; eventually he himself appears, and climbs over the parapet, carrying a bottle. He sees* **AGATA** *instead of* **PIA**, *but looks at her without surprise.*)

ANGELO: Look at all these things I've fished up. (*He indicates the bottle.*) There are a lot of these, a whole string of them, hanging from one of the hooks. I suppose they were left behind from Professor Ishi's time?

AGATA: Yes.

ANGELO: Is it sweet?

AGATA: It's juniper.

ANGELO: Was it made here? Do the peasants make it?

AGATA: Yes.

ANGELO: Do you mind if I have a drop? I'm exhausted. Are you the Professor's widow?

AGATA: Yes.

ANGELO (*pointing to* SILVIA, *who at this moment, comes in with* PIA): And this young lady must be your daughter . . . Miss Silvia.

AGATA: Yes.

ANGELO: Pretty. Young. Forgive me: I must dry myself, otherwise I may catch cold.

(PIA *hands him a towel. He begins to dry himself.*)

I'm a strong man: very strong. But I'm delicate as well. I get ill very easily, if I overstrain myself . . . (*He holds out an elbow to* PIA.) You: come and take hold of my elbow. (*to* SILVIA) And you come and take hold of the other one. (*They obey shyly.*)

Now, I'll put my hands together, as though I were praying. Like that. Now: pull as hard as you can, both of you, and see if you can pull my hands apart. Go on! Pull. (*They do so, without effect, and then laugh and stop.*) You can't, can you? No, and four men couldn't either. I'm very strong. All the same, I have to take care; I have to have my meals regularly. I'm clean, too. (*He laughs.*) Why, it's a pleasure to have me in the house, I'm so clean!

PIA (*teasingly*): Your skin's as white and soft as a woman's.

ANGELO (*pleased*): Yes, you wouldn't think I'd been through so many hardships, would you? But the good thing is: I always sleep very well. That's because I never do anybody any harm.

PIA (*teasing*): And those pretty curls: they make you look like a pet lamb.

ANGELO: Well, if it comes to that, you three have very fine skins too . . . from what I can see of them. Not like the women of my country: their faces are all covered with freckles. And they get great breasts much too early for my liking. Though I'm bound to say they're pretty good at giving a man what he wants. They know how to satisfy you when you make love to them; they know what you like.

AGATA: You were a prisoner, I gather?

ANGELO: Yes. But whatever happens to me I always say: never mind! I expect that'll make you think I'm frivolous. I'm not: I'm a very thoughtful type of man, as it happens. You'll be saying I talk too much about myself; the reason is that I have to make people understand me. And deep down, what I most need in life is affection. That was what I felt the lack of so badly in the prison camp.

(*He shakes his head, and laughs, then he holds up his hand with the thumb sticking up; he pretends to seize it with the other hand and tear it off; but he is only closing it in his hand; he shows the hand which now appears thumbless, and laughs again.*)

AGATA: Have you been free for long?

ANGELO: Yes. (*He still speaks with simple dignity.*) I've been rather a long time getting here, simply because of the money; I had none. I've sometimes had to make good the deficiency by rather unpleasant methods. Still, what's it matter? Why's a man given the gift of cunning, if he's never to use it? And certainly, I'm cunning enough. But I've worked as well, sometimes.

PIA (*goodnaturedly teasing him*): Ah, that *is* bad news.

ANGELO: Yes; I worked in a large mill: I used to keep the account books. But I soon grew tired of that. The people were such illiterate fools, and always covered with flour. And besides, I couldn't get this house off my mind.

AGATA (*coldly*): Why?

ANGELO: Because I'd heard so much about it. The house with the three women. All women. (*He laughs.*) Why, it smells of women! (*seriously again*) What was the use of my earning money at the mill and buying myself a smart gray tweed suit, if my soul was sunk in gloom the whole time? What I love most of all is to sit and think: to reduce complicated things to their simplest terms. And I love to read: to close the book with my finger still between the pages. Perhaps even to fall asleep over the book and then wake up and realize how my thoughts have gone wandering on by themselves. A charming habit, reading; I know the young lady is fond of it too. Aren't you?

SILVIA (*rather embarrassed*): Yes.

ANGELO: And what about the shutter? I know the shutter robs the young lady of her slumbers. Eh? I know a lot, don't I?

SILVIA (*as before*): Yes.

ANGELO: And what about your studies? How are they going? The university must cost a lot of money?

SILVIA: Yes, it does rather.

ANGELO: Still, it's good to learn why things are as they are, isn't it? I suppose you're on holiday at the moment?

SILVIA: I've not been very well this year; mother wanted me to stay at home and get better.

ANGELO: Which you seem to have done, to judge from the color in your cheeks. (*to the others*) But more than anything else in the world do you know what I like? Talking.

PIA: So we've noticed. You haven't stopped for a single second since you came in.

ANGELO (*gently*): Yes, I'd willingly go without food in order to talk. Arguments, beautiful conversations! Talking; discovering how well you agree with other people. And even if you disagree at first, if you just go on talking and questioning and answering, never raising your voice, never protesting, keeping your wits about you, slipping in a little joke every now and then, do you know what you eventually discover? That you have really been in complete agreement from the very start. Do you know why?

PIA (*mockingly*): Tell us.

ANGELO: Because men agree with each other by nature—and women of course, even more so. We agree, without realizing it. We are all brothers and sisters. (*He takes on the voice of a severe inquisitor.*) "Ah, brothers and sisters, eh? Brothers and sisters. And what about sin? How do you manage to explain sin, if we're all brothers and sisters?" (*as though replying*) Sin? . . . well, yes, sin does get born, certainly it does. The earth's black yeast ferments. I'm a very great sinner myself. The black yeast of the earth lures me more and more, even in a single day, toward woman; yet I despise it all. My soul craves simply for the innocent intimacy of a brother and sister. And if the innocent intimacy turns into sin? Well, it isn't the end of the world, even if it does. The One who created us created the material world that it might delight the eternal soul in us which craved for desire and love, and needed an object for its passion. And sin, sin, what is it, after all? It's the means by which we satisfy and thereby conquer this infatuation of the soul. Women find these things difficult to grasp, I know, even educated women. But one thing is certain: our salvation lies in sin; and it's only our damnable pride that dares think otherwise.

SILVIA: But were you really out there with my father?

ANGELO: Certainly I was.

SILVIA: Forgive me for asking. So many families have been taken in.

ANGELO (*with a sudden, unexpected burst of anger that makes his voice sharp and falsetto*): Do you doubt my word? Do you doubt my word?

SILVIA (*timidly*): But did you really talk to him?

ANGELO (*gently once more*): The whole time, for three long years.

SILVIA: What did you talk about?

ANGELO: Ah, many, many things: all the things you need to talk about if you're to get through every day for three long years. He opened his heart to me. It was he who told me to come here. When he saw at last that he himself would never be able to come back again, he seemed to want me to come in his place. (*silence*) So I started out. I've seen the most wonderful places in the whole of Africa and Europe, but it was this house that always kept beckoning to me. I'd like to have come here better dressed than this. I also know that a stranger isn't a stranger if he comes bearing gifts. People make you much more welcome when you bring them presents. (*to* **PIA**) And in fact, when I was in Algiers, I picked out a silk dress-length for you, in one of the finest shops I could find. And what silk! The shopkeeper sighed at the mere thought of parting with it. You couldn't really call it expensive even. (*to* **SILVIA**) And I decided to bring you two huge gilt bottles of scent from Paris; everyone told me they were the best you could get. (*to* **AGATA**) And for you, because you're the mistress of the house, I had to find an even more valuable present: so I chose a pair of earrings, with beautiful black stones set in them. And then . . . Well, I thought I ought to bring some cakes, the kind that stay fresh and soft for months. And I felt you'd like to have some sort of little animal in a cage, a quiet tame little creature, the kind you see nibbling nuts, holding them between their little hands. Oh, yes I took the greatest possible care I could to pick the sort of things you'd like. I chose them with great care . . . but of course I never actually bought them, because I was completely unprovided with cash! I hope you'll take the desire for the deed. (*He laughs at great length, amused at his joke, which however fails to amuse the others.*) Please forgive me for joking, but I always think it's a man's duty to keep women cheerful. When a man makes a woman laugh, she feels somehow protected. You three must have been very melancholy here without a man to laugh and joke with you, especially with the shutter disturbing you at night! (*He laughs again.*)

AGATA: You'll forgive me, but would you mind talking seriously? Had you any particular reason for coming here?

ANGELO: Yes, an important one.

AGATA: You were actually present when my husband died?

ANGELO: Yes, I was there.

AGATA: Did he give you any message for us?

ANGELO: Yes.

AGATA: Then suppose you tell us what it was.

ANGELO: I'd have done so before now, only I'm afraid it doesn't concern all three of you.

AGATA: Whom does it concern?

ANGELO (*after a pause*): You.

(*There is a silence:* PIA *and* SILVIA *rise and go out.*)

AGATA (*looking at the ground*): What can my husband still want of me?

ANGELO: I'm sorry you should be so distressed.

AGATA: I am not distressed.

ANGELO: Are you frightened of something?

AGATA: I am not frightened. So you really don't know?

ANGELO: Know what?

AGATA: You are here on my husband's behalf. But I am quite sure he can't have told you the truth. He rarely did tell the truth; even when he thought he did.

ANGELO: What do you mean by the truth?

AGATA (*almost indifferently*): It is simply that I have reasons for feeling resentful toward my husband, and I would prefer not to hear anything more about him.

ANGELO (*curiously*): That I was unaware of.

AGATA (*after a moment*): Do you know why my husband went away from here, and was taken prisoner and died, out there?

ANGELO: The war.

AGATA: No. My husband wanted to run away from me. (*almost derisively*) I am a woman who has been . . . "left." Though, in fact, I was alone even while he was here; I realized that afterward.

ANGELO: You dislike your condition here: the continual loneliness of it?

AGATA: No. I still have relatives; I could go to them, no doubt, if I wanted to. I just don't want to; that's all. Things have turned out as they have; and life doesn't begin over again.

ANGELO: What was your husband's reason for leaving you?

AGATA (*indifferently*): He was ashamed of himself. He was a liar; rhetoric was the only language he knew.

ANGELO: Why did you marry him?

AGATA (*as before*): I believed in him. I shared in his work. I married him against everyone's advice. (*ironically*) Oh, all his female students adored him. He was almost a saint down in the city.

ANGELO: However did you both come to live here?

AGATA: That was my doing. It's a long story. It was my doing. Perhaps you ought to know. Enrico was beginning to come up against a certain amount of opposition . . . I was proud of the fact to begin with: the two of us, against the world. Then I began to notice that all the trouble, the spite, the petty worries, were beginning to waste and tarnish something between us also. It was my doing. (*sadly*) Ever since I was a child I have wanted all or nothing. If I made a blot on a page, I preferred to tear it right out; a victim of rhetoric. I suggested to him—I had a little money of my own—I suggested we should leave everything behind: the city, the risks we ran. A revenge against the world. He kissed me; it was all very moving. And what a farce it all was! The two of us: alone, far away from everything. Our aspirations, our fondness for each other, our sincerity. So we came here. That was how it was.

ANGELO: And here?

AGATA: Wilderness—and silence.

ANGELO: How?

AGATA: Every day exactly the same, the absence of any kind of distraction. Perhaps even one's feelings, if they're left to themselves the whole time, begin to wear out. They burn themselves up and become empty. I began to notice that my husband hardly ever worked any more.

ANGELO: What did he do?

AGATA: He used to stay in bed. We fell into the habit of hardly ever speaking to each other. Hours, days, without a word. We no longer had anything to say to each other. Everything became . . . terrifyingly simply: daytime, evening, supper, silence: and the two of us. My husband began to avoid me. The loneliness, the distance from everything, the wind . . . (*She laughs.*) . . . and the goats.

ANGELO: The goats?

AGATA: Yes, all we could hear in the silence was the goats bleating. Goats are very important here; we earn our living from them.

ANGELO (*interested*): The milk and cheese, I suppose? And the kids?

AGATA: Yes. Goats. Their eyes are . . . unfriendly and melancholy at the same time. They actually stare at you.

ANGELO: They recognize people. There are a lot of goatherds' places where I come from.

AGATA: As I said, my husband and I hardly spoke to each other. After a time, it became . . . complete silence. Complete silence fell on us. I believe even thought has need of words; it runs along on words, as though along a thread. If you get out of the habit of words, something dark and shapeless forms in their place. The only words I was beginning to hear . . . (*with the ghost of a laugh*) were the bleating of the goats. I could hear them, hour after hour, as I used to lie stretched on the turf. (*pause*) Until one day my husband ran away, and I never saw him again. He ran away. Everyone thought he'd merely gone away for a time. I've never told anyone the truth; I was too proud.

ANGELO (*curiously*): What is it you blame him for?

AGATA (*indifferently*): For having deceived me. For making me believe in things he didn't believe in himself.

ANGELO: Deceiving you. But you wanted to be deceived. You wanted to marry a man who was your intellectual superior.

AGATA (*dropping her voice*): You don't know what my husband did after he left here. Former . . . attachments, low women . . . degrading intrigues. That was what he wanted. (*with a sudden tremor in her voice*) But the thing that still shocks me most is my own immense credulity, the great faith I had in him. A whole life! The whole thing sacrificed! And now . . . this: just waiting for the years to pass.

(*A pause.*)

ANGELO: But the dead forgive us and we have to forgive them.

AGATA (*with gloomy indifference*): I don't believe in such things. In nature there is no forgiveness. (*with a shadow of a smile*) It's a chemical matter. When a body becomes half-an-ounce too heavy it sinks, and that's the end of it. And God: it's difficult to imagine Him as an impulsive old gentleman; first of all getting very angry and after a time calming down again. No, everything is final and ordained.

ANGELO (*almost amused*): Hell?

AGATA (*half smiling*): I have imagined it ever since I was a child. I still do . . .

ANGELO: Even now?

AGATA: Rather than chaos, I still prefer to think of punishment. A punishment, inescapable, too. So that one doesn't have to think about it any more.

ANGELO: You suffered a great deal over all this, in fact?

AGATA: No, not really. That is what is so curious. I assure you I never suffered. It was something else. My faith had been shaken.

ANGELO: Faith . . . ?

AGATA: It's difficult to explain. On one occasion . . . (*She pauses.*)

ANGELO: Yes?

AGATA: It was after my husband had left. I was lying on the grass, as I often do. The goats were cropping round about, looking at me, going "beh" . . . It was a very peaceful day. I wasn't watching the goats; I could just hear them round about me: "beh" . . . I could smell them . . . I wasn't sad, I just felt indifferent . . . Do you understand? I realized how very little it mattered to me about my husband running away and dying; I no longer even cared about the house here, or the walls falling down, or even about my daughter. Nothing mattered any longer. I didn't care any more. And then, at last, I felt at ease, there, stretched out on the grass. I had ceased to think; yes, I had even ceased to think.

I felt a sense of repose . . . And I was happy simply to feel my own weight on the ground; and there was nothing else in the whole world. And then . . . I felt a curious wish. You know the absurd ideas that suddenly occur to you when you're completely alone? I suddenly wanted to go "beh" myself, "beh . . . beh . . . ," and to munch the grass like the goats. One of them stared at me, and I went "beh." (*She laughs.*) Well . . . (*She pauses.*) I don't know why I'm telling you all this; it's all nonsense, of course.

ANGELO: Lady . . . you must prepare yourself for a surprise. Did you know that, in spite of all you say, your husband's thoughts centered continuously on this place and on this house? Yes. He talked of it so much that after a while I even came to feel as if I had lived here myself. And he realized he could trust in me. It was he himself who said to me: "Go there, Angelo: those three women are alone, go and help them; go back in place of me."

AGATA (*coldly*): Do you think that's enough to earn you your board and keep?

ANGELO: Lady: I was only repeating your husband's words. A man would be very useful here. Your husband also spoke of his books and his work. He thought I might be able to go on with them.

AGATA: And is that the "surprise"?

ANGELO (*after a pause*): No, the surprise was something else. I was trying to find some way of telling you that would not offend you.

AGATA: I can imagine what my husband must have told you about me. "A fool of a woman, unbearable."

ANGELO (*laughs*): No, lady. Your husband actually told me a lot about you. He talked more about you than he did about the house, or his daughter, or anything else. I could almost say he never talked of anything except you. However, he never once spoke to me of the things you have spoken of. My dear good lady . . . those things are unimportant; they are trivialities. He talked of other things. (*with a change of tone*) Listen, lady, memories are like flagstones, time and distance work upon them like drops of acid. Your husband had completely forgotten certain aspects of you. Others he remembered completely. Just think: two men alone: as though on an island; I know nothing of you, you know nothing of me. It becomes permissible to talk about anything. The most intimate things. In any case, there's always a way of embarking on subjects that are particularly delicate: you laugh, you pretend they're of no importance. And then somehow you find you can say the most amazing things. Perhaps when your husband talked, he didn't always say it was you he was talking about. He spoke simply of a woman. He was cunning, but I was cunninger still. I merely observed, and pieced everything together, till I understood it all. It was you. Always you. Your husband did nothing but talk of you; it was as if he were . . . ill.

AGATA (*in a low voice*): Well, after all that: what did he say about me?

ANGELO: Well . . . (*He laughs shyly.*) Lady: out there, you were not . . . clothed. Forgive me saying it, but between us you were naked. The only thing your husband remembered of you was what you'd been to him on certain occasions, which he remembered with extraordinary clarity. The recollection made beads of sweat stand on his forehead. Your slightest breath: there it was. I'm bound to say that I was . . . interested. We were shut off from women and talked a good deal about them; everyone did. But in our case, it was different. (*He laughs.*) Coming in here, I had never seen your face before, but the rest of you . . . I had. I see that you are thinking I have insulted you.

AGATA (*contemptuously*): I know that among certain types of men there is always a certain type of conversation.

ANGELO: But this was different. Lady: a man and a woman embrace and make love to each other. And after a little . . . there's no world any longer, no longer any memory, no longer anything! For one moment, each of them becomes something anonymous and isolated. As a stone might be. And out of the stone there breaks a kind of cry. It is as though a stone were painfully making a confession. It is something extraordinarily lonely, lonely, a secret—the act of love—meant to be unheard and unremembered. Your husband, however disloyally, spied that out in you and told me of it.

AGATA: It's disgusting to listen to you. What are you trying to suggest?

ANGELO: Simply that I *know* you. You yourself don't know who you are, but I do.

AGATA: And who am I?

ANGELO: Why do you suppose your husband, as he approached his end, ignored the woman you were by day and remembered only the other? Because one was true and the other not. Up to now you have behaved like a dead child in a coffin.

AGATA: And how ought I to behave?

ANGELO (*he laughs as though he were ashamed of himself: and says, as though quoting*): "Love runs through the forest with hair on end, calling on the monstrous black boar." (*He laughs.*) There's no religion on earth that hasn't its legends on that subject. I've studied these things. In your countries you call her Pasiphae; she turned into an animal and gave herself to the bull. It isn't a matter of the senses, understand, it's the soul! The raging unquiet soul, which craves to tear itself to pieces and cure itself of being human. That is sacred, it's not a matter for shame. (*There is a long pause: he lowers his voice.*) And that is you.

(**AGATA** *stands for a long moment motionless; then she takes one of the soaking rags and slaps him across the face with it.* **ANGELO** *puts his hand to his cheek, and speaks slowly, without anger.*)

ANGELO: I shall pay you back for that. I have thought of you unceasingly; I have desired you all this time. That is the reason I have come all this way to find you; I would have been unhappy in any other place. Night after night you approach my bed, undress, and we are together. We shall continue to be so, here. It is right; it is sensible. And you wish it too.

AGATA (*calls*): Pia! Silvia!

(**PIA** *enters and looks at them; a moment later* **SILVIA** *follows her.*)

PIA (*taking a bowl and placing it on the table*): You'll be hungry; there's some milk and cheese, if you'd like some. And bread.

ANGELO (*coming to the table and sitting down*): Certainly I'd like some. I'd have asked you for them myself. But what about the rest of you? Aren't you having any supper? It's getting dark.

PIA: We eat very early here; we've become very countrified. In another half-an-hour we shall be in bed.

ANGELO (*tapping the bottle*): Still, surely you'll have a drink; aren't you going to try this with me? (*eating*) Bring some glasses; it won't do you any harm for once in a while. It was put down by my friend, he'll like the thought of our drinking it together.

PIA: Shall I really bring some glasses?

ANGELO: Certainly.

(PIA *goes to fetch them.*)

ANGELO: (*still eating*) And light a lamp as well.

(SILVIA *lights a lamp and brings it to the table.*)

ANGELO: It doesn't matter if you haven't a room. (*He points to the heap of goat skins.*) I can sleep on those perfectly well; it'll be better than a bed, if you'll just spread them out a bit for me. I'm used to far worse than that. (PIA *has uncorked the bottle.*)

(*pouring out*) Drink, my dears. You were a little flock without a shepherd weren't you? You already find the voice of a man in here comforting. What good cheese this is; excellent! (*turning to* AGATA, *who remains apart*) We've innumerable, endless tales about goats and goatherds in my country, you know, lady. I was thinking about what we were saying a while ago. They say that when goatherds have been away for months and months alone with their animals, they actually grow tired of the language and habits of human beings. So, when there's no one about, only the goats, in the big grazing-grounds, the goatherds themselves take to bleating. Yes. They keep it a secret, of course, but you can soon tell, because when they do talk with human beings afterward, they are always rather bewildered. And gradually—did you know this?—the goats themselves fall in love with the goatherd? They keep their eyes fixed on him, and never move away from him, they . . . butt him gently. Yes. And eventually the shepherd begins to understand, and after a little while they . . . make love, there in the meadows, pressing close together, closer than a man and women even . . . However, they say the best goatherd is the devil. (*He tastes the wine for the first time.*) This is good. Why aren't you others drinking?

(PIA *and* SILVIA *drink.* ANGELO *drinks again; then he goes over to the parapet of the well, and speaks down into it.*)

Thanks, Enrico, the bottle was excellent. We'll have a go at the others, all in good time.

(*He turns to the women, winks, and turns back to the well.*)

It's true, Enrico, isn't it? You do want me to stay here, don't you? At least till the hay is all in? (*He pretends to wait for a reply.*) He says "yes." Now we can put the top on. (*He does so.*) How on earth have you managed without a man here? What about the heavy work? And the winter? And what do you do for company? (*He suddenly bursts into song.*)

> *Esevi uttu sehe*
> *Bi be bo*
> *Esevi uttu sehe*
> *Bi be bo.*

That's one of the songs we sing in my country. It's a very, very long one. It means: if a man comes to your house, you, woman, must take his boots off and wash him; and after you've washed him you must dry him. And after you've dried him, you must make him eat. And after you've made him eat, you must make him drink. And after you've made him drink, you must make him lie down. And so forth . . . Come on: you sing it too, all of you: join in the chorus. (*He begins again.*)

> *Esevi uttu sehe . . .*

(*He signs to them to join in the refrain.*)

PIA (*with him*):

> *Bi be bo.*

ANGELO: What about you, Silvia? Come on, sing up . . .

> *Esevi uttu sehe . . .*

PIA *and* **SILVIA** (*with him*):

> *Bi be bo.*

AGATA (*coming forward and interrupting*): Look: I'm sorry to have to say that we can't possibly let you stay here. I've no doubt what you've told us is the truth; I know you must have been a friend of my husband's. But we haven't the resources here, and we have nowhere for you to sleep. You've had a rest, you've had some supper, and now I must ask you to leave.

ANGELO (*after a pause*): I see . . . So I have to go?

AGATA: Yes. You told us your presence in this country is illegal. You might get into trouble.

(**ANGELO** *says no more, rises, dusts himself down, and goes toward the door; here he turns, and says politely:*)

ANGELO: Good night. (*He disappears.*)

(*After a pause,* **AGATA** *goes to the door, closes it, and puts the chain across it.*)

SILVIA: We couldn't have let him stay. It's too cut off. There have been horrible cases: tramps and deserters coming into people's houses, and murdering them, or setting the place on fire. I didn't feel comfortable with that man in the house.

PIA (*lighting another lamp, and moving toward the door*): Go to bed, Silvia. (*She pauses, and her voice becomes shrill.*) I'd like to know why we don't go back to the town! (*to* **AGATA**) It's your fault, I'm tired of it. I don't want to be a servant here, working with my hands all day long. If that's what you want, you do it: you're the mistress here. But I'm leaving, do you understand? I shall find enough to live on . . . (*She pauses.*) What's that? (*She returns from the door.*)

AGATA (*stands looking at* ANGELO'S *sack*): He's left his sack behind. He's done that on purpose, so that he can come back. He will come back here.

(*Instinctively she turns to the door.* SILVIA *does the same.* PIA *runs to the window.*)

PIA: No, there's no one there now. (*She turns back.*) He's gone away. (*She approaches the sack and rummages in it.*) Just a couple of rags. They stink of sweat. How disgusting! (*In an outburst of hysterical revulsion, almost breaking down.*) How disgusting! How disgusting! It makes me feel sick! . . . (*She goes out.*)

SILVIA (*as she goes out with one of the lamps*): Good night, mother.

AGATA: Good night.

(*She stands for a moment motionless. Then she takes the lamp and goes out. For some time, the stage remains empty. But the light of the lamp does not disappear; it still shines from the next room. Then someone reenters cautiously, into the half-dark. It is* AGATA. *She advances into the room; and stands motionless for a long time, listening. Then she goes to the door, takes off the chain, and opens it. She comes slowly back. Then she goes over and sits on the pile of skins and waits.*)

CURTAIN

ACT 2

AGATA *and* PIA *are busy sewing. In front of them, comfortably seated, is* ANGELO. *A considerable time has elapsed. The well is covered.*

ANGELO: Have I ever told you that story about the bottle of Greek wine! The precious Greek wine? (*He smiles reminiscently.*) Well, I once happened to pass by a shop: a wine shop. There was a notice outside it, saying: "Exquisite Greek Wine: Why not try it?" etcetera . . . So of course, I thought: "Good, this means me." However, I didn't want to have to pay for it . . . being completely out of funds, as usual. (PIA *laughs, immoderately.*)

So I went into the shop and said very grandly to the man: "Oh, ah, wine-merchant . . . I'd like to purchase a couple of dozen bottles of your Greek wine," I said. "I . . . ah . . . naturally, I should like to try a glass of it before I actually order it . . ." The old devil behind the counter (I can't tell you how bloody ugly he was) took one look at me: "You see what the notice says?" "But I . . ." "*Samples on payment only,* that's what it says." "But . . . but surely," I said, "surely a purchaser of a large quant— . . ." "If you want to sample that wine, you've got to pay for it," he said. And he sent me away, pff, just like that.

(PIA *again laughs rather more than the tale deserves.*)

ANGELO (*going over to the window*): Between that old villain and me, from that day on, it was a fight to the death. Hasn't Silvia come in yet?

PIA: No.

ANGELO: Do you know where she's gone?

PIA: No.

ANGELO: Well, I let three weeks go by. Next time I went there, I went dressed as a kitchen-boy. (*imitating*) "Please sir, I've come from the Governor, and the Governor's butler has sent me to buy two or three crates of Greek wine for the Governor. So if you please, sir, will you kindly telephone the palace of the Governor, so that I can ask whether it's three, or four, or five crates he wants."

(**PIA** *laughs.*)

ANGELO: And I saw the man was mine. He looked up the number himself, rang through to it for me, and passed the receiver over to me—oh, so affectionately! I'm bound to say the sounds I heard at the other end of the telephone were extremely strange and offensive. But I ignored them. Every time I answered I pretended I was speaking to the Governor's butler. And all the time the wine-merchant was watching me with adoration in his eyes. "Have you spoken to the Governor's butler?" he said, when I'd finished. "Yes," I said. "It's five crates, they want, five . . . But first of all . . ." "First you'll want to taste it," he said, "won't you? Of course you will, I'll see to that for you, I'll give you a nice glass of it so you can really try it. Yes." And right there, on the counter, was the bottle with the label: saying: "Exquisite Greek wine. Why not try it," etc. But the wine man said: "No, no, not that, not that. I want to give you a drop of fresh I've specially uncorked for you." He ran into the room behind the shop, and came back with another bottle, and put it in front of me. And still he kept looking at me. He was just about to pour it out, when I stopped him: "Is it cold?" I said. "Cold," he said. "Greek wine," I said, "just opened?" "Greek wine," he said, "just opened." "Ah, then I'd like some ice in it," I said. "Ice?" he said. "Ice," I said. "You . . . you want some ice as well?" he said. Another minute and he'd have thrown his arms round me. "Bravo! Well done!" he said. "Ice in it. Straight away. I'll run and get it." He flew into the back room, I heard him breaking up the ice, back he came, and filled the glass right to the brim and placed it in front of me . . . and still he kept looking at me. I drank . . . Then I wiped the sweat off my face. "Like it?" he said. "Yes," I said. "Would you like another glass?" he said. I hesitated . . . It was then the brute exploded: he shouted at me in the most terrifying voice you ever heard, that either I had to drink another glass or he'd send for the police. So I drank another glass, and then I observed: "M'm it's not bad . . ." "Hahahaha! Being clever, eh?" he said. "Coming in here to try and catch me out, eh? Well you've just fallen in your own trap, see, my lad! That wasn't the Governor's telephone number, it was my sister-in-law's, the midwife's! That isn't Greek wine you've been drinking! That's seven year old vinegar!"

(**PIA** *laughs.*)

"It's worse than sulfuric acid that is!" he shouted. "You'll be in hospital tonight! You'll be in the churchyard tomorrow!" (*He pauses: then, in flute-like tone.*) "Do you think I might have another glass?" I said. (*a dramatic pause*) "Another glass?" "Yes." "Do you want to commit suicide?" "Yes." So I drank. And I drank again. Then I seized the bottle, emptied it, kissed the wine man tenderly on the forehead . . . and departed. (*solemnly*) After a few moments, I heard a tremendous row behind me. The brute had just discovered that while he was in the back room getting the ice, I'd changed the two bottles over. (*pause*) He had a stroke, and died on the spot.

PIA (*laughs and then says*):   You're a fraud, Angelo.

ANGELO: Why?

PIA: Not one of these things you tell us has ever happened to you. You're a rogue.

ANGELO (*pathetically*):   Yes, I'm a rogue. I'd be the first to admit it. You surround me with comforts, work for me, feed me, even look after my clothes and polish my shoes . . . while I (*He breaks off.*) Haven't you even seen her?

PIA: Who?

ANGELO: Silvia.

PIA (*sharply*):   No.

ANGELO (*continuing*):   And do you know what you really ought to do? You ought to take a whip and thrash me.

PIA: Of course we ought.

ANGELO: Of course you ought. Because I'm lazy. I waste time doing all sorts of useless things; and I'm a bit of a liar as well.

(*He rises and goes to look out of the window; then comes back and sits down again.*) I'm a parasite.

PIA (*shrilly and aggressively*):   Yes, you are! You're an idle good-for-nothing!

ANGELO (*gently*):   Never mind, my dear: everybody knows that some people are cut out for work, and others aren't. This morning I went out to chop the wood. Suddenly, I felt I had to have a rest for a minute, I sat down, and . . .

(**SILVIA** *has appeared in the doorway; the women turn and look at her; he goes on as if he had not seen her.*)

In a few moments I was deep in my own thoughts . . . thoughts so lovely, so delicate it would have been a crime to chase them away . . . merely to go back and chop wood. I'd been traveling in great ocean liners where even the plates and dishes were made of gold. Well . . . What's the point of it all? Here I am, thinking of America, thinking of eternity. There isn't an eagle could fly as swiftly. That's one's soul. Yes. Don't you agree with me, Silvia dear? Of course you do. I've noticed lately that whenever you come in, everything lights up: I always think that, every time I see you. But today you're even more . . . vivid and attractive than usual. What's the matter, my dear, don't you feel well? Perhaps you didn't sleep well last night? (*to the others*) Yet she looks perfectly well, doesn't she?

PIA (*sharply*):   Say something, you silly little thing!

(**SILVIA** *has come forward without looking at anyone, and as though she heard nothing.*)

ANGELO (*still affable and imperturbable*):   We were worried about you, knowing you were out in this heat. It's dangerous, you know. Ah . . . now I can see you properly: you've been out there too long. Of course you have. (*to the others*) This girl spends too much time out of doors! I'm beginning to suspect there must be something in the house she doesn't like. In which case . . .

PIA (*as before*):   Can't you open your mouth, you little fool!

ANGELO: . . . In which case, we'll all be ready and glad to do anything that may be necessary to put it right, won't we? Tell her so Agata. And you, Pia! Tell her.

(**PIA** *rises with deliberate hostility and goes toward the door.*)

ANGELO (*with sudden anger*):   Pia! I'm speaking to you.

(**PIA** *goes out.*)

ANGELO (*amiably once more*):   I allowed myself to speak like that, though of course I'm only a mere underling here, because I've been very sorry to hear that these are the last few hours our little Silvia will be with us. She's going away, leaving us. This very day, almost any minute, so I gather. I'm very distressed to hear that. Studies . . . the university.

AGATA (*to her daughter*):   Have you let old Edoardo know?

SILVIA: Yes. He's going to blow his hooter from the road, I'll go down with my bag.

AGATA: Is everything ready?

SILVIA: Yes.

ANGELO (*from the door, very quietly*):   But in any case old Edoardo will not be here until this evening. And we'd all be very glad if between now and then our little Silvia were persuaded to change her mind. (*He goes out.*)

(**SILVIA** *comes slowly forward and points to something among the garments that* **PIA** *and* **AGATA** *have been sewing.*)

SILVIA: I remember that jacket; Father used to wear it to go hunting in.

AGATA (*evasively*):   Yes, I think he did.

SILVIA (*with strange placidity*):   You'll have a lot of work to do on it. Angelo is fatter than father was.

AGATA: These things were getting moth-eaten. Now they'll be of some use to somebody at last.

SILVIA: There was something else in father's wardrobe. But it wasn't anything of any use to the rest of you. I've taken it.

AGATA: What was it? What do you mean? What was it you took?

SILVIA (*does not reply at once: then, suddenly, affectionately*) Mother, I was bound to have to go away. I ought to have gone long ago, because of my classes. And . . . besides . . . it's so stiflingly hot here . . . and so lonely . . . I can't bear it any longer. The other night, there was that shutter again: I hardly closed my eyes. If I went on staying here, I know I'd be ill again . . . (*She has begun to show signs of agitation.*)

AGATA (*who clearly wishes to avoid talking to her*): Yes, darling, I can see it will do you good to go away for a time and be with your friends again. (*She is moving toward the door as she speaks.*)

SILVIA: Where are you going?

AGATA: There are some things I must get ready for you to take with you.

SILVIA: No, mother, wait. I came in specially to talk to you. There's something I must say to you before I go.

AGATA (*without looking at her*): Very well, I'm here.

SILVIA: Mother, listen: these last few days we haven't spoken to each other very much. Perhaps we haven't had the opportunity. (*She speaks with difficulty.*) You know that there's . . . something we've never mentioned. Oh, mother, things have been happening here which I . . . can't . . . Oh, I've been so miserable and uneasy! Surely you know what I mean.

AGATA (*not looking at her*): You don't approve of that man being here, I suppose?

SILVIA: No.

AGATA (*evasively*) We needed a man here. There are some things here a woman can't do.

SILVIA: But this man . . . doesn't do anything, anything at all.

AGATA: He probably needs a little time to get used to the place.

SILVIA: But he'll never do anything, mother.

AGATA: How do you know? If that's the case, we shall send him away. As soon as the hay's been got in.

SILVIA: But this man will never go away; he'll never go away.

AGATA: What makes you think that? In any case his staying in this country at all is an irregularity. We could have him arrested if we wanted to. We've no cause to worry.

SILVIA: Mother . . .

AGATA: What is it?

SILVIA: The other morning I went down to the post office and then on to the village shop.

AGATA: Well?

SILVIA: Everyone looked at me.

AGATA (*pretending to be patient*): Why?

SILVIA: And I had a talk with old Edoardo.

AGATA: You shouldn't have done that; he's an old fool.

SILVIA: He told me that everybody is gossiping about us and this man.

AGATA: What are they saying?

SILVIA: They say we're running ourselves into debt in order to keep him here.

AGATA: That's ridiculous. You know it is.

SILVIA: They say . . . it isn't nice, for three women to keep a man here in the house.

AGATA: Those people said exactly the same kind of thing when I sent you away to study in the city. A girl, they said, all by herself in the city, among all the men; that wasn't respectable either, they thought. In any case you're going away; your reputation at least will be safe. And I really don't know why the whole thing worries you so much. (*going* *toward the door*) As for those people down there, we all know how silly and nasty they are. They can think and say what they like; I don't care.

SILVIA (*sadly*):   Wait a minute, mother, wait! You don't care about those people. Don't you care about me either?

AGATA (*comes back slowly and sits down again: with a kind of weariness*):   Why do you ask?

SILVIA: Surely you care, you must care, if you see things making me suffer, mother? (*cries out*) Mother, I don't like that man to wear father's clothes like this! I don't like him to sleep in father's bedroom!

AGATA: You don't expect him to sleep on the floor, do you?

SILVIA: I don't like it! I don't like it! It's because of father; it used to be as though we were still expecting him to come back one day. It isn't like that any more.

AGATA (*her eyes on the ground*):   I see: it's because of your father. Yet I seem to have heard you laughing a good deal about the place these last months. Or haven't I? I thought you were the first to forget him.

SILVIA (*almost a cry*):   But I'm only his daughter!

AGATA: And I'm his wife, you mean? So I oughtn't to forget him? Is that it? (*with a change of voice*) My dear child: the life a man and woman live together, my duties toward your father and his toward me, are a difficult problem, too difficult for an outsider to grasp. And sons and daughters are outsiders in these matters. They know nothing. Their judgments are only the conventional ones. Suppose we say no more about it, Silvia, shall we? In a very short time you'll be far away from here, and you'll find that many things here will seem very small and remote to you then. (*trying to be friendly*) You'll see all your friends again, you'll have plenty of amusements. You'll be well again there.

SILVIA (*with unwonted rebelliousness*):   My health! That's what you mean, my health! Mother! I've been wanting to speak to you for days. For days now, I've felt . . . frightened and worried . . .

AGATA (*almost with harshness*):   Go on then. You've been worried. What about?

SILVIA (*after a long silence*):   Pia.

AGATA: Pia?

SILVIA: Yes. She spends her whole time watching that man. I know she does.

AGATA: You think so?

SILVIA: Yes. I know I'm not mistaken.

AGATA (*after a pause*):   Well, Pia is rather like that. It's nothing to make a fuss about.

SILVIA (*agonized*):   Mother, it's the loneliness, the isolation here that frightens me . . . being here the whole time like this, bound and chained to the same thoughts the whole time. The most incredible things begin to seem . . . ordinary, close at hand . . . inevitable . . . as if one were dreaming . . . I think that is the way all those horrible things happen that one reads about in the . . .

AGATA (*not looking at her*):   But you're going away tonight, darling.

SILVIA: It's a net, mother: it's a net . . . ! And we shall all of us be caught in it.

AGATA (*her eyes lowered*):   All of whom?

SILVIA: Mother . . . I'm sure that that man . . . I'm sure he and Pia . . .

AGATA: What do you mean?

SILVIA (*dully*): You know what I mean.

AGATA: I don't think so. Angelo can't resist teasing people. (*suddenly*) Silvia, I don't want to listen to any more of this!

SILVIA (*calmly, dully*): I've spied on them.

AGATA (*in an outburst of exasperation*): Why? Why did you do that? Why? Why? (*controlling herself*) In any case . . . it's all nonsense. I don't believe you.

SILVIA: I've heard them. Don't you know what I mean?

AGATA (*roughly persuasive, and determined to break off this conversation*): No, no, my dear. I tell you no. You've made a mistake. You've made it all up; it's all out of your own head. You must stop, Silvia; I beg you. Please don't let's waste any more time on it.

SILVIA (*stares at her in silence for a moment*): Mother, from the minute I came into this room you've been pretending not to understand what I've been trying to tell you.

AGATA (*bitterly*): Very well then, what is it?

SILVIA (*almost weeping*): You know perfectly well what it is, mother. That man . . . why, you yourself don't even take the trouble to hide it . . . You and that man! . . . You and that man! Why do you go on trying to pretend!

AGATA (*sadly*): I haven't been pretending. I begged you. I begged you to spare both of us words that never ought to be uttered between a mother and daughter. But you wouldn't have it. Why?

SILVIA: I've seen you! You and that man! A stranger. A tramp. That's the reason I'm going away, surely you see that?

AGATA: Exactly: You're going away. You could easily have gone away and said nothing. (*a pause; sadly*) Silvia, we ought never to have started this conversation. You grew up, and so did I, in a world in which a great many facts and a great many ideas are taken for granted. Our books, our education, our friends, have made us used to accepting certain things. I have never asked you what you do with your time in the city. You are not a child any more. You're responsible for yourself. I haven't ever asked you anything, have I?

SILVIA (*after a pause*): You are right. I've been silly. There's just this, mother; there are other things we haven't said yet. Do you think I'd have asked to talk to you if it hadn't been necessary?

AGATA: Silvia, Silvia: surely there's such a thing as good manners, even between a mother and daughter, isn't there? Surely there's one threshold where even those that are dearest to us have to pause and turn back . . . And whatever you have to say, I can't believe these things really matter so much. (*bitterly*) They're only trivialities.

SILVIA: Mother.

AGATA: Will you be quiet! Leave me alone, be quiet. Surely we all have the right to be left alone, haven't we?

(*There is a pause. When* **AGATA** *goes on, it is more in the hope of bringing the conversation to an end, than in the expectation of being believed.*)

You've got everything wrong. You've misinterpreted things.

SILVIA (*suddenly, with great gentleness*):   Oh mother, how you must have been suffering ever since I started to talk to you. To think of you: pretending, lying, humiliating yourself, anyone as proud and honest as you. Mother, what has happened, how can it have come about? You asked me what right I have to be talking to you like this. I'm your daughter. You are my mother.

AGATA (*pale, her eyes lowered*):   Your mother. A signed document: a receipt. Your mother. And because of that, no longer alive. Your mother. Quietly embalmed.

SILVIA (*gently, as before*):   No, mother, that's not true. I remember when I was little. I was in love with you, I'd like to have given up my whole life for you. I used to turn over the pages of your music for you and look up at you every now and then and watch the lamplight in your hair.

AGATA (*bitterly*):   It is a pity everything couldn't have stayed like that, like a picture, quietly yellowing with age, and no one would ever have thought of it again. (*pause*) Yes, it's a pity; everything has changed, I'm no longer the same woman. (*pause*) And neither are you, Silvia; I remember things too. I remember your sweet little voice. But no, no, you've grown up, Silvia, you're a woman, you're another person, I don't know what you are. You've no longer any need of me, and the sound of your voice even annoys me. Sometimes when a little bird grows up, its mother drives it from the nest and pecks at it till it flies away. Nature is honest; we are not; we embalm our dead.

SILVIA: But to me you've always been the best thing in the world! Everything on earth was sweet and clean when you were there!

AGATA: And what did any of you know about me? I was alone. I've always been alone. Have any of you ever looked at me, or spoken to me, ever once wondered what I was thinking about when I was there, with the lamplight in my hair, or at night when I lay awake? Were you all so sure you knew me?

SILVIA: But your life here, mother, your beliefs . . .

AGATA (*bitterly*):   Beliefs. I've listened to lies, and I've told them. I've been cheated, and I've cheated back. Were you all so sure you knew me? (*almost desperately*) Were you all so sure you knew me? (*silence*) Stop tormenting me Silvia, stop!

SILVIA: And Pia? (*almost shouting*) What about Pia?

AGATA: What has Pia to do with it?

SILVIA (*stares at her in silence; then suddenly, and almost frantically*):   "What has Pia to do with it?" You know as well as I do. You've known it from the start! You even accepted that! You've let this horrible thing happen, you've let that man degrade you and Pia so that you're—like two mares in the same stable! You've been willing to cast aside whatever it is that makes you human! And if it were my turn tomorrow, you'd allow that too!

AGATA (*low-voiced and commanding*):   Lower your voice, Silvia! Pia's certain to be eavesdropping somewhere about; it only makes the whole thing even sillier.

SILVIA: I've seen it all, I've known all about it, I've watched you both panting there, like . . .

AGATA (*with harsh vehemence*):   What claptrap, what a ridiculous fuss over something so small and petty! (*suddenly in despair*) What do you want of me? Leave me in peace, keep away from all this! Why are you behaving like this? Why are you here?

SILVIA (*imploring*): Don't speak to me like that, mother.

AGATA: Whatever I am or do, what do I matter to any of you? Yes, what? Half my life, probably, I inflicted a kind of paralysis on myself. Well, it was all a mistake; I wore myself out, and all for nothing. The lies we told! The important thing is to know what you are and to be it, and then everything is simple. (*as though letting her thoughts wander*) Like when you're tired and falling asleep, and you let all your thoughts slip away from you one by one; they drift far away, and you feel relief from them, because you know they are foolish! Foolish and useless, all of them! And then at last: peace! The same peace that the grass knows, and animals, and stones. That is what I want: to be quiet. The rest can take care of itself.

SILVIA (*in a low, frightened voice*): Don't talk to me like that, mother . . .

AGATA: I shan't take the slightest notice of anything you've said. Words, words: I heard them long ago from your father—and you are just like him. But even you don't matter to me, Silvia. You were wrong to make me speak; I never have in my life before now. All this wearies me, wearies me, and bores me, I can't bear any more of it. Go away!

SILVIA: Mother, what has happened to you? It's he who's done all this! He came in here like a beastly animal . . .

AGATA: Darling: suppose I enjoyed . . . obeying him? His voice persuades me.

SILVIA (*shivering*): I know. I've heard it: his voice; and yours. Do you think I don't realize? For three months now I've had to live through all this. You were unable to say no to him.

AGATA (*with bitter defiance*): Exactly: I was unable to say no to him. Whatever he asked. And one thing is much the same as another, after all. Deep down, that was what I wanted: I was alone, the wind carried me away. Others called to me, but I didn't reply . . . It's all so simple, isn't it? It was what I wanted.

SILVIA: No, no, no, mother! This is unbearable! Oh, mother, I can't bear it!

AGATA: And who's asking you to bear it? What is it to do with you? Go away!

SILVIA (*suddenly*): Mother, do you know what they are saying down in the village? They're saying it about me as well! About me as well, can't you understand? They say we're his little flock: the three of us. It's driving me out of my mind, I can't bear it! A little while ago I looked in papa's drawer. His revolver was there, I took it, I've got it here with me, here, in my bag.

AGATA (*shaking her*): Go away, I tell you, Silvia! It's nothing to do with you! Your troubles are easily solved; all you have to do is go away!

SILVIA: I can't go away now! I've seen your face when you've gone into his room . . . And Pia's face . . . and your voices . . . You frightened me, I couldn't think of anything else . . . You've made me ill again! I'm ashamed for anyone to look at me! I can feel the stain of it on me, even when I'm asleep. (*She is on the ground, her arms round her mother's knees.*) Mother, let's go away, come away with me!

AGATA (*freeing herself*): No.

SILVIA: Come away, I beg you, I beg you!

AGATA: No. Let me go.

SILVIA: I'll put an end to it all. (*staring before her as though at a vision*) I will kill him, mother. I've thought it all out, every detail. I shall call him in here, I shall tell him to look down, there, where father's clothes are: I shall make him bend over them. And then, from behind, close up to him, I shall shoot, right in the back of his head. I have the revolver.

AGATA (*looks at her, with intense calm*): No, you won't shoot him; you won't do that; I know you won't. (*suddenly*) Silvia, what's really the matter with you? What is it? Why did you come in here, why have you been talking like this? Why have you been spying, why have you been shouting in this way? Why didn't you go away, why don't you want to go away now? Why? Why? (*She runs out of the room.*)

(**SILVIA** *still on her knees, continues to look at the door, her eyes wide and staring. Then she turns.* **PIA** *is standing before her. She has entered some moments earlier and has slowly advanced while the scene between* **AGATA** *and* **SILVIA** *has been in progress.*)

PIA: You look pale, Silvia. Is something the matter?

SILVIA (*absently, rigid*): No, nothing. Do you know where Angelo is?

PIA: Do you want to speak to him?

SILVIA: I have something to say to him.

PIA: Now? This minute?

SILVIA: Yes, now.

PIA (*lowering her voice*): Do you know what you're going to say to him?

SILVIA: Yes, I know. (*Her gaze drops to her handbag.*)

PIA (*following her gaze*): Sit down Silvia. You're shivering. I'll go and call him.

(**PIA** *makes* **SILVIA** *sit down.* **SILVIA** *obeys mechanically.* **PIA** *goes out; her voice is heard calling.*)

Angelo! Angelo! (*receding*) Angelo! Angelo! (*farther off still*) Angelo! Angelo . . .

(**SILVIA** *shakes herself.* **ANGELO** *is at the other door. He advances cautiously.*)

ANGELO: Ah, Silvia dear, I didn't know I should find you here. Someone was calling me; I'm sure it wasn't you. Let them go on calling me. We do nothing but run after one another in this house. But I run about much more than your mother and your aunt; I'm just like a pussy cat. (*He laughs.*) Silvia, my dear, I'd no idea I'd find you here; though to tell you the truth, I was very much hoping I would.

(**SILVIA** *slowly gets up from her chair.*)

What are you getting up for? Are you going away already? No, stay in here; this is nice. Silvia: I've been wanting to talk to you for a long while. Silvia dear: I'll confess it frankly and with all my heart: I was looking for you. I was waiting till you were alone. I so very much wanted to talk to you before you went away. Oh, yes, I know you despise me, and you're right. And I know you are proud, and you're right to be that too. Still, I can see you are hurt and unhappy, and you're too young and sweet for me to allow that. That's why I came in. I felt I had to talk to you.

SILVIA: So did I.

ANGELO: You too? Ah, then: I'm glad. We both wanted to. Dear Silvia, tell me: I'm very anxious to know what you've finally . . . (*He breaks off.*)

(SILVIA *goes rather stiffly to the table where her bag is, and picks it up.*)

Silvia dear: I think you have a few complaints you want to make about me. Very well: I'll accept them and try and not deserve any more. I know I've been at fault . . . in some ways. Or is it your mother and aunt that have been at fault? Even they can make mistakes. We'll try to correct them, shall we? Dearest Silvia, I'm sure you don't really mean to go away. What is it you don't like here?

(SILVIA *stretches out a hand, and points to her father's clothes.*)

What? Your father's clothes? Yes, you're right. You're quite right, my dear. It was unfeeling of me to think I might wear them. It's made you unhappy. My dear Silvia, they shall still be your father's. I won't touch them. Is that what you wanted? Is that all?

SILVIA (*breathing heavily; pointing to the clothes*):   Down. Bend down, and look at them. Look at them closely.

ANGELO (*surprised*):   Is there something there? Something I've not seen? (*He bends over them, picks up one of the garments, and turns to the girl.*) I can't see anything there.

(*He resumes his inspection of the clothes, and goes down on his knees.* SILVIA *approaches him, with her hand in her bag; she is standing over him.*)

PIA (*outside*):   Angelo! Angelo!

(SILVIA *moves away.* ANGELO *gets up from his knees and also moves away.* PIA *comes running in. She stops short, and looks at them: then she goes over to* ANGELO.)

ANGELO: What's the matter?

PIA (*whispering*):   She wants to kill you. She has the revolver.

ANGELO (*with a gesture, bids her be quiet; he stands reflecting for a few seconds without looking directly at* SILVIA, *then he says in a loud friendly voice*):   Thank you, Pia. What you've just told me is very important; it was a good thing you ran and told me. Now you can go.

(PIA *remains motionless, watching. He turns once more to the clothes, looks at them and bends over them, but in a very different way.*)

(*Slowly and amiably.*) Dear Silvia, I was just saying: I couldn't find anything among your father's clothes; I'll look closer, shall I? Like this. Is that better? Or must I bend lower down? Ought I to go down on my knees? Ah yes, I see now what it is I ought to find here. A sudden death. The death of a bull in the slaughterhouse. (*in the same amiable tone*) Did you want to kill me?

(SILVIA *stares at him fascinated.*)

ANGELO: (*suddenly at the top of his voice, furiously, in falsetto*): You wanted to kill me? (*in the same voice to* **PIA**, *who does not move*) Go away Pia, you can leave us. (*to* **SILVIA** *in the same angry scream*) You wanted to kill me?

SILVIA (*almost voicelessly*): Yes.

ANGELO (*lower*): You had a revolver.

SILVIA: Yes.

ANGELO: Give it to me.

(*She hands it to him. He takes it, still staring at her; then, to himself, as though unable to understand.*)

She wanted to kill me, to take my life. (*in tremendous surprise*) She hates me! (*to* **PIA**) She hates me, do you see? So long as she's alive my life's in danger. Do you understand? She hates me. She hates me.

(**SILVIA** *is suddenly shaken by sobs.*)

(*in the grip of a real terror*) Oh, oh, oh, do you see, Pia? I might have been lying there smashed to pieces by now. She'd thought it all out, splendidly. (*imitating it all, in a kind of pantomime*) I was here . . . I was down on my knees like this . . . and she . . . Yes! You! Where did you intend to hit me? On the back of my neck, was that it? Here, here. And I'd have been there, like that! My face on the stones, my teeth broken in; like that, like that! and then, with my head, like a smashed egg, a mass of blood and brains . . . (*suddenly, with tremendous fury, in falsetto, like some extraordinary trumpet*) You beastly, filthy insect! You dirty little whore! Dirty little whore! (*He runs at the girl, strikes her, seizes her by her blouse and hair, and throws her to the ground, shrieking and babbling.*) You filthy little whore! You could do that . . . ! . . . You could do that! You wanted to kill me! Filthy little whore! Filthy little whore! (*He lets go of her.*)

(**AGATA** *has appeared; uncertainly, overcome, she goes to her daughter.* **SILVIA** *is lying on the ground.*)

SILVIA (*through her sobs*): I wish I were dead.

(*There is a silence.*)

ANGELO (*suddenly, almost sadly*): I've given way to violence! And been unjust as well! I'm ashamed, what a dreadful thing to have done . . . (*to* **AGATA**) Our poor Silvia wanted to . . . (*His teeth are almost chattering.*) She's sick. Really and truly sick. We must do something; we must make her get better. Oh, I'd give anything in the world, yes, my own life even.

SILVIA (*as before*): I wish I were dead.

ANGELO: I couldn't believe it: but this poor girl actually hates me. It comes of being lonely; you have to be very strong to be able to bear loneliness. If you're not strong, a poisoned thought can worm its way in . . . and run through all your veins. You turn into a machine, and finish up by committing . . . Silvia might have done that . . . I escaped by a hair's breadth. Poor Silvia. She's too frail for this sort of life.

SILVIA (*sobbing, still prostrate*): I wish I were dead.

ANGELO (*dropping his voice a little*):   She wishes she were dead, she says. And out of pity for her you could almost wish . . . Poor Silvia, poor delicate little thing, gnawed by such a terrible disease. Poor Silvia, the best of us all: and in spite of that, fated to go on through the years, rotting away and befouling herself! Yes, rotting away and befouling herself! Cheated and mocked at; swollen, fat, and sinful. One could almost rather wish that she . . . that some mysterious pity would bend down and pluck the flower, gather it before it collapses into the mire and dirt. Gather it, and save it, so that it shan't be lost. (*a pause*) I don't know whether I have dreamt it, or whether it was only a thought; it seemed to me that it was evening, as it is now, and that our Silvia was weeping. She was saying . . . that she couldn't bear for a single night longer the awful noise of the shutter rattling; whang, whang. That noise at night has always been our dear girl's night-mare. And suddenly she says: "I'll go and tear the shutter down." And I say to her: "But dear Silvia, that would be very dangerous, you might meet with an accident." And she smiles. Upon my very word, she smiles; and she says: (*He lowers his voice.*) "Dear Angelo, let Fate decide. Whatever happens, I shan't have to hear the noise of the shutter any more. And then I can sleep in peace."

(*A silence. Dusk is beginning to fall.* **SILVIA** *half-rises from the floor, slowly.*)

SILVIA: Mother!

AGATA (*agitated*):   What do you want to say to me?

SILVIA: Mother, one day I was filled with despair and revulsion. I went to his room, because I wanted to drive him away, drive him away from the house . . . Mother, I am already lost!

(**AGATA** *turns slowly and moves away from her.*)

Mother!

(*Silence.*)

AGATA (*without turning round to face her*):   I loved you so much when you were little. You were so delicate, you filled me with pity.

(**SILVIA** *rises to her feet; slowly; a little stiffly, she moves to the door and goes out.*)

PIA (*in a low voice*):   Where is she going, now?

ANGELO: Why do you ask, you liar? You know as well as I do. It's always been more than likely that sooner or later she'd jump off that damned balcony. (*He looks up at the ceiling.*) It might be happening at this very moment. (*He looks toward the clothes.*) And at this very moment too, I might be lying there . . . with the flies already buzzing round my corpse. (*He looks up at the ceiling.*) Have we the right to interfere? It is destiny, itself, that must answer . . . yes or no. (*He listens.*) You, Agata, you, what do you say? It's you who should speak. Say something, for God's sake! She's your daughter.

(**AGATA** *stands motionless, gloomily.*)

Or perhaps we are only playing with fancies? . . . Besides, I . . . There. (*He looks up and listens.*) Oh, of course nothing's going to happen. But I can still scarcely breathe; I feel shaken. What ought we to do? How difficult it is to keep ourselves innocent and human . . . and alive. Why, why did our Silvia have to . . . How could she think of anything so monstrous? Why? Why has she done this?

PIA (*exasperated, with a cry*): Angelo, what a fool you are!

ANGELO: Why?

PIA: I think your fright must have put you out of your mind! Why do you think the girl did this? (*contemptuously*) Because she was in love with you.

ANGELO (*stands there, fascinated by this new thought*): How mysterious human actions are. Sometimes a single sail can be blown upon by two different winds. I often think . . . (*suddenly, frantically, to* AGATA) Call your daughter. Go and fetch her. (*shouting*) Go and fetch her! Quick! Call her! (*He runs to the door.*) Silvia! Silvia! Silvia! Silvia!

(*He has gone out; his voice recedes in the house; then, from a change of tone, it is clear that he has found the girl, and is leading her back. He reappears holding her up, almost carrying her. She is half-fainting.*)

Bring a chair. She's shivering with cold, she can't stand up. Take hold of her, bring her round; moisten her lips; make her drink something.

(AGATA *and* PIA *bend over her;* ANGELO *stands for a long moment regarding them.*)

Ah, look! Yes, look! To see you all three there, close together like that, in love and harmony! How soothing and calming that is . . . Indeed, indeed, we've all been blind. And all the time it was so simple.

AGATA (*turning to him*): What was simple?

ANGELO (*vaguely*): Everything.

AGATA: What do you mean?

ANGELO: I mean our dear little girl isn't going away after all: tonight or any other night. Edoardo is coming; he'll go back by himself again, awful old man. (*a pause*) The four of us. (*silence*)

(PIA *suddenly begins to laugh, shrilly and hysterically, her teeth chattering.*)

Would you have liked it better if there'd been bloodshed here? Or there, outside, under the balcony? Pride, always our pride, our damnable pride. The four of us. Why should we spoil everything, what reason have we to hate each other?

PIA (*still howling with convulsive laughter*): Angelo, you're insane . . .

ANGELO: I never even let myself tread on an insect. Whatever lives is delicate and lasts for only a short time, why do we have to behave cruelly to anything? Whatever our soul desires is always innocent. It is like a child stretching out its hand.

PIA: You're a fool, a fool! Agata, can you stand there and listen to him? (*wildly*) I'll go and throw myself off the balcony. I'll kill myself! I'll be the one! You filthy beast, you've ruined us! (*She is suddenly silent.*)

ANGELO: Pia, go and get my bag for me. It's I who am going away. I'll be able to go with old Edoardo: a good thing he's coming, after all. It will solve everything.

PIA: You! . . . Go away? (*screaming*) Yes! Likely, likely, likely, isn't it?

ANGELO: Do you think I'm joking? I don't want to stay here any longer, surrounded by mischief-making and spite . . . and my life in danger (*He moves toward the door.*) I shan't be long. I've only a few old rags to fling together, that's all. (*He is at the door.*)

AGATA: Angelo, what are you doing?

ANGELO: I'm going away.

AGATA (*pleading*): Wait.

ANGELO: No, I never turn back once I've made up my mind.

AGATA (*imploring*): But we hadn't decided anything yet, Angelo. Please wait.

ANGELO: No, I want to go away. I must look after my life after all; I must try and protect myself. You're all too much occupied with your own spite and jealousy to bother about me. I'm going.

AGATA (*still imploring him; her increasing distress is appalling to watch*): No Angelo, wait. We shall be able to explain everything.

ANGELO: We've already explained everything! It's a miracle I'm still alive. And you're all still suspicious of me, you all want to humiliate me.

AGATA: But no one is humiliating you . . .

ANGELO: Ingratitude; malice . . .

AGATA: I implore you, Angelo. I beg you. You can't go away like this. You've been here for months . . . Come . . . wait a little . . .

(*A pause.* **ANGELO** *comes slowly back into the room.*)

PIA (*suddenly cries*): But what on earth are you all doing? What is it? Are we all going mad? (*She throws herself on* **ANGELO**.) You swine! You cheat! You miserable sponger!

(*Almost calmly,* **ANGELO** *smacks her hard across the face. She is suddenly silent. In the distance the noise of* **EDOARDO'S** *car horn is heard.*)

ANGELO: There it is, Silvia. Old Edoardo, with his truck. Now it's stopping. It's up to you. You're free, Silvia. I won't take advantage of what happened between us a few moments ago. You are free to go or to stay. You can choose. Listen . . . He's stopped; he's blowing his horn.

(*It is heard again.* **SILVIA** *suddenly walks toward the door.* **ANGELO** *stops her halfway; he says calmly to* **PIA**:)

You, Pia: shout to him: tell him she's not going, we'll talk about it all later.

PIA (*goes to the window, and calls*): She isn't coming! She isn't coming!

(*The truck is heard departing. A silence.*)

ANGELO: Well, that was all very simple. (*amiably, to* **SILVIA**, *as he lets her go*) It's not that I forced you to stay, you know, Silvia? We were all agreed from the start, really. Only you all three wanted to . . . to feel yourselves a little compelled in some way; that's to say, guided, protected. So here we are: the four of us. There's nothing wicked or sordid between us is there? We're brothers and sisters. We've shouted and squabbled a good deal, and now . . . how nice and peaceful it is. It's evening, the moon is coming up.

AGATA (*suddenly under her breath begins softly to sing, without words, the tune of the song*):

Esevi uttu sehe . . .

ANGELO: Close the doors, Pia. Shut them all up, and put the bolts across. What's old Edoardo matter to us—what's the whole world matter if it comes to that? It's from outside that mosquitoes and doubts fly in. Close the place up.

(AGATA *and* PIA *do so,* AGATA *continuing to sing.*)

Out with them all. Ourselves alone. As if this house were a walnut, black outside but sweet within. No, not a walnut; an island, rather; in the sea; an island margined with silver, and we four quite, quite alone on the wonderful grass, and in every blade of grass the wind whistling lightly . . . and over us the clouds . . . and . . . (*a pause*) No one but ourselves. Free. Free! And tonight we must celebrate! Let's put all the best food in the house on the table! I'll go down the well and fetch some bottles up. There are still some left. You get everything ready, Agata; light the lamps. And you help her, Pia. Quickly, quickly. (*He points to* SILVIA.) This little sister of ours mustn't let us see she's been crying. Go and comb her hair, wash her face, tidy her up. Why, she's the reason we're having the party.

(*The two women begin to carry out his orders, at first a little uncertainly, but after a few moments with some alacrity.* ANGELO *gets ready to go down the well.*)

ANGELO: Get out the very best tablecloth, and the best glasses. My dear sisters! If one of you is in pain, the sun itself turns dark for me. Quick, Pia, take Silvia, and make her tidy herself up. (*gaily*) We all know Pia is a jealous girl, and she's been known to speak a little sharply at times, but all the same she's the most useful one of you about the house, and very obedient. Silvia is the flower . . . (*as* PIA *and* SILVIA *go out*) Pia, make her put on that dress she was wearing the day I came! And you, Agata . . .

(AGATA *is preparing the table; he is arranging the rope-ladder over the side of the well.*)

AGATA: Me? I'm old.

ANGELO: You are the one that matters. I came for you from far away; it's because of you I stay here. Whenever I look at you, I always remember that, where I come from, the women are never let out alone at night in the countryside.

AGATA (*pausing in her preparations*): Why not?

ANGELO: Because they might meet the devil. Everyone knows that all women want to make love with the devil . . . It's the devil who plays hard-to-get. (*He laughs.*)

AGATA (*interested*): Well?

ANGELO: Well, sometimes, of course, you have to send them out alone at night—to fetch the doctor, say, or on some other errand.

AGATA: Well?

ANGELO: Well, as they're going along, suddenly, if there's a moon, at the side of their own shadow they see there's another one. It's a traveler, who's decided to go the same way.

AGATA: What does he say?

ANGELO: Nothing. He just sniffs at them.

AGATA: Sniffs at them?

ANGELO: Yes. To see if they smell of smoke. Smoke is the smell of human beings; no other creature lights fires and boils pots on them. He sniffs.

AGATA: And what if they do smell of smoke?

ANGELO: Oh, he makes off at once. He knows they're just tarts or housewives: tearful little creatures; the devil can't stand them. Still, every now and then, just once in a while, he does meet one that doesn't smell of smoke.

AGATA: What does she smell of?

ANGELO: Nothing at all. In my country they say: she smells of the wind. The Almighty made a mistake over them. Something got mingled in their makeup that was intended for some other sort of creature, something stranger, more important, nearer to God. That's the reason why women of that kind are always melancholy. They are like you, Agata, hating it where there's smoke, hating it just as much where there isn't. Men love these women passionately, they say to them: "Soul of my soul!" But these women have often been known to poison their men. Nothing's right for them. Nothing at all, not even paradise. Those are the women the devil waits for at night. They have no fear; and off they go with him . . .

(*The last words come from the well;* **ANGELO** *is going down into it.* **AGATA** *stands thinking; suddenly she starts. A noise has been heard in the well.*)

AGATA: What's the matter?

ANGELO (*from inside the well*): Nothing, the ladder has fallen in, that's all; it came off the hook.

AGATA: What shall I do?

ANGELO: Throw me a rope down, will you?

AGATA: Yes, straight away. I won't be a moment.

(*She finds the rope, and goes toward the well with it; halfway there she pauses irresolutely, and lays the rope down.*)

ANGELO: Have you got it?

AGATA: I'm just getting it; wait just a moment, will you?

(*She turns.* **SILVIA** *comes in. She is gaily dressed, with flowers in her hair.* **PIA** *follows her, with a lamp.* **AGATA** *looks at her for a long moment.*)

They have dressed you up nicely, Silvia, haven't they?

PIA (*lifting the lamp in her hand, so that it shines on the girl*): Angelo; where's Angelo gone?

AGATA: He's gone down the well. (*motionless, averting her gaze*) We have to throw this rope down to him.

CURTAIN

ACT 3

(*It is still dark, just before dawn. The lamp is still burning on the table. **AGATA** is seated alone, in the half-dark. She sits there motionless for some time. Then **SILVIA** enters on tiptoe; she halts in the doorway.*)

AGATA (*in a whisper*): Did you want something?

SILVIA (*also in a whisper*): Mother, haven't you slept?

AGATA (*still with lowered voice*): I never sleep very much.

SILVIA: Aren't you coming into the other room? We are going to have something to eat.

AGATA: Later on. Was there something you wanted?

SILVIA: No, nothing. Mother, why don't you come in there with us?

AGATA: Later on. What's the matter with you, aren't you very well? These mornings are chilly. Go on; go back to Pia. There's no point in your coming in here. (*a silence*) Have you everything you want, in there?

SILVIA: Yes?

AGATA: Has anyone been for the milk? (*after a pause*) One of these days we shall have to do some washing. (*There seems a great sense of peace in her voice.*)

SILVIA: Yes. (*a further silence*) Mother, I'm rather frightened.

AGATA: You know it's only a joke, surely?

SILVIA: Yes, I know. (*a pause*) But why don't you come into the other room? We can't even talk in here.

AGATA: Later on. (*a silence*) Do you know what I've been thinking about? College: the professor of divinity: the words he used to use whenever he tried to describe to us the idea of eternity. He used to say: try to imagine a butterfly which every so often flutters its fragile little wings. It is placed upon a bronze globe. Now think how much time it would need for that butterfly, moving its wings every so often, to make a tiny mark on that bronze globe. And then think how long it would take for those weak wings to wear the whole of that bronze globe away. And then imagine that that bronze globe was as big as the earth and the sun together, bigger even than that, as big as the entire universe. And the little butterfly on that terrifying globe has to wear away the whole globe till nothing remains of it. And when it has worn away the whole of that, it has to wear away other globes, so many that you cannot count them. And when it has destroyed every single one of them . . . even then, eternity will still not have begun. The idea of eternity eludes human thought. Or perhaps it is the opposite idea that eludes human thought.

SILVIA: Mother: hasn't he spoken again?

(*For the first time, she casts a glance in the direction of the well.*)

AGATA: No. Only a few words. Nearly two hours ago.

SILVIA: Do you think . . . ?

AGATA: If you go very close and wait till your ear gets accustomed, you can hear him perfectly; you can hear him breathing.

(SILVIA *takes two or three cautious steps toward the well.*)

He's only quiet because he's sulking at the moment. He does sulk every now and then. (*She laughs quietly.*)

SILVIA: He was still talking up to two hours ago wasn't he?

AGATA: Yes.

SILVIA: What did he say?

AGATA: Nothing. He seemed a little impatient. He was making rather a noise. (*She laughs quietly.*)

SILVIA: What is he doing now?

AGATA: Thinking.

SILVIA: And before: why was he making a noise?

AGATA: He hadn't understood; he didn't quite realize.

SILVIA: Realize what?

AGATA: Oh, that it's . . . just a joke, a little game.

SILVIA (*rather frightened*): A game. I've been thinking: it's two days and two nights now . . .

AGATA: Not quite, it's less than that. Besides, you others agreed; you laughed, when I suggested it.

SILVIA: Yes, of course.

AGATA (*laughing quickly*): What are two days and two nights? And what about when he was in the war? That was much worse. And besides, there are plenty of bottles down there for him to pass the time with.

SILVIA: Bottles? What about them?

AGATA: Every now and then I hear him break the neck of one of them.

SILVIA (*with a laugh*): And does he drink it?

AGATA: Yes. I've heard him. He said so, too.

SILVIA (*laughs again*): Is he getting drunk? Down there?

AGATA: I think so. That's how he's passing the time. You've no need to worry; he isn't too badly off down there.

SILVIA: Are you sure?

AGATA: Quite sure.

SILVIA (*a little worried*): There's nothing to be afraid of. After all . . . two days and two nights . . . two days and two nights . . .

AGATA: Less than that. He can stay there much longer than that.

SILVIA: It will teach him a lesson; he deserved one, didn't he?

AGATA: Of course he did.

SILVIA: Of course: he deserved it.

AGATA (*vaguely*): There was something wrong here. We weren't quite at our ease. Oh, he's already changed, just a little. When he calls up from down there sometimes, he almost makes me want to laugh at him. (*a silence*)

SILVIA (*suddenly*): Mother, why don't you call to him? Just to hear him? To hear what he says. Call to him, mother.

AGATA: No, better not. I've noticed he begins to get rather lively when he knows there's someone here. He begins to talk, and shout. He hopes someone will answer him. But when he can't hear anybody . . . I've taken my shoes off. If he can't hear anybody . . . it's then that he begins to be a bit frightened . . . (*There is again the note of peace in her voice.*) That's what we want. We must wait till he begins to be a bit frightened.

SILVIA: Frightened of what, mother?

AGATA (*evasively*): Oh, just frightened. Besides, you're speaking quietly, too, and going about on tiptoe, aren't you? Why is that?

ANGELO (*suddenly from the well: hollow, echoing, and much magnified*) Silvia!

(**SILVIA** *moves back from the well, frightened.*)

ANGELO (*calmly*): Silvia. I know you are there. Answer me. I heard you, you know. Answer me. Go on, answer me.

SILVIA (*to her mother, whispering*): You answer him . . .

ANGELO (*calmly*): Pia, is that you, Pia? I can hear you splendidly. You've been going about on bare feet, all of you. Pia! Silvia!

(*A long silence. Then his voice begins to sound slightly angry.*)

Pia! Silvia! Pia! Silvia! Pia! Silvia!

PIA (*coming in, and whispering in an agonized voice*): I can't bear to hear him any more! We mustn't wait any longer. It's dangerous. Throw the rope down to him, and have done with it.

AGATA: You throw it to him.

PIA: I'm frightened. He sounds so fierce; he sounds like a madman. I'm frightened.

ANGELO: Pia! Silvia!

PIA: I can't go on hearing him call out to me like that!

AGATA: Why did you come downstairs then? I told you to stay up there, you can't hear anything upstairs.

PIA: You can hear upstairs; you can hear everywhere. And from the road too. If anyone goes by, they'll be sure to hear him.

AGATA: I don't think so. In any case, no one goes by.

PIA: All through the night, he's gone on . . .

AGATA: That's not true; it's just that you want to hear him. Even when he's quiet.

ANGELO (*as though discouraged*): Pia! Silvia! Pia! Silvia!

SILVIA: Why does he only call us? (*in sudden anger*) Why does he only call us, and not you?

AGATA: Because he knows you're easier to deal with; you're younger than I am.

ANGELO (*in normal tones*): Pia! Silvia!

AGATA: If you like, we can put the cover on the well. The lid is there.

SILVIA: Yes, of course we could . . .

AGATA: You wouldn't hear so much of him then.

SILVIA (*suddenly penitent*): No, no, don't let's cover it . . .

ANGELO (*quietly; too quietly*): Ah, so Agata's there, as well, is she? I know. (*Silence: then a long amiable echoing laugh; and now his voice is cordial and amused.*) Clever girls. There are times when I get angry down here. But then I see the funny side of it too. Schoolteachers: a schoolteacher's joke. I have to give it to you: clever girls. They once played a joke like this back in my own country, on a man I knew; it all ended up with a supper party, it was a wonderful evening; ah, yes, I remember it. A magnificent dinner; I was at that too.

AGATA (*gasping slightly*): There. You hear him? What sort of voice is that?

SILVIA (*surprised*): A quiet one.

AGATA: Do you know what it means?

SILVIA: What?

AGATA: Fright. It's beginning. The chill of fright. (*with an odd note of sadness*) He realizes he's in danger and refuses to admit it. He is trying to master himself, and to master us.

ANGELO: My dears, you've been keeping me in after school a bit, haven't you? . . . Never mind, I deserved it—I was getting to be too cheeky. (*He laughs.*) I'm growing such a thick beard; there's no razor down here. Luckily there are a few bottles, however. I'll bring any that are left up with me. (*He laughs.*) You'd better hurry up though, or I shall empty the whole cellar and get really drunk. Do you mind if I sing? (*He begins to sing "Esevi uttu sehe," but after a few bars the song becomes fainter.*)

AGATA (*strangely compassionate*): Oh, God! He really is frightened.

(*The song has broken off.*)

PIA (*distressed and aggressive*): Why are we doing this to him? Why?

AGATA: He's told you himself. He was getting to be too cheeky. We were all agreed about that, I think?

SILVIA (*almost as though in a dream*): But we've done enough to him, we can let him come up now, can't we?

AGATA (*laughing*): Yes!

PIA: Now! At once!

AGATA (*laughing*): Yes!

ANGELO (*suddenly, terrified, imploring, unrecognizable*): Silvia . . . for pity's sake . . . the rope . . . throw the rope down to me for pity's sake . . . They want to kill me . . . Your mother . . . she wants me to die down here . . . Quickly, I've no strength left, I'm going to faint. If I faint, I shall drown. Quick . . . Silvia . . . Pia. I'll leave you, I'll go away. I'll do whatever you tell me. Don't make me die down here . . . for pity's sake. (*He breaks off, pause.*)

(*Suddenly **SILVIA** runs and seizes the rope and carries it over to the well, struggling to free it from* *various entanglements.* PIA *runs to help her; now they are at the side of the well, and both suddenly stop.*)

    His voice suddenly rising to a wild epileptic shriek, savage and utterly inhuman): Murderers! (*pause*) Murderers! I'll come up and rip your insides out, I'll tear you all three to pieces! (*pause*) I'll get you condemned to death! I'll see you hanged! Hanged! Hanged! Murderers!

(PIA *and* SILVIA, *terrified, run away from the well; the rope has fallen from their hands.*)

ANGELO: You all plotted it! Murderers! You'll all three pay for it! You unhooked the ladder yourselves! You, you, all of you.

AGATA (*almost to herself*): It isn't true. It just happened.

ANGELO (*now horrifyingly raucous*): Murderers! I'll have you hanged! Murderers! I'll rip your insides out! I'll tear you to pieces!

(*It is no longer a voice, but an atrocious howl, alternating with convulsive babbling.*)

PIA (*terrified, and forgetting to speak quietly*): The cover! Let's put the cover on, quickly!

SILVIA: He's climbing up . . . Oh God, I'm frightened.

PIA: Let's throw something . . . drop something on top of him . . . a stone . . .

(*The noise from the well has died away into a kind of death rattle, then into a heavy breathing. Then silence returns.*)

SILVIA: He's fallen.

AGATA (*after listening for a moment*): He's breathing. (*to the others, with a return of the same sadness of voice*) He can't climb up. He tried to climb up earlier, during the night.

PIA: He tried?

AGATA: Yes, several times. I heard him. He can't get a grip on the stones.

PIA: But sometimes people who are mad . . .

AGATA: No. As time goes on, he gets angrier. He also gets weaker. If he hasn't managed it by now . . . I don't think he ever will . . .

SILVIA (*her teeth chattering*): But then . . . what are we to do?

(*A silence.*)

AGATA (*in a very low tone*): Nothing. There is nothing to do.

(*The light of dawn has begun. In a little while it will be daylight.*)

SILVIA: But what will happen then?

AGATA: Nothing.

SILVIA: What do you mean, nothing?

AGATA: I'm afraid it's already . . .

SILVIA: Already . . . what?

AGATA: Too late.

SILVIA: Too late . . . What do you mean?

AGATA: Oh, I don't ever expect to see him come up out of there again! Why, it would be like seeing . . . something monstrous coming up out of the earth . . . the devil. He'd tear us to pieces; I'm sure he would, he'd denounce us to the police, he'd get us hanged, all three of us. Nothing could save us. Surely you see that?

SILVIA: What then?

AGATA (*in a monotone*): But I don't think he'll ever manage to get up again. (*pause*) You two go in the other room; try and eat a little. I'll come as well, now.

(*A silence.*)

PIA (*stammering*): It isn't my fault. I had nothing to do with it. I've done nothing.

AGATA: None of us has done anything. It just happened. (*a silence*) He happened to come here. Who asked him to come? The ladder happened to slip off the hooks. Nobody touched it; it happened by itself. And he gets the idea into his head that it's our fault. What can we do to help him? . . . What a strange chain of events . . . It was obvious things were not right here. It was all confusion; insecurity. It couldn't go on. (*a pause*) It was as though he'd discovered for each one of us . . . a sort of root between us and the earth: a piece of gut, a bloody navel-cord, and he twisted it round his fist and dragged us along by it. He almost had us on all-fours, growing hair like goats. However, it was none of our choosing. It had to happen. And now it has happened.

SILVIA (*shivering*): Mother, you knew it would happen. You could have prevented it.

AGATA (*half lost in thought*): No. I couldn't.

SILVIA: But you'd realized . . .

AGATA: And you hadn't, I suppose? It's happened. And now one of us has to stay here quietly and think. It's an ungrateful task; I take it upon myself. (*shaken for a moment*) Do you think it doesn't horrify me too? (*controlling herself; in a whisper*) We shall leave here. It won't be long before the house and the well both collapse. There was a foreigner here; people will think he's gone, just as he one day arrived. In the meantime you can both go away.

SILVIA (*with a cry*): But . . . I can't bear . . . This thing, down there . . . I can't bear it!

AGATA (*harshly*): There are a lot of things you can't bear, aren't there? Fortunately, I'm here to bear them. Besides, in a little while, he'll have quieted down; there comes a point when things are seen to be inevitable and after that we do become quite calm once again. (*lost in thought*) Everything will happen very quickly. Dizziness; the water, though there's so little of it, will close over everything . . . and then be still again.

PIA (*hysterically*): Oh, my God . . . Oh, my God . . . Oh, my God . . . I'm going away! I'm going away!

AGATA: Good. You go too, Silvia. Nobody will ask you anything.

PIA: I won't stay here a minute longer! My things are already packed. This house has always been a prison!

AGATA: Yes, my dear; go to Vienna. Go and dine out in your evening frock.

PIA: Yes, I am going! You frighten me!

ANGELO (*suddenly*): Throw her on the ground, tie her up, she's mad! Pia, Silvia: don't let her do this. It's a crime! She's always laughed at you and despised you. Help me, help me; I can feel the cold of death on me. She was the one; she was responsible! It's her doing!

PIA: Yes, yes, it was Agata!

SILVIA: It was you, mother!

ANGELO: You! You!

AGATA (*suddenly, almost with a shout*): Very well, then! Yes. It was I. I've been lying all this time.

PIA: It's been you all along! You unhooked the ladder!

AGATA: Yes, yes. It was what I wanted. Someone had to put a stop to all this. Like when a window keeps banging at night. Someone has to get up.

ANGELO: No! Silvia, she did it out of jealousy! Jealousy of you!

AGATA: Possibly . . . Before long this man would have tired of me, and humiliated me. For your sake, Silvia. (*almost ironically*) Rivals. And as you see, I've won.

ANGELO: Silvia! She killed your father! She killed him more surely than if she'd strangled him.

AGATA: Even that may be . . . He had cheated me and oppressed me. It was a long gloomy farce. Today I can breathe, at last. A pity that you lie out there now, under the earth, in Africa, dear Enrico; you cannot see the results.

PIA: I've always been frightened of you. You horrible, evil creature! You've killed the happiness in everybody.

AGATA: And in myself most of all. Perhaps I could have done better, if there'd ever been anyone in the whole world who needed me. But there never has been.

ANGELO (*suddenly*): You gave yourself to a stranger, without a second thought, on a heap of goat skins.

AGATA: Yes.

ANGELO (*louder*): And then sent your sister-in-law to sleep with me.

AGATA: Yes.

ANGELO (*louder still*): And after that, your daughter! All three of you!

AGATA: I might protest a little there perhaps, but never mind; it's as true as makes no matter.

ANGELO: All three of you! All three of you!

AGATA: Yes. It was clear that it couldn't go on. (*a silence*) This is something that must end today.

SILVIA (*hoarsely*): Mother.

AGATA: What is it?

SILVIA (*a whisper, but gradually louder*): I can't go away and leave him here. Nothing matters to me any more: myself, nor you, nor anyone else. I want him to come back up. I can't bear to live without him.

AGATA (*forcefully*): That isn't true, Silvia. You two did nothing but follow after me, it was I who led you astray. Perhaps I wouldn't have let you stay immune. I feel sorry for you. (*lowering her voice*) And a little disgusted.

SILVIA (*passionately*): I want him to come up! When he calls to me I want to leave every-thing else on earth! I want to obey him!

AGATA: Those were my words, not yours. It is I who've infected you.

SILVIA: I want him to come back! I'll throw myself down there to him! (*weeping*) Mother: perhaps at this very moment . . . I may be . . . I may . . .

AGATA (*seizing her and shaking her desperately*): Be quiet, you silly girl! You're out of your mind. "I may be pregnant": that's what you're trying to say, isn't it? Well, that happens to women, and you're a woman. I was once pregnant with you; I was disgusted at the fact. (*a pause*) It's not true, Silvia, you're hysterical, you're out of your senses. Oh, why are you alive, why did you ever grow up? You were so affectionate . . . why didn't you die that summer when we all expected you to? (*controlling herself*) Be quiet and go away. (*in a voice that gradually rises, with melancholy authority*) There's nothing but disorder here, nothing but chaos. I'm the only one who keeps my head and thinks. I'm calm. I can take everything on myself. He's realized by now, we've all realized, there's nothing more to say or do. It's too late now. This is something that must end today.

(*A silence.*)

ANGELO (*suddenly, with unexpected calm, almost with sadness*): Agata, I want to talk to you.

AGATA (*she, too, is suddenly quiet and gentle*): I can hear you, Angelo. Go on.

(*A silence falls on the room.*)

ANGELO (*as before*): Agata, must I resign myself to this?

AGATA (*as before*): I too am resigned to it, Angelo.

ANGELO: It was you that wanted this.

AGATA: I hardly know. I seem to have been simply obeying.

ANGELO: Am I to stay down here and die?

AGATA (*lowering her voice*): I think things cannot be altered now, Angelo.

ANGELO: It's painful; it's terrifying to have to die down here, here in the dark. I was still young.

AGATA: Do you think it is any less painful for me?

ANGELO: I beg you, Agata. I implore you to come and free me. You have in your hands everything in the world that was good and pleasant to me.

AGATA: Yes. And I would even like to set you free.

ANGELO: Then why don't you, Agata? You liked seeing me; you liked obeying me.

AGATA: Yes. Nothing else mattered to me.

ANGELO: Without me, your life will become nothing again.

AGATA: Yes, nothing.

ANGELO: Then why don't you fetch me out of here? Why are you doing this?

AGATA: Because . . . I was frightened, and I could no longer bear it. I know that worse would have happened, if things had been allowed to go on.

ANGELO: But all that could be altered.

AGATA: *I* couldn't be. Nor would I ask to be. Once a drop of water has fallen, or a thought been thought, they remain so throughout eternity. (*a pause*) Angelo, one can never turn back. I could not bear to see you go away.

ANGELO: But now you are committing the worst crime of all.

AGATA: It had to be. So that we should be at peace again.

ANGELO (*still quietly*): You will never be at peace again! Poor Agata! You will be damned and cursed for all eternity!

AGATA: But that is the very thing that brings me peace: to receive what is my due.

ANGELO (*his voice dying away*): Poor Agata . . . Poor Agata . . .

AGATA: I do not believe in a divine mercy: I would be bewildered by it, I would be a black stain in the light. I love my burden. (*meditatively*) There is a point when we choose what we are to be. It is at the very beginning; when nothing so far exists, and everything is free for us to choose, and our eyes look upward in joy and thanksgiving. Or downward . . . That is the starting point. However, there is always a kind of peace in being what we are, and being it completely: the condemned man has that blessing. I accept. (*a pause*) Silvia: one day—you were only so high—the goatboy brought in here a sweet little kid that he had to kill. (*as though she saw the scene before her*) He slit its throat, just there, on the stones, sticking the knife right in. He skinned it, and opened it up, and fetched out its entrails; near by, there was a basin of steaming black blood. I helped him; my hands were bloody; the creature's eyes were still open. And suddenly I turned to the door . . . (**AGATA** *herself is terrified by what she is saying.*) . . . and you were there, Silvia, there, at the door; you'd been there for the last half hour! You stood there stiff and white, your eyes wide open, staring. You'd never seen anything of the kind before, you were too little. You began to cry: oh God, how you cried! I couldn't comfort you, I didn't know what to do; at first I couldn't even put my arms round you, because my hands were still . . . You went on crying for hour after hour; I begged you not to; I promised you all sorts of foolish things, I went down on my knees before you, I told you it wasn't true . . . Till at last you fell asleep. And then it was my turn to shake and tremble—my turn! my turn to weep!—in sweat and terror. I hardly know what it was I vowed to myself, what I cried out! But it was this: that you, my child, should not know this! My child should be clean. My child should be safe. The bloody hands should be mine alone, mine alone the bowl of blood, and the death, and the flesh, and the earth; mine alone the shuddering and the damnation . . . the smell of beasts . . . the well. And the child: away from here, safe, far away. Go away, Silvia. And if it's true that you are . . . (*She breaks off, and, going up to her daughter, caresses her tenderly.*) I was rather sorry when I saw you grow up and change. We always hope our children . . . we hope everything will be better for them . . . That is what children mean. (*She breaks off.*)

(*The three of them turn toward the well. The sound of panting can be heard from it, the scratching of nails, a noise. Suddenly* **PIA** *screams like a madwoman:*)

PIA: He's climbing up! He's climbing up!

(*The noise is heard increasing, rising, becoming desperate, near, enormous; they all expect in a moment to see a hand grip the edge of the parapet.*)

The three women stand there staring, as though turned to stone. Suddenly, there is a break in the heavy breathing. Not a cry. The noise of something falling. There is a long silence.

Loud, distinct and repeated, the sound of a truck hooting is heard. PIA *runs to the door and calls wildly:)*

PIA: Edoardo! Edoardo! Come up here! Quickly! Come up!

(There is a prolonged pause, until the old man EDOARDO *at last appears in the doorway.)*

EDOARDO *(coming into the room):* What is it?

*(*SILVIA *breaks into sobs.)*

What's the matter?

PIA *(breathing heavily):* Look, you're thirsty. Don't you want a drink of water? *(She repeats hysterically: it is almost a shout.)* Don't you want a drink? There. *(She points to the well.)* There. Draw yourself some water, out of there.

EDOARDO *(bewildered):* 'Course I'm thirsty; 'course I am. *(He approaches the well, speaking in the melancholy tones of someone repeating something he has said hundreds of times before.)* I'm getting too old to go dragging that broken-down truck all over the place in this heat. 'Course I'm thirsty.

(He has reached the well, and automatically bends over to look down it.)

AGATA *(who has come close up to him: quietly):* Here.

(She is just behind the old man, and hands him a glass of water, which she has poured from the jug. He turns, takes it, and drinks; and asks again:)

EDOARDO: What's the matter?

AGATA: My daughter is leaving; and my sister-in-law is going with her. Will you wait for them down below? They are quite ready.

EDOARDO: What about their things?

AGATA: They're being sent on later.

EDOARDO: And what about you?

AGATA: I'm staying here.

EDOARDO: And the foreigner?

AGATA: Gone away.

EDOARDO *(moving toward the door):* It's not only the sun, it's the air. And this wind: it burns; it burns right into you. *(to* PIA *and* SILVIA*)* Then I'll wait down there for you. Don't be too long, will you? *(He goes out.)*

AGATA *(suddenly, almost fiercely, cries):* Go away!

*(*PIA *rushes out after* EDOARDO.*)*

(to SILVIA*)* Go away, both of you! Leave me alone.

*(*SILVIA *rushes out also, terrified. Her footsteps are heard receding.* AGATA *stands listening; as soon as the silence is complete, she runs to the well.)*

Angelo! Angelo! Angelo! Wait!

(*She turns back frantically, seizes the rope and throws one end of it down into the well.*)

Catch hold of it! Take it! Angelo! Angelo! (*Gradually her voice begins to sound as though it were coming from a long distance.*) Angelo! Angelo! Angelo!

(*She straightens herself, and stands motionless; her hand lets go of the rope; she goes slowly to the window, and then to the door, bolting them both. It is dark inside the room. She seats herself calmly near the lamp, which is still burning on the table. She speaks to herself, quietly.*)

Dearest Angelo, do come. Do come, even if it's only to punish me, if you want to. There's all the time in the world, now.

(*The sound of the truck hooting is heard in the very far distance. Silence again.*)

Now there are only the two of us. How simple that makes everything. You will certainly never be able to go away now, and neither shall I. We shall go on calling to each other and fighting with each other through all eternity.

CURTAIN

THIRTEEN

ALBERTO
SAVINIO

Introduction

Alberto Savinio is a pseudonym for Andrea De Chirico, the younger brother of the painter Giorgio De Chirico. He was born in Athens on August 25, 1891. In his artistic and critical works he encompassed many fields of art. Much of his youth was spent abroad, in Athens, Munich, and Paris, where he made a name for himself in the avant-garde before World War I. In 1925 he was among those who helped found the Teatro d'Arte in Rome, which was headed by Pirandello, and he staged *La morte di Niobe* (The death of Niobe), a mimed tragedy, for that theater. Early in 1926 he married Maria Morino, an actress in the Teatro d'Arte, and they moved to Paris. In a 1927 exhibit of his art work that Jean Cocteau introduced, Savinio achieved major recognition for his painting. Nevertheless, he did not put down his writing pen. During World War II, he wrote his most important work and from 1946 on he was able to participate in the reconstruction of Italy, exercising all his creative abilities in his theatrical endeavors: as playwright, director of musical works, and set designer. Those were intensely active years for him. He died in Rome, May 5, 1952, leaving two children, Angelica and Ruggero.

It was only in the mid-1970s, more than twenty years after his death, that his work began to be rediscovered and given recognition for its place in twentieth-century Italian culture. It is, above all, to Leonardo Sciascia that credit for this reevaluation is due. Sciascia called Savinio "the greatest Italian writer since Pirandello"[1] and thus stimulated renewed publication of his work. Savinio's importance within the compass of European literature and art still needs to be clarified, particularly as regards his influence on the French avant-garde.

The youthful Savinio matured within an international cultural context, as did Piran-dello, but his sensibility was very different indeed from that of the great Sicilian. Savinio allowed himself to be influenced by Nietzsche and Schopenhauer, but he never forgot his solid classical education or abandoned Socratic irony. One must keep in mind that he was born in Greece and made constant references to Greek culture.

From 1910 to 1914 he lived in Paris. Possibly influenced by futurist musical experiments as well as by Max Reger's ideas about "musical prose," Savinio made his mark as a composer and as a promoter of new ideas in music. He wrote several operas and ballets prior to 1913 when he met the poet and critic Guillaume Apollinaire, an admirer of Alfred Jarry's *Ubu Roi* and one who inspired the surrealist movement. Apollinaire introduced Savinio to other proponents of the antirealist movement in the arts—Pablo Picasso, Francis Picabia, Paul Guillaume, Max Jacob, and Jean Cocteau—and in 1914 he published Savinio's *Les chants de la mi-mort: Scènes dramatiques d'après des épisodes du "Risorgimento"* (The songs of semi-death: Dramatic scenes based on episodes of the "Risorgimento") in *Les Soirées de Paris*[2] and invited him to give a performance of the work in the journal's meeting hall. It was in this piece that the Mannequin appeared that would become the symbol of the metaphysical paintings of his brother. This Parisian debut, at little more than twenty years of age, was dazzling. The audience was excited and hugely entertained by the ardor with which he attacked the piano to make every chord vibrate.

In 1915 Savinio's ideas reached America: some musical scores and some of his thoughts about the "new music" were published in *291*, a pre-Dada New York journal edited by the photographer Alfred Stieglitz. During World War I, while on military duty at Ferrara, Savinio continued his journalistic activities. In 1916, "Un vomissement musical" appeared in Tristan Tzara's journal, *Dada*, and "Atlas Italie" in Paul Reverdy's *Nord-Sud*. After the war, Savinio began to collaborate on many other journals—both Italian and French—writing about art, reviewing French surrealist writers, reviewing films, theater, and music, and writing about provincial life. This journalistic activity was to continue throughout his life, and his articles have been collected by Rosanna Buttier in a volume entitled *Savinio giornalista* (Savinio the journalist).[3]

At the same time he wrote short stories and novels: *Tragedia dell'infanzia* (*Tragedy of Childhood*, 1920), *La casa ispirata* (The inspired house, 1920), *Angelica o la notte di maggio* (Angelica or the May night, 1927), *Dico a te, Clio* (*Speaking to Clio*, 1939); *Infanzia di Nivasio Dolcemare* (*Childhood of Nivasio Dolcemare*, 1935–1941). He was also to write several film treatments, among which were *Didone abbandonata* (Dido abandoned, 1942), *Vita di Mercurio* (Life of Mercurio), *La notte della mano morta* (The night of the dead hand), and *San Francesco* (Saint Francis).

Savinio modified his dramaturgy over the years, moving from the surrealist provocatory style of his first works to a more sober and reflective style in his last scripts, but the theme of death dominates all his works for the stage. "Very few know how to die," he writes. "That is to say: very few die; because dying is an act of energy that very few people complete as such. . . . It is all a matter of reaching death in triumph." And just like death, theater "is able to complete what remains incomplete in life."[4] Some of his works, among them *Les chants de la mi-mort* and *Capitano Ulisse* (Captain Ulysses), were not simply influenced by what was happening in the world's avant-garde capital of Paris in the 1920s and 1930s, but themselves had a strong influence—more so than critics have realized till now—on other artists of the period, as is shown by documents indicating that Roger Vitrac had an interest in the Italian artist, as did Antonin Artaud ("a play by Savinio" was on the program for the Alfred Jarry theater, although it was never performed). In addition, André Breton included Savinio, the only Italian he selected, in his 1938 *Anthologie de l'humour noir* (Anthology of black humor).

Savinio's theatrical ideas, like his writing and his philosophy, were not destined for great success among his contemporaries. *Capitano Ulisse*, a three-act play Pirandello commissioned for the Teatro d'Arte in 1924, was not published until 1934 and was not staged until 1938 when it received a modest production at Anton Giulio Bragaglia's Teatro delle Arti under the direction of Nando Tamberlani.[5] In the intervening years, Savinio had made ties, and then dissolved them, with Pirandello's Teatro d'Arte. He respectfully put a distance between himself and the "gloomy" theater of the Sicilian writer and counterproposed his own idea of theater as a "colorful adventure."[6] Rather than a theater that dreads death and decline, he preferred one that reveals the incomplete death, or semi-death, caused by one's attachment to material objects, a metaphysical theater that accepts humankind's errant—in the sense of both wandering and morally straying—destiny and inherent predisposition for a "glorious" death.

In his one-act play *La famiglia Mastinu* (The Mastiffu family, 1940), adapted from his story with the significant title *Morte ammazza noia* (Death kills boredom), the death of the Grandmother constitutes the one vital shock to the asphyxiating routine of the petit-bourgeois family with its symbolic last name: *mastino*, or mastiff, denotes a fierce animal in its common usage, and it originates in the Latin word *mansuetus*, meaning "domesticated." The reactions of the encephalitic son, Michelino, make apparent the uneasiness of this "domesticated humanity, whose bestial nature peeps out through the folds of a very recent, and too sudden, civilizing process, creating overpowering grotesque effects."[7] The play was first staged in Bologna in 1953, shortly after Savinio's death, and then in Genoa in 1990 by Egisto Marcucci, who has contributed in a major way to the revival of Savinio's work.

After World War II, Savinio hoped that the theater would be rejuvenated, that the means and forms of production, which were so old-fashioned that they were condemned by the surrealists, would change. But this hope was not completely fulfilled. When Savinio's *Alcesti di Samuele*, a tragedy in two parts, was first produced at Strehler's Piccolo Teatro in 1950, it was treated as a marginal production. The most conservative reviewers criticized its avant-garde aspects and the young director, Giorgio Strehler, was censured both for his experimental staging and for the heavy language, which was deemed more philosophical than mimetic.

The protagonist of *Alcesti di Samuele* is Teresa Goerz, Jewish wife of Paul, who has committed suicide to rescue her husband from Nazi persecution. Teresa accepts resurrection as the only way to join in death with her beloved husband. Her ties to Paul hold her suspended in a state of semi-death until they can finally reunite in all or nothingness and she becomes Alcesti-Teresa, wife and mother of the beloved.

Savinio's transposition of myth into a petit-bourgeois reality using a surrealistic mode—one that did not however follow the dictates of Breton and that was, if anything, more connected to the *imagérie* of Jean Cocteau—did not impress the cultural powers who only wanted to see realistic reflections on the stage. And his musings on death were intolerable for a society striving to exorcise its social contradictions and anything else that might alarm it, in order to concentrate exclusively on economic growth.

The theme of death appears again in *Emma B. Widow Jocasta*.[8] In this monologue, the theme is in Freudian dress. Emma is awaiting her son, who she believes is coming home, after fifteen years of separation, defeated in life, in a state of despair, and emotionally dead. As she prepares to receive him, she realizes that he is the real man in her life, and thus she conceives of incest as a means of reversing the traditional woman's role; through incest she will dominate the male, her son.

Savinio's particular philosophy of life, with its stoic and mystic elements, is a philosophy that does not exclude social concerns but is not content to conceive of material things as the ultimate goal in life. Fundamental to it seem to be a rejection of organized religion in favor of an eclectic and personal mysticism, a search for knowledge through experience, an acceptance of the negative as a dynamic aspect of creation, and a view of life as a process of transmutation. He developed a specific symbolism in his paintings and his set designs with, for example, his use of the gnostic third eye and cabalistic circles, but his mystic bent has perplexed critics. While Ugo Piscopo, in the first in-depth study of Savinio's work, declared that Savinio's writings were "among the most significant documents in Italian literature of the 1940s for their depth and for the new cultural themes they embrace,"[9] Emilio Cecchi, seizing on the centrality of a typically baroque theme, the intermingling of love and death, to Savinio's drama, suggested that here was Metastasio again, played in a cubist key.[10]

A. A.

Trans. J. H.

Notes

1. Leonardo Sciascia, "Testimonianza per Savinio" (Testimony to Savinio), *Scena* 1:5 (1976), p. 36.

2. (August 1914).

3. Rome: Bulzoni, 1987.

4. Alberto Savinio, *Autunno* (Autumn), in *Opere*, Leonardo Sciascia and Franco De Maria, eds. (Milan: Classici Bompiani, 1989), p. 837.

5. It has been restaged in recent years. Particularly noteworthy is the 1990 version by Palermo's Teatro Biondo, directed by Mario Missiroli. This production came to New York in January 1991. The most accurate version of the text is that edited, with a "Comment," by Alessandro Tinterri (Milan: Adelphi, 1989).

6. Alberto Savinio, "La verità sull'ultimo viaggio" (The truth about the last voyage), introductory note, in *Capitano Ulisse* (Rome: Quaderni di Novissima, 1934); reprinted in *Capitano Ulisse*, ed. Alessandro Tinterri (Milan: Adelphi, 1989), p. 18.

7. Alessandro Tinterri, "Nota a *La famiglia Mastinu*" (Commentary on the Mastiffu family), in Alberto Savinio, *Alcesti di Samuele e atti unici* (Alcesti di Samuele and one-acts), ed. A. Tinterri (Milan: Adelphi, 1991), p. 349.

8. This monologue was first produced in Rome in 1952. In 1981, Egisto Marcucci revived it with the actress Valeria Moriconi playing Emma.

9. Ugo Piscopo, *Alberto Savinio* (Milan: Mursia, 1973), p. 241–42.

10. Emilio Cecchi, "Alberto Savinio," in *Letteratura italiana del Novecento* (Twentieth-century Italian literature), ed. Pietro Citati (Milan: Mondadori, 1972), p. 874.

■

EMMA B., WIDOW JOCASTA

A monologue

(*Emma B. vedova Giocasta*, 1949)

Translated by Martha King

■

The living room in Signora Emma's house. One door upstage and another on the right. The door upstage leads to the bedroom, the other to the hallway. On the back wall, to the right of the door, a pendulum clock. On the left of door a console table with drawer. Above the console table, a large mirror. On the left of table top, in a standing frame, a photograph portrait of Millo, son of Signora Emma, as a student. Against the left wall a large clothes wardrobe with two doors. An armchair between the wardrobe and the console table. The hallway, as seen through the open door, is lit. SIGNORA EMMA, *her back to the audience, standing in front of the door, which she partially hides, is speaking to the maid,* ANGELINA, *who is invisible in the hall. In her left hand* SIGNORA EMMA *holds a letter. She has the appearance, behavior, and dress of an elderly woman.*

SIGNORA EMMA: Thank you, Angelina. I don't need anything . . . All alone? What do you think I'll do? I'll be waiting. I'll rest. In the chair . . . Not on the bed, no. I'm not that tired. In the chair. I'll have a look at the paper. With all I've had to do this morning, I haven't even looked at the headlines . . . His room is ready. The dining room, too. Did you fix the pilot light like I told you to? . . . Good. All I'll have to do then is light it . . . I may not even need to. He might eat on the train . . . He doesn't say in his letter. He only says: "I'll arrive around eleven" . . . What time is it?

(She looks at the clock on the wall.)

Ten. Just an hour . . . A little more for the time it takes to come from the station. He'll take a taxi. Let's say it'll be eleven fifteen, eleven twenty . . . I would go to the station myself. But he didn't want me to. He says so in his letter. You know how impossible the station is with all the work that's going on there. Passengers coming out from three different exits. It's not easy to meet someone. A woman alone, at night, in that crowd . . . He's not even sure when he'll arrive. He could be late. He wasn't even sure he could get away. In the letter . . .

(She holds up the letter, turns it over, searching closely.)

Here: "I'll arrive Wednesday, around eleven. *(scans it)* If nothing comes up unexpectedly in the meantime." But I'm not worried. *(She forgets Angelina's presence and talks to herself.)* Nothing will happen. Nothing can happen. Nothing "more" can happen . . . *(At a question, presumably from Angelina, she comes back to reality.)* Why? . . . Just because. A thought . . . You're going to a movie? Over at the "Crystal" they're showing *Mother*. It's about a mother who finds her son after believing he was dead for fifteen years. Go see it. I've seen it. You'll like it. *(She laughs.)* In the neighborhood this evening they're having a celebration for mothers who've found their children again . . . Wait.

(She moves from the doorway, goes to the console, opens the drawer, takes out two bills; then, after hesitating a bit, another two. She returns to the doorway.)

I want to pay for your movie this evening . . . Are we being bashful, Angelina? . . . Come on! *(gives her the two bills)* And I want to pay for your sister too, if you go together. *(gives her the other two bills)* This evening it's my treat . . . How is your sister? Give her my very best . . . Have a good time, Angelina. Don't forget to turn out the hall light.

(She closes the door and immediately reopens it.)

What did you say? . . . No. He has the keys . . . I don't know. He said so in his letter. *(She holds up the letter. Reads.)*

"Don't bother coming to the door: I still have the keys to the outside door and to the apartment. I'll let myself in. At least I will if you haven't changed the locks." You see, Angelina? I have nothing to do but wait. To wait right here. What a silly boy! Why would I have changed the locks? . . . Good night, Angelina. Go on because it's getting late.

(*She begins to close the door and then reopens it to respond to something the maid has said.*)

Not at all! I'm sure about that. And I can tell you, Angelina: I want him to find me alone when he comes. Just think! I haven't seen him for fifteen years! Yes, when the Germans were here . . . But only for a few hours. We hardly even exchanged two words. He ran off right away . . . Fifteen years. He has never written. I followed his life, from a distance. I knew . . . Yes . . . He wasn't happy. He kept running after happiness, trying to find it . . . If only he had asked me! I would have told him. I would have said: "You, Millo, were not made for happiness. It's pointless for you to run after it. You weren't made for 'that' happiness. For the happiness that you believe in, the kind you're looking for." . . . But he would have thought badly of me if I had talked to him like that. He would have thought I was saying it for a purpose. For my own personal advantage. And he would have hated me even more. Because he did hate me. Yes: my son hated me. He went away because he hated me. He went to another town. He thought that I, his own mother, was keeping him from being happy . . . It was out of hate for me that he got married. He married that woman while he was still a student . . . And he kept at it. First with that one, his wife. Then with another one. Then with still a third one. Always searching . . . searching for something he couldn't find. Something he'll never find . . . And then this morning, all of a sudden, after fifteen years, this letter! The first! . . . But I was expecting it. For fifteen years I've been expecting it. I knew that it would come sooner or later . . . The first . . . Yes, there were other things from time to time . . . but were those letters? Could those be called letters? . . . And this morning, suddenly, eight pages from him, from my son. An outpouring. His first. The first time my son has opened up to me. He was always silent. Closed up. Hostile. I wasn't to interfere with his life. I would ruin it. As if I were his worst enemy . . . And now, all of a sudden, this letter! (*She raises her hand, brandishing the letter, the flag.*) This letter announcing his arrival. This evening. In an hour . . . Now . . . After fifteen years of separation, distance, coldness . . . My son's coming home . . . He's coming home . . . Because he's not happy. Because only I, his mother, can understand him, can comfort him . . . He says so himself. Here. In the letter. It's taken him fifteen years to understand that! . . . No, Angelina, I'm calm . . . I've never been so calm. I'm happy . . . It's something deeper. It's a . . . what should I call it? . . . it's a victory. "My" victory. I have won, Angelina. I feel like I've won. That's what makes me happy. Makes me proud. And deeply satisfied. I know now that I was right. I knew it before, but he didn't, he didn't know it. He did everything, in fact, to prove the opposite. And now he knows it. Even he knows it. Even he has realized . . . No. Don't worry, Angelina. Go on. I need space. I need space for my joy.

(*She starts to close the door, but is interrupted this time by an idea that comes into her head.*)

Are you going to the movie with your sister? . . . If it gets late just go ahead and sleep at her place.

(*She closes the door, moves to the middle of the living room.*)

Nothing to do now but wait . . . How long?

(*She looks at the clock.*)

Forty-five minutes . . . And I've been waiting for fifteen years!

(*A suspicion enters her mind. She returns to the door. Opens it. Looks out: the hallway is dark.*)

She's gone. (*She closes the door and returns to the middle of the living room.*) A good woman. But what a nuisance!

(*She looks around.*)

Alone! (*She raises her arms and stretches.*) Alone! Alone! (*She looks at the wall, under the clock.*) What a shame I sold the piano! (*She hums to herself and tries out a dance step. Awkwardly. Like an old woman.*) If only I had my poor old piano.

(*She stops, concentrates.*)

Who was that man so continually oppressed by outsiders, even by his family, that when he was finally alone in the house he felt so light he started to walk on the walls? . . . Although I wish her the best, poor thing! I could have thrown her down the stairs.

(*She inhales deeply, exhales with "freedom."*)

Ah! . . . (*She returns to her previous recollection.*) But where did I read that story? . . . One day—it says—his wife and children were leaving for the country. He opens the door, they go out with suitcases, dog, canary cage. He closes the door. And then, all at once he feels so unburdened, so free, that he takes off running, flies across the hallway, starts up the wall, and falls on his face.

(**SIGNORA EMMA** *partially acts out what she is saying. From the door where she is standing she crosses the living room on the run, bumps up against the opposite wall. She stops out of breath.*)

What a fool! . . . At my age . . . (*She moves wearily toward the armchair.*) I'll sit down. I'll skim the paper . . . Oh, yes! Fine shape I'm in for reading the paper tonight!

(*Suddenly she remembers:*) Of course! I read that story in a book by Savinio. (*She has a new thought.*) How does he happen to have the house keys? . . . (*searches her memory*) It must be that day he turned up here . . . In forty-four . . . January of forty-four. When the German's were here . . . The doorbell rang. I went to open the door myself. Before me stood a bearded man with glasses . . . Him! Starving. Older. A skeleton. He was on the run. He was hiding. I fed him. Such a lot. Then he slept. He slept all day. He slept all night. The next day we didn't go out. He read. There was no way to talk to him. I couldn't get a word out of him. Suddenly there was a pounding at the door. The electricity was off so the bell didn't work. Bang! Bang! Bang! They kept on pounding. (*She indicates, beyond the door, the invisible entrance way to the house.*) I understood immediately what that pounding meant. Even if Angelina hadn't come running to warn me . . . She looked as white as a corpse. Denounced by the doorkeeper. We immediately believed the doorkeeper was the spy. Poor Vincenzo! But at a time like that who keeps their head? Angelina couldn't speak. "The police!" She belched up the words. She had seen them through the little window on the stairs. She ran to open the back service entrance. She motioned for us to escape, him and me. "Are you crazy, Angelina? Don't lose your head." They kept on knocking. "Go open it. Let them in. And above all, treat them very politely." She didn't understand. I had to push her into the hallway. With another push I had him in the bathroom. He looked like death, too. He didn't understand, either. And he wanted to escape. Escape through the back service stairs. Onto the roof. How did I get the idea that came to me? . . . Just like that. Like poetry. He was as white as chalk under that ridiculous beard. Imagine if they were to see him looking like that; with that face! His eyes were popping out behind his steel-rimmed glasses. I whispered in his ear: "Stay here, behind the door, close to the wall. And don't move! Don't breathe!" I closed the bathroom door behind me. I went to sit on the toilet.

(*To illustrate her words, she goes to sit on the edge of the armchair, elbows on her thighs. She spreads her legs.*)

He and I. I didn't look at him. But I felt him looking at me as I sat there quietly, my skirt pulled half-way up my legs. Was he curious or only afraid? . . . Who knows? He was as white as chalk. I don't believe he was thinking about anything, was feeling anything. Those men were walking through the house. They were muttering. They stopped at the bathroom door. One asked: "What's in here?" I heard Angelina answer: "The bathroom." What could I do? I hadn't washed yet that morning. I hadn't put on my underwear yet. Was I to save him or preserve my modesty? . . . I didn't think twice. I pulled up my clothes. Up to my belly. My thighs were exposed. One of the men stood in the doorway. He stammered: "Oh, excuse me!" Or rather, "Pardòn!" And he closed the door again. I felt a tickle in my throat. I pulled out the roll of toilet paper, tore off a large piece and made a ball to stuff in my mouth to keep from laughing. But the men were leaving. The door to the house slammed shut. And I was still sitting there, feeling the cool air on my belly. The slam of the door was like a fist in Millo's stomach. Poor boy! He gave out a kind of sob. Like a turkey gobbling. He was next to the bath tub. And instead of turning he vomited on himself. Standing up. On his trousers. On his shoes. He was reeling.

(*She rises from the armchair.*)

He didn't stay an hour longer. He left the same day. We haven't seen each other since. Our last meeting. But what a significant one!

(*Looks at her son's photograph on the console.*)

That meeting saved your life. And you, my son, had a view of your mother, which children . . .

What an imbecile that policeman was! He was so young. A boy. And handsome. Blonde. You don't think of policemen as being blonde. He opened the door, and behind it was the man he was looking for. He had only to turn his head. One glance. But how could he guess? How could he imagine that standing in front of that woman sitting on the toilet with her skirt pulled up, was a man: her son? . . . That policeman will never know the effect his inspection had on my home that day . . . I went to sit on the toilet.

I was clearheaded. Inspired. In a state of grace. I saw through walls. I was an artist. Inflamed by art. But my hands were like marble. Heavy. Nothing could move them. One hid my face and the other weighed down my skirt. But all of a sudden I was an artist. A flash. An idea illuminated me. Completely. That certain attitude of "modesty," that certain attitude of someone who "knows she's being seen," would have given me away; worse: it would have given you away, my poor Millo. They would have realized that I was not alone . . . then the inspiration! Like closing my eyes on myself. There, inside, I was alone. Truly alone. I didn't have anything to hide from anyone. That was the idea I had to get into my head . . . And, suddenly, my hands were free. They became light. They pulled up my clothes, they bared my thighs, my belly . . . The truth! The truth! . . . I didn't find the strength to look at you. But why look at you? I shouldn't look at you. *You weren't there.* Well, yes, I was looking at you. But with other parts of me. I was conscious of you. I sensed, through that other self I became at that moment, at that interminable moment, I sensed that you were looking at me . . . "How" were you looking at me? I couldn't grasp it. But you were looking at me. I could sense it. Then, suddenly, thirty years of my past disappeared. The cow found its little calf. The mare found its colt. The mother found her child . . . Clothes (*she looks at what she is wearing*) seem like nothing, but they are walls. They keep one from speaking the truth. The truth of our skin, the truth of our flesh, the truth of our viscera. That truest, most sincere, most profound language of all. With the slam of the house door when the police left, the wall between you and me instantly returned. We never mentioned what happened between us there in the bathroom during the police inspection. How can one speak of something that happened in a different life? . . . It would take a different language. And we didn't have the time to speak about it anyhow. You left immediately. You didn't want to stay one moment longer. Now my house was dangerous for you. You said so yourself. It was the only thing you said. As though accusing me of a new fault. That time it had gone well because of a miracle . . . I remember: that was the word you used: miracle. You were careful, however, to say that I had performed the miracle. And what a miracle! It's natural for God or the saints to perform miracles: it's their business. But for me to perform a miracle, a miracle of thought and action, and without the basics, without the tools for miracles, just like that, with a toilet, my thighs bared . . . Look, Millo, it's a great thing, it's an extraordinary thing, it's truly miraculous . . . You left right away, on the pretext of danger, of prudence . . . But how could you not feel that no one would find you now? How could you not believe that no one could hurt you now? How could you not feel, now, that my protective wall around you was impenetrable? . . . What should I have done? What should a mother do, what should she do to make herself understood, to make her own son appreciate her? . . . You left. You went back there . . . Not to your wife . . . I knew you had nothing left to share with your wife. Some satisfaction! You hadn't left your wife for me but for that other woman. I knew who she was. I've never told you. I've even seen her. I went to Genoa secretly just to see her. And I saw you together. I even knew who she was, what she did . . . A midwife. The person who came to give me this information acted like it was

something funny. "Do you know who Millo is going with? . . . Guess! With a midwife!"
And she laughed. A midwife! My son took a midwife for a lover! But I understood. I
understood, and I didn't laugh. I felt that this . . . what? . . . This . . . choice masked
a deep secret. A man, a mature man, an adult who feels attracted to a woman who is
employed as a midwife . . . I was about to say, a man who "feels in need of a midwife."
. . . You went away. We didn't see each other again. We had never written to each
other. So there was no reason to now . . . What did we have to say to each other
anyway? What does a son have to say to his mother? Except to sometimes ask for money.
But now, for me, it was not like before. After that drama of ours, that tremendous
drama in the bathroom, me sitting on the toilet with my thighs bared, and you standing
behind the door, white with fear; the truth, the truth of skin, the truth of flesh, the
truth of viscera had spoken. And in spite of all our care, in spite of all our efforts to
pretend nothing happened, in spite of my attempts to convince myself that I had not
heard that voice of truth, I haven't been able to forget it. And you, too, you must have
heard that voice of truth. You gave no sign, but surely you felt it. You went away mute,
blind, as if that scene had never taken place, and yet I knew; I felt that the truth of skin,
the truth of flesh, the truth of viscera had awakened something irrepressible in you too
. . . I waited. There was nothing left to do but wait . . . You steered clear. More distant
than ever. Like a wild beast fleeing from fire. Wild animals run from fire, but at the
same time they're attracted to it, fascinated by it. I knew that you were keeping your
distance. But I was ready and waiting. Even if I've had to wait longer than I thought I
would . . . I knew anyway—my informers were very vigilant, thoughtful—I knew that
you had left the midwife and had taken up with another woman . . . And who was she?
. . . Guess! . . . I didn't have to guess. A nurse. My informers—see what impeccable
service!—even managed to get me a photograph of your new flame. I looked at it . . .
A veil, a veil hiding human frailty lifted before my gaze. Her eyes were close set, your
nurse . . . Hers, too! Now, when proof is presented three times, you have no more
doubts; you can have no more doubts; you don't have the right to have doubts. Your
other lover, the midwife, she also had close-set eyes . . . Your wife had close-set eyes
too . . . and I have close-set eyes . . . So, Millo, what are you looking for? Who? . . .
How difficult it is to say the word "mother," except in certain circumstances!

(**SIGNORA EMMA**, *surprised by her words, remains silent. Then, with a change of mood and attitude,
she continues.*)

From that moment on my perspective changed . . . Or rather: a new perspective
opened up. The *right* perspective. A curtain lifted. The wall that had stood before me
suddenly disappeared and a street was in its place: a wide open street with no end in
sight. Where did the street go? . . . Where would I take you down that street? . . .
Where would you take me? . . .

(*She turns toward the wardrobe and takes a long look at it. She points an index finger at its door.*)

My son is here. Inside this wardrobe. Only here. This is my son. Only this. I made my son's museum. Just like museums are made for a vanished race. This is all I had of him. And I had to be satisfied with this and no more. But I was resigned to it. What could I do? What could I have done? I reduced my desire to the minimum. To expressionless, voiceless, lifeless forms . . . Except for the life that I put into these forms myself . . . so much life! And it animated them, enlarged them, expanded them . . . When my son, all of my son, was here, right here, hanging in his clothes on the line strung across the room, I was in the company of giants. (*She approaches the wardrobe.*)

My son is here. Inside this wardrobe. My son's history is in here. (*She opens the two wardrobe doors slowly, with profound respect, as though they were the doors to a sanctuary.*)

My son's history: from the first day of his life . . . to that day he went away . . . The walls and ceiling closed in around me. I retreated into childhood. And I saw things as I wanted them to be. Like children do. And I was actually happy . . . Yes, happy . . . Now I don't understand how I could have been. But I was happy. Yes, I remember clearly. I was happy. Happy in the fulfillment of my desire. My one desire . . .

(*She takes a rope from the wardrobe. At each end is a loop. A hook is in the wall right of the wardrobe, higher than the doors. Another hook at the same height is in the jamb of the door leading to the bedroom.* **SIGNORA EMMA** *hangs one loop on the hook near the wardrobe and the other on the hook on the door. The rope, between the wardrobe and door, makes a diagonal in the air.*)

I reconstructed my son. The part of him I could arrange in place. I reconstructed him through his clothes. Each day. Some days more than once.

Now it's over. I won't have to do it any longer; I won't have to reconstruct my son like some excavated statue. He'll be here in flesh and blood. (*She shivers with joy.*)

Emma! Emma! You, the martyr of waiting, you are now an actress, a consummate actress. (*She looks at her watch.*)

Yes. I still have time . . . And now, play. Play, Emma. Play with the one who made you suffer.

(*From the wardrobe* **SIGNORA EMMA** *takes her son's first garment: a tiny linen shirt on a tiny hanger.*)

Your first little shirt. Made in one piece. Without any seams. They would have hurt your oh, so soft skin. (*She hangs the little shirt on the line near the hook next to the wardrobe.*)

They put me to sleep when Marta was born in Paris. That stupid doctor kept telling me: *"Poussez! Poussez!"* . . . Yes! What do you mean, *pousser?* That stupid woman didn't know anything. They had to give me ether and go inside with forceps. When I woke up and that stupid woman put on a sad face and told me: *"C'est une fille, Madame,"* I nearly had a fit . . . Yes, I was happy when Marta was born. But a daughter, a woman, is always attached to someone. She' a "dependent." Always. In one way or another. Your sister got married. From dependence on me she went to dependence on her husband. Who sees her any more? She belongs to another. She has been absorbed by the life ray of another . . . You were born in Italy. I was awake when I had you. I was myself when I brought you into the world. Birth pains, yes, but they're never too great when you're bringing a son into the world. You I saw right away. There's something else . . . Between you and your sister . . . that difference . . . how should I put it? . . . that anatomical difference . . . I felt, as I did so many years earlier, as a girl, my incompleteness as a woman, but at the same time I felt that I, an incomplete creature, I, a creature needing a complement, I felt I had created, had given life, had brought a complete being into the world.

(She pulls out from the wardrobe a vest and a teeny pair of knitted shorts on a hanger.)

I took you out in a carriage. Every day. In every kind of weather. Rain or shine. Always. For hours and hours. *(She hangs the vest and knitted shorts on the line. Pulls out a sailor suit.)* Your little sailor suit. *(hangs it on the line, pulls out a school uniform)* Your first long pants. *(She hangs the school uniform on the line.)* "Transition" clothes, let's say. *(She pulls out a man's suit and hangs it on the line.)*

The last suit you wore while you were still with me. Your first man's suit. It was your father's. I had it turned and cut to your size. I saw you in it . . . At first I didn't understand . . . At first I didn't see. At first I wasn't able to see . . . Then, little by little, like in the movies after a man is knocked unconscious by a fist in his face, and the darkness slowly turns to light like milk poured into ink. So, little by little, when I saw you emerge from the darkness, when I saw light around you, I thought: "It's him" . . . But which "him"? . . . For a moment there, standing before me, you were your father . . . That's how I saw you. With everything that went with him, with everything that "he" brought with him, with everything that frightened me . . . terrified me. I felt that disturbance, that distinctive "signal" of trouble . . . It was he, then; I wasn't mistaken . . . There was that confusion, that coldness, that "tensed up" feeling that he gave me . . . As if I had done something wrong; as if I were guilty, always guilty, and he were the warden, dark and silent; as if I never knew my lesson, and he were my examiner, dark and silent . . . I felt overcome by aversion . . . And paralyzed . . . He fascinated me, he did. I didn't want to look at him, and I was forced to look at him, as if my eyes were attached to him with steel wires . . . I stared at him . . . and then, little by little, the dark and silent man began to grow clear . . . A crow that turns white. Cracks that smooth over . . . My protective armor, my aversion, began to melt. I felt that I could move, that I was free. I felt soft . . . I saw you being "born" there before me. Born "fully clothed" . . . You, my son . . . No longer "only" my son . . . Behind you, above you, like smoke carried away by the wind, the dark and silent man separated from you and went away, went away . . . That man went away . . . He went away . . . "My" man . . . stood there before me . . . A year later "that man" died. Died also physically. More than died: vanished. He was completely gone from my life . . . What had "that man" been to me? . . . Nothing. I understood it better after he disappeared. And I understood who my man, my real man, was. That man was a stranger. He came from outside. From far away. He took command over me. The master. The one who put me beneath him. In every sense. He crushed me. In every sense. In every sense, Millo, in every sense. You, on the other hand, are not a stranger. You didn't come from outside, from far away. I made you. You were born from me. You came from me like a flower from a plant . . .

My man, my real man . . . Who can say it's not true? Who dares deny it? . . . You, my man. And now I can tell you. Now I'll be able to tell you. Freely. Without fear. Without reticence. Without shame . . . My man! . . . That other one disappeared. Completely. If he hadn't gone, I would take you by the hand and lead you to his shadow, to his fettering shadow, to his suffocating shadow, and I would say: "Millo, take that shadow away. Remove that shadow. Clear my way." Clear "our" way. I would have given you the means myself . . . Hate? . . . No. Oh, no! . . . There's something less than hate, and at the same time more effective than hate: irritation, boredom. And there's something else even more effective: indifference. Flaccid. Impalpable. But it gets in your pores. It fills you up. It spreads through your body. It slithers like a worm through the labyrinths of your brain. What anger makes you do suddenly, in an outburst at exceptional moments, indifference can make you do at any time, at the calmest, most switched off, "best" moment. It makes you do it "indifferently." . . . Remove this shadow for me . . . Not for another—what "other" could there be now between you, me, and that shadow?—not for another, but because nothing must stand between me and my man anymore. Nothing . . .

(*She looks at the clock.*)

Oh, God! Ten after eleven. (*She looks at the hallway door.*) He'll come through there. That door will open and my man will appear. Inside a frame of darkness. The man I brought into the world. The man I have suckled. The man I have raised. The man I have educated . . . And he, while still a student, took a wife. Against my will. Against my advice. And he went away. And didn't write again. For fifteen years. Far away. Far from me. And he was unhappy. The first. The second. The third time. He was unhappy with the first, the second, the third woman. And this morning, after fifteen years of distance, silence, hate, this morning he suddenly writes and says: "Mamma, you are the only one for me." . . . And now he will come. Through that door.

(*She steps backward in the direction of the wardrobe, continuing to stare at the door as though to better visualize his entrance.*)

Through that door, through that door my man will come, my little bull.

(**SIGNORA EMMA**, *as she moves, passes the mirror. She notices her reflection. She suddenly stops. Quickly, she goes back and stands in front of the mirror. She points a finger at her reflection.*)

My man, my little bull will enter, and see . . . you . . . old? . . . No! It can't be! It mustn't be! . . . What a foolish thing I was about to do. What insanity! . . . (*She looks at the clock.*)

Still a few minutes . . . What a crazy thing I would have done! (*She straightens up before the mirror. Touches her face with her hands.*) And these wrinkles? . . . These awful eyes?

(*She opens the console drawer, takes out various objects that she names as she places them on the top of the console.*)

Powder . . . powder puff . . . cream . . . lipstick . . . rouge . . . eye shadow . . .

perfume . . . Just wasting away in the drawer. Things I thought I'd never use again. (*She applies the cream to her face, makes up her eyes, lips, cheeks. She powders her face.*)

And this hair? . . . This bird's nest? . . .

(*She takes a comb from the drawer; rearranges her hair; fluffs it up. She continues to gaze at herself in the mirror. She takes a box of blue powder from the drawer and applies it to her hair. She then looks at the dress she is wearing.*)

And this dress? . . . This rag? . . . My man, my little bull comes and who does he find? . . . A bag lady? . . . What a sight! (*She tears at the buttons from neck to waist.*) Can I possibly let him see me like this? . . .

(*She opens the door leading to the bedroom; turns on the light. The doorway remains open. Through the door we hear* **SIGNORA EMMA'S** *voice.*)

Clothes—he says—are frivolous. They don't interest him. They aren't at all important to him. What counts in women—he says—is the inner life, the spiritual life . . . Lies! He even said it to that woman, to his wife. Yes! But what dress would suit that goose, that scorpion fish?

(**SIGNORA EMMA** *reenters the living room. She is in a low-necked evening gown, transformed, magnificent. She looks in the mirror.*)

There. Now my man can come. (*She goes to the hallway door, opens it. The darkness in the hallway is seen through the open door.* **SIGNORA EMMA** *moves upstage toward the back of the living room. She looks into the darkness of the hallway through the open door.*) I am ready.
(*She shudders.*)
No . . . If he comes in and sees me right away, like this . . . No! No! . . . It's better if he doesn't see me right away.

(*She moves toward the bedroom door, noticing Millo's various suits handing on the line as she passes. She stops to look at them.*)

Millo of the past! Millo of my desires, good bye! . . . (*She starts to go into the bedroom. She stops once again.*) Better to switch off the light in this room . . . Have a light on only where I am . . .

(*She crosses to the wall near the hallway door and flips the switch. The living room falls into darkness.*)

Only that light on in there.

(*The two doorways remain open: the one to the hallway lies in darkness, the one to the bedroom streams with light. Between them the dark living room.*)

And now . . .

(*Pause. The line holding the clothes breaks from the hook. All the clothes fall to the floor.* **SIGNORA EMMA'**s *voice from the bedroom:*)

Is that you, Millo? . . . (*Pause. Silence.*) I'm in here. Come in.

(*Pause. The door to the dark hallway slowly closes by itself.*)

CURTAIN

■

Bibliography

■

Since it is beyond the province of this anthology to give a complete listing of articles and books in English on Italian theater and playwrights, the reader is referred to the following:

ENCYCLOPEDIAS, DICTIONARIES, BIBLIOGRAPHIES

d'Amico, Silvio, and Sandro d'Amico, eds. *Enciclopedia dello spettacolo.* Rome: Le maschere, Sansoni, 1954–1968. ONE OF THE FINEST ENCYCLOPEDIAS ON THEATER.

Attisani, Antonio, ed. *Enciclopedia del teatro del '900.* Milan: Feltrinelli, 1980.

Bondanella, Peter and Julia Conaway Bondanella, eds. *The MacMillan Dictionary of Italian Literature.* London: Macmillan, 1979; also called *The Dictionary of Italian Literature.* Westport, Conn.: Greenwood Press, 1979.

Bondanella, Peter. "Italian Drama" and all Italian playwright entries in *McGraw-Hill Encyclopedia of World Drama.* 5 vols. 2d ed. Ed. Stanley Hochman. New York: McGraw-Hill, 1984.

Carpenter, Charles A., ed. *Modern Drama: Scholarship and Criticism 1966–1980: An International Bibliography.* Buffalo, Toronto, London: University of Toronto Press, 1986. SEE SECTION ON ITALY.

De Sanctis, Francesco. *A History of Italian Literature.* 2 vols. Trans. Joan Redfern. New York: Basic Books, 1959.

Donadoni, Eugenio. *A History of Italian Literature.* 2 vols. Rev. ed. Ed. Ettore Mazzali and Robert J. Clements. Trans. Richard Monges. New York: New York University Press, 1969.

Lunari, Luigi. "Italy." In *The Reader's Encyclopedia of World Drama,* edited by John Gassner and Edward Quinn, pp. 474–87. New York: Crowell, 1969.

MacClintock, Lauder. *The Age of Pirandello.* Bloomington: Indiana University Press, 1951.

———. *Contemporary Drama in Italy.* Boston: Little, Brown, 1920, 1923.

May, Frederick. "Italy." In *The Oxford Companion to the Theater,* 3d ed., edited by Phillis Hartnoll, pp. 480–99. London: Oxford University Press, 1967.

Whitfield, John H. *A Short History of Italian Literature.* 2d ed. Westport, Conn.: Greenwood Press, 1976.

Works by and Selected Articles and Books
on each Author

ANNUNZIO, GABRIELE D'

Plays in Italian

d'Annunzio, Gabriele. *Il teatro di Gabriele d'Annunzio*. 2 vols. Ed. Renato Simoni. Rome: Mondadori, 1940.

Plays in English Translation

The Daughter of Jorio: A Pastoral Tragedy. Trans. Charlotte Porter, Pietro Isola, and Alice Henry. Boston: Little, Brown, 1907; New York: Greenwood, 1968.
Daughter of Jorio. Adaptation by Michael Strange. New York Rialtoservice Bureau, 19——. Type-
script. Billy Rose Research Library, NYPL Lincoln Center.
The Dead City. (1) Trans. G. Mantellini. Chicago: Laird and Lee, 1902; New York: McGrath, 1902;
(2) Trans. G. Mantellini. In *The Eleonora Duse Series of Plays*. Ed. Oliver Sayler. New York: Bren-
tano, 1923; repr. Freeport, N.Y.: Books for Libraries Press, 1971; (3) Trans. Arthur Symons.
London: Heinemann, 1900.
A Dream of an Autumn Sunset. Trans. Anna Schenck. In *Poet Lore* 8, no. 15 (1904): 6–29.
A Dream of a Spring Morning. Trans. by Anna Schenck. In *Poet Lore* 8, no. 14 (1902–3): 6–16.
Francesca da Rimini. Trans. Arthur Symons. New York: Stokes, 1902.
Gioconda. Trans. Arthur Symons. New York: Russell, 1901; Chicago: Dramatic Publishing, 1913;
London: Heinemann, 1902, 1913.
The Honeysuckle (*Il ferro*). Trans. Cecile Sartoris and Gabrielle Enthoven. London: Heinemann,
1915.

Other Works, in English Translation

The Child of Pleasure (*Il piacere*). Trans. Georgina Harding. Verses translated by, and with an introduc-
tion by, Arthur Symons. Boston: St. Botolph Society, 1898.
Episcopo and Company (*Giovanni Episcopo*). Trans. Myrta Leonora Jones. Chicago: Stone, 1896.
The Flame of Life (*Il fuoco*). (1) Translated with an introduction by Baron Gustavo Tosti. New York:
Collier, 1900; (2) Trans. Kassandra Vivaria. New York: Neal & Liveright, 1900; New York:
Modern Library, 1900, 1919, 1932; New York: Fertig, 1974; (3) as *The Flame*. Trans. Dora
Knowlton Ranous. New York: The National Alumni, 1907.
The Intruder (*L'innocente*). Trans. Arthur Hornblow. New York: Richmond, 1898.
The Maidens of the Rocks (*Le vergine delle rocce*). New York: Richmond, 1898.
Prose Works: Selections—Nocturne and Five Tales of Love and Death. Translated with preface by Raymond
Rosenthal. Marlboro, Vt.: Marlboro Press, 1988.
Tales of my Native Town (*Le novelle della Pescare*). Trans. R. Mantellini. Garden City, N.Y.: Doubleday,
Page, 1920.
The Triumph of Death (*Trionfo della morte*). (1) Trans. Arthur Hornblow. Introduction by Burton

Rascoe. New York: Boni & Liveright, Modern Library, 1923. (2) Trans. Georgina Harding. New York: Fertig, 1975; Sawtry, England: Dedalus, 1990.

The Victim (*L'innocente*). Trans. Georgina Harding. London: Heinemann, 1899; repr. Sawtry, England: Dedalus/Hippocrene, 1991.

The Virgin of the Rocks (*Le vergine delle rocce*). Trans. Agatha Hughes. London: Heinemann, 1899.

Books and Selected Articles About in English

For this author, the reader is also advised to investigate works on Eleonora Duse.

Carlson, Marvin. "Duse and d'Annunzio." In Marvin Carlson, *The Italian Stage from Goldoni to D'Annunzio*, pp. 192–99. Jefferson, N. Carolina: McFarland, 1981.

D'Annunzio: Outstanding Contributions by Seventeen Scholars from America and Europe Ushering in the Fiftieth Anniversary of this Poet's Death, 1938–1987. Notre Dame, Ind.: Annali d'Italianistica, 1987.

Griffin, Gerald. *Gabriele D'Annunzio: The Warrior Bard*. Port Washington, N.Y.: Kennikat, 1970.

Gullace, Giovanni. *Gabriele D'Annunzio in France*. Syracuse, N.Y.: Syracuse University Press, 1966.

Jullian, Philippe. *D'Annunzio*. Translated from French by Stephen Hardman. New York: Viking, 1973.

Klopp, Charles. *Gabriele D'Annunzio*. Boston: Twayne, 1988.

MacBeth, George. *The Lion of Pescara*. London: Cape, 1984.

Rhodes, Anthony R. E. *The Poet as Superman*. London: Weidenfeld & Nicolson, 1959.

Symons, Arthur. *Eleonora Duse*. New York and London: Blom, 1927, 1969.

Valesio, Paolo. *Gabriele D'Annunzio: The Dark Flame*. Trans. Marilyn Migiel. New Haven: Yale University Press, 1992. SEE THIS RECENT BIOGRAPHY FOR A COMPREHENSIVE BIBLIOGRAPHY.

Weaver, William. *Duse: A Biography*. New York and London: Harcourt Brace Jovanovich, 1984.

BETTI, UGO

Plays in Italian

Teatro. Preface by Silvio d'Amico. Bologna: Cappelli, 1955.

Teatro completo. Preface by Silvio d'Amico and Achille Fiocco. Bologna: Cappelli, 1971.

Teatro postumo. Preface by Achille Fiocco. Bologna: Cappelli, 1955.

Plays in English Translation

Corruption in the Palace of Justice. Trans. Henry Reed. In *The New Theatre of Europe*. Vol. 1. Ed. Robert W. Corrigan. New York: Delta Books, 1962; and in Alvin Kernan, ed. *Classics of Modern Theatre*. New York: Harcourt, Brace & World, 1965.

Crime on Goat Island. Trans. Henry Reed. Introduction by G. H. McWilliam. San Francisco: Chandler, 1961; and in Robert Corrigan, ed. *Masterpieces of the Modern Italian Theatre*. New York: Collier, 1967.

The Gambler. Trans. Barbara Kennedy. Library Congress Catalog No. 66–15902. See also *Ugo Betti: Three Plays*, below.

The Queen and the Rebels. Trans. Henry Reed. In *Three European Plays.* Edited with an introduction by E. Martin Brown. London: Penguin, 1965.

The Queen and the Rebels. Trans. Henry Reed. Ed. Michael Marland. Contributions by Ronald Eyre and Dame Irene Worth. Press reviews by Kenneth Tynan and the dramatic critic of *The Times.* Glasgow, London: Blackie, 1966.

Three Plays: The Queen and the Rebels. The Burnt Flower-bed. Summertime. Translated with a foreword by Henry Reed. London: Gollancz, 1956. New York: Grove Press, 1958.

Three Plays on Justice: Landslide, Struggle Till Dawn, The Fugitive. Translated with an introduction by G. H. McWilliam. San Francisco: Chandler, 1964.

Two Plays: Frana allo Scalo Nord (Landslide), L'aiuola bruciata (Burnt Flowerbed). Edited with introduction, notes, vocabulary by G.20H. McWilliam. Manchester: University Press, 1965.

Ugo Betti: Three Plays. The Inquiry, Crime on Goat Island, The Gambler. Edited with an introduction by Gino Rizzo. New York: Hill and Wang, 1966.

Books About in English

Licastro, Emanuele. *Ugo Betti: An Introduction.* Jefferson, N. Carolina and London: McFarland, 1985. SEE THIS VOLUME FOR A COMPREHENSIVE BIBLIOGRAPHY.

BONTEMPELLI, MASSIMO

Plays in Italian

Nostra Dea e altre commedie: La guardia alla luna, Siepe a nordovest, Minnie la candida. Ed. Alessandro Tinterri. Turin: Einaudi, 1989. THIS IS A SUPERB CRITICAL EDITION THAT INCLUDES AUTHOR'S NOTES ON THE PLAYS AND EXCELLENT COMMENTARIES BY TINTERRI.

Teatro. 2 vols. Ed. Massimo Bontempelli. Milan: Mondadori, 1947.

Other Works in English Translation

The Lady of the Hennaed Hair. In *This Quarter,* vol. 4, no. 2 (April—June 1930): 585–603.

CAMPANILE, ACHILLE

Plays in Italian

Campanile's theatrical works were published haphazardly, in revised editions, with changes of titles, partial reprintings, and as adaptations of narrative works. All this makes it difficult both to create a complete list of his plays and to fix the dates of first production and publication.

L'inventore del cavallo e altre quindici commedie, 1924–1939. Turin: Einaudi, 1971.

Teatro: I. L'Amore fa fare questo e altro, Il Ciambellone, Centocinquanto la gallina canta, L'Inventore del cavallo, e 38 Tragedie in due battute. Milan: Treves, 1931.

Tragedie in due battute. Milan: Rizzoli, 1978. CONTAINS 192 OF HIS MORE THAN 500 MINIATURE "TRAGEDIES."

Other Works in English Translation

Alcyone. Trans. J. G. Nichols. Manchester: Carcanet, 1988.
The Inventor of the Horse and Two Other Short Plays. Trans. Francesco Loriggio. Montreal: Guernica, 1994.

DE FILIPPO, EDUARDO

Plays in Italian

For a comprehensive bibliography of De Filippo's published and unpublished works in Italian, the reader is referred to the bibliography in Anna Barsotti, Eduardo drammaturgo (fra mondo del teatro e teatro del mondo). *Rome: Bulzoni, 1988. Most of his plays are collected in* Il Teatro di Eduardo: Cantata dei giorni pari (*Sung on even days*). *Turin: Einaudi, 1959; new and revised editions, 1962, 1971, 1979; and* Il Teatro di Eduardo: Cantata dei giorni dispari (*Sung on odd days*). *3 vols. 1st vol. 1951, 2d vol. 1958, 3d vol. 1966; new and revised editions 1971, 1979. Turin: Einaudi, 1951–1982.*

SOME TEXTS ARE COLLECTED IN: *I CAPOLAVORI DI EDUARDO.* 2 VOLS. TURIN: EINAUDI, 1973–83.

MANY PLAYS MAY BE FOUND BY TITLE, AS SINGLE VOLUMES, IN EINAUDI'S COLLEZIONE DI TEATRO, EDITED BY P. GRASSI AND G. GUERRIERI. PLEASE SEE ANNA BARSOTTI, *EDUARDO DRAMMATURGO* FOR FURTHER INFORMATION.

Plays in English Translation

Filumena: A Play. Trans. Keith Waterhouse and Willis Hall. London: French, 1978.
Filumena Marturano. Translated with an introduction by Eric Bentley. In *The Genius of the Italian Theatre*, ed. Eric Bentley, pp. 439–510. New York: American Library, Mentor, 1964.
Four Plays: The Local Authority; Grand Magic; Filumena Marturano; Napoli Millionaria. Translated with an introduction by Carlo Ardito. London: Methuen Drama, 1992.
Inner Voices. (1) Trans. N. F. Simpson. Oxford: Amber Lane, 1983; (2) *Italian Theatre Review*, vol. 6, no. 2 (1957).
Oh, These Ghosts! Trans. Marguerita Carrà and Louise H. Warner. *Tulane Drama Review* 8 (1964): 118–62.
Saturday, Sunday, Monday. Trans. Keith Waterhouse and Willis Hall. London: French, 1974.
Sik-Sik, The Masterful Magician. Trans. Robert G. Bender. *Italian Quarterly* 11 (1967): 19–42.
Three Plays: Grand Magic, The Local Authority, Filumena Marturano. Trans. Carlo Ardito. London: Hamilton & St. George's Press, 1976.

Other Works in English Translation

The Poems of Eduardo De Filippo. Trans. Frank J. Palescandoli. Turin: Einaudi, 1988.

Books and Selected Articles About in English

Acton, Harold. "Eduardo De Filippo." In *The Genius of the Italian Theatre*, ed. Eric Bentley, pp. 551–63. New York: Mentor, 1964.

Bender, Robert G. "A Critical Estimate of Eduardo De Filippo," *Italian Quarterly* 11 (1967): 3–18.

——. "Pulcinella, Pirandello, and Other Influences on De Filippo's Dramaturgy." *Italian Quarterly* 12 (1968): 39–71.

Bentley, Eric. "Son of Pulcinella." Chapter I, Part IV. In *In Search of Theatre*. New York: Alfred Knopf. 1953.

Eduardo De Filippo: *Filumena Marturano*, Introduction." In *The Genius of the Italian Theatre*, ed. Eric Bentley, pp. 439–52. New York: American Library, Mentor, 1964.

Ciolli, Marco. *The Theatre of Eduardo De Filippo*. New York: Vantage Press, 1993.

Codignola, Luciano. "Reading De Filippo," *Tulane Drama Review* 8 (1964): 108–17.

D'Aponte, Mimi Gisolfi. "Eduardo De Filippo: Moralist and Social Critic," *Nemla Italian Studies* 13–14 (1989–90): 81–87.

——. "Encounters with Eduardo De Filippo." *Modern Drama* 16 (1973): 347–53.

Mignone, Mario. *Eduardo De Filippo*. Boston: Twayne, 1984.

MARINETTI, FILIPPO T.

Plays in Italian

Marinetti, Filippo Tommaso. *Teatro F. T. Marinetti*. Vols. 1, 2, 3. Edited with an introduction by Giovanni Calendoli. Rome: Vito Bianco Editore, 1960.

Plays in English Translation

Kirby, Michael and Victoria Nes, eds. *Futurist Performance*. New York: PAJ Publications, 1986. THIS VOLUME CONTAINS A GOOD SELECTION OF FUTURIST *SINTESI* AND MANIFESTOS IN ENGLISH TRANSLATION AND HAS EXCELLENT COMMENTARIES BY THE EDITORS AND AN ANNOTATED BIBLIOGRAPHY.

Other Works in English Translation

Let's Murder the Moonshine: Selected Writings. Ed. R. W. Flint. Preface by Marjorie Perloff. Los Angeles: Sun and Moon, 1991.

Marinetti: Selected Writings. Ed. R. W. Flint. New York: Noonday, 1972; London: Secker & Warburg, 1972.

"Futurism and the Theatre," *The Mask* (January 1914): 188–93. Reprinted in *Total Theatre*. Ed. E. T. Kirby. New York: Dutton, 1969.

The Futurist Cookbook. Trans. Suzanne Brill. Edited with an introduction by Lesley Chamberlain. San Francisco: Bedford Arts; London: Trefoil, 1989.

Stung by Salt and War: Creative Texts of the Italian Avant-Gardist F. T. Marinetti. Translated and edited by Richard J. Pioli. Bern, Switzerland: Peter Lang, 1987; New York: Lang, 1987.

Marinetti, F. T., Emilio Settimelli, and Bruno Corra. "The Synthetic Futurist Theatre." In *Art and the Stage in the Twentieth Century*, edited by Henning Rischbieter. Greenwich, Conn: New York Graphic Society, 1968.

Articles and Books About in English

Cheshire, David F. "Futurism, Marinetti, and the Music Hall," *Theatre Quarterly* 1 London (July–September 1971), p. 54 and refs.

Clough, Rosa Trillo. *Futurism: The Story of a Modern Art Movement—A New Appraisal.* New York: Philosophical Library, 1961.

Dashwood, Julie R. "Futurism and Fascism," *Italian Studies* 27 (1972): 91–103.

Deak, Frantisek. "The Influence of Italian Futurism in Russia," *The Drama Review* vol. 19, no. 4 (Winter 1975): 88–94.

Durgnat, Raymond. "Futurism and the Movies," *Art and Artists* (February 1969): 10–15.

Kirby, E. T. *Total Theatre.* New York: Dutton, 1969.

Kirby, Michael and Victoria Nes, eds. *Futurist Performance.* New York: PAJ Publications, 1986.

Lista, Giovanni. *Futurism.* Trans. Charles L. Clark. New York: Universe, 1986.

Rischbieter, Henning "Futurism and the Theatre." In *Art and the Stage in the Twentieth Century*, edited by Henning Rischbieter. Greenwich, Conn.: New York Graphic Society, 1968.

Taylor, Christiana. *Futurism: Politics, Painting, and Performance.* Ann Arbor, Michigan: U.M.I. Research Press, 1979.

Wynne, Marjorie G. *F. T. Marinetti and Futurism.* Catalogue of an exhibition in the Beinecke Rare Book and Manuscript Library, Yale University, New Haven. February, 15 to May 10, 1983. New Haven: Beinecke, 1983.

PETROLINI, ETTORE

Works in Italian

Opere, 1: *Teatro: Macchiette, Venite a sentire, Nerone, Amori de notte, Romani de Roma, Acqua salata, Gastone, Il padiglione delle meraviglie, Benedetto tra le donne, Chicchignola, Il metropolitano; 2: Memorie.* 2 vols; *3: Immagini di Petrolini.* Ed. Annamaria Calò. Venice: Ruzzante, 1977.

Articles, Books About in English

Longman, Stanley V. "The modern *Maschere* of Ettore Petrolini." *Educational Theatre Journal* 27 (1975): 377–86.

PIRANDELLO, LUIGI

Plays in Italian

Pirandello, Luigi. *Opere: Vols. 4 & 5: Maschere nude* (Naked masks). With an introduction and notes by Alessandro d'Amico. Milan: Mondadori, 1956, 1971. INCLUDES BIBLIOGRAPHY.

Play Collections in English Translation

Collected Plays: Luigi Pirandello. 3 vols. Ed. Robert Rietty. London: Calder; New York: Riverrun Press, 1987–.

Each In His Own Way and Two Other Plays. Trans. Arthur Livingston. New York: Dutton, 1951.

Limes from Sicily, and Other Plays. Trans. Robert Rietty. Leeds: Arnold, 1967.

Mountain Giants and Other Plays: The New Colony, When Someone is Somebody. Translated with an introduction by Marta Abba. New York: Crown, 1958.

Naked Masks: Liolà, It Is So (If You Think So), Henry IV, Six Characters in Search of an Author, Each in his own Way. Ed. Eric Bentley. New York: Dutton, 1958. SEE THIS WORK FOR VALUABLE BIBLIO-GRAPHICAL MATERIAL.

Pirandello's Major Plays: Right You Are, Six Characters in Search of an Author, Emperor Henry, The Man with the Flower in his Mouth. Trans. Eric Bentley. Foreword by Albert Bermel. Evanston, Ill.: Northwestern University Press, 1991.

Pirandello's One-Act Plays. Trans. Gilbert Murray. Garden City, N.Y.: Anchor, 1964; London and New York: French, 1977.

Right You Are! (If You Think So). All for the best. Henry IV. Trans. Frederick May and Henry Reed. Edited with an introduction by E. Martin Browne. Harmondsworth: Penguin, 1962.

The Rules of the Game, The Life I Gave You, Lazarus. Edited with an introduction by E. Martin Browne. Harmondsworth: Penguin, 1959.

Sicilian Comedies: Cap and Bells; Man, Beast and Virtue. New York: PAJ Publications, 1983.

To Clothe the Naked and Two Other Plays. Trans. W. Murray. New York: Dutton, 1962.

Single Plays in English Translation

As You Desire Me. Trans. Marta Abba. New York: French, 1948.

Cap and Bells. Trans. John and Marion Field. New York: Manyland Books, 1974.

Diana and Tuda. Trans. Marta Abba. New York: French, 1960.

"*Dream, But Perhaps Not.*" Trans. Samuel Putnam. In *This Quarter* vol. 2, no. 4 (April–June 1930): 605–29.

Enrico IV. (1) Translated and adapted for the American stage by John Reich. Hollywood, Ca.?: S. French?, 1978. (2) Trans. Robert David MacDonald. London: Oberon, 1990; (3) *Henry IV.* Trans. Julian Mitchell. London: Eyre Methuen, 1979; (4) *The Emperor.* Trans. Eric Bentley. In *The Genius of the Italian Theatre,* ed. Eric Bentley, pp. 372–438. New York: Mentor, 1964.

The Jar. Trans. Frederick May. In *Four Continental Plays.* Edited with an introduction by John Piers Allen. London: Heinemann, 1964.

Man, Beast, and Virtue. Trans. Charles Wood. Bath, England: Absolute Press, 1989.

The Man with the Flower in his Mouth. Trans. F. May. Leeds: Pirandello Society, 1959.

No One Knows How. Trans. Marta Abba. New York and London: French, 1963.

The Rest is Silence. Dramatization of the short story *Sgombero.* Translated and dramatized by Frederick May. Leeds: Pirandello Society, 1958; Norwood, Penn.: Norwood Editions, 1978.

Right You Are. Stage version with an introduction and notes by Eric Bentley. New York: Columbia University Press, 1954.

Sicilian Limes. Trans. Isaac Goldberg. In *Plays of the Italian Theatre by Verga, Morselli, Lopez, Pirandello*. Boston: Luce, 1921.

Six Characters in Search of an Author. (1) Trans. Frederick May. London: Heinemann, 1954; (2) Trans. John Linstrum. London: Methuen, 1989.

To Find Oneself (Trovarsi). Trans. Marta Abba. New York: French, 1943.

Tonight We Improvise. Rev. and rewritten by Marta Abba. New York: French, 1960.

Tonight We Improvise and Leonora Addio!. Translated with an introduction and Notes by J. Douglas Campbell and Leonard G. Sbrocchi. Biblioteca di Quaderni d'Italianistica, vol. 3. Ottawa: The Canadian Society for Italian Studies, 1987.

When One Is Somebody. Trans. Marta Abba. New York: French, 1963.

The Wives' Friend. Trans. Marta Abba. New York: French, 1949.

Other Works in English Translation

Better Think Twice About It and 12 other stories. Trans. Arthur and Henri Mayne. London: Lane, 1933; New York: Dutton, 1934–35; Plainview, N.Y.: Books for Libraries Press, 1976.

Bitter Waters. Translated and adapted by Frederick May. Leeds: Pirandello Society, 1962.

The Captive. In *Story: The Magazine of the Short Story*. Trans. Arthur and Henri Mayne. (May–June 1941): 71–82.

A Dream of Christmas. Trans. Frederick May. Leeds: Pirandello Society, 1959.

Horse in the Moon: Twelve Short Stories. Translated with an introduction by Samuel Putnam. New York: Dutton, 1932.

The Late Mattia Pascal. (1) Trans. Arthur Livingston. New York: Dutton, 1923; (2) Trans. William Weaver. Garden City, N.Y.: Doubleday, 1964; and Hygiene, Colo.: Eridanos; New York: Distribution by Rizzoli, 1987; (3) Translated with an introduction and chronology by Nicoletta Simborowski. London: Dedalus, 1987; New York: Hippocrene, 1987.

The Medals and Other Stories. New York: Dutton, 1939.

The Merry-go-round of Love. New York: New American Library, 1964.

The Naked Truth and 11 Other Stories. Trans. Arthur and Henri Mayne. New York: Dutton, 1934.

The Notebooks of Serafino Gubbio, or Shoot!. Trans. C. K. Scott Moncrieff. Sawtry, England: Dedalus, 1990. SEE *SHOOT!* BELOW.

The Old and the Young. 2 vols. Trans. C. K. Scott Moncrieff. London: Chatto & Windus, 1928; New York: Dutton, 1928.

On Humor. With an introduction, translated and annotated by Antonio Illiano and Daniel P. Testa. Chapel Hill: University of North Carolina Press, 1974.

One, none, and a hundred-thousand. (1) Trans. Samuel Putnam. New York: Dutton, 1933; (2) *One, no one and one hundred-thousand*. Translated with an introduction by William Weaver. Boston: Eridanos, 1990.

The Outcast. Trans. Leo Ongley. New York: Dutton, 1925.

Shoot! The Notebooks of Serafino Gubbio, Cinematograph Operator. (1) Translated with a bibliography by C. K. Scott Moncrieff. London: Chatto & Windus, 1927; New York: Dutton, 1926; (2) as *The Notebooks of Serafino Gubbio; or (Shoot!)*. Trans. C. K. Scott Moncrieff, with chronology by Nicoletta Simborowski. New York: Fertig, 1975; Sawtry, England: Dedalus, 1990; (3) as *Shoot!*. The Garland Classics of Film Literature, vol. 24. New York: Garland, 1978.

Short Stories. Trans. Lily Duplaix. Introduction by Frances Keene. New York: Simon & Schuster, 1959.

Short Stories. Translated with an introduction by Frederick May. London and New York: Oxford University Press, 1965; London: Quartet, 1987.

The Sounds of the Girgenti Dialect and Their Development. Translated with an introduction by Giovanni R. Bussino. New York: Lang, 1992.

Tales of Madness. Translated with an introduction by Giovanni R. Bussino. Brookline Village, Mass.: Dante University of America Press, 1984.

Tales of Suicide. Translated with an introduction by Giovanni R. Bussino. Boston: Dante University of America Press, 1988.

Selected Articles and Books About in English

Abba, Marta. "Introduction." In Luigi Pirandello, *Mountain Giants and Other Plays*, pp. 1–29. CONTAINS DIRECT QUOTATIONS IN ENGLISH TRANSLATION FROM PIRANDELLO'S CORRESPONDENCE WITH MARTA ABBA FROM 1926–36.

Alessio, A., D. Pietropaolo, and G. Sanguinetti-Katz, eds. *Pirandello and the Modern Theatre*. Ottawa: Canadian Society for Italian Studies, 1992.

Bassnett, Susan, comp. *File on Pirandello*. London: Methuen Drama, 1989.

Bassnett, Susan and Jennifer Lorch, eds. *Luigi Pirandello in the Theatre*. Philadelphia: Harwood Academic Publishers, 1993.

Bassnett-McGuire, Susan. "Art and Life in Pirandello's *Questa sera si recita a soggetto* (*Tonight We Improvise*)." *Drama and Mimesis*. Ed. James Redmond, pp. 81–120. Cambridge: Cambridge University Press, 1980.

Bassnett-McGuire, Susan. *Luigi Pirandello*. London: Macmillan, 1983; New York: St. Martin's, 1983.

Bentley, Eric. *The Pirandello Commentaries*. Evanston, Ill.: Northwestern University Press, 1986.

Bermel, Albert. "The Living Statues: *Six Characters in Search of an Author.*" In Albert Bermel, *Contradictory Characters*, pp. 122–43. New York: Dutton, 1973.

Bishop, Thomas. *Pirandello and the French Theater*. New York: New York University Press, 1960.

Bloom, Harold, ed. *Luigi Pirandello*. New York: Chelsea House, 1989.

Cambon, Glauco, comp. *Pirandello: A Collection of Critical Essays*. Englewood Cliffs, N.J.: Prentice-Hall, 1967.

Caputi, Anthony F. *Pirandello and the Crisis of Modern Consciousness*. Urbana: University of Illinois Press, 1988.

Dashwood, J. R. and J. E. Everson, eds. *Writers and Performers in Italian Drama: From the Time of Dante to Pirandello*. Essays in Honor of G. H. McWilliam. Lewiston, N.Y.: Mellen, 1991.

DiGaetano, John Louis, ed. *A Companion to Pirandello Studies*. Foreword by Eric Bentley. New York: Greenwood, 1991.

Gassner, John. "Pirandello and the Illusionism of the Italian Stage." In John Gassner, *Masters of Modern Drama*. 3d. rev. and enlarged ed., pp. 431–45. New York: Dover, 1954.

Giudice, Gaspare. *Pirandello: A Biography*. Trans. Alastair Hamilton. London and New York: Oxford University Press, 1975.

Matthaei, Renate. *Luigi Pirandello*. New York: Ungar, 1973.

Oliver, Roger W. *Dreams of Passion*. New York: New York University Press, 1979.

Paolucci, Anne, special ed. *Pirandello*. Review of National Literatures Series, vol. 14. New York: Published for the Council on National Literatures by Griffon House, 1987.

———. *Pirandello's Theatre*. Carbondale: Southern Illinois University Press, 1974.

Papers on Pirandello's Enrico IV. Whitestone, N.Y.: Griffon House, 1989.

Ragusa, Olga. *Luigi Pirandello*. Columbia Essays on Modern Writers, vol. 37. New York: Columbia University Press, 1968.

———. *Luigi Pirandello: An Approach to his Theatre*. Writers of Italy Series, vol. 8. Edinburgh: Edinburgh University Press, 1980.

———. "*Six Characters*, 1921–1925 and Beyond." *Pirandello. 1986*. Eds. Gian Paolo Biasin and Nicolas J. Perella, pp. 19–30. Rome: Bulzoni Editore, 1987.

———. "*Tonight We Improvise*: Spectacle and Tragedy." *A Companion to Pirandello Studies*. Ed. John Louis DiGaetano, pp. 245–58. New York: Greenwood Press, 1991.

Sogliuzzo, A. Richard. *Luigi Pirandello, Director: The Playwright in the Theatre*. Metuchen, N.J.: Scarecrow Press, 1982.

Starkie, Walter. *Luigi Pirandello, 1867–1936*. London: John Murray, 1937. 3d. ed. rev. and enl. Berkeley: University of California Press, 1965.

Stone, Jennifer. *Pirandello's Naked Prompt*. Ravenna: Longo, 1989.

Thompson, Doug. *An Introduction to Pirandello's "Sei personaggi in cerca d'autore"*. Hull: Department of Italian, University of Hull, 1985.

Vittorini, Domenico. *The Drama of Luigi Pirandello*. Foreword by Luigi Pirandello. 2d. ed. New York: Russell & Russell, 1969.

ROSSO DI SAN SECONDO, PIER MARIA

Plays in Italian

Teatro. 3 vols. Ed. Luigi Ferrante. Introduction by Francesco Flora. Rome: Bulzoni, 1962; 2d ed., 1976.

Teatro, 1911–1925. Ed. Luigi Ferrante. Introduction by Francesco Flora. Rocca San Casciano: Cappelli, 1962.

Plays in English Translation

The Staircase. In *Eight European Plays*, edited and translated by Winifred Katzin. Preface by Barrett H. Clark. New York: Brentano's, 1927.

SAVINIO, ALBERTO. PSEUDONYM FOR ANDREA DE CHIRICO

Plays in Italian

Alcesti di Samuele. Milan: Bompiani, 1949.

Alcesti di Samuele e atti unici. Ed. Alessandro Tinterri. Milan: Adelphi, 1991.

Capitano Ulisse. Edited and with a "Note" by Alessandro Tinterri. Milan: Adelphi, 1989. THIS IS THE MOST ACCURATE VERSION OF THE TEXT.

Dramatic Adaptations by Others

Since the 1970s, many texts that Savinio did not intend for the stage have been adapted and produced in Italy. Among the most memorable are:

La partenza dell'Argonauta (The Argonaut departs) derived from his 1914 novel *Hermafrodito* (Hermaphrodite) by Memè Perlini who presented it at the Florence May Musicale in 1976.

La nostra anima (Our breath of life), adapted and directed by Luca Valentino at the Chieri Festival, 1988, and revived by Egisto Marcucci and Valeria Moriconi during the 1991–92 season.

Il coturno e la ciabatta (The cothurnus and the slipper), directed and acted by Paolo Poli in 1990. Poli and his collaborator, Ida Omboni, adapted the script from *Narrate, uomini, la vostra storia* (Narrate your story, you men), *La verità sull'ultimo viaggio* (The truth about the last journey), and *La nostra anima* (Our breath of life).

Other Works in English Translation

Capri. Translated with a preface by John Shepley. Marlboro, Vt.: Marlboro Press, 1989.

Childhood of Nivasio Dolcemare. Trans. Richard Pevear. Introduction by Dore Ashton. Hygiene, Colo.: Eridanos Press, 1988. New York: Distrib. by Rizzoli International Publications.

The Departure of the Argonaut. With illustrations by Francesco Clemente. New York: Petersburg Press, 1986; and New York: MOMA, 1986.

Isadora Duncan. Trans. John Shepley. Parma: Ricci, 1979.

The Lives of the Gods. Trans. James Brook and Susan Ellinger. London: Atlas, 1991.

Operatic Lives. Trans. John Shepley. Marlboro, Vt.: Marlboro Press, 1988.

Speaking to Clio. Trans. John Shepley. Marlboro, Vt.: Marlboro Press, 1987.

Tragedy of Childhood. Trans. John Shepley. Marlboro, Vt.: Marlboro Press, 1991.

Books About in English

The Dioscuri: Giorgio de Chirico and Alberto Savinio in Paris, 1924–1931. Exhibition; part of Italy on Stage. Texts by Maurizio Fagiolo dell'Arco, Paolo Baldacci, and Fabrizia Lanza Pietromarchi. Translated by Shara Wasserman and Martha A. Davis. Milan: Mondadori, Edizioni P. Daverio, 1987.

ITALO SVEVO. PSEUDONYM FOR ETTORE SCHMITZ

Plays in Italian

Opere: Edizione critica delle opere di Italo Svevo. 4 vols. Ed. Bruno Maier. Pordenone: Ed. Studio Tesi, 1985.

Opera omnia. Ed. Bruno Maier. Milan: Dall'Oglio, 1966–69. 1. *Epistolario* (Letters), 1966. 2. *Romanzi* (novels). 3. *Racconti, saggi, pagine sparse* (Tales, critical writings, miscellany) 1968. 4. *Commedie* (Plays), 1969. VOLUME 4 CONTAINS AN INTRODUCTION AND NOTES BY UMBRO APOLLONIO.

Plays in English Translation

The Broken Triangle (*Terzetto spezzato*), anonymous translation, *Atlas* 1 (1967): 42–51. Also translated by Beno Weiss in "*Terzetto spezzato*: Svevo's Spiritistic Fantasy," *Italica* 55 (1978): 211–24.

A Husband (*Un marito*). Trans. Beno Weiss. In *Modern International Drama* 6 (1972): 43–88.

Inferiority (*Inferiorità*). (1) Trans. P. N. Furbank. In *Essays on Italo Svevo*, edited by Thomas F. Staley, pp. 131–51. University of Tulsa Monograph Series No.206. Tulsa, Okla.: University of Tulsa Press, 1969. (2) Also, trans. Beno Weiss, "Svevo's *Inferiorità*," *Modern Fiction Studies* 18 (1972): 45–51.

Regeneration. A Comedy in Three Acts. Trans. P. N. Furbank. In *Further Confessions of Zeno*. Trans. Ben Johnson and P. N. Furbank. The Uniform Edition of Svevo's Works, vol. 5. Berkeley: University of California Press, 1969; London: Secker & Warburg, 1969.

Other works in English Translation

As A Man Grows Older. Trans. Beryl de Zoete. New York: New Directions, 1949; repr., Westport, Conn: Greenwood, 1977; London: Secker & Warburg, 1980.

Confessions of Zeno. Trans. Beryl de Zoete. 2d ed. Harmondsworth, U.K.: Penguin Books with M. Secker & Warburg, 1964, 1982; Westport, Conn.: Greenwood, 1973; New York: Vintage, 1989.

Further Confessions of Zeno. Trans. Ben Johnson and P. N. Furbank. Berkeley: University of California Press, 1969; London: Secker & Warburg, 1969.

The Hoax. Trans. Beryl de Zoete. London: L. & V. Woolf, Hogarth Press, 1929; New York: Harcourt Brace, 1930.

James Joyce. Trans. Stanislaus Joyce. A lecture delivered in Milan in 1927. New York: New Directions, 1950; Milan: Esperia, 1950.

A Life. Trans. Archibald Colquhoun. New York: Knopf, 1963, 1982; London: Secker & Warburg, 1980.

The Nice Old Man and The Pretty Girl and Other Stories. Trans. L. Collison-Morley. Introductory note by Eugenio Montale. London: L. & V. Woolf, Hogarth Press, 1930.

Short Sentimental Journey, and Other Stories. Trans. Beryl de Zoete, L. Collison-Morley, and Ben Johnson. The Uniform Edition of Svevo's Works, vol. 4. Berkeley: University of California Press, 1967; London: Secker & Warburg, 1967.

Books about in English

Fonda, Carlo. *Svevo and Freud*. Ravenna: Longo, 1978.

Furbank, P. N. *Italo Svevo: The Man and the Writer*. London: Secker & Warburg, 1966.

Gatt-Rutter, John. *Italo Svevo: A Double Life*. Oxford: Oxford University Press, 1988.

Lebowitz, Naomi. *Italo Svevo*. New Brunswick: Rutgers University Press, 1978.

Moloney, Brian. *Italo Svevo and the European Novel*. Hull: University of Hull, 1977.

———. *Italo Svevo: A Critical Introduction*. Edinburgh: Edinburgh University Press, 1974.

Ragusa, Olga. "'The Light is split in the Prism . . .': Svevo's Unfinished Play *Con la penna d'oro*." In

Olga Ragusa, *Narrative and Drama: Essays in Modern Italian Literature from Verga to Pasolini*, pp. 109–21. Paris: Mouton, 1976.

Russell, Charles C. *Italo Svevo: The Writer from Trieste–Reflections on his Background and his Work.* Ravenna: Longo Editore, 1978.

Staley, Thomas F., ed. *Essays on Italo Svevo.* Tulsa, Okla.: University of Tulsa Press, 1969.

Subrizi, Lilia Ghelli. *Svevo: A Fascination with Melancholy.* Florence: Il Candebio, 1984.

Svevo, Livia Veneziani. *Memoir of Italo Svevo.* Trans. Isabel Quigly. London: Libris, 1989.

Weiss, Beno. *Italo Svevo.* Boston: Twayne, 1987.

———. *An Annotated Bibliography on the Theatre of Italo Svevo.* University Park: Pennsylvania State University Libraries, 1974.

FEDERIGO TOZZI

Plays in Italian

Teatro. Vol. 3 of *Opere.* 7 vols. Ed. Glauco Tozzi and Giancarlo Vigorelli. Rome: Vallecchi, 1970. THIS CONTAINS TOZZI'S FOURTEEN PLAYS AND TWO PLOT OUTLINES WITH MARVELOUS COMMENTARIES BY HIS SON GLAUCO AND ADDITIONAL NOTES BY GIANCARLO VIGORELLI.

Other works in English Translation

Eyes Shut: A Novel. Trans. Kenneth Cox. Manchester: Carcanet, 1990.

Ghisola (Con gli occhi chiusi). Translated with an afterword by Charles Klopp. Conclusion by Giose Rimanelli. Garland Library of World Literature in Translation, vol. 18. New York and London: Garland, 1990.

Three Crosses. Trans. R. Capellero. New York: Moffat Yard, 1921.

Books and Articles About in English

Klopp, Charles. "Federigo's Ark: Beasts and Bestiality in Tozzi." *Italian Quarterly*, vol. 21, no. 81 (Summer 1980): 55–62

———. "Metaphor and Psychology in Tozzi's *Gli egoisti*." *Italian Culture*, vol. 5 (1984): 141–55.

Pacifici, Sergio. Introduction to *From Verismo to Experimentalism: Essays on the Modern Italian Novel*, edited by S. Pacifici, pp. xv–xxxvi. Bloomington, Ind.: Indiana University Press, 1970.

———. *The Modern Italian Novel from Capuana to Tozzi.* Carbondale, Ill.: Southern Illinois University Press, 1973.

Pedroni, Peter N. *The Anti-naturalist Experience: Federigo Tozzi.* Tallahassee, Fla.: De Soto Press, 1989.

———. "Federigo Tozzi: Autobiography and Antinaturalism." *Italica*, vol. 60, no. 1 (Spring 1983): 10–23.

Rimanelli, Giose. "Federigo Tozzi: Misfit and Master," *Italian Quarterly* 14 (1971): 29–76.

RAFFAELE VIVIANI

Plays in Italian

Teatro. Vols. 1–5. Ed. Guido Davico Bonino, Antonia Lezza, and Pasquale Scialò. Naples: Guida, 1987. THESE LOVINGLY COLLECTED FIVE VOLUMES OF VIVIANI'S PLAYS CONTAIN MUSIC, NOTES, AND COMMENTARY BY THE EDITORS.

Teatro di Raffaele Viviani. 2 vols. Ed. Lucio Ridenti. Preface by E. Possenti. Biographical introduction by Alberto Spaini. Critical commentary by Vito Pandolfi. Turin: ILTE, 1957.

■

Contributors

■

Antonio Attisani   is associate professor of theater history at the School of Literature, University of Venice. From 1989–1993 he was also artistic director of the International Theater Festival at Santarcangelo di Romagna. Among the books he has written are
Breve storia del teatro, Teatro come differenza, and *Il teatro di Tibet.* He also edited *Enciclopedia
del teatro del '900* and from the mid-1970s has directed the journal *Scena.*

J. Douglas Campbell,   Associate Professor of English and coordinator of extra-
curricular theater at Carleton University, Ottawa, Canada, is also a theater director and
professional actor. He has directed Euripides, Shakespeare, Ibsen, Mayakovsky, Joe Orton,
Pirandello (*Right You Are If You Think So, The Man with the Flower in His Mouth, When You're a
Somebody*), and early Italian works: Aretino's *The Marescalco* and *La Cortegiana* (both co-
translated with Leonard G. Sbrocchi), and Gianlorenzo Bernini's *The Impresario.* He performed Dr. Hinkfuss in the production for which this translation of *Tonight We Improvise*
was prepared.

Mimi Gisolfi D'Aponte   is on the theater faculty of the Graduate School and University Center, City University of New York, and Professor of Speech, Baruch College.
Her articles have appeared in *Italian Theatre Quarterly, Modern Drama, TDR,* and *Western European Stages,* for which she serves as contributing editor. Other publications include *Teatro
religioso e rituale della Penisola Sorrentina e la Costiera Amalfiana* on Italian ritual theater, and
chapters in *A Companion to Pirandello Studies* (Greenwood, 1991) and *Made by Hand, Played
by Heart: Ethnic and Folk Culture in Queens* (Cooper Union Press, 1994). In 1982 Studia Hu-
manitatis published *Shepherds' Song,* her co-translation with her husband of *La cantata dei
pastori* by Andrea Perrucci.

Paul Feinberg   is a theater artist and properties master with Berkeley Repertory
Theater in California. He received his M.F.A. from Temple University in 1989 and was
previously a puppeteer with Italy's foremost company of Sicilian puppets for several years.
This is his first translation effort.

Jane House   was director of the Theater Project in Columbia University's Institute
on Western Europe (1985–1991) and is presently teaching theater at N.Y.U. and Lehman
College, C.U.N.Y. She has contributed articles to *Western European Stages* and *Slavic and East
European Performance* and edited *Political Theatre Today.* As an actress, she has appeared on

Broadway, regional theater, television, and film. She translates from French as well as Italian.

Martha King   received her Ph.D. in Italian from the University of Wisconsin and has lived in Tuscany since 1979. Among the Italian writers she has translated are Cesare Pavese, Pier Paolo Pasolini, Dacia Maraini, Grazia Deledda, and Giacomo Leopardi. She edited *New Italian Women: A Collection of Short Fiction* (Italica Press, 1989) and is presently working on a biography of Grazia Deledda.

Anthony Molino   has translated works by poets Antonio Porta and Valerio Magrelli and has received a National Theater Translation Fund grant to translate Manlio Santanelli's award-winning play, *Uscita d'emergenza*. A Fulbright grantee to Italy in 1980, Mr. Molino has been awarded three grants by the Pennsylvania Arts Council for his translations. He lives in Philadelphia where he is a practicing psychoanalyst.

Anthony Oldcorn,   who translated the plays by D'Annunzio, Bontempelli, and Svevo, is an expatriate Britisher who holds degrees in Romance languages from Oxford, Virginia, and Harvard. Professor and chair of Italian studies at Brown University, he has published scholarship and criticism on a number of Italian authors. His version of Carlo Goldoni's *Villeggiatura Trilogy* received one of the 1993 Kayden Translation Awards.

Paola Quarenghi   is a researcher at the Department of Music and Entertainment of the University of Rome "La Sapienza." She has published various articles on Eduardo's theater and edited the volume *Lezione di teatro* (Torino: Einaudi, 1986), which documents the work of a lecturer at the University of Rome from 1981 to 1983.

Henry Reed (1914–86)   was best known as a radio-dramatist; his adaptation of *Moby Dick* (1946) featured Ralph Richardson and Cyril Cusack. Other texts have been published in *The Streets of Pompeii and other Plays for Radio* (1971) and *Hilda Tablet and Others*. His poems, which appeared mainly in the *Listener* and *New Writing*, are collected in *A Map of Verona* (1947) and *The Lessons of War* (1970) and were published by Oxford University Press in 1991. Besides *Crime on Goat Island*, Reed translated Ugo Betti's *The Queen and the Rebels, Burnt Flower-Bed, Summertime,* and *Corruption in the Palace of Justice*. In addition, he translated Balzac's *Père Goriot* and *Eugénie*, poems by Leopardi, Pirandello, Montherlant, and Natalia Ginzburg's play *The Advertisement*.

Leonard G. Sbrocchi   is a professor of Italian at the University of Ottawa, Ottawa, Canada. His essays on Italian writers have appeared in such journals as *Lettere Italiane, Lares, Critica Storica, Il Veltro, Rivista di Studi Pirandelliani, Italica, Canadian Modern Language Review, Quaderni d'Italianistica* as well as in dictionaries (*Columbia Dictionary of Modern European Literature, Dictionary of Literary Biography*) and in anthologies. He has written monographs on Pavese and on Fucini and has co-translated into English *The Comedies of Ariosto*, Aretino's *Marescalco* and *Cortegiana*. As editor of the monographic series Biblioteca di Quaderni d'Italianistica, he has published *L'enigma Pirandello, Pirandello and the Modern Theatre*, and *Tonight We Improvise*. In the field of language teaching and methodology he has also published

I verbi italiani (and their English and French equivalents), has co-edited *L2 and Beyond* (Legas, 1993) and is associate editor of the journal *Il Forneri.* He is also director of the publishing house Legas.

Laurence Senelick is Fletcher Professor of drama at Tufts University, former Fellow of the Institute for Advanced Studies, Berlin, and twice Fellow of the John Simon Guggenheim Foundation. His most recent books include *The Age and Stage of George L. Fox, National Theatre in Northern and Eastern Europe 1743–1900,* and the two-volume *Cabaret Performance: Europe 1890–1940.* His translations of plays from the Russian, German, French, and Italian have been widely performed in this country.

Copyright Acknowledgments